C000141029

Nick Harris was born in Derby
Southampton supporter. He has
Japan and has been a sportswriter
He lives in Scotland with his wife a...

Praise for *The Foreign Revolution*

THE FOREIGN REVOLUTION

HOW OVERSEAS FOOTBALLERS CHANGED THE ENGLISH GAME

NICK HARRIS

This edition first published 2006 by
Aurum Press Limited
25 Bedford Avenue
London WC1B 3AT
www.aurumpress.co.uk

First published as *England Their England* by Pitch Publishing
in 2003

A catalogue record for this book is available from the British
Library.

ISBN-10   1 84513 159 2
ISBN-13   978 1 84513 159 3

10 9 8 7 6 5 4 3 2 1
2010 2009 2008 2007 2006

Designed and typeset in Minion and Helvetica Neue by
SX Composing DTP, Rayleigh, Essex

Printed and bound in Great Britain by Creative Print and Design,
Ebbw Vale

CONTENTS

AUTHOR'S NOTE AND ACKNOWLEDGEMENTS

As the title of this book suggests, only England's history of foreign players is considered, although some of Scotland's legionnaires are mentioned in passing. Every overseas-born player to have appeared in at least one English Football League or Premier League match since 1888 is included in the appendices, although some non-League players are mentioned in passing in the narrative. Some of the players in the appendices are overseas-born Britons but are included for the record.

Foreign players, for this book's purposes, are defined as those born outside Britain and Ireland. Though Scotland, Wales, Northern Ireland and the Republic of Ireland are all distinct from England in international football, they share a heritage and role within English football as old as the game itself. In that sense, they are not considered foreign. On a practical level, including them would have trebled or quadrupled the size of the book.

I am grateful to hundreds of people in dozens of countries for their help and cooperation. First and foremost all the players, managers and other football folk who gave freely of their time and their memories. They include Ossie Ardiles, Jimmy Armfield, Brendon Batson, Clyde Best, Craig Brown, Keith Burkinshaw, Barry Davies, Lindy Delapenha, Alec Eisentrager, Sir Tom Finney, Eddie Firmani, Denis Foreman, Steve Gibson, John Giles, the late Ron Greenwood, Johnny Haasz, John Hewie, Hans Jeppson, Juninho, Graham Kelly, Joe Marston, Gary McAllister, Lawrie McMenemy, Steve Mokone, Jan Molby, John Motson, Michael Parkinson, Ces Podd, Claudio Ranieri, Sir Bobby Robson, Graham Taylor, Peter Taylor, Bert Trautmann, Martin Tyler, Rolando Ugolini and Howard Wilkinson.

I am also indebted to Michael Joyce and his database of every match in English football history. That marvellous piece of software deserves a wider audience and has been pivotal in compiling the statistics and keeping them updated. Mike's website can be found at http://allfootballers.com and is a mine of information about all players – not just foreigners – to have featured in the English Leagues since 1888.

My thanks also go to all the other statisticians and historians who helped compile the appendices, and to all the supporters who provided anecdotal colour for the narrative. Space does not permit me to list every one, but you know who you are.

Thanks especially to Colin Jose, a fountain of knowledge about the game in North America; Colin Cameron of Charlton, who has been tirelessly helpful; Jack McInroy, for his painstaking research into the life of Hassan Hegazi; Leigh Edwards, for his encyclopaedic knowledge; Tom Egbers, for helping to throw light on the complicated life of Steve Mokone; and my good friend John Roberts for his generosity, experience and unstinting enthusiasm. I am also grateful to the varied expertise of Steven Bridge, Alex Fynn, Miriam Sutter, Brian Sears, Jo Hathaway, Karen Hobden and Bill Swallow. And to all those journalistic colleagues whose work has in turn informed and inspired, not least Richard Williams, Phil Shaw, Glenn Moore, Henry Winter, James Lawton, Grahame Lloyd and Paul Hayward. Thanks also to everyone at Aurum for having faith.

Above all thanks to Helen, Daisy and Isabel, who never fail to inspire.

Nick Harris
May 2006

INTRODUCTION: ARRIVEDERCI ISOLATION
An overview of the reverse
colonisation of English football

GIANLUCA VIALLI COULDN'T understand the fuss. There he was, sitting at a small table in the pokey post-match pressroom at The Dell on Boxing Day 1999, expecting to give his thoughts on how his Chelsea side had beaten Southampton 2–1, and all the questions were about his team selection.

'Was it deliberate?' asked one of the assembled journalists.

'Did you know it's never been done before?' asked another.

'How do you feel to be the first manager ever to pick a team entirely made up of foreign players?'

That afternoon, after 111 years, three months and 17 days of Football League history, when British players had featured on both sides in every one of its 150,000-plus fixtures, the Italian had become the first manager to select a team with none. His goalkeeper was a Dutchman and his defenders hailed from Spain, Brazil, France and Nigeria. His midfield quartet included a Romanian, a second Frenchman, a Uruguayan and a Swiss-born Italian. Another Italian played a support role in attack to a Norwegian. His historic team sheet read: De Goey; Ferrer, Thome, Leboeuf, Babayaro; Petrescu, Deschamps, Poyet, Di Matteo; Ambrosetti, Flo.

'We had a few players out,' shrugged Vialli. 'Unfortunately, some of them were English.' He said that nationality was 'not important'.

Within a generation England had become the most cosmopolitan footballing nation on earth, which was both apt and extraordinary. Having given football to the world in the nineteenth century, England then spent more than 100 years being institutionally opposed to foreign players. In the early decades of the League, foreign players were often reviled and stigmatised – by the authorities if not the fans.

Then the English FA actually changed its rules to keep them out. This effective ban stayed in place between 1931 and 1978.

Navel-gazing logic was consistently applied to support this stance. What did foreigners know about football? Very little. What could they teach? Nothing. What could they bring to the English game? Job losses and confusion. What would an acceptance of foreign players say about England? That England could not produce enough good players of her own.

The ban was only lifted when the European Community forced the FA's hand in 1978. A ripple of exotic faces arrived, most prominently at Tottenham, who made the extraordinary double signing of the Argentinian World Cup winners, Ossie Ardiles and Ricky Villa. Yet a decade later, in the 1988–89 season, it was still absolutely normal that Arsenal should win the League title without using a single foreign player all season. They were the last team to do so, and it is unlikely that any team will ever again win it using players solely from Britain and Ireland.

It was only after the advent of the Premier League, in 1992, that foreign players became unexceptional, at all levels. The growth was exponential, and Chelsea's all-foreign XI for that Boxing Day match at The Dell a perfect illustration. Seven years before, on the opening weekend of the 1992–93 season, there were only 10 foreigners in total among 242 players in the 22 starting line-ups. 'Whoever we play, wherever we play and in whatever competition, everyone – British or foreign – must be capable of adapting,' Vialli said at The Dell in 1999. 'We are an English team made of English and foreign players. It doesn't matter as long as we speak the same language on the field.'

Vialli's starting XI represented a defining moment in the reverse colonisation of English football, yet it was flagged in the next day's newspapers with little import. Subsequent landmarks have drawn less attention still. The decline of English players in England's top division reached 'tipping point' in the 2001–02 season, when, for the first time, less than half of all the players who appeared (262 from more than 550) were qualified to play for England. In 1992–93, the corresponding figure had been 391. By 2005–06, it had fallen closer to 200.

The first all-foreign match squad – as opposed to Chelsea's mere all-foreign starting XI – arrived on 14 February 2005, when Arsenal started with 11 foreign players and had another five on the bench against Crystal Palace. In that season, 82 per cent of the players fielded in first-team matches under Frenchman Arsène Wenger hailed from outside Britain or Ireland. The corresponding figure at Chelsea, under the Portuguese José Mourinho, was 67 per cent, while at Liverpool, under the Spaniard Rafael Benitez, it was 61 per cent, and at Manchester United, under Sir Alex Ferguson, it was 48 per cent.

Overseas influence has stretched way beyond the touchline. Foreign managers dominate the Premiership and the chase for other major trophies. Foreign billionaires, in the shape of Roman Abramovich and Malcolm Glazer, bought Chelsea and Manchester United. Tycoons, hucksters and wannabes from Thailand, Africa, America and the Middle East have made bids for a variety of clubs. In turn an increasing number of clubs have looked East to try to milk the markets of Asia, believing that a boom in the popularity of the English game could somehow be turned into plentiful revenue. In every sense, foreign players – on the field, in the dugout and in the boardrooms – have led a revolution that has changed the English game.

While Chelsea's all-foreign XI in 1999 was by no means the start of it, that occasion still acts as the perfect point from which to trace the genesis. Glenn Hoddle, one of the most stylish and creative midfielders of the 1980s with Tottenham and England, was appointed as Chelsea's player-manager in summer 1993. He was one of the rare Englishmen to have had success abroad, in his case in France between 1987 and 1991 with Monaco. It was there, under the tutelage of Wenger, that Hoddle first thought of himself as management material. And there that he gained Continental experience as part of a blended multi-national squad. In July 1995, Hoddle's Chelsea signed Ruud Gullit, a 32-year-old former European Footballer of the Year with his own ambitions of management and a bulging contacts book. The seeds were sown.

In summer 1996, Hoddle left to manage England. Gullit took the reins in one hand and opened the chequebook with the other. In came a torrent of foreign talent. Vialli and Gianfranco Zola were among those brought to Stamford Bridge before Gullit was sacked in February 1998. Vialli took up the baton, signing another 13 foreign players between his appointment and December 1999, by which time an alien XI was almost inevitable.

Flo scored both Chelsea's goals on Boxing Day 1999, one laid on by Poyet, his captain for the day, and the other by Didier Deschamps, a 1998 World Cup winner. Southampton, whose starting line-up was slightly more typical of the lesser top-division sides of the day – a Welshman, six Englishmen, two Norwegians, a Moroccan and a Latvian – pinched a late consolation through their Sheffield-born forward, Kevin Davies.

Far away from the Premier League's made-for-TV world of exotic names and seven-figure contracts, Chelsea's team was seen as astonishing. 'Imagine if the Baltimore Orioles came out to play at Camden Yards with not a single American in the starting line-up,' wrote one columnist in the *Washington Times*. 'Sounds crazy, doesn't it? . . . Chelsea's 30-man roster reads like the United Nations, with players from 12 different nations, including seven Italians and four Frenchmen.'

It was ironic that observers in America, a nation as distant from England as it gets in footballing geography, should seem alarmed. By 1999, even in melting pot America – home throughout the twentieth century to a series of leagues based on imports, often from Britain – there were limits. Teams in the Major Soccer League had a ceiling of four foreign players.

Chelsea's approach, of attempting to jigsaw together from myriad nations a team capable of fighting for honours, at home and in Europe, was pioneered enthusiastically by Ken Bates, the club's chairman. 'There is a suggestion that so-called foreign mercenaries are driving out English footballers, destroying the grass roots,' Bates had said in 1997, a year when Chelsea won the FA Cup, their first major silverware since 1971. 'What actually happens is that the foreign players bring new ideas, new ways of living and new attitudes to training which brush off on the youngsters.'

Certainly by 1999, the cream of the imports had made their mark, domestically and in Europe, not least in Arsenal's Double-winning team of 1998 under Wenger, in Chelsea's European Cup Winners' Cup-winning team of the same season and in Manchester United's unique treble-winning side of 1999. Imports had also made a clean sweep of the Footballer of the Year award for five consecutive years, from Tottenham's Jürgen Klinsmann in 1995 to Manchester United's Eric Cantona in 1996, Zola in 1997, Arsenal's Dennis Bergkamp in 1998 and Tottenham's David Ginola in 1999.

But these were just a handful among the 800 foreign players who had entered the English game's four professional divisions during the 1990s alone. This particular influx – the biggest if not the first –

started with a couple of dozen foreign players in 1991, becoming 100 by 1995 and more than 200 by the end of 1996. Another 450 new faces arrived in the three years before Vialli picked 11 of them to face Southampton.

A multi-national Premiership

In one sense, the 1990s influx originated in the 'dark days' of English football in the 1980s. Hooliganism – 'the English disease' – was commonplace, at home and abroad. Fans were taken for granted. Facilities were terrible.

The 1985 European Cup final between Liverpool and Juventus at the Heysel Stadium in Brussels on 29 May became an irrelevance after 39 people, mostly Italians, died when a wall collapsed on them during a riot involving supporters. Eighteen days earlier, on the last day of the domestic season, 56 people died when a fire, possibly caused by a discarded cigarette, swept through the aged, wooden main stand at Bradford City's Valley Parade ground. And then, on 15 April 1989, at the semi-final of the FA Cup between Liverpool and Nottingham Forest at Sheffield Wednesday's Hillsborough ground, came Europe's worst ever football tragedy. Errant policing and poor signposting led to a fatal crush in a fenced terrace pen that cost 96 people their lives.

The official report into the Hillsborough disaster was published at the end of January 1990. English football, it said, was blighted by old grounds, poor facilities, hooligans, a lack of adequate leadership and a frequent disrespect for the people who funded the industry – the supporters. It was recommended that terracing be banned from all grounds, starting with the top clubs. Within months the Football Association, under the stewardship of a new chief executive, Graham Kelly, was considering other fundamental steps forward.

By August 1992, English football was radically reshaped. The leading 22 clubs – each housed in or planning refurbished or new all-seater stadiums – embarked on their inaugural season in the Premier League, the new breakaway top division, funded by television receipts from Rupert Murdoch's Sky TV. England's performance at the 1990 World Cup, drenched in the tears of a young Paul Gascoigne, had already reawakened a wider interest in the national game. Now the cash paid by Murdoch to the Premier League clubs – up to £304 million between them over five years from 1992 – enabled a round of unprecedented spending on transfer fees and wages.

Déjà vu . . . with spending power

The advent of the Premier League, crucial though it was in attracting foreign players, was actually only the stimulus for a *revival* of imports after a hiatus that effectively spanned most of the 1980s because of the state of the English game. Foreign footballers had been effectively excluded from playing in England between 1931, when the FA introduced a two-year residency rule to deter imports, and 1978, when European Community legislation dictated that national associations could not, by law, ban players from Common Market countries. This 47-year period was not without imported players, many of them prominent, some of them involved in momentous matches in English football history. They came and played in England despite the insular mentality of the game's rulers and the government, either because they arrived before 1931, or came from colonial territories, or were refugees or amateurs or prisoners of war who never went home. But the period between 1931 and 1978 was nonetheless an era when all obstacles possible were placed in the way of aspirant immigrants.

From 1978–79 onwards this was no longer the case. The English authorities were forced to open their doors and did so to players from outside Europe as well. Ardiles and Villa arrived at Spurs. At Ipswich, Bobby Robson signed the Dutchmen Arnold Muhren and Frans Thijssen. Manchester City signed Poland's most-capped international, Kazimierz Deyna. Southampton signed Ivan Golac, a Yugoslavian international defender. These half-dozen were joined the same season by others from around the world following moves that a year before would have been outlawed by the authorities' isolationist rules. And they came not for money per se but because English football was seen as a vibrant and potentially successful place to work.

It was during the 1978–79 season that Trevor Francis became Britain's first £1 million footballer after a move from Birmingham to Nottingham Forest. Kevin Keegan, then with SV Hamburg in Germany, won the European Footballer of the Year award and would soon return to England. Nottingham Forest won the European Cup, the second of six consecutive successes by English clubs in the competition and one of 11 European trophies won by English clubs between 1976 and 1985.

Foreign internationals arrived steadily in the early 1980s – and mostly at top-division clubs – from Argentina and Poland and Yugoslavia, from Belgium and the Netherlands and from across Scandinavia. But by the mid-1980s, when hooliganism was rife and English clubs were indefinitely banned from European competition because of the Heysel tragedy, the attraction of England had dramatically diminished. Why come when you couldn't aspire to European football? To dodge policemen as they tried to break up crowd disturbances at the final whistle? To play in front of dwindling crowds in crumbling stadiums?

Not until the European ban was lifted in 1990–91 was there again any real incentive for a foreign player to come to England. The close of the following season saw the end of the old Football League structure and the start of the Premier League. The international players started to come back, only this time circumstances meant they came in numbers.

Back in Europe, back on track

English football was being screened, live via satellite television, to a wider international audience than ever before. The marketing men projected a fan-friendly environment that had shaken off its grubby, thug-ridden image of a decade before. There was no ban on English clubs playing in Europe, so players could move with legitimate hopes of international club football as well as good money. And the money, of course, was an incentive in itself, not only to the players but to agents. The most infamous of the 1990s, the Norwegian Rune Hauge, saw profits to be made – legitimately and otherwise – and personally brokered the transfers of countless players, mostly Scandinavians. Agents proliferated at a global level and so did the moves to England, where home-grown players became increasingly more expensive than imports.

By December 1995, the imports of the early 1990s were already well established. The Norwegian defender, Henning Berg, had been part of a title-winning team with Blackburn in 1995. The Danish midfielder,

John Jensen, had featured as Arsenal won the FA Cup and Coca-Cola Cup in 1993 and the European Cup-Winners' Cup the following season. Stig Inge Bjornebye, Liverpool's Norwegian defender, had helped his side to the Coca-Cola Cup in 1995. Peter Schmeichel, the Danish goalkeeper, and Andrei Kanchelskis, the Ukrainian winger, had both won two League titles with Manchester United, the second as part of a League and FA Cup double in 1994. That quintet of players, incidentally, had all been represented by Hauge during their moves to England. A third foreign player at Manchester United, France's Eric Cantona, had been part of the club's recent triumphs as well as a title-winner with Leeds in 1992.

The Bosman ruling

Yet it wasn't until the end of 1995, and the so-called 'Bosman ruling' in the European courts, that overseas markets became the primary source of talent, including for clubs lower down the leagues. Like Murdoch and Hauge before him, Jean-Marc Bosman, a journeyman midfielder from Belgium, was to become another outsider who would never play football in England yet influence the landscape of English football dramatically.

His legal action began when he took the Belgian FA and his club, RC Liège, to court in 1990 after they had combined to stop him moving to a minor French side, US Dunkerque. His contract with Liège had expired, but they wanted to retain him on a quarter of his former salary. Unemployed but unable to move to Dunkerque because his registration had not been transferred, as was mandatory, he took action through the local courts. The process led, almost five years later, to a momentous decision in the European Court of Justice in Luxembourg. Out-of-contract players became free agents, no longer at the mercy of clubs, who had previously been allowed to stop them moving unless fees were paid.

On the face of it, the decision was a boon for footballers across Europe. They could see out their contracts and then move for nothing to another club who would, in all probability, pay higher wages because there was no transfer fee payable. In a sellers' market, the wage spiral cranked ever higher. New Premier League deals with Sky TV and the BBC in 1996 – worth £743 million over four years from

1997 – gave the clubs yet more money. This in turn enticed more players from overseas. And as foreign managers, including Wenger at Arsenal, Gérard Houllier at Liverpool, Jean Tigana at Fulham and Claudio Ranieri at Chelsea became more prevalent, so the number of foreign players rose ever faster. The international market, revitalised by the formation of the Premier League, fuelled by Sky and staffed by Bosman, was well and truly open.

England's gift to the world

England first codified the rules of football and then played an integral part in its global dissemination. It should have been the natural home for a heterogenous footballing culture during the twentieth century. Yet throughout those 100 years the game's governors and administrators – often with the assistance of the government – had done almost everything in their power to stop it being so.

Never mind that codified football had spread around the world since the English FA had formed in 1863 and lain down its rules. Nor that, after the English Football League kicked off in 1888, clubs and leagues with British roots were hastening the development of a truly international game. If Empire was ultimately about expansion of territory to utilise resources, English football's hierarchy wanted none of it. It was a blinkered approach based on the ignorant supposition that football should be controlled from the centre and that the centre was England.

Not that such attitudes curtailed expansion. In the Netherlands, where English textile workers took the game in the 1860s and clubs still carry names marking their British roots (Go Ahead Eagles in Deventer and Gronigen's Be Quick, for example), there was an FA by 1889. By 1889 there was also an FA in Denmark, where that country's first club, KB, had been started by Englishmen 11 years before. By 1908 the Danes had the strongest international side outside the British Isles, a fact illustrated by their progress to the Olympic final of that year. They reached the next Olympic final too, where they again met Great Britain, and lost.

In Switzerland, a playground for wealthy British students in the latter half of the nineteenth century, the St Gallen club was formed in 1879 by locals who had learnt the game from English visitors. The same team eliminated Chelsea from the UEFA Cup 121 years later. History is littered with such Continental wins over English clubs by teams started by Englishmen a century or more before. Another Swiss team, Grasshoppers, was founded by Englishmen in 1886, the same year that a footballing pioneer, Vittorio Pozzo, was born in Italy. He later played for Grasshoppers on his travels in search of football knowledge across Europe, which included time in Manchester. He was Italy's coach as they won the 1934 World Cup on home turf and retained it in France four years later.

Italy's oldest club, the Genoa Football and Cricket Club – which like AC Milan, retains its English spelling in testament to its founders – was started by Englishmen in 1893. The same year, Argentina established the first FA in South America. The game had been taken there in the 1860s by English sailors, leading to the formation in 1867 of Buenos Aires FC, the first constituted club outside Britain or North America. By 1898, when Italy founded an FA, the first club in Spain, Athletic Bilbao, was being formed in the wake of the game's intro-duction there by British businessmen. The Spanish took the game to Mexico, where the first league in North America started in 1902.

By the start of the twentieth century, football had spread through-out Europe. Germany formed an association in 1900, some 20 years after Bremen had been formed under English influence. One early team in Hamburg, a forerunner of the SV Hamburg of today, kept their minutes in English. Uruguay's FA was also formed in 1900, where 18 years earlier English students had started the first club. In Hungary, where an FA was formed in 1901, the game's dissemination was largely down to pioneer Karoly Lowenrosen, who had lived for years in Britain.

In Austria, the Vienna Cricket and Football Club was formed by English expats, soon to spark a rival, First Vienna, staffed by locals but retaining the English spelling. Direct English influence came through Mark Nicholson, a defender in West Bromwich Albion's FA Cup-winning side of 1892. He moved to Vienna to work in the city's Thomas Cook travel agency and was instrumental in the formation of the early Austrian FA.

So the game was passed on, invariably by Englishmen and Scots and then from neighbour to neighbour. To Sweden, Finland, Russia, Brazil, Portugal, just a few of which had associations before the First World War. Often, as in France, the game took hold many years before any formal organisation was formed to administer it. France's FA was formed in 1919 but its first club, Le Havre Athletic Club, was founded by English students in 1872. By the turn of the century there were numerous clubs in Paris, including The White Rovers, primarily made up of Scotsmen, and Standard FC, a British invention and such a success that citizens in the Belgian town of Liège copied the name.

Football was, by any measure, a truly international game and arguably the only one. And it had come largely via England. And yet, in official terms, there was little more than arrogance, distance and superiority from the country where it started. Indeed when the idea was first mooted in 1904 by broadminded nations to establish FIFA, an international association, the English dragged their heels to such an extent that they missed the boat. There was one early English FIFA president, Daniel Burley Woolfall, between 1906 and 1918, but England and the other home nations had a sporadic and fractious relationship with FIFA until after the Second World War. Indeed England did not enter the World Cup, organised by FIFA, until 1950.

The voice of little England

If there was one voice that epitomised England's isolationist stance, it was that of Charles Edward Sutcliffe, a driving if not universally popular force within the Football League for some 45 years from the 1890s onwards. No one would disagree he was dedicated to the game although few could agree where his priorities lay. A solicitor from Lancashire, he was renowned for his blunt manner. He was the chairman of Burnley, and also a leading Football League official, influential in England international matters, an FA councillor and later the League's president.

'Who does he represent?' someone once asked Sutcliffe at an international match, pointing to another FA official, a buttonholed, white haired, revered figure of the Stock Exchange.

'The Public Schools,' said Sutcliffe.

'Who do we represent?' asked his companion.

'The public houses,' came the reply. And yet Sutcliffe was a lifelong teetotaller.

The contradictions stretched to his relations with players. He was a thorn in the side of the Professional Footballers' Association for years despite having been a player once himself. He fought consistently to keep wages down and campaigned vigorously against foreign players, whom he maintained would cost English footballers their jobs. Some said he typified a generation of power barons and mill owners who wanted nothing but to profit from the game. And yet there are anecdotes that portray him as a man of honour striving to maintain the principles of sport. One Christmas Day in the 1890s he is said to have cancelled his family's festivities at short notice to make a six-hour round trip on a slow, freezing cold train to stand in as referee for a game at Darwen. When the hosting secretary came to pay him, he said he never pocketed such fees and asked that it be put in the players' box.

What was never in dispute was Sutcliffe's authority, actual or perceived, nor his ability to send out messages about what the FA, or the League, believed to be the final word. As the author John Harding noted in his official history of the PFA, *For The Good Of The Game*: 'He was a one-man propaganda machine on behalf of the League and his influential and prominent articles in popular magazines helped shape the outlook of the average fan and thus, in turn, the attitude of the general public towards the professional player.' What Sutcliffe said and wrote carried weight. So the view below, expressed on 14 January 1928 in his column for the weekly sports paper, *Topical Times*, where he was regularly billed as 'C. E. Sutcliffe, The Famous Football Legislator', can be taken as official FA policy on international matters:

Continental football has no appeal to me. It takes me all my time to study things at home and the clubs have enough on hand to keep things going here and bring about the necessary improvement in the game without wasting time by overseas worries.

I don't care a brass farthing about the improvement of the game in France, Belgium, Austria or Germany. The F.I.F.A. does not appeal to me. An organisation where such football associations as those of Uruguay and Paraguay, Brazil and Egypt, Bohemia and Pan Russia, are co-equal with England, Scotland, Wales and Ireland seems to me to be a case of magnifying the midgets. If central Europe or any other district want to govern football let them confine their powers and authority to themselves, and we can look after our own affairs.

A fortnight later, writing about the disagreements between the home nations' associations and FIFA, Sutcliffe asserted:

I can foresee nothing other than a lot of Associations who are still learning the game and with little experience of government, and of no concern to us, seeking to make laws and lay down the law, to play the game and make the laws of the game, no matter whether we approve or not. The British Associations previously severed their connection with the Federation and then joined up again and though the Continental Associations talk of a desire to respect our wishes and work amicably, they have the power to do as they like; and my experience is that inexperience with power leads us to the improper exercise of such power.

Referring to the fact that many English teams enjoyed touring overseas, and disregarding the possibility that some clubs and supporters might enjoy or benefit from overseas contacts, he added: 'I think the clubs of this country have done more to reduce their efficiency by Continental tours and picnics than many of them are aware of.' Two weeks after publication, the British associations officially withdrew from FIFA.

Such an insular mentality was being displayed at a time when football's other nascent powers in Europe were spreading their recruitment nets, and not just to neighbouring countries. Hundreds of South American players were taking their skills and knowledge from Argentina, Brazil and Uruguay to Europe, especially to Italy and Spain. The only players born in Argentina, Brazil or Uruguay to play in England before the 1970s were sons of Britons who had temporarily migrated for work. Barriers had been erected, by the League, the FA, the PFA and various government departments, to keep any others out.

Against the tide

Those foreign-born players who did get into England often paid a price, as later chapters will show. Max Seeburg, born in Germany in 1884, came to London as a child and went on to play for Tottenham. He suffered for his nationality into adulthood. Nils Middleboe, a renowned Olympian who played for Chelsea before the First World

War, was forbidden from earning from his labours. Hassan Hegazi and Tewfik Abdallah, Egyptian internationals who played either side of the First World War for Fulham and Derby respectively, found themselves torn between studies and football. Gerry Keizer, a Dutch international goalkeeper who played briefly for Arsenal in the 1930s, saw his move lambasted via one of Charles Sutcliffe's columns. It is no surprise he did not stay long. There were others who were refused even entry to the country by immigration officials.

The Second World War went some way to dismantling the barriers. English football was every bit as much in need of manpower as the rest of society. But with the FA's two-year residency rule in place and no willingness on the part of the League or FA to consider paying professional foreigners to play, the imports were restricted largely to refugees and amateurs. Or in the case of Bert Trautmann and Alec Eisentrager, German POWs who stayed on after the war to forge long and contrasting careers at Manchester City and Bristol City respectively. Needless to say, they encountered discrimination from opponents and fans, and not only those of the opposition.

Other imports who had largely successful experiences in the 1950s before eventually hankering for their country of birth were Joe Marston, an Australian lifesaver who swapped the beaches of Sydney for Preston, and George Robledo, a World Cup star for Chile in 1950. Other notable international players were denied long-term contracts due to the rules. Albert Gudmundsson of Iceland had played in Glasgow for Rangers during the war but his time at Arsenal was limited. Milan were more than happy to make him a professional. Hans Jeppson of Sweden, who like Robledo had starred in the 1950 World Cup, was another who found fame and vast fortune in Italy because the English authorities would not allow a change in amateur status.

Sources of foreign talent were largely limited to territories with colonial ties. South Africa alone provided a stream of talented players between the 1930s and the 1950s. Charlton recruited dozens of South Africans, many of whom made League appearances in that period.

Throughout the twentieth century there were also players from the West Indies and Africa who, because they were black, faced not only the travails of migration but the psychological lacerations of racial prejudice. 'Darkie' was a common nickname for any black player into the 1960s. The language of the 1950s, peppered with phrases defining what were or were not 'Negro sports', typified the age. Monkey chants were the norm, not the exception, well into the 1980s. As for the logic of the racist supporter, it stretched little beyond theorising that 'the blacks' couldn't function in cold weather and had no place in the game.

Given the laws of the land and the restrictions of the football authorities, it is little surprise how few native players, relatively, came to England from colonial territories. The appendices in this book list every player born outside the British Isles who has played at least one game in the Football League; in the case of a few countries (India being the best case in point) the majority were born of British parents working overseas either in the military or in commerce. Despite the expansionism that saw such people work overseas, Britain has always been reluctant to accommodate the indigenous from her conquered territories. Clearly they had nothing much to offer. Other nations have traditionally taken a different view, as a brief glance at the birth certificates of numerous French and Dutch footballers to have played in England would confirm. They are almost as likely to read Senegal or Surinam as Marseille or Maastricht.

Cometh the hour, cometh the Swede

But despite there never having been any prospect that an England team would be staffed primarily by players born in India or Kenya or Hong Kong, the colonisation of the domestic game by other players from overseas has been completed. Even the English international team has had a foreign manager in Sven Goran Eriksson, who led his charges to two World Cup tournaments, including that in Germany in 2006. The Swede had accepted the job six years earlier, at the first time of asking. 'As for my heart, it will become more and more English,' he said in early November 2000, presumably meaning he would become more attached to his life and work in England as opposed to more insular and suspicious.

The *Sun*, a newspaper owned by Rupert Murdoch, the man who bankrolled the multi-national Premier League, was scathing that England should appoint a foreign manager. 'What a climb-down. What an admission of decline. What a humiliation. What a terrible, pathetic, self-inflicted indictment. What an awful mess.' Jeff Powell of the *Daily Mail* waded in with: 'We've sold our birthright down the fjord to a nation of seven million skiers and hammer throwers who spend half their lives in darkness.'

In the twenty-first century, it seemed, in a multi-cultural Britain where foreign experts were managing or administrating in all walks of life from the London Underground to the Stock Exchange to Marks & Spencer to the Royal Ballet, it was still too much to expect wholehearted approval of a foreigner in charge of an England football team. Sushi had become a supermarket staple and Cuba a common destination for holidays. Britain's champion rowers were coached by a German, England's cricketers by a man from Zimbabwe and the head of the Lawn Tennis Association was French. But a foreigner in charge of the English football team? Perish the thought.

'Bobby Robson was persecuted for his white hair, Glenn Hoddle for his beliefs, Terry Venables for his business dealings, and Graham Taylor for just about everything. Welcome to the world's toughest job, Svennis,' said the Swedish newspaper, *Aftonbladet*. With this Eriksson set out on his own voyage of discovery, and ultimately bitter disappointment at the 2006 World Cup, another footballing foreigner in England's long, long line.

1

PIONEERS AGAINST THE TIDE

THE LONGEST MATCH report in *The Times* on Monday 10 September 1888 made no reference to any of the teams in the new Football League, which had kicked off two days earlier. Instead, its small section on football was topped by news from Glasgow of an international touring side. One of the players involved, born and raised in Canada, later became the first foreign player in the League.

The Times' front page from the morning of the game provides a snapshot of the era. Sport is nowhere. Social announcements, personal ads and miscellany take priority. 'A Lady' advertises that she would 'be glad to travel abroad. Has spent two years in Italy. Expenses only. Highest references.' There are plenty of distractions for the hoi polloi, including an afternoon at Alexandra Palace to witness Professor Baldwin's 1000ft jump from the clouds at 5.30 p.m. 'The Press of Great Britain, the Continent and America unite in describing this feat as the most remarkable of this or any past century. One shilling.'

This was the England of Queen Victoria, in her 52nd year on the throne. London, a sprawl of seven million people, lay at the heart of a burgeoning empire. And the 'Latest Intelligence' in *The Times* dedicated as much space to news from overseas as it did to events at home. The 'Sporting Intelligence' section on 8 September was short and dealt solely with horse racing and cricket. The previous day, Dr W. G. Grace had opened the batting for Lord Londesborough's Eleven against the Australians at the Scarborough Festival. 'Extraordinary cricket has been a frequent occurrence this season,' the report said. 'However, yesterday's play must certainly rank among the most remarkable events of the summer. In the Colonial innings, 90 went up with only two wickets down; yet the whole side was out for 96 . . .'

But the first round of matches to be played in the new Football League were not mentioned at all. The competition was untried and untested. No impartial observer would have had any idea that the new structure, retaining the same fundamental shape, would evolve to such an extent over the next 100 years that its cast of players would one day infiltrate all sections of most newspapers. And while football had grown in popularity since the widespread adoption of the Saturday half-day holiday, the League in 1888 was the preserve of a northern clique, and not necessarily an attractive one. Not so long ago, football had been just a game. Now, in the minds of gentlemen amateurs, it was becoming slightly vulgar.

Until 1888, football clubs had largely relied on local tournaments and friendly matches for their income, the exception being ties in the FA Cup, which had steadily grown in popularity since the inaugural tournament in 1871–72. The legalisation of professionalism came on 20 July 1885 after 18 months of bitter arguments between the largely amateur south and the predominantly reformist north. This paved the way for the formation of the League, which would guarantee the major fixtures necessary to pay the players. Thus when William McGregor, an Aston Villa committee member, sent a letter floating the idea to a select band of clubs in March 1888, the response was positive.

The number of free weekends in the season dictated that membership be limited to 12 clubs. Six were selected from Lancashire and six from the Midlands. Thus Accrington, Blackburn Rovers, Bolton Wanderers, Burnley, Everton, Preston North End, Aston Villa, Derby County, Notts County, Stoke, West Bromwich Albion and Wolverhampton Wanderers became the founder members of the Football League. From being a game played solely for fitness and recreation by amateurs, and dominated by Oxbridge gentlemen of the south, its power base had shifted to the industrial north.

It was into such a footballing landscape that Walter Wells Bowman, born in Ontario in August 1870, first set foot in Britain in August 1888, as a forward in the Canadian side. Primarily a right-sided player, he was good enough to represent his country and is recorded playing internationally, including against the United States in East Newark, New Jersey, on 25 November 1886. The US beat Canada 3–2. Bowman had just turned 16.

By 8 September 1888, Bowman's Canadians had already played four games on their tour, all in Ireland. The first, on 1 September, was against County Antrim. The visitors won 6–2. The result filtered back across the Atlantic at the same time as reports of the third in a series of gruesome murders in London's Whitechapel district.

By the time the Canadians began their fifth tour fixture, in Glasgow on 8 September, Jack the Ripper had struck again. *The Times*, on the Monday, carried lengthy reports of the savage dismemberment of the latest victim, Annie Chapman, a prostitute. The 'Sporting Intelligence' was dominated again by horse racing and cricket (another 'startling' collapse for the Australians) but there was also lawn tennis, with news of the annual tournament at Devonshire Park, Eastbourne. Finally, there was football.

The first League matches were there, as single-sentence reports, mixed together with other football games of the day, from both the rugby and association codes. The report of the first League meeting between two of the Midlands' major teams read: 'Aston Villa v Wolverhampton Wanderers – played on the ground of the latter at Wolverhampton and ended in a tie, with a goal to each side.' This was listed above York v Hull – 'played under Rugby Union rules at York. Hull won by a goal and a try to a try' – which in turn was listed higher than West Bromwich Albion v Stoke: 'The winners of the National Cup visited Stoke and gained a victory over the home side by two goals to none.' The leading item in the section, consisting of the fixture in capital letters plus three whole sentences, was dedicated to the touring internationals:

THE CANADIANS v GLASGOW RANGERS – Having played four matches at Belfast, three of which they won, the Canadians on Saturday engaged in a contest with the powerful Scotch club, the Glasgow Rangers, at Ibrox Park. After some spirited play the result was a tie match, each side kicking a goal. The Canadians continue their tour with a match at Aberdeen today.

In Scotland, the game was discussed in two lengthy articles in the Monday edition of the *Glasgow Herald*. One writer, no doubt mindful of the start of the English League, a competition that would lure the best Scots south, noted that 'our national pastime, instead of being on the wane, as some captious critics would have it, is in as flourishing a condition as ever.' There had been 'considerable misgiving' before the match whether the tourists would have anything to show. But they secured their draw 'after displaying form which was admitted on all hands to have far exceeded expectations. They play the game as it should be played, in a true, gentlemanly spirit, and in every respect they will prove themselves foemen worthy of the steel of any organization.'

And so, tentatively, the concept that alien footballers might actually be able to play football began to evolve. As *The Globe*'s pseudonymous tour reporter, The Parson, wrote after the game with Rangers: 'The eyes of all the football world are on us – we feel it and our chests protrude about 2½ inches accordingly . . . The idea that Canada can produce something in the way of football worth going to see is growing gradually on the mind of the canny Scotchman.'

As Bowman and co. progressed south, so illusions were shattered about their talents and countenance alike. After the Canadians beat Lincoln City 3–1 on 29 September, The Parson wrote:

> Some queer ideas have been dispelled as to the colour, language and manners of the inhabitants of Canada as shown by its representatives on the football team. In this old fashioned city of Lincoln, one of the ministers told the secretary of the city club that he was going to see these blacks play football. On being told this it was suggested that we blacken our faces for the first half-time then come out from the dressing room like the Nigger boy that used Pears' soap. Everywhere we are called Yankees and told that we speak through our noses. What a sad blow to the swell members of the party to be told that they speak with a down-east Yankee twang! And [that despite] trying to acquire the English accent, not to mention the frequent use of that peculiarly English word, 'jolly'. . .

In Nottingham, at the start of October, the tourists took a break from the delights of the famous Goose Fair – 'menageries and side shows; shows where fat women, skeletons and "real" American cowboys could be seen, all for the small sum of a penny. Fakirs and thieves of all kinds were in abundance' – to head to the Trent Bridge grounds and face the Notts County team. They lost 2–0 but not without heart. Then at Newton Heath – who would later become Manchester United – the Canadians won 2–0, with Bowman on the score sheet. The game was watched by 7000 spectators and the post-match banquet was hosted by a knight called Ferguson, Sir James to be precise, the Political Secretary at the Foreign Office.

Other opponents came from both sides of the amateur–professional divide, from Blackburn Rovers to Oxford University, from Aston Villa and West Bromwich to the Old Carthusians, concluding, on 31 October 1888, with a 1–0 defeat to the Swifts at the Kennington Oval, with the Prince of Wales in the crowd. After 23 matches in two months, the visitors had won nine, lost nine and drawn five. And as observers even in the heartland of the League acknowledged, they had given a decent account of themselves. 'Before the Dominion team came over their chances against our best English teams appeared rather remote,' the *Blackburn Telegraph* reported. 'But the visitors have given ample proof that they know how to play clever and scientific football out in Canada . . . There is an impression abroad that the Canadians are merely imported Scotchmen but that is a fallacy for we are able to state positively that every man in the team was born in Canada.'

Historic first

Despite the success of the tour, Bowman's League debut did not come quickly. *The Globe* reported that he and two team-mates, Kranz and Brubacher, headed next to 'the Fatherland'. All their roots were in mainland Europe. Bowman was the son of Daniel and Wilhelmina, and was known as a child as Walther. Genealogical research suggests that his family originated in Thun in Switzerland in the seventeenth century, and that their original surname was Bauman. Walter's ancestors moved from Thun to Pennsylvania, and later, as part of the Mennonite emigration, to Ontario. In Walter's absence, FC Thun took a long time to make an international impact. It was only in 2005–06 that they defied their minnow status to reach the Champions League group stages.

After Bowman's 1888 sojourn in the Fatherland he went back to Canada, but returned to England on a second tour in 1891. After this voyage he signed for Accrington, and it was for Accrington, on 23 January 1892, that he first played – and scored – in a League match as his side beat West Bromwich Albion 4–2. An alien player, born and raised to adulthood in a country so far removed from Britain that some people were unaware what colour its inhabitants were, let alone that they played international football, had started the process of reverse colonisation.

Bowman's time with Accrington was brief. He played five games and scored three goals at the tail end of the 1891–92 season. By the start of the next season he had joined Ardwick, and scored on his debut on 18 February 1893, in a 3–1 win over Crewe. Although Ardwick were later forced into bankruptcy, Bowman remained with the club as they re-emerged in 1894 as Manchester City. In seven years, he played play 47 League games for them.

Among Bowman's most notable games was Ardwick's record defeat, 10–2 at Small Heath – later Birmingham City – on 17 March 1894. There was also an 11–3 win, then a record for Manchester City, against Lincoln City on 23 March 1895. By that time Bowman was playing alongside the legendary outside-right, Wales's 'Wizard of the Wing', Billy Meredith. And towards the end of his time at City, the club signed Jimmy Ross, previously with Burnley and Liverpool but best remembered as a member of the Preston North End 'Invincibles' who won the first ever League and FA Cup Double in 1888–89 without losing a match.

To keep such company, Bowman was evidently a decent player. He was also versatile. Records even show him turning out as a goalkeeper, in an emergency capacity, against Newton Heath in a reserve match in November 1898. The result was 1–1. It was one of his last appearances in English football.

Little is known about Bowman's life away from football, nor what work he undertook outside the game. It is known, however, that he eventually returned across the Atlantic and settled in America. He was last heard of in Butte, a copper mining city in western Montana. Entries in a residents' directory for his most probable neighbourhood during the period throw up two possible theories. One shows a Walter Bowman, a chef, married to a woman called Dixie. Given Bowman's advancing years, he would probably have retired by then. Another shows a widowed teacher, Marie Bowman, whose deceased husband had been called Walter.

Captain of history

While the final resting place of Walter Bowman is uncertain, it is known where another significant overseas-born player, Edward Hagarty Parry, is buried. He never played League football – his career came too early for that – but his place in English footballing history warrants a mention.

Like Bowman, Parry was born in Canada, in Toronto on 24 April 1855. The son of Edward St John Parry and Lucy Susanna Parry (née Hagarty), he was baptised in St James' Cathedral in Toronto on 10 June 1855. His grandfather, Thomas Parry, a former missionary, once served as the Bishop of Antigua, typifying the nomadic lifestyle of the era's travelling classes.

Unlike Bowman, Parry left Canada with his family when he was young and moved to England. A fine scholar and sportsman, he attended Charterhouse School and later Oxford University, where he was formally admitted on 17 October 1874. He obtained second-class honours in Classical Moderations in 1876 and third-class honours in Modern History in 1878. In between, he played for Oxford University in the 1877 FA Cup final as they lost 2–1 to the prolific winners, Wanderers.

Parry, who played at inside left, was a fast dribbler with a fair shot. He went on to play three times for England but it was in the 1881 FA Cup final, when the Old Carthusians beat the Old Etonians 3–0, that he secured an historic first. The significance of Parry's role is clearly marked, both in the London publication *Bell's Life*, on the morning of the game, 9 April 1881, and in the match report in *The Times* on the following Monday. Both list the teams and identify Parry as the captain. So it was, more than 100 years before Eric Cantona was widely claimed to be the first foreign-born captain of an FA Cup-winning side, that Edward Parry actually became the first overseas-born player to achieve the feat.

Parry was later a teacher, becoming a headmaster in Slough between 1892 and retiring in 1918. He died on 19 July 1931 in West Bridgford, Nottingham, aged 76. His funeral was held at Plumtree, a few miles outside the city, and he was buried there, in the village churchyard, where he remains today, alongside his wife, Amelie Marthe.

Opening the door

It took three seasons from the League's inception for Bowman to take his bow as the first foreigner, but overseas-born players became more common as the nineteenth century drew to a close. James Dalton, a team-mate of Bowman's in Canada's 1891 touring side, stayed on in

England and eventually signed for Sunderland. The extent of his career was a few League games in the 1893–94 season. As such, he was an early example of a transient visitor who either didn't make the grade or decided England wasn't for him.

The 1893–94 season also saw the League debut of Arthur Wharton from Ghana. Thanks to a detailed biography, *The First Black Footballer* by Phil Vasili, we know much about his triumphs, troubles and ultimately depressing end, although the title of that book no longer strictly applies.

The first black footballer now commonly accepted to have played for a League club in Britain was Andrew Watson, a Guyana-born warehouseman. He started playing in Glasgow in 1874 – pre-dating Wharton's football career by about a decade – and later went on to play for the famous Queen's Park club. He also represented Scotland three times. But it was only in recent times that curators at the Scottish Football Museum at Hampden Park discovered nineteenth-century references to Watson as a 'coloured gentleman'. 'For years, I had looked at our pictures of Watson in his Queen's Park and Scotland strips but never had the facts to back up the evidence of my own eyes,' Ged O'Brien, the museum's director, said.

The census of 1881 shows Watson living in Govan, the working-class shipbuilding district of Glasgow that later produced Sir Alex Ferguson. There is no record of why or when Watson came to Britain but his birth date on the census is given as 1857 and the place as Georgetown, Guyana, which was then a British colony. Watson was therefore, as far as has been established, not only the first black player but the first foreign-born player of note anywhere in Britain. But despite records showing he also ventured south of the border, he never played in the English Football League. Indeed he would have been ending his career as it started.

Keeping up appearances

The same was not true of Arthur Wharton, born in 1865 in Accra (then in the Gold Coast), the son of the Rev. Henry Wharton, a Wesleyan Methodist missionary from Grenada. Arthur's paternal grandfather was a Scottish merchant. Arthur's mother, Annie, also had Scottish ancestry, being the daughter of another Scottish trader, John Grant, and Ama Egyiriba, a Fante royal.

Wharton's middle-class background meant he had the benefit of a good education. Some of it came in London in the late 1870s, and then, after time back in Ghana, at two missionary schools, in Cannock and Darlington, where he studied to become a missionary teacher. He was a remarkable all-round athlete, running and boxing particularly well, who came to prominence as a sprinter in the 1880s, winning the national sprint title at Stamford Bridge in 1886 in a time of 10 seconds flat. He would have been deemed the fastest man in the world if official international records had been kept at the time. Speed was evidently Wharton's forte, but all his football was played in goal. He made his League debut for Rotherham in the 1893–94 season, playing for them 19 times before stints at Sheffield United, Rotherham (again) and non-League Ashton North End. He returned briefly to the League with Stockport County in 1901–02.

One of Wharton's legacies was the spirit of entertainment he brought to football. He was eccentric, and known to hang from the crossbar to catch the ball with his feet. He was a fine puncher – as any good boxer would be – although opponents' heads were as likely as the ball to feel the weight. There are also recorded incidents of him lying on the goal line during quiet spells only to jump up at the last moment to foil an approaching attacker. But while such buoyancy of spirit gave him and his supporters some good times, his essential 'otherness' – his phenomenal talents as well as his origins – worked against him. Black people were not supposed to excel, let alone enjoy doing so.

Wharton's private life was also complicated. He fathered one, possibly two, children by Martha, the sister of his wife, Emma Lister. In later life, he became a landlord and a heavy drinker, and his sporting achievements were rapidly consigned to history. He spent some of the remains of his working life as a haulage hand at Yorkshire Main Colliery, Edlington, and died, aged 65, after a lengthy illness, on 12 December 1930. Two causes of death were noted on his death certificate, syphilis and epithelioma (a form of skin cancer). He was buried in a municipal cemetery in the local pit village. Only in 1997, after a memorial campaign was launched by the 'Football Unites, Racism Divides' campaign, was a headstone provided. The largest single donation came from the Professional Footballers' Association.

Success and skulduggery

Around the turn of the century came the League debuts of various other players who, like Wharton, were 'firsts' from their countries of birth. Cornelius Hogan, the first player from Malta, joined New Brighton Tower in 1899. Wilfred Waller, a goalkeeper, was the first South African to join the League when he played for Bolton from 1899.

The second South African, Alec Bell, had more of an impact. Born in Cape Town in 1882 of Scottish ancestry – which later earned him a Scotland call-up – he played 278 League games for Manchester United from 1902 onwards. He was part of the first United team to win the League, in 1907–08, and also won the inaugural Charity Shield in 1908, the FA Cup in 1909, and a second League title in 1911. The last of those triumphs was a fitting way for United to mark the end of a first season in their new home, Old Trafford. The following year the League was won by Blackburn Rovers, for whom Bell played briefly before ending his career as the most successful foreign-born player of the era. Not long after Bell left, United signed George 'Cocky' Hunter, one of 20 Indian-born players to feature in the League before the Second World War. Needless to say, none of them were Indian.

Among the other 'firsts' of the era was John Cuffe, born in Sydney in 1880. He was the first Australian in the League, a full-back who had a lengthy career at Glossop from 1905. He also played cricket for Worcestershire. Billy Andrews, born in Kansas City in 1886, was the first League player born in the USA, although he had Irish roots and was capped by Ireland.

Another early player with connections to America was Tom Wilcox, the only League player known to have been born at sea. This son of a sea captain entered the world on board the four-masted *Grassendale* en route to America in 1879. His ability as an athlete became apparent across the Atlantic, where he reportedly excelled at punchball. He made his League debut for Blackpool in 1906–07. He was a non-playing member of Manchester United's first championship-winning squad in 1907–08 and played for them twice the following season. After serving in the First World War, he ran a tobacconist's shop in Preston before retiring to Blackpool, where he died in 1962.

Most of the earliest foreign-born players – Wharton excepted – faced few, if any, problems with prejudice. For all the distance they had travelled they were white, they spoke English and they could mostly claim links to Britain or her Empire. This was not true of the first League player from Continental Europe, Max Seeburg.

Going Continental

Seeburg was born in Leipzig, Germany, in 1884, and moved to London as a boy. Yet his country of birth would affect him throughout his life. His father, Franck, arrived in England in the late 1880s to work as a furrier at a shop within sight of Tower Bridge. The family settled in Tottenham, where young Max soon showed talent on the pitch. Despite his father's disapproval of a career in the game – he felt his son, an apprentice carpenter, would be better served by a 'proper' trade – Max began playing for local side Cheshunt. Later he moved to Chelsea, then Tottenham, where he made his League debut in 1908–09. His other clubs in a nomadic career included Leyton, Burnley, Grimsby and Reading, who were then in the Southern League.

Seeburg's daughter, Margaret, was born in 1923, some 10 years after he hung up his boots to manage a pub. Yet in her eighties she could still recall with clarity her father's stories of his time in the game. Grimsby had been a special place, she recalled. 'My parents weren't far from the sea, so they could get in the water and strengthen their legs. There was none of these gymnasiums in those days.' And settling in Reading after moving around the country for years had been a source of relief to her mother, Ellen. 'She was quite delighted when they eventually came back to stay. She wasn't enthralled by the life, moving from town to town, finding somewhere new to live all the time.'

The first repercussions for Seeburg of his birthplace came shortly after the start of the Great War. 'Father had assumed that he and his brother, Franck Junior, had been naturalised but they hadn't,' Margaret recalled. 'Franck was already fighting for Britain in France when they came and took Dad away. He said to mother "I've got to go" and he was taken to the POW internment camp in Newbury. The police in Reading knew him well and he was well liked so they sorted it all out quickly. He only stayed there a week before being released.'

But the damage had already been done. Despite his good relations with his employers and neighbours, the week he spent in Newbury cost him his job. 'They lost the pub and everything,' said Margaret. 'Tipped out, because my father had been born in Germany. Mother was absolutely shattered. Because of this blessed business with the war my parents spoke very little of the past. They blocked it out, the fact he was born a German.'

Some 20 years later, in 1939, Margaret applied for her first job, at Berkshire County Council. 'I remember going to the post box with my application one evening. The next day, the very day it arrived, there was a policeman on the doorstep asking for Father's naturalisation papers.'

Seeburg, who died in 1972, owned a succession of Reading pubs including the one in Kings Road where Margaret was born. 'I used to go with him in the old days to watch Reading. He was always there and I took an interest, when football was football. I wouldn't go now. In those days you mixed with the people you saw playing.'

Flair from afar

Arguably the most flamboyant import of the pre-1915 period was Hassan Hegazi. Born in Kremlah, on the east side of the Nile delta, in September 1891, he was the spoilt son of a wealthy rural aristocrat, Mohammed Bey Hegazi. As a member of National Sporting Club, he spent his mid-teenage years competing against teams drawn from the British army bases and government offices stationed in the Middle East.

He arrived in London in the summer of 1911 to study engineering at University College and joined Dulwich Hamlet FC as a forward. His approach to the game was a revelation. Central attacking players at the time were, typically, burly individuals who hung around the goal. Finesse was an affliction. Bundled conversions were the norm. Hegazi was different, agile and quick. He was a sprinter, playmaker and dribbler. His ball control was superb, his passing second to none. True, he had an inclination, on occasion, to wander around and indulge his gifts. He would have been known perhaps, in later parlance, as 'a luxury player', the kind who would seemingly be doing nothing until a shimmy, a flick and a shot ended with a bulge in the net. Hegazi ran the show and his goals were sweet and plentiful. 'The way he makes openings for himself and his wing men shows much brain work,' said the *South London Press* in September 1911. 'He should make quite a name for himself.'

He did, and it wasn't long before Fulham of the Second Division saw his potential. Their manager, Phil Kelso, asked him to play in a League match against Stockport County. The date could not have been more auspicious: 11 November 1911. Hegazi opened the scoring in a 3–1 win and was asked to play at Leeds the following week. The authorities at Dulwich, not best pleased at potentially losing their man, went to see Hegazi at his lodgings in Gower Street, Bloomsbury.

'I was in a difficulty,' Hegazi told the local newspapers. 'For I wanted to play very much in League football, and at the same time I did not want to leave Dulwich Hamlet who have been very good to me. So I have decided to play for the Hamlet. I am sorry if Fulham are disappointed.' Pa Wilson, the esteemed Dulwich manager, said that Hegazi's decision made him 'as honourable a man as ever stepped onto a football field'. And with that his League career was over.

Two days after his solitary outing for Fulham, a report on the match, with a photograph of the player and a few biographical details, appeared in the *Athletic News* under the headline 'An Egyptian Centre Forward'. His goals were lauded as 'brilliant'. The following week, the same publication's resident bard penned a long poem in dedication. It began:

> Hussein Hegazi, by birth an Egyptian,
> Djinn of the leather and wizard of wiles,
> Do not imagine, though, by this description,
> That he is fictive, and not in these isles . . .

Fulham's attempt to secure Hegazi's full-time services provoked an intense debate about the poaching of players. Although, in all the furore, his nationality was not an issue, it was only a matter of time before players such as Hegazi provoked not awe but suspicion.

Hegazi remained with Dulwich until 1913 and returned to Egypt in the summer of 1914. Within weeks of his departure, Lord Kitchener, the Proconsul of Egypt, returned to London to take up his role as Secretary of State for War, in which he masterminded the recruitment drive with his 'Your Country Needs You!' campaign. Virtually every one of Hegazi's British male friends – students and fellow footballers – were to be involved in the Great War. Many lost their lives.

Hegazi continued his football career at home, going on to play for his country in the Olympic Games of 1920 and 1924. In 1932, at the age of 40, he hung up his boots. In his later years, when married with five children, he developed a reputation as a socialite and ladies' man on account of his affairs with women such as Naima Almassreya, a prominent actress of the day. Hegazi died in Egypt in 1958 and has a street named after him, Sharia Hassan Hegazi, in the Garden City area of Cairo.

A first Great Dane

Two other players with international pedigrees also played in the League before the First World War. Isaac Van Den Eynden of Belgium played for Clapton Orient in the 1913–14 season. And Nils Middleboe, of Denmark, was attached to the Casuals and Newcastle before playing League football for Chelsea. He played 41 times for them from the 1913–14 season onwards. Photographs from the time show an awkward, apparently shy man with long skinny arms and a concave chest. But as his lengthy international career and authorship of coaching manuals showed, he lacked nothing in skill or mental application. He came to the attention of English clubs through his involvement in the Olympic tournaments of 1908 and 1912. At the first, in London, the hosts prevailed, beating Denmark – and Middleboe – in the final. By the 1912 Games in Stockholm he was captain, playing in the final as Denmark lost again to England.

The resumption of organised football after the Great War saw more 'firsts' but most were by dint of colonial connections. Jack Butler, born in Sri Lanka, had a lengthy career with Arsenal. Frank Burton, born in Mexico, where his father had been working, played for West Ham. Francisco Enrique Gonzales (aka Frank Peed), born in Argentina of a native father and Wolverhampton mother, played for a succession of clubs in the 1930s. And Edward Laxton, born in Brazil, the son of a British engineer, made his League debut in 1920–21 for Norwich City. The next Brazilian-born player to arrive in England was Mirandinha at Newcastle in the late 1980s.

A Cantona for the 1920s

An exception among these 'colonial link' players of the time was the French international, Eugene Langenove. Exhaustive non-League records are lacking, so it is impossible to chart the movement of every player at every level around the world. But certainly numbers of Englishmen crossed the Channel to play professionally in France early in the twentieth century while Frenchmen played in England below national level around the same time. Goalkeeper Georges Crozier at Fulham, before their elevation from the Southern League, was among them. But it was Langenove, one of the star players of the French giants Olympique de Paris from 1919 to 1921, who was the first Frenchman in the Football League. Like one of his most eminent successors, Eric Cantona, he was a man with a soupçon of attitude. A right-sided defender, he won two caps for France in 1921. In that eventful year he also played in the French FA Cup final against Olympique's Paris rivals, Red Star, in the Stade Pershing. Then, in July, he was suspended for three years for kicking another player in the eye during a friendly match.

Undeterred by his sentence, he had a one-game trial with Le Havre in 1922, in the hope of an amnesty that never came. Banned from playing in France, he made his way across the Channel to find another employer. Walsall, then a Third Division (North) side in the tough industrial West Midlands, took him on near the start of the 1922–23 season. His debut came on 7 October 1922 against Crewe in a 1–1 draw, in which he played at inside-right. Possibly the position did not suit him, and after he played there again the following week against Rochdale, he was dropped.

He returned to France, where another year was added to his suspension for having played professionally in England. He eventually resumed his career in 1925–26 with Red Star. Not a chap to learn his lessons quickly, he kicked another opponent during a friendly in March 1926. Red Star expelled him. But as football history has shown time and again, bad behaviour is not necessarily a hindrance to a player as long as he does the business on the pitch. Langenove went on to play for SC Draguignan, AS Cannes and Nice before ending his career with a string of minor clubs around the suburbs of Paris. He left behind no record of speeches about seagulls, trawlers or sardines.

The Pyramid effect

Throughout the 1920s, the trickle of colonial-born players from South Africa and India continued, and the second Egyptian arrived. Tewfik Abdallah was the last international from his country to play for a League club before Ahmed Hossam (aka Mido) arrived at Tottenham 85 years later.

Born in Cairo in 1897, Tewfik moved to Derby, aged 23, in 1920. His main aim in migrating was to find experience in the engineering trade but his arrival caused a stir. The front cover of the *Topical Times* in November 1920 featured a photograph of him grinning as he ran with a ball. This cheery-looking chap was set against a line-drawn backdrop complete with a pyramid, the Sphinx and palm trees. 'Derby's Dusky Dribbler' said the billing. There was a brief mention of him inside, but only in passing in a news item about the 'new fashion' of 'going far afield for players'.

Sheffield United had just secured the services of a young Canadian outside-left, Jack Coule, who had resigned from his job as a Mountie to travel to the steel city. Clearly, the appreciation of Canadian football had grown since Walter Bowman's day even though Coule ultimately failed to make the grade.

Tewfik had what it took, although it would be later, in America, that he was most appreciated. An inside-right of no little technical ability, he made his Derby debut at home to Manchester City in October 1920. He was the subject of numerous jibes about his quirky style and trademark chewing – which earned him the nickname 'Toothpick' – not to mention his struggles with the language. One probably apocryphal tale of his first game saw him take to the field asking: 'Where's me camel?' Mick Hamill, it transpired, was an Irishman making his City debut. Tewfik had been assigned to mark him.

Derby won the game 3–0, with Tewfik scoring. It was first of 15 appearances for the club but his first and only goal. Derby were relegated and he was sent on loan to Cowdenbeath in the Scottish Second Division. The fans took him to their hearts, nicknaming him 'Abe'. According to local legend, he won the ultimate accolade when a prominent local miner named his greyhound 'Abe' in his honour. Hampered by injury, he lasted a season before moving to non-League football in Wales with Bridgend Town. His last League club in Britain was Hartlepools.

The American dream

In the summer of 1924, Tewfik left England for the American Soccer League, which was causing quite a stir in Britain. The British economic downturn in the early 1920s had already seen waves of workers head west to America. Now the offer of good prospects and hard cash was enticing 'freebooter' footballers to join the rush. 'Is American Football Menace Real?' asked one typically hysterical headline of the day. The threat of a talent drain was regarded seriously because the United States was not bound by any international agreements on transfers.

One high-profile migrant was the aforementioned Mick Hamill of Manchester City and Ireland. Tewfik and Hamill both went to clubs in New England, the Providence Clamdiggers and Boston Wonder Workers respectively. Tewfik played in the ASL until 1928, first with the Clamdiggers, where he scored a goal every other game, then the Fall River Marksmen, Hartford Americans and New York Nationals. He also played for the ASL all-star team against Nacional of Montevideo at the Polo Grounds in New York on 2 April 1927. Tewfik was later a coach himself, in the US, although it is thought he finally left America after becoming disaffected at the racial divide. Being black, he was often not allowed to stay in 'white hotels' with his team. It is thought he returned to Egypt, although the Football Association there has been unable to confirm what became of him.

Tewfik's time in Britain, and his subsequent move to America, were illustrative of the growing international market in players. Even though the United States had passed an Immigration Act in 1921, the first real attempt to ration the number of people coming in, football was different. The British were not only about to intensify the rules governing players going out but also to tighten the regulations to stop foreigners coming in.

Banning foreigners

The pivotal event that spurred this action was an attempt by Arsenal to sign an Austrian goalkeeper, Rudy Hiden, in summer 1930. The Gunners' manager, Herbert Chapman, and Hiden's club, Vienna, had agreed a fee and a two-month contract was prepared that included the option for an extension. Arsenal had even found Hiden suitable supplementary work as a chef. His boat duly arrived in England, where he was promptly refused admission to Britain. Hiden's was not a unique case. The Ministry of Labour said allowing such people into the country would restrict employment opportunities for Britons.

Signs that the authorities would not back Hiden's cause had first come, resoundingly, in the *Topical Times* column of the game's most vocal administrator, Charles Sutcliffe, earlier in August. He said that the Management Committee of the League would discuss the matter, if it arose, on the 25th of that month. Under the headline 'This Foreign Player Business', he wrote:

If and when a registration form with the accompanying memorandum of the contents of the player's agreement arrives at the league office, the Management Committee can then take such action as it thinks fit and consistent with its rules.

I hope we may be spared giving an official opinion, not because I fear anyone would shirk it but merely because I feel the idea of bringing 'foreigners' to play in league football is repulsive to the clubs, offensive to British players and a terrible confession of weakness in the management of a club.

If the report of the Arsenal's intention is accurate, I cannot see why the authorities should refuse admission to players engaged or proposed to be engaged by three other clubs and then favour the Arsenal. If such importations are allowed, where will it end? The difficulties are innumerable and if the opportunity arises I hope the Management Committee will decline to register Continental players.

Sutcliffe, and by extension the authorities, could not have made their stance clearer. Sure enough, when the Football Association's various committees met at the FA's Lancaster Gate HQ on Monday 25 August, the opinion was voiced that the Government should be encouraged to stop imports before they became common. This became official policy, as laid out in the minutes of the FA's International Selection Committee meeting of that day. Minute No. 11 was as follows:

Alien Professional Players. The Committee having considered a letter from the Minister of Labour, decided to make the following recommendation to the Council:– In reply to an enquiry of the Minister of Labour, the Council of The Football Association is not in favour of granting permits for alien players to be brought into this country for the purpose of being employed as football players and would desire a continuance of the present practice of the Minister of Labour.

The minute was submitted to the FA Council that day and the recommendation immediately adopted. Sutcliffe used his *Topical Times* column of 6 September 1930 to explain precisely how united the authorities and the government had been on the issue. 'The Football Association have sounded the death-knell of the proposal to engage alien football players,' he trumpeted. He quoted the Minister of Labour as saying: 'Why should an alien be permitted to land to keep a Britisher out of a job?' He claimed the Players' Union, which also represented coaches, was initially afraid that stopping foreign players might see retaliatory measures that would limit opportunities for British coaches abroad. And yet he said the PFA ultimately resolved: 'We don't care, keep the aliens out.'

Sutcliffe ended his piece with a double flourish. 'It may now be assumed that the Austrian will finish his chef education in another country . . . It will be a bad day for club managers when they have to cultivate team spirit in a team of players where some would not understand a word said to them.'

The matter did not finish there. Arsenal, having been thwarted in their attempt to sign Hiden, had secured the services of another foreign goalkeeper already resident in England. His name was Gerry Keizer and he became the first Dutch international at Highbury some 65 years ahead of Glenn Helder and Dennis Bergkamp in 1995. Charles Sutcliffe was almost apoplectic as he wrote his column for 13 September 1930. Not only had Arsenal already played Keizer but they had circumvented the spirit of the FA's new 'anti-professional foreigner' stance with a bizarre arrangement. Keizer, it seemed, had been offered a professional contract and accepted it. But Arsenal, knowing the authorities would refuse a work permit, had torn it up. Instead, Keizer was offered terms as an amateur and duly received a permit to play without pay.

Sutcliffe wrote: 'Thus we had a club of untold wealth who could well afford to get a professional [British] goalkeeper, who, in turn, would make room for another unemployed [British] professional, playing a player with an alien permit and without pay.' With barely concealed disgust, he added that he was 'British to the bone' and that if the time ever came when the country could not find British players for its teams there would be 'something seriously amiss'.

In the event, Keizer, who had a reputation for being something of a bruiser, only played 12 times for Arsenal, moving down a division to join Charlton the next season.

In the months following Hiden's non-arrival at Arsenal and Keizer's appointment, the debate intensified within the FA about what could be done to stop foreign players. The Government was on side but that would not necessarily be permanent. In any case, the authorities wanted control of their own affairs. By December 1930, the FA Council was considering a proposal that would ban non-British players from playing in FA Cup matches. This could effectively be achieved by introducing a two-year residency rule to deter impulse buying. But by the time the FA came to formalise this notion, in June 1931, the game's authorities took more draconian action still. They changed the Rules of the Association. The following amendment to the rules concerning the eligibility of players was formally approved by the FA Council at Lancaster Gate on 1 June that year: 'A professional player who is not a British-born subject is not eligible to take part in any competition under the jurisdiction of this Association unless he possesses a two years' residential qualification within the jurisdiction of the Association.'

To much of the world, the door was closed. Between 1931 and 1939, only players with colonial ties came in. Alf Charles was notable as the first player from Trinidad. A magician by trade, he played League football for Southampton. The biggest single country of origin for imports to England was South Africa, with 24 League players arriving between the wars. Some were sons of British servicemen. Others were born and raised to adulthood in South Africa and were either spotted by British teams, many of whom toured that popular location, or came to Britain on tours themselves and stayed on.

Liverpool's Arthur Riley, a goalkeeper, and Gordon Hodgson, who would become one of Anfield's greatest ever goalscorers, arrived by the latter route after a Springbok tour to the UK and Europe in late 1924. Hodgson scored 232 goals for Liverpool in 359 League games, all in the First Division, an astonishing ratio in any era. It was no surprise he was capped by England. He also played cricket for Lancashire and football for Aston Villa and Leeds before turning his hand to management with Port Vale. After taking charge in 1946, he oversaw the club's move to their current stadium, Vale Park, in 1950. He died the next year, aged 47.

And so these 'non-foreign' overseas players came throughout the 1930s to Liverpool, Aldershot, Fulham, Millwall, Southampton, Chesterfield and elsewhere. Umpteen destinations from few ports of origin. What a difference another war would make.

2

BACK IN BUSINESS

SOCCER kicked off after seven years in pelting rain, on slippery grounds – and with sensations in plenty. Wolves routed Arsenal 6–1, Brentford took away points from Everton. Villa lost at home to 'Boro. Bury piled up seven against Fulham. Luton trounced Sheffield Wednesday. Newport v. Southampton was postponed through floods . . .

CROWDS of close on a million saw the League games. Highest was at Chelsea – 61,461. Everton drew 55,000. Sunderland 53,000. Wolves and Villa 50,000. A Third Division match drew 25,000 to Frank Buckley's Hull City. Gates closed at Chelsea, Millwall, Swansea. Total for League matches, 847,000. Add the few smart ones who dodged the turnstiles . . .

GOALS a-plenty. Jesse Pye, Wolves' capture from Notts County, got three. So did Barnsley's Robledo.

Daily Mirror, *Monday, 2 September 1946*

A DEBUT HAT-TRICK. What a way to bid adios to the war. Seven years on from the last official League matches in England, 16 months on from VE Day and 363 days since VJ Day had marked the cessation of hostilities in the Pacific, football was back in business. On 'F Day', as the tabloids dubbed Saturday, 31 August 1946, the national game returned to its feet. And George Robledo, born in Chile, ended his first 90 minutes in the League with three goals to his exotic name.

Robledo wore the no. 9 shirt for Barnsley of the Second Division that afternoon. Their match against Nottingham Forest at Oakwell drew a crowd of 17,317. Forest scored twice, but Robledo went one better by himself in a 3–2 win. He scored another two in a 4–2 win at Sheffield Wednesday in his next game, just two days later. Two outings, five successful strikes, four points.

Robledo played 42 games that season and racked up 23 goals. Before his time as a Tyke was up, he made 114 appearances and scored 47 goals. Later, with Newcastle – 164 games, 91 goals – he scored the winner in the 1952 FA Cup final. It was his second FA Cup success in two years, in the second of six consecutive FA Cup finals that featured landmark contributions by players born overseas.

In August 1946, football in the post-war era faced exactly the same crises as society at large. Manpower was insufficient, rebuilding was the key. Many of the men walking onto pitches for the 3.15 p.m. kick-offs had never played League football before. Numerous players had been killed in the war. Others had been more fortunate, losing only the best years of their careers.

Britain was not devoid of war-time competitions, in which visiting players were often the participants, but as *The Times* noted in the countdown to 'F Day', war-time football 'served its purpose [but] was unreal and may be forgotten gracefully'. Now it was back to points and prizes; promotion, relegation, honours; the drama of the FA Cup, and all without a reservoir of youth upon which to draw. The League, resuming with the same teams in the same divisions as during the abandoned 1939–40 season, was facing the sternest test in its history.

There were signs that wider society was returning to some kind of normality, albeit after a process of re-evaluation. Comedian Charlie Chaplin was again able to make the front pages, even if it was to announce that he was throwing away his moustache, bowler hat and walking stick 'because the funny little man I always portrayed has no meaning to the present generation'. But the world at large was still distracted by post-war dilemmas.

Even popular adverts required amendments for the times, with Cadbury's taking extra space to inform consumers: 'Although milk chocolate is one of the most nourishing foods made from milk, Cadbury's are allowed only a very small proportion of the surplus summer milk allocated each year to manufacturers. This is why Cadbury's milk chocolate is in short supply. When you are lucky please save it for the children. There's a glass and a half of full-cream milk in every half pound.'

Talent from another planet

Football was on the verge, through necessity, accident and circumstance, of its most multi-national era to date. The rules and regulations designed to keep foreigners out would remain in place – and indeed be strengthened yet again – but the League soon featured 'firsts' from Bermuda, Jamaica, Hungary, Italy, Iceland, Latvia, Norway, Poland, Sweden, Spain and Switzerland. Some of this new wave were refugees, others civil servants, students, servicemen or businessmen. Some were professionals, others amateur. Some stayed a few games, others for decades. What George Robledo did, on 31 August 1946, was announce their arrival in emphatic fashion.

'I just thought he came from another planet, another world,' recalled Sir Bobby Robson, a boyhood fan of Robledo. 'Thick-set, swarthy, he had a Chilean countenance, half sunburnt. Good-looking chap actually. Compact, solid player, a goalscorer. He got in with the centre-forward, he saw the crosses, he got in the box. He worked very hard, he could turn on the ball, he could play the good pass.' Robson was in attendance at Wembley, as a fan, for both Robledo's FA Cup successes in 1951 and 1952. 'He was a bit like Alan Shearer, a good solid body, good legs, strong thighs, he got up and down and he played in that attacking half. He could turn on the ball and he was adept in the air.'

Robledo's mother, Elsie, was born and raised in South Yorkshire. Aged 18, she travelled to Argentina to work as a governess to the children of an English mine manager. When her employer was transferred to northern Chile, she moved too. It was there, in Iquique, that she met Aristides Robledo, an accountant, and had three children. George was born in 1926 and Ted, who also played for Barnsley and Newcastle, in 1928. Not long after the arrival of a third son, Walter, in 1932, Elsie decided to return to England. Aristides stayed behind.

Elsie and the boys settled in West Melton, Yorkshire, where George, having developed into a fine athlete, played amateur football for Huddersfield and Barnsley in the war. He joined the latter professionally in April 1943, the month of his 17th birthday. Three years later he made the national papers with his debut League hat-trick. He went on to become a huge favourite with the fans, even inspiring a local poet to immortalise him in verse.

Relentlessly he surges on; Intrepid, fearless, cool,
The foeman cannot stem the tide; Engulfed in this whirlpool.

With desperation in their hearts; They give a cry of pain,
Then – crash – the ball is in the net; Robledo strikes again.

Such prowess in front of goal was bound to attract attention. In January 1949, Newcastle United tempted George to the north-east. They paid £26,500, George making a condition that Ted move too.

George, or 'Pancho' to his team-mates, formed an attacking partnership with Jackie Milburn that was to become the country's most feared. By the end of the 1949–50 season, his form earned a call-up to the Chilean national side for the 1950 World Cup in Brazil. He played in all Chile's group matches, including a 2–0 defeat to an England team featuring Alf Ramsey, Tom Finney, Stan Mortensen and Wilf Mannion. In Chile's third and last match of the tournament, George opened the scoring in a 5–2 win over the USA, who three days earlier had pulled off one of the greatest ever World Cup shocks by beating England 1–0. Returning as a hero in both Chile and England, George helped Newcastle to fourth place in the League in 1950–51.

The season was crowned when Newcastle beat Blackpool – a side boasting Stanley Matthews and Mortensen – in the FA Cup final. Milburn scored both goals, George providing the crucial opener five minutes into the second half.

The following season Newcastle finished eighth in the League but scored more goals – 98 – than any other team. They scored another 15 in the Cup. George scored 39 in all competitions, with 33 in the League, making him the country's leading marksman. By this point, Ted was also in the Newcastle team and the brothers played together in the FA Cup final of 1952, against Arsenal.

The match was remembered for the Londoners' valiant display after being reduced to 10 men after 27 minutes by an injury to Walley Barnes, their right-back. 'We have won the cup but the glory is yours,' said Stan Seymour, the Newcastle director-manager, to the Arsenal players afterwards. But the glory was also George Robledo's, having been the man who, five minutes from time, attached himself to a cross from Bobby Mitchell and headed home the decisive goal.

In the 1952–53 season, Arsenal won the League and Newcastle finished seventh from bottom. After repeated approaches from

Chilean clubs, George and Ted joined Colo Colo of Santiago. The chance of playing in their country of birth, not to mention earning salaries that far exceeded the kind of money they could earn in wage-capped England, proved irresistible. The brothers went on to win League titles with Colo Colo and regularly played for Chile, where they were known as 'Jorge' and 'Eduardo' despite having been baptised with anglicised names.

After his playing days were over George went into coaching and later teaching. Ted returned to England for a brief spell with Notts County and later worked on oil rigs, only to die in mysterious circumstances in 1970 after going missing from a ship in the Persian Gulf. 'I heard Ted was on a banana boat,' Bobby Robson said. 'The body was never found. I think he was thrown overboard. Disappeared off the boat. Obviously murdered. That's the message I got.' No one, in fact, was ever found guilty of Ted's murder. Although the captain was charged with murder, he was acquitted.

George died in Chile of a heart attack in 1989, aged 63, never knowing what had happened to his brother. George's Chilean widow, Gladys, stayed in touch with Bobby Robson and travelled to Newcastle at the end of 2002 to unveil a plaque at St James' Park in honour of her late husband.

The Robledos made the kind of footballing contribution to the post-war years that would later be held up as the trademark of the best foreign players. Their professionalism was unquestioned, on and off the pitch. They trained well and looked after themselves as full-time athletes, not twice-weekly entertainers who could spend five nights a week in the pub. They sought new experiences, and ultimately better money, befitting their talents. George was an innovator, and was a rarity in using the 'bicycle kick'. Through their looks, style and George's flair, they compelled people to pay good money to walk through the turnstiles and watch them play, in hope of magic.

Journeymen and trailblazers

Arnold Woollard could not claim to have had quite such an effect but he won many admirers. He was the first Bermudan to play in the League – the first to play anywhere in the world professionally – after joining Northampton in 1949 on the recommendation of Bermuda's

High Commissioner. After being converted from a winger to a full-back, he moved to Peterborough. Newcastle, impressed by his displays in the giant-killing FA Cup run of 1952–53, then signed him for £4000, a record fee to a non-League club. He played only 10 times alongside the likes of the Robledos and Milburn but considered his time at St James' Park, which included the successful FA Cup run of 1955, a highlight in his career. He later gave long service to Bournemouth, where he played a part in FA Cup upsets over Wolves and Tottenham, before a second short spell with Northampton, helping them win the Third Division. He returned to Bermuda to work in a bank. In 1964, aged 33, he was a member of his country's first international side ever to play outside Bermuda. They lost to Iceland.

Newcastle did not have a monopoly on foreign players in the north-east of the 1950s. Sunderland had two South Africans, Ted Purdon and Don Kitchenbrand, and an Australian-born goalkeeper, Willie Fraser. Middlesbrough also had an overseas goalkeeper, Norman Malan from South Africa.

Another, more significant foreign-born goalkeeper at Ayresome Park was Rolando Ugolini, the first Italian to play in the League. And strictly speaking, despite having moved to Glasgow with his parents as a toddler, he *was* Italian when he played his first League match for Boro against Chelsea at the start of the 1948–49 season. He had never been naturalised – quite why, Ugolini was never certain. It may have been because his father wanted Rolando to retain that key part of his Italian heritage. Alternatively, it may have been that Ugolini senior did not feel especially predisposed to British officialdom, having been interned on the Isle of Man during the Second World War because he was Italian. 'It was only for three months,' Rolando recalled. 'Although during that time me and my mother were sent to live in an unprotected area of Glasgow where we spent every single night in a bomb shelter as Clydebank was blitzed.'

Whatever the reasons, Ugolini was officially Italian when he first played for Middlesbrough. That meant the football authorities deemed him to have broken their anti-foreigner rules. Why? Because his first major club were Celtic, who sold him to Boro in May 1948 for £7,000. Therefore, when he made his Boro debut not only was he an Italian, but he had not lived within the jurisdiction of the English FA for two years before playing a League game. And as the FA rules stated at the time, he was therefore ineligible to play in any competition within the jurisdiction of the English FA. His time in Scotland did not count.

Matters only came to a head before the third round of the FA Cup in the 1948–49 season. Possibly the protectionist FA had taken its eyes off the ball before then. Thus this 'foreigner', born in Lucca but raised almost entirely in Britain, had been allowed to slip through the net. But come the FA Cup, and no doubt a flurry of media interest in Ugolini's fine and often theatrical displays, the authorities decided to clamp down. It was clear evidence that despite the labour situation of the post-war period, the anti-foreigner stance was still well and truly in place. 'It was approaching the first Cup tie I was due to play in and the FA said that I could only play if I was British,' Ugolini said. 'They said I wasn't British, and until I was, I wouldn't be able to play.'

Middlesbrough, faced with an intransigent FA while an important Cup match loomed on 8 January 1949, did the only thing they could. 'They put me in a taxi, sent me up to the appropriate office in Linlithgow in Scotland and got me to become a naturalised British subject.' As FA Cup luck would have it – bad luck, in this case – Middlesbrough of the First Division went to Brentford of the Second Division, and lost 3–2.

Winging in from Jamaica

Most of Ugolini's time at Middlesbrough was spent in the same team as Lindy Delapenha, the first Jamaican ever to play League football and the first black player to be part of a championship-winning team, with Portsmouth in 1948–49. Born in Kingston in 1927, the young Delapenha excelled at school in a variety of sports, winning trophies at youth level in athletics, cricket and tennis. 'But football was what I liked,' he recalled. 'Academically I wasn't going to be a doctor or a lawyer so when my sports master said he thought I might make something as a player, I thought I'd give it a go. And England was the only place I could try.'

The 18-year-old's parents funded the cost of a one-way ticket, £40. It bought a berth on a ship transporting British POWs on a circuitous route home after years of captivity at the hands of the Japanese. 'Most of them had had an awful time, but they looked after me and gave me some good advice,' said Delapenha. 'I knew I wouldn't be able just to go over and start playing football straight away so the idea was to join the army, the physical training corps, spend some time playing football there and see what happened. I arrived in November 1945 in Southampton. My first night was spent in a Nissen hut made for five thousand people. I was the only one there. I hadn't really thought about the situation I'd find but it wasn't that – being in Jamaica one minute and then in this strange place, washing in freezing water the next.'

Part-time enlistment was not possible. That left two options: find a club immediately despite having no experience, or sign up full-time in the army and take his chances down that route. 'I did service for two years at a barracks in Brentford and then got posted overseas. It was a blessing in disguise. I blossomed in the heat of Egypt, played football, cricket, ran 10.1 seconds for the 100 yards. I made a bit of a name for myself. During one game against the Egyptian national side, a scout spotted me and said I might be useful to Chelsea or Portsmouth. He wrote me a letter of recommendation. When I was demobbed in 1948 I had nowhere to live but I had a friend who lived not far from Portsmouth who said I could stay with him. That's why I went to see the Portsmouth manager, Bob Jackson. I gave him the letter. He said he'd give me a trial to see what I was worth. We went to Bristol Rovers with the reserves. He signed me at half-time. He said he'd seen enough.'

That was in April 1948. In the 1948–49 season, Portsmouth, in their golden jubilee season, won the first of their back-to-back League titles, ahead of Manchester United in second place. In 1949–50, they won again, finishing level on points with Wolves but taking the League by dint of a better defensive record. The second title-winning side involved, for five games, the Swedish international forward Dan Ekner, the first man from his country in the League. He moved to England to study business at college and was only allowed to play short-term as an amateur. He went on to forge a long, lucrative professional career in France, Italy, America, Spain, Germany and The Netherlands.

Like Ekner, Delapenha only featured sporadically in Portsmouth's championship-winning seasons but he did enough to earn the chance of moving centre-stage elsewhere. He went to Middlesbrough in April 1950. Delapenha favoured the inside-right position in the forward line, but on arrival at Ayresome Park he found himself in the reserves. 'You're not playing me in the first team,' he told Middlesbrough's manager, David Jack, who didn't need to point out that he already had a decent inside-right in Wilf Mannion. Along with four other giants of the era – Stanley Matthews, Stan Mortensen, Tommy Lawton and Tom Finney – Mannion was a member of the 'Famous Five' England forward line, the best attacking line-up that England ever fielded.

'Can you play outside-right?' Jack asked Delapenha, who replied that he'd give it a go. Some go. His combination with Mannion brought the house down. Delapenha became Middlesbrough's biggest name of the mid-fifties, and their highest-paid player. In 270 games he scored 93 goals, a magnificent return for a winger.

His favourite memories revolve around games where for one reason or another he succeeded despite not being expected to do well. The notion that a man from Jamaica would struggle in snow irked him. 'When it was so cold and snowy that the lines had to be marked out in blue, I set out to be extraordinary,' he said. 'And I was. I remember one cup-tie against Derby, January 1952, which we drew at Ayresome Park and then won the replay away in four climates – frost, sun, quagmire, wind, the lot.'

He was also an asset to his team-mates, introducing skill drills and head-tennis tournaments after regular training, which was often tedious in the extreme. One of the players to benefit was a young man called Brian Clough, then progressing into the side. 'We never saw a ball from one week to another,' Delapenha recalled. 'So the head tennis especially became popular. At one stage, word got around that we were doing this and me and Brian Clough were invited to go on stage at the local Empire Theatre and do it as a routine in support of a fella who was doing a Houdini-style variety act. We did it every night for a week.' Delapenha was the only Boro player at the time who had a car, and he was enlisted to take Clough and his wife-to-be, Barbara, to buy their engagement ring in his Morris Minor.

There were also difficult times, not least the abuse he received because he was Jamaican. 'My complexion is quite light, maybe that's why I didn't get all that much,' he said. Certainly there were no problems with home supporters or team-mates, among whom he counted Clough, Ugolini and Peter Taylor – later Clough's assistant in the glory years at Derby and Nottingham Forest – among his closer friends. But it did happen, and often it came from opponents. 'You got called names. It happened a lot. Remarks about going back where you belong. But my greatest asset was to take it all, on all occasions, and then turn around and laugh straight at whoever said it. I'd smile and then say: "It's OK, I'll be on the next banana boat home." I did that over and over.'

The message soon got through that he wasn't going anywhere, except up the right wing and onto the score sheet. After Middlesbrough, Delapenha moved to Mansfield, where he played 120 games and scored 27 goals. He had a spell in non-League football, playing for a time at Burton under Peter Taylor, before returning to Jamaica in 1964 to coach a sugar estates team. 'But sugar went bad and they paid me off. They gave me a ticket to England but I didn't really fancy the weather any more.' He sold insurance for a while before carving out a new career as a commentator with the Jamaica Broadcasting Corporation.

Refugees and soldiers

Along with Delapenha, Ekner and Ugolini came a group of other 'firsts' in the post-war years. Emilio Aldecoa was the first Spaniard in the League, playing for Coventry in the 1946–47 season. He arrived in England in 1937 as one of 4000 Basque refugee children fleeing General Franco's fascism in the Spanish Civil War. He played wartime football in attack for Wolves, then moved to Coventry in 1945 as a winger. He played one season of League football before returning to Spain, where he starred for Atletico Bilbao, Real Valladolid and Barcelona, where he won two league titles. He was capped by Spain shortly after he returned there from England. Two other refugees from 1937, the Gallego brothers, Tony and José, also played League football after the war.

The first Polish players also made League debuts in 1946–47. Outside-left Eryk Kubicki and goalkeeper Edouard Wojtcazk, a former tank commander and champion ice skater, were members of the Second Polish Army Division stationed at Sand Hutton, near York, after the war. The pair impressed in a friendly game when a Polish side beat York 7–3 in October 1946. Both went on to play for

York that season. Stan Gerula, a Polish amateur international goal-keeper, made 30 League appearances for Leyton Orient around the same time. He later played for Walthamstow Avenue as they twice won the Isthmian League and earned national attention by taking Manchester United to an FA Cup replay. Two other Poles, Konrad Kapler and Adam Wislewski, had short spells with Rochdale. A third, at Northampton, was Felix Starocsik, a winger who played 50 times and scored 13 goals. He later settled in Bedford, where his son became a local golfing celebrity.

The first Icelandic player also made his League debut in 1946–47. Albert Gudmundsson, born in Reykjavik in 1923, had already played as a forward for Rangers in Scotland, where he had been studying marine biology, before he moved to Arsenal. But as with a variety of others in the era, he was only allowed to play amateur football in England. He played just twice in the First Division before seeking paid employment elsewhere. He went on to play professionally for Milan in Italy and for Nancy and Racing Club de Paris in France before an illustrious career in business, politics and football administration. He was the president of the Icelandic FA between 1968 and 1973. There is no knowing what he might have achieved had he stayed in England, but the authorities were in no mind to find out. His son, Ingi Bjorn Albertsson, who was born in 1952, might have ended up a British citizen and been in contention for honours in an adoptive country rather than in Iceland, where he became one of the most prolific strikers of the 1970s. But it was never to be, because of the effective ban on professional foreigners via the two-year residency rule.

Amateurs, so the rationale went, would only come to England if they had a primary purpose other than football. Why would they stay if they could not earn from the game, as they could elsewhere? Thus, Gudmundsson, Ekner and others plied their trades in other countries and the English game passed up chance after chance to allow the possibility of fresh ideas from outside.

Amateur dramatics

Another international player with a short League career was the defender Willi Steffen, the first Swiss in the League, with Chelsea in 1946–47. Again, he was an amateur and he stayed for just one season.

Clearly he was a player of note, appearing in the famous 'Match of the Century' at Hampden Park, Glasgow, on 10 May 1947, when the return of the British associations to FIFA was celebrated with a game between Great Britain and a Rest of Europe XI.

Other 'firsts' in the decade after the resumption of football included Arthur Atkins, born in Japan, albeit of British parents. He played for Birmingham and Shrewsbury. (The first Japanese national did not debut in the League until November 2001, when Yoshi Kawaguchi played in goal for Portsmouth.) Eddie Freimanis was the first Latvian in the League, in 1948–49 at Northampton. He came to England to work as an interpreter after the war. He later changed his name to Freiman and then Freeman. Moving into the mid-1950s, Mauno Rintanen, the first League player from Finland, joined Hull from HJK Helsinki in September 1956. Finland's international goalkeeper and a former Finnish Player of the Year, he was only allowed amateur terms with Hull and stayed just a few months.

The first League player born in Hungary was Mick Nagy, very briefly with Swindon in the early 1950s. Next came Bela Olah at Northampton, from December 1958, and then Johnny Haasz, in the early 1960s with Swansea and Workington. Olah and Haasz were both among the 21,000 Hungarians who fled their country following the 1956 uprising against the Communist regime.

Prior to leaving Hungary, Haasz had been involved in some gruesome guerilla activity against the Soviet occupiers. On the run he once found himself hiding in a graveyard, inside an occupied coffin. Despite having been a footballer at home, he was unable to play immediately in his new country because the Hungarian FA deemed such players 'deserters' and banned them. FIFA decided to uphold the Hungarian FA's ruling and helped to enforce the edict internationally. Olah escaped a ban, not having been a prominent footballer before his escape from Hungary.

Puskas, the impossible purchase

In some cases, after lobbying from the Communist nations, FIFA extended the bans. Such a fate befell the legendary Ferenc Puskas – the captain of the Hungarian side who beat England 6–3 in astonishing fashion at Wembley in 1953 – after he fled Hungary in 1956. Matt

Busby, the manager of Manchester United, considered trying to sign Puskas when he was rebuilding his team after the Munich air disaster of February 1958. The possibility was ultimately ruled out. The maximum wage and the FA's restriction on foreign players would make such a move impossible. So Puskas ended up in Spain, with Real Madrid. His enforced lay-off was followed by an awesome renaissance capped with four goals in the European Cup final of 1960. That match, a 7–3 crushing of Eintracht Frankfurt at Hampden Park, Glasgow, was Real Madrid's fifth European Cup win in the five years since the tournament began. Things might have been quite different but for FIFA's rules and the English authorities' barricades.

Haasz returned from his own ban in the less rarified surroundings of Swansea Town. 'There were never any problems as far as the locals were concerned,' he said. 'The government found us refugees jobs. We were warmly received and quickly accommodated.' Another foreign player who settled in England before Haasz even arrived was the first post-war Belgian, Marcel Gaillard, who played for Crystal Palace soon after the war and later for Portsmouth. A classy winger, he played more games for Pompey than Lindy Delapenha and Dan Ekner combined, appearing in 58 League games and scoring seven goals in the First Division. He also played in six FA Cup games in the 1951–52 season, scoring six goals in a run that ended in the sixth round. The 4–2 home defeat when Portsmouth were eliminated came – in a thrilling encounter – at the hands of the Newcastle side of George Robledo, who scored the winner to lift the trophy that May.

From Down Under to Deepdale

For some imports of the 1950s, England provided years of rich memories but not a lifelong allure. Australia's Joe Marston was such a player. After George Robledo in 1951 and 1952 and Bill Perry in 1953, the first Australian to appear in the Wembley showcase, Marston, in 1954, graced the FA Cup final with a foreign presence for a fourth consecutive year.

Marston was doing his shift as a lifesaver on Whale Beach on Sydney's north shore on 31 December 1949 when he received a message to get in touch with Percy Sewell, a scout from England who'd settled in Australia. Sewell had seen Marston, a sturdy centre-half, playing for Leichardt Annandale in Sydney. Impressed with his attitude and composure, he'd written to Blackpool and Preston with a recommendation.

'Blackpool said they were fixed up for centre-halves,' Marston recalled. 'Then Percy told me Preston wanted to give me a trial. They paid the fares, £665 one way for me and my wife Edith. We flew on BOAC Qantas and it took four days. We stopped in Singapore, where we stayed at Raffles, then Karachi, in another wonderful hotel, and then Cairo.'

The couple landed at Heathrow on 2 February 1950, where two directors from Preston met them and whisked them straight to Windsor for a look at the castle. 'The deal was effectively tied up before I arrived and I went straight into the reserves after a week,' Marston said. The weather took some getting used to – he'd never seen snow before – and the English landscape differed markedly from his preconceived idea. 'On the train to Preston, I couldn't believe how much vacant land there was – farms, rural areas, quite an eye opener.'

His starting wages – £7 a week, £2 bonus for a win, £1 bonus for a draw – were lower than he'd earned at home in a paint factory. But football came first and these were small quibbles. He made his League debut, in October 1950, at right-back, where he failed to make an impression. Fate then intervened when Preston's regular centre-half, Harry Mattinson, broke his leg and Marston was switched to replace him. He went on to make 185 League appearances and be a Preston ever-present between 1951 and 1954.

'I don't think there were any bad times,' he said. 'A footballer's life, even then, was on a higher level. People thought of you as something special, you got recognised. They were good times.' The high points included being part of the side that won the Second Division title in 1950–51, and being ever present in the 1952–53 team who had a neck-and-neck battle with Arsenal for the League championship.

Over the following season, yearning for the beach and more sunshine, Marston considered going back to Australia. But then someone offered him tickets to go and see the 1953 FA Cup final, which turned out to be a classic. 'I went with Edith. After seeing all that razzmatazz and the rendition of "Abide With Me", I turned around to her and said "Wouldn't it be amazing if we were here again next year, only with me playing?" As it turned out, we were.'

In 1954, Edith watched proudly from the stands while Joe, alongside team-mates who included Tom Finney, took to the pitch to face West Bromwich Albion. Despite a spirited performance in which Finney, who had been voted Footballer of the Year that week, was man-marked out of the action by two opponents, Preston lost 3–2. 'I'm not one for big emotions,' Marston recalled. 'But I did have to take a few really big breaths out there at the end to cope. It was a bitter pill, actually.'

The day was also memorable for the post-match sentiments of team-mate Willie Forbes. 'He was a heavy smoker, Willie, and he took out his match box and emptied it onto the floor. Then he used it to scrape the mud and bits of turf off his boots and he stuffed the box with the proceeds. "This is what I'll keep, this is my souvenir from today," he said. He was right. We all took something away.'

The following season was Marston's last in England. Before he left, though, he was party to another big occasion, being selected to play for the English League against the Scottish League at Hampden in March 1955. The Scots won 3–2, thanks to an own goal by Joe. His abiding memory of the trip was sharing a room with Duncan Edwards, the young Manchester United and England wing-half, later to lose his life in the Munich air disaster. Many believed he would have gone on to be one of the finest footballers the world had ever seen. Marston remembers him most fondly as a mate with whom he saw a Frankie Vaughan concert on a free night in Glasgow in March 1955.

By 1955, Joe and Edith had a young daughter, and for all the good times, they missed Australia, their families and the weather. They went home, where Marston continued playing and coaching.

A struggle for identity

Another notable Antipodean – the first Australian of Aboriginal descent in the League – was Peter Baines, who played at Wrexham during and after the war, and later, briefly, for Crewe, Hartlepool and New Brighton. He is not recalled in great detail by any Wrexham archives. At one time, a (now deleted) reference on the club's official website said, in its entirety: 'Peter "Darkie" Baines is believed to be the first coloured player to have represented the club, making 55 appearances and scoring some 35 goals during and just after WW2. Unfortunately, soon after his professional career was over Peter was sent to prison at Manchester Crown Court for receiving stolen goods – the first of many appearances before the courts.'

Baines's story was infinitely more complex than those two sentences relate. Even his birthplace is a subject of conjecture. Some sources claim he was born in Manchester, where he was raised in an orphanage. But it seems he was actually born in Australia and only later transported to the orphanage as a result of the repugnant 'Make Australia White' policy. This official government programme was in place in Australia in 1919, the year of Baines's birth, and saw mixed-race children with one Aboriginal parent forcibly removed from their families and taken to institutions – religious or otherwise – to be raised as 'civilised' members of society. In most cases, the father was white.

By taking those children and effectively making them orphans (their mothers were left behind, their fathers were mostly unwilling to have anything to do with them), the powers-that-be made headway towards their aim of a segregated society and shortened the odds of embarrassing the fathers in the process. It is possible that Baines was the product of a relationship between an Aboriginal woman and a white man who would have been embarrassed if any knowledge of his illegitimate half-Aboriginal son had become public. Official records at the time were regularly fudged to protect white men who preferred others not to know of their associations with black women. If Baines's father fell into this category, it could be that strings were pulled to send Baines as far from Australia as possible, in his case to Manchester. It was there, after his playing career fell apart, that he turned to crime, served his prison sentences, and ultimately died, in 1997.

Benchmark for a trusty Scandinavian

Alienation for Baines and other black players would long be a common experience in England. Conversely, it was players from nations of cultural and linguistic proximity who often fared best and stayed longest. In the 1930s and the 1950s, such individuals mostly came from South Africa and Australia. By the 1990s, the biggest recruitment ground was to be Scandinavia, where most professionals spoke English and followed the English game. They became seen as good value, adaptable and dependable. All these qualities were found in Viggo Jensen of Denmark, who did much to propagate such an image in the immediate post-war years.

Jensen was born in Skagen in 1921 and was working as a Danish government official when he signed for Hull City in October 1948 as an amateur. Although he was an established Danish international at the time – he played for Denmark against Great Britain in the 1948 London Olympics – these were the only terms Hull were allowed to offer. After spending two years living in England, however – thereby fulfilling the criteria set down by the anti-foreign FA – he was able to sign professional terms in December 1950. He was a mainstay in the Hull side, in a variety of positions, from 1948 to 1956.

Jensen's longevity at Hull was matched by his versatility. He started his career at left-back, ended it at right-back and played in positions across midfield and attack en route. His Hull career featured one hat-trick, in February 1949. The club won promotion that year to the Second Division under player-manager Raich Carter, one of England's greatest players. Jensen scored on both his League and FA Cup debuts and there was only one season, 1950–51, when he did not score at all. His best-remembered goal came in a fifth-round FA Cup match in 1954 against Tottenham, who'd been First Division champions in 1951 and runners-up the following year. Hull played most of the game with 10 men after they lost a player through injury. Spurs took the lead but Hull equalised with a Jensen penalty. Hull lost the replay but many of those in the 47,000-strong crowd say the original tie was among the most memorable ever staged at Boothferry Park. Jensen retired from playing in late 1956 and returned to Denmark as a coach. 'He can be regarded as a truly great player in the annals of Hull City but, equally as important, he will be remembered as a gentleman as well,' said Mike Petersen, a club historian.

Hats off to Hans

Another Scandinavian who had an enormous impact around that time was Hans Jeppson, albeit in a short spell at Charlton. The Swedish centre-forward had scored against England on his international debut, a 3–1 win, in 1949. He had also made a splash at the 1950 World Cup – being part of the team who shocked Italy 3–2 in their opening game of the tournament – before his arrival in London in January 1951 for a three-month business course. Jimmy Seed, Charlton's manager, knew about Jeppson's trip because he had been informed by Sigge Anderson, the secretary of a Swedish side that Charlton had played against during a 1938 tour. Jeppson knew something about Charlton because a family friend, a Mr Borg (father of the tennis legend, Bjorn), had started following the London side's fortunes after the same tour.

Charlton were in the mire at the wrong end of the First Division. Seed knew Jeppson wanted to play in the League, as an amateur, while studying. He also knew Arsenal were interested and that Jeppson had arranged a meeting, at the FA's headquarters, to discuss his options. Seed turned up unannounced and persuaded the Swede to share lunch. Jeppson was initially unsure about moving to The Valley but Seed asked him to go and meet Charlton's vice-chairman, Stanley Gliksten, even though Gliksten was in bed with flu. He got up pretty quickly when Seed told him Jeppson was downstairs. A short-term amateur contract was signed the following day.

Charlton's transformation during Jeppson's sojourn was extraordinary. He played only 11 League games but scored nine goals, including a hat-trick at Highbury against Arsenal. He remains one of an elite band to have achieved that feat. 'Now It's Hats Off To Hans', said the headline in the *Daily Mirror* on 26 February 1951, the Monday after the game. The accompanying article noted: 'Hans left the ground with the white ball used in the second half. It was inscribed: "To Hans Jeppson with congratulations on a great game at Highbury, Tom Whittaker" . . . Hans will take the ball back to Sweden when he returns home on April 1 on completion of a salesmanship course here. He certainly seems to have learned how to sell the dummy.'

Jeppson stored the ball for safekeeping in his summer house in Sweden, where it remains. He also scored vital winning goals against Sheffield Wednesday (an 89th-minute strike on his debut), Liverpool and Chelsea. He scored two against Wolves in a 3–2 win and four in a 5–1 friendly win over West Ham. In short, he saved Charlton from relegation and provided thrilling entertainment in the process.

By the time it came for Jeppson to return to Sweden, Gliksten had become so enamoured with the 'Handsome Swede' that he tried to charter a helicopter to whisk him away from his final game. He failed, but instead paid 30 guineas to transport him in a launch along the Thames to Tilbury docks, where he boarded the Swedish ship, *Suecia*, that took him home.

'I was only at Charlton for three months,' Jeppson said. 'But I worked well with my team-mates, people like [legendary goalkeeper] Sam Bartram and [club captain] Benny Fenton. I had some proposals that were seen as fantastic. Like keeping the ball on the ground. Or playing one-twos with my centre-half that left defenders confused. Players marking me had no idea where I was going. Little tricks like that worked well. It was a special time in my career.'

For the football authorities it had been a little too special. The Football League, unhappy that Charlton had imported a foreign player to save their season, subsequently refused an application by Hull to sign Jens Hansen, a compatriot of Viggo Jensen, even on amateur terms. By December 1952, temporary transfers of 'foreign well-known players' had been banned under League rules. Not until European law dictated, in 1978, that the two-year residency rule be dropped and the ban be lifted could such high-profile foreign players think about returning to England.

Not that this mattered to the talented, genial Jeppson, who turned professional on the back of his exploits in London, securing a lucrative move to Italy with Atalanta. He received a signing-on fee of £18,000, a huge amount of money at the time. Later he moved to Napoli for a record 105 million lira fee – about £60,000 – of which he received another £18,000 signing-on payment. It was the first time anyone had moved for a fee of more than 100 million lira and Jeppson was reputed at the time to be the highest paid footballer in the world. The English game, as ever, was unable to compete. And the authorities, of course, were unwilling to let it happen.

3

FROM SOUTH AFRICA TO THE VALLEY AND BEYOND

Buying in bulk

IN THE IMMEDIATE post-war period, one manager above all others decided that his staffing problems could be solved by importing from abroad. Charlton's Jimmy Seed identified South Africa as his hotbed for recruitment.

Fifty-two footballers born there made League debuts between 1946 and the end of the 1950s alone. A quarter of those did so at Charlton. This influx bears examination for several reasons, not least the sheer numbers involved, which caused more eyebrows to be raised in the players' country of origin than in England. The individual players' stories represent a cross-section of migrant experiences, from those who spent less time playing football than in transit to those who went on to fame and fortune at the highest level.

Seed found the transitional season after the war hard. Charlton finished 19th in the First Division in 1946–47. After three consecutive top-four placings in the seasons before the war, that was unsatisfactory. In his 1958 autobiography, Seed wrote: 'I realised something had to be done to strengthen the side. The war had left the country short of young and ambitious players. I discovered sadly that my happy hunting ground in the north-east of England, which had provided me with so many youngsters in the 30s was now barren soil.'

He enlisted the help of George Brunton, a South African defender, and Frank Bonniwell, a scout, both men he had known since touring the Union as the captain of England in 1929. Word soon came back that Syd O'Linn, a Cape Town inside-forward and also a South African Test-level cricketer, was a player worth considering. He agreed to travel to London for a trial if his friend, Dudley Forbes, could travel with him. That first pair arrived in England on 6 December 1947. Players often came two by two. 'And just for their boat fare,' Seed was fond of saying, time and again.

At the end of the 1948–49 season, Seed travelled to South Africa, ostensibly to look at Johnny Hubbard, an outside-left. He decided against taking him and Hubbard went on to play for Rangers in Glasgow. Seed did return, though, with another player he'd seen on the same trip. Norman Nielson was a big defender who didn't stay long at The Valley but went on to play for Derby, Bury and Hull. And Seed also scouted Bill Perry, a 'go-ahead, speedy and goal-scoring winger'.

In a meeting with Seed, Perry said he wanted to come to England but needed time to think about the move. Seed went back to England, leaving behind a furore about the poaching of South African players. Undeterred, he and his chairman, Stanley Gliksten, who was originally from South Africa, went back to Johannesburg in September 1949. That trip made the front pages in England and they were mobbed by local journalists on arrival. By the time they touched down, the South African Football Association had already made a statement saying Seed's arrival was the worst possible news for the country's footballers. 'At the moment we are powerless to stop South African footballers being taken away, but we are determined to fight tooth and nail against this latest threat.'

Undeterred, Seed contacted Perry again, who told him he was awaiting a call from Blackpool. The next time the pair met was when Charlton lost 3–2 to Blackpool – and Perry – at The Valley in December 1950. Perry signed for the seaside club in November 1949. The highlight of his time at Blackpool was scoring the winning goal in the most famous FA Cup final ever, the so-called 'Matthews Final' of 1953. The world's most famous footballer, Stanley Matthews, finally won the medal that had eluded him as Blackpool beat Bolton 4–3. Bolton were 3–1 ahead after 55 minutes before Stan Mortensen made it 3–2. Mortensen's equaliser came, like much else that afternoon, through Matthews's persistence and passing. In the last minute of normal time, after a pass from Matthews, Perry converted the decider from 10 yards.

Seed's September 1949 trip was not without dividends. He scouted a 16-year-old Cape Town schoolboy, Stuart Leary, who was recommended by Syd O'Linn. He also picked up a 21-year-old defender, John Hewie, who signed within minutes of meeting him in a Pretoria café. That deal was overheard by the restaurateur, a local football official, who reported it to the authorities. The next day it was announced that any player wanting to leave the country would need to give seven days' notice of his intent. If he failed to do so, he could face being banned from South African football in future. Hewie travelled anyway, disembarking at Southampton on 14 October 1949.

Before returning to England, Seed moved on to Cape Town to see Leary in action again. The teenager scored twice in a 9–2 win and the other seven goals were scored by another 16-year-old, a forward called Eddie Firmani. Impressed with both youngsters, Seed talked to the boys' parents and promised that if they were allowed to travel to England they could both turn professional for Charlton. They arrived in February 1950. It was only then that Seed 'discovered' they were both still short of their 17th birthdays and were not yet allowed to sign professional forms. He signed them both anyway, earning nothing more than a warning from the English FA for his 'impulsive' behaviour.

In the following years, Charlton also enticed Ken Chamberlain, Peter Firmani (Eddie's brother), Ron Oosthuizen, Brian Tocknell, Cliff Durandt, Leslie Fourie, Henry Griesel, Kenneth Kirsten and Karel Blom. Some made the grade, others did not, but all were born and raised in South Africa. As a sign of how significantly the influx was regarded, Seed was invited by the Scottish FA to select a South African XI to face Scotland at Ibrox in the 1955–56 season. A crowd of 50,000 turned up to watch Scotland nick a 2–1 win.

Fantastic Firmani

Of all the South Africans at Charlton, three – Eddie Firmani, Stuart Leary and John Hewie – stood out for their broad achievements. Firmani set a British transfer record when he moved from Charlton to Sampdoria in Italy. He remains the only player to have scored 100 League goals in both England and Italy. He later returned to Charlton twice more as a player and then as manager. Later still he managed in the USA, at one stage for the famous New York Cosmos side that included Pelé and Franz Beckenbauer.

'Cape Town to England was a long way to travel,' said Firmani, recalling his first journey aboard the Union-Castle liner. 'My mother didn't want me to go. My father convinced me I should. In the end the boat trip was like a two-week holiday for Stuart and I, entering the daily sporting competitions, training on the deck every day.

'I didn't have any preconceptions about England. I just wanted to do my best. When I got off the boat and took the train to London, George Robinson [Seed's assistant, whose daughter Pat would become Firmani's first wife] was waiting at Waterloo station. He had a taxi to come to fetch us. As we drove through London, we didn't know what we'd let ourselves in for. Bomb damage, ruined houses, barricades. We wondered what the hell we were coming into. It was like a desolate area. In South Africa we'd had green grass and then in England we had slush and rain, heavy pitches. But Charlton was the right club, absolutely. Very close. It was a family club, a family team, no bickering, no fighting, no animosity.'

Firmani made his first-team debut in 1951 but after an error did not get another chance until November 1952. Charlton lost 5–1 at Manchester City. 'I thought that was the end,' he said. But Seed kept faith with his team. The following week Firmani scored a hat-trick in a 5–1 win over Stoke. 'That was the beginning,' he said. From then on he stayed at inside-left, with Leary at centre-forward.

During his first spell with Charlton, Firmani played 100 League games and scored 50 goals, a strike rate that attracted admirers from Italy. In July 1955 Seed called Firmani into his office and told him that Sampdoria wanted to sign him. A meeting was arranged at Claridges hotel with officials from the Italian club. Firmani had his first-ever glass of wine at that lunch but it was the numbers that really made his head buzz.

Sampdoria paid Charlton a £35,000 transfer fee, then the record amount received by an English club. Firmani got a £5000 signing-on fee and a weekly wage of £18, double what he was earning in London. The bonuses were phenomenal. In England they were £2 for a win and £1 for a draw. At Sampdoria it was £50 for an away win, £25 for a home win or away draw and £12 10s for a home draw. There was also assistance with a flat and a car and the promise of more bonuses if he received an international call-up. He did, for Italy, the land of his grandfather's birth. Firmani went on to play in Milan for Internazionale, who paid £88,000 for him, and for Genoa before being sold back to Charlton, in October 1963, aged 30, for £10,000.

Firmani later played for Southend before a final playing spell at Charlton from March 1967. This ended when he was offered the manager's job, which he kept until being sacked in 1970. Some time away from the game, selling insurance, was followed by a managerial career in the USA and elsewhere, including the New York Cosmos, where he managed the likes of Pelé, Beckenbauer and Carlos Alberto.

He also spent six years in the Middle East. Most dramatically, in 1990, he returned home to Kuwait just as Saddam Hussein's Iraqi army was invading. Using his football contacts, he was helped to Baghdad by a former Iraqi international and secured a visa to flee to safety. He went on to work for Field Turf Inc, a company that sells artificial pitches to sports stadiums around the world and to Premier League academies in England.

Such a rich tapestry of experience, as a player and manager, gave Firmani a rare perspective. He recalled the differences between English and Italian football in the 1950s and how those differences remained apparent into the twenty-first century. 'In England the training was hard, very hard, the aim being to instil toughness. If someone hit you, you needed to get up and get on with it. Develop resistance. Increase your stamina. In Italy there were more exercises, more stretching and drills. We actually trained with the ball as you would in a match. And Italy was where I learned about tactics.

'English soccer was a different game. It was about being strong and powerful and playing at the very highest speed, getting long balls to the forwards. In Italy they passed the ball on the floor. It was better to watch along the floor too. In Italy we played possession football going forward. We played to feet, not to zones unless someone was making a specific run into that area. In England they played fast, too fast. They still do. When you consider the time that's elapsed, it hasn't changed a hell of a lot.'

Hewie the hard man

If one player embodied the application of strength and power in the 1950s it was John Hewie. By his own admission, he was such a rough diamond when he got off the boat in 1949 that Jimmy Seed didn't want to play him in the first team in case he damaged himself or, more likely, an opponent. And yet, after making his breakthrough, he was rarely out of the side for almost 15 years, making 495 first-team League appearances and scoring 37 goals from defence. Capped for Scotland by dint of his ancestry, he took his first ever trip to that country to make his international 'B' debut. He later played for Scotland in the 1958 World Cup.

He wasn't a bulky player but he was tall, rangy and resolute. Watching him in action would give the impression he was a hard man, a persona apparently affirmed by his memory of leaving South Africa. 'The Northern Transvaal association suspended me for leaving without notice, not that I gave a damn because I had a contract in England. Jimmy Seed organised the ticket for the boat. I got an overnight train to Cape Town to catch it. That was it.'

But away from a football pitch, he was a different, quieter person. 'I was an introvert when I arrived in England. So shy that for the whole two weeks on the boat, the *Athlone Castle*, I did not speak a single word to anyone at all until the day before we docked. I went for meals alone, walked around deck by myself. And I slept. The day before we docked I saw someone who seemed in a similar position and went up and said hello to him. He was Italian. He didn't speak a word of English.'

As with Firmani, the taxi ride across London came as something of a shock. 'The only thing I'd heard about London was that there were pickpockets and prostitutes all over. I was told "Keep your hands in your pockets".'

He soon settled in, lodging with a Mr Wright, a former steam-train driver, and his wife. He caught the bus from Bexleyheath to training and back. He hung out with the other South Africans, playing snooker or going to the cinema in his free time. And he tried to tame his game, so he'd have a chance of playing in the League.

'I was in the third team for one and a half seasons, I didn't even get a reserve game. I was too wild. Anything that moved, I kicked it. A person, a ball, whatever. That'd been the way I'd played in South Africa. I was wild, rushing about. Raw and crude. Really quite physical. And then at Charlton I was told "If you keep flying into tackles like that you'll get hurt". I was still quite shy off the pitch and I gradually calmed down when I was on it. That got me into the reserves.'

In August 1951, Hewie got his chance in the first team. 'Jock Campbell, our full-back, was injured. I got in. And I stayed in, for 15 years, never out of the team unless I was injured.' His debut was away from home, against Portsmouth. He was played as a right-back and given the job of marking Pompey's Belgian winger, Marcel Gaillard. 'He was a decent player,' Hewie said. Portsmouth won 1–0 and Hewie didn't enjoy defeat.

Over the next decade and a half, he gained a formidable reputation. Sir Bobby Robson rates Hewie among the best foreign defenders ever to play in England: 'He was at Charlton the same time I was at Fulham. He was a big guy, very tall. A very good defender. What amazed us at the time was how he'd come from South Africa, not really a footballing nation, and how they should supply somebody like him. Good defender, long legged. I wouldn't quite say like Jackie Charlton but he was tall and slender like Jackie Charlton. Good in the air, and a really combative player. He took no prisoners, he didn't. He rattled you. Very combative. Good solid defender. Didn't like playing against him. Didn't like him. I liked him because I didn't like him. You went past and he kicked you.'

Such a style, in the physical combat of 1950s football, gained Hewie admirers, including the England manager, Walter Winterbottom. 'England were grooming me, Winterbottom was interested and I played three games for an FA team. But then our club physician, Dr Montgomery, noticed my father had been born in Scotland. He told the Scots and I was drafted in for a "B" game in Edinburgh.' His first full cap came in a 1–1 draw against England in 1956. He played for Scotland 19 times, including for Scotland at the 1958 World Cup in Sweden.

There were umpteen matches where Hewie kept attackers at bay, and not just as an outfield player. Due to a goalkeeping crisis in 1961–62, he played four consecutive First Division matches between the posts. Charlton won two and drew two. Hewie also played in one historic game whose scoreline, 7–6 to Charlton, at home against Huddersfield in December 1957, remains one of the most incredible in League history. Indeed, no team before or since has scored six goals away from home in the League and lost. The outcome is more fantastic still when you know that Charlton were losing 5–1 at half-time, having been reduced to 10 men by injury.

Derek Ufton, a centre-half, was the player who went off after only 15 minutes. With no substitutes in those days and the defence weakened, it was a one-sided contest until the interval. The second half was one-sided too, in the other direction. And as forward Johnny Summers started clawing back the deficit – he scored five times, all with his right foot, his 'wrong 'un' – so every Charlton fan in The Valley and every one of their players believed they would achieve the impossible. 'It was the most remarkable game of my life,' said Hewie.

The whole team, led by Summers, were asked afterwards to climb to the directors' box and take their applause. As Summers explained to newspapermen who found him the next day, celebrating with his family and team-mates in the Arrow, his local pub: 'I just hit the ball and the goals went in . . . I'm a great one for singing a song and after I'd said thanks to the fans they asked me for a tune. But I was so choked that I couldn't even give them my favourite, "I'm Going to Sit Right Down and Write Myself a Letter".'

The match was obviously the talk of the weekend although an Arsenal player, Danny Le Roux, was also gaining a few headlines for his performance in a 3–0 win over Sunderland. 'Dan Le Roux, a strong, fast right-winger from South Africa is Highbury's new pin-up boy,' said one report. 'He made two of Arsenal's three goals even though he didn't get the service he deserved. Le Roux goes straight, cutting out all unnecessary frills and follies. He's a favourite with Arsenal fans.'

Le Roux would play only five League games for the Gunners. Genuine longevity was the preserve of men of granite, like Hewie. Among all the overseas-born players in the history of the League, no outfield player has yet made more League starts for one club than Hewie's record of 495 for Charlton.

Hewie's stay at The Valley, despite the rough-and-tumble start, was happy. 'Moving to England meant I was playing in front of 30,000 or 40,000 people. When I played at Hampden that could be 120,000. It brought me out of my shell. I lost the shyness. I just wanted to be a Charlton player and gave my best to be one.' The Charlton South Africans faced no problems with discrimination although Hewie recalled one match at Bury when he was abused. 'Someone shouted "Get back to South Africa you black bastard." I thought it was a strange thing for someone to be shouting. It was even stranger because I'm not black.'

The legend of Leary

While Firmani and Hewie both played international football, and the likes of Brian Tocknell gave Charlton great service – almost 200 League games – many Charlton supporters of the 1950s regard Stuart Leary as the most naturally gifted footballer of them all. Leary, a marvellous all-round athlete, scored more League goals for Charlton than any player before or since. He also played cricket for Kent for 20 years, scoring 16,517 first-class runs, including 18 centuries, and taking 146 wickets. He once took a record six catches in one innings in 1958.

His footballing statistics tell their own story. He played 376 League games for Charlton and scored 153 goals. Leary's prowess as one of the country's finest centre-forwards meant he could have spent his prime at a higher level. Yet he stayed with the club from 1950 until 1962 even though, when he was 24 in 1957, Charlton were relegated. In the summers he played first-class cricket for Kent. He amassed his thousands of runs with a light but stealthy touch. He took most of his wickets with leg breaks and was also a brilliant fielder.

But that was just part of it. On a football pitch he appeared to have more time and space than anyone, his mind ahead of the game so he'd already have stolen an advantage by the time his feet caught up. Not that he was slow. He delighted in running to the corner flag as the clock ran down, seemingly time-wasting, only to turn and flick the ball across to a team-mate. His touch was teasing, patient, light. His passing was divine, and he was great in front of goal.

In January 1954 he was picked for the England Under-23 team to face their Italian counterparts in Bologna. What should have been, by widespread consensus, the start of a long international career for his adopted country turned out to be his last appearance in an England shirt. The FA introduced a ruling that stated that a player's father had to be born in England for that player to represent England. Leary's international career was over. A barrage of criticism, led by the press, had no effect. Why, they wondered, could a man who had willingly done national service, as Leary had in the RAF, be asked to be ready to fight for England but not be allowed to play football for her? It was to no avail.

Leary stayed with Charlton until 1962, when he fell out with his manager, Frank 'Tiger' Hill. He moved across London to Queen's Park Rangers, where he played until 1965–66. He continued to play cricket for Kent until 1971, with a benefit year there in 1967. He received proceeds of £9,100, then a Kent record. Sir Alf Ramsey contributed to one of the programmes issued in connection with Leary's benefit. He wrote: 'Leary will be remembered as one of the stylish forwards of his day . . . As a player, he graced the game with a combination of skill, intelligence and hard work. His behaviour on the field speaks for itself and is an example to all who play football; in 16 years he was never suspended or sent off. He contributed a great deal to our game.'

Leary returned to South Africa to do some coaching work. In August 1988 it was reported that he had been missing from his home and that his car had been left near the base station of the cable-car system that ascended Table Mountain. Poor weather and high winds hampered the search for him. His body was eventually found five days after he disappeared. At the summit, from which he jumped, there is a plaque in dedication.

'In my opinion, Leary was the best player, of any nationality, to have worn a Charlton shirt, certainly since the war,' said Colin Cameron, a lifelong fan and also the club's official historian. Another fan, Ian Burden, who left Bexleyheath for Sydney in 1967, wrote: 'I lived for Saturday afternoons, to stand on the vast terrace at about the halfway line and watch Stuart Leary lead the team out to "Red Red Robin". There was a touch of class about him, his appearance, his demeanour. I remember being in the queue at Bexleyheath station one Monday morning waiting for my train ticket. Stuart was in front of me in the line. He was suntanned and smart. Even in a ticket queue he looked too good for the rest of us.'

Golden glory, journeymen and cricketers

The most successful South African player of the 1950s, in terms of medal-winning feats, was Eddie Stuart, a defender who travelled from Johannesburg to sign professional terms with Wolverhampton Wanderers in January 1951. He played a part in three title-winning campaigns, a triumphant FA Cup run and one of the most famous European club matches of the decade.

Alongside all their domestic success of the 1950s, Wolves won admiration for their performances against European opposition, not least during their floodlit friendlies at Molineux in the mid 1950s. The popularity of these matches, against some of the Continent's leading sides, helped lead to the establishment of the European Cup.

Wolves' most significant win, for English football as well as the club's supporters, came in December 1954 with the visit of Honved of Hungary, who were billed at the time as the best club side in the world. Their players included six internationals, Ferenc Puskas and Sandor Kocsis among them. That pair were both in the Hungary side who had beaten England 6–3 at Wembley a year before and then 7–1 in Budapest six months later. Although Wolves went 2–0 down within 14 minutes, they staged an epic comeback to win 3–2 in front of an ecstatic crowd of almost 55,000. The result made headlines around Europe and Stuart played his part. Old photographs show him leaving the pitch afterwards, shaking hands with Puskas.

Another long-serving player of the era was Denis Foreman, who stood on a ten-gallon drum in Cape Town to get a peep of a touring Wolves side in the late 1940s and vowed to play in England one day. He achieved it, with Brighton, and stayed for good. He recalled: 'My mother had said I couldn't go on the boat to England because I couldn't swim and I walked in my sleep. She thought it was a fatal combination. But Paddy O'Connor, one of the Christian Brothers at my school who taught football, told her not to worry. He had a few words at the quayside with some people who were sailing on the same boat. I went down to dinner on the first evening and found myself sharing a table with nine priests, returning from mission stations in the Belgian Congo.'

After 14 days under their watchful eyes, Foreman arrived in England on 15 February 1952. News of his arrival made a paragraph in the papers, although it was somewhat overshadowed by the blanket coverage of King George VI's funeral. As Foreman came down the gangplank, carrying four cricket bats – he would play cricket for Sussex for 16 years – his new manager, Billy Lane, chirped up: 'I hope you realise we're a football club.'

Foreman, a winger, played more than 200 times for Brighton before a knee injury curtailed his career. After hanging up his boots, he became a cricket coach and sports teacher. He retired, aged 60, in 1993, to spend his days coaching football and cricket in Brighton. His most memorable Brighton moments include a trip to Anfield in September 1958, a few months after Brighton had won the Third

Division (South) title. They travelled with high hopes of an encouraging result at their new higher level. Liverpool won 5–0.

They were bittersweet times for many players, as summed up by Eddie Firmani. He described the day in February 1955 when he scored five goals for Charlton in a 6–1 win against Aston Villa. No other player, before or since, has ever scored five League goals in a top-division game for Charlton. 'I was very proud that I went to England and did the things people expected me to do. I made the grade and that's the best you can do.'

As he talked about that game at length, half a century later, he recalled that it was the first and last time his parents were ever able to make the trip from South Africa to watch him play at The Valley. 'It was one of the highlights of my life to see them in the stands.' He paused for a long time, overcome with emotion, before saying very quietly: 'I should've gone home more often.'

4

TWO POWS AND ONE WORLD CUP QUALIFIER

Whatever success I have enjoyed in English football could not have been achieved without the co-operation, tolerance and sympathetic encouragement of the man who represents the backbone of your great national game – the chap on the popular side with his cloth cap and muffler, and penetrating voice. To him and his lady I owe more than I can hope to repay . . . Thank you to supporters all over the country for their many kindnesses to a German stranger in what was once an alien land.

Bert Trautmann, Footballer of the Year, 1956

AT NEWCASTLE UNITED'S Christmas party in 1998, some 53 years after the end of the Second World War, the German midfielder Dietmar Hamann unwrapped a gift from his colleagues – a copy of *Mein Kampf*.

Other presents handed out that day also reflected the humour of the dressing room. The Italian defender Alessandro Pistone was handed a sheep's heart, fresh from the butcher's and still dripping with blood. He was told: 'Here's a heart because you haven't got one.' How he laughed, all the way to arbitration. Alan Shearer, the local hero, was given a Mary Poppins doll to reflect his 'goody two shoes' image. Stuart Pearce, another England veteran, then aged 36, was given a Zimmer frame. Duncan Ferguson, a former Scotland international who once served time in prison for an on-field assault, was given a convict's outfit. Dietmar Hamann's defining characteristic, the elementary peg on which his gift was hung, was his nationality. What a thoroughly modern Premiership.

Hamann left Newcastle after less than a year. While he was there he played in an FA Cup final, only the second German to do so. But the period was otherwise marked down to unpleasant experience. At his next club, Liverpool, he was part of the team that won a treble of domestic and European trophies in 2001, and then, quite astonishingly, the European Cup of 2005. In the final against Milan, he only entered the field of play as a second-half sub, by which time Liverpool were 3–0 down. Yet at the end of an extraordinary night in the Ataturk Stadium, Istanbul, Liverpool stormed back to 3–3 at full-time and then won the penalty shoot-out 3–2, with Hamann firing home Liverpool's first spot kick. Years before, he had secured another significant victory, scoring the only goal for Germany against England at Wembley in a World Cup qualifier in October 2000. The old stadium's last ever international fixture also signalled the end of an era for Kevin Keegan, who promptly resigned as England manager. It was the latest dramatic episode in the history of Anglo–German football relations.

Antipathy within the Anglo–German relationship has been mirrored in football since the first decades of the twentieth century. In some cases history has served only to instil discord into events where there was none originally. To this day, the famous antique photographs of a German Graf Zeppelin flying over Wembley are routinely captioned to reflect menace. The craft is invariably described as 'looming', 'hovering', 'ominous', as if to hint at sinister encroachment on the heart of English football, indeed England. Such presentation is distortion. Yes, the Zeppelin was used in bombing raids in the First World War. Undoubtedly it had been a token of German aggression. But the photographs were taken in 1930 on the day of the FA Cup final. By then, the Zeppelin was a commercial aircraft on a legitimate peacetime pleasure flight. It was not unfamiliar. The pilot descended to 2000ft to give his passengers a better view as Arsenal beat Huddersfield Town 2–0.

But to acknowledge that would be to diminish the hostility still inherent in English society everywhere from tabloid caricature to jibes about Germans and their sun-loungers. Even the language of stereotype has been crafted from the rhetoric of battle. German efficiency is still invariably 'ruthless'. Implementation is 'clinical'. Resistance is 'stubborn'. These terms are applied across all walks of life, from finance and business to politics and sport, more than 60 years after the end of the Second World War.

*

Bert Trautmann and Alec Eisentrager were two Germans who arrived in England as prisoners of that war but went on to have long careers in English professional football. On his arrival in England, Trautmann was officially classified as a Nazi. More than any other footballer in England before him, he had to rally against being defined by what he represented as opposed to who he actually was. He defied his critics, not only as a great goalkeeper for Manchester City but as an innovator in a team that took risks in search of progress. He was part of the team that won the FA Cup in 1956, playing for the last 15 minutes with a broken neck. Six weeks before that he was voted Footballer of the Year, the first foreign player to win the award, and one of only two Germans to date. Jurgen Klinsmann was the other, in 1995, and he also had to overcome English antipathy.

Trautmann became a hero far beyond the boundaries of Maine Road, offering the ultimate proof that nationality need never be a bar to becoming a fans' favourite, whatever the prevailing political and social conditions. But he also paid a price for his nationality. He endured hostility, suspicion and cynicism throughout a career that was also littered with personal traumas and tragedy. Had he been an Englishman, he would have been one of the most celebrated figures in British sporting history.

Eisentrager's story is less well known outside the West Country, where he enjoyed immense popularity, playing hundreds of times for Bristol City. Trautmann arrived in England as a hardened, 21-year-old 'Nazi' veteran; Eisentrager, who arrived first, was a 17-year-old novice soldier when captured. His classification, as an 'ordinary' combatant, was less severe. He had his ups and downs – some because he pined for home, some because he was German – but his ascension to League football and his innovation when he got there were barely noticed when set against Trautmann's exploits.

Most of the reasons were self-evident. Trautmann was tall, blond, strapping, tough, single-minded and vociferous, the epitome of the stereotypical German soldier. He also moved to a big club and made a big impression on the biggest stages. Eisentrager was 5ft 6in, slight, cheeky, brown-haired, boyish. He played in the Third Division (South). Promotion to the Second Division was a pinnacle for him. His personal life was unsensational. Yet ultimately, it was their formative years and wartime lives that led to Trautmann and

Eisentrager's different classifications on arrival, and their experiences in England.

Battling to Bristol

Eisentrager was barely out of his childhood when he left the family home to fight. The son of a Polish mother, Appolonia, and a German father, Oscar Johannes, the young Alois – later anglicised to Alec – only ever wanted to play football. He was a junior with SV Hamburg, the biggest club in his home town. He would have stayed there into adulthood if the war hadn't happened. 'My mother said it would be better to enrol voluntarily in the air force than wait to be conscripted to the infantry,' he recalled. 'She said if I was conscripted they'd probably send me to the Russian front. But if I joined the air force then they'd have to teach me to fly, and by the time they'd done that the war would be over!'

But in July 1944, the week before his 17th birthday, he was called up and sent on a three-month infantry pioneer course. Eisentrager wasn't cut out for soldiering. He was immediately in trouble, for licking a gherkin container. He spent three days in the cells. He celebrated his release with a cigarette. He smoked it in a barn full of hay, earning another six days in the slammer. Later, in a billet full of soldiers, a potential target for bombing, he neglected to extinguish his lamp overnight. Another two days in detention. Not that any of these slip-ups meant he would avoid the hostilities. He was dispatched to defend the front line in Belgium in October 1944. Less than two weeks later his war was over – he was captured near Breda in The Netherlands.

'All the best troops had been sent back to Germany to defend the Rhine. The rest of us had been told to defend the line with our last bullet. But we had a smart lance-corporal who said, "I'm responsible for you, I want to make sure you come home with your lives. When the British come I'll put out the white flag." And he did. 'There were ten of us. The British soldiers were very good with us on the front. The further back we got, the more they pinched everything we had – cigarettes, photographs. It didn't seem fair, even the pictures of my parents were destroyed.'

After a short stay in a POW camp in Belgium and four months in a holding camp in Ostend – 4,000 prisoners held in open kilns in a derelict brick factory – he was taken to Tilbury Docks in the hold of a ship. Naturally, the war was dominating all aspects of life in England. A photo-story on the front page of the *Daily Mirror* in January 1945 summed up the English attitude towards Germans. The caption read: 'This German soldier was wounded by American shelling in Belgium. He fell into the snow and the bitter cold stiffened his upraised arm as he died.' It was accompanied by a picture of a dead German soldier, as described, with the headline: 'Heil Hitler!'

But Eisentrager's first impressions were not of hostility. 'We were amazed at the quality of the trains,' he said. 'We weren't used to it, second-class seats with upholstery. We thought "Blimey, this is smart". The other thing we couldn't understand was women smoking on the streets – amazing! In Germany, some women smoked but not on the streets. But the most surprising thing when we got to the next holding camp, at Kempton Park, were the hot showers. The first one I had was like someone giving me £1,000.'

Football was the main activity at all his prison camps, first in Nottingham, then in Ashford, Kent. On official release in 1948, he took up the offer of civil agricultural work in Herne Bay, where he played a few times for the local football side. And then in summer 1948 he was transferred to Chippenham in Wiltshire where he was assigned to hay-making. 'I cut all the wrong things so they put me in the kitchens. I wasn't any good there either. I never wanted to do anything except play football.'

The chance emerged through the efforts of a fellow former prisoner, Bert Meyer, who designated himself as Eisentrager's agent and wrote to the most prominent local team, Trowbridge Town. Word got out and the local newspapers carried reports that Ted Long, the Trowbridge manager, wanted to sign a German. The Wiltshire FA intervened to say Long was not allowed to sign an alien. Long appealed to the Football Association in London, who said that Eisentrager could join them as long as he was only an amateur.

A deal was struck. Officially, Eisentrager was an agricultural worker and paid £4 10s per week for his labours, playing football in his spare time. 'But Trowbridge actually fixed it that I didn't have to work on the land. I trained full time.'

The investment paid dividends. Eisentrager, a forward, scored 38 goals in the 1948–49 season. He quickly attracted attention. A job offer arrived from 1860 Munich, one of Germany's biggest clubs, as early as October 1948. News of Eisentrager's progress had been reported in newspapers and magazines back home. Although Munich officials could not offer much of a salary, a letter sent to Eisentrager said he could be otherwise compensated. 'I'm thinking in terms of a coat, a suit, shirts, etc and in addition a one-off sum direct to you of DM 1,000 [about £80],' wrote Robert Engels, a senior club official. Engels also offered to help Eisentrager find a house and a job in his chosen profession. 'I think I can promise you'll do well here. The players of the first team are all good, decent people. One is a builder, another a shopkeeper and others are office workers . . . I hope you'll soon be coming back to your native land.'

But Eisentrager had settled well at Trowbridge and was happy in his digs and with the surrogate parental attentions of his landlady, Mrs Sartin, and her husband. They'd lost their own son, a pilot, in the war. It seems plausible that they responded so warmly to Eisentrager because of that fact, not in spite of it. 'They treated me like their own son,' he said. Life at the football club was also good. The management and directors were eager to keep their prolific young talent happy, even paying for his parents to make a trip from Hamburg to visit him. The supporters too showed, from day one, that they backed him. Ted Long initially put Eisentrager in the reserves because he was afraid of a negative reaction to fielding a German in the first team. A deluge of letters to the club and the local press rapidly brought his promotion.

With Eisentrager in such good form, it was inevitable a League club would come in for him. That club was Bristol City. 'A scout came along and said did I want to join them. He said they'd see me right. I had no formal links to Trowbridge in terms of a contract so I went. After the way I'd been treated so well I did feel guilty, like I'd done the dirty on them. But City sent a team down for a friendly and Trowbridge got a crowd of 6,000 for that.'

So it was, in June 1949, that Alec Eisentrager, on an amateur contract with Bristol City, became the first German national, born and raised in Germany, to join a League club. He played as an amateur until 1950, by which time he'd been a civilian resident for two years and could sign professional terms. He stayed with the club for a further eight years, playing 229 League games and bringing something new to the supporters in the process.

*

Many fans had fears that such a diminutive figure would not last long in the tough environs of the League. But what Eisentrager lacked in stature he made up for in application. He could control the ball in a manner rarely seen at that level, picking it smoothly from the air with his foot and stopping it dead. He was a dribbler, a schemer and liked to shoot from a distance. And his pièce de resistance, a version of the bicycle kick, was something most observers had never seen. 'It was like a scissor kick,' he said. 'I remember we had instruction films from the FA telling us not to use it because it was dangerous and not very effective. The FA policy was to wait and hit the ball on the volley. But I always felt you were quicker to the ball with the scissor. And it was pretty accurate. I scored goals with it. I even passed with it.'

During Eisentrager's time there, Bristol City's greatest success was winning promotion to the Second Division in 1955. His personal high point had come early, in September 1949, when he scored four in a 6–0 win against Newport County.

Away from the pitch he was hugely popular. Photographs of his wedding to a local girl, Olwyn, show large crowds of fans, draped in City colours and scarves and showering the couple with confetti. His nationality was no problem for his wife's family although four of her brothers were ex-servicemen and one of them had been a former POW under the Japanese. 'I think there was more compassion in people then, full stop,' Eisentrager said. 'People had had a hard time in the war and they knew that others had had a hard time too, wherever they came from.'

Eisentrager eventually left Bristol to play non-league football in Wales before retiring from the game in the 1960s. He later worked as a salesman and in printing and then spent 19 years as a machinist with a Bristol engineering firm. He retired in 1988 and stayed in the area, where his sons have since been heavily involved in West Country football.

'I had ups and downs,' Eisentrager said of his career. He mentioned sporadic examples of prejudice: the opposition fans at Trowbridge who had persisted in saying he 'fiddled with the ball' because of who he was; an opponent at City who would sometimes run past and say 'I'll get you, you little Hitler'. He recalled how he got on well with his team-mates despite their regular jokes about him paying for the bomb damage to their city. And he talked about the time when he walked into a pub in London and someone started having a go at him because he was German. 'But I can honestly say I had no problems because of my nationality,' he said.

The making of a legend

Bert Trautmann did, both en route to the League and when he arrived in England. Trautmann was born in Bremen in 1923, the son of Carl, who worked in a chemical plant, and Frieda, a housewife. He excelled at sport, especially Volkerball, a throwing game where the basic aim was to hit a member of the opposing team with a ball. His agility allowed him to dodge incoming shots – a key element in the game – while his power and accuracy gave him a useful throw. He also played football, either as a forward or a defender, both positions where his height and strength were advantageous.

When he was nine he joined Tura, a publicly funded club where young people were encouraged to play a range of sports. The same year he joined the Jungvolk, a boys' organisation where hiking, organised games and lectures on a variety of subjects prepared him for full entry to the Hitler Youth movement at 14. It was a natural progression for Trautmann and his friends to make, unaware of the political significance of their actions.

After leaving school, Trautmann began a two-year apprenticeship as a motor mechanic which ended in early 1941. By then he was 17 and Adolf Hitler had invaded Poland, starting the Second World War. Many of Trautmann's friends had already joined the forces and in March 1941 he followed suit. He volunteered for the Luftwaffe as a wireless operator and was posted to Schwerin-in-Mecklenburg near the Baltic Sea. The following month he was reassigned to a paratrooper unit in Berlin and four weeks later was sent to Zamos in Poland. Germany then declared war on Russia, and at 4 a.m. one morning in June 1941 his unit was dispatched to western Ukraine. He spent three years on the Russian front.

It was early in this period that Trautmann was court-martialled for sabotage, for tinkering with a military vehicle that his unit did not want another group to commandeer. He was sentenced to nine months in prison, later reduced to three on the grounds of his youth and inexperience. Shortly after his incarceration, he was diagnosed with acute appendicitis and underwent emergency surgery. The doctor told him he had been within an hour of death. Trautmann spent the rest of his sentence in the hospital.

He emerged to the routine horrors of war. He killed, and saw comrades killed. He was caught by the Russians but escaped. He got drunk one Christmas and punched a staff sergeant. He avoided a second court martial only after an unofficial overnight incarceration in a potato-storage pit. His experiences, he said, were no worse and no better than those of millions of others. 'There was tragedy and there was humour, as there was on every battle front.'

In 1944, serving in France as part of the Odenwald paratroop unit, Trautmann was captured by French Resistance fighters. After 30 hours tied up in a forest, he wriggled free. He described it as 'an effective but unspectacular exit'. A more dramatic escape came that October, around his twenty-first birthday. The Allies launched a bombing raid on the German town of Kleve. Trautmann sheltered in a school, as did many others, including children. He was among a handful of people who survived. Hundreds died. A month earlier he had been at Arnhem as countless Allied paratroopers fell from the sky into a hail of bullets. The slaughters, that day and in Kleve, diminished any appetite for further battle.

The grim winter of 1944 turned into the no-more-hopeful spring of 1945. The Germans were in permanent retreat and Trautmann's regiment had split up. He was part of a small detachment stationed near the German town of Krefeld. By March, desertions were commonplace, as were the subsequent executions, meted out by the SS. Morale was non-existent. Trautmann decided to make the 100-mile journey north to his home town. Finding his way home proved difficult. He ended up hopelessly lost and fell into the hands of some American soldiers. He was questioned and then led into a field under moonlight, told to stand against a tree with his hands on his head. He heard guns being cocked and then a shout in English. No shots came, and so he fled without looking back. He ran across fields. He jumped over hedges. And then he landed in the middle of a British field-telephone unit having a tea break. After four years of combat when he was honoured five times for bravery, including with the Iron Cross (First Class), his war was over.

Classified a Nazi

Trautmann spent two weeks in a derelict brick factory near Ostend before being moved to Kempton Park, where his status was classified. Prisoners were put into three categories: A, B and C. Those who could prove they were ideologically opposed to Nazism were 'A' prisoners. Those who were judged to be essentially non-political and non-Nazi were 'B' prisoners. Soldiers who had known nothing but Nazi indoctrination from childhood, most of them SS or paratroopers, were 'C' prisoners. Trautmann was, officially, a Nazi.

After a week at Kempton Park, Trautmann was transferred to a camp in Cheshire, where 3300 prisoners, all German, were divided into two sections, East (non-Nazi) and West (Nazi). Football was the major pastime. The camp's only pitch was on the East side so all the West's games were played away from home. Even in kickabouts, adversity dogged Trautmann. In early June 1945 he was moved again, this time to a camp in Ashton-in-Makerfield in Lancashire, where he lived until his release in March 1948, working as a driver for the camp's commanding officer. It was in Ashton-in-Makerfield that he first played as a goalkeeper, deputising for an injured team-mate. He was a natural and was soon the regular no. 1 in a camp team who faced local sides, including Wigan, Orrell and Haydock, in charity fixtures.

Through these games the Germans forged friendships with local people, whom they were allowed to visit on Sundays, as long as they remained within a three-mile radius of the camp. This was how Trautmann met his first girlfriend, Marion Greenall, although the relationship ended in acrimony when Marion fell pregnant and Trautmann declined to marry her. The paternity suit over the baby girl, Freda, was one of many personal issues he had to deal with in England.

Trautmann was officially released from captivity in February 1948. Like Eisentrager, he took up the option of doing civil agricultural work in a nation short of labour. He had no immediate prospects in Germany so he decided to stay and was posted to a farm in Westmorland. It was during a visit back to Ashton-in-Makerfield during this period that he was invited by a local friend, Cliff Knowles, to attend a trial at St Helens Town football club.

The St Helens manager, George Fryer, asked him to play in a Liverpool County Combination game. He was an instant hit, and commuted to matches every weekend until late 1948. At Christmas that year Jack Friar, the secretary of St Helens, invited Trautmann to meet his family, including his daughter Margaret. She announced that she did not like Germans and would go out if he came round. She kept that pledge but later became Trautmann's first wife. However, her objections to his nationality were eventually to resurface.

At the start of 1949, Trautmann moved to Huyton near Liverpool as a member of a bomb-disposal squad. It meant he no longer had to travel so far at weekends to play football and he became a regular face around St Helens. He was evidently already popular. At the end of January, the British government paid for all former prisoners of war to make a trip home to see their families. Before Trautmann departed, the St Helens supporters' club invited him to a meeting. He was presented with an envelope containing £50 and a trunk full of sugar, cakes, ham and other items that were scarcer in Germany even than in England.

On returning to England in March 1949, he moved in with the Friars, briefly, before being posted to a new bomb-disposal unit in Bristol. It was there that he and Alec Eisentrager had their one and only meeting. It did not last long, as Eisentrager recalled: 'Bert Trautmann came along to Bristol City, where I'd just started playing. I got a message that some German fella wanted to speak to me and that he'd like a trial. Would it be possible for me to ask the manager to see him? I went to the club secretary to say that he was there but he told me "We've got three keepers on our books already. We don't need any more." And that was it. They lost out on the best goalkeeper in the world.'

With Trautmann soon pining for Lancashire, and St Helens keen to find a goalkeeper who lived closer to home, Jack Friar engaged the help of his local MP to get Trautmann posted back to Huyton. He signed another amateur contract, for the 1949–50 season, but it quickly became apparent he was heading to a higher level. Trautmann had a formidable physical presence with big, capable hands. His agility, despite his size, also marked him out, and he also had an innovative approach to the game. The goalkeeper's traditional remit was to stop shots and then hoof the ball away as far as possible. Trautmann, remarkably for the time, read the game ahead of him and actually tried to aim his clearances. Doncaster, Wrexham, Bolton, Grimsby, Liverpool and Everton were among clubs who made inquiries. Manchester City were also seeking a replacement for their veteran custodian, Frank Swift.

Public debate

Before officials from St Helens had even met their counterparts from City, the newspapers in Manchester began receiving letters of protest. 'As a Jew, I feel very sore that Manchester City should contemplate signing on a German,' wrote one correspondent in a letter that appeared in the *Manchester Evening News* on Thursday 6 October. 'The Germans killed six million of my brothers and sisters in the last war and the English public must have a very short memory if they can forget the thousands of women and children killed in air raids in this country . . . I have sent a telegram to the directors of the Manchester City Football Club informing them that if they sign this German goalkeeper I will organise a boycott . . . I myself have been a City supporter for 45 years.' Another correspondent, who'd served in the Second World War and had used his rare leave to watch City play wartime football, wrote: 'I did not think that one day Frank Swift's place would be taken by an individual who was at that time an enemy.' Such sentiments were echoed over and over again.

City were undeterred, and signed Trautmann anyway. With the transfer official, the story took on wider significance. It made the front pages of the national newspapers. They reported that former servicemen were threatening a boycott of City, that representatives from Manchester's sizeable Jewish community had made their opposition clear. City were taking an enormous risk, they said.

The letters pages reflected the divide in public opinion. Large numbers of people believed there was no place for a Nazi in English football. Others felt the bitterness of the war should be set aside. If Trautmann was a good goalkeeper and seemed to be a good man, why not allow him to make his living in peace? 'I don't give a damn what you are or where you come from as long as you can play football and can put some life into this City team,' wrote one supporter in a personal letter. 'Best of luck, and take no notice of these miserable buggers.'

The official view from City was similar. 'People can boycott or not, as they like,' said Bob Smith, the club's chairman. 'I am very glad we have signed Trautmann. From what I have heard of him he is not a good goalkeeper, he is a superb goalkeeper. We had to get him in quickly or other teams would have taken him from under our noses.'

Trautmann met his team-mates, including the City captain, Eric Westwood, who had served in Normandy during the war, on 11 October. His career in League football was under way.

His debut for the City reserves was on 15 October 1949 in a 1–0 defeat at Barnsley. One national newspaper reported: 'Berg [sic] Trautmann, the young German goalkeeper, gave a promising show. One cat-like leap had the stamp of class, although there were other times when his handling and impetuosity did not inspire complete confidence. With coaching he should do well.'

He made five reserve appearances before his League debut at Bolton on 19 November 1949. City lost 3–0 but Trautmann, who heard the first 'Heil Hitler' chants ring out that afternoon, took heart from Frank Swift's assessment. 'Good lad, you'll do,' said the outgoing keeper. From a man who'd served City since 1933 and was about to embark on a new career as a respected newspaper correspondent, it provided solace.

'In some ways I'd been lucky when all the controversy broke about me joining City,' Trautmann recalled. 'I'd been in St Helens, away from the centre of it. And I'd already been playing for St Helens so I knew that it was possible that supporters could take to me. St Helens showed a lot of kindness. They showed friendship.

'That game at Barnsley was the first time I actually saw people protesting against me. But within a month, a lot of those same people who'd been against me were having a go at anyone having a go at me. It changed very quickly. When I signed for City the papers were full of discriminating headlines along the lines of "If City sign a Nazi, what next?" And then people realised I'd been digging unexploded bombs in their country. They started to see me as a person with a mother and father. It was all about the human touch.'

Trautmann's first few months saw some contrasting results. His home debut ended in a 4–0 win over Birmingham. The following week, City lost 7–0 at Derby. But the match that long stood out for

Trautmann came on 14 January 1950 when City travelled to Fulham and he played in London for the first time.

The capital still resembled a giant bomb site, destroyed by years of German attacks. More than the inhabitants of any other English city, Londoners were faced, on a daily basis, with the evidence of conflict. Throw in the traditional north–south rivalries of football and two sides struggling for consistency and the easiest target for abuse was the German goalkeeper.

'Jack Friar, who was about to become my father-in-law, told me before I left for London how important the game would be for me personally,' Trautmann recalled. 'He said I needed to play better than ever because I'd be the focus of all the attention. He said I wasn't just playing against Fulham, I was playing against London. I needed to make a good impression to get the national press on my side, and he told me he expected we could lose 7–0 or 8–0.'

Trautmann gave the performance of his fledgling City career against a backdrop of abuse that grew quieter with every brilliant save in a 1–0 defeat. At the end, led by the home side, all the players formed a line of honour and applauded him down the tunnel. The crowd began to join in. 'In London, at that time, that was a testimony,' he recalled of a day he still remembers as one of the proudest of his life.

The 1949–50 season ended with relegation for City but Trautmann, personally, had settled. Away from the pitch, he had married Margaret Friar, who was expecting the couple's first son, John. On the pitch, his goalkeeping was often the only thing that had kept some of City's scorelines respectable. He was also developing a reputation as a penalty specialist, something confirmed by career statistics that showed he saved six in every ten.

When City dropped to the Second Division, manager Jock Thompson departed. He was replaced by Les McDowall, an Indian-born son of a British church minister. McDowall had been the captain at City before the war. He had an immediate impact as manager. City started the 1950–51 season by going 10 games unbeaten and ended it promoted in second place behind Preston. Trautmann played every League game, earning £5 a week for doing so. The law dictated that former prisoners were only allowed to play football if they also had another job, so technically his wages were for his other job as a mechanic in a local garage.

Trautmann's pay increased to £12 per week at the start of the 1951–52 season as McDowall began to build his team in earnest. The most significant move was the purchase of the inside-forward Don Revie from Hull for £29,000, a huge sum at the time. Revie was a tactician, as was Trautmann, and although at the end of their first season playing together the team finished mid-table – and with Trautmann starting to wonder whether his future lay in Germany – it would be a key acquisition.

Plotting an exit, asking for trouble

In the summer of 1952 City toured Spain, playing against the likes of Barcelona, Seville and Zaragoza, the last of those managed by a Hungarian, Emilio Berkessy. 'He was a man with revolutionary ideas who would have made his presence felt in England,' Trautmann noted. In the late 1950s, Berkessey agreed to take up a position in England, with Grimsby Town, but the move fell through because he was refused a work permit on the grounds that he would be taking the job of a British worker.

Trautmann ended the 1952 summer tour with a trip home to Germany on a mission that would have lasting repercussions. He held unofficial talks with a club there, Schalke 04, who offered wages of £100 a month and also a garage business for Trautmann to run. But City refused to let him move, and Schalke officials told the media the stumbling block was a £20,000 transfer fee – an unprecedented price for a goalkeeper.

For Trautmann it was a turbulent time, partly of his own making. Margaret was livid. City were outraged because they were roundly criticised for stopping Trautmann, who had served them well in difficult circumstances, from leaving. He continued to play, making progressively less noise about moving. By April 1953 the fuss had died down. Trautmann had decided to stay put and City escaped relegation by a whisker.

Alec Eisentrager also wanted to leave England at one point but was more straightforward in the way he tried to engineer the move. He spoke to a Hamburg newspaper, a strategy that he correctly assumed would have no repercussions in England if his bid to leave was unsuccessful (as it turned out to be). The resulting feature, which appeared in Germany after he'd been with Bristol City for five years, was spread over several pages and carried the headline: 'Homesick for Germany, but will he be successful?' The plea for a new club could not have been more direct. 'I would like to go back to Germany. The finances are looking better there,' he told the Hamburg paper. 'A German club could offer me a better job and raise my income.'

The feature was accompanied by a series of photographs of Eisentrager, including one of his mother in Hamburg awaiting his return and one of him doing the dishes at home in Bristol. The latter carried the caption: 'Doing the dishes without being asked points to good honour in a husband. Just like Alex [sic] Eisentrager. Wife Olwyn is happy about that. By the way, husbands in England are much more natural with the dishes than ours.' There was even a quote from Olwyn saying: 'I would like to live in Germany. The Germans are much funnier – they know how to live.'

Ultimately, the ploy failed, just as Trautmann's attempted move to Schalke had failed. Both players stayed put to become part of winning teams. In Trautmann's case, it was in dramatic fashion as an indirect result of an event a few months after his doubts of the 1952–53 season had been resolved. That event, significant for English football as well as for Trautmann personally, came on 25 November 1953. The 'Magical Magyars' of Hungary came to Wembley and won 6–3, handing England their first ever home loss against Continental opposition.

Inspiration for the Revie Plan

The result was achieved, above all, through the individual brilliance of Hungary's key players, the forwards Ferenc Puskas, Nandor Hidegkuti and Sandor Kocsis, and the mainspring right-half, Jozsef Bozsik. But it was the way that their collective talents allowed their coach, Gustav Sebes, to deploy Hidegkuti as a 'deep-lying' centre-forward that left a lasting impression and would ultimately help Manchester City to their 1956 FA Cup win. The England–Hungary match has taken on an almost mythical status, as if it were a singular turning point for the game. In fact it was about some exceptional Hungarian players, with only one man deployed unconventionally, playing fluid, varied, communicative football to the best of their abilities. Still, watching the game on the television in Manchester, Bert Trautmann and Don Revie were as stunned as any other football fans.

'That game mattered,' Trautmann said. 'Before then managers had made assumptions about how opposing players were going to behave. They'd say "The player in that position will play like this and therefore you need to try doing that to stop him". They did not think how to counter individual styles.'

Nor did managers do much to encourage players to use them. McDowall was about to, inspired by what he'd seen. He began to experiment with a system based around a deep-lying forward in City's reserve team during the 1953–54 season. At the start of the 1954–55 season he tried it with his first team. Because Revie played the Hidegkuti role, McDowall's experiment became known as the Revie Plan in the national media, who were keen to follow its progress.

The debut of the plan was inauspicious. City lost 5–0 to Preston. But McDowall was adamant that his best team had not been available that day and he needed to persevere. In the next game, City beat Sheffield United 5–2 and suddenly the plan wasn't so stupid after all.

Trautmann's role became more and more important. He could throw the ball a long way with accuracy and because the plan's effectiveness was reliant on quick progression forward, via accurate passing, a goalkeeper who could get involved from his own line was a huge bonus. Gyula Grosics in Hungary's goal had played similarly.

City topped the table for a while before ending in seventh place, only two points adrift of the runners-up spot. Trautmann had a personal disappointment when he was suspended – for a week – for the first time in his career. He'd taken exception to the referee in a game against Charlton and when he was booked for derogatory comments about the official, he gave his name as Stanley Matthews. But the season also brought a good FA Cup run all the way to the final.

City beat Derby, Manchester United and Luton on the way to a sixth-round meeting at Birmingham. During City's 1–0 win Trautmann made two saves that were heralded as among the best of the season. The semi-final, against Sunderland at Villa Park, was again settled with a single goal. Trautmann was on his way to Wembley to face Newcastle in the final on 7 May.

The teams emerged from the tunnel after the traditional rendition of 'Abide With Me' and lined up to meet the Duke of Edinburgh, in attendance with the Queen. Roy Paul, the City captain, made the introductions, telling the Duke that Trautmann was the first German ever to play in a Cup final at Wembley. '*Sehr gut,*' said the Duke, shaking the goalkeeper's hand. Trautmann was so stunned that he began bowing, much to his team-mates' surprise.

The jollity lasted for all of 50 seconds once the action started, Newcastle's Jackie Milburn heading his side into the lead. City's attacking game-plan was already in disarray even before a nineteenth-minute injury to their right-back, Jimmy Meadows. He couldn't continue, and City were reduced to 10 men for more than 70 minutes. Somehow Bobby Johnstone equalised after some accomplished goalkeeping by Trautmann had kept his side in contention. But two second-half Newcastle goals meant the Cup was going back to St James' Park for the third time in five years.

Trautmann spent the evening at a gala dinner at London's Café Royal, where his parents, who had been flown over from Germany by the *Manchester Evening Chronicle*, were special guests. They also attended the civic reception at Manchester Town Hall on the following Monday, where they were overwhelmed at the reaction their son received. His father, Carl, seemed strangely quiet. Trautmann asked him if anything was the matter. 'They seem to be very fond of you and you must never forget them and what they have done for you,' he told his son. 'Hitler never had a reception quite like that.'

Putting the boot in

The 1955–56 season followed a similar pattern to the previous campaign. It began with innovation, albeit only the introduction of a new boot for Trautmann. A friend from Germany, Adolf 'Adi' Dassler, asked him if he'd be interested in becoming a sales agent for his sportswear range. Trautmann declined, but he was still the first player in England to wear the company's boots.

City had another decent season in the League, finishing in fourth place. Trautmann was outstanding but courted fresh controversy when accused of a foul on Tottenham's outside-left, George Robb, in the FA Cup semi-final at Villa Park. City won 1–0 but Robb was denied a penalty after Trautmann grabbed his leg. The incident led to a renewal of abuse about his nationality, not least in sackloads of letters from London, though balance was provided by an equally large correspondence from people who believed his 'honest accident' version of events. The people of Manchester made their feelings clear by voting Trautmann their Player of the Year. Shortly afterwards the prestigious Football Writers' Association voted him Footballer of the Year.

So to another FA Cup final. There were fewer than 15 minutes left when Peter Murphy, Birmingham City's inside-left, surged forward towards the Manchester City goal. Birmingham had reached the final as favourites by winning five consecutive away games, scoring 18 goals and conceding only two. But now, in the last act of the Wembley showpiece, they trailed 3–1.

The ball was headed into Murphy's path. He was inside the box, seemingly certain to score. Trautmann thought otherwise. He was in no mind to lose two finals in two years. He threw himself forward and to the right and somehow took the ball in his hands. Murphy's left leg was outstretched and the full weight of his body was on course for a collision. There was no chance of avoiding the goalkeeper.

Trautmann lost consciousness still holding the ball. The first words he heard as he came round were from the City trainer, Laurie Barnett: 'Only fourteen minutes left.' 'That was the last thing I remember,' Trautmann told reporters after the whistle, having continued, dazed and in pain. It took four days of inaccurate diagnoses before the extent of the injury was confirmed.

'Trautmann's neck was BROKEN,' said one typically incredulous headline. Trautmann's second vertebra had cracked in two while the third vertebra had wedged against it, holding the pieces together. Surgery was required to bore two holes in Trautmann's head and calipers bolted through to support his spine and neck, which was encased in plaster. He stayed in hospital for two weeks.

Almost as soon as he was released disaster struck. Having been confined to bed for a fortnight he'd decided he deserved a break and accepted an invitation to be a special guest at a Germany versus England game in Berlin. His son John was knocked down and killed in a road accident while he was away.

Such tragedy on the back of his existing misfortune inevitably took its toll, not least on Trautmann's already troubled marriage. It took years to fall apart completely but even at this time it was not abnormal for Trautmann's wife to make derogatory comments about his nationality. He was not a perfect husband but such occurrences, combined with the continuous suspicion surrounding him – for years he underwent 'routine' post-war debriefings and assessment by intelligence officers – would have affected anyone's state of mind.

And yet by December of 1956, Trautmann was back playing reserve football, a month after having his calipers removed. The following season, 1957–58, he played 34 games as City finished fifth from top, the first team ever to score and concede 100 goals in the same season. English football was overshadowed that year by the Munich air disaster. The death of Trautmann's predecessor and City hero Frank Swift, on the plane on assignment with his newspaper, was among the first to be confirmed. Another of those killed was Eddie Colman, the best friend of Steve Fleet, who had covered for Trautmann during his rehabilitation.

But Trautmann, who had proved time and again he was made of stern stuff, was nowhere near the end of his career. He played on until 1964. His final League game at Maine Road was a 5–0 win over Norwich that March. He played his last League game the next day in a defeat at Preston. The official attendance at his testimonial match in April 1964 was stated as 48,000 but was probably closer to 60,000. Trautmann banked £9000 and started thinking about the future.

Initially it lay in general management at Stockport County of the Fourth Division, between 1964 and 1966, by which time relations with the club owner had become strained. A summer spent as the official attaché to the German World Cup squad brought some relief but by October 1966 Trautmann had resigned. Having been relegation fodder when he arrived, Stockport went on to win the Fourth Division a few months after Trautmann left. Two spells in management with minor German teams followed, exacerbating Trautmann's domestic problems. Margaret stayed in England with the couple's two boys, both born after John's death. The marriage finally broke down in 1971.

At one stage Trautmann went missing and Interpol were involved in the search for him. He ended up working in a friend's garage in Germany before joining a German FA scheme that sent managers to Third World countries to assist with the development of the game. He spent accomplished stints in Burma (where he met his second wife,

Ursula), Tanzania, Liberia and Pakistan before a spell back in Germany. There he split up with Ursula and met Marlys, who later became his third wife, before spending the mid-1980s working in Yemen and Malta. He retired in 1988 and settled in Valencia.

'This German-born player owes so much of his popularity to his cheerful demeanour on the field and his determination to do well whatever the odds,' wrote Sir Stanley Rous, then the secretary of the FA, in the foreword to Trautmann's 1955 autobiography, *Steppes to Wembley*. Without irony, Rous added: 'It is typical of football in this country that not only have we accepted Trautmann as a player but we have come to praise his splendid goalkeeping and to admire his rich personality.'

More than 40 years after his playing career with City ended, Trautmann felt that his good times in England exceeded the bad. But he remained unsure whether the Anglo–German relationship had progressed, or whether in fact it had actually always been too intimate, and therefore hostile. 'England and Germany are like two poles pushing each other away,' he said in one of several interviews for this book. 'But even in those days [the 1940s and 1950s] you had to ask whether this was because they were actually so similar.'

English football belatedly honoured Trautmann in 2005, inducting him into the Hall of Fame at the National Football Museum in Preston. He was only the second foreigner to be inducted, after Eric Cantona. In 2004 he was awarded an OBE by the Queen at a ceremony in Berlin for his work in fostering good relations between Germany and Britain. He also established the Trautmann Foundation to pursue the same aims via football.

Trautmann remained a regular visitor to Maine Road into retirement and took a keen interest as compatriots including Hamann, and before him Jürgen Klinsmann, made their impact in England. In 1995, when Klinsmann won the Footballer of the Year award – the second and last German to date to do so – Trautmann was the guest of honour at the presentation dinner. He was also the City of Manchester's guest of honour during Euro 96, when Germany were based there during the tournament. By that time Klinsmann was Germany's captain.

Klinsmann

Jurgen Klinsmann's two spells with Tottenham, for the duration of the 1994–95 season and the second half of 1997–98, were an unqualified success for the player and a boon for the club. This was entirely down to Klinsmann's ability to turn a potentially awkward situation around very quickly and persuade potential detractors of his value before they even had the chance to criticise.

The backdrop to his initial move to White Hart Lane from Monaco was not promising. He had shown exquisite form in the 1994 World Cup but had a reputation in England as a 'dirty' Continental who was expert in the dark arts of diving. He had also been an integral part of the winning German team who'd ended England's interest in the 1990 World Cup, which hardly endeared him to the average fan. Nor did Spurs' off-field situation in the summer of 1994 inspire confidence. After being found guilty of financial irregularities by the FA, they'd been docked 12 points and banned from the FA Cup before the season even kicked off. These punishments were subsequently rescinded but when Klinsmann signed in July 1994, the day before his thirtieth birthday, they seemed threatening indeed.

Klinsmann won respect, with a little self-mockery, before a ball was kicked. 'Is there a diving school in London?' he asked the assembled media in his first press conference. In his first-team debut, in the opening game of the season, he scored the winning goal, a stunning header, in a 4–3 win at Sheffield Wednesday. He celebrated by diving to the ground with a huge grin. His team-mates promptly copied and then mobbed him.

He scored seven goals in his first seven Premier League games, and 20 altogether in 41 League games that season, which was disrupted by the sacking of manager Ossie Ardiles. He added four more in the Coca-Cola Cup and another five in an FA Cup run that went as far as the semi-finals. Away from the pitch he was a complete professional in every sense of the word. He trained well, he ate well, he was a good example to his young – and not so young – team-mates. He turned up, on time, for interviews. He was engaging company. And there was nothing flashy about his lifestyle, despite the assumption that he was the highest-paid player in England at the time. He drove a VW Beetle because he'd always driven one and he liked it.

At the end of the season, Spurs finished seventh, which meant they failed to qualify for the following season's UEFA Cup. Klinsmann said he wanted to leave because there was no prospect of European football and moved to Bayern Munich. Spurs' chairman, Alan Sugar, made public his disgust by throwing Klinsmann's shirt away on television. Even two years later, berating what he saw as a general trend of money-grabbing foreigners, Sugar said: 'They come here for a year to better themselves and for personal gain because they saw what happened with us and Jürgen Klinsmann.'

Many Tottenham fans begged to differ in Klinsmann's case. He returned to England for Euro 96, captaining Germany to success in the tournament, although he missed the semi-final against England through injury. And he rejoined Spurs as a player in December 1997, a surprise not least because it was Sugar, on a breakfast TV show, who made the announcement. During this stay Klinsmann played in only 15 Premier League games but scored nine times to end the season as Spurs' top scorer in a dire year. In the penultimate game of the season, when a victory against Wimbledon was needed to all but ensure safety from relegation, he scored four times in a 6–2 win.

After the 1998 World Cup Klinsmann retired from football and moved to California. 'I still feel a great affinity with the fans in England and the Spurs fans in particular, who were the best I ever played for,' he said later. 'Many of the greatest experiences of my career were in London where I was very happy.' Klinsmann's business career went from strength to strength as he became the vice-president of a sports marketing consultancy. Through this, he also worked in Major League Soccer with Los Angeles Galaxy before his surprising appointment as the coach of the German national team on an initial contract running up to the World Cup finals on home soil in summer 2006.

Twenty-first century targets

If the experiences of German players in England have ultimately shown that nationality is no bar to hero status among fans, hostility remains in some quarters. During a Premier League game at Charlton in December 2002, Dietmar Hamann fell victim to the abuse of a Charlton follower who was subsequently charged in court with using 'racially aggravated threatening words and behaviour'. The perpetrator was a 30-year-old manager at a company that provided stewards and security at several of London's football clubs. He was found guilty of racially abusing Hamann, given a three-year conditional discharge and ordered to pay £50 in costs. By the time of his court appearance, Charlton, a family-orientated club with a friendly reputation, had already banned him from their ground for life. They were surprised that the courts did not ban him from attending all football matches.

The case showed once again how a German player was targeted for abuse simply because of his nationality. There is ultimately no bar to whom supporters will adore. It just makes it easier if they're not German, or, if they are, that they're like Klinsmann, and not only confound the stereotype from day one but are tremendously successful on the pitch as well.

Another sign of how slowly things change – and how long hostility endures – came in the run-up to the 2006 World Cup. The British government said it would give its full support to German police to arrest any English hooligans caught making Nazi salutes during the tournament. 'It's not a joke, it's not a comic thing to do,' said Charles Clarke, then Home Secretary. Which is, more or less, where we came in.

5

EXTREME PREJUDICE

A number of key themes emerged:

1) Racism is evil and needs to be eliminated
2) Its origins lie outside football in wider society
3) To extinguish it co-operation is needed from all interested bodies, inside and outside football
4) Long term planning is essential for success

FIFA's monthly news bulletin for the world's media, August 2001, summarising findings from a Conference Against Racism that summer

IN AUGUST 2001 the official news bulletin of FIFA, football's world governing body, carried an article about the 'Conference Against Racism' that FIFA had organised in Buenos Aires. Hundreds of delegates from FAs, confederations and NGOs had gathered to debate ways to eliminate racism from football. FIFA's president, Joseph S. Blatter, congratulated the conference on addressing the problem. He concluded, arguably 30 years late: 'Now the moment has come to start working on this issue.' The FIFA bulletin highlighted the 'key themes' that had emerged from the conference, reproduced at the top of this page. The headline said: 'Approved resolution to eradicate widespread evil'. If only.

In March 2006, five years after that conference, FIFA announced new directives, supposedly to come into force around the world immediately, to stamp out racism and other 'contemptuous' acts. The new rules stipulated that if any player or fan was found to have indulged in such an act, their team would be docked three points for a first offence, six more for a second, and be relegated for a third. FIFA stated it was the responsibility of national associations to police and enforce the rules. Many observers, including anti-racism campaigners, had doubts quite how effective this would be. Taking a stance is all well and good, but it needs to be meaningful and practical, rather than bold but token.

Black players are still subject to episodes of racial abuse. Some England players have been so severely abused that they considered leaving the pitch, as against Spain, in Madrid, in the 2004–05 season. Shaun Wright-Phillips and Ashley Cole in particular were subjected to monkey chants. This came not long after Spain's national coach, Luis Aragones, had referred to Arsenal's French striker, Thierry Henry, as a 'black shit' (for which he was fined 3000 euros by his FA), and not long before he called Henry's team-mate, Jose Antonio Reyes, 'a gypsy'.

And this in 'enlightened' times when anti-racism initiatives have been funded and backed solidly for years by the likes of the Professional Footballers' Association, the Kick It Out campaign and the FA.

The careers of English football's non-white pioneers knew no such initiatives or understanding. To many people in the 1970s and earlier, racism was an alien concept – no pun intended – and political correctness was something to do with the House of Commons.

Many of those pioneers were born and raised in Britain. Walter Tull was born in Folkestone in 1888 and played for Tottenham in the League. He was the first black outfield player in England's top division and later the first black combat soldier to fight – and die – for Britain. He was killed in the First World War. Mike Trebilcock, born in Cornwall in 1944, was the first black player to score in an FA Cup final, when he did so twice for Everton against Sheffield Wednesday in 1966. And Viv Anderson, born in Nottingham in 1956, was the first black player to win a full England cap, in 1978 against Czechoslovakia. These home-grown players were all subject to the routine prejudice that came with the colour of their skin. For non-white players from overseas, there were also the added hardships and uncertainties of physical displacement in a foreign land.

The incredible Kalamazoo

The career of Steve 'Kalamazoo' Mokone, the first black South African footballer to play outside that country, offers one extraordinary example. Mokone was born in Doornfontein in March 1932, the son of Paul Mokone, a Methodist minister turned taxi driver. Paul Mokone hoped his son's studies would keep his mind away from football but before Steve was 16 he was making a name for himself with Bush Bucks FC. At that age he played for a black South African XI and was attracting attention from touring English managers.

Stan Cullis of Wolverhampton Wanderers, who steered his side to FA Cup victory in 1949 and three League titles in the 1950s, was one who was rebuffed. 'My father said no, I was too young, I had to finish at school first,' Mokone recalled. An offer from Stan Seymour of Newcastle, the FA Cup specialists of the era, was also turned down. It was only in the mid 1950s, with the intervention of Charlie Buchan, that Mokone left South Africa.

Buchan was a prolific striker either side of the First World War, playing for Sunderland, Arsenal and England. He remains Sunderland's all-time leading goalscorer. When his playing days were over he found a new career as a journalist, publishing *Charles Buchan's Football Monthly* for many years. It was in that capacity that he met Mokone and helped fund his passage to England. 'He came to see me and said that a lot of teams were interested,' Mokone said. 'He knew people at Coventry and thought it might be a good place to start. They were in the Third Division and the idea was I could work my way up.'

It took more than a year for the South African authorities and police to make what they deemed sufficient investigations into Mokone's past to issue a passport. Under the apartheid regime initiated in 1948 by Daniel Malan's National Party, any black person wanting to travel overseas was viewed as a threat. When the passport was issued in 1955, Mokone went to collect it and was told: 'Stay out of politics, or else.' It was assumed that anti-apartheid activity was always one aim of such trips.

In one sense, for Mokone, it was. He was not overtly political but knew some senior figures in the African National Congress, including Dr William Nkomo, a close associate of Nelson Mandela. 'The night before I left South Africa in 1956, Dr Nkomo, who was like a second father to me, said that every goal I scored would be one more goal towards independence. As the days drew closer to leaving I became a bit sceptical about what I was doing. There were doubts and fears. But this was the chance of a lifetime to show that South Africa was not a bad place.'

He found himself in a different world as soon as he stepped off the plane in London. 'I'd never been in an all-white environment before. I had no one to talk to, no one to confide in. It was a very lonely experience to begin with. Even the hotel I found shocking. It was the first time I had ever stayed in a hotel and I remember it clearly, the Strand Palace Hotel. There were white people serving me in the restaurant and white people making my bed. It was a total culture shock.'

During his first few days in London, Mokone had the chance to meet another black South African sportsman, the boxer Jake N'tuli, better known in Britain as Jake Tuli. The fighter was the first black South African to win an Empire boxing title, at flyweight, in his first fight abroad in Newcastle in 1952, and was rated among the best in the world of his era. Tuli was training in London when Mokone arrived and provided a friendly face for a few hours. But even their meeting ended with panic.

'After walking Jake back to his tube station at Piccadilly Circus I went to buy a newspaper and got lost. I emerged at the wrong exit. I couldn't work out where I was. I saw a policeman but there was a psychological block to approaching him and asking for help. In South Africa as a young black man you developed a scent for policemen. It was an almost instinctive ability to sense danger, to know there was a police vehicle a street away.'

Eventually Mokone approached the policeman and announced he was lost.

'What's the name of your hotel?' asked the policeman.

'I don't know.'

'That's bloody helpful, that is. How will I know where your hotel is if you don't even know its name?'

A supervisor was called, and after making a few inquiries, discovered Mokone's arrival in England had been covered in the media, and had mentioned the Strand Palace.

The surprises kept coming, including the television set in Mokone's hotel room. Britain had been hit by television hysteria over the previous four years, with church leaders, doctors and even the BBC becoming alarmed at the effect it was having on ordinary folk as they sat by their firesides. Some viewers were confusing characters with real people. Some actors and TV personalities had received death threats. Mokone had never even seen a television. 'I didn't know how it worked or even how to switch it on.'

More confusing was the concept of room service. 'There was a lady who came to make the bed and she took my shoes away afterwards. I thought "Why the hell is she taking my shoes away?" But I couldn't say anything because she was white and because I was afraid of the implications of confrontation. When the cleaning supervisor came round I told her that my shoes had been taken away. They were brought back but the next day they were taken away again. I just could not understand why they were doing this. The cleaning lady told me they took them away to polish them and I didn't believe her. After that I took them and hid them under the bed. I just wasn't sure.'

Mokone spent a long time contemplating whether he was being subjected to racism. 'In one sense I expected it. I assumed all white people were racist. But because I wanted to play football, I thought England would give me that chance.'

There weren't many – if any – prominent black sportsmen in Britain. The USA had produced some who were well known in Britain, most often boxers or track athletes. But there were few others outside this narrow range. The mere presence on the women's tennis tour of the black American, Althea Gibson, was still newsworthy in 1956, the year Mokone arrived in Coventry. When Gibson became the first black woman to win Wimbledon, in 1957, it was a defining moment. Yet comparable success for black footballers in the English game was still many years away.

Coventry confused Mokone. The city seemed less proud of its football than its statue of Lady Godiva. Her longevity and resilience were constant talking points. The first weeks were disconcerting. 'I was homesick. Children ran up to me and touched me and ran away. The first time I went to a Coventry game people just stared at me. It made me uncomfortable. When they started smiling it only made me more suspicious. But I said to myself that I've got to make it.'

Coventry found him lodgings with a devout Christian family who were involved in the anti-apartheid movement. 'It still felt uncomfortable, using the same cups and the same toilet as a white family. But I know now that these were problems of my own making. That was my cultural baggage and it was not their fault in any way.'

Mokone judged with hindsight that moving to Coventry was 'a terrible mistake', if only because the approach to the game was so different. 'If you start in a poor division, you only make things more difficult for yourself. It worked against you all the time, trying to use skill and thought when the standard wasn't great. It didn't work and you didn't make progress.'

His ability became a potential burden from day one. After one of his first training sessions, he noticed a group of players practising penalties against goalkeeper Reg Matthews. One of the local newspaper reporters suggested Mokone have a go, which he did, reluctantly, unsure how his new team-mate might react if beaten. Matthews, despite playing in the Third Division South, was the England goalkeeper at the time. Mokone stepped up to the ball and feigned as if to hit it to Matthews's left – Matthews dived in that direction – but actually placed the ball to his right.

The delighted reporters laughed and asked him to do it again. He did the same thing, reversing the feint. Two–nil. More laughter. The reporters asked for one more shot, as did Matthews, and Mokone scored a third time. Uncomfortable, he refused to take any more penalties and headed for the bath. Matthews found him and congratulated him to ease his anxiety. Later, he was the only player to invite Mokone to his house. Few of the others showed such warmth.

Mokone's closest associate in Coventry was the Irish boyfriend of a West Indian woman who lived in the area. He felt it was natural to make their acquaintance because the woman was black. 'One day this Irish guy got badly beaten up in pub. A few days later he went back to the same pub. I was very naïve. I said "Why on earth are you going back to the same pub? Why don't you go somewhere else?" I'll remember his reply for the rest of my life. He said "It won't make any difference. The fucking English discriminate against the Irish." I just could not understand what he was saying. It confused me absolutely. I thought blacks had a monopoly on being discriminated against.'

Back at the football club, Mokone was soon elevated to the first-team squad. An outside-right, he possessed the pace and dribbling skills that good wingers required. What marked him out was his touch and trickery, exemplified elsewhere to best effect later in his career. Such artistry was of limited use in the hurly-burly of the Third Division. And when he did do well, he was often unsure whether his team-mates were too impressed. He recalled one practice game when he scored twice although the pitch was shrouded in fog. 'In the dressing room afterwards someone said well done for my goals and then another player, I did not see who it was, said "You should have

had a hat-trick. It was so murky out there no one would've seen you."
It was a huge joke that I interpreted as racism whether it was meant
that way or not.'

Not long afterwards, a newspaper reporter who had been following
Mokone's progress suggested in conversation that the player was
worth a lot more than £5 a week, which was less than half his team-
mates' earnings. When he went to the club with his proposition he
was told: 'That's the trouble with you people, you're never satisfied.'

'The phrase "you people" had so many connotations for me,'
Mokone recalled, certain in his own mind that he was being treated
differently because he was black. The ultimatum paid dividends,
however. He was offered a better contract the following day. Signing
it proved to be about as good as things got. He played just four League
games in the 1956–57 season, scoring one goal.

Even a good relationship with Coventry's coach, George Raynor,
did little to improve matters. Raynor was well-travelled and broadminded. A former player, he was a physical training instructor for the
British army in Iraq during the Second World War. His work at
Aldershot FC soon afterwards led to a recommendation to the
Swedish FA, who appointed him as their national team manager. He
led Sweden to the Olympic title in 1948 and took them to third place
in the 1950 World Cup. Hans Jeppson, later of Charlton, played
under him in that tournament. Raynor then coached in Italy at
Juventus and Lazio before becoming the coach at Coventry under
Harry Warren. He would later take charge of Sweden again, leading
them to the 1958 World Cup final on home turf, which they lost 5–2
to Brazil and their emerging superstar, Pelé.

But in the 1956–57 season, Raynor's remit was to mould a team to
cope in the Third Division South. 'My style just didn't fit,' said
Mokone. 'It was the long-ball game and I was used to short passing. I
felt I had a good awareness of where people were and how to build
play. And if I couldn't find a way forward then I'd pass backwards.
But at Coventry I was told not to do that. And some of the training I
couldn't understand at all. We had to climb ropes like we were in the
marines. We could only train with the balls one day a week. We were
told they were like fish and chips. If you had them Monday, Tuesday,
Wednesday, Thursday and Friday you'll have no appetite for Saturday
when you're meant to enjoy them. I found it completely baffling.' A
year that started with paranoia and culture shock stretched into one

of isolation, frustration and loneliness. Coventry said Mokone could leave without a transfer fee.

In the summer of 1957, he was considering returning to South Africa but was made aware that other European clubs had shown interest. Mokone travelled to Spain to investigate the possibility of a trial with Real Madrid. 'But I couldn't speak a word of Spanish. They told me it wouldn't be a problem because they had a secretary who spoke English but when I was introduced it was obvious she only spoke movie English. She just had phrases like "See you later, alligator".' In fact he never saw her again.

Back in London, a telegram arrived from a Dutch club, Heracles, saying they were interested in meeting him. Heracles, based in the small town of Almelo, about 10 miles from the border with Germany, had once been a leading Dutch side, winning the country's top division in 1927 and 1941. But by 1957 they had tumbled to the Second Division, which was the third tier of the Dutch game. They were intent on reviving their fortunes. 'Heracles said they wanted to play me in a trial that weekend in a pre-season game against Eintracht Frankfurt. They offered me $1000 [then worth £360] for one game.' He played and scored twice in a 4–3 win. Heracles asked him to stay and play again the following Sunday for the same fee. He did, and scored again.

His appearances were good for business, and a lucrative contract was rapidly offered and accepted. It was worth upwards of £3500 a year but proved good value for Heracles. The population of Almelo was only 35,000 people but in the 1957–58 season, the club regularly drew crowds of 20,000, travelling from far and wide to see Mokone play.

His first season was sensational. He played almost every match and scored 15 goals from the wing, a decent return from any wide player. He also provided countless assists to the striker Joop Schuman, who scored an astonishing 43 League goals that season. Heracles won the Second Division title and Mokone's place in the club's history and the annals of Dutch football was secure. His second season, in the First Division in 1958–59, was also a success, although an ankle injury limited his appearances.

Mokone's time in Almelo was recounted in detail in *De Zwarte Meteoor* (The Black Meteor), written by the Dutch football journalist Tom Egbers in the late 1990s. The book was made into a film in 2000. There is also a street named after Mokone in Almelo and one of the stands in Heracles's Polman Stadion is named after him.

Three factors contributed to Mokone's decision to leave Heracles. First, he believed that he could play at a higher level. His reputation led to bigger clubs inviting him to play for them as a guest in major one-off friendlies. Second, he had a disagreement with Heracles about his terms of employment. Most of the players were semi-professional and had other jobs. Mokone worked as an entertainer and singer in the local theatre. Heracles said that he should stop, and concentrate on his football. He did not agree. Third, and most improbably, Mokone received an invitation to return to the Football League, with Second Division Cardiff City. 'I'd been disappointed not to achieve something at Coventry and still hoped be able to make it in the English League,' he said.

Mokone's nomadic career ultimately showed he was not destined to settle in one place for long, but neither did British football seem intent on encouraging him to do so. He made his League debut for Cardiff on 22 August 1959 at home against Liverpool, scoring the opening goal in a 3–2 win. In the next match, four days later against Middlesbrough, he played well in a 2–0 home win but sustained a knock to his ankle. Having damaged the same leg at Heracles he was reluctant when picked for the trip to Charlton three days later, but was selected and told he should get on with it.

'My ankle was hurting like hell. I didn't do well in the game and got criticised. I said "What do you expect when I'm not fully fit?" They weren't happy and it was all downhill from there.' Mokone did not play for Cardiff again, seeing out the rest of the 1959–60 season from the sidelines. Cardiff won promotion almost entirely without him and he left the Football League for a second time.

His next deal saw another strange twist. 'I agreed to join Barcelona but because they already had their full quota of foreign players, was loaned indefinitely to Marseille,' he said. He never made an appearance for either club, but occupied himself in the south of France by running a small factory that made football boots, sold under the brand name 'Mokone'. At the end of the 1960–61 season, one of little playing activity, he ended up back in England, where he joined the third and final Football League club of his career, Third Division Barnsley. It was the briefest of associations. Mokone made one first-team appearance, in a first-round League Cup win against Southport on 13 September 1961.

There was one other significant event during Mokone's time in England, his marriage to Joyce Maaga, a South African he met in London. After the couple had spent a year in Rhodesia, where Mokone played for Salisbury, they moved in autumn 1962 to Italy, where he played for his last European team, Torino of Serie A.

He made an early impact, as was his forte. In one match against Verona, he scored four goals, leading to a huge front-page headline that compared him favourably with the great Eusebio, a European Cup winner and later the leading goalscorer at the 1966 World Cup finals. Yet ask about Mokone in modern-day Italy, even in Turin, and it is likely you will be met with scepticism that he ever played there at all. Only by physically searching the shelves in the archives at newspapers such as *Gazzetta Dello Sport*, where an old envelope of cuttings about Mokone sits gathering dust, can you be certain he even passed through. By the mid 1960s he had also passed through Canada, where he ended his football career, before settling in the United States.

His story took another series of extraordinary twists. In 1966, he and his wife had a daughter who became the subject of a bitter custody battle in the mid 1970s. By that time Mokone had gained a degree, a master's degree and a doctorate and was an assistant professor of psychiatry. His wife was a nurse who lived in hospital digs. Steve won custody.

Three violent assaults followed. Mokone himself was attacked in a parking lot by three unidentified assailants. Next Joyce's lawyer was attacked with acid. Then Joyce herself was attacked in an almost identical assault. Mokone was arrested, charged and faced separate trials for the attacks on each of the women. He maintained his innocence but was convicted and sent to prison in New York for a term dictated as '8 to 12 years'. He served eight and was released in 1988.

Numerous people offered support. One was the Reverend Desmond Tutu, alongside whom Mokone had studied at college in South Africa in the early 1950s. Tutu wrote to the New York Supreme Court in 1984 to plead Mokone's case and ask that he be set free. He described Mokone in his letter as 'a gentle man. He speaks for kindness and compassion among humans.'

Another believer in Mokone's integrity was Tom Egbers, who only discovered Mokone's history as a convicted criminal after he had written *De Zwarte Meteoor*. Having spent a lot of time talking to

Mokone and establishing what he assumed was a solid friendship, he was 'stunned' to be informed that Mokone had been convicted of two assaults. 'Steve had never mentioned it,' said Egbers. 'I confronted him, only to be told that he did not want to talk about it. Steve said he was innocent and that he would rather leave it behind him. It was in his past.' But Egbers wanted to know, for his own peace of mind, what had happened. He went to America to investigate.

His findings were published in 2002 in the book *Twaalf Gestolen Jaren* (Twelve Stolen Years), which, like *De Zwarte Meteoor*, was only published in Dutch. Egbers uncovered evidence, including previously undisclosed documents and tapes relating to the cases, that made the verdicts questionable. This evidence included a suggestion that a key prosecution witness had been coerced to testify against Mokone and that the jury in the second trial had seen prejudicial material from the first.

Egbers also unearthed letters of the period from the shadowy Department of Internal Affairs in South Africa and the American CIA, calling for Mokone to be brought to heel. He concluded there was a strong case that Mokone had been framed. In the mid-1970s Mokone had pre-existing ties to the ANC and in the USA his outlook and writing had become increasingly political. He had been blacklisted as a member of the ANC, which was held to be a terrorist organisation. In 2002, Egbers took his findings to all the protagonists in the cases who were still alive. Some of them, including one lawyer, claimed never to have heard of Mokone or the case. 'I know I wasn't guilty,' said Mokone, but in the eyes of the law he remained so.

After Mokone left prison he worked for four years, retiring with heart trouble in 1992. He continued in his duties as a goodwill ambassador for the South African tourist board in New York, a task he was offered after leaving prison, and helped found a charitable institution that assisted young South Africans with a talent for sport to find places in further education abroad, including America.

Mokone's story is one of a gifted footballer who ultimately found that English football could not accommodate him. His talents were better utilised where foreign players and new ideas were more welcome. Unlike English football, he moved on.

Barefoot and brilliant

Teslim Balogun, the first Nigerian to play in the League, stayed slightly longer. He first visited England in 1949 as part of a Nigerian touring side who earned plaudits for their flair and gasps of wonder for the fact they played in bare feet. The lanky forward – 6ft 2in in his non-stockinged feet – spent the next six years back at home, winning the Nigerian Challenge Cup with three of the six teams he played for. He was then asked back to England in 1955 for a trial with Peterborough United of the Midlands League. He stayed with them a year as a regular in the reserves, simultaneously working for a printing firm to gain experience in a useful trade.

Balogun was popular with the Peterborough fans and it came as a surprise when he was released by the club in 1956. Unsubstantiated rumours of recreational drug use had been doing the rounds but no reason for his departure was ever made public. He ended up at QPR, and stayed for one season. London was not to his liking and he headed back to rural Lincolnshire with non-League Holbeach. His best performance came in a match against Peterborough reserves when he scored four times against the club who had let him go. Within a year he was back home in Nigeria and by his early thirties was establishing himself as a coach. He returned briefly to England in 1964 to take a Football Association coaching course and went on to become one of the most influential figures in Nigerian coaching in the 1960s. He died in 1973, aged 42, although his legacy lives on today, with a stadium in Lagos named in his honour.

The second Nigerian in the League was Elkanah Onyeali, who arrived in England in summer 1960 to study electrical engineering at a technical college on Merseyside. As with Balogun, his primary aim was to learn a useful trade but he also wanted to continue his football career. It was with this in mind, shortly after his twenty-first birthday, that he went to see Peter Farrell, the manager of Tranmere Rovers, then in the Third Division. Onyeali, an inside-forward, told Farrell he had played in all of Nigeria's international matches the previous season and had scored 14 of their 26 goals. The information was hard to verify. Even now, the Nigerian FA is unable to confirm such historic details, although other sources do mention Onyeali as a prolific goalscorer in the months after his reported Nigeria debut in October 1959.

Farrell was touched by the player's enthusiasm and organised a private trial match. Onyeali scored twice to earn himself a one-year part-time contract. A second trial game was opened to the public, who immediately took Onyeali to their hearts.

His reserve debut, against Stockport, was a revelation. The Tranmere supporters had rarely, if ever, seen a player try to juggle the ball and flick it during a game, let alone dash with such verve around markers. The slightly built Onyeali scored twice. On his next outing, three days later, he scored again, and the crowd started calling for his promotion to the first team. He made his League debut on 3 September 1960 at home to Bournemouth.

Tranmere were 3–2 down and seemingly heading for defeat when he effortlessly sidestepped his marker and picked his spot for the equaliser. When he scored his second, the winner, there were few doubts Farrell had got himself a gem. Two days later, Onyeali scored again, in a 2–1 win over Southend. He then surprisingly announced that his studies were his priority and that football must not be allowed to get in the way. He continued to play for a while but his studies then took him off to the USA.

Another player who ended up across the Atlantic, in Canada, was Gerry Francis, the second black South African in the League after Steve Mokone. He'd paid his own way to England with money earned repairing shoes in Johannesburg, and joined Leeds as an amateur. He became a pro in 1957 and made his first-team debut in October 1959. He did not feature prominently in that campaign, which ended in relegation. The following year, 1960–61, he made the large share of his 46 League appearances for Leeds, scoring some fine goals from the right wing. Of more significance that season was the part he played in orchestrating Leeds's signing of his compatriot Albert Johanneson, another black winger, in April 1961.

The pair were close friends – Johanneson was the best man at Francis's wedding – but their appearances together were limited. They attracted huge attention for becoming the first pair of black wingers in the same League side, when Leeds drew 0–0 with Stoke in the month Johanneson joined. But within six months, Francis was transferred to Fourth Division York City. He played 20 times then moved to the non-League game. In the 1970s he emigrated to settle in Canada.

Johanneson spent considerably longer at Elland Road than Francis, staying from 1961 until summer 1970, when he too moved to York

City. His time at Leeds can be split into two distinct periods, before and after the 1965 FA Cup final, when he became the first black player to appear in the showcase event.

His best years unquestionably came in the first half of his stay. The statistics tell their own story. From April 1961 to May 1965 he played an average of 33 League games per season. He scored most of his 48 League goals in that period. Between the 1965 Cup final and his departure he played an average of eight games a season. This was, to some degree, due to the emergence in 1965 of a rival in his position, Eddie Gray, who went on to become one of Leeds and Scotland's most admired players. But the Cup final marked a symbolic downturn for Johanneson. He was physically sick before the game. As his former team-mate John Giles recalled: 'The occasion got to him. He just didn't play.'

Leeds went into the final, their first, as favourites. They lost to Liverpool, who took their first FA Cup, 2–1. All the goals came in extra time.

Johanneson's decline, argued Giles, had really started when Leeds won promotion in 1964. In his first two full seasons he'd been a firm fixture in Don Revie's resurgent team in the Second Division. He was Leeds' top scorer as they won it. 'He was a fairly orthodox winger,' recalled Giles. 'He had good control, pace, he was well balanced, he could beat people at close quarters and he finished well. I remember playing with him in my first match and seeing him go for a ball where he was clearly second favourite. He got it. Even in the cross-country he'd leave the rest of us standing. When we won promotion he played brilliantly. I thought he was going to be a real star.

'I think he had difficulties with the First Division. It was only my impression, I never talked to him about it, but I think the grounds and the crowds, the bigger names, places like Manchester United, got to him. He just didn't play as well. It seemed partly his mind, a psychological barrier. And maybe partly it was the absence of the usual transition that other players had. He wouldn't have been brought up with the same background in terms of joining a youth team [at a League club], staying there a few years, moving to the reserves, acclimatising there, breaking into the first team. He went into the first team, did brilliantly in the Second Division and then couldn't seem to cope with the First Division.'

Johanneson's problems on the pitch followed him off it. He drank too much towards the end of his playing days and more than too much when they ended. It cost him his marriage and children. He planned to return to South Africa as a coach and spent a short time back there exploring the possibilities. But he returned to Leeds, lost his battle against alcoholism and died alone, aged 53. It was several days before his body was discovered in his flat in a tower block in Headingley.

England's exclusive agenda

The experiences of Steve Mokone, Gerry Francis and Albert Johanneson in English football ultimately proved dispiriting but the decades since have seen numerous successful black South African-born footballers. The prolific forward Mark Stein played from 1984 onwards for a host of League clubs. With the dawning of post-apartheid South Africa and its re-emergence on the international stage in the 1990s came the likes of Phil Masinga and Lucas Radebe, following Francis and Johanneson at Leeds. Others included Shaun Bartlett at Charlton and Quinton Fortune at Manchester United.

South Africa aside, however, the majority of nations with colonial ties are not, and never have been, major providers of non-white players to Britain. This is most evident when considering the Indian subcontinent, which has had close ties to Britain for centuries and is home to a fifth of the world's population. Football has never been especially popular in India (or Pakistan or Bangladesh in their various incarnations since partition in 1947) for numerous political, social, cultural and historical reasons. But it remains statistically remarkable that the first Indian-born player without parental links to Britain to play in the English League arrived only in the last months of the twentieth century, when Bhutia Baichung signed for Bury of the Second Division.

And only a smattering of Indian-born players with any Indian heritage at all had played League football before him. Among them were Roy Smith, born in Rawalpindi, then in India, who played at West Ham from 1955 and later with Portsmouth. Bud Houghton, born in Madras, signed for Bradford from non-League Cambridge in 1955 and also played for Birmingham, Southend, Oxford and Lincoln. Kevin Keelan, the goalkeeper son of a British army officer and an Indian–Portuguese mother, played at Aston Villa, Stockport and Wrexham before embarking, in 1963, on a 17-year career with Norwich. He made 571 League appearances for them. No overseas-born player has ever made more appearances for one League club.

Keelan's family had left India in 1948, discontent with post-partition uncertainty. Wilf Heppolette, whose son Ricky became a star at Preston in the late 1960s, moved to England from Delhi for similar reasons in 1952, when Ricky was three. Heppolette junior, a feisty midfielder, grew up in Bolton and signed for Preston as an apprentice at 15. He played 149 League matches for them before moving on to Orient, Crystal Palace, Chesterfield and Peterborough.

The main reason for the dearth of non-white players from former colonies was British officialdom's attitude to non-white people. In the years between 1952, when the Football Association's non-racial but stringent anti-foreigner regulations were tightened again, and 1978, when the effective ban on foreign players was lifted, around 120 foreign-born players made League debuts in England. The majority were white and hailed from nations with colonial ties such as South Africa, Canada and Australia. They had no trouble entering Britain. Others were born in European nations like Italy or Germany but had either moved to Britain as children or were the sons of servicemen. A few more were refugees. Some came to England for other reasons and qualified to play via residency. Others were allowed to play under short-term amateur deals, having been deemed of sufficient insignificance as to merit no threat.

And then there was a group of black players from countries with colonial or Commonwealth links. They arrived, often with their parents, in a society undergoing profound change. It was a period that started with the self-interested inclusiveness of the 1948 British Nationality Act but then witnessed growing institutional aversion to non-white immigrants. Football mirrored what was happening in society. When the 1948 Act was passed, enshrining the right of Commonwealth citizens to enter the UK, settle, work and bring their families, it quickly became apparent that the Government had never actually intended to be welcoming. The arrival at Tilbury of the *Empire Windrush* in 1948, carrying 492 Jamaicans, signalled the start of pronouncements and legislation to prove the fact.

In 1949, the Royal Commission on Population argued that immigrants should only be encouraged if they were of 'good human stock'. Another sign of the times came in 1950, when a Private Member's Bill to outlaw racial discrimination failed. Another bill, to outlaw racial discrimination in public, failed in 1956. Six years later, the Government effectively reversed the 1948 Act by passing the 1962 Commonwealth Immigrants Act. This restricted the admission of Commonwealth immigrants with the introduction of employment vouchers. Cabinet papers from 1961 detail how these vouchers were conceived by the Conservative Government specifically to restrict non-white immigrants. The scheme was presented as non-discriminatory on the grounds of race and colour but in practice operated on non-whites almost exclusively.

Racial tension was evident in Britain either side of the 1962 Act, from violent street attacks on black people in Nottingham and London in the late 1950s to the election slogan of one Conservative candidate in Birmingham in the 1964 election: 'Nigger for your neighbour? Vote Labour'. A few years later Enoch Powell talked of 'rivers of blood' if immigration continued, and three years later the implicit aim of the 1971 Immigration Act was to end primary migration.

Bermuda's Best

It was against this backdrop that footballers such as Ces Podd, born in St Kitts, and Brendon Batson, born in Grenada, grew up. Racism was an issue for players like Mokone and Johanneson but it became more widespread, blatant and vitriolic for their successors. Podd and Batson both arrived in England as boys in the early 1960s and first played League football in the early 1970s. Before either of them debuted came Clyde Best from Bermuda, who arrived in 1968, aged 17, with the sole intention of playing professional football. Their stories are significant not just because of the longevity and direction of their careers – Podd and Best both became international managers, and Batson the most high-profile black administrator in English football – but because of the doors they helped to open for later generations of non-white players.

'It was only a long time after I left England that I came to appreciate what my time there meant to other players later,' said Best. 'Players like Cyrille Regis, Ian Wright, they've specifically told me what I meant to them, how I made it easier, saying they're grateful that I played.' Best was recommended to West Ham's manager, Ron Greenwood, by Graham Adams, the English manager of the Bermudan national side. 'Ron Greenwood deserved a lot of credit over many years, for his football and his humanity,' said Best. 'If he hadn't given me a chance then perhaps there'd be a lot less black players now.'

Other black players at West Ham at the time included the Charles brothers, John and Clive. Best lived as part of their family when he first arrived. In seven years with the club, he played 188 League games and scored 47 goals. He endured constant racial abuse, which had become widespread during the previous decade, on and off the pitch. His footballing approach, despite being 6ft 1in and powerful, was built around technique rather than traditional brawn. This also earned him criticism from those who thought he just wasn't tough enough to cope.

'What people forgot to realise was that just because you couldn't run through a brick wall didn't mean you couldn't play. Give some of those big guys the ball and they didn't know what to do with it. They'd have failed abroad in a more sophisticated environment. My technique was as good as anyone's. People said that I wasn't strong enough or willing to assert myself physically. They also said that black players couldn't play in cold weather. Total nonsense. Every time I went on the field I tried to give it 100 per cent. I looked at players like Billy Bonds and I tried to emulate his work rate. He'd run himself into the ground. I worked hard to do the same. The West Ham fans were knowledgeable people and they liked people who worked.'

The racist abuse was worst at away matches. 'It was a bit more brutal,' said Best. 'But you couldn't let them upset you. You can't be selfish in those situations. If it affects you, you let people down. If there'd been no one to consider but myself then maybe I wouldn't have stuck it out. But I was also playing for people at home, the people behind me. I was lucky because Mrs Charles took me in and treated me as part of her family. "Don't listen to it," she said. "It happens. Don't dwell on it. Look what you're trying to achieve. Be conscious of what you're doing." I also thought that people of colour had dominated world football for so long – Pelé, Garrincha, Eusebio – that abuse and ignorance wasn't going to stop me playing football. All sorts of things go through your head but you have to stick it out.'

He stuck it out until 1976, by which time he'd helped to dispel the myth that a black footballer couldn't cope with life in the top division. What he couldn't cope with, in the end, were the off-field pressures. More accurately, he made a conscious decision that he shouldn't have to cope any more. He moved to America, where he played for the Tampa Bay Rowdies and the Portland Timbers. 'I'd visited America before 1976 and I liked the lifestyle. The standard of living was better in the US, there was less pressure. In England, you couldn't go to a chip shop or a pub without people bombarding you. I didn't mind too much if it was people asking for autographs but if you're having a meal with your wife and they come up and start having a go, it gets a bit much.'

When Clyde Best's playing days were over he settled in California. He maintained a close interest in the game, not least in Bermuda, where his success was an inspiration. In 1997, he was asked to return home and become the national team manager. He went, staying in the post three years before being sacked for failing to achieve the Bermudan FA's unrealistic targets of regional dominance. Best, the son of a prison warder, then followed in his father's footsteps, working in a halfway house in Bermuda, helping to rehabilitate offenders.

A Bradford hero

Cyril 'Ces' Podd, like Best, played when racism in football was an everyday occurrence. He moved to England from St Kitts in 1962, aged nine, with his mother and father, Georgina and Cyril senior, and his five brothers and sisters. Cyril senior had been employed as a clerk in St Kitts but worked on the buses in the family's new home town, Leeds. Ces recalled with laughter one of his early pre-occupations in England: 'I remember at school sitting in class looking at other kids flicking their hair. I just sat there thinking "Mine won't move".' But the fact he was black meant he was a target for racism. He described it as 'persistent casual abuse', from direct name-calling to being expected to laugh at television jokes about black people, invariably 'niggers'.

'Either you became strong and ignored it or you fought it. I became strong. I didn't talk to anyone about it. I kept it to myself. I didn't want to upset my parents. I didn't tell them to protect them. Without realising it, I was dealing with a lot more than I should've been at that age. Having said that, there were lots of good people in our neighbourhood who completely accepted us even though we were the only black family.'

Podd had 'hardly even heard of football' before coming to England, let alone played in an organised team. That quickly changed. He was soon playing for his school and the local church team. And after watching Albert Johanneson at Leeds United in the early 1960s, he decided a career was possible. 'Johanneson was an inspiration, just the fact that he was black and playing.'

While playing for the church team Podd was spotted by a scout for Wolverhampton Wanderers. They offered him a trial. 'I was the only black kid, and the only kid who didn't get a follow-up. The same thing happened at Manchester United.' At a trial with Bradford City he was also the only black kid. 'I was a right-winger but the only position available at the trial was at full-back. I said "I'm a full-back." I got in.'

He stayed in, as a defender, making 502 League appearances between 1970 and 1984. No overseas-born outfielder has played more for one club. 'I went through some tough times,' said Podd, recalling the abuse that occurred systematically in the 1970s. 'Everything was thrown at me, from bananas to saliva. I almost got arrested once for reacting to a situation at Crewe. It was the end of a game, I was absolutely shattered, walking off the pitch taking gulps of air. My mouth was open and this guy spat in it.'

After leaving Bradford, Podd played for Halifax and was assistant manager at Scarborough. He moved on to Leeds, where he played an integral part in setting up their innovative community programme. By the late 1990s, it offered a wide range of educational and outreach projects to local children.

After the 1998 World Cup, and the success of Jamaica's 'Reggae Boyz' in reaching the finals, the Football Association of St Kitts & Nevis asked Podd if he could be the architect of another Caribbean dream. 'Everyone wants to manage their own country. I took the job.' He was in charge of the 'Sugar Boyz' for two and a half years from 1999, blending a team of talented locals with players from Britain and Europe who he discovered were qualified to play for him. They won the Leeward Islands championship and more importantly progressed through the early regional qualifying rounds for the 2002 World Cup.

For a country with only 46,000 people it was a decent achievement. But failure to make the World Cup finals was deemed a failure by an over-expectant FA and Podd resigned. He returned to England to work for Leeds-based HN Sport, a management agency for professional footballers.

Gotta lotta bottle

Brendon Batson, like Podd, played the majority of his football in the 1970s. He arrived from the Caribbean, also aged nine, in 1962. He and his elder brother lived with their uncle and aunt in Tilbury until their mother and sister moved over to join them two years later. 'We came over in April and I remember it was bloomin' cold,' Batson said. 'Having never seen snow before I was really looking forward to the winter of 1962–3. It turned out to be the worst winter in thirty years. There was so much snow I hated it. I still do. Other than that it was a big adventure. Kids are quite resilient, I took it in my stride.'

Batson stood out in the town. Indeed all the Batsons stood out. 'We were the only black family in Tilbury. When you went out no one needed to ask your name because you were a Batson. Everyone knew it. My aunt was a midwife and she'd delivered half of Tilbury.'

Like Podd, Batson was subjected to persistent casual racism. He fought against it, often literally, into his teens. By then he'd fallen in love with football, a game he never saw before moving to England. He was spotted playing Sunday football by Arsenal, signed as a schoolboy and became intent on making his way as a player. 'Arsenal was a fantastic club to grow up in. Football was the dominant factor in my life. And Bertie Mee, the manager, had a way of developing people not just players but as men.'

Batson progressed to the first team but only made six starts in an Arsenal shirt. He felt he 'hit a brick wall' in terms of his progress and asked for a transfer. In 1974, he moved down to the Third Division with Cambridge United, where manager Bill Leithers was soon replaced by Ron Atkinson. When Big Ron progressed to West Bromwich Albion in 1977, Batson followed soon afterwards.

At The Hawthorns he was one-third of the black trio Atkinson famously nicknamed his 'Three Degrees', the others being Cyrille Regis and Lawrie Cunningham. Batson recalls the label as a publicity stunt typical of his ebullient manager. (Atkinson's subsequent career as pundit came to a crunching, shameful halt in 2004 when racist comments he made about Chelsea's Marcel Desailly – thinking he was off air – were broadcast around the world. Atkinson was heard saying: 'He's what is known in some schools as a fucking lazy thick nigger.')

Batson best remembers his times at West Brom for getting on with his job in an exciting era for the club. 'I don't think we realised the impact or significance,' he says of his position as a role model and forerunner to generations of non-white players. 'I was just a player making my way. You were aware of a constant whispering campaign about black players, people saying "They don't like training, they're lazy, they've got no bottle." I just wanted to prove people wrong.

'I thought as the number of black players increased the abuse would ease. It got worse before it got better. You got it in all forms, monkey chants, bananas. I was surprised by nothing except the scale of it. If you're walking down the street and someone says something it's bad enough. If you're running down a football pitch towards a whole bank of supporters shouting things, it's something else. That deterred a lot of people coming to games. Even today you don't see the percentage of black players reflected among the supporters. That all stems back. The time to capture those supporters was then but they were lost to football.'

The same was undoubtedly true of some players, although between the late 1970s and the mid 1980s the number of prominent black players increased and colour slowly became less of an issue. Others who made an impact at that time included Luther Blissett, born in Jamaica, and Regis, born in French Guyana, both of whom starred for England. Another full international of the era was Nigeria's John Chiedozie. His father, fleeing the Biafran war, moved to east London to work in a car plant. Chiedozie joined him in 1972, aged 12, his childhood having been disrupted by war. He was unable to speak English and couldn't write. Four years of intensive assistance from a sympathetic teacher remedied that, although it took less time to make progress on the pitch. Spotted playing for a Sunday team at 14, he went on to have a lengthy professional career involving five clubs, including Tottenham in the era of Hoddle, Ardiles and Crooks. When he retired from the game, he moved to Hampshire to run a children's

entertainment company. He also started a coaching programme for
local children.

After Batson's playing days were curtailed by injury in the early
1980s, he went on to work for the Professional Footballers'
Association, becoming deputy chief executive to Gordon Taylor.
From his experiences as a player and with the PFA, where he worked
on numerous anti-racism campaigns, he believed football in the early
years of the twenty-first century was 'a good example of an integrated
industry', albeit one that mirrored society and must guard against
any complacency.

The PFA, he added, was a progressive organisation when Taylor
asked him to be his deputy and it remained a progressive
organisation. Taylor remained the PFA's chief executive. He had held
the post since 1978, and it was in that year that English football
underwent one of the biggest changes in its history.

6

THE BARRIERS COME DOWN: 1978–79

World Cup final
Sunday, 25 June 1978
Monumental, Buenos Aires
Argentina (1) 3 Netherlands (0) 1 (after extra time)
Attendance: 76,609

KEITH BURKINSHAW, THE manager of Tottenham Hotspur, was sitting in his office at White Hart Lane a few days after the 1978 World Cup final. He had less than two months to prepare for the start of the new season. Spurs were returning to the First Division after a year away. Bill Nicholson, Burkinshaw's most eminent predecessor, the man who'd overseen Spurs' glory days of the early 1960s, had joined him for a chat. There was plenty to discuss. While they were talking, the phone rang. Nicholson answered it.

'Hello Bill, it's Harry Haslam.' Haslam, a friend of Burkinshaw, was the manager of Sheffield United.

'Hello Harry, what can we do for you?' asked Nicholson.

'Would Keith be interested in signing Osvaldo Ardiles?' said Haslam.

Nicholson turned around to Burkinshaw. 'Harry Haslam's on the phone and he wants to know if you're interested in signing Osvaldo Ardiles,' he said.

'Is he pulling your leg or what?' said Burkinshaw.

Ossie Ardiles, a 25-year-old midfielder, had been one of the stars of the World Cup. Defying the stereotype of the bustling, long-haired Latin, he was 5ft 6in, slightly built, and had a short coiffure that resembled a beret. He could also play like a dream. A right-sided midfielder with his Buenos Aires club, Huracan, he'd been the perceptive, thoughtful architect of much of Argentina's best play. Not that he dawdled, he could ease past opponents. And his ball control and passing were brilliant.

He was there in the starting line-up on 2 June as Argentina took to the pitch amid a blur of flags, lights and tickertape for their first World Cup finals match on home soil. Argentina beat Hungary 2–1. He was there again, darting nimbly past defenders, as they beat France 2–1 in the next game. He did well in the defeat to Italy, and then excelled next time out against Poland, setting up the second goal with his playmaker's touch. Against Brazil, he lasted only 45 minutes, replaced by his friend Ricardo 'Ricky' Villa. And he missed the 6–0 win over Peru, a result that smelt of a fix but saw Argentina to the semi-finals on goal difference at the expense of Brazil. But he was back for the final, part of the team who brought rapture to a nation living in the shadow of a military junta.

Ardiles was selected in almost every pundit's team of the tournament, including that of Ron Greenwood, the England manager. Greenwood was only in South America as a spectator, England having failed to qualify for the World Cup finals for a second time in succession. It seemed incredible that Harry Haslam was suggesting Ardiles was available for a move to north London. But he was. Over the next 12 months there was to be a revolution in the English game. The barriers preventing foreign players from moving freely to England came down. Established international names from Europe and further afield brought their talent to the League.

These players entered a tough, physical environment and found a tactical approach that was often one-dimensional. The emphasis was on bravery and strength and getting the ball upfield quickly. The tempo was helter skelter. 'Fitness regimes' meant laying off the booze the night before a game. 'Dietary sophistication' was the timing of your pre-match steak and chips. There was never any prospect that a few dozen imports could achieve radical transformation overnight, or even in a season or two. But from 1978 onwards, English football did start to appreciate and utilise a more Continental approach. Midfield became a place to pass through not bypass. This required better technical ability, which players like Ardiles possessed. Mental application became more important, which again suited Ardiles. He regarded the game as an intellectual exercise as well as his sporting passion.

The Football League had not been without British-born thinkers and players of extraordinary technical ability. Herbert Chapman was a visionary coach and an astute tactician at Huddersfield and Arsenal in the 1920s and 1930s. Stanley Matthews, the Wizard of the Dribble, the first ever European Footballer of the Year, in 1956, was football's first global star. He also took care of himself, playing until he was 50. John Charles of Wales, known as the 'Gentle Giant' in an Italy he mesmerised, earned lifelong adulation with his delicate, sumptuous style. Jimmy Greaves possessed a speed of thought to match his feet and was his generation's most natural goalscorer. Northern Ireland's George Best, who at his peak was the greatest British player ever, had it all.

But such giants of the game marked themselves out as exceptional. They were not products of a system that deliberately set out to encourage and nurture their genius. They and other home-grown innovators either swam against the tide because they believed wholeheartedly in progress, like Chapman, or were uniquely gifted, like Matthews and Charles, or were trend-bucking mavericks with all the good and bad that entailed, like Greaves and Best.

It was not until later that coaches began to move in numbers towards a holistic approach where detail mattered, from diet to training to sports science to technique to instilling a sense that foot-ball could be a genuinely intellectual as well as a physical profession. But if Arsène Wenger at Arsenal set new standards of excellence in this way in the late 1990s, the seeds were sown for him to do so in 1978. There were a few kicks and screams along the way – not least from the government and the PFA, still edgy about the consequences of a 'foreign invasion' – but still there were glimpses of what the best of football's travellers could bring, to the pitch and to attendance figures alike.

The political decision that ultimately allowed them to come was taken on 23 February 1978 in an anonymous meeting room in Brussels. The European Community declared that all football associations within the EC must modify their regulations to fall in line with the Treaty of Rome. 'According to the new EC ruling, there may be no restriction in future on the number of players from EC states signed on by clubs in other EC states,' announced the official monthly bulletin of UEFA, the governing body of the European game, in March 1978, reporting the EC's February decision. The news nestled at the bottom of page 18 of the bulletin under the headline 'EC lifts restrictions on foreign players'.

The EC's purpose in introducing this new legislation was to extend to football the scope of the Rome Treaty regarding workers' freedom of movement. At its AGM in the summer of 1978, the Football League had no choice but to accept the decision and amend its rules, thereby reversing the effective ban on foreign players that had been implemented in 1931 and strengthened in 1952. Foreign players, and not just those from Europe, the League decided, were free to come to England. The only stipulation was that no more than two foreign players be fielded in one team. Over time, such quotas would expand and in most cases disappear.

'I said to Bill "Is he pulling your leg or what?"' Burkinshaw recalled of that June day in 1978. 'I'd watched the World Cup on TV. Of course the Argentinians were a very good team. Ardiles took my eye and there was one game when Ricky Villa came on as a sub and I thought what a big strong lad he was. But that was it. I hadn't actually been out to see it.

'I went on the phone for a chat. Harry said he was going out to Argentina to look at some players. He couldn't afford Ardiles but he knew he was available. I said I couldn't believe it was true, that I'd just be able to go there and sign someone of that calibre, but I said I'd go along. I had nothing to lose.'

Sensational signings

Harry Haslam's interest in South Americans stemmed from contacts built via one of his senior coaching staff, Oscar Arce, an Argentinian. Burkinshaw knew this, and that Haslam already had a rudimentary scouting network in place across in Argentina. He was still a little taken aback when he disembarked in Buenos Aires on Saturday 8 July 1978 to be met off the plane by Antonio Rattin.

Rattin had captained Argentina in the most notorious game of the 1966 World Cup finals, the ill-tempered quarter-final against England. During the first half-hour of the game, which England won 1–0, Rattin committed a series of fouls, contested almost every decision and spat in front of the referee. He was sent off after 36 minutes but refused to leave the pitch. There was uproar as he stood his ground and it took eight minutes to persuade him to go. He tried to sit on the touchline and was eventually escorted away by the police. Alf Ramsey, England's manager, described the Argentinians as 'animals'. The infamy of Rattin and his team was sealed.

'But Rattin was a tremendous guy,' Burkinshaw said of their 1978 meeting. 'We were there for four or five days and he was a great fella. He escorted us everywhere, he made all the introductions, he was wonderful.'

Burkinshaw met Ardiles at a Buenos Aires hotel within hours of arriving in Argentina. Considering the impact the deal would have, it was concluded more smoothly than Burkinshaw could ever have anticipated. 'I asked Ossie if he'd be interested in signing for Tottenham. He said yes, but he'd have to come back with his wife, Sylvia. Twenty minutes into that second meeting he said "Give me the form and I'll sign it." Then he said "Would you like to sign Ricky Villa?" I rang Tottenham. The chairman told me to go ahead if that's what I wanted. I met Ricky the next day and five minutes later he was a Tottenham player.'

News of the signings reached England on Monday 10 July. 'Sensational' appeared in numerous headlines. Bookmakers responded instantly by cutting Tottenham's odds of winning the First Division from 66–1 to 25–1. Tottenham's chairman, Sidney Wale, went public on the reasons for his purchases: 'The [financial] situation is certainly right for signing players out there.' The pair cost around £750,000 between them. Ardiles, already the holder of more than 40 caps, cost £325,000 from Huracan; Villa, despite having less international experience, cost marginally more from Racing Club.

Not everyone was convinced. Burkinshaw arrived back in London on Wednesday 12 July to find objections from the players' union. 'It is a situation that cannot be dismissed lightly,' said Cliff Lloyd, secretary of the PFA. 'Seeing these two could whet people's appetites and we could be caught up in something that is detrimental to the game in this country as a whole ... One has got to consider the game in this country at all levels, right up to the England team and what sort of effect it will have.'

Interviewed for this book, Ardiles explained he and Villa signed for Spurs because Tottenham were the first European club to make an offer. 'It had never crossed my mind for a second that I might go to England. I'd thought about maybe Spain, Italy or even France, people had talked about this around the World Cup. But when we got home there was nothing whatsoever. The first person who came out to Argentina to see us was Keith Burkinshaw. Suddenly he was there. He wanted me and Ricky, he put the offer on the table. The rest is history.' Neither player, on arrival, knew much about the English game beyond some basic knowledge of the international team. They knew most about Kevin Keegan, who was playing in Germany for SV Hamburg. Otherwise they could name only Bobby Charlton, Bobby Moore and Gordon Banks, all from the 1966 World Cup team, as examples of prominent English players.

The Argentinians' arrival received plenty of positive coverage in the newspapers on Tuesday 18 July. It was rare, at the time, for such news to spread beyond the sports pages but the pair soon found themselves on the news and features pages. There they shared space with other items of international interest, including the imminent birth of the world's first test-tube baby. There was news of the 60th birthday of Nelson Mandela, who'd spent a third of his life in prison. Mandela's wife, Winnie, said that her husband, locked away on Robben Island, was inspired by the hope that he might live to see black South Africans free from apartheid. It seemed an unlikely aim.

The barriers come down

Within two days of Tottenham's transfer coup came news that a third Argentinian, Alex Sabella, was coming to England. Harry Haslam signed the 23-year-old midfielder from River Plate for £160,000, a record fee for Sheffield United. 'I've seen him play and he has a lot of skill and flair,' said Haslam. 'I think he can fit in well at Bramall Lane.'

Gordon Taylor, a member of the PFA's executive committee, reacted by saying: 'If a trickle of foreign players becomes a flow, it would be detrimental to our members.' His statement did nothing to deter other clubs from looking abroad. Manchester City confirmed they were interested in signing Legia Warsaw's Kazimierz Deyna, Poland's most capped player. Birmingham were interested in an Argentinian, Alberto Tarantini, and Southampton had already done a deal to sign the Yugoslav defender, Ivan Golac. Lawrie McMenemy, Southampton's manager at the time, recalled: 'The same time I signed him, Tottenham were getting all the publicity for their big-money Argentinian deals. It overshadowed my little fifty-thousand-pounder. But Ivan was a terrific fella and terrific value for money.'

There were still some hurdles to clear before these transfers could be rubber-stamped with long-term work permits. Although the

Football League accepted the registrations of Ardiles, Villa and Sabella on 30 July, the government, at the behest of the PFA, then stepped in. From 31 July, League clubs were temporarily banned from buying non-EC players.

The ban lasted until 28 September, when a compromise plan was drawn up by the Sports Minister, Denis Howell, and the Minister of Employment, John Grant. To allay the PFA's fears, they and football's governing bodies agreed that only 'established' foreign players would be given work permits. 'Established' meant players who had been capped by their countries and who could make a 'distinctive contribution to the national game'. English football was attracting some famous foreign names and was on the verge of some landmark events. Kazimierz Deyna completed his move to Maine Road in November, the same month that Gordon Taylor stepped up to become chief executive of the PFA. Kevin Keegan of Hamburg became European Footballer of the Year in December, the first Englishman to do so since Bobby Charlton in 1966. Trevor Francis became Britain's first £1m footballer when he moved from Birmingham to Nottingham Forest in February 1979. This came a few days before Ipswich signed a second Dutchman, Frans Thijssen, from Twente Enschede, following the earlier arrival of Arnold Muhren.

Other foreign signings that season included Middlesbrough's purchase of the Yugoslavian striker Bozo Jankovic and Chelsea's acquisition of the Yugoslavian goalkeeper Petar Borota. Bristol City signed the Dutch winger Gert Meijer and the Finnish midfielder Pertti Jantunen. Bolton signed the Polish winger Tadeusz Nowak. Decades later, in the Premier League era, such signings would become so routine that a player's nationality would not be an issue. When Bolton fielded their first starting line-up entirely of non-British players, in March 2003, it warranted the merest of mentions. But in 1978–79, every foreign signing was worthy of special scrutiny.

Before that season was finished, there were signs that the newcomers would not all acclimatise. Birmingham, heading for relegation, sold Tarantini back to an Argentinian club, Talleres, after only six months and 23 League games. (And even that was a successful tenure compared to that of another Argentinian, Pedro Verde, the uncle of Juan Sebastian Veron, who played only 10 League games for Sheffield United in 1979–80.) But there were also signs that the foreign players were bringing benefits. Ardiles and Villa attracted huge crowds as Tottenham finished 11th in the table. Ipswich enjoyed a purple patch after signing Thijssen, winning 10, drawing six and losing only one of their 17 League games after his arrival. They also reached the quarter-final of the European Cup-Winners' Cup and were not disgraced in defeat to Barcelona, the eventual winners. Manchester City did not have the best of seasons in the League, but reached the quarter-finals of the UEFA Cup, with Deyna scoring during their European campaign. Like Ipswich, they were defeated by their competition's eventual winners, Borussia Moenchengladbach. English football was confirmed as a vibrant place to work when Brian Clough's Nottingham Forest won the European Cup on 30 May, the winning goal scored by Trevor Francis.

Two days later the AGM of the Football League decided that out-of-season loans of English-based players to the North American Soccer League were to be banned. In the summer of 1978, England had provided 129 players to the NASL – more than any other nation, including the USA. Trevor Francis was one of them. It meant that he'd only arrived back in England for the start of the 1978–79 League campaign a few hours before kick-off. Evidently it hadn't done him any harm but it fuelled a season-long debate about conflicts of interest. The outcome was clear. England was now an importing nation, and it also wanted to hold on to its own.

Glory and war: Tottenham's Argentinians

Impact, honours and legacy are the hallmarks of any successful career. Ossie Ardiles and Ricky Villa provided White Hart Lane with all three during playing tenures that lasted a decade and five years respectively. They also brought glamour, a convergence of cultures, and drama. This was never more intense than in the successful FA Cup runs of 1981 and 1982. In the first they both featured to the point of memorable triumph. In the second Spurs ultimately retained the trophy without them in the wake of the Falklands War.

The pair made their first appearances for Tottenham on 8 August 1978 in a pre-season friendly in Belgium against Royal Antwerp. 'It was crazy,' said Burkinshaw of that pre-season tour. 'We had to be escorted everywhere by the police. The ground was absolutely packed.

There were people standing on the roof. Everyone wanted to see Ossie and Ricky.'

The same was true on their Football League debut, away to the defending champions, Nottingham Forest, on 19 August 1978. The crowd at the City Ground was so large that kick-off had to be delayed while the pitch was cleared of an overspill.

Ricky Villa scored the equaliser in a 1–1 draw after Martin O'Neill had put Forest ahead. The headline-grabbing start was not maintained, not for winning reasons at any rate. On the Argentinians' home debut four days later, Spurs suffered a 4–1 drubbing against Aston Villa. Three days after that they were held 2–2 at home by Chelsea and in their next match, in the League Cup, they could only draw at Third Division Swansea. Before the replay, which ended in an embarrassing 3–1 home defeat to the Welsh side, a rampant Liverpool crashed seven goals past Spurs in the League at Anfield without reply.

But taking these results in isolation, or even Tottenham's League placings of 11th, 14th and 10th in the Argentinians' first three seasons would be to miss the point. Their very presence spoke of ambition. Their flair and individual brilliance said that Burkinshaw wanted to revive the glory days in glory fashion. 'Tottenham spectators were always looking for top technical players,' he said. 'They enhanced what we had at the time. They fitted in the way we wanted to play. I thought buying from abroad was a terrific idea at the time. I think what's gone wrong now is that there are so many, there are some teams with virtually no home-grown players. That's too many. They come for the money. Ossie and Ricky didn't come for the money. They were earning as much as our best players but that was it.

'We acquired a big house out near the training ground that took in the two lads and their wives and families and settled them down. Three or four months later they moved to their own houses next door to each other. Having them together made it a success. After six or eight months they had their own friends and settled well.

'Ossie was such a character. He was only small but on the field no one could boss him. His feet never stopped moving, making positions for himself to receive the ball. He was always very aware of where everyone was. And his passing was unbelievable. So accurate. I'd not seen the like of it before. He was a big influence. Ricky was the better technical player. Glenn Hoddle was the best but Ricky wasn't far behind. The only thing I'd say was he wasn't the most consistent. If he started a match well, I knew he'd have a good performance. If not then I wasn't so sure.

'The other good thing is they looked after themselves. It was good for the younger players to see how they behaved. It was a sportsman's life, not the culture of going out and knocking back the pints.'

Ardiles contends that it probably wasn't until the 1990s, and the arrival of the likes of Jürgen Klinsmann and Gianfranco Zola, that young home-grown players started to copy the best Continental habits in training and preparation. 'Certainly those players had a major influence. They brought in new diets, tactics, training, the whole lot. The bigger you are, the more influence you have. If someone like Klinsmann runs better, eats better, trains harder, doesn't drink and plays better for it, you copy him. You have to be stupid not to follow the best examples.'

But he also acknowledges that he and Villa were more aware of what they ate and drank than their British counterparts 25 years ago. 'When we arrived we never drank anything except Coca-Cola and water, maybe we had one glass of wine once a week with a meal. But the lifestyle of British players, what they ate and drank, I was very surprised. The food was terrible. It was chips, sausages, greasy things, it was awful. The pre-match meals were heavy. Steak and chips, bread and butter. And that was on top of a full English breakfast in the morning.'

He found the on-pitch fare almost as rudimentary. 'I came into a team that was not the best. We had some talented players, like Glenn Hoddle, who was almost South American in his approach, but the style in general was very direct. It was like all the other English clubs at the time, except Liverpool. It bypassed the midfield. English players were fit, never say die, they ran more than us definitely, but there was still a long-ball mentality. I don't think it was unique in Europe, but even within Europe you could differentiate these things.

'In 1978 England was very, very isolated. Italy and Spain were very open to influence from the outside, especially from South America and Brazil. Other countries were more sceptical. England was the head of the sceptics. It took a while for Tottenham to improve. We were pretty bad. But when we started doing it as an eleven we got better.'

The 1981 FA Cup final, which went to a replay against Manchester City, provided evidence of this, albeit after some drama. Ricky Villa was substituted in the initial 1–1 draw and left the pitch in tears. 'I took Ricky off and he didn't like it,' Burkinshaw recalled. 'I've said to him since "You were having a stinker" and he's agreed, "Yes I was." When it happened I went into the dressing room afterwards and told him straight away that he was playing in the replay and that he needed to be ready.'

Villa responded by scoring one of the most memorable goals in FA Cup history. His late winning strike came at the end of a powerful run where he rounded man after man before beating Joe Corrigan to make the score 3–2. It was the defining moment in a Tottenham career that Ardiles contends was only ever, in Villa's mind, going to be temporary: 'We were exotic and people loved us for that. And then we played well, and they loved us for that. I enjoyed it and I adapted myself a lot quicker than Ricky. Mentally he was different. People said before we came that he would be the one to survive and I'd had no chance because I was smaller.

'But Ricky had an approach where he always seemed to be getting ready for life back in Argentina while he was still in England. If I went out and bought a picture, for example, I'd be thinking "That'll look good on the wall of my house". I'd be thinking of my house in England, where I lived. If Ricky did the same he'd be thinking "That'll look good in my house in Argentina". He had a big farm there, cattle, it was his home. For me, once I'd arrived here, this was my home.'

Conflict and confusion

Ardiles's attachment to his adopted country made the fallout from the Falklands War ever more painful. Keith Burkinshaw recalled how he first heard news of the conflict, on the morning of 3 April 1982. 'We were due to play in the FA Cup semi-final against Leicester at Villa Park that day. When everyone went to bed in the team hotel the night before everything was fine. The next morning the two lads told me that our countries were at war. They'd been up literally all night talking to people back home. They'd hardly slept. I had to make a decision whether or not to play them.' In the event, only Ardiles was picked to start and Spurs won 2–0. Burkinshaw recalled that Ardiles got 'some terrible stick' from the crowd.

In the aftermath of the game there was intense media debate about whether or not it was right and proper for the Argentinians to continue playing for Tottenham while Britain was at war with their country. Matters were further complicated because Ardiles was due to return to Argentina to begin pre-World Cup training with his international side. When he left for Buenos Aires after the FA Cup semi-final, his departure was taken in some quarters as a political statement. Burkinshaw insists it was a pre-arranged move that had nothing to do with the Falklands. 'Before the semi-final, I'd already agreed that he could go home to prepare for the World Cup in Spain. The press said at the time it was because of the war. That was wrong. The decision had been made before the war even started.'

Villa, who was not involved in the World Cup, stayed in England and played on during the war, although he removed himself from contention in the FA Cup final, played on 22 May while the hostilities were still raging. Spurs beat Queens Park Rangers 1–0 without him.

In early June, Ardiles was back in Europe, although not in England. The doubts still lingered about his future and many observers felt he would never play for Spurs again. Burkinshaw travelled to the Continent to meet him at the training camp where Argentina were preparing for their opening World Cup match on 13 June. Ardiles told him: 'It will not be possible for me to play for Tottenham again. We're at war.'

It was an awkward meeting. Barely a month had passed since almost 400 Argentinian crew aboard the cruiser *General Belgrano* had been killed as their ship was torpedoed by the British outside the war zone, while sailing away from the islands. More recently, the battle of Goose Green had brought multiple deaths and injuries on both sides and reports of bloody hand-to-hand bayonet combat were filtering out. The Argentinians were also stepping up their air attacks on British landing craft, a policy that claimed dozens of lives.

'We're winning,' Ardiles told an incredulous Burkinshaw.

'I don't think you are,' Burkinshaw replied.

'I don't want to come back,' Ardiles said.

'Well I'm not going to sell you,' said Burkinshaw. 'You can go somewhere on loan for twelve months but I'm not letting you go.'

Burkinshaw recalled: 'It seemed obvious that he'd been given all kinds of false information back home. The propaganda in Argentina had been drilled into him all the time. And then the war was all over a few days after that. In the end we agreed a loan deal to let him go to

Paris St Germain but almost as soon as he got there he was on the phone saying "Come and get me".'

Ardiles recalls the period as 'an incredibly difficult time where it was hard to have an everyday life. Tottenham never wanted me to leave but I thought returning to England would be a bad thing to do. My wife wanted to come back, Keith wanted me to come back. But I thought the best thing to do was leave. The scars were open, people had lost sons on both sides. We compromised and I went to France. I don't regret going and I don't regret coming back.'

He returned to Tottenham in January 1983 and in his first match, away at Luton, he received vocal abuse from the home supporters. There was also criticism from Argentina. Within a couple of months, by early March, Ricky Villa had decided to leave England. Ardiles remained, and went on to play for Spurs until March 1988, after which he had a brief playing spells with Blackburn and QPR before embarking on a globe-trotting career in management.

He said the highlight of his time at Spurs – and the second best moment of his playing career, after the 1978 World Cup – was the 1981 FA Cup win. Although Spurs won the UEFA Cup in 1984, Ardiles only appeared as a substitute in one leg of the final against Anderlecht. And in any case, he says that the FA Cup, in 1981 at least, was 'the cup in the world. People always say it, but then it was really true. The FA Cup was better to win than the UEFA Cup. Now, it's unequivocally not. The European Champions League is the cup to win. But then the FA Cup was the most prestigious.'

Aside from the high point of 1981 and the low of the war, Ardiles picked out a third-round FA Cup replay win over Manchester United in 1980 as a particularly memorable moment. Many fans remember it best as the time when Glenn Hoddle was drafted in as an emergency goalkeeper in the second half. Ardiles remembers it for scoring the only and decisive extra-time goal, in the 118th minute.

Away from the pitch, he endeared himself to supporters with his polite and gentle manner and never flinched from extracurricular activity that might amuse supporters. No student of football songs is ever likely to forget that the 1981 FA Cup final was commemorated in verse beforehand in the genre 'classic', 'Ossie's Dream (Spurs Are On Their Way to Wembley)', sung by the squad and accompanied by Chas & Dave. No foreign player, before or since, has been honoured in such a way. The song began with the lines 'Ossie's going to

Wembley/His knees have gone all trembly' and contained the following verse, in which Ardiles memorably sang the final – heavily accented – line:

> In our ranks there's Ossie Ardiles
> He's had a dream for a year or two
> That one day he's gonna play at Wembley
> Now his dream is coming true
> Ossie we're gonna be behind you
> All together, man for man
> We know you're gonna play a blinder
> In the cup for Tott-ing-ham!

In retrospect, the verse that included the lines 'We are the boys from Keithy's army/And we're marching off to war/We're sending our soldiers to Wembley/Under General Burkinshaw' was never one that Ardiles would be singing a year later, but it seemed light enough at the time.

War was a recurring theme for Ardiles in 1981. It was also the year he starred in John Huston's cult football movie, *Escape To Victory*, with such venerable acting talent as Michael Caine and Sylvester Stallone and alongside footballers including Pelé, Bobby Moore, Mike Summerbee, Kazimierz Deyna and what seemed like half of Ipswich Town.

Legacy

Ardiles and Villa's footballing legacy was that they ushered in the era of the passing game. Keith Burkinshaw says: 'Now it's better than ever, more accurate, not just forwards but sideways and backwards, and with patience.' Ardiles agrees, although he says it took 'a long, long time' to happen. Burkinshaw adds: 'But there are other things we've lost. We've lost wingers, we've lost people with the ability to dribble, we don't run with the ball at people. At one time there'd be a lot of players like that, causing a threat.'

The greatest intangible legacy lies in the memories of supporters, both of Tottenham and of football at large. Keith Palmer, a lifelong Spurs fan, said: 'I look back at those years with extreme reverence – a meeting of two worlds, a meeting of two peoples. The strong, cold, physical world of the northern hemisphere, and the flamboyant, skilful style of two South Americans who will remain in the hearts of Tottenham fans all over the world forever. Individual games did not matter as much as the effect their mere presence brought with them, and in an era before the English Premiership became the world's largest temp agency.' Steven Bridge, a Charlton fan and chronicler of the game through his photography for several decades, said: 'I'll never forget the slow-motion footage of Ardiles doing this flick with the heel of his foot with the ball going up in the air. It was out of this world, and certainly not out of England. I'd never seen such a trick. Years later Ossie was to repeat it in *Escape To Victory*.'

Bridge recalled going to a Charlton match away at Everton in August 2000. One of the other Charlton fans travelling with him was a 17-year-old, Pete Underwood, who'd recently seen a video of Ardiles's party piece for the first time.

> We arrived on the coach early. We saw loads of kids playing football on Stanley Park. We fancied a bit of footy before the real thing, and so we challenged five teenagers to a game. During the game, at full speed, Pete did the Ardiles flick over their goalkeeper, rounded him, only to hit the post with his shot. But twenty years on, Ardiles's South American magic lived on and his influence was felt by a lad not even born when Ardiles entered English shores. I'm a Charlton fan through and through but I went to Ardiles's testimonial at White Hart Lane in 1986, paid good money to see a great player grace our game in England. Ardiles signed my programme. That's the test. I went the extra mile to get the autograph.

Bobby Robson's double Dutch

Bobby Robson had already transformed the fortunes of Ipswich Town by 1978, winning the FA Cup that year having forged a successful team who regularly finished in the top six in the First Division. His side boasted England internationals including Mick Mills, Brian Talbot, Paul Mariner and Trevor Whymark as well as the youthful but experienced Scots, George Burley and John Wark. The club played regular European football from 1973 onwards and there was plenty of evidence that Robson was becoming one of the leading managers in the country.

Yet their style of play was still essentially English, with an emphasis on getting the ball as quickly as possible from the defence to the attack. 'Total football' it was not, but as a keen follower of the Dutch game, where Rinus Michels pioneered that philosophy based on fluid movement and versatility, Robson aspired to try something new.

'I built some good teams at Ipswich but we did play quite direct football, from back to front, quite often,' he recalled. 'Get the ball up to Mariner, get the ball up to Whymark. That was all right but it used to break down a lot of the time so we used to bypass the midfield. I knew for us to improve and be a better team altogether we had to play a different form of football than we'd ever played. Through the midfield, passing the ball in sequence and get it up to the strikers in a better, more controlled way. And to do that you need to have top-class midfield players who can command the ball.'

His solution, once the transfer barrier came down, was to turn to the Netherlands, to Frans Thijssen and Arnold Muhren, two midfield players he first saw in action when they played against Ipswich for Twente Enschede in the UEFA Cup in 1973–74 and 1974–75. The Dutchmen offered Ipswich something different in their approach, mentally, physically and technically. England had few home-grown players with such lavish technical gifts and those that did exist, like Glenn Hoddle at Tottenham, were expensive. Muhren and Thijssen also brought dedicated professionalism and good training and dietary habits.

'I thought they were wonderful players,' said Robson. 'Highly technical players. Muhren was a beautiful passer of the ball, very educated left foot. Not a great defender but in possession he was outstanding. He could hit every pass in the book. Thijssen was a great dribbler. They were just what I needed to make my team.'

Robson made his approach for Muhren after a lengthy period of solo clandestine scouting. 'I didn't tell anybody, just got on a plane and went to watch Dutch football. So I saw them play independent of our games against them.'

Money was a significant factor in the transfers. 'I saw those two would be ideal players. And they were cheap. I sold [Brian] Talbot to Arsenal for £450,000, which was a large sum of money then. We'd just beaten Arsenal in the FA Cup in 1978 and Talbot had been outstanding. Terry Neill wanted to buy him and in the meantime I'd identified these two players. We paid £150,000 for Muhren and

£200,000 for Thijssen and put £100,000 in the bank and we brought two crème de la crème players to the club.

'They were sensational. They adapted themselves to the English style of football, which was a bit more rugged, a bit more competitive. They loved the English way of life, the English way of training. They adapted very well. They spoke English, as most Dutch people do, so that wasn't a problem. So their adaptation into the town wasn't too difficult. They just went straight in.

'They were two big pieces in a jigsaw. They were two players we couldn't get in England anyway. We didn't have two players like that in England. And if there was anyone else of that quality in the market, we couldn't afford it.'

In the season before the Dutch pair moved to Suffolk, Ipswich finished 18th in the First Division. When Thijssen arrived, they were 13th but rallied to finish in sixth. They finished third in 1979–80. The following season they were runners-up behind Aston Villa, won the UEFA Cup and reached the semi-final of the FA Cup before elimination by Manchester City. Ipswich players made a clean sweep of the end-of-year awards, with Thijssen winning the football writers' Footballer of the Year award, the first foreigner to do so since Bert Trautmann in 1956.

Robson recalled: 'In 1981, that lovely Ipswich side that I created was brilliant but those two were marvellous architects of the way we played. They brought a different dimension to our game, a different way of playing. They were terrific pros. They were non-drinkers, they were great trainers, they conducted themselves very well.

'Arnold Muhren could speak six languages. He could speak Dutch, English, German, French, Italian and Spanish. And he could switch from one language to another just like that. I said, "How do you do that?" He said, "My upbringing." . . . I wasn't conscious of what we were doing in the grand scheme of things. I didn't know it would be the beginning of a fleet of players.'

Ipswich achieved another runners-up spot in the First Division in 1982, this time behind Liverpool, before Robson became manager of England and Muhren moved on to Manchester United under Ron Atkinson. There, he was part of the FA Cup-winning side of 1983, scoring a penalty in the replay of the final against Brighton. He demonstrated his longevity by returning, aged 34, to the Netherlands, where he won the European Cup-Winners' Cup with Ajax in 1987.

He was also an integral part of the magnificent Dutch team – including Marco Van Basten and Ruud Gullit – that won the European Championship in 1988, beating England 3–1 along the way. He subsequently became a coach.

Thijssen left Ipswich in 1983 for a brief spell with Nottingham Forest before moving to Canada with the Vancouver Whitecaps. He returned to the Netherlands in the mid-1980s and continued playing until 1991, later becoming a manager.

A Pole apart

The most prominent Pole to arrive in England in 1978–79 was Kazimierz Deyna, Poland's World Cup captain. His transfer was unwittingly inspired by the words of the BBC television commentator, Barry Davies, and the intervention of a Manchester-based football reporter, John Roberts. Roberts was working for the *Guardian* at the time of the 1978 World Cup, a tournament he watched on television in England. During one of Poland's early games Davies made an off-the-cuff comment that Deyna would be interested in playing club football in Western Europe. Roberts thought nothing more about it until he saw a news agency report, a few days after the World Cup, linking Manchester City with a possible move for Ossie Ardiles and Ricky Villa. To check out the story, he consulted City's chairman Peter Swales, who explained he'd been given an option to buy Ardiles and Villa but had not been entirely happy with the deal and had let it pass. 'He told me City were looking for a midfield player and asked if I knew any who might be available,' recalled Roberts. 'I mentioned Deyna because I'd heard that BBC commentary.'

Swales was interested. The Poles had established themselves as an international force since ending England's hopes of qualifying for the 1974 World Cup finals. Swales also thought their style was similar enough for a smooth assimilation. He asked Roberts how City could go about making an approach and Roberts offered to talk to the Polish international coach, Jacek Gmoch. Roberts had met Gmoch when the latter had travelled to Manchester United to study training methods.

Gmoch confirmed Deyna's interest. He told Roberts: 'I know Deyna would like to move and Manchester City seems to me to be the kind of club which would suit him. In my opinion, Deyna has enough stamina and ability to be able to offer at least two seasons in the highest grade of football anywhere in the world.'

City thus called upon the services of another Pole already at the club, a catering manager called George Bergier, to act as a go-between and interpreter. A complex series of negotiations began. City had to deal with, in turn, the Polish FA, the Polish government and the Polish army. The army had to agree to demobilise Lieutenant Deyna, a member of the army club, Legia Warsaw, for whom he had scored almost 200 goals in nearly 500 games. He moved to Manchester in November 1978 in a deal that cost City around £100,000, comprising photocopying machines, medical instruments and US dollars, which the Poles used to send their athletes abroad to prepare for the 1980 Moscow Olympics.

There was no doubt that Deyna was a skilful player. He was technically accomplished and had won a record 102 caps for his country at a time when the team was respected throughout Europe. But the bagatelle style in England did not suit him; nor, ultimately, did City. When Malcolm Allison returned to Maine Road as manager to succeed Tony Book, who'd signed Deyna, the Pole found himself playing in the reserves. This prompted him to say: 'City play ping-pong football. I don't need Malcolm Allison to tell me I am a great player. Pelé told me I am a great player.'

Although he outlasted Allison, who departed in 1980, the next manager, John Bond, also rejected his talents, selling him to the San Diego Sockers in January 1981. As Alan Durban, then the manager of First Division Stoke, said at the time: 'The problem is, Deyna's on a different wavelength. He's tuned to Radio Four, and the others are on Radio Luxembourg.' Deyna continued to play professionally until 1987 before becoming a coach in the US. He was killed in a car crash in California in 1989.

The Yugoslavs

A cluster of Yugoslav players arrived in England in the wake of Ivan Golac, the first player from that country in the League when he joined Southampton. The attraction for the clubs was that they were hiring proven players at affordable prices. The lure for the players was partially money – they could earn more in England – but also the opportunity for career advancement. This often came within football, as the subsequent coaching careers of several showed, but also in other professions. Many of the migrant Yugoslav footballers were highly educated men, and several went on to pursue careers as lawyers.

Bozo Jankovic and Petar Borota were joined in England in the late 1970s and early 1980s by fellow internationals Raddy Avramovic and Raddy Antic. Jankovic, a striker, joined Middlesbrough in February 1979. He was Boro's leading scorer in 1980–81. He later moved to France with Metz before becoming a coach back home and then the president of his first club, Zeljeznicar. He had trained to be a lawyer throughout his playing career but had to abandon his law practice in war-torn Sarajevo in the early 1990s. He died in 1993.

Borota, an extrovert goalkeeper, joined Chelsea from Partizan Belgrade in March 1979. He broke Peter Bonetti's record of 16 clean sheets in a season in 1980–81. He was also voted Player of the Year, twice, at Stamford Bridge. But his unpredictability was sometimes a little unsettling for his team-mates. He was even known to backheel the ball to a team-mate in his own box to liven up a dull match, or move upfield for corners. Avramovic, another goalkeeper, joined Notts County in August 1979 and was a key figure as they regained their First Division place in 1981 after an absence of 55 years. He later played for Coventry but was sacked after some poor displays and returned home to become a lawyer.

Raddy Antic, a midfielder, joined Luton Town in 1980 and helped them to win the Second Division title in 1981–82, then scored their winner at Manchester City on the last day of the following season to preserve their top-flight status at City's expense. When his playing days were over, he embarked on a managerial career which included a short stint at Barcelona in 2003.

But Ivan Golac stands out, not just for his success with Southampton but for his later managerial success in Scotland. The high points in his career at the Dell included reaching the League Cup final of 1979, being voted the club's Player of the Year in 1980–81 and being part of the Saints' most successful ever League season, in 1983–84. He was pivotal in that campaign, albeit at the end. He'd returned to Yugoslavia in 1983 but rejoined Southampton during the title run-in. The team were in fifth place on the day of his first game back but his return to the defence inspired eight clean sheets in the last 11 games, and only one goal conceded in each of the other three. Southampton finished second in the League, three points behind champions Liverpool.

Lawrie McMenemy, who signed Golac for Southampton, recalls the 1978 World Cup as a time 'when everyone was getting a flavour for international football. It just seemed to have more impact'. McMenemy worked on the BBC's expert panel during the 1978 tournament. Shortly after it ended, he took a call from a friend, Tom Lawrence, who was an agent. 'Except he wasn't a football agent, they hardly existed in those days. He was a travel agent. He had this company offering tours abroad and he had a connection with a fella in Yugoslavia. The football system over there dictated that players couldn't leave until they were 28 and they also had to be inter-nationals. Golac fitted the bill.

'He came over and played in a pre-season friendly and I more or less had to make my mind up on that one game. I knew at half-time that I'd take him. He cost £50,000. By the end of the game we'd pretty much sorted out all the paperwork.'

McMenemy recalls the post-match meal when Golac and his representative – who wore a cream suit and was therefore nicknamed 'The Ice Cream Man' – came over to his table and 'stood to attention'. 'They asked if we could go out for a walk to discuss things. It was very amusing, so formal. But it made an impression. Nowadays people take a lot of chances buying players but I always put a lot of store by character. Ivan had a wife and kids, was a good family man, you weigh all those things up. He was totally in awe of the British game. And he had one of the best record collections around. He loved pop music.'

Aside from Golac's quality on the field, the value for money he gave Southampton was also significant: 'The first day we went up to training we were driving past some houses in town. They were basic terrace houses with six-inch gardens and Ivan said how he impressed he was. I thought "He'll not be hard to please". It didn't take long for the standing to attention to wear off and his taste in houses soon changed but we never had any problem with his contracts. He was delighted just to come to England and he didn't get massive money for it. Pound for pound those players were better value than nowadays. Now there are players being pushed all over Europe and they're often mercenaries. The English Premier League is popular among players, but don't let's kid ourselves, it also pays well.'

Golac's managerial career began with Partizan Belgrade, whom he steered to the Yugoslav league and cup double in 1989. He briefly managed Torquay in 1992 before making history in 1993 when he took over at Dundee United, the first coach born outside Britain or Ireland to take charge of a Scottish League side. He won huge acclaim from the fans by guiding his side to their first ever Scottish FA Cup win in 1994, when they beat Rangers 1–0 in the final. He also endeared himself to the players, fans and media alike with his novel approach. On one occasion, after a 5–0 defeat, he fined every member of his team, and himself, £100 for the poor performance. He encouraged his team to 'smell the flowers' during training, and claimed to have learnt English by listening to the Rolling Stones. He was sacked in 1995 but went on to coach elsewhere in Europe, including in Iceland, Serbia – where he also ran a chocolate factory – and Ukraine.

If the British careers of players such as Golac and Raddy Antic ultimately prepared them for management, they also helped inspire later generations of east Europeans to move to England. Such players included Sergei Baltacha of the USSR, who became the first Soviet in the League when he moved to Ipswich in 1989. Baltacha's son, Sergei junior, who grew up in Suffolk and Scotland, has since played for the Scotland Under-21 side. His daughter, Elena, was ranked no. 1 in British women's tennis for a time.

Ipswich also had the first Bulgarian player in the League, Bontcho Guentchev, in 1992. Other 'firsts' from eastern Europe and the Balkans included the Czech Republic's Ludek Miklosko, who entered the League with West Ham in 1990, Romania's Stefan Iovan (who arrived at Brighton in 1991), Croatia's Igor Stimac (Derby, 1995), Georgia's Georgi Kinkladze (Manchester City, 1995), Slovakia's Vladimir Kinder (Middlesbrough, 1997), Slovenia's Ales Krizan and Macedonia's Georgi Hristov (both Barnsley, 1997) and Moldova's Ivan Tistimetanu (Bristol City, 1998).

By the start of the twenty-first century, the English Leagues were the most diversely staffed in the world thanks to the process that started in 1978. Foreign players no longer stood out simply because they were foreign. They had to make a special impact to do that, as the following chapters show.

SEVEN SHADES OF ERIC

'When the seagulls follow the trawler it is because they think sardines will be thrown into the sea.'

Eric Cantona, March 1995

'If a Frenchman goes on about seagulls, trawlers and sardines he is called a philosopher. I'd just be called a short Scottish bum talking crap.'

Gordon Strachan, a former team-mate, in response

ERIC CANTONA POLARISED opinion like no other footballer before him. Devotees were in thrall to the reader of Rimbaud who painted expressionist artworks and quoted the great philosophers. They adored his unique talent, both as a player and as the inspiration who underpinned a glorious decade at Manchester United. They appreciated that he eschewed the trappings of success to live in modest accommodation with his wife and two children. They warmed to his generosity and humility.

Cantona's critics said he was a pretentious, garbage-spouting lout, too volatile to be reliable. They claimed he couldn't tackle and was useless in the hothouse of European football, that he was a head-case who deserved a jail sentence because he couldn't control his temper. They asked why, if he was really so humble and uninterested in cashing in on his fame, he exploited Rimbaud in Eurostar commercials and accepted the Nike dollar with such gusto. And as for humility, they asked 'What humility?'

It was a trait not widely attributed to a man, nicknamed 'Le Dieu', who took to the pitch with upturned collar, the epitome of arrogance. A different story is told by those who got close to him. Alex Fynn worked for Saatchi & Saatchi and was involved in the blueprint for the

Premier League. A writer on the business of football, he also worked as a consultant for Manchester United, and was asked to help Cantona with two projects in 1996.

'Eric was obliged to produce a book and a video as part of his contract with Manchester United,' Fynn recalled. 'My job was to make it as painless as possible for him. I hired a commercials director to do the video, which took a couple of afternoons. For the book, *Cantona On Cantona*, I sat down with him and asked him questions, in French. He replied and the answers were translated later.'

It was a simple enough exercise and was proceeding steadily when Fynn wondered whether Cantona was enjoying the process. 'In the middle of the conversation I stopped and asked him "Do you like me?"'

Cantona, slightly nonplussed, replied: 'Yes.'

'Is it because you've found someone who speaks French worse than you speak English?' Fynn asked. Cantona was not renowned for his use of English. He could speak it, certainly, although former team-mates tell how he would underplay his ability if he felt uncommunicative. It had been, at times, a touchy subject. 'But he just laughed,' Fynn said. 'Some people had this image of a pompous individual but he wasn't like that.'

At a later meeting, Fynn discovered that Cantona seemed genuinely reluctant to milk his image for cash. 'He was such a commodity it would have been easy for him to transcend the game. I did one presentation for him about how he could become a brand, much the same way Ayrton Senna had become a brand, popular well outside the boundaries of his own sport. After the presentation we had a discussion and Eric said he didn't need the money or the hassle.'

Regardless of the divergence of opinion, there is no doubt that during Cantona's five years at Old Trafford the landscape of English football changed beyond recognition and that he was a major catalyst. His first season at United, 1992–93, ended in triumph with the club's first title for 26 years. His second, 1993–94, ended with United's first League and FA Cup Double. Had he not kung-fu kicked an opposition supporter in January 1995, earning himself an eight-month worldwide ban, United would most likely have won back-to-back Doubles. Instead the second Double came in 1996, followed by another League title in 1997. It was Cantona's fifth title in six years because he also won the League with Leeds in 1992.

The hard facts of his influence were plain to see, domestically at least. His playing record, examined in detail later in this chapter, shows that United were a better team when he was on the pitch. They were more likely to win. They scored more goals per game. They conceded fewer. Those margins matter in football and Cantona was influential by a margin. Even in the period after his ban, when the statistics show his ability to turn a game was on the wane, one purple patch saw him almost single-handedly drive United to the 1996 Double with goal after match-winning goal.

Manchester United's torrent of success established them as the no. 1 football club in England and the most valuable in the world. It was a heady transition. As recently as 1989, the self-styled 'millionaire property tycoon' Michael Knighton had been on the verge of buying United for £20 million. The deal fell through because the money failed to materialise but it acted as a marker of where United – and football – stood in the immediate post-Hillsborough era. A decade later, after years of success, kick-started by Cantona, United were the most successful club in the world's richest league and were being courted by billionaires, Rupert Murdoch among them. They were on the way to being the first £1 billion sports club in history.

'He was born to play for United,' Alex Ferguson once said of his French captain. 'Some players, with respected and established reputations, are cowed and broken by the size and expectations. Not Eric. He swaggered in, stuck his chest out, raised his head and surveyed everything as if to ask: "I'm Cantona, how big are you? Are you big enough for me?"'

Cantona was not the first Frenchman in the League, nor even the first to land a ban for hot-headed kicking. Eugene Langenove met both those criteria in the 1920s. But he was the first Frenchman to win anything in England. And he was the first foreign player ever to be voted Footballer of the Year by his peers when he won the PFA award in 1994. He brought a new dimension to the English game. He blazed a trail for French football, which became the largest provider of foreign players to the League. His achievements proved that a gamble on a foreigner could pay massive dividends.

The irony of his success in England was that he only ever crossed the Channel because he felt unable to function in France. He rebelled against the system that went on to produce a golden generation of

World Cup and European champions. Instead he took the burning desire of his singular approach to the English game. It collided with a monolithic culture and won.

Shades of Eric no. 1: Accommodating l'étranger

'Eric gives interviews on art, philosophy and politics. A natural room-mate for David Batty, I thought immediately.'

Howard Wilkinson, manager of Leeds, after hiring Cantona
in 1992

'We're a team who shout a lot and at the moment Eric is not getting all the messages. He's an excellent player – it's just a pity he wasn't born in Barnsley.'

Howard Wilkinson, on adjusting to Cantona

'Eric likes to do what he likes, when he likes, because he likes it, and then fuck off – we'd all like a bit of that.'

Howard Wilkinson, post-Cantona

Cantona arrived in England with a reputation for trouble. Only his first three seasons, from his debut for Auxerre, aged 17 in 1983, until his last year there were largely uncontroversial. He built a gritty reputation – attributed in part to his Marseille upbringing – that earned the first of 43 French caps in 1987, the year he paid his first heavy fine. His crime was to punch a goalkeeper in the face, giving him a black eye. The fine would probably have been bigger if his victim hadn't been his own goalkeeper.

He moved to Marseille in July 1988 for a then-record fee of 22 million francs (£2.2 million). Despite a decent start he was left out of Henri Michel's next France squad. Cantona reacted by calling Michel a 'sack of shit'. It would have been wiser not to do this on television. He was suspended from the French team for a year.

Five months later he was suspended indefinitely by Marseille after a tantrum in a European game against Torpedo Moscow. After being substituted, he kicked the ball into the crowd, took off his shirt, threw it to the ground and left the pitch with his head held high. He joined Bordeaux on loan, briefly, before transferring to Montpellier for a seventh of the fee that had taken him to Marseille.

A series of disputes at Montpellier culminated in a 10-day suspension after Cantona smashed his boots into the face of a team-mate, Jean-Claude Lemoult. The pair put the incident behind them, and Montpellier won the French Cup that year, although Cantona returned to Marseille soon afterwards. He made a good start to the 1990–91 season, scoring nine goals in 12 matches under the coaching guidance of Franz Beckenbauer. A knee injury then curtailed his season and when he returned to action, he found himself on the bench, from where he watched Marseille lose the 1991 European Cup final on penalties.

In 1991 he moved to Nîmes, newly promoted to the French First Division. He was attracted by the prospect of joining a dynamic young team but poor results frustrated him. On 7 December in a match with St Etienne, he flew into a rage after what he perceived to be a poor refereeing decision. He threw the ball in the official's face, walking off the pitch before the inevitable red card was shown. He was banned for three games. At his disciplinary hearing, he walked up to each member of the committee in turn and said 'Idiot'. His ban was increased to two months and he announced his retirement from football.

His exile did not last long. By January 1992 he was in England, having a trial with Sheffield Wednesday. His rationale was that a new country would give him a chance to wipe the slate clean. He had been at Hillsborough for a week when the manager, Trevor Francis, suggested he spend another seven days being assessed. He promptly left to join Leeds, managed by Howard Wilkinson.

Cantona made his League debut on 8 February 1992. Leeds, who were in a neck-and-neck battle for the title with Manchester United, lost 2–0 at Oldham. He went on to make 15 consecutive appearances until the end of the season. Manchester United faltered, losing three of their last four games, to finish runners-up. Leeds won the title. In Cantona's first season in England they were the last team, to date, to win the title with an English manager.

At the start of the inaugural season of the Premier League in 1992–93, Cantona scored a hat-trick in the Charity Shield and then six more goals in 13 games in the League. His relationship with

Wilkinson soured, however, and by December 1992, Cantona had been sold to Manchester United for £1.2 million.

Shades of Eric no. 2: Becoming an Old Trafford talisman

'One minute I'm thinking "Who's that ugly, French, one-eyebrowed git?" Then one trip over the Pennines and suddenly there's this dark, brooding, Heathcliff-type figure on the horizon.'

Lizzie from Bolton, a Manchester United fan, in an article entitled 'One for the Ladies', in the United fanzine, Red Issue

'He certainly deserves the captaincy of France as far his talent is concerned but I'm not sure about his cultural knowledge, which seems pretty basic to me.'

Claude Simonet, president of the French FA, 1994

'The only English I've heard from him is "Goal!"'

Steve Bruce, team-mate of Cantona at United

'No one should have any doubt about the massive influence made by Eric Cantona. He brought priceless presence and style to the team.'

Alex Ferguson, manager of Manchester United

At the end of one of his first training sessions with Manchester United, Cantona approached Alex Ferguson and asked if he could borrow a couple of players. He wanted to continue practising and it was helpful to have someone crossing the ball and someone in goal to make the session a little more realistic. It was a key moment in the manager's relationship with his new player, the moment he felt vindicated about his potentially risky purchase.

Within days of his first extended training session, Cantona was being accompanied not by youngsters drafted in to help him, but by volunteers including David Beckham, Ryan Giggs, Paul Scholes and the Neville brothers, who went on to form the spine of United's team in the 1990s. 'Players like myself, the Nevs, Butty, Scholes and Becks stay behind and practise, things like free-kicks and shooting,' said

Giggs in an interview the year after Cantona left United. 'We've always done it because that was what Eric always used to do. We just learned from his actions, the way he played and trained.'

As Ferguson wrote in his autobiography: 'Many people have justifiably acclaimed Cantona as a catalyst who had a crucial impact on our successes . . . but nothing he did in matches meant more than the way he opened my eyes to the indispensability of practice.' It said much about the English game in the early 1990s that one player should stand out so prominently simply by doing more than was required in training. But then he also made a huge impact on the pitch, at domestic level at least. Specifically, what stood out was his imagination, his control, his passing, his long-range shots, his clinical touch close up and his ability to squeeze the best from a small amount of space in no time at all. Not to mention his utter commitment to winning. The backheeled passes, the chips, the lobs and the volleys on the turn were a bonus.

Ask Manchester United fans to name special or important goals between 1993 and 1997 and several of Cantona's 80 will almost certainly feature. A breathtaking volley against Wimbledon in the FA Cup run of 1994, perhaps. Or his two penalties in the final against Chelsea the same year. Or the two goals in the first Manchester derby of that season, that helped turn a 2–0 half-time deficit to a 3–2 full-time win. Or both goals in the reverse fixture, which ended 2–0 to United. There was a delicate chip that defied the wind of Bramall Lane against Sheffield United the following year. Cantona stood, a trademark statue, as the home fans watched in disbelief.

The downside was Cantona's disciplinary record and occasional lapses into reckless, even callous, challenges. Bookings were frequent and he was the only player in United's history up to 1997 – the year of his departure – to be dismissed in consecutive matches. That pair of red cards came against Swindon, when he inexplicably stamped on John Moncur, and then against Arsenal, for two bookable offences. He also saw red in Europe, at Galatasaray, after calling into question the referee's honesty. His most notorious transgression, however, arguably the most notorious English football had ever seen, involved neither a player nor an official.

Shades of Eric no. 3: The kick

Four minutes into the second half of Manchester United's League game at Crystal Palace on 25 January 1995, Cantona kicked an opponent, Richard Shaw, and was sent off. Walking towards the dressing rooms, he suddenly jumped into the crowd. He leapt feet first in kung fu style, kicking an abusive Palace supporter, Matthew Simmons, a 21-year-old double-glazing fitter, in the chest. As soon as he was back on his feet Cantona started raining punches on Simmons, until dragged away. The event and its repercussions became headline news around the world for weeks.

The following day, Simmons made an official complaint against Cantona to the police, leading to a charge of common assault against Cantona. The Football Association released a statement saying it was appalled by the incident, which it said brought shame on those involved and on the game. Cantona was given 14 days to answer charges of bringing the game into disrepute.

Former players, pundits, commentators and even people who knew nothing of football began calling for the Frenchman to be banned from the English game for life. 'Pressure was no excuse,' said Sir Stanley Matthews, who was never booked during his career. 'I would take any amount of personal abuse for £10,000 a week.' 'He's nothing more than a brat,' said Jimmy Hill. 'He's a genius but there is this other side to him,' said Chris Waddle, who'd played alongside Cantona at Marseille. 'Maybe he needs someone to examine him, a psychiatrist or something.' 'What I don't understand is how a Frenchman can be playing for Manchester United,' said Lord Denning, formerly one of Britain's most senior judges. 'He's not even from England. They employ him to play football for them, not to go round hitting people.'

The reaction in France varied from philosophical to disgusted. An editorial in *Le Monde* said: 'In leaping the barrier, boots first, Eric Cantona attacked English football in its most sensitive spot. The British have succeeded in eliminating football violence to the point where the hideous metal fences supposed to protect the players have disappeared from their grounds. Now they have to acknowledge that the hooligans are on the pitch, threatening the public.' Another newspaper, *Le Provençal*, stated: 'We're no longer interested in his escapades, his pseudo philosophical bragging, his crudeness and the state of his soul. He lives his life and we live ours and we don't miss him.'

Manchester United maintained their silence until 27 January, when they announced that they had suspended Cantona for four months, until the end of the season, and had fined him the maximum allowed, two weeks' wages, or £20,000. The same day, the French FA announced Cantona had been stripped of his captaincy of the national side. Simmons, meanwhile, who had been revealed as having a conviction for assault and close ties to far-right groups, was banned from Crystal Palace for the season.

Cantona's disciplinary hearing with the FA was on 24 February 1995. He had already written to the FA, giving his side of the story, saying that Simmons had insulted him racially, causing him to react impulsively. He asked the FA to take into account his regret and his club's punishment.

Simmons, during his own later trial for using threatening language and behaviour at the Manchester United game, claimed: 'I was shouting "Off, off, off!", and I was pointing towards the dressing room 'cos that's what you do at football games. At no time was I doing anything else than pointing. I did not use any language of this kind. At no stage did I swear and I am quite certain of that. As far as I am concerned I was doing nothing wrong to deserve these actions. I was teasing Cantona but there is a big difference between a criminal offence and what you would call banter at a football match.'

Simmons was subsequently found guilty of two charges of using threatening words and behaviour during the Cantona incident. When he appeared for sentence he was jailed for seven days for contempt of court for attacking a lawyer during those proceedings. As police overpowered him, he tried to attack the prosecuting counsel. He shouted: 'I am innocent. I swear on the Bible. You press. You are scum!'

It was never officially established what Simmons actually said to Cantona, although it was thought to be derogatory about his nationality, and rather 'industrial'. A friend of Simmons was quoted in the *Guardian* as saying: 'He [Cantona] should be deported. We were giving him verbals. It was just the usual stuff about him being French. That's why you pay your £20.'

None of this had any bearing on Cantona's FA hearing. The FA commission's task was simply to consider the evidence before them in

February. Graham Kelly, the FA's chief executive and an admirer of Cantona's football, was acutely aware that the spotlight was on his organisation and how they handled the issue. He did not, however, want to see Cantona lost to the English game so he contacted him privately before the hearing. He advised Cantona that he had to make it clear that he was sorry. Although he did not say so to Cantona, there could be no repeat of the 'Idiots' situation years before in France.

The hearing commission included a director of Oldham, Ian Stott, who caused mirth among the Manchester United contingent at one point by asking Cantona: 'Isn't it a fact that you're a kung fu expert?' Cantona was confused by the question but his representatives stepped in to say that no, he was not.

More than three hours after the start of the hearing, Cantona was called to speak. Kelly recalled how Cantona said that he wanted to apologise to all concerned, including Manchester United, his team-mates, the United fans and the FA. And then, right at the end, in a gesture that showed he wasn't quite ready to bow and scrape completely, he added: 'And I want to apologise to the prostitute who shared my bed last evening.'

The commission doubled the ban that United had handed out to eight months. They also fined Cantona £10,000. A month later, at his court case for assault, he was sentenced to two weeks in jail. He was bailed pending appeal, which he subsequently won. His sentence was commuted to 120 hours' community service on 31 March. On hearing the news he hosted a press conference. He sat down, composed himself, and then began, with quiet purpose, to speak.

'When the seagulls,' he said, stopping to sip water for dramatic effect, 'follow the trawler, it is because they think sardines will be thrown into the sea.' He added 'Thank you' and departed.

It was a surreal afternoon – a French anti-hero, who'd kicked a loutish fan, having a jail sentence rescinded, then talking nonsense and leaving. The final bizarre touch came when a 13-year-old boy, a fan from Kent called Sebastian Pennells, handed Cantona a greeting card on his way out. Inside was the message: 'Eric is an idol, Eric is a star, If my mother had her way, He would also be my Pa.' Cantona the enigma marched on.

After some doubts over whether he would stay in England, he signed a new three-year contract with United on 28 April 1995, a couple of weeks before United ceded the League title to Blackburn

Rovers on the final day of the season by a single point. Blackburn actually lost their last match against Liverpool but United, without Cantona, could only draw at West Ham and failed to overtake them. A Cantona-less United also lost in the FA Cup final that year, 1–0 to Everton.

'Nobody in the history of football has been punished as hard as Eric but he has never said a word about it or complained. He is so mild mannered when the volcano is not erupting inside him.'

Alex Ferguson, during Cantona's ban

'Wasn't it good to see Eric Cantona back in action? Let's hope this time he remembers that kicking people in the teeth is the Tory Government's job.'

Tony Blair, as leader of the opposition, addressing the Labour Party conference of 1995, shortly after Cantona's ban ended

'I'd hesitate to say that what happened was a mistake, or that it was foolish or silly. It was far too complicated to be characterised in such a way.'

Cantona, 1996, reflecting on 'The kick'

Shades of Eric no. 4: Renaissance

Between 22 January and 5 May 1996, Manchester United played 15 Premiership games, winning 13, drawing one and losing one. Cantona played in every one, scoring in nine of them. At one stage he scored vital goals in six consecutive League games. He also played in all seven of United's FA Cup games between 6 January and 11 May, scoring in five of them, including the only goal of the final against Liverpool.

In May 1996, Cantona was voted the Footballer of the Year by the Football Writers' Association, becoming the fourth foreign player – and the first Frenchman – to win the award.

A purple patch for the King – 20 games in 1996

Date	Comp	Scoreline	Cantona	Goals
22 January	PL	West Ham 0	Man Utd 1	1
27 January	FAC (4r)	Reading 0	Man Utd 3	1
3 February	PL	Wimbledon 2	Man Utd 4	2
10 February	PL	Man Utd 1	Blackburn 0	–
18 February	FAC (5r)	Man Utd 2	Man City 1	1
21 February	PL	Man Utd 2	Everton 0	–
25 February	PL	Bolton 0	Man Utd 6	–
4 March	PL	Newcastle 0	Man Utd 1	1
11 March	FAC (6r)	Man Utd 2	Southampton 0	1
16 March	PL	QPR 1	Man Utd 1	1
20 March	PL	Man Utd 1	Arsenal 0	1
24 March	PL	Man Utd 1	Tottenham 0	1
31 March	FAC (sf)	Chelsea 1	Man Utd 2	–
6 April	PL	Man City 2	Man Utd 3	1
8 April	PL	Man Utd 1	Coventry 0	1
13 April	PL	Southampton 3	Man Utd 1	–
17 April	PL	Man Utd 1	Leeds 0	–
28 April	PL	Man Utd 5	Nottm Forest 0	1
5 May	PL	Middlesbrough 0	Man Utd 3	–
11 May	FAC (final)	Liverpool 0	Man Utd 1	1

PL = Premier League match; FAC = FA Cup match

Shades of Eric no. 5: Statistics, success and the sticky issue of Europe

Throughout Cantona's time at Old Trafford, Manchester United played a total of 250 games in the Premiership, the Coca-Cola Cup, the FA Cup and in Europe. Cantona played in 182 of them, scoring 80 goals, or 0.44 goals per game. In his peak season in the Premier League, 1994–95 before his ban, he scored 0.57 goals per game. He eclipsed that figure in the FA Cup, scoring 0.59 goals per game over four years in 17 matches, only one of which United lost. His worst season in the Premier League was his last, when he scored 0.31 goals per game, the same strike rate he achieved in European competition.

Statistically, Cantona was a positive influence over the length of his United career. During that time, the club won 5.8 per cent more games when he played, drew 3.6 per cent more and lost 9.4 per cent fewer. They scored 0.26 goals per game more when he played and conceded 0.06 goals per game fewer.

The effect of his ban can be broadly seen by United's statistics 'pre-kick' and 'post-kick'. Between signing for the club and that day at Selhurst Park, United won 12.6 per cent more games when Cantona was in the team, drew 9.2 per cent more and lost 21.8 per cent fewer. They scored almost half a goal per game more and conceded almost a quarter of a goal per game less. After his return, the 'Cantona effect' was actually slightly detrimental overall, although the 'post-kick' era also contained the purple patch of 1996. But the following details should give some indication of quite how valuable Cantona was to United.

Manchester United's Record During The Cantona Era

The summary

Premier League winners: 1993, 1994, 1996, 1997

Premier League runners-up: 1995 (Cantona suspended from Jan 1995 to end of season)

FA Cup winners: 1994, 1996

FA Cup runners-up: 1995 (Cantona suspended)

Other FA Cup runs:

1992–93, United were knocked out in fifth round by Sheffield United (Cantona was not playing)

1996–97, United were knocked out by Wimbledon in a fourth-round replay (Cantona played. It was the only FA Cup match he lost from 17 contested)

Coca-Cola Cup runners-up: 1994 (Cantona played five of the six Coca-Cola Cup games of his career during that season. The defeat in the final to Aston Villa was his only Coca-Cola Cup defeat)

European Cup/Champions' League

1993–94: Second-round exit to Galatasaray (Cantona was sent off at the end of the second leg)

1994–95: Eliminated after group stage (Cantona was serving a European suspension for four of six games)

1996–97: Semi-final exit to Borussia Dortmund (Cantona played 10 games during the campaign)

UEFA Cup

1995–96: First-round exit to Rotor Volgograd (Cantona was not playing, still suspended after 'the kick')

The statistics

OVERALL: Premier League, FA Cup, Coca-Cola Cup, European Cup

	P	W	D	L	F	A	
Man Utd	250	154	58	38	469	225	
without Cantona	68	39	14	15	115	64	
with Cantona	182	115	44	23	354	161	(80 Cantona goals)

	% Won	% Drawn	% Lost	Goals per game	
without Cantona	57.4	20.6	22	F: 1.69	A: 0.94
with Cantona	63.2	24.2	12.6	F: 1.95	A: 0.88
The Cantona effect	+5.8	+3.6	−9.4	+0.26	−0.06

PREMIER LEAGUE

	P	W	D	L	F	A	
1992–93							
Man Utd	25	17	6	2	49	19	9 Cantona goals =
with Cantona	22	15	6	1	44	16	0.41 goals per game
1993–94							
Man Utd	42	27	11	4	80	38	18 Cantona goals =
with Cantona	34	23	10	1	72	31	0.53 goals per game
1994–95							
Man Utd	42	26	10	6	77	28	12 Cantona goals =
with Cantona	21	13	5	3	40	17	0.57 goals per game
1995–96							
Man Utd	38	25	7	6	73	35	14 Cantona goals =
with Cantona	30	19	6	5	58	27	0.47 goals per game
1996–97							
Man Utd	38	21	12	5	76	44	11 Cantona goals =
with Cantona	36	20	11	5	73	42	0.31 goals per game

FA CUP: Five seasons, 1992–93 to 1996–97 inclusive

	P	W	D	L	F	A	
Man Utd	27	20	4	3	55	18	10 Cantona goals =
with Cantona	17	14	2	1	34	8	0.59 goals per game

COCA-COLA CUP: Cantona played during two seasons, 1993–94 and 1995–96

	P	W	D	L	F	A	
Man Utd	16	10	1	5	28	19	1 Cantona goal =
with Cantona	6	4	1	1	10	6	0.17 goals per game

EUROPEAN CUP: Three seasons, 1993–94, 1994–95 & 1996–97

	P	W	D	L	F	A	
Man Utd	22	8	7	7	31	24	5 Cantona goals =
with Cantona	16	7	3	6	23	14	0.31 goals per game

Before and after 'the kick'

Before 'the kick'	P	W	D	L	F	A	
Man Utd	126	81	29	16	242	112	
without Cantona	31	17	5	9	49	33	47 Cantona goals =
with Cantona	95	64	24	7	193	79	0.49 goals per game

	% Won	% Drawn	% Lost	Goals per game	
without Cantona	54.8	16.1	29.1	F: 1.58	A: 1.06
with Cantona	67.4	25.3	7.3	F: 2.03	A: 0.83
The Cantona effect	+12.6	+9.2	−21.8	+0.45	−0.23

After 'the kick'	P	W	D	L	F	A	
Man Utd	124	73	29	22	227	113	
without Cantona	37	22	9	6	66	31	33 Cantona goals =
with Cantona	87	51	20	16	161	82	0.38 goals per game

	% Won	% Drawn	% Lost	Goals per game	
without Cantona	59.5	24.3	16.2	F: 1.78	A: 0.84
with Cantona	58.6	23	18.4	F: 1.85	A: 0.94
The Cantona effect	−0.9	−1.3	+1.8	+0.07	+0.1

The sticky issue of Europe

	P	W	D	L	F	A	
Man Utd	22	8	7	7	31	24	5 Cantona goals =
with Cantona	16	7	3	6	23	14	0.31 goals per game
without Cantona	6	1	4	1	8	10	

	% Won	% Drawn	% Lost	Goals per game	
without Cantona	16.7	66.6	16.7	F: 1.33	A: 1.67
with Cantona	43.7	18.7	37.6	F: 1.44	A: 0.88
The Cantona effect	+27	−47.9	+20.9	+0.11	−0.79

Cantona played in 16 European matches for Manchester United over three European Cup campaigns, in 1993–94, 1994–95 and 1996–97. There is no doubt he failed to make his mark, as his goal contribution, let alone his performances, shows. The first of those campaigns saw an aggregate preliminary-round win over Kispest Honved (in which Cantona scored), and then a defeat, on away goals, to Galatasaray. The second leg of that tie saw a lacklustre Cantona display and ended with him being sent off after the final whistle. A four-game ban from Europe followed.

By the time he returned to the European stage, United had already played four games from six in the Champions League group stage of the 1994–95 competition. They had won one, drawn two and lost one, making the next match, against Gothenburg, crucial. Cantona was ineffective, meaning that even though the last game ended in a 4–0 win, United were eliminated on goal difference.

Cantona did not play in Europe the following season as United were knocked out of the UEFA Cup by Rotor Volgograd. He was still serving his ban for 'the kick'. That left only one other European campaign in his United career, the 1996–97 European Cup, when his side reached the semi-final.

In the group stage, he scored twice, once at home to Rapid Vienna and once away in Fenerbahce. The latter goal was scored in what was probably his best European performance. At least United played as expected against moderate opponents and Cantona played his part. But in four other games in that year's competition, he played below par. Two of them were in group-stage losses to Juventus. The other two, crucially, were in the semi-final against Borussia Dortmund. He featured as a marginal figure in the 1–0 away leg and was hustled off the ball for the Germans' goal. In the home leg, which United also lost 1–0, he was sluggish and missed chances he would normally have been expected to convert.

In short, in the key games, against Galatasaray, against Gothenburg and especially against Dortmund, he failed to make an impact. It was to his great credit that he rarely, if ever, failed to make an impact domestically and to United's regret that he failed to make that impact on Europe's biggest stage. His exclusion from his national side, which coincided with his worst displays in Europe, probably had something to do with his inability to cope in international club football.

Alex Ferguson admitted that there was 'perhaps some kind of mental block' that stopped him from playing at his best at the highest level. 'There was an element in his nature that seemed to prevent him from realising the full potential of his incredible gifts.'

Shades of Eric no. 6: Departure

The morning after Manchester United's European Cup semi-final defeat to Dortmund, Cantona told Alex Ferguson he wanted to retire from football. As the season drew to a close, Ferguson leaned towards agreement with the decision. As he wrote in his autobiography: 'Seeing the dullness in his eyes, and the changing outline of his physique, I had to acknowledge that perhaps he was right to terminate his career before blatant decline became an insult to the fierce pride that burned in him.'

Cantona made his decision final a few days after United won their fourth title in five years. The club announced the decision on Sunday 18 May 1997. Cantona had gone before the news broke, leaving only a note. It said: 'I have played professional football for 13 years, which is a long time. I now wish to do other things.'

Ferguson faced the press, telling them: 'It's a sad day for United that he has decided to retire. He has been a fantastic player.' The Cantona era was over.

> 'The danger with games is that you can get tired of them. That's why I swapped soccer for cinema in the way a child takes up playing Cluedo when he is sick of Monopoly. But I'm still interested in football. It is like when you leave a woman and you don't cry when she goes off with someone else.'
>
> *Eric Cantona, 1998*

'He's a footballer, a thug and he's French.'

Gavin Stamp, art critic, on why there would be no portrait of
Cantona in the National Portrait Gallery, 1997

Shades of Eric no. 7: Legacy

In a BBC documentary several years after his retirement, Cantona accused Manchester United of treating him 'like a shit'. Ferguson said in his autobiography that Cantona had given two reasons for his departure: that he felt he had become a pawn of United's marketing department, and he felt there was a lack of ambition by the club's board in the purchase of players.

Ferguson's explanations need to be digested with care. First, his autobiography was originally published in 1999, a time when the manager was flexing his muscles in his own struggles with the board. Any suggestion that a club hero such as Cantona had said the club was not ambitious enough would only serve to back his argument in wrangles over transfer cash. Second, Cantona apparently did not acknowledge to Ferguson when he quit that he felt his influence on the pitch was waning. He was under no obligation to do so, of course, but to suggest that marketing quarrels were more influential than a slipping of his own high standards seemed strange. And anyway, later in 1997, in an interview with *GQ* magazine, Cantona said: 'I stopped playing football because I'd done as much as I could.'

This was backed up in April 2003, on the day he was named the Overseas Player of the Decade at a ceremony to mark the first 10 seasons of the Premier League. 'I loved the game,' he said of his retirement, 'but I no longer had the passion to go to bed early, not to go out with my friends, not to drink, and not to do a lot of other things – the things you like in life.'

The exploitation of his image while at the club had clearly rankled, however. In the BBC documentary he said that he had agreed a deal whereby he would share the profits for the use of his image: '[But] I signed a contract and they did not respect anything. At that time they thought that merchandising was more important than the team and players. When the business is more important than the football I just give up, rather than be treated like a pair of socks, a shirt or a shit. I am not a shit at all.' The current generation of players, who looked up to Cantona and learned from him, would testify to that. As would the supporters.

Cantona remains one of the truly iconic figures in Old Trafford history. He also continued to air fans' concerns after his departure, as when Malcolm Glazer took a controlling interest in the club in 2005: 'I feel far less close to United today. I love this club for what it is and for what it has given me. But I fear that economics will now become the real priority. United have existed for more than a century. It has always been with a philosophy, an identity and a very solid youth system. This is a turning point in the history of the club but it is not in the right direction. We are getting away from the idea that I have of football.'

United fans can still be seen wearing Cantona shirts and plastic face masks, waving French flags, even carrying toy parrots that say: 'Ooh Aah Cantona'. Many have travelled around the world to watch their hero, now pursuing a film career, play on the international beach football tour. 'Without exception, he always has the time to talk and thank those travelling,' said Oli Swinton, a United supporter. 'Everything about him was different.'

'1966 was a great year for English football. Eric was born.'

Advert for Nike

'Cantona is a great player, but only in the context of English football.'

Robert Louis-Dreyfus, president of Marseille, 1997

'For my next film role I would love to play a psychopath or an unpleasant person.'

Cantona, 2000

8

NORTHERN ROCKS AND MURKY MIDDLEMEN

SCANDINAVIA HAS PROVIDED England with some of its most durable, popular and successful foreign players, as well as with one of the most notorious agents in the game, and with England's first foreign national manager. The agent, Rune Hauge, was central to one of the English game's most damaging episodes – the bungs scandal that cost George Graham his job at Arsenal in 1995. But at times in Sven Goran Eriksson's tenure with England, between 2001 and its shambolic end in Germany five years later, you could have been forgiven for thinking that he was a greater villain than Hauge, who had been corrupt, not merely clueless.

Partly this was down to Eriksson's turbulent private life, which led to criticism that it impinged on his ability to do his job. It was seen either as a distraction, as with his affair with his celebrity compatriot, Ulrika Jonsson, or damaging to the very fabric of the FA, as with his affair with FA secretary, Faria Alam. That particular liaison led to the resignation of the FA's chief executive, Mark Palios, as well as a witch-hunt in some quarters for Eriksson's head, and, indirectly, to the Government demanding a review of the FA's structure.

Partly the coolness towards Eriksson was due to his own coolness, especially towards his job. Entering talks with Roman Abramovich in 2003 about a possible vacancy at Chelsea was seen almost as treason, not as a professional exploring his options. The same could be said of his remarks to undercover *News of the World* reporters in 2006, when he was admittedly naïve in the extreme to fall for a so-called 'fake Sheikh' sting and admit he might be interested in taking over at Aston Villa.

He rarely exhibited much outward passion or excitement. He was easy to parody for the nothingness of his post-match comments. 'We did a good job' and 'We played football' was about as animated as he got. Even when stirred by losing 4–1 to Denmark in a friendly in 2005, his claim that 'I'm angry . . . it was a disaster' was delivered with no discernible fury.

The bottom line for a manager's acceptance or otherwise is always results. Eriksson guided England to the World Cup finals in 2002, where they suffered a limp quarter-final exit, to the eventual winners Brazil, that prompted the first serious questions about his tactical nous. England reached the quarter-finals of Euro 2004, losing to hosts Portugal, who reached the final. And they also made it to the 2006 World Cup in Germany, albeit via some stumbling and shambolic qualifiers, in which Northern Ireland inflicted one especially embarrassing defeat.

With England possessing what was widely regarded as the most talented squad in a generation, Eriksson's ultimate goal was always success in 2006, to end 40 years of World Cup hurt. He entered that tournament knowing that even success would be greeted, by some, as nothing less than many others could have achieved with the resources available, and that failure would mark him out as an alien who never really got what it meant. Such are the pressures that come with being the England boss, especially if you're foreign.

In their own ways, Hauge, a Norwegian, and Eriksson, a Swede, stood as symbols for their respective eras within the story of foreign 'players' in England. The English game was so hungry for cheap, exotic talent when Hauge entered the scene that it often failed to discern between good deals and dodgy ones. By the time Eriksson arrived, foreigners were common, and embraced when they thrived, yet nationality was still among the first reasons cited if they stuttered. Among actual players, it was a Dane, Peter Schmeichel, whose achievements, not least in a decade of dominance with Manchester United, set him apart.

Safety (and in numbers)

Some 300 footballers from the so-called 'Northern Countries' of Denmark, Sweden, Norway, Finland and Iceland have played in England's professional leagues since the first, Nils Middleboe, in 1913. Other notable Danes included Jesper Olsen, bought by Manchester United in 1984. Having made his name at Ajax and scored for his country against England, he played in United's FA Cup-winning side of 1985. Although his impact declined as the tempo of the English game took its toll, he stayed at Old Trafford until moving to France in 1988. He later became an agent.

Sweden's Roland Nilsson, a cultured right-back, won promotion with Sheffield Wednesday in the same year, 1991, that his club won the League Cup. He was also part of the side who lost both domestic cup finals to Arsenal in 1993 and later played for, and briefly managed, Coventry. His compatriot Tomas Brolin moved to Leeds United in 1995 for £4.5 million from Parma. He was dogged by injury, his weight fluctuated and he became a figure of fun at Elland Road and later at Crystal Palace. When news came through in 1999, after his retirement, that he'd been involved in a non-serious road collision with an elk, it only cemented the image. He said, without irony: 'I am very lucky not to have been injured.'

Given the huge number of Scandinavians who've worked in the English game, it is not surprising there have been flops. But they have been consistently outnumbered by cheap, jobbing professionals who rarely had problems with the language, the climate or the style of play. In the post-Bosman years, the migration across the North Sea only intensified. The sheer numbers and specific successes tell their own stories, from Thomas Gravesen at Everton to Freddie Ljungberg at Arsenal.

Iceland provided English football with the likes of the prolific striker Eidur Gudjohnsen and the stalwart defender Hermann Hreidarsson. That country also provided Stoke City – owned by an Icelandic consortium – with a squad list featuring the likes of Gudjonsson, Gunnlaugsson, Gunnarsson, Danielsson, Dadason, Gislason, Kristinsson, Thordarson and Marteinsson. Almost every team shirt had a 'son' on its back, if not a son of the City inside it. Similar influence – from Norway – saw a comparably Nordic feel to team sheets at Wimbledon and Hartlepool around the same time. From the end of the 1990s, Finland started exporting players to England in numbers, notably no. 1s. At one stage three Finnish goalkeepers – Jussi Jaaskelainen, Peter Enckelman and Antti Niemi – were playing simultaneously in the Premier League.

Norwegians have made a big impact, on and off the pitch. The dealings of Rune Hauge became notorious, while the service provided by some of his compatriot clients, including Henning Berg, Ronny Johnsen and Ole Gunnar Solskjaer, was more glorious. That trio are among the most prolific medal-winning foreign players ever to play in England, each having been involved in multiple title successes as well as domestic and European Cup wins.

But no single Scandinavian in England has yet eclipsed the value for money, the durability, the professionalism or the single-minded will to win of Peter Schmeichel, Manchester United's northern rock.

Bringing home the bacon

When Schmeichel's playing career drew to a close in 2003, the goalkeeper from Gladsaxe could justly be regarded as one of the greatest custodians football has ever seen. In a 19-year, six-club odyssey that started in 1984 with Hvidovre in his native Denmark and ended with Manchester City, he won 15 major trophies with his clubs as well as a European Championship with his country and an assortment of personal awards. He retired because his 39-year-old body had taken – and given – enough. Amid a barrage of eye-catching statistics from Schmeichel's career, one stands testament to his influence. During the most successful decade in Manchester United's history they won 10 major trophies. Schmeichel had a pair of big hands in them all.

If Eric Cantona was a catalyst for success, and Ireland's Roy Keane later the thundering heartbeat who sustained it, Schmeichel proved to be the bedrock, as United's long-time failure to find a replacement of similar stature later showed. His contribution to the cause was massive in all senses. At 6ft 4in, his physical presence between the posts was enhanced by his foghorn exhortations to his team-mates. His shot-stopping ability was second to none. He was unrivalled in the one-on-one, capable, as all great goalkeepers are, of 'making himself big' in the eyes of an oncoming striker. Schmeichel was also possessed by an attacking instinct that manifested itself in his own penalty area and the opposition's. Like Bert Trautmann at Maine Road in the 1950s, he understood the value of the long, accurate throw as a crucial starting point for assaults on goal. Not that he always stayed back to attack. In his last game for Manchester United, his madcap run into Bayern Munich's area in the dying seconds of the 1999 European Cup final helped spread the confusion that led to United's crucial equaliser.

At Manchester United he won five Premier League titles, three FA Cups, a League Cup and a European Cup. Only one other foreign player to date has won more medals in England. That was another goalkeeper, Bruce Grobbelaar, who won 13 major honours with Liverpool. But Schmeichel also won three league titles and an FA Cup in Denmark before arriving in England, as well as a Portuguese title with Sporting Lisbon in 2000. He also played a crucial part in Denmark's European Championship win in 1992.

Bargain of the century

Schmeichel was approaching his 28th birthday when Alex Ferguson signed him for £505,000 in the summer of 1991. Ferguson first spotted him training in Spain, where United used the same warm-weather training facilities as those used by Brøndby, Schmeichel's club at the time. Ferguson's scouts soon confirmed what a special talent he was.

The people of Denmark already knew. After starting at an amateur team with his hometown club, Gladsaxe, Schmeichel made his debut for Hvidovre in 1984. He stayed three years, scoring six goals in the process to prove he was no ordinary keeper. In 1987 he signed for Brøndby, where he won three league titles, the Danish cup and the first of his 129 international caps. In 1990 he was voted Denmark's Footballer of the Year.

At the start of the 1991–92 season, Schmeichel went straight into United's team as a replacement for Jim Leighton. He played 40 games in the League that year as Leeds United took the final title of the pre-Premier League era. He also played in six of United's eight matches in the League Cup, at a time when the spark still existed in the tournament. Winning it was a cause for celebration, even for a club of United's pedigree.

The summer of 1992 brought another title for Schmeichel, when his nation won the European Championship. Denmark only played as eleventh-hour replacements for Yugoslavia. Schmeichel was a key figure in the success. England and the Netherlands were among those thwarted en route to the final against Germany, which saw some vital saves in a combative match.

Back in England, in the first season of the Premier League, 1992–93, Leeds sold Eric Cantona to Manchester United, who won the title. Schmeichel played in every match. His team lost their first two games of the season – 2–1 at Sheffield United and 3–0 at home to Everton – but lost only four more in the next 40, and never by more than a single goal. Schmeichel kept 18 clean sheets in the League.

The following season brought another title, with United losing only four League games, one at home. Schmeichel kept 15 League clean sheets. United reached two domestic cup finals. Without Schmeichel – who was suspended – United lost the League Cup 1–0. They won the FA Cup 4–0 against Chelsea.

A remarkable match at Liverpool the same season became the focus of intense debate on the day and well beyond. United quickly established a 3–0 lead only to capitulate and draw 3–3. When Bruce Grobbelaar, Liverpool's goalkeeper that day, was later accused of match-fixing, that fixture, and the three goals he conceded, became the focal point of the jury's attention. The three goals Schmeichel conceded became the focal point of his manager's anger immediately after the game.

'He wasn't just livid, he was absolutely hysterical,' Schmeichel said later of Alex Ferguson's reaction. 'He didn't just criticise my kicking, he more or less heaped derision on just about everything I had done in the entire game.' Schmeichel hit back with a tirade of his own. 'It reached such a personal level that neither of us was interested in, or capable of, backing down. I said the most awful things. I questioned his capabilities as a manager. I accused him of having a suspect personality. Ferguson did not keep anything back either and at one point he threatened to throw a cup of tea in my face.'

Ferguson decided the only appropriate course of action was to sack his goalkeeper for impudence. Such steely resolve was a feature of his management style, as later players, such as Jaap Stam, found out. Despite being a formidable presence in the heart of defence in the treble-winning side of 1999, the Dutchman was quickly sold by Ferguson soon after publishing an autobiography which included an anecdote about his manager's temper.

Schmeichel survived because he apologised to his team-mates for his outburst, an act of contrition that Ferguson overheard. There is no doubt that the goalkeeper's value to the club was also taken into consideration.

That value was apparent when Schmeichel was absent due to injury for an eight-game stretch in the League in the middle of the 1994–95 season. Those eight games included a 2–1 home defeat to Nottingham Forest, a 1–1 home draw with Leicester and a 2–2 draw at Southampton. Something was missing. A single extra point from any of those matches would have handed the title to United. They eventually lost out by one point to Blackburn, who had an inferior goal difference. The evidence suggests that with Schmeichel present the extra point necessary would have come from either the home game against Forest or the one against Leicester. United conceded goals in both of these, something they were not in the habit of doing at home when Schmeichel was between the posts. He did not concede a single League goal at Old Trafford between 23 April 1994 and 7 May 1995. In fact, United only conceded four at home in the whole of the 1994–95 season, and three of those hit the back of their net when Schmeichel wasn't in front of it. Even the fourth, on 10 May against Southampton, which brought the Dane's astounding run of home invincibility to an end, came in a 2–1 win for United.

Ferguson's problems continued almost as soon as Schmeichel returned from injury – Cantona kung fu kicked his way to an eight-month ban shortly afterwards. United certainly missed the French-man's influence, both in the title run-in and the FA Cup final defeat to Everton, but Schmeichel's temporary loss had also taken its toll.

The defining moments in a goalkeeper's career tend to be the crucial saves in the biggest matches. Schmeichel was no different, but his involvement in the opposition box also proved memorable. The most significant – and final – upfield foray of Schmeichel's career ended in a goal, the injury-time equaliser in the 1999 European Cup final. Though he did not score it, his presence in the penalty area helped create confusion in the Bayern Munich defence. David Beckham's corner flew into the box and fell to a rattled Thorsten Fink, who could only scramble a clearance to Ryan Giggs. The Welshman's shot was steered in by Teddy Sheringham.

In the absence of Roy Keane, Schmeichel was the United captain that day, in his last match for United. After the equaliser he barely had time to settle back on his own line before United had scored again to complete the most astonishing last-gasp comeback the European Cup has ever seen. 'Not even Hans Christian Andersen could have written a fairytale like that,' he said.

Norway's Ole Gunnar Solskjaer scored the winner that day after coming on as an 80th-minute substitute. Waiting on the bench for most of the game, only to enter the fray and deliver this kind of crucial input, was Solskjaer's trademark. Earlier that season, in February, he had made his appearance as a substitute 18 minutes from the end of a League game at Nottingham Forest. He scored his first goal on 80 minutes and added another three before the final whistle, claiming the record for the fastest ever hat-trick (let alone four-goal haul) by a substitute. 'Good job they didn't put him on earlier,' said Ron Atkinson, then Forest's manager, who'd just watched his side lose 8–1.

If the European Cup final and the Forest game exemplified the essence of Solskjaer, then Schmeichel's United career was encapsulated by 45 minutes at St James' Park on the evening of Monday 4 March 1996. The occasion pitted the League leaders Newcastle, under the irrepressible guidance of Kevin Keegan, against second-placed Manchester United, a team in transition. Key figures from a year before, including Paul Ince, Mark Hughes and Andrei Kanchelskis, had gone. The likes of David Beckham, Paul Scholes, the Neville brothers and Nicky Butt were in their first full season as regular starters. Schmeichel needed to be a big presence.

The match was pivotal in the title race. Keegan's side had let slip a seemingly unassailable 12-point lead at the top of the table but were still six ahead of United before kick-off. A win would reopen the gap to nine, a defeat would leave the visitors with only three to catch up and a game in hand. Keegan's starting XI was typically brimming with attacking options, with Les Ferdinand and Faustino Asprilla a potent Anglo-Colombian blend up front, supplemented by the scampering of Peter Beardsley and the flair of David Ginola.

Newcastle had not lost at home for almost a year and they showed why by laying siege to their visitors' goal with mesmerising waves of attack. They were thwarted by one man. Specific saves included marvellous reaction stops to shots by Ferdinand, Ginola and Robert Lee. Time after time the Dane narrowed the angle, made himself big, refused to countenance that he could be beaten. A Newcastle goal seemed inevitable. It never came. Eric Cantona scored, making it 1–0 to him and Schmeichel, whose sheer belief gave his team-mates the confidence to hold out.

Another notable performance – specifically one save – also came in 1996, in the away leg of a Champions League match against Rapid

Vienna in December. Somehow, after a seemingly unstoppable shot from Rene Wagner, Schmeichel reached the ball after diving to his right. He spooned it over the bar. It was reminiscent of Gordon Banks's save from Pelé in 1970.

Yet another memorable stop came in the FA Cup semi-final of the treble-winning season against Arsenal in the best semi-final in the Cup's history. The football was bewitching: drama, tension, a sending off, and a last-gasp extra-time decider by Ryan Giggs that was one of finest goals in the tournament's history. But he only had a platform for his 70-yard, 13-touch wonder goal because Schmeichel had saved a penalty during stoppage time at the end of the regulation 90 minutes. Having already denied Dennis Bergkamp with a full-stretch save in open play, he produced a world-class save from the Dutchman's spot kick. That, and his marauding in the Bayern Munich penalty box soon afterwards that helped to win the European Cup and complete the unprecedented treble, were fittingly significant ways to end his days with United.

Wheeling and dealing: Rune Hauge

Rune Hauge had a role in the majority of the deals involving the move of Scandinavian players to England in the early 1990s. He represented some of the key figures of the era, Schmeichel included. There is no suggestion that Schmeichel's move from Brøndby to Manchester United, or indeed many others involving Hauge, were 'dodgy' in any way. But several transfers did involve irregular payments, leading to the 'bungs' inquiry that cast a shadow over the game in the mid-1990s and beyond. In essence, Hauge paid money to various people to smooth some of the transfers involving 'his' players. The buying clubs were the losers because money they believed was going to the selling club was actually being paid as 'palm-greasers' to other parties.

Hauge's first big-money deal with an English club involved brokering the move in the late 1980s of a Norwegian goalkeeper, Erik Thorstvedt. Hauge initially offered the player to Arsenal, who thought the £60,000 fee was good value. The London side could not obtain a work permit, however, because Thorstvedt was not an international. He moved instead to Sweden with IFK Gothenburg, and in December 1988 – after a year and an international call-up – to Tottenham, then managed by Terry Venables, for around £600,000.

In 1989 Hauge enlisted the services of Steve Burtenshaw, who would later become chief scout at Arsenal, to introduce him to English managers, coaches and scouts. Burtenshaw signed a deal with Hauge's firm, Proman, that would pay him 25 per cent of the profits from any business he put Hauge's way, net of any 'paybacks' (undeclared payments, or bungs) that would be necessary to facilitate those deals. Through Burtenshaw, Hauge forged links with more than 20 managers, coaches and scouts in England. To most of them, Hauge was just another agent, albeit one with a good eye for a valuable player, and they dealt with him accordingly.

From late 1989, Hauge was involved in a string of player moves to England. The Norwegian defender, Erland Johnsen, moved to Chelsea in December 1989. In the same month, a suspect deal brought Toddi Orlygsson, an Icelandic midfielder, from Akureyri in his native country to Nottingham Forest, then managed by Brian Clough. It was later revealed during the bungs inquiry that Ronnie Fenton, Clough's assistant, had received a £45,000 backhander as part of the Orlygsson move. Fenton collected the money in Hull, where it arrived on a trawler stashed in a fish box.

In 1990, Hauge was involved as Anders Limpar moved to Arsenal. In 1991, he oversaw Schmeichel's move to Manchester United, and before that, helped in the negotiations that led the winger, Andrei Kanchelskis, to move from Shakhtar Donetsk in Ukraine to Old Trafford, initially for £650,000. United paid Hauge a £35,000 fee for 'professional services', one of which was helping with the Schmeichel and Kanchelskis transfers. This breached the rules on payments to agents but an FA inquiry established no bungs had been paid.

The Kanchelskis move evolved into a saga – not involving Hauge – so murky that it even made Hauge's transgressions look tame. When Kanchelskis signed in 1991, United's deal with Shakhtar included a clause which said United would pay additional sums, amounting to an extra £550,000, depending on the player's appearances and whether he renewed his contract. United later paid this money in good faith into a Swiss bank account but it did not reach Shakhtar. The club's president, Aleksandr Bragin, was suspected of diverting the money. He and five bodyguards were killed by a remote-controlled bomb triggered by persons unknown in October 1995.

Whether the events detailed below contributed to that assassination will never be known but suspicions about Bragin had built up during the previous year. Kanchelskis had signed a new contract at United in 1994, brokered by an agent, Grigori Yesaulenko. A clause in that contract stated that Kanchelskis would receive one-third of any sell-on fee if he left United. Shortly after it was signed, Yesaulenko handed £40,000 in cash in a wrapped box to United's manager, Alex Ferguson, in a hotel car park. Ferguson, shocked upon opening the box, reported the matter to his club. The money remained in United's safe for almost a year until Yesaulenko next visited Old Trafford. As Ferguson wrote in his autobiography: 'If I had been able to foresee the dramas that were still to be enacted in the Kanchelskis saga, I might have wondered if the cash was meant to be not so much a thank-you for past assistance as an encouragement towards co-operation in the future.'

That 'co-operation' was probably expected by Kanchelskis's connections in 1995 when he announced he wanted to leave Old Trafford. This presented United with two problems. The player's 1994 contract said he was entitled to a third of the sell-on fee. Additionally, a clause in United's original 1991 contract with Shakhtar had stipulated the Ukrainian club was also entitled to a third of any sell-on fee.

United clearly did not want to sell Kanchelskis and then give away two-thirds of the proceeds. After their chairman, Martin Edwards, had said as much, he received death threats. He explained to Yesaulenko that he just could not sanction a sale if United had to pay Shakhtar a third. A fax on Shakhtar notepaper, dated 13 July 1995, waiving this payment, arrived soon afterwards. Kanchelskis was then sold to Everton for £6 million.

The matter was still not closed. In September 1995, United received a letter from Bragin and his deputy saying that the author of the July fax, a director called Kolotsei, had not known what he was doing. They wrote: 'Mr Kolotsei signed . . . text in the English language prepared by Mr Yesaulenko . . . only because Mr Yesaulenko requested and explained that this fax was necessary exclusively for helping Andrei Kanchelskis to solve private problems . . .'

It was only when other senior figures associated with Shakhtar started looking into the Kanchelskis deal that they realised the club had been due £550,000 in performance payments under the 1991 contract and that the money had never arrived. Bragin was killed shortly afterwards for reasons unconfirmed. Shakhtar remained in dispute with United over monies due to them until March 1996, when United made a £770,000 settlement payment. Both parties signed a confidentiality agreement relating to the deal.

After the Kanchelskis and Schmeichel deals, Hauge's next major sale to an English club was that of Pal Lydersen, a Denmark-born Norwegian defender, to Arsenal in November 1991. After the deal went through Hauge gave Arsenal's manager, George Graham, £140,000 in used £50 notes.

In August 1992 came the deal that would prove to be Graham's undoing. Hauge arranged the transfer of the Danish international John Jensen to Arsenal for £1.57 million from Brøndby. The bungs inquiry report would later conclude: 'From a transfer fee of £1,570,000 paid by Arsenal, Brøndby paid approximately £392,500 to HSV Hamburg [Jensen's former club], approximately £739,433 to InterClub Ltd [Hauge's company] and retained approximately £438,067. From the amount InterClub received, we know it paid £285,000 into a bank account opened for Mr Graham's benefit.'

The scam was initially uncovered by a Danish reporter, Henrik Madsen, although Graham was actually accused as a result of an Inland Revenue inquiry following a tip-off. Graham always maintained that the two payments he received from Hauge were unsolicited gifts. Hauge backed him up. The authorities did not agree and in 1995 Graham was banned from football for a year and fined £50,000. He repaid Arsenal the total amount of his 'unsolicited gifts' from Hauge, plus interest. Hauge was banned by FIFA for life from being an agent, a punishment that was commuted to a two-year ban on appeal.

Hauge brokered a raft of other deals, before and after his ban. The most prominent and longest-serving Scandinavians involved included Stig Inge Bjornebye, Henning Berg, Lars Bohinen, Alf-Inge Haaland, Gunnar Halle, Ole Solskjaer, Ronny Johnsen and Tore Andre Flo. With the exception of Haaland's move to Nottingham Forest in 1994, after which Ronnie Fenton received another £45,000, there was no evidence that any of the deals were anything but legitimate, above-board moves. George Graham even had the confidence to use Hauge's services to provide players for him at Leeds after their respective bans elapsed.

Seventeen games of wonder (then a decade of despair)

Football and money have never mixed well but few deals have led to such a catastrophic outcome for one club than that which took Allan Simonsen to Charlton in 1982. The bare facts hardly convey the enormity of the move. Simonsen, a Danish forward, had been European Footballer of the Year in 1977. By 1982, he was playing at Barcelona when he swapped the Nou Camp for Charlton, then mid-table in the English Second Division. An equivalent move in 2006 might have seen Michael Owen, European Footballer of the Year five years before, swap Newcastle United for QPR (mid-table in the division below the Premier League). Unthinkable.

Charlton's chairman, Mark Hulyer, was able to persuade Simonsen to move by offering a lucrative two-year contract worth £82,000 a year, an enormous sum at the time. Hulyer believed that Simonsen would not only increase attendances dramatically but help lift Charlton to the top division. He also agreed to pay Simonsen a share of sponsorship deals he was sure would materialise through the Dane's presence. The attraction for Simonsen – 29 at the time and not past his peak – was that he was struggling to hold his place in the Barcelona side. Crucially, Charlton also had a former Denmark international coach, Ernst Netuka, working for their manager Lennie Lawrence. Two other Danish players, Viggo Jacobsen and Johnny Ostergaard, had recently had spells at the club. On-off negotiations between Charlton and Barcelona dragged on through the late summer and early autumn of 1982. Simonsen eventually moved in November for a fee of £324,000, not that Charlton were able to pay it all up front. With hindsight, it was obvious they could never afford the deal in the first place.

Steven Bridge, a 'long suffering' Charlton fan even before 1982, was among the crowd when Simonsen made his first appearance in a Charlton shirt. It came on 10 November 1982, in a reserve match against Swansea City: 'It was such an event that I took my wife. Simo had scored for Borussia Mönchengladbach against the winners Liverpool in the 1977 European Cup final and he'd won the European Cup-Winners' Cup with Barcelona only six months before signing for Charlton.

'The average attendance for a Charlton reserve game was 419 at the time. Me and my wife were two among the 2578 who went to see if it really was true. Then in typical Charlton let-you-down style, Simo wasn't in the team. Nor was he on the bench. He wasn't there. An announcement was made that he was stuck in traffic. He made it for a second-half appearance. The wait until his first-team debut was unbearable. Three days. I was like one of the disciples of Jesus waiting for the resurrection. The restoration of Charlton's fortunes, that's what it was going to be.'

The first-team debut came on 13 November 1982 at The Valley against Middlesbrough. Simonsen scored once in a 3–2 defeat in front of 10,807 people, which was about double the usual attendance. His next game was on 4 December against Newcastle, who also had a former European Footballer of the Year on their books. Kevin Keegan did not play that day, Charlton won 2–0 and Simonsen scored again. He played another 14 League games and one FA Cup match, scoring nine times altogether.

But despite Mark Hulyer's best intentions, crowds settled to average around 5000 (half the level anticipated), there were no major sponsorship deals and, crucially, no vast improvement in Charlton's on-pitch fortunes. Nick Riley, a Charlton fan since 1965, recalled: 'Simonsen was so good it was frightening, but the players around him were very poor, it didn't do us any good. Simonsen could spot things the other players just didn't read. Exquisite defence-splitting passes went nowhere. Magical runs into space went unnoticed by his colleagues. He was some player but completely wasted at Charlton at that time.'

Another supporter, Dave Rodden, recalled: 'Supporting Charlton for 40 years has produced many a surreal moment, but watching one of Europe's all-time greats line up alongside the likes of Les Berry took the proverbial hobnob. The defining moment of this bizarre episode came in a match at The Valley against Leicester. With the exception of the incredibly talented Simo, we had a remarkably average team, and perhaps the most average of the ingredients was a certain Don McAllister. Twenty minutes in, with Simonsen yet to see a ball played to him within viewing distance, let alone along the ground, the ball was lobbed towards McAllister in the right-back position, tight on the touchline and with Simonsen ten yards in front of him. Don, with that sturdy right boot of his, smashed the ball on the volley, at 150 mph, straight at the diminutive Dane's thyroid. An average player would have been killed. A really good player would have got out of the way. Simonsen, astonishingly, caught the ball on his chest so that it dropped to his feet, took a quick look up, and rolled it back along the ground to McAllister. He swung that trusty right boot again, and sliced the ball viciously into the main stand. You knew at that moment that this was never going to work out.'

The transfer quickly took its toll on the club's balance sheet. Simonsen's wages were becoming a burden and Charlton failed to pay him on time. On 26 February 1983, the Dane refused to board the team bus before a game at Burnley. After persuasion he relented but Charlton lost the game 7–1. The next day Charlton announced that signing Simonsen had been a 'costly error' and that he would be sold. Barcelona were also pressing for £180,000 still owed on the transfer. Simonsen was put up for sale at that price. His last game was on 19 March and then he headed back to Denmark, joining Vejle BK for an undisclosed but probably small sum.

Charlton's financial problems ended in bankruptcy. In 1985, they lost their ground, playing in exile for seven years at Crystal Palace's Selhurst Park and West Ham's Upton Park. Extinction was a real threat and it was only after years of faith and dogged campaigning by fans that the club returned to The Valley in 1992. Rightly, no one ever blamed Simonsen, it was not his fault. But his time at Charlton tipped the club over the edge.

Despite the years of turmoil, few if any Charlton fans have anything but positive memories of Simonsen himself or of the kudos that his astonishing cameo briefly brought. Simonsen returned to London six months after he left, but only to represent Denmark against England in a European Championship qualifier at Wembley. He scored the only goal of the game. When his playing days were over, he moved into management. He spent eight years as the national coach of the Faroe Islands before moving to the equivalent post in Luxembourg.

Liverpool legend: a Danish Scouser

In contrast to Simonsen's four months at Charlton was the 14-year League playing career of his compatriot Jan Molby, who moved to Liverpool from Ajax in 1984. In his prime, he was, as his former Liverpool team-mate and manager Kenny Dalglish said, 'one of the finest midfield players of his generation'.

His first successes with Liverpool, and arguably his greatest, came with the Double in 1985–86. The FA Cup final that year, the first all-Merseyside final, became a showcase for his major strengths, which were his vision and his passing. Everton took a 1–0 lead through Gary Lineker but Molby exerted his influence to turn the game on its head. He created the equaliser, setting up Ian Rush. He provided the cross for Craig Johnston to make it 2–1. He also started the attack that led to Rush getting his second of the game for 3–1. Dalglish, in his first season in management, had done the Double. The Liverpool team that day included three overseas players who are still, to date, among the most successful foreigners, by medal count, ever to have played in England. Johnston, a South African-born Australian striker, won nine major honours. When his playing career ended he embarked on a successful business career that included the invention and development of the Predator football boot.

Bruce Grobbelaar, who produced a world-class save in the 1986 FA Cup final, won 13 major honours with Liverpool between 1982 and 1992. Grobbelaar ended his time in England with a tarnished reputation.

Born in South Africa in 1957, Grobbelaar was a Zimbabwean citizen and represented Zimbabwe internationally. He started his professional career in Canada with the Vancouver Whitecaps before a first spell in England in 1979–80 with Crewe. He returned to Canada before Bob Paisley bought him for Liverpool for £250,000 in March 1981 as an understudy to the England goalkeeper Ray Clemence.

When Clemence left for Tottenham that summer, Grobbelaar became Anfield's no. 1. 'He was a phenomenal athlete,' recalled Jan Molby. 'He was quick off his line, he provided good cover for crosses, he was always very fit. As a person he was a character twenty-four hours a day. He had fun. He enjoyed himself. He made some high-profile mistakes, as all goalkeepers do, but he made some fantastic saves as well.'

Although Grobbelaar's clowning became a trademark, his record speaks for itself. He made more than 600 appearances in 13 years with Liverpool and went on to play for Stoke, Southampton, Plymouth, Oldham, Bury, Lincoln and in the non-League game, finally hanging up his boots in his early forties. Arguably his most successful piece of theatrics came in the 1984 European Cup final against Roma, which ended with a penalty shoot-out. Steve Nicol hit Liverpool's first kick over the bar. 0–0. Roma scored. 1–0. Phil Neal scored. 1–1. Roma missed. 1–1. Graeme Souness scored. 1–2. Roma scored. 2–2. Ian Rush scored. 2–3. Then as Roma's Francesco Graziani stepped up to the spot, Grobbelaar stood on his line wobbling his legs like manic spaghetti. Graziani missed, meaning if Ray Kennedy scored the game was beyond the Italians. He did.

But if Grobbelaar's on-field antics were controversial for their eccentricity, they were nothing compared to the match-fixing accusations levelled against him by the *Sun* in November 1994. The newspaper had secretly filmed Grobbelaar in a meeting with a former business partner, Chris Vincent. It was alleged that Grobbelaar had conspired to fix specific matches dating back to 1992. Malaysian betting syndicates were said to be behind the scam. These matches included games when Grobbelaar was playing for Liverpool and Southampton, not least the 3–3 draw in 1994 between Liverpool and Manchester United that had earned Peter Schmeichel his massive rollicking from Alex Ferguson.

The *Sun*'s claims led to two trials in 1997, when Grobbelaar, plus fellow players Hans Segers and John Fashanu, and a businessman, Richard Lim, were acquitted. Grobbelaar sued the *Sun* for libel and won £85,000 in damages in 1999. 'It was not the money I was after, I was just trying to clear my name in football,' he said. In January 2001, appeal court judges sensationally overturned the 1999 verdict, saying the jury's verdict had been 'a miscarriage of justice'. Grobbelaar then asked the House of Lords for permission to appeal.

In October 2002, he won that appeal but his original damages were cut from £85,000 to £1. Lord Bingham, who presided over the Law Lords, said: 'It would be an affront to justice if a court of law were to award substantial damages to a man shown to have acted in such flagrant breach of his legal and moral obligations.' It was judged that Grobbelaar had accepted bribes but that the *Sun* had failed to show that he actually let in goals to fix the matches under scrutiny.

Undoubtedly Grobbelaar accepted money from Vincent. By doing so his legacy in England was soiled. But there were – and remain – plenty of people within football who never thought that Grobbelaar had actually thrown games. As Jan Molby said: 'Not in a million years.'

England, his England

After Molby won the 1986 Double, he added another League title in 1990, having played a bit-part role in the title of 1988 in between. He also won another FA Cup winners' medal in 1992 and played in the successful Cup run of 1988–89, although not in the final. His clinical penalties – he had a success rate of 40 from 42 – earned him a place in the record books in November 1986 with a spot-kick hat-trick against Coventry in a League Cup game. Molby's other major acquisition was his remarkable Scouse accent, which did much to endear him to fans in Liverpool and beyond.

When he left Anfield, he embarked on a managerial career, first with Swansea from 1996, and then with Kidderminster, whom he steered to promotion from the non-League Conference to the Football League in 2000. For that he won the Conference Manager of the Year award and a new four-year contract. He resigned from Kidderminster in 2002 and took up a short-lived post at Hull City soon after. In a pressured environment where immediate promotion from the Third Division was expected, he was sacked after 16 games. He went to his 'native' Liverpool, doing media work and waiting for an opportunity to get back into the game.

'Settling in England was never a problem for me,' he recalled. 'Liverpool was a very relaxing place, a great club to go to. The difficult part was the football, at least to start with. It was different to what I'd been used to, more physical. There were a lot of old-fashioned sides around whose aim was just to get the ball forward however they could. That wasn't true of Liverpool but we still had to cope against teams who did it. Having played in Holland for two years that took some getting used to, as did the pace. There was pace in Dutch football but only in the final third.'

Molby described the 1986 Double as unexpected, not least because Everton were a 'super side' that year. 'And really we should have done the Double again, in 1988 and 1989.' Instead Wimbledon beat Liverpool's 1988 League title winners in the FA Cup final that year and Arsenal pipped Liverpool's FA Cup-winning side of 1989 in the final dramatic game of that League campaign.

Such sporting setbacks were put firmly in perspective for Molby by other events in his time at Anfield. He fought a constant battle with injuries and then, as a result of a series of subsequent lay-offs, with his weight. Grahame Lloyd, who collaborated with Molby on his 1999 autobiography, *Jan the Man*, noted: 'It's often said that Jan Molby peaked too soon and achieved too little.' It was something that many, including Molby, agreed with. His wife, Mandy, described as 'heart-breaking' watching her husband cope with injuries, put on weight, lose it, hope the next season would mean a fresh start and then be thwarted again. Molby himself admitted: 'I wasn't as careful with food and drink as somebody of my size should have been when not playing. I thought I could lose weight as easily as I'd put it on and I now regret not taking much more care of my body.'

Ironically, one of the times his Liverpool team-mates saw him at his slimmest and fittest was after he had failed to take care elsewhere. He was arrested in 1988 for reckless driving and spent six weeks in prison as a result. He felt he was victimised because he was a high-profile footballer with a flashy car. The press vilified him and there were calls for him to be sacked and even banished from England. Some of his fellow prisoners were given cameras and offered large sums of money to snatch photographs of him for the newspapers. It was, he said, 'the worst time in my life, not just my career'. He served his time and got back to his football.

Within a few months, in April 1989, came a tragedy on a scale that English football had never seen before. Ninety-six people lost their lives at Hillsborough. Molby was there, as he had been at Heysel in 1985 when 39 people were crushed to death by a falling wall at the European Cup final: 'Immediately after Hillsborough happened on the Saturday, we players were a bit distant from it, we got on the coach back to Liverpool, went home. Then the magnitude of what happened began to dawn. People came to see you, relatives, a father or a daughter of someone who'd died, just to talk about it. There was no hiding place, and no one wanted to hide.'

Liverpool made sure that at least one player, past or present, attended the funeral of every victim. Molby went to eight. 'All of those players at the time feel a particularly strong bond to the city. Not many cities would have responded in the way that Liverpool did. There was unity from everyone, Liverpool, Everton. It brought home that there's nothing more important than your football club. I thought people who'd lost relatives might've said "That's it, I'm never going back." But they turned to their football club for support and inspiration. People came in their hundreds of thousands just to walk around the pitch and lay flowers. The players and Kenny Dalglish, we just did whatever we could. We had to, and wanted to. It was the least we could do.'

Despite everything – because of everything? – Molby remained a resident of Liverpool. 'Without actually being English,' he said, 'you couldn't be any more English than me.'

9

SAMBA ON TEES

'It would be strange to play in England but not play for Middlesbrough.'

Juninho, February 2003

SHORTLY AFTER 11 A.M. on Monday 16 October 1995, a private jet en route from London to Teesside dipped beneath the clouds and made its final approach to the runway. Its exotic cargo, small but priceless, leaned into the window and took a look at his new home town below. No transfer to the Premier League had ever resonated with such possibilities. Juninho, Brazil's no. 10 and Pelé's heir, was just 22. Now, with his best years ahead of him, he had swapped South America not for Madrid or Milan but Middlesbrough. Had he joined Arsenal or Manchester United, the move would still have been huge news. But he hadn't. If unfashionable, unsuccessful, unloved Boro could lure so lavish a talent to the banks of the Tees, then what limits were there for the rest of the English game?

True, Juninho was not the first big-name foreign signing to the cash-rich League. In the summer of 1995 Arsenal had paid £7.5 million to Internazionale of Italy to make the Dutchman Dennis Bergkamp their record signing. And Jürgen Klinsmann had already come and gone at Tottenham, taking the Footballer of the Year award with him. But Arsenal were a rich club with a history to match and Spurs had used all their heritage as well as a huge salary to attract a player aged 30 on arrival. Both those clubs had also used the playground of London as enticement.

Juninho's move to Middlesbrough – who had never won a major trophy – was widely instructive for several reasons, not least why he migrated there, how he settled and how he forged such a bond that even when he was forced away – twice – he kept coming back for more. The details of the transfer, and how it almost collapsed, throw light on the complexities of the international market and the pitfalls for a club on the rise.

The move said that Premier League football, for its own sake, could persuade a golden boy from Brazil, the most glamorous and successful nation in the world game, to England. It said that talent would go to the most unlikely places to be part of it. It said that money needn't be the be-all and end-all. Juninho was handsomely rewarded for decamping to north-east England, but he could have pocketed much more elsewhere. And the affinity he would develop with Teesside would show that a player's horizons don't always shift with the weight of cash stacked upon them.

The move also showed that there wasn't necessarily an unbridgeable gulf between contrasting footballing cultures. In 1995, much was made of the contrast between the sun-drenched Copacabana and cold, grey Teesside. Never mind that Juninho actually came from Sao Paulo, a city every bit as industrialised as Middlesbrough, and much poorer. But even the salient point in the argument, that a Brazilian would struggle with the physical, sometimes crude, approach in England, ended up being disproved by the slightly built Juninho.

On the other hand, the move did emphasise other less palatable facts. Juninho shone because he was brilliant but also because most of those around him in the League weren't from the same school, let alone in his class.

Moreover, by the end of his first spell (of three) at the club, Middlesbrough had found success elusive. In fact they were relegated from the Premier League and defeated in two Wembley cup finals. Worse still, instead of being universally applauded for their coup, the club and its town felt a nasty backlash of 'told you so'. Middlesbrough was painted by some not as a place trying to make good, but a town acting above its station. Even as the League sought to attract an international cast, the parochial bickering remained. Juninho's story, and that of Middlesbrough from the mid-1990s onwards, says much about the impact that one foreign player could make.

Precedents

Only three Brazilian-born footballers had played in England before Juninho. Two of them, Edward Laxton and Marques Isaias, weren't even Brazilian. The birthplace of Laxton, who played for Norwich from 1919, was down to his father's work as an engineer. Isaias, who joined Coventry in the summer of 1995, was raised in Portugal and was a Portuguese national.

The only previous bona fide Brazilian had been Mirandinha, who'd spent two seasons with Newcastle from August 1987. On arrival, he was heralded as a prolific striker. Though popular with fans, the evidence was sporadic. He scored 20 goals in 47 League starts before falling out with his manager, Jim Smith. He departed when Newcastle were relegated.

A couple of Brazilians had been employed in the Scottish League but neither had made an impression. The first, who joined St Mirren in 1965, was Fernando Jose de Azvedo Parreiras Horta, also known – to the great relief of the stadium announcer – as Nando. He played a couple of matches and livened up a few half-time breaks with some ball juggling before finding the climate too harsh and going home. In 1994–95, Dundee United signed a forward, Sergio, who played 15 first-team games that season. He was prevented from returning for the 1995–96 season by a passport problem, which was spotted in Portugal after a pre-season training trip. He never made it back to Scotland. Such experiences made the capture of Juninho all the more remarkable.

Pre-Juninho Middlesbrough

In May 1992, Middlesbrough won promotion from the old Second Division to become north-east England's only representatives in the inaugural season of the Premier League. Their home was Ayresome Park, a shabby old ground, and their team was mediocre at best. They lasted a season before being relegated.

The pattern of non-achievement irked Steve Gibson, a local businessman and lifelong fan, and he yearned to do something about it: 'I felt that the club had always had this history of mediocrity and we needed to make a statement to the town and the football world that we had ambition and we meant business.' Backed by the millions he'd accrued from his haulage business, he took over as chairman, aged 36, in September 1993. Boro were attracting crowds of less than 7000 as they languished in mid-table in the First Division.

Gibson's revolution involved a new manager, Bryan Robson, the former captain of Manchester United and England, who was hired in May 1994. Robson led Boro to promotion in his first season. The next step was a new £20 million stadium, the Riverside, built during the promotion year. With perfect timing, it was ready for life back in the Premier League in 1995–96, which only left a squad to grace it. Enter Juninho.

'To bring in Juninho, the rising star of world football, was symbolic for us,' Gibson said. 'It was only afterwards that we realised the wider significance of him coming to England rather than an Italian or Spanish club. The English could finally compete. No Italian or Spanish player of consequence had ever played in England and suddenly we had Juninho, Brazil's Player of the Year, at Middlesbrough. In retrospect it was probably the start of the reassessment of English football.'

Signing Boy Wonder

Oswaldo Giroldo Jnr, aka Juninho, was born in Sao Paulo in February 1973. He started his career at a junior club, Ituano, where Tele Santana spotted his potential. Santana was the manager of Sao Paulo FC, the big boys of Brazil in more ways than one. Juninho, when he signed in 1993, was 5ft 1in and skinny. On Santana's advice, he expanded his diet to six meals a day. He grew four inches, filled out – to eight and a half stone – and waltzed to his first batch of honours. In 1993, he helped Sao Paulo win the Recopa, the Super Copa and the World Club Championship, Milan being vanquished in the latter.

The next year Sao Paulo won the Recopa again and then the Conmebol Cup, with Juninho, as bedazzling as he was committed, taking the Golden Boot. As his mother Lucia later recalled, there had only ever been one game for her son: 'We'd give him toys, model cars, you name it, but he never touched them. All he ever played with was a ball. I'm so proud of him, that God gave me a son like this. He's a simple boy and humble.'

In 1995 Juninho was voted Brazil's best player and made his first visit to England. The occasion was the Umbro Cup, a four-nation tournament featuring the host country plus Japan, Sweden and Brazil. Juninho dazzled as his side beat Sweden 1–0 and Japan 3–0 but it was against England that he really caught the eye. At the time, Bryan Robson, while Middlesbrough's manager, was acting as an assistant to the England coach, Terry Venables. He watched from the bench as Juninho scored a sensational free-kick in Brazil's 3–1 win over England.

'Bryan was absolutely mesmerised by him,' said Gibson. 'He thought "What a player!" We went and watched him play for his club in Brazil and decided to make a move for him.' Robson and Boro's chief executive, Keith Lamb, flew to Sao Paulo in July 1995. 'I had no idea of the wheeling and dealing of the clubs out there,' Gibson said. 'Oswaldo senior appointed an Italian guy as Juninho's agent. It was long-winded. First we had to deal with Sao Paulo, but they didn't own all of his registration, so there was the previous club to consider as well. Then there was the father, the agent and the player. We had to deal with this cauldron of ties. But we entered negotiations and bit by bit by bit it started to stack up.'

It wasn't until September 1995 that Juninho finally decided he wasn't going to renew his contract at Sao Paulo. Robson and Lamb flew to Brazil again at the start of October. Neither had yet had a one-to-one meeting with the player. They spent days around the negotiating table with a multitude of interested parties. Matters became more complicated when Arsenal and Internazionale both faxed confirmations of firm interest. But by the evening of Friday 6 October, Sao Paulo had agreed to sell Juninho to Middlesbrough. Robson met Juninho for the first time a few hours later.

'It was surprising for me that after only two years with Sao Paulo I was able to move to Europe,' Juninho recalled. 'No one in Brazil really knew about English football because we didn't watch it much on television. People said to me "Don't go, it's too hard, it's hard football. They play mostly long balls over there and that will make it difficult for you." I was also being told by people at home "Wait, wait until tomorrow, wait until the next day, because agents are talking to other clubs that could be better for you." I said to them: "The most important thing for me is the manager, not the president, not the directors." And after talking with Bryan, I just said to them "I'm going. I'd like to play in England."

'I'd only seen videos of Bryan before but I knew that he was a big name in English football, he'd been the captain of the national team and of Manchester. He took trouble to come to Brazil to see me and show me how he wanted me to play. That's why I made my decision. I didn't ask him about the place because the most important thing for me was the football. If you are happy with the way the team's playing, never mind the place, you can adapt to the place.'

Juninho's only prior knowledge of Boro was that they were based somewhere in rainy northern England and that the team played in red, his lucky colour. 'I didn't know much about Middlesbrough but Bryan told me how we were going to play. He showed me the ambition of the club and I moved because I trusted Bryan. I was young and when you're young you're just thinking about playing, and that's all. Once I'd decided to move to England I never thought I wasn't going to adapt. People said it would be cold, very different weather from Brazil. But I think it's better to play in the cold than the heat. It's easier to warm up than cool down.'

Juninho's family was an important factor. Middlesbrough cared for them en masse: mum and dad, sister, granny, and a variety of visiting friends. 'And then there was the security that we were offering,' Gibson said. 'When you look at the average income, we were making Juninho and his family secure for life.'

Contract details at Middlesbrough, as at all English clubs, are private matters. Gibson has never breached that privacy to reveal details. But it is thought Juninho was earning £13,000 a week in 1995, an era when the £10,000-a-week pay packet was still a rare thing, even in the Premier League. Juninho also received 15 per cent of the transfer fee, a lump sum of around £660,000. The transfer fee was around £4.4 million. The deal overall was an eye-opener for Gibson: 'They had grooming schools there where players are taken at an early age and a guy owns 10 per cent [of a player]. One club owns something, another owns something, [the player] owns something. So where it [the fee paid for Juninho] all ended up, I can't be certain . . . We paid it all into the Brazilian FA and then it was distributed wherever by the Brazilian FA. But that was none of our business really.'

On the brink

One startling aspect of Juninho's transfer was never made public. The whole deal was almost scuppered at the eleventh hour by a winding-up petition served on Middlesbrough. Such petitions are legal tools used by creditors to exert pressure on debtors. The tacit aim of using one is to force a suspension of trading. They necessarily disrupt business. They lead to bank accounts being frozen and can force companies to the wall. A winding-up petition was hanging over Boro when they signed Juninho, although the club's fans and the media were oblivious at the time.

The man who issued the petition was Albert Dicken, a local businessman. Dicken, by his own admission, had never been a huge football fan. He'd been involved with a small-scale sponsorship deal at Boro in 1986–87 but had no special affinity with the club. His attentions were primarily focused on his business interests, which included a chain of DIY stores and some retail outlets in the north-east. He became involved with Middlesbrough again in the mid-1990s because he saw it as a good way to boost the profile of his DIY chain.

Boro did a deal by which Dicken would sponsor the club in the 1994–95 and 1995–96 seasons. The deal was agreed while Boro were in the First Division and before the Riverside stadium – which was central to Steve Gibson's grand plan for the club – was built. After Bryan Robson made such a successful start to his tenure and as the stadium became reality, Boro's ambition grew. Gibson was pouring millions into a venture that was boosting local morale. He wanted to continue building the dream, of which Juninho would become a crucial part: 'The deal in financing the stadium was that we brought in a top-quality sponsor, not a local parochial guy who could pay us tens of thousands but a club sponsor who would sponsor the shirts and the stadium and would pay the club millions. And we pulled off this deal with BT Cellnet which was a fantastic deal.'

British Telecom agreed to pay £3 million for 'naming rights' to the Riverside so that its Cellnet brand would become synonymous with the venue. The company agreed to pay another £1 million a year for five years to sponsor Middlesbrough's shirts. The only problem for Boro was that the deals needed to start with the 1995–96 season and Dicken already had a deal for that year.

Boro approached Dicken in May 1995 to ask him, 'in the interests of the community', to waive his right to sponsor the club in 1995–96. They offered him substantial compensation, far in excess of his original investment of around £35,000 a year. Dicken, interviewed for this book, said he had disagreed with the notion that Boro's expansion was being pursued for the good of the community: 'It was business.' He added he was 'very concerned and upset' about being asked to step aside. 'You should always honour your contracts, regardless.' He entered a process of tough negotiation to secure as big a pay-off as possible. Gibson said Boro's opening offer was £250,000. Dicken declined to say precisely how much he eventually settled for but said it was 'compensation we were happy with'.

In September 1995, he was evidently still not happy with Middlesbrough. After negotiating his sponsorship pay-off he claimed the club had reneged on a deal to rent space in some of his retail outlets. On 25 September 1995, his lawyers issued a winding-up petition. Dicken said that the petition sought a 'substantial' six-figure sum from Boro.

Steve Gibson believed that Dicken was trying to make as much money from Boro as possible and that the imminent Juninho transfer was being used as a lever: 'What we wanted was a surprise announcement [about Juninho] but these things never stay private. It began to leak. Because of the press speculation, Mr Dicken decided to put as much pressure as possible on Middlesbrough Football Club.' Dicken said he was unaware at that time that his legal action would jeopardise the signing of Juninho. He also said he had been unaware of the precise measures his lawyers had taken against Boro.

The winding-up petition was issued against Middlesbrough on 25 September 1995 in a court in Newcastle. 'Immediately that happens you have to appear in court,' Gibson said. 'But that court thing can take 14 days and in that 14 days the banks have no option other than to freeze your accounts. Mr Dicken could see we were about to make a major coup by signing Juninho. The whole town was up for it, all the community supported it. We'd delivered Bryan Robson, we'd delivered promotion to the Premiership, we'd delivered on the new stadium. We'd brought in Nick Barmby for five and half million and strengthened the team and we were riding high, seventh in the Premier League. To bring in Juninho would just keep that momentum going. And this guy comes along and sticks a winding-up petition on the club.'

On 6 October 1995, the football world thought that Juninho's transfer had been sealed. It was actually far from complete. Boro's accounts had been frozen and the transfer fee had not been paid. Only after Boro took swift legal action to free their finances could the deal be rushed through before Juninho's unveiling. The petition had almost thwarted the biggest signing in Boro's history. 'It nearly stopped us signing Juninho,' said Gibson.

The petition was subsequently 'struck out' by a court in Newcastle on 2 November 1995, effectively underlining that it had been an invalid claim. Dicken and Boro remained at legal loggerheads until 1999, when they resolved their differences. Dicken said Boro made a donation to a local hospice as part of the settlement.

The episode underlined some of the hazards of the football business. Dicken had almost ruined a transfer that, as Gibson rightly asserted, had led to many people reassessing English football. Amid all the excited gossip about Juninho's arrival, very few people had been aware of the price Gibson was paying. Boro, thinking big, had been stymied by a bloke who owned the local DIY store.

A one-man band

Juninho eventually flew into Teesside on 16 October 1995. The following day Boro threw a welcoming party in his honour. The samba band was fake but the pint-sized messiah was the real deal. As a 50-piece ensemble from the local Stockton and Billingham College knocked out tunes on upturned bins, some 4000 fans turned the Riverside into a sea of adoring yellow. Brazilian flags and shirts were as numerous as wide-eyed kids playing truant. Some schools had closed until lunchtime and those that hadn't weren't surprised by their absentees. They knew their pupils would be learning an important lesson at the Riverside: Middlesbrough had something to shout about.

The local papers had been shouting for weeks. The signing had 'brought the town to life', said the *Evening Gazette*. Juninho was front-page news day after day before he'd even put pen to paper. There were huge queues for season tickets, prompting Boro's spokesman, Dave

Allan, to announce: 'Juninho-mania is underway. I would recommend that any supporters who want to watch the team regularly should buy a season ticket because if they don't they risk disappointment. Credit is available and fans can pay monthly if they wish.'

The club increased its season-ticket quota to 26,500, equivalent to almost 90 per cent of capacity. They sold out. Local shirt suppliers ran out of Brazil shirts. The *Gazette* ran beginners' guides to Portuguese, telling its readers how to communicate with Juninho with such phrases as 'I like football', 'Is this your first time in England?', 'Would you like to come to dinner?' and 'I have three sisters'. Juninho had demonstrated the extent of his English in an interview with the *Independent* newspaper before he left Brazil. He'd mastered just one phrase – 'You is beautiful. I love you, sweet honey'.

In later years, he became fluent enough to recall the welcome he'd been given that October day. 'It was incredible. I didn't know that people would know me. I had a great reception, even before I'd played. Each country has a different presentation of players and what happened in Middlesbrough was a surprise to me. In Brazil they just introduce you to the press and that's it, you don't get introduced to the supporters. In Spain it's different again, there's a game to introduce you to your team-mates and the fans. England was great for me because I'd never had an opportunity of being welcomed like that. I'll never forget it.'

Steve Gibson will never forget his first meeting with Juninho on the day the player arrived on Teesside. 'I couldn't believe it when I met the guy, he was so small. We even had to get special boots that were small enough, something like size five or six. I said to Bryan Robson "Are you sure about this? He looks so small he'll get kicked to death in the Premiership." But Juninho proved he could cope. I remember watching him with the ball. The tricks, the confidence. He was quite charismatic in a very quiet way. He could never be described as extrovert but he was a presence.'

That presence had done enough to stir jibes from elsewhere, not least London and the *Evening Standard* newspaper, which had a dig at Teesside after Arsenal had failed to win Juninho's signature. The gist of what was said can be gleaned easily enough from the response in Middlesbrough. 'Don't believe a word of it' an *Evening Gazette* front-page headline told Juninho. The story said: 'Proud Teessiders today rounded on a London newspaper after an astonishing attack on our area. The *Evening Standard* article commenting on Boro's coup in signing Brazilian soccer superstar Juninho MOCKS the way we speak, IMPLIES our women are unattractive, DAMNS the area as polluted and ugly.'

Though the *Standard*'s attack was probably tongue-in-cheek, it touched a nerve and had repercussions. 'Something that was so positive – getting a Brazilian international to come to Middlesbrough – actually worked the other way for us,' said Gibson. 'It was great PR within the town but outside the town people concentrated on the things that were wrong. Comments along the lines of cloth caps, whippets, coal miners, ugly women. It was horrid. It became a negative factor for the club for quite some time. But the fact is Juninho had come to Middlesbrough and people adored him.' The affection became mutual.

Middlesbrough offered Juninho a choice of four houses. He opted for a property in Ingleby Barwick, a village within easy reach of the club. He shared it, at various times, with his mother and father, his sister Gislene, his grandmother Rosa, and an assortment of friends and relatives who travelled from South America for a taste of the English countryside.

'In Brazil I lived in a big city, 20 million people, so of course it was different but I ended up getting on very well with the local people,' Juninho recalled. 'Whenever I went out they were very welcoming to me. I never thought I wasn't going to adapt. And anyway it's impossible not to adapt to a place where the people are so polite. My family decided to come with me because we're close and because it was good for me. I didn't go out that much but we got on well with the neighbours. Everyone was nice to me.' Steve Gibson added: 'Possibly because of the bad press the whole town was more motivated to make the whole family feel welcome.'

One of the main concerns for the family, not least Juninho's mother and grandmother, was food, and specifically a supply of decent coffee and the right pulses to make an authentic *feijoada* (pork and bean casserole), Juninho's favourite dish. A small community of expat Brazilians who worked for a local Brazilian-owned engineering firm was on hand to offer advice. Supply lines were soon established.

Middlesbrough's priority was to keep the family happy. Doing so would keep Juninho happy. Gibson enrolled them all at the language-learning unit at the local headquarters of ICI, then a major shareholder in Boro. They received one-to-one tuition and help with any day-to-day problems. 'It's relatively easy for foreign players to settle because they're busy,' Gibson said. 'It's more difficult for the families because the wives and children don't speak English and they're trying to settle into a new culture. How do they get a plumber if they need one? What if they need help with a bank account? You need to take care of all that.'

A routine was quickly established. Juninho went to work, his week filled not only with training and playing but a whole range of engagements befitting the most popular man in town. The number of requests to Middlesbrough for him to make public appearances outstripped the total for the rest of the squad combined. He visited schools, hospitals, coaching clinics. He was the guest of honour at numerous functions and would rarely if ever say no to a shirt-signing session. 'There were a lot of invitations and I did my best to talk to everyone,' he said.

'Off the pitch, he never said no,' said Gibson. 'It got to the stage where we had to protect him, ask him not to do so much because nearly all the requests were for him. Left to himself he'd have done them all.'

Juninho played 21 League games during the 1995–96 season, scoring only twice as he got to grips with England and its rough-and-tumble game. But if that bedding-in period was pocked with inconsistency, so was Middlesbrough's form. At one stage they lost eight consecutive games in a 13-match winless run that ruined any hopes of qualification for Europe the next year. There was still no doubting the Brazilian's work rate nor his repertoire of speed, trickery and skill. 'He worked his socks off in training,' Gibson said. 'And he had a willingness and a desire to learn. And this in someone who had skills that you can't coach. They were God-given, natural talent.'

Juninho himself had no doubts that he would be able to cope, despite his size, once he'd spent time acclimatising: 'You have to be strong. Never mind your size. Your legs have to be strong. My legs have always been strong so I don't need to be tall to play. If it was basketball or volleyball, sure you need to be tall. But not with football. You have to know how to play. You have to be quick and then you don't have to try to make contact with the other players.

'I knew that for one-on-one challenges for the ball I was going to lose out on size alone. But I try to get there first, make my feet do the work beforehand. It was incredible at first because, when you're watching English football on television, you think there is no space to play. But when you compete you can find space when you're on the pitch. To me there's a very big difference between watching and playing.'

Triumphs and tears

No Middlesbrough supporter is ever likely to forget the 1996–97 season. It was the year in which their club was relegated despite having won enough points to stay up. It was the year their team reached two Wembley finals and lost both. It was the year that a posse of foreign players arrived but one made his mark above everyone. For better or worse, it was Juninho's year. 'My enduring memory of that year was whereas one or two of the other foreign players looked to blame everyone else for the club's plight, Juninho just gave it everything he had,' said Steve Gibson. 'And that's what the fans loved about him as well. He gave everything he could for the football club.'

The season started with a bang when Boro's new £7 million Italian striker Fabrizio Ravanelli scored a hat-trick on his debut on the opening day against Liverpool. The only downside was that Liverpool also scored three times to take a point. Boro's next match ended in defeat, 1–0 to Chelsea. That was followed by a 1–1 draw at Nottingham Forest, Juninho getting the goal.

Ten more goals followed in three games as Boro beat West Ham 4–1, Coventry 4–0 and Everton 2–1 at Goodison Park. Juninho, starting to sparkle, scored twice against Coventry and the winner at Everton. He was establishing himself as a danger in the area and the creative hub of the side. His portfolio of jinking runs, twists and turns, bursts of speed and slide-rule passes were the key to Boro's best performances.

Though Juninho was standing out, the team then faltered, securing only four points from four draws, in their next dozen League games. Juninho was absent, injured, for three of them, including the season's biggest defeat, 5–1 at Liverpool. On his return to the side on Boxing Day 1996, he scored twice in a 4–2 win over Everton.

A few days earlier Bryan Robson had made a decision that would, unbeknown to him, prove fatal to Boro's season. Due to an injury and illness crisis that sidelined 23 players – Juninho included – Boro unilaterally cancelled their game at Blackburn on 22 December. The following month, after a Premier League inquiry, Middlesbrough were docked three points and fined £50,000 for this 'illegal' act. At the end of the season, the three-point deduction meant they were relegated, in 19th place on 39 points. Without the deduction, they would have had 42 points, enough for a 16th-place finish and safety.

That did not become apparent until later, of course. Juninho, in the interim, illuminated the season in the three domestic competitions. Aside from his intrinsic entertainment value, he provided 38 goal assists, mostly for Ravanelli, as well as scoring 15 times himself. He scored a dazzling 90th-minute goal against Sheffield Wednesday after a lightning dribble from the touchline. He was instrumental in four successive League wins in March as Boro beat Derby 6–1, Leicester 3–1, Blackburn 2–1 and Chelsea 1–0. He scored in the last three of those games, including Boro's goal of the season against Chelsea, a move he orchestrated from midfield and finished with a diving header.

Two cup runs led to two Wembley finals. In the Coca-Cola Cup, Hereford were despatched 10–0 on aggregate, before Boro beat Huddersfield, Newcastle, Liverpool and Stockport en route to the final. That match, against Leicester, went to a replay and ended in defeat. In the FA Cup Boro beat Chester 6–0, then non-League Hednesford, Manchester City (Juninho scored the only goal), Derby (Juninho scored) and Chesterfield, after a replayed semi-final. The final, against Chelsea on 17 May, ended in another defeat.

Six days earlier had come the most poignant of the season's reverses when Middlesbrough were relegated following a 1–1 draw at Leeds. The home side had taken a 77th-minute lead through Brian Deane. Juninho equalised two minutes later. A win – and another two points – would have been enough for safety. It was not to be. At the final whistle, Juninho sank to his knees and wept.

The season had been a personal triumph and was recognised as such when Juninho was voted Premier League Player of the Year by the tournament's sponsors and runner-up in the Footballer of the Year award handed out by the Football Writers' Association. He was also the Middlesbrough fans' Player of the Year, with 98 per cent voting for him. (A search party is still looking for the other two per cent.)

But as Juninho knelt on the Elland Road turf, he knew his time at the Riverside was over. 'He didn't want to leave but he was pressured into leaving by the Brazilian national team coach Mario Zagallo following relegation,' said Keith Lamb. 'Zagallo knew how desperate Juninho was to go to the World Cup in 1998 and said, "If you're not playing in the Premier League it will put severe pressure on my ability to pick you for the Brazilian squad." And so he was almost forced away from the club. I'm sure he would have been the first to stand up to get us back into the Premier League from the First Division. It wasn't as if he hadn't given his all.'

Juninho's tears had been genuine, a fact still evident years later, when he could recall how upset he'd been that day. 'I was, I was. I'd learned to love the club. They'd been very good to me. I was very involved with the club so I didn't want to leave. I was happy. Maybe if we'd won one of the cups it would have been different. It was an incredible season because we went twice to Wembley and that meant a lot to the supporters. But at the same time we went down. The fans still say it was the best season ever but it should've been better. We had a lot of opportunities to stay up and we didn't do it. That was the little punch.'

Once the decision had been made that Juninho was leaving, Boro needed to secure the best move for themselves and the player. That meant finding a top-flight club somewhere in Europe. Tottenham's chairman, Alan Sugar, wanted it to be Spurs and he made an offer.

'Spurs fans were quite cynical about Alan Sugar's approach but I know it was genuine,' Gibson said. 'Alan Sugar rang me and made me a significant offer and the offer was actually better than the one we eventually received from Atletico Madrid.'

Juninho went to Madrid and not Spurs for two reasons. After a season of such raw emotion, he could not envisage playing in England for a team other than Boro. And Boro preferred that he went abroad. That would make it easier to negotiate a first option on a buy-back later. It would also reduce the chances that Juninho would ever have to play against Boro. 'We had a preference not to have him staying in England,' Gibson said. 'Alan Sugar acted with integrity and made an offer acceptable to Middlesbrough Football Club [but] there would have been quite a lot of pressure on us, locally, if we'd allowed him to go to another English club. When Atletico made a derisory offer, I told them we had another offer. In the end they matched it. Actually it fell short, but only just short, and Juninho went.' Atletico paid around £12 million and agreed to give Boro first refusal if they decided to sell Juninho later.

Within five months of leaving England, Juninho was back, briefly, playing for Atletico in the UEFA Cup against Leicester. The Brazilian gained a small measure of revenge for his Coca-Cola Cup final defeat five months earlier by scoring as the Spaniards ended Leicester's European adventure. It was a rare positive moment in a wretched time in Madrid. Juninho had rearranged his life to suit Zagallo but then suffered a broken leg in Spain that kept him out of the 1998 World Cup anyway. The injury, the result of a tackle by Celta Vigo's Michel Salgado, effectively ended his career at Atletico Madrid. By the time he was recovering, the manager who'd signed him, Raddy Antic, was gone. Juninho was overlooked by Antic's successor, Arrigo Sacchi, and by Sacchi's replacement, Claudio Ranieri.

Trouble and strife from across the Atlantic

Although Juninho had an unhappy time in Madrid, Spain has always had a good record of assimilating Brazilians and other South Americans. The same has not been true of England. The appendices of this book tell their own story of hit-and-miss flings with players from a variety of nations. It is especially evident that players from South and Central America have struggled to settle (or been tough to accommodate).

Middlesbrough found out as much with three other Brazilians in the late 1990s. Branco, a vastly experienced international defender, played only two League games. He failed to settle or impress and left eight months before his contract was due to expire. Emerson, a huge – and hugely talented – midfielder, played for the best part of two seasons, including all of 1996–97. At one stage he went AWOL in Brazil after his girlfriend had described Middlesbrough as a 'strange, terrible place'. He was reluctantly sold.

Then there was Fabio, Emerson's girlfriend's brother-in-law. He was ostensibly brought in, along with his wife, as company for

Emerson and his partner. He was also given a trial. He'd played a bit of local football in Brazil and had a Spanish passport, which made signing him easy, and he ended up getting a chance in the first team. He was outstanding in his only match, a First Division game against Huddersfield in October 1997. He never hit such heights, or indeed played, again.

Newcastle fans delighted in the two-year stay of Faustino Asprilla between February 1996 and January 1998. The flamboyant Colombian striker possessed all the attacking verve associated with Kevin Keegan, the manager who signed him. He was part of the side who finished as Premier League runners-up in 1997 and his personal high point came with a European hat-trick against Barcelona. But his ultimate return of nine goals in 48 League matches was a moderate tally and he left for Parma.

The football-crazy north-east witnessed a farcical postscript to the Asprilla story in the 2002–03 season when Darlington of the Third Division said they were going to stun the football world by signing the Colombian. Darlington's owner, George Reynolds, appeared live on television to announce the great news. Asprilla even appeared with him, smiling and laughing. Within hours he'd boarded a plane and fled, leaving Reynolds understandably fuming. The episode did nothing to dispel the notion that players from the region were something of a gamble.

It was a theory that had been bolstered by numerous signings across England. Sunderland signed the Honduran Milton Nunez for £1.6 million in March 2000 in the belief he was coming from a top-flight Uruguayan club. He'd actually played for a small Third Division team. He made one substitute appearance at Sunderland before being released for nothing. Derby paid around £1.9 million for an Argentinian, Esteban Fuertes, in 1999 after protracted negotiations. He scored once in eight League games. Passport irregularities were then discovered at Heathrow Airport as he returned from a mid-season break in Portugal. Fuertes was deported, his English sojourn over.

In 2001, Aston Villa paid a club-record fee of £9 million to buy the Colombian international striker Juan Pablo Angel. It proved a poor investment initially as he struggled to live up to his transfer fee. Agustin Delgado, a striker from Ecuador, was even more of a dis-appointment at Southampton. He made one League appearance in his first season after joining in November 2001. By the summer of 2004, dogged by injuries and under a cloud after a series of spats and walk-outs, he was gone after two League starts (and one goal) in almost three years.

One of the most high-profile signings of the early Abramovich-backed era at Chelsea was Hernan Crespo, the prolific Argentinian striker who once commanded a world record fee of £37 million when moving from Parma to Lazio in Italy. Chelsea signed him from Internazionale in 2003. Soon afterwards, he explained to reporters from back home how cultural differences were making life tough. His comments perhaps explained why so few leading South Americans considered England a more attractive European alternative than Spain or Italy. 'I have to go to the baker's, I have to go shopping, the electrician is coming round, I have to get the car serviced, and for all these things I have to go and speak in English,' he said. 'They might seem silly little things, but in reality it's not so easy. We're Latins, and all through our lives we're used to someone giving us a hand. But that's not the Anglo-Saxon way. The cultures are different.'

After one unspectacular season under Claudio Ranieri, Chelsea hired Jose Mourinho, and Crespo, apparently surplus to require-ments, was loaned to Milan for a year. He thrived, scoring two of Milan's three goals in their ill-fated Champions League final of 2005 against Liverpool. Mourinho, having failed to lure another big-name striker for 2005–06, recalled him to London, hoping a second shot at English culture would work.

A popular boy from Brazil

There have been some heroes in England from South America, but mostly local heroes, cult figures at their clubs and not much beyond. Into that category came the Brazilian striker, Edinho, who joined Bradford City of the First Division in 1997. Though his goals were important – he was joint top scorer in 1997–98 – his relationship with the supporters cemented his place in local lore. He was known to drive through town, honking his car horn and waving when he saw someone in a Bradford replica shirt. Costa Rica's Paulo Wanchope was briefly adored at Derby County after joining in March 1997. He scored on a memorable League debut as his side inflicted a rare defeat on Manchester United at Old Trafford. His gangling, almost random, runs endeared him to fans although he fared less well after moving to West Ham and later Manchester City.

Of the South Americans who arrived at the Premier League's leading clubs from the late 1990s, Uruguay's Gustavo Poyet was among the most productive. He joined Ruud Gullit's Chelsea legionnaires in the summer of 1997. He excelled as a probing, attack-minded midfielder who maintained consistency at a club renowned for doing the opposite. Poyet's influence was underrated and he was badly missed when absent. This was never more apparent than in the middle of the 1998–99 season, when Chelsea's first League title since 1955 seemed attainable. On Boxing Day 1998, with Chelsea at the top of the table, Poyet fell victim to a horrible, damaging tackle by Patrick Colleter, a French Southampton defender. The resultant injury kept him out for 10 games. When Poyet returned, Chelsea were third, having dropped vital points in various games, including those against Manchester United and Arsenal. Those teams eventually finished first and second in the title race, five and four points ahead of Chelsea.

Recovery for Poyet – and Chelsea – came too late on that occasion but the Uruguayan helped win silverware before and after. He was part of the European Cup-Winners' Cup-winning team in 1998 and the FA Cup-winning team of 2000. And on Boxing Day 1999, back at Southampton with Chelsea a year to the day after the Colleter tackle, he was part of the first all-foreign XI ever to start a League match in England.

While a few other South Americans enjoyed qualified success – such as Brazil's Gilberto Silva, a World Cup winner in 2002, at Arsenal – others came and went without hitting any heights. Argentina's Juan Sebastian Veron, who became British football's record signing when he joined Manchester United for £28 million in 2001, never found a role that best utilised his undoubted abilities and moved to Chelsea in 2003. After a year and only five League starts there, he went back to Italy, with Inter. Similarly Uruguay's Diego Forlan, who became an Old Trafford striker in January 2002, saw his chances to strike quite limited. Of his 63 League games for United, 40 came as a sub, and after only 10 Premiership goals in two and a half years, he moved to Villarreal in Spain, where his career took off again.

Juninho's second coming

Juninho endured his own period of frustration, in Spain at Atletico Madrid, while recovering from his broken leg. By the start of the 1999–2000 season, he was desperate to get back to fitness and felt he needed to be playing matches. Middlesbrough had kept in touch and Steve Gibson, Keith Lamb and Bryan Robson flew out to Spain to meet Oswaldo senior. He indicated his son wanted to move back to Boro and a short-term loan, from September 1999 to May 2000, was arranged with Atletico.

Back at the Riverside, some things had not changed. Juninho resumed occupation of the same house in Ingleby Barwick and took up where he left off in his rapport with the fans. But the Boro squad – and approach – had seen some significant alterations. Brian Deane, who'd scored for Leeds on Juninho's first Middlesbrough debut and then again on the fateful day in 1997 when they were relegated, was wearing the Brazilian's no. 10 shirt. Fabrizio Ravanelli was long gone, as was Emerson. The new-look squad – less cavalier, more intent on solidity – now featured the likes of Paul Ince and Gary Pallister, both former Manchester United men like Bryan Robson.

Steve Gibson's assessment was that Juninho had less freedom to show his flair in a side primarily concerned with re-establishing itself in the Premiership. Certainly he did not thrive as in 1996–97. Robson also felt the recovery from the broken leg was not as it should be. The skill was still there, but the pace and final touch were not back to their best. After nine months, 28 League games and four goals, Juninho's second spell at Boro came to an end.

Renaissance, Ronaldinho and glory

Juninho returned to Atletico in May 2000. Still out of favour, he went home on loan to Brazil's Vasco da Gama. It was the perfect move, leading to success in the Mercosur Cup and more importantly, a recall to the Brazilian squad. By the 2002 World Cup, he was firmly re-established as an international regular. 'When we arrived at the World Cup our mental [attitude] was very sharp. The press didn't know that so they thought we wouldn't do so well. They were surprised when we played our first three games. And then they started to believe us that we could play very well. Because our mentality was strong.'

Brazil won all their group games, beating Turkey, China and Costa Rica; Juninho featured in each match. They beat Belgium in the second round, with Juninho playing for 57 minutes before being substituted with a non-serious knock. The quarter-final pitted Brazil against England. Ronaldinho reduced David Seaman to tears with his brilliant winning goal, a free kick from 40 yeards. Brazil beat Turkey in the semi-final, for which Juninho was rested, and then Germany in the final. Ronaldo, the former World Player of the Year, capped a tournament of personal salvation by scoring both goals in a 2–0 win. After a few unhappy years himself, Juninho – on the pitch as a late substitute for Ronaldinho – achieved his own personal redemption.

Before the World Cup had even started, Steve Gibson had decided he wanted Juninho back at Middlesbrough. The subject had been discussed with Steve McClaren, Robson's successor as manager, who agreed that if Juninho had recovered to be anywhere near the player he'd been in 1996–97, he was worth buying. Gibson thus organised his hectic schedule to combine some business with a trip to the World Cup. He made contact with Juninho's father a couple of days before the quarter-final with England. The conversation started with small talk and catching up on family news. Then Gibson told Oswaldo senior: 'The reason I'm ringing you is because I'm interested in bringing Juninho home.'

Juninho's father said his son could be interested. It was all Gibson needed to know so he could make an official approach to Atletico Madrid, to whom Juninho was still contracted. The deal was done and the player moved 'home' to Teesside for around £6 million. 'When I was in Spain I always said I wanted to go back to English football,' said Juninho.

His third term at Boro had an inauspicious start. He sustained serious knee ligament damage in a friendly before the 2002–03 season and was sidelined for seven months. But he recovered, and was again an instant hit. His comeback in a reserve match against Bradford at the Riverside on 25 February 2003 drew a staggering 20,000-strong crowd, a record for a second-XI match. He scored once in a 9–0 win. Three days later he made his Premier League reappearance, against Everton. It was his first competitive match since the World Cup final and his first League match for Middlesbrough since 14 May 2000. The opponents that day too had been Everton and Juninho had bid farewell with a goal. He scored against them again to mark his return.

'It would be strange to play in England but not play for Middlesbrough,' he said around that time. 'That's why I'm here for the third time. And this time I deserve to win something.' This time he did. In February 2004 he played at the Millennium Stadium as Middlesbrough beat Bolton in the League Cup final to win the first major silverware in their history. At the end of the 2004–05 season, he joined the Glasgow giants, Celtic, but he was not a first-choice pick for manager Martin O'Neill, and he soon returned to South America.

It's possible, sometime around the year 2020, that someone in England could be showing an interest in Juninho's son. Lucas Giroldo can already claim to have made the most important debut of his life in Middlesbrough. He was born at the town's James Cook University Hospital in October 2002, shortly after Juninho signed for Boro for a third time. Lucas's first family home was in Yarm, Teesside, where Juninho moved when he returned, bringing his wife, Juliana, and a daughter, Brunna, with him. Juninho had specifically wanted Lucas to be born in England. 'That was Juliana's present for me.' As for the future, Lucas will be qualified to play for England. 'Yes,' said Juninho, grinning. 'If he's not good enough to play for Brazil.'

10

SUBLIME AND RIDICULOUS

DIAMOND TALENT GLINTS in various shades, from the brilliant orange of Dennis Bergkamp to the rhapsody in blue of Gianfranco Zola. The Dutchman played a pivotal role in trophy-winning teams at Arsenal. The Italian, as enduring as he is magical, set new standards for his Chelsea team-mates, on and off the pitch. The impact, honours and legacy of that pair are examined later. But such stars have been hugely outnumbered by other, less stellar, legionnaires. Some have been farcical, others fictional. Many have been ordinary, others simply mercenary. Some have been good enough to shine in major international tournaments but not deemed good enough to rise to England's top division. Others have evidently not been good enough to play there but have managed to do so anyway.

Of course there have been good and bad home-grown players at all levels of the game as long as football has existed. Why should it matter now where players come from, that foreign players are no longer primarily big names at big clubs but routine acquisitions at every club from Carlisle to Wigan, Burnley to Scunthorpe, Millwall to Bournemouth to Plymouth?

On one level, the PFA would argue, it matters because the quest for cheaper, more exotic, crowd-pulling labour has changed the make-up of the player pool too radically. In 1990, of the country's 3000 professionals, a few dozen came from overseas. Thousands have followed. To the displaced natives and their union, that's simply too many. They say mediocre imports have taken the jobs of home-grown players, that this will damage the long-term development of the domestic and international game.

On another level, the influx matters because of the effects of its rapidity and scale. The clubs have contributed to this, wittingly and otherwise. They have paid enormous salaries to lure leading players from overseas. This has been necessary in many cases to compete with the richest Continental clubs. And there is nothing wrong with paying the going rate if you can afford it and you think you're getting value for money. But many clubs have paid high, unsustainable wages to ordinary players, justifying that expenditure with claims that in the post-Bosman era, savings have been made on transfer fees. These claims have been made throughout the divisions. In reality, any savings have often been cancelled out by the costs of higher salaries. Worse, by paying high wages – either to lure players or because no transfer fee was paid – clubs have helped create crippling wage inflation.

This wage inflation has only increased the attraction of England as a place of work, not just for players but for middle men and agents. If their clients are earning more, they are earning more. And if their clients are moving around, so much the better. Fees to agents for a few days' work arranging a move can run to hundreds of thousands of pounds.

So the range and number of newcomers have continued to grow, leading to fundamental changes in the recruitment process. These are intrinsically linked to the process of dealing with foreign markets. Clubs rely, more heavily than ever before, on third-party brokers. Basic information on background and ability is often left to people with vested interests to verify on trust. Sometimes such details are never verified at all. Haphazard hiring, sometimes solely on video evidence, is far from unknown. The process that has brought some wonderful, innovative footballers has also brought some absolute duds. It has brought hoaxers, whose antics can be seen as amusing, and shadowy opportunists whose mendacity, scamming – and occasional threats of violence – cannot.

In 1999 Gordon Taylor, chief executive of the PFA, revealed that up to one-fifth of foreign players seeking working permits in England had had their requests refused in the previous five years because of suspicions that deals were being brokered by unscrupulous agents. 'I'm talking about players from places such as Eastern Europe, Africa and South America. With those deals, I'd estimate that in 10 to 20 per cent of cases there have been too many grounds for caution to allow the deals to go through.' Taylor said the PFA had been concerned that buying clubs had been asked to pay fees to third parties rather than to the selling clubs. 'If we're not careful, the game will be run by agents. Without proper controls, you can't be sure who's getting paid for what.'

Anecdotal evidence within the game suggests such problems have not gone away. The difficulty for investigators, not least the football authorities, is that the evidence has remained mostly that – anecdotal. Administrators and senior club figures, interviewed anonymously for this book, talked about offers of bungs and corrupt middle men, including one agent who showed up with heavies and threatened extreme violence unless his client was allowed to move. A chairman and a manager at one club had both been offered bungs, which they said were declined. One senior executive talked about going overseas to negotiate a deal. An agent mistook him for another middle man instead of the major shareholder he was. 'This guy said he'd open a Swiss bank account for my slice of the action. I told him he was suggesting I nick my own money. Then I told him to eff off.'

So did all these incidents get reported? No. The reason? Lack of evidence. As one executive said: 'If you're in the clear yourself and you don't get involved in that, how can you prove something that didn't happen? And if you did report it, there's the possibility that it gets out that you're helping with an investigation. And then everyone thinks you're "at it" anyway.'

But back to the players. Into the blend of the sublime and the ridiculous, you can throw plenty of decent jobbing professionals, of myriad nationalities, who have simply tried to make their way. They have arrived in England, settled happily in towns and cities up and down the country, become firm local favourites and played, productively, for years. The whole ensemble has helped to change the English football landscape.

What can never be known for certain is whether a newcomer will settle, whether he will succeed, whether he will have that X factor that wins games and hearts. This is as true of those who have already been successful and famous elsewhere as it is of those who are unknown. Players who have cost millions have flopped. Others who have cost nothing have excelled. But every new arrival, on debut day at least, speaks of hope: for the clubs, for the fans, and for the players themselves.

Movers and fakers

Southampton's Ali Dia played one game for the club in 1996. He had apparently been recommended to Saints' manager, Graeme Souness, by Liberia's George Weah, a superstar at Milan and the World

Footballer of the Year. According to some of Southampton's players, including Francis Benali and Matt Le Tissier, Dia had seemed strangely reluctant to exert himself in training. No one made a big issue of the fact. Weah wouldn't recommend duds, would he? Anyway, it was reasoned, Dia hadn't been at the club long and was probably still acclimatising. Souness put him on the bench for the Leeds game on 23 November.

The match was 32 minutes old when Le Tissier suffered a groin strain and limped off. Dia was sent on in his place. Within seconds he had a first opportunity for glory. Eyal Berkovic, Southampton's Israeli playmaker, surged forward from the halfway line. Dia ran ahead of him and peeled off to the right. Berkovic slipped a pass to his feet, all of 12 yards from goal. With time and space to pick his spot, Dia kicked the ball straight at the goalkeeper, Nigel Martyn.

It was the high point in Dia's afternoon. In the second half it became obvious he was out of his depth. He struggled for position, wasted possession of the ball and tired quickly. This was a problem and it became serious when Leeds' Gary Kelly scored the first goal of the game in the 82nd minute. If Southampton wanted to take anything from the contest they needed to score. Dia was clearly not going to do that. The substitute was substituted five minutes from the end. He had been on the pitch for 53 minutes. He was replaced up front by Ken Monkou, a defender. Leeds scored again, the game finished.

Little fuss was made the next day. A poor debut was an unremarkable event. According to newspaper reports, which concentrated on the simple details of Dia's identity, the newcomer was a 30-year-old Senegalese international striker. (He was actually 31.) It was reported that Dia had been available on a free transfer after leaving Bologna in Italy, and that he'd been a former team-mate of Weah's at Paris St Germain. Souness was quoted as saying: 'When someone the calibre of George Weah calls to recommend a player you tend to sit up and take notice.'

It took a few weeks for Dia's true credentials to be revealed. Several lower division clubs, having seen him on TV against Leeds, announced they'd been approached before Southampton. Second Division Peterborough and Bournemouth had both considered him because he had a French passport and a move would have been free of red tape. Trials proved unconvincing.

First Division Port Vale admitted they'd been surprised to hear from Weah but weren't the kind of club to look a gift horse in the mouth. They had actually played Dia in a reserve match in September before deciding he wasn't going to fit in. Tony Pulis, the manager at Second Division Gillingham, was more forthright in his appraisal. He'd also taken a phone call from Weah and given Dia a trial. 'The lad was rubbish.'

Belated checks into Dia's past revealed he was not an international. George Weah, asked about the player, said he did not know anyone of that name and had certainly not made calls on his behalf. Bologna and PSG had never heard of him. The whole background was fabrication. Dia, whose professional experience stretched no further than a few months with Lübeck in Germany, said he was innocent, that an agent he'd employed in England had been claiming to be Weah without his knowledge. After a few setbacks, it had been relatively simple to get a game in the Premier League.

Dia subsequently moved to non-League Gateshead, where he scored two goals in 10 games in a three-month stay. He later took a business degree at the University of Northumbria, graduating in 2001. Weah himself played briefly for Chelsea and Manchester City in 2000, making more impact than Dia had done at Southampton. But not that much more.

While Dia's appearance in the League was the result of a few lies and some institutional complacency, at least he had existed in the real world. The same wasn't true of Didier Baptiste, who seemed on course for a move to Liverpool in 1999. At least that's what readers of *The Times* could have been forgiven for thinking. In the daily round-up of Premier League news on 23 November 1999, the newspaper reported: 'Liverpool are interested in signing Didier Baptiste, the left-back, who is a France Under-21 international and plays for AS Monaco. He would cost £3.5m.'

The story had been taken from a seemingly authoritative source, Liverpool's Clubcall service, an official premium-rate telephone hotline that promised the inside line from Anfield for 60p a minute. Unfortunately, the inside line had been anything but. Clubcall had taken the story from the previous day's *News of the World*. On 21 November 1999, the newspaper had told its readers: 'Liverpool boss Gérard Houllier wants Monaco's £3.5m rated French U-21 international Didier Baptiste after losing out to Manchester United in his bid to sign Mikael Silvestre earlier this season. But he faces stiff competition from Arsène Wenger who wants a long-term replacement for Nigel Winterburn at Arsenal.' On the same day, the *Observer* reported: 'Liverpool are close to signing French U21 star Didier Baptiste from Monaco.'

The story had been taken in good faith from a news agency, Hayter's. The agency had acquired it, also in good faith but without independent checks, after it had appeared on an unofficial website. Baptiste, it seemed, had confided that he might be moving to play 'in England for a French manager'.

Herein lay the problem. Baptiste was not real but a character on *Dream Team*, Sky TV's football soap opera. In the storyline he was moving from Monaco to fictional Harchester United. Tom Redhill, the actor who played Baptiste, had indeed uttered the line about playing in England for a French manager. But in the fantasy land of English football, a false whisper to a news agency had become hard news.

Two Sunday newspapers had picked it up and run with it. Liverpool's Clubcall service had no reason to doubt such voices of authority. *The Times* had no reason to doubt Liverpool. News outlets around the world had no reason to doubt any of them. That's why a paper as far removed as the *Waikato Times* in New Zealand found itself having to tell readers on 26 November 1999: 'Oops. Now here's a trap for New Zealand-based soccer fans who try to bring you the latest UK news.'

The Baptiste affair, amusing and harmless though it was, was illustrative of the state of the game. In an industry where hundreds of stories each week linked unknown players to clubs, fiction could pass as fact. The cross-border trade had made verification not only tricky but evidently, in some cases, unnecessary. Arguably the Baptiste error was only spotted – and gloated over by those not involved – because it was prominent and could be traced. There was irony in the fact that *The Times* and the *News of the World* were both owned by the same company that owned Sky TV, which made *Dream Team* and had exclusive rights to Premier League football. But if another fictional name had been inserted into a similar story about a less high-profile club and nothing had come of it, it's easy to believe it would have passed largely unnoticed.

Believing what you're told is not abnormal. Southampton believed Ali Dia was a peer of George Weah. Sunderland believed Milton

Nunez was a top Honduran player. West Ham believed, on the basis of an edited video, that Marco Boogers was worth an investment in his £1m transfer fee and wages. The Dutchman's signing is still held up as one of Harry Redknapp's least prudent investments. He played just four times, all as a substitute, and West Ham lost all four games. Third Division Bury believed, in 1993, that David Adekola was an experienced Nigerian international striker with 16 caps and a good track record in the French league. It seemed touching rather than bizarre when he said he wanted to join Bury rather than Marseille because his girlfriend lived nearby.

Unlike Ali Dia later, Adekola made a great start to his League career. Bury won six of the first seven League matches he played for them. He scored in his second game and got two more in his fourth. He scored again in his fifth and nabbed a hat-trick in his sixth. This was ample reason for the fans to delight in the coup.

Adekola went on to play a total of 48 League games while attached to six different clubs over four years. Thirty-five of those appearances came for Bury, where his early blaze of form petered out by his second season. Only later, after investigations by the *Observer*, did it emerge that Adekola's caps could not be traced and that clubs in France who he had supposedly been attached to had never heard of him. Did it matter to the Bury fans, who'd warmed to his character and relished his goals? Not really.

Trouble at Palace

The story of Crystal Palace in the 1998–99 season provided one of the most emphatic examples of what can go wrong when scrutiny is thrown out the window. The hiring of a posse of foreign players was a significant part of the problem. Indeed when the club went into administration in March 1999 with debts of £20 million, contractual liabilities alone – not least to 'star' foreign names – stood at around £14 million. Another £5.4 million was owed to foreign clubs in unpaid transfer fees. And the owner of Palace, Mark Goldberg, who ended up bankrupt, was still pondering quite how he'd managed to sanction some rather bizarre signings.

Goldberg first showed an interest in owning Palace in 1997, when the then owner, Ron Noades, placed an advert in the *Financial Times* seeking interested buyers. Goldberg phoned Noades and told him he was a lifelong fan and had plans to transform the club. Noades had never heard of Goldberg but discovered he was a moderately wealthy businessman who owned a recruitment company, MSB, that mainly dealt with IT specialists.

Noades did a deal whereby Goldberg would buy 10 per cent of Palace for £3 million in November 1997 with an option to buy the rest when he'd raised the money. He struggled to do so and sold more than £20 million of shares in MSB to raise the funds. He paid Noades £22.8 million for the club, but this did not include Palace's ground, Selhurst Park, to which Noades retained the freehold. As even Noades acknowledged: 'It was a stupid deal for him to do.'

Even before Goldberg had taken a controlling interest, he helped to broker a deal which took the Italian midfielder, Attilio Lombardo, from Juventus to Palace on a contract worth an astronomical £14,000 per week. Goldberg thought that by assembling a glittering array of international names he'd be able to steer Palace to the upper echelons of the Premier League and market the Palace brand worldwide.

By the time Goldberg had completed his takeover in the summer of 1998, Palace had been relegated, taking Lombardo (and his wage bill) into the First Division. Undaunted, Goldberg hired Terry Venables as his new manager. He offered the former England manager a package including a salary worth £750,000 a year after tax, an unsecured interest-free loan of £500,000, a house worth £650,000 and a Mercedes. It was little surprise that Venables accepted.

Between July and November 1998, Palace signed nine foreign players. They included an Australian defender, Craig Moore, signed on a four-year contract on a starting wage of £10,705 per week; a Yugoslav defender, Gordan Petric, who signed on a four-year deal that paid £5000 a week; an Israeli defender, David Amsalem, signed on video evidence, on a three-year contract worth £6500 a week; a Swedish forward, Mathias Svensson, signed on a four-year contract worth £3500 per week; and Craig Foster, an Australian midfielder, signed on a weekly wage of £3000, contracted to rise to £4000, plus an annual loyalty bonus of £100,000.

To give some idea of how big these deals were, a survey of footballers' salaries in April 2000, compiled by the *Independent* in association with the PFA, showed the average wage in the First

Division was less than £2500 per week. Yet Palace had been paying, in some cases, up to four or five times as much 18 months earlier.

Three of Palace's other foreign signings in the period July–November 1998 caused ripples that went beyond the balance sheet. They were those of the Chinese pair, Fan Zhiyi and Sun Jihai (who had initial wages of £3500 a week each), and the Argentinian Walter Del Rio (£2500 a week). Goldberg's grand plan behind signing Fan and Sun was to make Palace a force in the enormous market of China. This never happened. Some of Palace's games were screened there but the money from the rights deals wasn't huge and anyway went into a central Football League pot for distribution to all the 72 clubs below the Premier League. There was no Chinese stampede for Palace shirts and souvenirs, there were no lucrative spin-off deals and no Palace-mania. Goldberg was soon on his way out of Selhurst Park, having blown some £30 million.

The original deal to bring Fan and Sun to London had been troublesome. In August 1998 Palace agreed to pay £1.35 million for the two players. In November 1998 it was revealed that the authorities in China were expecting only $1.5 million, or £400,000 less than the figure Palace were paying. Somewhere in the deal, that £400,000 seemed to be unaccounted for. Shijun Liu, the London-based Chinese representative in the deal, said he could not comment because of a confidentiality clause.

In mid-November, Palace released a statement saying: 'At today's board meeting, it was confirmed that the board had requested an FA-assisted inquiry into the destination of monies paid by the club to a Chinese FA bank account in London, authorised by its London representative Shijun Liu, for its two Chinese players.' No action was taken after an investigation and the two sides reportedly resolved their differences. No explanation of what happened to the missing money was ever made public.

Another transfer that Goldberg was unhappy with was that of David Amsalem. Aside from the player's wages of £6500 per week, Palace had agreed to pay a fee of £850,000 for him, about £600,000 more than Goldberg thought he was worth. The gamble didn't pay off. After six League starts and four substitute appearances Amsalem was released. His original move had been problematic after the selling club, Maccabi Neve Alom, had complained they hadn't received all the money they thought was due. It was around this time that

Goldberg said he would support any moves within the football industry 'for improved regulatory procedures governing the transfer of foreign players'.

If one single move summed up the era at Palace it was that of Walter Del Rio. The transaction whereby he moved from Argentina in the summer of 1998 was typically convoluted. His arrival was announced in the club programme along with that of two young compatriots, Pablo Rodrigues and Cristian Ledesma. Rodrigues subsequently failed a medical and went home while Ledesma was unhappy with the deal he was offered and left without playing too. Del Rio remained, alone, although how much he cost was uncertain, even to those within Palace's hierarchy.

In 1999, a leaked letter from Palace's former chief executive, Jim McAvoy, who had resigned in dismay at the club's situation earlier that year, said: 'The Argentinian escapade cost £448,769 in agent fees and £187,000 in transfer fees.' No transfer fee should have been payable for Del Rio because he was out of contract when Palace signed him. English football clubs are loath to disclose how much they pay for players or how much agents receive. It was subsequently revealed that a British agency, First Artist, had made £91,000 commission on the Del Rio deal. But as with the Chinese transfers, Palace never explained publicly the full facts surrounding the Argentinians.

Del Rio's personal plight showed the insecurity and pitfalls of being a young player abroad. A 22-year-old squad player with Boca Juniors in Buenos Aires, he'd gambled on his future and eight months later found himself with no job and no income, living in Croydon, south London. Instead of coaching sessions at home that had featured guest appearances by his hero, Diego Maradona, he ended up excluded from Palace training and running around a field by himself to keep fit. During an interview at the time, Del Rio said he had only travelled to England after being told Venables had been impressed by watching a video of him in action: 'I was very excited to have the chance to play for Crystal Palace.' He made his debut in a 4–0 defeat at Barnsley in September and was used as a late substitute in the next game against Sheffield United. The club's coach, Terry Fenwick, went onto the pitch afterwards, put his arm around Del Rio, and said: 'You did very well today. Well done.' It was Del Rio's last appearance. 'But no one ever talked to me or told me why,' he said.

In March 1999, with Palace in a parlous financial state, Del Rio received a two-sentence letter signed by the club secretary, Michael Hurst: 'This is to confirm that Crystal Palace Football Club have given you a free transfer. You have the club's authority to seek future employment with any other club.'

Del Rio was not paid that month. A second letter, dated 13 April, said: 'I, as secretary, acting with the authority and on behalf of the Club, hereby give notice that the Club will cancel your contract on 30 June 1999.' It too was signed by Hurst. The club had every right to cancel the contract – it was only due to run a year – but Palace had also stopped paying him. He went to training every day so they could not claim that he'd failed to turn up. He ran around by himself.

'I'm very worried,' he said at the time. 'It's very difficult. I sent my last pay home and now I have no money.' Del Rio's wages made a big difference to his widowed mother and two brothers. At the time he also feared the bailiffs might arrive to evict him from his flat in Croydon, which the club paid the rent for, or his car might be repossessed. In the end he went home, returning to British football the following year with Dundee.

One of the most ironic aspects of that era was how much was actually done to meet the needs of the Palace players. Among other personnel, Goldberg hired a broadcasting manager, an IT manager, a human resources manager, an Internet specialist, a variety of PR executives, a full-time doctor, a fitness expert and team of three personal trainers, a nutritionist, five physiotherapists, a masseur, extra office staff and a cook. But no one specifically to meet players from the airport. Or see them off again.

Local heroes

The converse of the unhappy, short-lived stays of the likes of Walter Del Rio can be found in the stories of men like Alex Calvo-Garcia from Spain. 'He's considered to be something of a local hero,' said John Staff, an historian and lifelong fan of Scunthorpe United. 'He was the first foreign player to join us who had no previous ties with England. He came over because he wanted to make it in the Football League. When he arrived he spoke limited English but with a lot of hard work, on the pitch and in the language classroom, he made it into the first team.'

In 1996 Calvo-Garcia, a midfielder, was playing for a small club, Eibar, located in northern Spain between Bilbao and San Sebastian. He was 24 at the time and felt he wanted to try living abroad. His agent told him Scunthorpe were holding trials. He knew nothing about Scunthorpe, or indeed where it was, but he travelled anyway and was immediately offered a contract.

He ended up staying for eight years, until the end of the 2003–04 season, becoming Scunthorpe's longest-serving player at that time. He made more than 200 League starts and scored some vital goals. None was more important than the only goal of Scunthorpe's Third Division play-off final at Wembley Stadium in 1999. 'There was even talk of naming a street after him after that,' said Staff.

Although Calvo-Garcia broke his leg during the 1999–2000 season, spending a long and painful year on the sidelines, he fought back to fitness and returned to the side. Away from the club, he bought a house in the town with his Spanish wife, Leira, and took up snooker as a hobby. It wasn't a game he'd ever played at home but a lot of his Scunthorpe team-mates played. 'He's extremely popular with the fans and can easily be spotted around town,' said John Staff during Garcia's final season. 'But then his car is the only one in Scunthorpe with a Spanish registration plate.' Despite standing out, Calvo-Garcia believed England to be a more peaceful place to make a living than Spain. 'The fans are more loyal,' he said, 'and it is easier to go about daily life without being pestered all the time.'

Another player who acclimatised well was Canada's Carlo Corazzin, a striker. By the end of the 2002–03 season, his last in Britain, he'd spent almost 10 years in England providing decent service at each of his four clubs, Cambridge, Plymouth, Northampton and Oldham. He'd made more than 300 League starts and scored more than 100 goals. Despite never making it into the Premier League, he'd enjoyed a triumphant career as part of the most successful national side in Canada's history.

In February 2000, while making a living at Third Division Northampton Town, he won the Golden Boot at the Gold Cup, an event that Canada won after beating the likes of Mexico and Colombia. He scored in the final against the latter and received his award from Sir Bobby Charlton afterwards. 'Winning it was an honour but it was almost as much of an honour to be presented it by him,' he said. After the tournament Corazzin went back to Northampton and ended that season by helping them win promotion to the Second Division. He hoped at the time that an offer might come in from a First Division club – or even one of the smaller Premier League sides – but nothing materialised and he moved to Oldham.

Corazzin's international colleague, Jason De Vos, a defender, spent the 2002–03 season not far away, at Wigan, and later moved to Ipswich. De Vos had previously played at Dundee United. Before that he'd been at Darlington, where he gave locals something to celebrate by becoming the first player in the club's history to win international honours while attached to them. He achieved the feat when he played for Canada against Iran in August 1997. It probably wasn't the kind of fixture that many Darlo followers would have imagined would excite them a decade before, but it showed the positives of the foreign invasion.

Other full internationals who have played hundreds of times for English clubs without ever making it to the top division include Australia's Andy Bernal (Reading) and Shaun Murphy (Notts County, West Brom, Sheffield United and Crystal Palace); Bermuda's Kyle Lightbourne (nine different clubs); St Vincent's Rodney Jack (Torquay and Crewe); and at least half a teamful of Trinidad & Tobago's 2006 World Cup finals squad. Numerous others have started at lower clubs and worked up – including Australia's Lucas Neill and Tim Cahill, and the United States' Kasey Keller – while many more will undoubtedly follow. Others have gone in at the top with the sole intention of staying there, not least a brilliant Dutchman and a pint-sized Italian.

Brilliant orange

The Netherlands has been one of the leading providers of foreign players to England since the mid 1990s. Some enjoyed their peaks in other countries and only ventured from mainland Europe late in their careers. Patrick Kluivert spent a so-so year at Newcastle from summer 2004, while Edgar Davids joined Martin Jol's resurgent Tottenham, aged 32, in 2005. Others came with bags of youthful promise, like Arjen Robben, the talented winger from PSV Eindhoven, who joined Chelsea for £12 million, aged 20, in 2004, and was one of the most exciting elements in a side who lifted Chelsea's first title for 50 years.

Ruud Van Nistelrooy was 25 when he joined Manchester United with a hunger for goals that made him Europe's leading marksman for a while. At the end of the 2002–03 season, his second at United, he'd won a Premier League winners' medal, a Golden Boot and broken or equalled several records. By scoring against Everton on the last day of that season, he'd taken his Manchester United tally for the season to 44. Twelve of those had come in the Champions League (a tournament record) and 25 in the Premier League (which won him the Golden Boot). His goal at Goodison Park made him the first United player to score in 10 consecutive games – eight in the League and two in Europe – and equalled his own record of scoring in eight successive Premier League matches. His scintillating form had brought two goals for the Netherlands, meaning he'd racked up 17 goals (including two hat-tricks and one brace) in the final 12 matches of his football year.

These were remarkable feats even by his own standards. In the 2001–02 season, his first at United after recovering from a serious injury, he'd scored 'only' 35 goals, including 23 in the Premier League (enough for the Golden Boot) and 10 in Europe (the highest in the competition). A strike ratio in the Premiership of more than a goal every two games at United over a succession of seasons is a record few have matched.

Of the other Dutchmen, Ruud Gullit's best days were behind him when he arrived at Chelsea, although he was still influential both as a player and manager. Bryan Roy and Pierre Van Hooijdonk made impressions at Nottingham Forest in the 1990s, although Roy's was not lasting and Van Hooijdonk's tenure ended in farce when he went on strike and walked out.

Marc Overmars was a key figure in Arsenal's 1998 Double but departed after 100 League games. Jimmy Floyd Hasselbaink had a terrific strike rate at Leeds in the late 1990s but left on terrible terms. His return to England with Chelsea in the summer of 2000 showed he could still be influential, as did his move to Middlesbrough in 2004. It also showed he could still be temperamental, as several 'Will he stay?/Won't he stay?' episodes showed.

Jaap Stam at Manchester United was the best example among many hard-working, no-nonsense Dutch defenders, playing a key role in Manchester United's 1999 treble. But he eventually departed after being erased from his manager's plans. The same fate befell the Dutch international goalkeeper Sander Westerveld at Liverpool. Westerveld won three major honours in 2001 only to find himself surplus to Gérard Houllier's requirements. But at least before Van Nistelrooy's arrival, of all the Dutchmen to have played in England – and there have been some 150 in the League to date – it was Dennis Bergkamp who undoubtedly made the biggest impact.

The non-flying Dutchman

Dennis Bergkamp, who by 2005–06 was Arsenal's longest serving player, outdid them all, at least in terms of staying power and consistent achievement at one club. He moved to Highbury in 1995. It is a tribute to both his own efforts and those of the elite educational establishment that nurtured him at Ajax. He was well aware of the standards required when he entered their youth system as a 12-year-old. This was a club who'd been captained to a hat-trick of European Cups by Johan Cruyff in the early 1970s under the managerial guidance of Rinus 'Total Football' Michels.

Cruyff was back as manager by the time Bergkamp made his debut. The young player knew that making the grade would be tough and that 100 youngsters would fall by the wayside for every one who made it to the first team. But he was utterly dedicated, realising from his teenage years onwards that going to bed early and staying away from off-field distractions would make him a better footballer. 'What's so great about smoking, drinking and partying?' he later wrote on his website.

As he matured into his teens, it was clear he had outstanding technical ability – a prerequisite at Ajax. He made his debut in European competition at 17 and won a European Cup-Winners' Cup medal in 1987 three days before his 18th birthday. He came on as a substitute in the final against Lokomotiv Leipzig, a game won by a single goal from Marco Van Basten. Bergkamp later won another European trophy with Ajax, the 1992 UEFA Cup, with Liverpool among those eliminated en route.

After scoring 103 goals in 185 games in seven seasons with Ajax, he moved to Internazionale in Milan in the summer of 1993. In hindsight it was an error. Inter had promised they'd make other adventurous signings and change the way they played to accommodate him. But instead of becoming exponents of free-flowing football – which had never been likely in the land of defensive strategy – they stayed truer to *catenaccio* tradition, locking up at the back when ahead.

The move to Italy's Serie A did not work out, even though Inter won the UEFA Cup in 1995 with Bergkamp their leading scorer in Europe. He scored just 11 goals in two years and critics said he had failed. Away from the easy pickings of the Dutch League, they claimed, he couldn't make his mark. Bergkamp himself admitted that in such a stifling football culture – on the pitch where defending was an art form, and off it where footballers were public property – he found it tough.

His move to Arsenal in 1995 was his road back to freedom of expression. Arguments will always rage about the essential characteristics of English football. One man's high-tempo, rough-and-tumble pinball is another man's merit-heavy, attack-based entertainment. But there is no doubt it suited Bergkamp, who was soon finding plenty of space in which to make his runs and lots of chances to craft delicious, tricksy goals.

He also got himself into trouble, resorting on occasion to a tough physical approach, including crude tackling and a forceful use of his arms or elbows. This landed him several red cards, an FA fine of £5000 for improper conduct and criticism from various opponents, pundits and managers (although never, in public, from Arsenal's Arsène Wenger). Depending on your point of view, his misdemeanours were either a result of hot-headed petulance or the over-stretching of a necessary application of force to cope with the conditions. The truth probably lies somewhere in between. It's arguable that several of England's leading foreign imports have been able to 'mix it' when necessary, not least Patrick Vieira, one of the best and most influential midfielders in the world in his heyday at Arsenal. But Bergkamp was always capable of a burning sense of injustice when things didn't work out the way he planned. He admitted as much when talking about his reaction to being the victim of a foul.

'I accept that I do quite often sit on the ground after a foul, with my hands in the air calling on the referee to make a decision my way. It must be frustrating for the fans when they see that because even though I've been fouled, they must wish I could just get on with it. But it's so frustrating because you have the whole picture of the move in your head and then you get pushed or pulled and no one sees it.' These are the words of someone who eats, sleeps and above all thinks about the game, right down to how he's going to finish a move once he's split a defence or found a gap in which to work.

Arsenal's Double-winning campaign of 1997–98 saw him at his peak. Although he missed the FA Cup final, injured, he ended the season as Arsenal's leading scorer in the League and in both domestic cups. Some of his goals were mesmerising and he achieved a unique treble when a hat-trick against Leicester secured him first, second and third places in the BBC's Goal of the Month competition. He also achieved a personal 'double' by being voted player of the year both by his peers and by the Football Writers' Association. He then capped a decent World Cup at France 98 by scoring a breathtaking 89th-minute quarter-final winner for the Netherlands against Argentina. Not only was it a classy volley under pressure but it was Bergkamp's 36th international goal and broke the Netherlands' record tally of 35, reached by Fas Wilkes in 1961.

Bergkamp chose in 1995 to give up travelling by plane, a decision that remains intriguing to many, if not the player himself. He said that it bored him and annoyed him when well-intentioned people offered advice about how his fear can be conquered. As far as he was concerned, he made a decision for his own reasons and that was the end of the matter. If it affected his chances of playing in faraway locations, so be it. All he ever said publicly on the subject is that he reached a point when the thought of flying was affecting him so much his game was suffering. He would worry for days before a flight to a game. On the pitch he would fret about the flight home. Around the time he moved to Arsenal, he decided never to fly again. 'I felt free again after I'd made that decision. I believe it's not a coincidence that I've played the best football of my career at Arsenal, since I made that decision.'

So where did the fear originate? It is a question worth asking if only because Bergkamp is convinced that removing the fear – by eradicating the possibility of it – had such an effect on his game. He has never said why he stopped flying. In fact he's said that there was no specific reason. Various theories have done the rounds, including one that he was shaken by an on-board bomb scare while in America at the 1994 World Cup. But privately he says this was not the reason.

There are few other clues, although one entry in his old website biography did make interesting reading. It came in a section where he wrote about his favourite goals at Ajax and a particular goal against RKC on 4 October 1992: 'It was a very good goal for me even though it wasn't an important goal because we were already four or five goals ahead. The movement leading to it was excellent and the goal itself was a great chip. That's my speciality . . .' It wasn't mentioned in the biography but he actually scored a hat-trick that day in a 5–0 win.

On the day of the game, an El Al Boeing 747 crashed into an Amsterdam apartment block shortly after take-off from Schiphol Airport. Forty-three people were killed, most of them on the ground. Bergkamp's diary entry ends: 'I have mixed memories of that day because straight after that match, we heard about the infamous 747 plane crash in Amsterdam. I tend to remember those two things together so I have a great memory from the goal but a bitter, sad memory of the plane crash.'

Whether that incident had any effect on him is open to speculation. It's quite possible it didn't, although his reminiscence does confirm a strong link between the game and that day's events. Did he somehow subconsciously equate on-field brilliance – the scoring of a wonderful goal, one of a hat-trick – with air disaster? That's one for the shrinks to argue over.

But Bergkamp did not score another hat-trick for almost six years, until after he'd given up using planes.

Rhapsody in blue

Gianfranco Zola flew for all his footballing life, from the day he made his debut aged 18 for Nuorese of the Italian Fourth Division to a thrilling 2002–03 season when he continued, aged 36, to defy the years and shine for Chelsea before leaving English shores. At 5ft 6in, he was a giant in a diminutive frame. His passion for football, and the example he set to others, made him one of the most valuable foreign players England has ever seen.

His body of work, measured strictly by honours, is impressive enough. He won the Italian title and Super Cup with Napoli, where he became Diego Maradona's successor. He won the UEFA Cup with Parma, for whom he scored 49 goals in 102 matches in the tight

Walter Bowman (standing, fourth from left, No. 3) first came to the British Isles with this 1888 Canadian international touring side, and later became the first foreign player in the English Football League, with Accrington. He also played for Ardwick, who became Manchester City.

Hassan Hegazi, an Egyptian international forward, came to London in 1911 to study engineering. He joined non-League Dulwich Hamlet as a forward, and his dazzling array of playmaking skills soon attracted the attention of Fulham, for whom he briefly played League football.

Arthur Wharton was born in Ghana in 1865 and became the first black footballer in the League when he made his debut for Rotherham in 1893. A superb all-round athlete who at one point was the fastest man in Britain, he played all his football in goal, also appearing in the League for Sheffield United and Stockport.

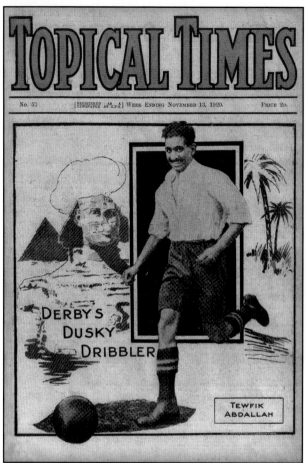

No. 57   [REGISTERED AS A NEWSPAPER AT G.P.O.]   WEEK ENDING NOVEMBER 13, 1920.   PRICE 2D.

DERBY'S DUSKY DRIBBLER

TEWFIK ABDALLAH

left: Tewfik Abdallah came to England in 1920 to seek experience in the engineering trade, and played League football for Derby and Hartlepool. His arrival in the game caused such a stir that he was put on the cover of the *Topical Times* news magazine. He also played in Scotland before pursuing a coaching career in America.

bottom left: Eugene Langenove was the first French player in the League when he appeared for Walsall in 1922. He was a full international, capped as a right-sided defender, and he only came to England because he'd been banned from playing in his home country for violent behaviour.

bottom right: Nils Middleboe first came to the attention of English clubs when he played for Denmark in the Olympic football tournaments of 1908 and 1912, where his country met England in both finals, and lost. He played League football for Chelsea from the 1913–14 season onwards, and later wrote authoritative coaching manuals.

Bert Trautmann (holding the back of his head) is accompanied off the pitch at the end of Manchester City's 1956 FA Cup final triumph over Birmingham. Trautmann, a former German POW, earned widespread respect for his wonderful goalkeeping and his bravery. In the 1956 final he broke his neck but played on. He was the first foreigner to win the Footballer of the Year award.

George Robledo of Chile (right, in action for Newcastle against Fulham in 1951) was the first South American to make any impact on the English game. He played League football for Barnsley and then Newcastle, with whom he enjoyed back-to-back FA Cup wins: he set up the winner in 1951 and scored himself in 1952.

Alec Eisentrager (bending backwards, about to kick the ball) arrived in England in 1945 as a German prisoner of war and had a long career at Bristol City. He made headlines back home for his success, and one newspaper feature carried evidence of his domestic bliss – Alec doing the dishes with his British wife, Olwyn.

Eddie Firmani travelled from his native South Africa to join Charlton in 1950. He commanded a British record transfer fee of £35,000 when moving to Sampdoria in 1955 and remains the only man ever to have scored 100 professional goals in both England and Italy.

Steve Mokone was the first black South African to play professional football outside that country, with Coventry City in the mid-1950s. In the course of a turbulent, extraordinary career, he also played for Cardiff and Barnsley, won honours in the Netherlands, and served a lengthy prison sentence in America for crimes he denied committing.

Dutch internationals Frans Thijssen (left) and Arnold Muhren were signed by Bobby Robson for Ipswich in the landmark season of 1978–79, when England's ban on foreign players was lifted. They helped to transform the way the game was played, with Thijssen later picking up the Footballer of the Year award.

Bruce Grobbelaar punches the air in celebration as Liverpool win the League Cup of 1983, one of 13 occasions when he lifted major silverware with the club. The South African-born Zimbabwean international goalkeeper's trophy haul makes him the most successful foreign player in English football history.

Peter Schmeichel, known variously as the Great Dane and the Northern Rock of Manchester United in the 1990s, won 10 major honours as the club's goalkeeper between 1993 and 1999. His final season at Old Trafford in 1998–99 culminated in the landmark treble of the League, FA Cup and European Cup.

The arrival of Juninho, then seen as Pelé's heir, at unfashionable Middlesbrough in 1995 helped to redefine perceptions of the English game. The brilliant Brazilian midfielder had three separate spells at The Riverside, enduring two lost Cup finals and relegation in his first stay, but left on a high after League Cup success – Boro's first ever trophy – during his third.

In Gianfranco Zola's six and a half years with Chelsea, where he played until the end of the 2002–03 season, the diminutive Italian won the FA Cup (twice), the European Cup-Winners' Cup and the League Cup. He also won the Footballer of the Year award in 1997 and was voted Chelsea's best player of all time in 2003 for his massive contribution, on and off the pitch.

Eric Cantona polarised opinion like no player before or since. Even his depiction as a deity in this 1997 painting by Michael Browne provoked controversy, with its message that some of England's brightest young players depended on a mercurial Frenchman for inspiration. Cantona was Manchester United's talisman as they virtually annexed the Premiership between its inaugural season in 1992–93 and 1997, the year of his sudden departure. The French striker won five League titles (one with Leeds and four with United) and two FA Cups, both as part of Doubles during his time at Old Trafford, in 1994 and 1996.

Thierry Henry (centre) celebrates an entire season unbeaten in the League in 'The Invincibles' season of 2003–04 along with, from right, his French international team-mate Patrick Vieira, the Brazilan Edu, the Dutchman Dennis Bergkamp, and England's Ashley Cole, one of the rare Englishmen to play regularly within that team.

Arsène Wenger (right), transformed the fortunes of Arsenal when he became the manager at Highbury in 1996 through his holistic approach, his attention to detail and his eye for promising talent, whatever the origin. His fellow migrant, Rafael Benitez of Liverpool, made a stunning start to his Anfield revolution by guiding his side to a dramatic European Cup success in 2005.

confines of Serie A. Six months after joining Chelsea in the 1996–97 season he was voted England's Footballer of the Year. By 2003, after six and a half years at Stamford Bridge, he'd won the FA Cup twice, the European Cup-Winners' Cup and the League Cup. Beyond that he'd also won admirers for his grace, his technique, his deceptive toughness and his sportsmanship.

'I've been watching Chelsea for 37 years and Zola, without doubt, is by far the greatest player ever to have graced the hallowed turf of Stamford Bridge,' said Billy Black, a Chelsea fan, in the year that Zola left. 'He is everything you would or could want from a player. He's got skill, motivation, integrity. He's got a gentle nature but can tackle strongly. He is the model that all players should aspire to. It's difficult to pick out one match that he made a difference to, because 99 per cent of his performances contain some moment most other players can only dream of.'

Evidently many Chelsea fans feel the same. In 2003, they voted him the greatest player, from any nation, ever to represent the club. Zola's team-mate, Frank Lampard said, shortly after that award was announced: 'You can talk about people like Dennis Bergkamp and Eric Cantona, and I think Cantona would be the one nearest to Franco for his influence on Manchester United as a club, but Franco is definitely the best. He's got individual skill, has helped Chelsea win trophies and the way that he holds himself makes people respect him. No one ever has a bad word to say about him. Franco is a great ambassador for kids to look up to and he always has time to sign autographs and help younger players. That makes him not only a great player but also a great man.'

What set Zola apart is that he also gained affection far beyond the fringes of partisanship. As Alex Ferguson once confided: 'I just love the wee man. Even some of the greatest players cheat, but he never does. Aye, I love him.' To paraphrase the famous Nike advert about Eric Cantona: '1966 was a great year for English football. Gianfranco Zola was born.' And he was born to last. Although only six weeks younger than Cantona, by 2003 he'd played at the top level until he was six years past Cantona's retirement age. Unlike Cantona, with Zola there was no dark side, no tortured exposition of the soul, no torn-apart heart on the sleeve. The Italian's heart was in his work, and in his tireless desire to play, in the most literal sense, with a smile on his face.

'Whatever you do, you have to do it with passion,' Zola told BBC Radio London in April 2003, as he pondered whether to extend his stay at Chelsea another year. (He left, and an offer to reconsider by the incoming billionaire owner Roman Abramovich arrived too late to sway him.) 'That has been the key to my success so far. I've done whatever I've done because I've enjoyed it so much that I've never felt tired with what I was doing. That will be the same when I do something else.'

The measure of any player's contribution is ultimately his legacy. As Lampard and numerous others have testified, Zola led by example. There are striking parallels listening to him talk about the players who inspired him. He named three who he especially admired in Italy: Zico, often called the best Brazilian since Pelé, who spent time at Udinese; Michel Platini of France, who played for Juventus; and Diego Maradona of Argentina, Zola's one-time teammate at Napoli and his ultimate hero. 'For me, I don't think there will be a player like him in the future,' said Zola. 'He was simply amazing, a great inspiration.'

The common thread is that Zico, Platini and Maradona, like Zola in England, were players from another country, another world. They inspired first and foremost through their ability. But they also inspired – Maradona above all – because they were shrouded in otherworldliness but were simultaneously down to earth. Here's how Zola explains the effect Maradona had on him.

'When you think of great games of football, like Real Madrid against Manchester United [in the 2003 Champions League quarter-finals], it was a game where you thought "I just have to go and play football". It was so good, it gave you a charge. Just watching Maradona training had the same effect for me. I wanted to go and do that. That's the feeling I got from him. He was a lovely guy . . . the first time I met him I was shaking and speechless, I didn't know what to say. But he was so easy to talk to, he put me at my ease. I've always been impressed by that.' Replace the name 'Maradona' with 'Zola' and history repeated itself for any number of young English players.

Talking of his admiration for England, he added: 'The thing I enjoy most is the way the fans live for football. I really like the passion they have for their club, no matter. If the club is successful, good, if not, they still keep close to the club all the time.'

Zola won admirers for making an effort all the time, be it in a pre-season friendly, a vital international or major European game. His work-rate was not swayed by arenas, it seems, only by the task in hand. And whichever task that was, it was always the most important. Three examples. He scored for Italy in 1997 as they inflicted England's first ever World Cup match defeat at Wembley. He scored twice for Chelsea against Reading in a pre-season friendly later the same year. He came off the bench to find the winner in the European Cup-Winners' Cup in 1998. It was hard to differentiate at any given moment in any of those games which meant more. The point was that they all meant everything.

'The moment which most sums the wee man up in my book came at the end of the 2001–02 season,' said Dan Davies, a Chelsea fan. 'We were playing West Ham at reserve level on a Monday evening. The crowd was sparse, it was a non-event. With two or three minutes to go, we were 2–0 up and I was making my way behind the goal that we were attacking on my way out of the ground. We got a throw-in level with the edge of the West Ham penalty area. Not only did Franco run across the box to receive the throw, he was jinking and turning, spinning in a desperate attempt to give him that half yard of space to receive the ball. Nothing came of the move, but to see the level of effort and application that he was putting in under such mundane circumstances said it all.'

In a class of his own

Set against Zola's benchmark, no other Italian in England has come close in terms of class or legacy. Giorgio Chinaglia, born in Italy and raised in Wales, played for Swansea in the 1960s but was not a star until he played prolifically for Lazio and later the New York Cosmos. Fabrizio Ravanelli scored goals for Middlesbrough but was temperamental and did little for his team-mates.

Chelsea's aristocratic Gianluca Vialli did plenty, as a player and manager, although his transformation from one to the other caused rifts that led to his leaving. Roberto Di Matteo secured a place in history with the fastest ever goal in an FA Cup final, scoring in 43 seconds as Chelsea beat Middlesbrough 2–0. He scored the winner in the 2000 FA Cup final too but his career was cut short when he sustained a broken leg in a European defeat to St Gallen of Switzerland.

Away from Stamford Bridge, the Italian who consistently grabbed most headlines during his time in the League was Paolo Di Canio, although often for the wrong reasons. A transient striker who pledged undying allegiance at various stages during a career at Lazio, Ternana, Juventus, Napoli, Milan, Sheffield Wednesday, West Ham and Charlton, his ability – a delight at times – was beyond question.

Di Canio was always a jumble of contradictions. Of Benito Mussolini, he wrote in his autobiography: 'What fascinates me, and this is probably where Mussolini and I are very different, is the way he was able to go against his morals to achieve his goals.' And yet, despite frequent talk of playing his heart out for his team, he was capable of behaviour detrimental to it. Late in his career back in Italy, he was still getting in trouble for fascist salutes.

On the pitch, his most notorious moment in England was when he earned an 11-match ban in 1998, while playing for Sheffield Wednesday, for shoving the referee Paul Alcock to the ground. And then there was 'fair play' Di Canio, the persona who won a FIFA prize for an outstanding act of sportsmanship in a game between West Ham and Everton in 2001. With a clear opportunity to score but with the Everton goalkeeper Paul Gerrard in obvious need of treatment, he caught the ball and stopped play.

But there was also street-fighting Di Canio, the character who grew up supporting Lazio and used to be a member of the club's notorious Irriducibili hooligan mob. (One recollection from his 'ultra' days was: 'So I kicked the Padova fan while he was lying on the ground. Two or three times, I don't remember how many . . . I was high from the adrenalin rush.')

Di Canio's footballing abilities meant that he was not the kind of player teams liked to face. But then his inconsistencies often made it tough for his managers to guarantee him a place. Zola, by great contrast, always worked for the team, setting an example while not stooping to judge those who had not followed it. Even in his less fruitful periods, such as the second season at Chelsea when injuries and squad rotation disrupted his flow, he remained patient and dignified. Again this set him apart. His raison d'être has always been to ask the most from himself and not be dissatisfied when others don't deliver.

English football can be grateful for his contribution, on that there is unanimous agreement. Gordon Taylor said at the end of the

2002–03 season, 'Pound for pound, foreign players hardly come much better than Gianfranco Zola. He has been absolutely brilliant, not just this season but ever since he arrived at Chelsea. He continues to be a joy to watch – a tremendous professional and a thoroughly nice gentleman to boot . . . He has shown this season that he is as good as anyone else on display in the Premiership and you could not find a better role model.' So said the chief executive of the English PFA.

11

FRENCH CONNECTIONS

ARSÈNE WENGER, THE master of minutiae, turned English football on its head by using his brain. And that, ultimately, is what English football's so-called 'French Revolution' was all about: attention to detail, studious application, and thought. The type of game played by Wenger's Arsenal at their peak, and indeed by the French sides that lifted the World Cup in 1998 and the European Championship in 2000, was characterised by the same guiding principles.

On the pitch there was a strong preference for progressive full-backs, an influential holding midfielder paired with a probing partner, pace on the flanks and creativity in attack. Whether the players lined up 4–4–2 or 4–2–3–1 or anywhere in between, was not as important as fluidity and ability to switch with the play. Off the pitch, minute attention was paid to all areas of preparation, from diet to training to individual mentoring. Technical improvements were hastened through physiological conditioning. As Wenger said: 'When you win a cup or a championship, it's down to very small things.'

He was talking about moments that can turn a game, for better or worse, be it using an extra half yard of pace, finding a few extra inches in a jump or possessing a split-second advantage in awareness. Such moments, as he'd said before, can be influenced by small things in preparation. And Arsène Wenger is a god of small things.

Not that grooming ends with the body. Wenger views football as a cerebral exercise. He wants his players to win, certainly, but he wants them to win by expressing themselves, by enjoying the pursuit of perfection, and self-improvement. 'Sometimes the job reveals a new facet of our personality or rather it reveals to us a facet of our personality that we were not yet aware we had, either because we lacked confidence or because nobody had ever allowed us to discover it,' he wrote in 2005. 'When you have inner resources, you grow into what is required to do your job.'

He was talking specifically about Patrick Vieira, his former talismanic Arsenal captain who by then had moved to Juventus. Yet his wider point, that constant self-analysis can lead to improvement via a proper understanding of one's failings, highlighted his thoughtful approach. 'I like the type of self-doubt that [Vieira] has because it produces some very positive questioning. It's not the sort that paralyses you during a game, instead it leads to a process of reflection which makes you self-critical.'

Wenger has always wanted his players to feel that every game is important but none is more important than the next one. When a game is gone, its only worth is what it has taught. By extension, when a career is gone it is too late to change it. So take care of yourself now. *Carpe diem*.

Wenger's other Latin motto, in practice at least, is the one historically inscribed on Arsenal's official badge: *Victoria concordia crescit*. Although this was dropped from the badge in 2002 after 'corporate re-branding', the sentiment lived on: Victory through harmony. And what harmony there was between May 2003 and October 2004, when Arsenal went unbeaten for 49 League matches, a Premiership record that encompassed the whole of the 2003–04 season. In achieving that remarkable feat, they became only the second club ever to finish an entire top-flight campaign unbeaten. The only team to do it before were the 'Invincibles' of Preston North End, back in 1888–89, the first season of the Football League when there were a mere 22 matches in a season.

Wenger's own Invincibles included a hugely significant trio of Frenchmen: Thierry Henry, Patrick Vieira and Robert Pires. This awesome team's typical line-up was Lehmann; Lauren, Campbell, Toure, Cole; Ljungberg, Vieira, Silva, Pires; Bergkamp, Henry. José Reyes and Cesc Fabregas were teenagers on the margins. That 2003–04 side played football for purists, easy on the eye, uniquely thrilling at its best. Alan Hansen, three times a European Cup winner with Liverpool and then a BBC pundit, echoed the sentiments of many when he said Arsenal of that vintage were 'the most devastating team in British history'.

For a season, at least, they undoubtedly were, and if one game exemplified not just their gold but the graft and nerve, it was at home against Liverpool on 9 April 2004. It was Good Friday, aka brilliant Friday, eventually. The day started with questions about Arsenal's supposedly crumbling season. A week earlier they'd crashed out of the

FA Cup, and then been knocked out of the European Cup by Chelsea. A potential treble was down to a singular aim – the Premiership, and at half-time against Liverpool, and 2–1 down at home, even that seemed to be in doubt.

But a second-half display of sheer determination and no little flair was crystallised in Thierry Henry's second goal and Arsenal's third. Henry ran at Liverpool, dodging past Didier Hamann, laying a dummy for Jamie Carragher and making one of Igor Biscan, who collided with a team-mate. Slipping the ball past Jerzy Dudek looked easy but required incredible composure. Henry then secured his hat-trick in the 4–2 win. This was the beautiful game, raised in France, transforming England.

One of the hallmarks of Wenger's career has been the promotion of a team ethic, an all-for-one and one-for-all mentality that starts at the top and works down. He never – ever – criticises his players in public, on the basis that what happens within a club stays within a club. Maybe this explains why he always claims not to have seen contentious incidents involving his players. The unity of the team is paramount. The development of his players – as men as well as athletes – is part and parcel of the same aim. In this respect he is not just a manager but a teacher.

Wenger's erudite approach was evident from the moment he started his debut press conference at Highbury in September 1996. He expounded a philosophy: 'I like real, modern football. Football made of compact lines, of zones, of pressure. And football of quick, co-ordinated movements with a good technical basis.' He laid down an agenda in clear and simple terms: 'I believe in discipline. But the best discipline is always when a player understands it's in his best interests. Success today relies on discipline on and off the field.' He tipped a nod to England's place in the history of football. 'The main reason for coming is that I love English football, the roots of the game are here.' Easy to say, but this detail was sincere and it mattered. It told his ultimate audience – the players and fans – that he came with respect for his new home.

And he acknowledged that his move to north London was also inspired by self-interest. 'For my career, it can be another improvement, a further step for my personal development.' It was a shrewd statement, a deliberate message. It said: 'My fate is tied to Arsenal's. I want Arsenal to improve under me.'

He added: 'There are two challenges. The first is for me to adapt to the team and the qualities of English players. The second is for them to adapt to my ideas. I want to improve the squad with my ideas.'

Ideas didn't so much as tumble out as queue up and stride forth. He wanted to blend an English fighting mentality with a sophisticated technical style. He wanted to bring players in who would be young and have their best years ahead of them. He said he wanted to do 'quality work' and after that 'hope for the best'. Some hope. Some realisation.

Wenger's 1996 press conference marked him out for several reasons. A bit like traditional English football, a traditional English debut press conference deals with the basics. Journalists, looking for a line, want an incoming manager to say 'This is the biggest challenge of my life' or 'This club has the potential to challenge for honours'. It is routine fare. It makes for easy headlines. If a manager will also throw in some information about his transfer kitty, the players he wants to buy and a prediction for where his team will be at the end of the season, so much the better. But you don't, as a matter of course, expect talk of compact lines, of zones, of discipline being in a player's interests, of the manager's personal development.

Of course it was different with Wenger because he was the first Frenchman ever to manage in England. Few people knew much about him and there was an element of starting from scratch. But Wenger also stood out because he was full of ideas and expressed them.

Revolutionary fruit

Measured by honours alone, the French have had an enormous impact in England since the mid 1990s. Wenger's Arsenal won Doubles in 1998 and 2002, another Premiership title in 2004, and further FA Cups in 2003 and 2005. Until 2006, his Arsenal side never finished lower than second in the Premier League. Gérard Houllier at Liverpool won a treble of the FA Cup, League Cup and UEFA Cup in 2001 and added a second League Cup in 2003. Between 1996 and 2006, the Footballer of the Year award went to Frenchmen in six years from eleven, the recipients being Eric Cantona (1996), David Ginola (1999), Robert Pires (2002) and Thierry Henry (2003, 2004, 2006). Cantona alone won five Premier League titles and two FA Cups. More than 30 other French players have played some role in winning at least one major domestic or European trophy with an English club in the last decade.

In terms of numbers, France has provided England with more players than any country outside of Britain and Ireland. By 2006, the figure stood at almost 250, the vast majority arriving since 1997. A bandwagon effect on the back of France's international successes in 1998 (in the World Cup, on home soil) and at Euro 2000 can account for journeymen Frenchmen at League clubs of all sizes – Barnet, Carlisle, Colchester, Darlington, Oldham, Orient, Swansea, Stockport and Tranmere to name a few. But there has also been a high number of internationals, past, present and in the making.

Eric Cantona raged and rampaged to brilliant effect. David Ginola skipped stylishly down the wing at Newcastle and Tottenham. They were followed by Patrick Vieira, who blossomed to become one of the world's best midfielders; Nicolas Anelka, who caused a stir, on and off the pitch; Emmanuel Petit, whose telepathic relationship with Vieira led to honours for club and country; and Marcel Desailly, one of the world's great defenders in his prime.

Others who have chosen England in their prime include Sylvain Wiltord, Pires and Henry at Arsenal, Mikael Silvestre at Manchester United, and Chelsea's William Gallas and Claude Makelele, who both played important roles in securing back-to-back Premiership titles in 2005 and 2006. Among those who still felt they had something to offer late in their careers were the likes of Laurent Blanc, Didier Deschamps, Youri Djorkaeff and Christophe Dugarry. The last two were influential in helping Bolton and Birmingham respectively to stay in the Premier League in 2003.

Without doubt the epicentre of England's French revolution has been at Arsenal under Wenger, whose annual battle with Manchester United's Alex Ferguson developed into one of the most compelling rivalries in British sport until the advent of Roman Abramovich. Without Wenger, would Arsenal have consistently pressured United for so long to raise their own standards to stay on top? Would the two-horse race for the title from the mid 1990s to 2003 actually have been more like a walkover for the northern reds?

But even if Wenger had never come to England, he would still have played his part in reshaping the English game. It was under his managerial guidance at Monaco in the late 1980s that Glenn Hoddle first had thoughts of becoming a manager himself. Hoddle later signed Ruud Gullit for Chelsea. Gullit made them multi-national, hiring, among others, Gianluca Vialli, who continued the trend and ended up fielding the first all-foreign XI in English League history.

By the same token, Wenger might have to claim some responsibility for Southampton's signing of the hoaxer Ali Dia, who only got a game by trading on the name of George Weah. And where did Weah blossom from being a rookie Liberian teenager into a sublime talent who became World Footballer of the Year, and later a presidential candidate, on a 'man of the people' platform in Liberia? At Monaco, under Wenger. 'Arsène is the best coach I have ever played for,' Weah said when Wenger joined Arsenal. 'He brought the best out of me as a footballer.'

Take your pick of any prominent French footballer of the last decade and many will echo the sentiment, not least Henry, Vieira and Pires. And if they don't cite Wenger, the chances are they'll mention Gérard Houllier, England's second French manager. It was under Houllier, at various points in time, that many of France's golden generation were nurtured. After his tenure at Liverpool ended in 2004, his record at Anfield was widely disparaged in England. But his reputation as a key figure in nurturing a generation of French players remained intact.

As well as managing France's senior and junior teams, Houllier long had close ties to the Clairefontaine national coaching centre, located south-west of Paris, which was the physical and spiritual heart of that country's footballing renaissance. Wenger, Houllier and the ethos of Clairefontaine have all helped reshape English football. So has another Frenchman, one who wasn't even born in France.

Genesis of a revolution

The French Revolution started not in France but in Algeria. Or more precisely in Kouba, a suburb of Algiers. That was the birthplace, on 1 October 1923, of Fernand Sastre, who pioneered the Clairefontaine project and later organised France 98, where the graduates of Clairefontaine lifted the World Cup. The story of how Sastre, the son of a *pied noir* farmer, masterminded those triumphs and others is instructive to English football. It speaks of inclusiveness, open-mindedness, long-term planning, attention to detail and thought. It tells how Sastre was influential not only at Clairefontaine but also, tacitly, in the careers of Houllier, Wenger and a generation of French players.

Without Sastre, it is possible that France would not have produced, in their contemporary forms, either Houllier or Wenger. Both men evolved as managers within a French footballing structure put in place largely under Sastre's administration. Both have benefited as managers from the players that that system has produced. And both, like Sastre, have been guided by principles that encourage freedom of expression, equality of opportunity regardless of background, and team spirit. (Or 'liberté, égalité, fraternité', as the French might say.)

Sastre, Wenger and Houllier all grew up believing that football was no mere distraction but an integral part of life. In doing so they followed in the tradition of another French football addict, Albert Camus – philosopher, writer, goalkeeper. He, like Sastre, was born into a working-class *pied noir* family in Algeria (in 1913) and was involved in local football. But whereas Sastre spent his twenties in coaching and development in Kouba, Camus concentrated on actually playing the game, for the Racing University club in Algiers (RUA) among others. Camus's days as a keeper were just ending as Sastre became involved with Kouba FC a few miles away.

One oft misquoted phrase from Camus states: 'All I know about morality and the obligations of man, I owe to football.' It was not quite what he said. His exact observation, made in an essay for *France Football* magazine in 1957 – the year, incidentally, that he won the Nobel Prize for Literature – was: 'What I most surely know in the long run about morality and the obligations of men, I owe to sport: I learned that at RUA.' Still, the message was the same: football, a moral and sporting conundrum.

Sastre, Houllier and Wenger all travelled widely to broaden their experience. Sastre, a tax inspector by trade, ascended to mainland France in 1962, the year Algeria gained independence. He later travelled extensively on government and football business. Houllier travelled to England in the late 1960s, to work as a teacher in Liverpool (where he watched football from the Kop) and then around the world as a coach. Wenger travelled to Cambridge, albeit briefly, to study English, and then around France as a coach before moving to Japan and then to Arsenal. Understanding how their careers converged at various times, and how they all influenced the French game, helps explain how they have been able to influence England's football history.

Sastre's involvement in the administration of the French game, from his arrival in the country in 1962 onwards, was a natural progression. He had worked his way up the ladder in the Algerian game, becoming an influential figure in Algiers. His rise in France was nonetheless swift. In 1969, after seven years in France, he became secretary-general of the French Football Federation; in 1973 he became its president. He retained that post until 1984, when he became an honorary life president.

France experienced some pivotal moments during Sastre's 11 years in day-to-day charge. On 27 June 1984, the nation won its first international competition, the European Championship, with a 2–0 victory over Spain on home turf at the Parc des Princes. The winning team included Jean Tigana and three-times European Footballer of the Year Michel Platini, who scored the first goal in the final to add to the eight others he'd scored in the tournament. Sastre, the chief organiser of the event, was among the first on the pitch afterwards to congratulate Platini, with whom he forged a long friendship based on mutual admiration.

Sastre delighted in Platini's brilliance as a footballing architect. Platini, a strategist in all areas of his life, appreciated Sastre's meticulous approach in mapping the future of the game, not least his proposal, put forward in 1976, that France needed a national training centre. Sastre also wanted a network of regional centres of excellence to work in coordination with it. This was long-term thinking, and took a long time to achieve, but 1976 was a significant year for beginnings.

The same year, Gérard Houllier, then 30 and a youth coach at Arras, took up his first job as a head coach, at Third Division Noeux Les Mines. He spent six years there, winning promotion with his senior side, several titles with his youth sides and a reputation as a shrewd developer of talent.

When Houllier took over at Noeux Les Mines, Arsène Wenger, heading for his 27th birthday, hadn't even made his playing debut at professional level, let alone taken up coaching. Like Sastre and Houllier, he was never an exceptional footballer. He grew up in an Alsace village, Duttlenheim, located outside Strasbourg. Of his prowess on the pitch, he later said, with self-deprecation: 'I was the best . . . in the village. And it was a small village.'

Wenger's priorities in life were academic. He gained a degree in economics and sociology from Strasbourg University and played amateur football for Mutzig, Mulhouse and Vauban before a brief professional career – less than a dozen first-team games – in the late 1970s with Strasbourg. He played three times in their title-winning season in 1978–79. It was only after that, as he hit 30, that he took a manager's diploma in Paris.

In 1982, by which time Wenger was youth coach at Strasbourg, the FFF, under Sastre's guidance, finally chose a location for a national training centre, at Clairefontaine. Houllier, meanwhile, moved from Noeux Les Mines to Lens, with whom he won the French title in 1986. By then Wenger's career was advancing swiftly, as was the Clairefontaine project. Wenger had become player-coach at Cannes in 1983 and then coach of Nancy in 1984. The FFF had put the final touches to their Clairefontaine designs, been granted planning permission and arranged funding. In 1985, as Sastre stepped down from the day-to-day presidency of the FFF, the first bricks were laid at the national coaching centre.

In 1987, as Wenger took over at Monaco, Clairefontaine was being fitted out and decorated. It opened for business on 1 January 1988, a few months before Wenger led Monaco to the French title. That summer Houllier was appointed as the technical director of the French national team, as an assistant to the French national coach, Platini. Their base was Clairefontaine.

The integrated revolution was under way in earnest. Promising young players were identified for enrolment at academies around the country, linked to Clairefontaine. A strong emphasis was put on uniform standards for players' development. Sastre's work was coming to fruition in the hands of his friend Platini as well as other national-level coaches like Houllier and club coaches like Wenger, who was constantly refining his own methods.

By 1992 those methods were paying dividends. Wenger's stock rose as he took Monaco to the final of the European Cup-Winners' Cup that year. Two months later Houllier was appointed manager of France, succeeding Platini, who moved into administration at the FFF. By November 1992, Platini and Sastre were co-chairmen of the organising committee for France 98.

After Monaco reached the semi-finals of the European Champions League in 1994, Wenger was offered the job of French national coach. Houllier had resigned in 1993 – after France missed out on qualifying for the 1994 World Cup – but stayed on as FFF technical director. Wenger was also offered a job at Bayern Munich. He turned down both the FFF and the Germans, saying he could not walk out on his Monaco contract. A few months into the 1994–95 season, he was sacked.

In January 1995, Wenger moved to Japan to become the coach of Nagoya Grampus Eight, where he turned his new club from relegation fodder into league runners-up and cup winners by 1996. The same year Houllier became the coach of the French under-18 team, which included the likes of Thierry Henry (who had played at Monaco as a 17-year-old under Wenger) and Nicolas Anelka. By 1997, when Houllier was coach of the French under-20 side (including Henry, Anelka, Mikael Silvestre and William Gallas), Wenger was manager of Arsenal. His recruitment drive included buying Anelka in March 1997, and Emmanuel Petit and Gilles Grimandi (who had both played for him at Monaco) that summer.

In the spring of 1998 Arsenal won their first Double of the Wenger era. Anelka, Petit and Patrick Vieira (signed in 1996 from his former club, Cannes) were all prominent. Houllier, meanwhile, was a few months away from a move to Liverpool but first spent the summer watching the Clairefontaine dream realised as France lifted the World Cup.

At the end of France's semi-final win over Croatia, the French manager, Aimé Jacquet, turned to Houllier and said: 'This is our victory.' By the time Brazil had been beaten in the final it really was. It was also Sastre's victory, Clairefontaine's victory and a victory for Wenger's players, past, present and future. Among the triumphant French squad were Henry, Vieira, Pires and Petit, who scored the third goal of the final, France's 1000th in international competition.

It was also a victory for the rainbow nation of France, featuring players born as far afield as Senegal (Vieira), New Caledonia (Christian Karembeu) and Ghana (Marcel Desailly) as well as Henry and other second-generation immigrants. And the talisman of the side, the scorer of France's first two goals in the final, was Zinedine Zidane, whose family roots lay in Algeria, the birthplace of Fernand Sastre.

Sastre had been overjoyed to bring the World Cup finals to France and was justifiably proud of his role – often in the background – in developing the team who won it. But he was not there to see Les Bleus lift the trophy. A few hours after their first match of the tournament, a 3–0 win over South Africa, he died, aged 74, his life's work done. His legacy lives on.

Wenger's way

The boozing had to stop. That was Arsène Wenger's most emphatic message in his first few weeks at Arsenal. 'I will not ban beer completely, because one pint helps relax people. But I do not want the players drinking 15 beers, because that is bad,' he said at the end of September 1996. 'A footballer's body is his work. If he then destroys that with bad habits like drinking, it's silly. My players will have to change their social habits.'

And with that, Wenger set about changing the culture of Arsenal. It needed changing. For every strength there seemed to be a damaging weakness. The club had an illustrious history and noble tradition but was reeling after the sacking of Bruce Rioch and the resignation of his temporary successor, Stuart Houston. Arsenal were comparatively wealthy and should have been at the forefront of innovation but they didn't even own their own training facilities. The team's famous defenders – Lee Dixon, Steve Bould, Martin Keown, Nigel Winterburn and Tony Adams – were the best in the business, their cohesion unrivalled, but the linchpin and club captain, Adams, had just admitted he was fighting alcoholism.

The club was replete with decent players but self-discipline was in short supply: in the same squad as the health fanatic Dennis Bergkamp, there was Paul Merson, who had problems with gambling, cocaine and alcohol, John Hartson, who was fond of his pints and his partying, and a group of others – Bould, Ray Parlour and Winterburn among them – who had been in trouble at one stage or another for drink-related misdemeanours. Ian Wright was also a loose cannon. Though the problems of Adams and Merson attracted huge attention, Arsenal were not atypical. English football had long been a professional game lacking a professional approach.

Wenger's ideas, utilised to rapid effect at both Monaco and Grampus, made all the difference at Highbury. What the players ate and drank was of great importance. 'I think in England you eat too much sugar and meat and not enough vegetables,' Wenger said. 'I lived in Japan and it was the best diet I ever had. The whole way of life there is linked to health. The people there are known to work harder than anywhere else and they have the highest life expectancy. Their diet is basically boiled vegetables, fish and rice. No fat, no sugar.'

Japan had a big effect on Wenger beyond the food he ate. In many ways he had more freedom to experiment with his philosophies and methods than in any previous job. The Japanese have always been happy to borrow ideas and then sell them back to the world. Grampus were really just borrowing a fresh perspective from Europe. They allowed Wenger the scope to do whatever he wanted. It helped that the J-League was in its infancy – and therefore everything was relatively new. It also helped that Wenger was a success.

In turn Wenger took away new ideas about food, about a work ethic, and about succeeding on his own terms in an environment traditionally suspicious of individuality. Japanese society, from the playground to the boardroom, is arranged to encourage conformity. The company is every salaryman's ultimate master. Something as simple as going out for a drink after work can become a minefield of manners. If you don't drink enough, it can be seen as a sign you're not on board. If you drink too much, you risk embarrassing the firm. There is always pressure to be seen to be doing the right thing.

In Japan, although most *gaijin* (foreigners) are subject to fewer of these pressures, they still exist. So the way Wenger coped was interesting. He worked tirelessly, which is the measure of a company man in Japan. And because he was bookish, multi-lingual, methodical and evidently very clever, he was viewed as something of a *sensei* (teacher). While every Japanese teacher is sensei (for instance Mr Sugimoto, the geography teacher, is known to his pupils as Sugimoto-sensei), the term sensei is also used in honorific fashion to show deep respect to any mentor. Wenger-sensei pulled off the tricky feat of doing things on his own terms, and succeeding, while maintaining – indeed increasing – the respect people had for him. Whether the experience strengthened his belief that he could impose his ideas in other arenas resistant to change (such as English football) is something only he knows.

Back to Arsenal's diet in 1996. Out went the steak and chips and booze. In came pasta, lean meat, fish, vegetables and plenty of water. As Ian Wright said at the time: 'He's put me on grilled fish, grilled broccoli, grilled everything. Yuk!' But it worked, as did the widespread introduction of vitamin injections and dietary supplements, such as Creatine.

Longer training sessions were introduced, their focus being drills and exercises to hone technique, tone specific parts of the body and build muscle memory. The stopwatch was never far from Wenger's hand as he controlled the precise length of sessions and monitored exactly how much his charges were improving. The importance of warming-up and warming-down was stressed, as was the need for enough rest. 'It's silly to work hard the whole week and then spoil it by not preparing properly before the game,' Wenger said. 'You can point out what is wrong. Some players act the wrong way because they are not strong enough to fight temptation. Some act the wrong way just because they don't know what the right way is. As a coach I can teach the players the things they're doing wrong without knowing it.'

After making it clear to the players that he expected them to look after themselves, Wenger made it clear to the Arsenal board that the club needed training facilities fit for champions. The hierarchy agreed and Wenger went on a fact-finding mission to borrow ideas from leading institutions in France, Germany and Japan to blend with his own. Arsenal invested more than £10 million in a brand new complex at Shenley in Hertfordshire. It opened in 1999 complete with 10 pitches (indoor and outdoor), a gym, a warm-up room, a steam room, a swimming pool, a hydrotherapy pool, treatment rooms, a doctor's office, a canteen serving all the right foods, and a common room. It became the heart of Wenger's Arsenal operation, a place if not of seclusion then of focus on excellence. Visiting international sides who have borrowed the facility – including Brazil – have come away with nothing but admiration.

That Wenger took such a hands-on role in the design said much about his attention to detail and obsession with his job. And he is obsessed, as he has admitted himself. These days, he says, he thinks about football for only 90 per cent of the time. He expects at least as much dedication from his players. How he has succeeded – or failed – to achieve that aim is best examined through the stories of his players.

The making of Vieira

Wenger has earned a reputation at Arsenal as a talent spotter par excellence. He is the shrewdest of traders, bringing players to the club who either become committed to the cause and offer superb value, or who end up leaving at a profit. Nicolas Anelka was bought for £500,000 and sold for £23 million. Emmanuel Petit and Marc Overmars were bought for £9.5 million between them and sold for £30 million. The trio all provided something on the pitch and then left something in the bank. So did Vieira, bought for £3.5 million and sold for almost £14 million after nine years of trophy-winning service.

Freddie Ljungberg (bought for £3 million), Thierry Henry (£10 million) and Robert Pires (£6 million) all fall into the category of players who had potential but only realised it fully under Wenger. Their values rocketed accordingly. Kolo Toure was a steal. Robin Van Persie, Philippe Senderos and Cesc Fabregas all came cheap (relatively) or free. And though some high prices were paid for young talents (£10 million for Jose Reyes, £5 million rising to £12 million for Theo Walcott), the hits outdid the misses. The latter were mostly British, like Francis Jeffers, the £8 million kid from Everton who never made it at Highbury and was sold at a £5.4 million loss. As David Dein, Arsenal's vice-chairman, was fond of saying: 'Arsène makes an average player into a good player, a good player into a very good player, and a very good player into a world-class player.'

Arsenal under Wenger also gained a reputation for lacking discipline, on the pitch. Vieira exemplified both Wenger's judgement of a player, and Arsenal's incautious approach. The two are not mutually exclusive. Vieira was signed because Wenger believed he could play in English conditions. By being tough on the pitch, he was hugely influential. Of course Wenger would have preferred that he hadn't got himself in so much trouble. But that's probably why he made Vieira his captain from 2002–03, and why the player matured so much since, 'as a player and as a man'.

'I go on the pitch with the same commitment but I had to improve the way I acted,' he said in early 2003. 'I made some mistakes and I learned. Now I am captain I don't react like I used to because I have to be an example. Tackles are part of the game. I give them and have to accept them.'

A précis of Vieira's charge sheet at Arsenal does not make light reading. He was twice charged with misconduct in 1998 and was fined £3,000 for a scuffle, then £20,000 for a gesture at an opposition crowd. In 1999 he was given a six-match ban and a £30,000 fine for spitting, and a two-match ban and a £15,000 fine for a confrontation with a police officer. He was charged with misconduct for kicking an opponent (in 2000), for an elbowing offence (in 2001, of which he was subsequently cleared), and, in 2002, for using 'abusive and/or insulting words' to a match official. (He told referee Andy D'Urso that he had no personality.) For the latter he received a two-match ban and a £25,000 fine. He was also sent off 10 times for Arsenal, eight times in the League.

And yet Vieira was consistently Arsenal's most influential player for six years, with Wenger's team almost always enhanced by his presence and weakened by his absence. His height (6ft 4in) and power were assets in themselves but it was his energy, his commitment to winning the ball and his distribution that made him special. He was signed at Wenger's behest before the manager even took over. He made his debut on the day that Wenger's arrival in London was officially confirmed and was at the heart of two Double-winning sides and the Invincible team who played some of the most attractive football Highbury has ever seen.

Even Vieira's history of hints at departure – which were rarely subtle and sometimes downright rude – could be offset against the amount of work he did. In the 2001–02 season, which ended with France's unsuccessful World Cup odyssey, he played 66 times in 11 months for club and country, often after long journeys abroad. As for his disciplinary record, statistics show that while he was no saint, he was more likely to be a victim than a perpetrator of fouls. Arsène Wenger was unhappy with his side's red card count for a long period but there is some evidence that opponents tended to take a physical approach to thwart and rile them. The seasons ending in 2001, 2002 and 2003 respectively saw three, six and three Arsenal sendings-off in the League, but their opponents collectively racked up seven, eight and nine.

Team-mates were always quick to praise Vieira. Thierry Henry called him the best defensive midfielder in the world. Wenger said Vieira was the umbilical cord connecting him with his team. And his disciplinary record improved after becoming captain, with only one red card in his first captain's season – and that for two bookable offences – and one in each of the next two.

Vieira was a natural fighter. Born in Dakar, Senegal, he moved, aged eight, to France, where he settled with his mother and brothers in Dreux, a small town 40 miles west of Paris. At the time Dreux was a National Front stronghold. Vieira developed a mentality – particularly strong among France's rainbow nation – of making the most of his opportunities. A recurring theme was that the opportunities mattered more because in childhood they were infrequent, even unlikely. Vieira's heritage was a common reference point, as was his desire to reflect the spirit of his country of birth. 'I'm a French product with an African's hunger,' he said in 2003.

Wenger was crucial in helping Vieira see his dreams realised. Milan saw enough potential in the 19-year-old to sign him from Cannes, his first club, in late 1995, but he played just twice in Serie A that season. Wenger bought him and moulded him into a World Cup-winning player. The key was letting his players know he believed in them, and that he would stand by them.

Enfant térrible

Nicolas Anelka was a month short of his eighteenth birthday when Arsène Wenger signed him from Paris St Germain in February 1997. He was a 20-year-old Double winner and a formidable striking talent when Wenger sold him to Real Madrid in August 1999 for a profit of £22.5 million. In Anelka's turbulent career it says a lot that his best – most consistent, most productive – playing days to date were those at Arsenal. And it says a lot that even after big-money moves to Spain (where he won the European Cup with Real), and France (where he had two mediocre years back at PSG), he yearned to return to England. Gérard Houllier ultimately decided not to sign him for Liverpool after a five-month loan in 2001–02 so he moved to Manchester City instead, for £13 million, and later to Fenerbahce in Turkey.

Anelka may have been 'Made in England', as the cover of *France Football* magazine proclaimed in January 2002, but he was not able to sustain himself at one club in England for years. 'Perhaps having a huge fee on his shoulders at the age of 19 was a bit too flashy for him,'

Wenger said during the player's time at Manchester City. 'That's maybe why it did not work out at Paris St Germain. But I have kept a check on Nicolas's career and I feel he has gone through a needed evolution. Mentally he has taken a big step forward now. He has matured. There has never been any doubt about his football ability.'

The question of Anelka's maturity has risen time and again. It earned him his Arsenal nickname of 'The Incredible Sulk'. Towards the end of his days at Highbury he became more and more outspoken about his team-mates. In February 1999, during a season in which he was Arsenal's top goalscorer, he made public his disdain for Marc Overmars. 'It's the absolute truth that Overmars plays exclusively for his own benefit and that he never gives a scoring pass,' Anelka raged to *L'Equipe* of the Dutch winger. 'Why shouldn't I say that? There's no reason why I should shut up about having to run like a bird-dog after the missiles that he aims out to the wings, where I'm left with no choice but to put them back into the centre so that he can take advantage of them to shine all by himself, which was his aim all along.'

Matters deteriorated to the extent that Anelka demanded he be allowed to leave. There was talk of him unilaterally breaking his Arsenal contract if he wasn't given a move. His brothers, Claude and Didier, who looked after the business side of his career, were portrayed as the puppeteers behind this perceived outrage but there was evidently something unsettled about the player himself. At Real Madrid he fell out with his coach, Vicente del Bosque, refused to train and was suspended by his club. He returned to shine in the Champions League success of 2000 (and in Euro 2000 for France) but struggled at PSG and then failed to persuade Houllier – who'd mentored him at junior international level – to give him a Liverpool contract.

After joining Manchester City, on another contract that did not last its course, Anelka himself said that he was happy in England, indeed happier than in any other country. As Wenger said: 'He realises that it is a paradise for footballers here. The big following, the commitment of the fans, you get it here more than anywhere in the world. Every player needs to be loved.' And maybe therein lies the reason why his early professional years were so turbulent. He knew he was valued, because the price on his head told him. But after two years' estrangement from his non-footballing friends while at Claire-fontaine, and a high-profile move to Arsenal as a 17-year-old, it's possible he felt more like a commodity than a kid who happened to be a good footballer.

He'd wanted to succeed. He'd accepted that leaving home at 13 was part of that. He knew his career was important to his parents, Jean-Philippe and Marguerite, who had swapped Martinique in the 1970s for a life in high-rise, south-west Paris. But none of that changed the fact that he was a teenager living in a strange country under a constant media spotlight.

Certainly there are those who can testify that even in his sulking phase at Highbury, he was still bemused by the attention and lifestyle his work handed him. Like every famous footballer, Anelka was bombarded with offers of free goodies by manufacturers eager to have their name associated with him. Patrick McAleenan was a PR consultant for one such company, a well-known clothing label. McAleenan, who knew nothing about football, had no idea who Anelka was when he was detailed to take the player shopping in 1999. He only found out when a workmate pointed out newspaper stories of Anelka's supposed attitude problem.

'He was actually quite shy,' McAleenan said. 'There was nothing remotely arrogant or stroppy about him. I think the clothes thing was something an agent had told him to do. He came along and we gave him some gear. He picked out a few things he liked, not huge amounts of stuff. And he was very grateful. He kept saying thank you. It was as though he was surprised that we were interested in working with him.'

One night in February

If one match on English soil summed up the French Revolution in progress at the end of the twentieth century it was the friendly fixture between England and France at Wembley Stadium on 10 February 1999. Nicolas Anelka scored France's first ever goal at the venue – and then the second – as the visitors won 2–0. Even to the most sceptical English minds it was obvious: France's World Cup win had been no fluke. The world champions really did have strength in depth. What other conclusion was there when Anelka, who hadn't even made it to France 98, had put England to the sword so stylishly?

Roger Lemerre, France's coach, said afterwards that the result had gone some way to dismantling the 'myth of Wembley': 'When I go to watch Arsenal, Liverpool, Manchester United and Chelsea the fervour is still there. But at Wembley it is not as great. When the crowd are all behind England it's 10 times harder. Perhaps in some way it's the myth of Wembley disappearing.' It was certainly the might of France being sustained.

Four names in the England starting line-up were notable: Seaman, Dixon, Keown, Adams. Aside from Chelsea's Graeme Le Saux at left-back, the home back five were from Wenger's Arsenal. And they were torn to pieces by Wenger's Anelka.

The rest of the French players in action that day were as follows: Barthez (Monaco), Thuram (Parma), Desailly (Chelsea), Blanc (Marseille), Lizarazu (Bayern Munich), Deschamps (Juventus), Petit (Arsenal), Djorkaeff (Internazionale), Zidane (Juventus), Pires (Marseille), Leboeuf (Chelsea), Dugarry (Marseille), Wiltord (Bordeaux), Vieira (Arsenal). With Thuram, Desailly, Blanc and Lizarazu solid at the back, a two-man central midfield pairing of Deschamps and Petit played distribution and holding roles. The pace of Pires, the genius of Zidane and the passing of Djorkaeff in the line ahead of them allowed incision with a touch of class. Anelka finished with poise, netting three times, one of which was disallowed. The substitutes were stylish window dressing.

With the exception of Thuram, Lizarazu and Zidane, every starting player and most of the squad played in England at some stage. Barthez and Blanc went to Manchester United, Deschamps to Chelsea, Djorkaeff to Bolton, Pires and Wiltord to Arsenal and Dugarry to Birmingham. The French squad that night was not a bad snapshot of France's influence in England. Desailly, who was at the very top of his game with Milan, was nonetheless an important figure at Chelsea afterwards. Significantly, he has been influential in the careers of William Gallas and a generation of young players at Stamford Bridge, not to mention Arsenal's Patrick Vieira (while he was at Milan). Desailly was also part of the Chelsea side, along with compatriots Frank Leboeuf and Didier Deschamps, who won the last FA Cup staged at the old Wembley Stadium, in 2000.

Petit, before and after 1999, was of great importance alongside his close friend Vieira in Arsenal's midfield, if not so great at Chelsea, via Barcelona, later. And then there was Pires, the star of the show in Arsenal's 2002 Double, at least until he ruptured the cruciate ligaments in his knee at the tail end of the season. Not that that stopped him achieving a personal Double of the PFA and Football Writers' player of the year awards.

Almost without exception, French players marvel at the spirit of the English game and the fact that supporters follow one club – and passionately, regardless of results – for their whole lives. Both those factors made an impression on someone who wasn't in the French team in 1999 but who became England's most prolific French goalscorer, and Arsenal's most prolific ever.

Va va voom

Thierry Henry moves around a football pitch with such ease that it sometimes appears his feet aren't touching the ground. Watch him from high in the stadium and his movement can mimic a tornado. It's not the speed per se that catches the eye, although there is that. And it's not the force because he looks so easy. It's the virtual certainty that whatever falls in his path he will find a way around it. In practice he drops a shoulder and then dips past on the other side, or knocks the ball beyond himself, loses his marker and catches up again. But it can be so fluid on occasion that it seems like he's levitating.

His timing is superb. He can stop a ball dead and then wait for the precise fraction of a second to pass before a lay-off or shot. He does a lot of lay-offs, and crosses, and running. He also scores a lot of goals, more than seven in every 10 games in the Premier League. He surpassed Ian Wright's record total of 185 goals for Arsenal in October 2005, and beat Cliff Bastin's long-standing club record of 152 League goals in February 2006. He was, by that time, the most prolific Frenchman ever to play for an English club by far. It was appropriate that in Arsenal's last ever game at Highbury, on 7 May 2006, just before their move to a new home, he should score a hat-trick in the final League game of that season, against Wigan, including the last goal ever seen at that prestigious venue. As he kissed the turf, no one was sure where his future lay. His subsequent decision to stay with the club, he said, had much to do with the passion of the English crowds, a defining characteristic of the English game cited by numerous foreign players as a reason to come to England or prolong a stay.

Henry's brilliance led to him being voted player of the year in 2003 by his peers, and in 2003, 2004 and 2006 by the Football Writers' Association. Among a strong cast of contenders, Henry is potentially Arsène Wenger's greatest success story. Patrick Vieira is way up there but Henry, a failure at Juventus, enjoyed a renaissance to become one of the best footballers in the world.

The rise has more than an echo of Vieira about it. Henry too was brought up in a Parisian suburb, the son of immigrant parents. Antoine, who came from Guadeloupe, and Maryse, who hailed from Martinique, instilled a work ethic in their son and made him determined that he would not let failure envelop him.

That he failed at Juventus is something he has admitted himself. Here, he is talking about the pain endured by childhood friends who also wanted to be footballers but failed to make the grade. 'No one thinks about the possibility of failure. That's why when you do fail it is so difficult mentally. You can have it in your mind from eight to 21 that you're going to be a professional. Thirteen years of dreams and then you fail. Your family crying their eyes out because you've failed. That feeling when you go home and say "Sorry, I didn't make it." Everyone fears that feeling. That's what drives me. That's why I'm running my socks off, not to have that feeling. I failed at Juventus. To lose I can accept but to fail I can't. Failure is at my front door every day. People should remember that.'

What Arsène Wenger did, in buying Henry for Arsenal, was restore the player's faith in himself and his ability. Wenger knew all about the latter, having been the manager at Monaco who fast-tracked a 17-year-old Henry into his side without even stopping off at the reserves. When Wenger was sacked and left for Japan he knew that one day, if possible, he'd be reacquainted with his protégé. In 1999 he was, and Henry will never forget it.

An Anfield academic

Aside from investment in French teenagers, Gerard Houllier's managerial tenure at Anfield had several parallels with Wenger's at Arsenal, if not sustained success. He took an academic and disciplined approach, cleared out the dead wood and boozers and set about building his own side. Like Wenger, he invested in a lot of foreign players. The roll call of hits and misses included Kippe, Ferri, Song,

Traoré, Hyypia, Camara, Henchoz, Westerveld, Smicer, Meijer, Hamann, Babbel, Diomede, Arphexad, Ziege, Vignal, Sjolund, Biscan, Riise, Litmanen, Dudek, Baros, Xavier, Diouf, Cheyrou, Diarra, Luzi and Diao.

At the end of 1999–2000, Houllier's first full season in sole charge (he started as co-manager with Roy Evans in an experiment that failed), Liverpool finished fourth in the Premier League, qualifying for the UEFA Cup of 2000–01. He signed a five-year contract in the summer of 2000 and embarked on his most successful season. On 25 February 2001, Liverpool won their first trophy in six years by beating Birmingham 5–4 on penalties in the League Cup final. On 12 May, they added the FA Cup after two goals from Owen were enough to see off the challenge of Wenger's Arsenal, 2–1. On 16 May an historic treble was completed when Houllier's side won the UEFA Cup, claiming it after a golden goal had given them a remarkable 5–4 win over Alaves in Dortmund. Three days later Liverpool secured third place in the Premier League behind Manchester United and Arsenal to claim a Champions League qualifying slot for 2001–02.

The treble-winning team had key foreign elements, notably Germany's Dietmar Hamann as a vital holding player ahead of a central defence of Sami Hyypia and Stéphane Henchoz. The English personnel – Owen, Gerrard, Heskey, Murphy, Fowler – were supplemented by the wise old Scottish head of Gary McAllister, who was hugely influential.

Liverpool and Houllier had a life-affirming 2001–02. After major heart surgery in October 2001, Houllier's mere return to work in March 2002 was a triumph. His team, in the hands of Phil Thompson, went on to finish runners-up in the League behind Arsenal, thereby consigning Manchester United to their first finish outside the top two since 1991. Houllier's side, it seemed, were ready for the final push to break the Arsenal–United duopoly at the top.

The 2002–03 season started well, Liverpool topping the table after 10 games, but then came a slump that ruined not only their title chances but their hopes of qualifying for the Champions League in 2003–04. It was a close thing, eventually coming down to one match at the end of the season against Chelsea, but the Londoners prevailed to win a place at Europe's top table.

As Houllier said in January 2003, when Liverpool hit the 'blip' that undermined their season: 'We have to keep strong. But this is an ideal opportunity to tell people that at the end of the season the strong will be even stronger, but the weak will have to go. The more difficult the period is, the more you get out of it and the strong personalities and top players will emerge stronger, bigger and more clever. The weaker ones will disappear – sometimes you need that sort of crisis to sort out what is going on. Over the last four years we have changed a lot of things at the club and managed to win five trophies. I would not jeopardise that for a blip that has lasted a couple of months.'

In the same week he said: 'I would be disappointed to leave this club without a championship trophy.' By the time he did leave, without that trophy, in May 2004, the French Revolution was simultaneously at its peak, and waning. Invincible Arsenal had won the title but would not sustain that domestic form. And over at Chelsea, Roman Abramovich was about to change his manager, and the landscape, once again.

12

SOLD OUT

ONE EVENING IN late June 2005, three men were going about their business in Manchester when they came under sustained attack from an angry mob. Between 200 and 300 people erected barricades on the streets to stop the men from getting away. Missiles were hurled. Chants of 'Die, die, die' rang out. More than 100 officers from the Greater Manchester force were required to get the three men to safety.

A couple of days later, Scott Sinclair, a 15-year-old footballer from Somerset, was officially registered on the books of a Premiership club in London. Until then he had been plying his trade with Bristol Rovers of League Two. At a later tribunal hearing, the 'buying' club, who had tempted Sinclair, and other boys from elsewhere, were ordered to pay £200,000 up front and agreed to pay another £50,000 when he made his debut, plus up to £500,000 more in other performance-related fees. They also promised a chunk of any future sell-on price to Rovers, who still felt they'd lost a prized asset on the cheap.

Those two incidents, both indicative of a new era in the English game, had something in common. Sinclair was lured by Chelsea, the first English club to be bought by a billionaire foreign businessman, Russia's Roman Abramovich. And the three men in Manchester – the American brothers, Joel, Bryan and Avi Glazer – were the sons of Malcolm Glazer, the second foreign billionaire to buy an English club, Manchester United. They were on their first trip to Old Trafford since Glazer senior had taken effective control and had just met a group of their future customers, known in a quainter era as 'fans'.

Abramovich's purchase of Chelsea in 2003 changed the landscape of English football at a stroke. He broke every spending record to buy players, and racked up record losses in world football by doing so. He fired a manager, Claudio Ranieri, who had taken Chelsea into the Champions League in his first season as owner, and replaced him with another, Jose Mourinho, who had already won that competition elsewhere. With the Portuguese maverick at the helm, the plutocrat from Saratov bankrolled Chelsea's first League title in 50 years in their centenary year, 2005, and a second, back-to-back, in 2006, the year in which he was listed as the richest Russian in the world. His estimated fortune by then was £10.5 billion, making him the eleventh wealthiest man on the planet.

Abramovich did not buy Chelsea for the love of the club. He wanted a club, any club, though preferably an English club in London. He almost bought Tottenham. Instead he snapped up Chelsea, because they were available. He paid £140 million up front to cover the purchase cost (£60 million) and to wipe out debts (£80 million). If Abramovich hadn't come along, Chelsea would have been in serious trouble, heading for financial collapse.

'It's not about making money,' Abramovich said in early July 2003, explaining his buyout. 'I have many much less risky ways of making money than this. I don't want to throw my money away, but it's really about having fun and that means success and trophies.'

At no stage did he pretend to be a Chelsea fan. He just wanted a club, and his goals were obvious. He was rich enough to have such a plaything. He wanted respectability in the West. He wanted a potential haven, in case the political situation back in Russia turned nasty. He even enrolled his children in English schools. 'I can afford to fly in and out of the UK and back to my job in Russia,' he said. He was also governor of the remote Chutkotka province back home. 'I enjoy England and I'd like to see every Chelsea game, though that may not be possible . . . I'm realising my dream of owning a top football club. Some will doubt my motives, others will think I'm crazy.'

The Glazers were viewed as crazy to visit Old Trafford that day, if not crazy to buy the club, which had long been England's most profitable. Their motive was more straightforward than Abramovich's. It had nothing to do with respectability, asylum or playthings. It was all about money. 'We're delighted to make this offer to acquire one of the pre-eminent football clubs in the world,' said Joel Glazer as his family's bid neared completion. 'We're long-term sports investors and avid Manchester United fans.' Joel was reputedly a United fan in his college days, when he had a Tottenham fan as a room-mate, but 'we are avid fans' was pushing things too far for many.

The animosity towards the Glazers was huge, at least among a core group of anti-takeover supporters. For Joel to claim an affinity for his whole family made things worse. Yet the main reason their takeover was reviled came down to money. The Glazers bought a profitable, debt-free club with large sums of borrowed cash and then loaded United with debt. Inevitably the fans would be the ones who would foot the bill, at first through higher ticket prices. Later, some feared, they would pay through the long-term destabilising of their club.

The foreign buyouts at Chelsea and Manchester United heralded a new era of English clubs as tools in multi-national franchise empires. Although Abramovich started out by saying it was fun, he was soon claiming Chelsea would become the biggest club in the world, a self-financing giant of world sport. And the Glazers never pretended that they were interested in anything other than United's pre-eminence as a brand, one to be marketed more aggressively worldwide than ever before.

This was evidence, on one level, that the Premier League, in little more than a decade, had made English football so attractive that foreign investors believed it could make them money. But at what cost to those clubs and the game in the long term? And bringing what benefits, if any?

One apocalyptic future saw Abramovich growing bored or coming a cropper or being forced, for reasons unforeseen, to abandon his interests along the Fulham Road. What then for Chelsea? A return to penury and the brink of pre-buyout collapse as they cut costs, sold players and tried to make ends meet without a billionaire benefactor? As the club racked up record losses for a second successive year in 2006, spokesmen and spin-doctors briefed that its future was secure, whether Abramovich stayed or not. But they gave no details.

In Manchester, the Glazers vowed to be 'long-term investors' but equally did not rule out, explicitly, a 'flipping', or selling on, of United at some stage if the bottom line dictated. As for the hundreds of millions of debt? The Glazers pronounced themselves 'happy' with it while not explaining how it would be repaid, especially if their on-pitch expectations of continued success were not met. In another apocalyptic future, they would fail to service their debts and sell Old Trafford, then cede partial control of the club to the hedge funds that lent them the money to buy United. Player budgets would be cut and wins would become more elusive. United would begin a spiral of decline that ended in calamitous collapse like that of Leeds United. 'It's a completely different situation to Leeds,' said one of the Glazers' team of financial advisors when this scenario was suggested. Yes, came the reply. Leeds only borrowed £60 million to get into their mess. The Glazers borrowed more than five times as much.

And what of a dream scenario, where Chelsea do indeed become the biggest club in the world, self-sustaining and even profitable? Or if not the biggest club, then one of the biggest, along with the thriving international brand of Manchester United. (And those of Barcelona, Real Madrid, Arsenal, Juventus, Milan, Bayern Munich and others who feel they have the same clout and are vying for a place in this same international market.)

Over at Liverpool in the spring of 2006, there was yet another round of takeover talk after a Spanish millionaire, Juan Villalonga, the former chairman of Telefonica, Spain's biggest telecom firm, became the latest potential foreign bidder for a stake at Anfield. He had spoken of 'a change from a domestically focused club into a global force'. It was the language of Abramovich and the Glazers and any number of wannabe tycoons who saw English football as an international currency. And maybe it is, or will be. And maybe not, not for all of them. Only history will judge whether these grand plans work out but into the second half of the first decade of the twenty-first century, foreign investors were already changing the way that English football operated, on and off the pitch, and within their communities, traditional and global.

Roman's empire

Roman Abramovich made his money through the privatisation of Russian state enterprises, sold off at knock-down prices by the regime of Boris Yeltsin. Abramovich was aged 25 in 1992 when he started his first businesses, and the state sell-offs had been under way for several years. Aided by his then friend, Boris Berezovsky, one of the major tycoons of the era and himself close to Yeltsin, Abramovich acquired a large stake in Sibneft, one of Russia's main oil companies. Berezovsky, a controversial figure, later fell from grace under the regime of Vladimir Putin and was given political asylum in Britain. Abramovich amassed holdings in one of the world's biggest aluminium producers, car manufacturers, a TV station and a variety of other firms. He was elected to the Russian parliament, the Duma, in 1999, becoming the governor of Chukotka in 2000. In late 2005, he sold almost 73 per cent of Sibneft for £7.4 billion to Gazprom, Russia's state-controlled gas company, in a move that was interpreted as firming up his own relationship with Putin. It also gave him some spare cash to pour into Chelsea.

In his first year after taking control on 2 July 2003, he spent more than £150 million on new players alone. Damien Duff cost £17 million from Blackburn, Wayne Bridge £7 million from Southampton, and Glen Johnson and Joe Cole together £12.6 million from West Ham. They were interesting buys if only because they were English and Irish, not foreign. Claudio Ranieri thought this important, as did Mourinho later. Self-evidently, so did Abramovich. It was rumoured that there had been input from Sven Goran Eriksson, then England manager, who controversially met with Abramovich in July 2003. (There were further rumours that Eriksson would be taking over at Chelsea in 2006.) Scott Parker later followed the early English quartet to Chelsea from Charlton for £10 million, and in summer 2005, Shaun Wright-Phillips arrived from Manchester City for £21 million.

Back in the first year, Ranieri's only one within the Roman empire, Abramovich also funded the purchase of Adrian Mutu for £15.8 million (later to be effectively written off after Mutu's sacking for cocaine use), Hernan Crespo (£16.8 million) and Claude Makelele (£16.6 million). Later, with Mourinho in charge, money remained no object with the hiring of, among others, Petr Cech (£7 million), Arjen Robben (£12 million), Paulo Ferreira (£13.2 million), Ricardo Carvalho (£19.9 million), Tiago (£8 million), Didier Drogba (£24 million) and Michael Essien (£24.4 million). Total expenditure on transfer fees alone by 2006 had reached almost £300 million. Wages, debt repayments, other executive salaries and new facilities meant Abramovich had, by spring 2006, spent more than £600 million in total and was showing no sign of closing the cheque book. Indeed, had any of his 'ultimate' player targets been available before then – like Arsenal's Thierry Henry – he might well have spent £100 million more. Proof came during the summer of 2006, when he committed much more than another £100m in fees and contracts for Michael Ballack, Andrei Shevchenko and a variety of others.

Mourinho had not needed them to land back-to-back titles. Abramovich had not needed them to feel safe in declaring, after less than two years as owner, his grand ambition for Chelsea. Gone was the pure notion of fun. In came the declarations of global dominance.

After they secured the Premiership title in 2005, he said: 'I view this title as the beginning of a new era for Chelsea and would like to reiterate my long-term commitment to the club. We want to build the most successful football club in the world . . .' By October 2005, the vision was not just planetary supremacy within a decade, but 100 years of joy. Writing in the foreword to an official Chelsea book, he said: 'Everything we have done so far is geared to [becoming the greatest club in the world]. I hope to carry this forward in the true blue tradition of Chelsea but also build even stronger foundations to last us the next 100 years.'

It is wrong to say Chelsea simply bought their titles. Money alone cannot buy success, as Ranieri, 'The Tinkerman', showed. But it is hard to argue that Chelsea would have succeeded in their swift annexation of the League and its transformation into a competition devoid of real competition without the cash.

As the second title-winning season drew to a close in 2006, Chelsea executives' talk about breaking even within a few years seemed fantasy. They announced that in the financial year to June 2005, the club had lost a staggering £140 million. That smashed the world record for losses by any football club in a single year. And the previous record holders were Chelsea themselves, in the 2003–04 season. The losses to June 2005 represented a 60 per cent increase on the £87.8 million net deficit accrued during Abramovich's first year as owner. Most worrying, from an accountant's point of view, was that Chelsea's income had dipped, year-on-year, from £152.1 million to £146.6 million. And this was before some lower than capacity crowds in 2005–06 led to the extraordinary situation where Chelsea had to advertise in the London *Evening Standard* to get people through the turnstiles.

Yet their expenditure had soared to £286.6 million, principally, they said, due to a series of 'one-off items'. Except there were four such items in that year alone. They had cancelled a sportswear deal with Umbro, written off the contracts of Mutu and Veron, and incurred the 'exceptional' costs of 'academy recruitment', which included hiring Frank Arnesen from Tottenham to head their youth programme.

While they argued that the Umbro deal had been replaced by a better contract with Adidas, that Mutu was a 'book cost' not real expenditure, and that the youth programme would reap its own rewards in the long term, it was still a lot of money to be leaking. As was an annual wage bill of almost £110 million. Chelsea's chief executive, Peter Kenyon, lamely argued: 'These figures reflect the continuing restructuring of the business which we began in 2003–04 ... In simple terms we have taken some pain now for long-term gain.'

That phrase 'long-term' recurred time and again. If phase one of the plan was to spend big initially to smash England's Premiership duopoly held by Manchester United and Arsenal, then phase two was to snare Britain's best talent early to save money later. Frank Arnesen laid out the plan in October 2005 when he spoke for the first time since being poached from Tottenham to oversee the youth development and scouting operations at Stamford Bridge. Capped 52 times for Denmark, he had a decent playing career in the Netherlands that peaked when he won the European Cup with PSV Eindhoven in 1988. He later worked as an assistant coach to Bobby Robson at PSV and then became general manager. He was credited with discovering and nurturing such talents as Brazil's Ronaldo, Iceland's Eidur Gudjohnsen and a trio of Dutchmen in Jaap Stam, Ruud Van Nistelrooy and Arjen Robben.

Arnesen's remit at Chelsea was to get the best young players, wherever they could be found, but with a preference for home-grown talent. 'Most of the recruitment will be here [in Britain],' he said. 'If we get tips, we send people out, I go out as well. I have always liked foreign players. I was one myself. But also the culture of the club and country is very important. England and the United Kingdom is my number one priority. And then from there we spot the best we can. If we have two similar players, I'd take the English guy. It's less risky taking players from home. No homesickness. But we'll go out for the best players.'

His aim, he said, was to provide one player per year for the first-team squad: 'Sometimes it can be two players one year and none the next. But in two years' time, the first has to have come through. We are looking for what all clubs are. First you have the talent, the technical skill, also physically, then the tactical, which you already start to see at 15, 16 years old. But what is more important is the mentality.'

Within a month of that press conference, Chelsea were attending a Football League appeals committee hearing to ascertain how much they would need to pay to three lower-division clubs for players, each under 16, who had been enticed to Stamford Bridge that year.

One of them was Scott Sinclair, who had joined in the summer from Bristol Rovers. Another was Ryan Bertrand, a prospect lured from Gillingham. He cost Chelsea an initial £125,000. The third was Stockport's Harry Worley, whom Chelsea had wanted for £90,000. They were told at the hearing to pay an initial £150,000, and promise up to £800,000 more depending on appearances.

In the spring of 2006, Chelsea made moves for two teenagers from Leeds, Tom Taiwo and Michael Woods, who rejected scholarship deals at Elland Road to move to the London club. In a market where the best young native talent drifts towards the money – though this was not always the case, as Theo Walcott's move from Southampton to Arsenal, not Chelsea, showed in 2006 – Chelsea, under foreign ownership, were using foreign cash to buy up England's best resources. The true impact of this would only ever be seen over time, but logically, it would restrict opportunities for some of these players to break through. Wherever supply exceeds demand, there is waste. In Chelsea's case, supply of young players risked exceeding demand of any given manager to use them.

If this is a hyper-critical analysis, then even in Chelsea's first-team squad in the first two title-winning seasons there were examples of players bought and then utilised evidently less well than they had been before. England's Shaun Wright-Phillips was a prime example, being used so infrequently in 2005–06 because of so many others ahead of him in the pecking order that he missed out on the 2006 World Cup. He was not playing enough club football to warrant Sven Goran Eriksson's faith in him.

The Chelsea plan did not stop with seeking a grip on home-grown talent. In March 2006, the club announced 'a unique long-term commitment to soccer in the United States'. They entered into a 'major strategic alliance' with AEG, a company that built stadiums Stateside and ran four Major League Soccer teams in America. This was due to start in the summer of 2007, and involve a direct tie-up between Chelsea and the then MLS champions, LA Galaxy. There was much talk of helping develop the game in America, an aim that can only be tested in the long term. No doubt a first call on some of America's best youngsters was an aim. Chelsea were rather more direct in admitting their commercial interest. 'By building the profile and interest in Chelsea in this way we are confident we can expand our business and build a platform for increasing our fan base, merchandising and sponsorship opportunities.'

At a time when all forward-thinking clubs, English and otherwise, were seeking to expand globally, this was good business practice, assuming it worked. But Chelsea were far from alone in seeking money from overseas. And their expansion, underwritten by a man of seemingly limitless resources who showed at least in his first three years that he would invest heavily, was eagerly welcomed by success-starved supporters. Elsewhere the reaction was not quite so enthusiastic.

Red Devils

The Glazer family's takeover of Manchester United became inevitable on Thursday, 12 May 2005, which was described in some newspapers the following morning – Friday 13th – as 'the blackest day in United's history'. Surely this was histrionic? The club had, after all, been functioning profitably as a PLC, a tradeable commodity, for years. Malcolm Glazer had simply kept trading up his stock until the fateful day when John Magnier and J. P. McManus, two Irish racing tycoons who had invested in previous years as speculators, finally decided to sell him their 28.7 per cent stake in the club. Added to the 29 per cent he already owned, that gave him instant effective control and triggered a formal offer for the rest of the shares. In turn that led to a total buyout and de-listing from the Stock Exchange.

That it was 'the blackest day' was, however, how many supporters felt. This had nothing to do with xenophobia, although the fact that the Glazers were American, perceived to have little understanding of football or United's history, or role within the community, was a problem to some. An alternative club, FC United of Manchester, was founded as a response. There were various reasons for this, all stemming from a disenchantment with the wider commercialisation of the game, but the Glazers' takeover was the catalyst. Having joined the North West Counties Football League, FC United stormed to the title in 2005–06, their first season, as they began their climb up the league pyramid.

The single biggest reason for opposition to the Glazers was that they borrowed huge sums of money to buy United. Loading the club with so much debt made its very existence vulnerable if the business plan – never explained publicly – failed. United's board had been in close contact with the Glazers over several years prior to the buyout and even they had rejected pre-buyout proposals from the Glazers as 'aggressive' and 'potentially damaging' to United in the long term. David Gill, United's chief executive at the time of the Glazers' stalking, even made a private verbal offer of funds to one anti-Glazer group, Shareholders United, before the takeover. No money ever changed hands, but the offer alone was to prove embarrassing for Gill. By the time it was revealed, he was working for the Glazers.

If Malcolm Glazer had been a bona fide multi-billionaire with a demonstrable ability and will to put massive sums into a club, like Abramovich at Chelsea, it is probable he would have faced much less opposition. As Oliver Houston, vice-chairman of Shareholders United, said at the time of the takeover: 'Chelsea was a club in crisis and had crippling debts. Roman Abramovich wiped out the debts. Glazer is a completely different animal. He's not a sugar daddy.' According to various rich lists, Glazer was a dollar billionaire, with an estimated $1 billion to his name, and perhaps a bit more according to United insiders at the time. But he did not buy United principally with his own cash, but with loans. Herein lay the problem for many fans.

The Glazers spent a maximum of £272 million of family cash, up front, to complete a £790 million takeover. The rest of the money came from initial bank debt of £265 million (loaded on previously debt-free United's books soon afterwards). This rose to £374 million with extra borrowing. The interest rates on that alone were estimated at up to £30 million a year, without capital repayments. All United's profits, in a very good year, with a bit added, might have come close to covering such a sum, but because the Glazers had no obligation to publish detailed financial information, even that was not clear.

But on top of the £374 million was another £275 million, borrowed from hedge funds. This was described as 'the ticking time bomb' debt, repayable at astronomical interest rates of up to 20 per cent per year. Again, because the Glazers did not reveal details, an element of guesswork was always necessary to establish quite how much interest would be payable to whom, or when. The Glazers said they were 'comfortable' with the debt, without revealing how this could be so. Many fans felt uneasy.

By the spring of 2006, United had been dumped out of the Champions League early, but finished in second place in the Premier League. Fears of meltdown or dramatic changes in the way the club would be run had, by then at least, proved premature, but not unfounded. It was always going to be the longer-term headaches that the fans worried about, if that mountain of debt became unsustainable. A leaked 'business plan' in late 2005, described by Glazer aides as 'not definitive or set in stone', suggested that the family planned to increase United ticket prices by 54 per cent within five years. The same plan made no mention of how the 'ticking time bomb' debt would be repaid, although there was always the option of selling the club's Old Trafford stadium (Joel Glazer said there were no plans to do so), or selling the family's American NFL team, the Tampa Bay Buccaneers (the family said there were no plans to do so). An alternative option was to borrow against future earnings to pay off the bank debt and then restructure the hedge fund debt in its place. By the end of the 2005–06 season, this still seemed the most likely option but was yet to happen.

The Glazers expected to increase United's total turnover by 52 per cent, to £245.6 million, by 2010. This was not an unattainable goal as long as Old Trafford continued to be full, at higher prices, and as long as United never failed to qualify for the group stages of the Champions League. Like Chelsea, United envisaged an increase in commercial revenue, and an expansion into overseas markets.

Experts who knew how the Glazers worked in America rejected the idea that cost-cutting on the team combined with price hikes for fans would be the family's formula for success. 'I don't think [Malcolm Glazer] is spending all this money to run a cut-rate team,' said Salvatore Galatioto, the president of Galatioto Sports Partners, a New York sports investment firm, who had worked for Glazer senior in the past. 'The Glazers are extremely innovative and very bright people. If they're doing this, they have a plan that has a high likelihood of success. My experience with them is that they know what they're doing.'

The family might have endeared themselves to fans had they been more accessible in the early days. Instead they guarded their privacy and little was done to present a human face to what appeared as a deal in which business came first, football second. Sources in America described Joel, Bryan and Avi Glazer respectively as 'a family man', 'an emotional movie buff' and 'a secretive dreamer'. 'They don't know that much about soccer, but they see a business opportunity,' said one source who had known the family for years through working with the Tampa Bay Bucs. 'They think there's a profit to be made, but don't expect them to tell you how. They trust no one but themselves.'

All three brothers had worked at some stage as vice-presidents of Glazer senior's First Allied Corporation, a property firm that made its money in investments ranging from trailer parks to shopping malls. Joel and Bryan were vice-presidents of the Bucs. Avi had no day-to-day role at the Bucs, and preferred to plough his own furrow, albeit with family money, controversially and unsuccessfully at times.

Joel was the key player in the move to buy United. 'He's a methodical guy, unemotional, logical,' said a Florida source. 'He's very steady, never loses his cool, he's a dedicated family man.' Bryan, who held de facto control at the Bucs, and also served on the board of another family company, the Zapata Corporation, was widely credited with revamping the Bucs brand, including the logo, and transforming them into a profitable business.

'He's a little more emotional than Joel,' said the source. 'He's single, and don't bet on that changing. He enjoys the nightlife. He takes regular trips to Chicago to see friends. And he likes going to the cinema. He's a movie buff, nothing frivolous. He likes realism, and dramas with punch.' Bryan was not thought to know or understand much, if anything, about football. 'He probably wouldn't know the difference between a free-kick and a throw-in,' said another source. Joel and Bryan both had 'extensive sports management experience', according to one official press statement, although that experience began and ended with the Bucs.

Avi, the eldest brother, was arguably the most intriguing figure of the trio. He was described as a 'maverick', 'a guy with eclectic tastes' and 'the most money-minded of all the brothers'. He had studied in China in the 1980s, then got a law degree in Washington. His business record was chequered – he lost money in the dot-com era – but he still held a key role in the financial side of the family's United takeover.

Towards the end of the family's first year in charge, there were no signs of United's on-pitch fortunes diving. The Glazers had not, as feared, tightened the purse strings completely, and had paid £4 million for Park Ji-Sung the previous summer, and £7 million for Nemanja Vidic and £5.5 million for Patrice Evra in the January transfer window. Sir Alex Ferguson stated that he was happy with the new regime and that it was easier to do business under the Glazers than under a PLC, when an array of permissions had been needed for any transaction.

If some fans were still unhappy – Shareholders United for example, who were no longer shareholders, and thousands of others who had taken their primary allegiance and custom to FC United – most remained, and the newly expanded stadium remained full. United did lose a shirt sponsor, Vodafone, replaced by the Glazers with a more lucrative deal. The Glazers did sack 23 non-playing staff to cut costs. Two fans' groups were banished from the Fans' Forum consulting group, which was odd for a club that had stated in Article 1.1 of its own Charter that it 'consults supporters on a regular basis'. And United were the most indebted club in British football history. But the Glazers remained confident that would not always be the case.

Tycoons, time-wasters and a Thai Prime Minister

Chelsea and Manchester United were both bought by foreign businessmen but were not alone in being seen as ripe for takeovers. English football was seen as such a prestigious international product by the early years of the twenty-first century that wannabe owners came flooding with buyout proposals.

Liverpool were targeted in 2004 by the then Thai Prime Minister, Thaksin Shinawatra. Realising that Premiership football was immensely popular in his country, he wanted to buy a stake at Anfield as an electioneering tool. He also wanted to secure Liverpool's commercial rights for Asia. At one stage he claimed he was on the brink of buying a 30 per cent stake but the deal never happened – partly because he was asking too much for his money, partly because he wanted seats on the Liverpool board and a degree of day-to-day control. It was never clear how he intended to fund his ambitions, which would have cost around £63 million. A national Thai lottery especially for the cause was suggested, and later dropped.

Richard Caborn, the British government's sports minister, entered the debate to say that clubs had a fundamental duty to try to retain links with their communities. He stopped short of saying the government could or would intervene to stop someone like Shinawatra, who had a dubious human rights record, from investing in an English club, but he made clear his preference for new investment from local sources: 'Football clubs are a little bit special, they're part of the community. So I think it's incumbent upon football clubs to make sure that they do have very strong roots into their community. I think that's what ought to be considered when any takeover bids or indeed investment is being made.'

It was a quaint idea, and one dear to many fans' hearts. Clubs as community, at the centre of communities, not of global business interests, run in franchise form like so many other sports in other countries. But actually the government could and would do little to intervene when foreign businessmen, be they Abramovich, the Glazers or pretty much anyone else, came calling with their chequebooks.

Liverpool were also of interest to the American Kraft family, who owned the NFL's New England Patriots, and to a couple of Los Angeles movie moguls. One of them, Mike Jefferies, the producer of the *Goal!* series of films, originally hailed from England. But these approaches had come to nothing by spring 2006.

Thai investors were also reported to be interested in Everton, Fulham and Manchester City, but details remained vague. West Ham attracted brief interest from a company called MSI, registered in the Virgin Islands and fronted by an Iranian-born businessman, Kia Joorbachian. MSI had previously invested in a Brazilian club, Corinthians, and was partly funded by Boris Berezovsky, who had helped Roman Abramovich make his fortune. But the West Ham bid came to nothing.

Aston Villa were reportedly a target for a consortium of Russian businessmen, but again nothing happened. At Newcastle, it was money men from Malaysia who were said to be circling. Things were different at Portsmouth, where Alexandre Gaydamak, the son of a Russian billionaire, Arcadi Gaydamak, became the joint owner in 2006, his motives unclear. Money was made available for players, though at nowhere near the levels provided by Abramovich, as Portsmouth narrowly escaped relegation in the spring.

Arguably the most bizarre stream of foreign aspirant owners was at Leeds during the depths of their financial crisis in 2003–04. Those involved included a Bahraini sheikh, Abdulrahman bin Mubarak Al-Khalifa, a Ugandan 'tycoon', Michael Ezra, and a Chinese multimillionaire, Xu Ming, who had had an interest back home in Dalian Shide. The sheikh's interest eventually came to nothing. Ezra claimed to have £90 million to save the club, but little was ever confirmed about how the self-styled 'property tycoon' made his 'fortune', and its size was unknown. He was not listed as the owner of any major assets in Uganda, nor had the £600,000 Lamborghini he reportedly imported ever been seen in public. Harvard University, where he claimed to have studied, had no record of any graduation. As a teenager in 1987, he had won the 'All Africa Disco Dance Championships', held in Kampala, and he had later represented Uganda at athletics, but this hardly enhanced his credentials to buy a football club. Xu Ming's interest, if indeed it was ever real, never hardened into a firm bid. Instead, in January 2005, the club was bought by Ken Bates, who 18 months earlier had sold Chelsea to Roman Abramovich. The Russian inherited Claudio Ranieri as his manager, not that the Italian was destined to stay for long.

13

SPECIAL ONES

BY THE END of the 2005–06 season, Manchester United had never had one, nor had Manchester City, West Ham or Everton. Port Vale had had one, the first in England. Stockport County had had two, including the second in the country. Liverpool had also had two, as had Newcastle, Portsmouth, Stoke and Cambridge. And Chelsea and Tottenham had each had four.

Given their limited number – 31 in English League history up to summer 2006 – every foreign manager has been a special one of sorts, for better or worse, if not *the* Special One, as José Mourinho styled himself. Those 31 individuals had held 44 separate posts, Ossie Ardiles, Danny Bergara, Ruud Gullit, Jan Molby, Gudjon Thordarson and Gianluca Vialli each managing at least two different English clubs.

The big-hitters at the top level in recent years – Mourinho and Arsène Wenger – are worth particular consideration because they have had the most positive impact on English domestic football, albeit using a minority of English footballers. Martin Jol is a distinctive case, having used more Englishmen than the others when excelling in his first full season at Tottenham in 2005–06; he attributes that partly to his own playing background in England, which the others never had. And Rafa Benitez, having worked wonders in his first season to win the European Cup with Liverpool, is an engaging figure whose rebuilding programme at Anfield continued apace in 2005–06.

But a survey of their predecessors emphasises English football's historical wariness of foreigners. Those who have thrived since the mid 1990s despite such wariness have hastened both the flow of foreign players to England and, in many cases, the acceptance of foreign coaches and managers through results and wider benefits to the game.

The alien boss – a short history

For a long time, the reluctance to hire foreign coaches was institutional. Foreign managers were no more likely to be allowed to work in England than foreign players, as Emilio Berkessy's case showed. The respected Hungarian, with a wealth of experience at club level across Europe, was prevented by Britain's labour laws from taking up the role of coach at Grimsby Town in the 1950s because he was foreign. The logic behind the refusal was that a British candidate could do the job. That sent out a message to others to forget even thinking about it.

The first five foreign managers in England all had long-established ties in the country and established residency. That's why they were allowed to work as managers, and also why none of them were innovators in management – they had all been immersed in English football for decades. South Africa's Gordon Hodgson, a star player with Liverpool, was the first foreign manager in the English game. He managed at Port Vale for five years in the Third Division (South) between 1946 and 1951. The second was Germany's Bert Trautmann, at Stockport in 1965. The third, in 1967, was South Africa's Eddie Firmani, at Charlton.

The fourth, in 1988, was Danny Bergara, a Uruguayan who had had a career in Spain as a striker. Having settled with his English wife in the early 1970s after his playing days finished, it was 15 years after his arrival in England when he got a manager's job, at Rochdale. Before that, he had coached at Luton, using a work permit that only entitled him to load lorries for the club's chairman. By the time the Rochdale job came up he was naturalised. He became Stockport's second foreign manager in 1989, and in 1992 made history as the first foreign manager to lead a club to Wembley, albeit in the Autoglass Trophy final, which his team lost to Stoke. The fifth foreign manager was another South American, Ossie Ardiles, at Swindon in 1989. By that time he had been in England for more than a decade.

Neither of the League's only two managers to date with Far Eastern roots – Frank Soo and Sammy Chung – are considered foreign, for the simple reason that they were born and raised in England. Both had one Chinese parent, but both men were British. Soo, born in Buxton, managed Scunthorpe in 1959 and 1960; Chung, born in Abingdon, managed Wolves in the mid 1970s and Doncaster in the mid 1990s.

The first foreign manager with no previous footballing experience in England was Dr Jozef Venglos, who also became the first in the top division when he took over at Aston Villa in 1990. The studious Slovak, who had coached Czechoslovakia to acclaim, lasted only a season at Villa Park. Villa finished 17th and he stepped down. The appointment was regarded as an unsuccessful experiment. Some fans nicknamed him 'Dr No' for his apparent reluctance to sign anyone. Others argued that he was given little money to do so, and that it takes longer than a season to rouse a sleeping giant.

Venglos remained the only foreign coach without previous experience in the English game to be hired by any English club up to September 1996. There *were* foreign managers between 1991 and 1996 but all had pre-existing ties. This was the case with Ardiles, who went from Swindon to Newcastle and then West Brom, Ivan Golac (a former Southampton player) at Torquay, Jan Molby (of Liverpool fame) at Swansea, Ruud Gullit at Chelsea (he arrived there as a player), and Bergara at Rotherham. Dr Venglos's successor – in the sense of arriving as a manager without previous ties to England – was an unknown called Wenger.

Others who subsequently arrived without any former grounding in England included Christian Gross and Jacques Santini, both flops at Tottenham; Claudio Ranieri, who tinkered with limited success as Mourinho's predecessor, then Mourinho himself; Gerard Houllier at Liverpool, although he had lived in the city decades earlier as a teacher, followed by Rafa Benitez; Jean Tigana at Fulham; and Velimir Zajec and Alain Perrin at Portsmouth, both for short stints.

The real success stories among them, in terms of winning trophies, have been Wenger, Mourinho and Benitez, who started with the European Cup in his first season, 2004–05. Before considering their contribution to English football, it is relevant to consider the importance of 2006 in the history of foreign footballers everywhere, with the introduction of UEFA quotas for home-grown players in European competition from 2006-07. Twenty-eight years after the lifting of restrictions on foreigners across Europe, and a decade after Bosman, the European governing body decided that not only were unlimited numbers of imports creating distance between clubs and their communities, but they were making football less competitive.

UEFA helps the 'home-growns'

In February 2005 UEFA announced firm proposals for quotas, to come into effect from the 2006–07 season. They would apply to all clubs, from all countries, competing in UEFA competitions, namely the Champions League and UEFA Cup. No quota system strictly based on a player's nationality would be able to withstand legal challenges, so a system based around 'club trained' and 'locally trained' players, regardless of nationality, was adopted. UEFA's rationale was stated as follows: 'Essentially football is not encouraging enough development of new talent and instead clubs are looking for "quick fix" solutions and opting to buy players rather than train them. In this kind of environment, football risks becoming more of a financial contest rather than a sporting contest.' The subtext was: 'We want to encourage the production of home-grown players who actually make it into first-team squads.'

The quotas rule stated that within each 25-man squad, at least two players must have been 'club-trained' by the club's own academy (defined as having spent three seasons at the academy between the age of 15 and 21). Two more must have been 'locally trained' by other clubs from the same association. For English clubs, this meant having at least two players from the club's own academy, plus two from another English club's academy. This so-called '2+2' rule for the 2006–07 season was scheduled to be increased to '3+3' for 2007–08, and '4+4' for 2008–09. In other words, by 2008–09, each 25-man squad should have at least four club-trained players and another four 'locally trained' by other academies in that country.

To the letter of the law, not one of them would actually need to be nationals of that country (for example, English players at English clubs), but in practice UEFA envisaged that 'a majority would be', particularly of the 'locally trained' players. Even if clubs imported ever younger foreign players to their academies in order to get them qualified as 'club trained' by 21, it was assumed that it would make more sense for clubs to meet the quotas for 'locally trained' players by developing these players themselves, of their own club's nationality, than lure other foreign but 'locally trained' players from other clubs within their own country.

Complicated? Certainly. But any system stating that 'you must have X number of players from your country' would fall foul of European laws on freedom of movement.

By summer 2006, it was not clear how many national FAs would adopt UEFA's quotas within their domestic leagues, though it seemed a majority would. The Premier League had no plans to put them in place for matches in England, though English clubs would still have to adhere to them in European competitions. This contrasted with the approach of the Scottish Football Association: 'We welcome the proposals and hope it encourages greater investment by clubs in home-grown players. It can only be to the benefit of football in Scotland.'

The background to this enthusiasm was that for much of the previous decade in Scotland, the two dominant clubs, Rangers and Celtic, had filled their ranks with foreign players. At the same time, the fortunes of the Scotland international side had dwindled. The simplistic but logical explanation was that Scotland's biggest clubs were failing to develop local players, leading to a dearth for the national side. At the same time Scotland's best Scots had little chance to play on the biggest club stages, hence further depriving the Scotland team of locals with high-level experience.

By 2006, with Gordon Strachan, a Scot, in charge of Celtic, that club's policy on recruitment and development was becoming notably more pro-Scottish again. In England, the major clubs, most of them managed by foreign managers, had club success as the priority, as would be expected. Why on earth *would* they want to promote English players for the sake of it?

Wenger's world view

As detailed in Chapter 11, Arsène Wenger inherited a core of English players in 1996 but his teams became gradually more foreign thereafter. He won his first Premiership title in his first full season, 1997–98, with the famous English back line comprising Seaman in goal and a combination of Dixon, Keown, Bould, Adams and Winterburn in defence. There was an Englishman on one wing in Ray Parlour, two Frenchmen in the middle – Patrick Vieira and Emmanuel Petit – and a Dutchman on the left, Marc Overmars. Up front, Dennis Bergkamp and England's Ian Wright were pushed for a starting berth by Nicolas Anelka. Of the side who went undefeated in the League in 2003–04, the first-choice team comprised just two Englishmen. Sol Campbell had been a free from Tottenham, and Ashley Cole was the only product of Arsenal's youth policy.

Fast forward again, to the team of 2006, the team who took the Champions' League by storm – the third built by Wenger and the first without Vieira – and even Campbell and Cole had faded from regular participation for a variety of personal and injury reasons. Hence the 2006 side, restructured to become a force much more rapidly than many imagined, contained no English, or even British players at all on a regular basis. Remarkably, when Arsenal faced Real Madrid in the Champions League in Spain in February 2006, Real with David Beckham and Jonathan Woodgate had two more Englishmen on the pitch than the English club. The side that later beat Juventus 2–0 in the Champions' League was typical: Lehmann; Eboue, Toure, Senderos, Flamini; Hleb, Silva, Fabregas, Pires (although Freddie Ljungberg could interchange); Reyes, Henry (and still Dennis Bergkamp on the bench).

This led West Ham's English manager, Alan Pardew, to comment, not unreasonably, and without malice: 'I saw a headline saying Arsenal are flying the flag for Britain. I kind of wondered where that British involvement actually was when I looked at their team. It's important that top clubs don't lose sight of the fact that it's the English Premier League and English players should be involved. Foreign players have been fantastic. We have learned from them and from foreign coaches. But, to some extent, we could lose the soul of British football – the English player.'

Wenger hit back at this perceived slight, effectively implying that Pardew was being racist. 'Racism is nothing to do with colour,' he said. 'It's only linked with where you come from or how you look . . . I feel responsible for the traditions of the club. We represent a football club which is about values and not about passports.' David Dein, Arsenal's vice-chairman, added: 'The fans want a winning team, and if we can get English players, that's a bonus.' This was a curious statement from a man who was also a vice-chairman of the Football Association, and whose responsibilities in that post included the England national team's well-being and future. But then conflict of interests, self-interest and sheer chutzpah in defending your own personal interests, as opposed to those the FA work for, is nothing new in football.

Pardew responded by explaining his position in more detail, although it seemed a clear and innocent enough sentiment the first time. 'When I said that [about Arsenal and flying the flag], I was not being racist or xenophobic, as Arsène Wenger has suggested. A manager who is married to a Swede and has signed players from all over the world cannot be called racist. Our multi-cultural approach to our squad [at West Ham] is something I'm proud of. But I care passionately about our game and will always give my views honestly and from the heart.'

Wenger could legitimately argue that he has tried to give English players a chance, but most of them have not worked out. In 10 years between 1996 and 2006 he signed six Englishmen of any significance. Campbell was free and an established international. He paid for the five others. The first four were Matthew Upson (who cost £2 million as a 17-year-old), Jermaine Pennant (£2 million as a 16-year-old), Francis Jeffers (£8 million as a 20-year-old) and Richard Wright (£6 million as a 23-year-old). They made a combined total of 38 League starts and all moved on, at a collective transfer loss of £8.9 million. The other English player signed in that time was Theo Walcott, who signed as a pro with Arsenal on his seventeenth birthday in March 2006.

That still leaves a question mark over why, Ashley Cole aside, Arsenal's youth system produced no English talent good enough for a sustained place in Wenger's first team in 10 years. Arsenal, and Dein, always argued that it was not through lack of trying, but Wenger's actions spoke louder than any words. He has sought instead to seek out the best youngsters not just from the rest of Europe but from across the world, especially Africa. An avowed citizen of the world who has lived and worked across Europe and in Asia, Wenger has long-standing ties with compatriots and other contacts in Africa, and genuinely feels football should be a game without borders.

He is also passionate about producing attacking sides with flair to thrill purists, and has often succeeded in doing so. Is it his job to provide a platform for English hopefuls? No. Is it his responsibility to spend Arsenal's transfer budget on inflated fees for home-grown stars when he get better value elsewhere? No. Should anyone, apart from Arsenal fans, worry if there are few or no English players representing Arsenal on a regular basis? From a neutral viewpoint, one that takes UEFA's quotas at the face value of trying to encourage local players, and create even a slightly more level playing field, yes.

Arsenal are precisely the kind of club, like their fellow European giants – and they will become more so as every season at their new 60,000-seat Emirates Stadium passes – who have the clout and money to lure young players from all over the world, even to 'hoard' them. So any headway they make, or are forced to make, in rearing more home-grown players – and not even English players – is surely a good thing. UEFA's quotas were hardly swingeing measures. They would not decimate squads as they stood around Europe in 2006, nor threaten to do so when all the players subjected to the quotas might actually be foreign.

Indeed Arsenal in 2006 already seemed to be shaping up for the new rules. Their academy, their reserve side and the fringes of the first team were all furnished with foreign teenagers on their way to eligibility as home-grown. In addition to the all-foreign 2006 Champions League line-ups detailed above, Arsenal had another group of players on the edge of the first team. Two were English – Walcott and Kerrea Gilbert. The rest were foreign: the likes of Vassiriki Diaby, Johan Djourou, Emmanuel Adebayor, Arturo Lupoli, Alexandre Song Billong and Robin Van Persie. None of them were older than 22 at the end of 2005–06. Several of them – and others – had already been within Arsenal's set-up for a year or more, and hence on the way to being 'club trained'. And although Arsenal's methods – like the controversial loans that funded a takeover at their 'feeder' club, Beveren in Belgium – raised eyebrows and caused controversy in some quarters, the fact they were judged to have done nothing illegal in funding a factory for Ivorian players showed they knew how to push the rules without breaking them.

Martin Jol – St George of the Lane?

In another part of north London in 2005–06, Martin Jol made the case, verbally and practically, that managers of English sides had some sense of duty to provide the best English players with a platform. Eight of his regular first-team players were English, and either established in the England team or knocking on the door. They were his goalkeeper Paul Robinson, defenders Ledley King, Michael Dawson and Anthony Gardner, midfielders Jermaine Jenas, Michael Carrick and Aaron Lennon, and striker Jermain Defoe. Other

Englishmen he had signed included Wayne Routledge and Tom Huddlestone. And while he also acquired foreign players in his first year – Finland's Teemu Tainio, the Netherlands' Edgar Davids and Lee Yong-Pyo of South Korea were all regulars in 2005–06 – he was not afraid to state that he wanted an English heart to his side.

This, he said, was because of the time he spent in England as a player with West Bromwich Albion and Coventry in the 1980s. 'I spent four years in England as a player a long time ago so I know how important it is to keep an English dressing room. That doesn't mean I'm critical of the foreign players because they've brought so much to the Premiership, an extra quality. But in the Champions League [when Arsenal were the only remaining English club in 2006], there wasn't a single English player involved and that's very strange. That's why I think everybody in England should get behind us and be proud that we have an English team, admittedly with some foreign players thrown in.'

Jol's attitude endeared him to the fans. 'No one would argue that overseas players have added to the game, especially at Tottenham when you look at our history,' said one lifelong Spurs fan, Jonnie Baker, towards the tail end of the 2005–06 season. 'Ardiles, Villa, Klinsmann. All great, no argument, and good for the game. But part of our appreciation of what Martin Jol has done comes from him using English players – our English players differentiate us from Arsenal.'

Young Big 'Ead

José Mourinho, frequently compared to the late, great Brian Clough for his mouth, motivational qualities and serial successes, first stormed into the consciousness of many football fans in England on 9 March 2004 when his Porto side stole a last-minute win in the Champions League last 16 against Manchester United at Old Trafford. Porto had a 2–1 lead from the home leg, but Paul Scholes had made it 1–0 to United on the night before having what seemed a perfectly legitimate second goal disallowed. Entering the final moments, United stood at 2–2 on aggregate and were through to the last eight on the away goals rule when Porto's Costinha popped up with a last-gasp winner to send the Portuguese side on their way to the final – and glorious success in Gelsenkirchen against Monaco that May.

A few days afterwards, Mourinho was dining on Roman Abramovich's boat, the 377ft *Pelorus*, one of the largest private yachts in the world. He arrived via helicopter from Monaco, then by speedboat, every inch the international jet-setter. By 15 August 2004, he was installed in the Chelsea dugout for the first game of that season, a home fixture against Manchester United. Chelsea won 1–0 and kept on winning.

By 2006 Mourinho had become a figure of almost mythical status in England. That is not to say he was widely respected. By the end of his second season the novelty factor had worn off and a certain chippiness surfaced, alienating many neutrals. But he had played a key role in smashing the duopoly of Manchester United and Arsenal, which in itself was enough to draw wide attention, not to mention six books published in England concentrating solely or largely on his life and sporting works.

But in assessing, however briefly, his impact within the story that this book is attempting to outline, it seems fitting to revert to the dossier style so beloved by Mourinho himself. Abridged maybe, but this much we know:

José Mário dos Santos Mourinho Félix was born in Setubal, Portugal, in January 1963, the son of a goalkeeper, Félix Mourinho, whose own playing career peaked with one substitute appearance for his national side. Mourinho senior went on to become a manager. Mourinho junior was never talented enough to make it as a professional player but prepared detailed dossiers on opponents for his father. His first big break came when he worked as Bobby Robson's interpreter (later technically becoming 'assistant coach' in acknowledgement of his astute input) at Sporting Lisbon, Porto and Barcelona. By this time, he had already made up his mind that he wanted to be a manager in his own right, and had studied in Scotland for his coaching badges. He made little impression on peers or tutors at this early stage.

When Robson left Barca, Mourinho stayed on, under Louis Van Gaal. Only in 2000, after redundancy from the Spanish club, did he take up his first full managerial position, at Benfica, but a change of president led to his departure and his next job was at Leiria. In January 2002 he was back at Porto, where his work began in earnest.

He shaped a winning team with an emphasis on detailed preparation, especially the physical robustness of his side. A 'pressing' approach, closing down opponents, trying to eke a lead and then guarding it, became his trademark there and again later at Chelsea. Deco, a Brazilian-born playmaker who switched nationality to represent Portugal (and later moved to Barcelona) was his talismanic flair player. In 2003, Mourinho guided Porto to their domestic league title as well as the Portuguese Cup and the UEFA Cup. The following season he impressively won the Portuguese title again, and the Champions League. The 'special one' arrived in England, and let everyone know it.

Mourinho deserves – and was given – immense credit for winning the Premiership title in his first season at Chelsea. Claudio Ranieri, his predecessor, had failed with the same resources at his disposal. Mourinho is utterly driven, meticulous, a perfectionist – and a terrible loser. Maybe it is because of the chips on each shoulder, one weighing him down because he never made it as a player, the other a burden because he was so rarely given much if any credit for his years as 'The Translator' under Bobby Robson.

As the Portuguese writer Alberto da Silva, a journalist with the newspaper *A Bola*, told the BBC after Mourinho had won the title in 2005: 'Arsène Wenger, Alex Ferguson and Benitez all have a more romantic view of football in a way that Mourinho doesn't. Arsenal, Manchester United and Liverpool wouldn't play with six men in defence, but if it means Chelsea win, then Mourinho is perfectly happy to do that . . . because of Mourinho, come three o'clock on Saturday for 90 minutes, Chelsea are better prepared and more determined. Not only that, they are better fighters. Mourinho is operating at a different level from the other managers. For Mourinho it's a matter of life and death. He tells the players: "I want that victory, I want nothing else." Of course there has been a lot of money for him to spend and he has a great squad at his disposal. But there is no other manager like him in the way he handles the millionaire players.'

Money cannot be discounted in the Mourinho story at Chelsea. Yes, he won the title while Ranieri did not. But while his counterparts at England's other leading clubs could afford to make the odd expensive mistake, they did not have the safety net of Abramovich's billions to keep on making them, if necessary. Didier Drogba could not be called a mistake but at £24 million he was not cheap. Nor was

Michael Essien at another £24 million or Shaun-Wright Phillips at £21 million. The latter was a huge price tag given that Mourinho started him in less than one-third of Chelsea's Premier League matches in 2005–06, the winger's first season at Stamford Bridge.

If Mourinho was engaging in his first title-winning season at Chelsea it was often because he gave good copy. He declared himself 'the special one' from the off. He remonstrated when Chelsea drew with Tottenham in September 2004: 'They brought the bus and they left the bus in front of the goal.' He complained when opponents like Blackburn's Robbie Savage got physical, but seemed as myopic as Wenger when his own side used force rather than flair on many occasions. He extolled his own virtues consistently, as when marching to that first title: 'We are on top at the moment but not because of the club's financial power. We are in contention for a lot of trophies because of my hard work.' And he said, time and again, that his aim in taking the attention away from his players was to relieve them of pressure.

Undoubtedly he forged a team spirit of rare intensity. He told the *Daily Telegraph* in April 2006: 'Sometimes I don't understand your culture. People have tried to explain it to me. I cannot judge people's feelings, because I am on the privileged side. I'm young, I do what I want, I have a wonderful family, I love my job, I earn a lot of money. When I stop football, I can have a very good life. I'm on the good side. If people on the other side of the picture get frustrated, they try to kill us with envy. They criticise people. Even if people are doing well, they only speak about the negative. Envy is the gun of the incompetent.'

This kind of 'us against the world' mentality was found in previous years in the Manchester United dressing room of Alex Ferguson. But it went too far at times at Chelsea, no more so than when Mourinho effectively accused referee Anders Frisk of colluding with Barcelona's coach, Frank Rijkaard, in the Champions League encounter of 2004–05 to get Drogba sent off. Frisk retired soon afterwards after receiving death threats and recriminations. Mourinho himself had fanned the flames: 'When I saw Frank Rijkaard entering the referee's dressing room I couldn't believe it. When Didier Drogba was sent off I wasn't surprised.' In fact he had seen nothing. He was fined £9000 and received a two-match touchline ban.

On a charge sheet of belligerence, misdemeanour and pure irritation you would also need to include Mourinho's grudging acceptance of Liverpool's win over Chelsea in the Champions League of 2005, his infamous 'shushing' of Liverpool fans during the League Cup final victory of the same year, and his involvement in the attempted tapping-up of Arsenal's Ashley Cole, albeit with Cole's compliance and the assistance of assorted officials and agents. Mourinho was fined £75,000 for his role in the latter. Then there was the spat with Arsène Wenger in which he accused the Frenchman of being a voyeur, the tacit approval of diving and theatrics, not least by Drogba, the refusal to shake hands with fellow managers when the mood took him, and the apparently pathological inability to concede that a better team won when it wasn't *his* team.

None of this is meant to diminish the achievements of a brilliant coach, a motivator par excellence, a strategist and schemer who can make a significant difference to his clubs. He is also genuinely funny – if tetchy – in a dry way that the English like. He is handsome, stylish, and attractive not just to non-footballing audiences but, because of that, to the multinationals who have paid him substantial amounts of cash on top of his £5 million-a-year Chelsea basic pay to sell their goods.

But good for English football? For Chelsea, yes. And for his significant role in breaking up the dominance of two clubs, and attracting fresh attention to the League. He also championed key English players within his ranks. As early as November 2004, he vowed to have English players at the heart of his side: 'We must only go abroad to buy what we don't have here. If you don't have a special player for a special position in the English market you have to look abroad. But the most important thing is to try and look for English players first.' He made John Terry his captain, and improved him as a player. Frank Lampard came on by leaps and bounds, as did Joe Cole. Shaun Wright-Phillips did not get such a great chance, in his first season at least. But Chelsea did start buying up a lot of other British youngsters, demonstrating they had the will to champion local talent if not the subtlety to do it sparingly.

But it was always hard to believe that a man so driven towards personal goals that he always envisaged certain targets at different stages of his life in different posts would remain to build multiple sides in the Wenger style, especially if Champions League success eluded him for too long at Chelsea. Or came to him, for that matter. Still, four league titles in four years at two clubs was an excellent record for the period between 2003 and 2006. But then, perhaps he was in the right place at the right time.

Only history will be able to judge if Mourinho really is a coach who operates at an altogether different level to other men of substance and achievement who have had success at multiple clubs in different countries. Men like Arsène Wenger, who raised the bar in England, and who set a benchmark for meticulous preparation – on and off the pitch – while Mourinho was still primarily an interpreter. Men like Rafa Benitez, who arrived in England with a UEFA Cup trophy freshly to his name and then masterminded Liverpool's astonishing European Cup win of 2005 as he set about revitalising a club too long in the shadows. Benitez proved astute in the transfer market, arguably more so than Mourinho given his – relatively – limited budget. The hiring of Mohamed Sissoko, Peter Crouch and Jose Reina, each of them ultimately thriving in 2005–06, was evidence. He also bought tactical acumen, and showed flexibility in switching systems against different teams. Again this was arguably more evident in Benitez than Mourinho. The Spaniard shared two major traits with the Portuguese. First, a desire to foster team spirit, starting with English as the language of the dressing room, not least for his compatriot imports in the playing ranks. Second, an intimate knowledge of his players, down to the exact heights and weights of virtually every player he had ever worked with. The biggest difference between Benitez and Mourinho was the extent of his self-regard.

Both men, and Wenger, and Jol and others have brought ideas, methods and players that English football could only dream of a generation ago. And for that, English football should be grateful.

14

NEW HORIZONS

Dateline: 19 March 2006, Fengtai Stadium, Beijing

THE RUMPUS IN the queue was caused by too many people and not enough sales windows. Two offenders were picked out and taken away without much of a struggle. It wasn't police or army business, although there were hundreds of each in attendance. Instead, a few of the many on-site security guards did the picking and taking. The message had been sent. The fans quietened down, slowly secured their tickets and made their way into the ground. It was Beijing's first home match of the 2006 Chinese Super League season, against Shanghai Liancheng. The venue was Fengtai because Beijing's normal home ground, the Workers' Stadium, was being renovated ahead of the 2008 Olympic Games.

The rumpus on the pitch was caused because the home side missed too many opportunities. They took an early lead through their Hungarian international striker, Krisztian Kenesei, one of the few non-Chinese players on the field. But Shanghai ran rings around their hosts thereafter, equalising just before half-time through Zhang Xiaorui, and snatching a last-gasp injury-time winner through their Brazilian striker, Tiago Jorge Honorio. 'You have no manners, and are of low culture,' chanted the Beijing fans – at their own players.

It was all good-natured, unlike another rumpus the previous summer among the wider sporting public in China and in the local press. The cause was two Western teams, Real Madrid and Manchester United, who 'toured' China to underwhelming effect. United's pre-tour hype included a statement from Anheuser-Busch, the parent company of Budweiser, one of the corporate giants with a stake in the venture: 'The soccer extravaganza will feature a galaxy of superstar players as the Red Devils take on the Beijing Hyundai team on July 26 in front of an expected sell-out crowd of 60,000 at Workers' Stadium in Beijing.'

In fact, despite the inclusion in United's squad of their young Chinese striker, Dong Fangzhou, and their recent South Korean recruit, Park Ji-Sung, only 23,000 people were lured through the gate. David Gill, United's chief executive, had to admit that the attendance was 'disappointing . . . The reasons behind that will have to be investigated . . . [but] I don't think we are waning in popularity.'

The issue – or rather illusion – of a staggeringly large fan base and the attractiveness of Chinese-language websites will be considered later. But in fairness to Gill, United's business in Asia on that occasion was not purely a 'smash and grab' raid for cash. Their whirlwind tour did concentrate on potentially lucrative markets in Hong Kong (one match), China (one match) and Tokyo (two, perhaps because Japan offered more immediate payback), but the club was also there on Unicef business. The charitable aspect included a £200,000 donation by United to help the United Nations Children's Fund's anti-child-trafficking programme in China. Sir Alex Ferguson, along with Ryan Giggs and Dong Fangzhou, also attended a press conference to show that they backed Unicef's Sport for Development, a scheme using sport to promote all aspects of youth development.

This was United's saving grace, at least as some locals viewed matters when comparing United with Real Madrid. The Spaniards had nipped in and out of Beijing on a three-day, one-match jaunt just a few days earlier, part of a trip that also took in Tokyo, Seoul, Los Angeles and New York. It was reported that Real asked for 6.5 million euros (£4.5 million) per game in Asia and received much if not all of this figure from the multinational corporations who wanted to increase their profile in the world's most populous nation. Real's one game in China was also against Beijing, in the Workers' Stadium, and attracted a crowd of around 30,000. The reception was not great, and there was much displeasure that Real's English superstar, David Beckham, did not feature. 'It was a really ugly match,' said one fan who was there, 18-year-old Zhang Ran. 'The organisers should have told us that Beckham would miss the match. It's like we have been cheated.'

This was not an isolated voice. One Chinese newspaper made a scathing point in cartoon form on its front page. It depicted a Chinese supporter shaking hands with a Manchester United player. Evidently, even without a capacity crowd, China still felt United had come for something more than money. But as the fan leant forward towards the United character, a Real Madrid player was depicted picking the fan's pocket.

There is a significance for English football in all the incidents above – the game between Beijing and Shanghai, the foreign tours to Beijing, and the bubbling animosity towards greedy foreign sides. There is a huge, if fickle, interest in football in China, which has a population of 1.3 billion and is growing inevitably towards being the biggest economy in the world. At some stage in the future there may well be a large audience with disposable income that might feel like spending it on following foreign football. They may even start buying merchandise at Western prices, like the genuine Chelsea and Real Madrid shirts on sale at £36 each in the Beijing club shop at the Beijing–Shanghai game, instead of buying cheap imitations, for little more than £1, like the Manchester United jersey sported by a teenager in the crowd that day. But China's domestic football in 2006 was a mess.

As Yin Mingshan, a club owner and an advisor to the Chinese government, testified, the domestic scene had been dogged by 'match-fixing, gambling, corruption, biased reporting, strikes, rude crowds, violence, drugs, prostitution, debts and falling standards'. The Super League, an updated version of the 1994 pro-league, was still badly run, effectively under state control, and the game on a widespread basis was in its infancy in terms of professionalism and marketing, even technically. Despite the queues at Fengtai on 19 March 2006, the crowd numbered about 20,000 in an arena built to hold more than 30,000. Top-class Chinese players, in 2006, were few and far between.

Yet already we have examples of how a Western, and especially an English desire to tap into this market can have direct effects on the English game, whether through the hiring of players, the choice of academy scholars, an emphasis on marketing over sporting excellence, or tiring summer tours during periods that would otherwise be breaks. China is used here as an example because it is the biggest potential market, but what follows might be applied equally to countries across Asia, a continent that will only become more influential on the English game, directly and indirectly. By summer 2006, the total number of Asian players in English football history numbered a few handfuls, with Chinese, Japanese and South Koreans leading the way. But in the future, the only question is the pace of change, not the fact that Asian football will evolve at all levels, and more players will move to England.

Bought for branding

Li Weifeng was a member of China's 2002 World Cup team. Playing in the tournament was a great achievement for the then 23-year-old, a defender with Shenzen Ping'an. But a few weeks after returning home he found out he'd achieved something equally fantastic without even knowing.

'Last night I had a good sleep, making no dreams. And this morning when I got up, I was told that I have been loaned to Everton,' he told local reporters on 18 July 2002. 'Even now I cannot calm myself down. When I was a child I dreamed that one day I could go to play in the Premiership. And now it suddenly comes true. I need some time to let it sink in.'

The move arose because Everton had signed a sponsorship contract with a Chinese company, Kejian, who made mobile phones. Everton would wear shirts with the company's name on the front and Kejian would pay Everton to do so. Additionally, Kejian would send a player to Everton for a year on loan. In fact, they sent two: Li Weifeng and Li Tie.

The logic was straightforward enough. If a Chinese player managed to get into Everton's team, it would be big news in China, where English games were screened live on TV. And if Everton were attracting a sizeable audience in China, then Kejian would be reaching new customers via the advert on Everton's shirts. That was always their main market – Chinese fans in China, via English football beamed there. English football was seen as a classy product, a mark of quality, unlike the Chinese game, where a sponsorship deal would have little kudos and no global visibility. The financial arrangements of the deal were not revealed because they were 'commercial secrets' according to the Chinese media. It is thought that Kejian paid Everton around £1 million, a typically moderate sum for a club outside the giants. Some of the money was spent on a loan fee to Li Weifeng's club and some on his salary.

By January 2003, after one appearance in the Premier League, Li Weifeng was back home. 'I lost my way, my confidence went when I was off the pitch and not playing in the first team,' he said. 'I am afraid I cannot get that back if I play for the reserve team for a long time, that is the reason why I would not come back. I really wanted to play for the first team, but there are a lot of quality players in the same position and it is very difficult to get into the side.'

In the summer of 2002 it seemed that David Moyes was not exactly thrilled at having two players imposed on him. Kejian's president, Hao Jianxue, had made it clear that Everton ultimately decided which player they wanted, but the bottom line was that Everton had to take a player as part of a commercial deal. Talking about Li Tie, Moyes seemed cool about the chances of either player actually getting a game: 'Li is, I feel, the best player that the Chinese national team has to offer but we really mustn't get carried away. He will have a great deal of work to do and progress to make if he's to break into our first team.'

In the event, Li Tie did, apparently, prove himself as a player who met Moyes's standards, for a while at least. He played 29 League games in Everton's midfield in 2002–03. At the end of May 2003, Moyes said he would like to sign the player permanently, but added: 'Li Tie's club seem to want too much for him now so we will try to get another year's loan.' Everton finally signed Li Tie on a three-year contract of some complexity whereby they paid only around a third of his fee, the rest being met by a group of sponsors. In 2003–04, the player's sporting fortunes took a downturn and he hardly appeared, making only four League starts before breaking his shin on international duty. He did not play in 2004–05, or in 2005–06. It was announced in March 2006 that he would undergo surgery, effectively ending his Everton career.

On the face of it, it makes commercial sense for any club to strike a deal like Everton's arrangement with Kejian, even if it does not always make sense for the players. The club makes money and cracks a new market, and the company gets exposure. Whether such details remain harmless as clubs seek to expand further into new Asian markets – primarily China, Japan and South Korea – remains to be seen. There seems an obvious risk of clubs hiring 'emerging market' players in deals that stipulate they must play in a certain number of televised games. The moment that happens, the game will lose what's left of its sporting integrity.

There is no suggestion that Everton's tie-up with Kejian involved any such agreement. The deal was a straightforward plugging opportunity for Kejian, as the company's chief marketing officer, Samuel Lam, told the *China Daily* newspaper in November 2002: 'It is a great breakthrough for Kejian to sponsor Everton as part of our brand strategy. It is expected that Kejian will become an everlasting and world-famous brand. Everton is a famous football club in the United Kingdom with a history of more than a century. In this respect, Everton matches Kejian's strategy in seeking to become a long-lasting brand.' The *China Daily* concluded: 'Everton matches are now a 90-minute advertisement for Kejian. The image and fame of Kejian have been dramatically boosted.'

When Everton's deal with Keijan expired, they entered another 'strategic' alliance, based on shirt sponsorship, with an Asian company. Chang Beer is Thailand's biggest brewery. This time no first-team players were imposed on Moyes, but a trio of young Thai hopefuls took up places at Everton's academy in 2004–05 as part of the package. The three youngsters – Rattapol Piyavutiskul, Sompong Soleb and Teeratep Winothai – were selected in a *Pop Idol*-style contest in Thailand involving 500 youngsters. Teeratep had previously spent a couple of seasons within Crystal Palace's youth set-up but he and his fellow trainees did not find their time at Everton, which also included an education course at Myerscough College, fulfilling.

They *were* featured alongside established Everton stars in a Chang TV advert that was screened back home in Thailand. English football is hugely popular there, and Everton and others feel there is money to be made. But it was as close as they came to action – or contact with Everton's big names. In fact by December 2004, they were home in Asia, Teeratep saying that his stint in England had been akin to being 'abandoned on a desert island'. The three youngsters said they had been led to believe that, if successful, they would have been given contracts with Everton. 'I dare say that from the very first day we reached there to the day we returned, we had only a chance to train in the Goodison Park,' said Teeratep. 'They abandoned us and our hopes.' Sompong said: 'Our trip this time was not a happy one. We had high hopes of sharpening our skills and developing our potential, since we badly want to become professional players. By contrast, Everton thought that we wanted to be professional coaches. It hurt our feelings.'

Chang Beer disputed the players' claims, saying there had been a misunderstanding and that their stint with Everton would have progressed to something more meaningful. It didn't. Teeratep never went back. Rattapol and Sompong did briefly return to Merseyside, and then bizarrely, a few months later, were being paraded around at League Two's Chester City, who announced the pair would sign for the club as part of a new initiative. The Thai FA and Chang Beer were involved in the venture. Fulham were among other clubs supposedly interested in similar projects. They never happened.

Missed opportunities, fresh risks

The headline in the English-language version of the *China Daily* newspaper in December 2004 hardly inspired confidence or gave any indication that the story was of major significance. 'Veteran Hao Haidong to join Blades for a quid', it said. The player was one of China's most famous stars, in his heyday, and he was about to sign for Sheffield United, for the token sum of £1. At one time Hao Haidong was known as 'China's Alan Shearer'. He was tall, tough, a striker who was, for years, head and shoulders above the best of the rest that China had to offer. He was capped 94 times and scored 37 goals for his country, a record. He played for China at the 2002 World Cup, and won a host of domestic honours with his main club, Dalian Shide.

He was 34 when he moved to Sheffield, in January 2005, and almost 36 when he finally made his first-team debut a year later in a third-round FA Cup match in early 2006. United, heading for promotion to the Premiership, were at home to Colchester of League One. The score was 1–1 when Hao came on as a 65th-minute substitute, and 2–1 to Colchester at the final whistle. There weren't too many people who expected their popular Chinese import to be making too many more appearances in the first team. That remained to be seen.

The reason Hao was purchased had little or nothing to do with what he might offer United's manager, Neil Warnock, on the pitch. Rather it was one part of a plan by United to break into China. Just a couple of weeks before Hao's debut, United announced they would become the first foreign club to buy a Chinese club. The club in question was Chengdu Five Bull, who played in the second tier in China. The deal, for 90 per cent of Chengdu, was done the week after Hao's debut, for an undisclosed sum that is understood to have been some way below $1 million (£600,000). Chengdu were immediately renamed Chengdu Blades, in honour of United's nickname. Hao, the marketing tool, had helped to smooth the first phase of Operation Chengdu. If the timing of his 25-minute first-team appearance was not mere coincidence, then no one at the club would attest to it. In any case, those close to the situation privately acknowledged that Hao was always going to be most useful as a bridge between United and their local Chinese community, and, more importantly, as a figurehead as they expanded their academy operations in China.

'We are taking the Blades global with the acquisition of the Chengdu club,' said Kevin McCabe, then chairman of Sheffield United plc, at the time of the deal. The club had already been involved in the Hainan Soccer Academy in southern China. But buying the club in Chengdu, a city of 10 million people and the capital of Sichuan Province (population 87.5 million) was a significant step up. 'Although I do not expect them all to become fans, this does present us with a huge potential fan base with which we develop both the Chengdu and Sheffield United brands.'

Around the same time it was anticipated that United would also take a second Chinese player, Zhang Yaokun, on loan, although it didn't happen. United could not secure a work permit because he had not played the necessary number of games for China's senior international team. Still, United sent coaching staff to Chengdu to help improve the standard of local football and envisaged a long-term involvement.

The logic behind the tie-up was clear enough. McCabe talked about expanding United's business interests in many fields in a variety of places, and specifically Chengdu: 'From a business point of view, there are numerous ways that we can enhance Chengdu's performance, and our initial focus will be on improving sponsorship and increasing attendance. We intend to establish a leisure-football shop in the stadium as well as a Blades bar in the city. In addition, we intend to sell Chengdu merchandise for the first time, encourage the growth of the fan base and create a new revenue stream.'

Here was the crux of the matter: revenue. It was reported locally that United would spend around £1 million investing in the Chinese club's infrastructure and team. While a large sum of money, it was less than they would pay for one player of any significance in England. But even to recoup this they would need to be taking something from Chengdu, and the question, in 2006 at least, was how. Analysts and observers of the football market in China wondered whether the deal had as much to do with Kevin McCabe's private business dealings – which involved property, including in China – as much as with a foothold for United in the country. An announcement by McCabe in March 2006 that he might scale down his day-to-day duties with United, or even step down as chairman, because of the demands on his time of his other businesses, did nothing to dispel this notion. When United won promotion to the Premier League in time for the 2006–07 season, their new prominence was expected to help their push in China.

The quest for revenue via football in China was not a new path for British clubs to tread but none had been very successful. In the wake of Manchester United's most successful season ever – 1998–99, when they won that unprecedented treble – their stock market value soared to £1 billion. They tried to cash in with themed restaurants and bars across Asia, including China. By 2006, only one remained open. Ironically it was in Chengdu, where Kevin McCabe was planning a rival establishment in Sheffield United's colours.

Around the same time as Manchester United's cafe foray, Newcastle United forged a link-up with Dalian Shide, and the Glasgow giants, Rangers, established a cooperation agreement with Shenzhen. A few years and no windfalls later, both partnerships lay effectively dormant. In the summer of 2005, it was announced that Everton, Bolton and Hull had entered into a joint arrangement, via an intermediary company, the Lynx Group, to forge a 'strategic approach to the rapidly expanding Chinese football market'. The idea was that each club would link with a specific, separate club or region and build a viable business over time.

Lynx's commercial director, Steve Bellis, had spent 14 years as marketing manager of League Two Stockport, who established links in China during his time there. A tie-up with Tiger Star, a club in Liaoning province, involved football schools and tours – and the Chinese club changed its name to Stockport Tiger Star. John Hollins was briefly their coach. When the regime at Stockport changed, the relationship faltered. Bellis started Lynx, attracting the trio of clubs by saying they could not expect easy revenue streams but that long-term benefits would accrue. Time will tell.

Also in 2005, Southampton entered a cooperation agreement with Qingdao, a club located in their Chinese twin-city port of the same name. But with relegation taxing minds and budgets at the St Mary's Stadium, nothing concrete was going to happen quickly. Similarly the English Football League's chairman, Sir Brian Mawhinney, revealed in March 2006 that the League was in preliminary talks with a provincial government in China about some official partnership between that province – it was not named – and the League. If anything was to happen, it would take a long time to establish.

Real Madrid, meanwhile, had been unperturbed by the hostility they encountered on their 2005 trip to Beijing, and on 10 November that year signed a 'collaboration agreement' by which they would support the 'sporting, technological, commercial and strategic aims, and the management and development' of Beijing's Super League club, and of Chinese football in general. The deal was done through CITIC, one of China's major corporations and the parent company of the club, whose official title when founded in 1992 was Beijing Guo'an. (For three years, until March 2006, they were more commonly known as Beijing Hyundai, but at the end of a sponsorship deal with the Korean car manufacturer, they officially reverted to Beijing Guo'an.)

The machinations behind Real's partnership with Beijing were complex, but undoubtedly intended to crack the Chinese market. CITIC's international portfolio of businesses includes banks, mining, communications, property and, crucially, television interests. It controls more than 20 cable networks in China, and by 2006, had more than six million pay-TV subscribers in 14 Chinese cities.

It was no accident that two days before Real Madrid announced their agreement with Beijing, they announced a record shirt sponsorship deal with BenQ Mobile. It was to run from the 2006–07 season until 2010, and was worth £14 million a year. As Jose Angel Sanchez, Real's marketing director, said at the time: 'Real Madrid will benefit from BenQ Mobile's presence in over 70 countries worldwide, especially its strong coverage in Asia will assist in strengthening Real Madrid's fan base . . . BenQ Mobile's nearness to the Asian market will help us to develop and expand our activities in this region.'

Hence Real had a deal with a shirt sponsor, aimed to help crack Asia. They also had a deal with Beijing, owned by a company that could provide access to people's homes, and theoretically their cash, via TV. And, intriguingly, Beijing Guo'an also appeared to be linking up with an Austrian company that had reportedly invested some money with one eye on a future shirt deal. The firm's name, BWin, did not make it clear that its primary business was internet gambling, or to be more precise, operating the internet gambling portal, betandwin.com. But then in China, a country where gambling was illegal and where the government had recently been clamping down hard on those who ran internet betting sites, it was sensible not to highlight the fact.

Yet gambling did offer a tantalising opportunity in China, where it was estimated in 2006 that up to £3.5 billion a year was being wagered online, illegally. The prospect of gambling being legalised in China, which in 2006 seemed a future possibility, meant that many football clubs were exploring ways to use their brands to entice punters to online casinos, poker and other betting. A Gibraltar-based online gambling company called Mansion wanted to use Manchester United in 2006 as a route to rapid fame (and market penetration) in Asia via a shirt sponsorship deal. Mansion executives were furious when United turned at the eleventh hour to a different sponsor, an insurance firm, AIG. The AIG deal, worth £56.5 million over four years to United, was worth less than Mansion offered (between £65 million and £70 million). But as United's chief executive, David Gill, said in April 2006 when United signed the deal: 'AIG has over 250,000 employees and agents in Asia alone – a region where we have an estimated 40 million fans.' You do not need to read too closely between the lines to understand's United's priorities. They preferred to piggy-back to potential Asian riches via AIG rather than let Mansion piggy-back to Asian prominence via United. Mansion instead became Tottenham's sponsors.

And what has all this to do with football? In the twenty-first century, more than any purist would want to believe. Money now drives the major clubs more than ever before, and finance may one day soon dictate not only financial decisions but more 'sporting' decisions, including the hiring of particular players. At Everton, Sheffield United and elsewhere, it's already happened.

The fallacy of quick cash

China's interest in football was beyond doubt when the national team rode the crest of a wave to the 2002 World Cup, the country's first and only appearance in the finals to date. The women's World Cup will be staged in China in 2007. And there is huge government backing for the men's and women's national teams, especially in Olympic competition, and never more so than in the run-up to the 2008 Olympic Games in Beijing. The general public are also keen on club football, and arguably more interested in foreign leagues than the mismanaged fare they have been served in recent domestic seasons. This might have more to do with foreign results being the basis for the national lottery (a kind of pools, played by 150 million people) than any urge to follow the ups and downs of individual clubs. But foreign football is certainly seen as more reliable and of superior quality. The *T!TAN* sports newspaper, the market leader, sells 5 million copies a week and its 32 pages regularly include as much coverage of Serie A, the Bundesliga, the Premiership and La Liga as of Chinese football. Serie A and the Bundesliga vie for TV ratings supremacy, with matches averaging between 13 million and 15 million viewers. The Premiership is not far behind, with Spain's La Liga trailing, hindered by evening kick-offs in Europe (the middle of the night in China).

But attempts to make a quick buck by foreign clubs and leagues have largely failed. Most Chinese access their live foreign football via free-to-air channels, often city sports stations that sub-licence from the regional rights holder. There is no proof that people are willing or able to pay very much for the privilege of watching. One reason is that the average income is low – less than £1000 a year in 2006 – and disposable income negligible for the majority. 'Football clubs have made a dash for cash but with little strategic thought,' said Dr Simon Chadwick, the co-director of the Birkbeck Sport Business Centre, which had conducted research in China on the subject, including Manchester United's tour of 2005. 'Teams have landed in China thinking "There's pots of cash to be made here" and then not found it. Outside the hot spots like Beijing, Shanghai, Shenzhen, it's still a fairly agrarian society. A lot of people have low or no disposable income, and even in the hot spots, there's massive competition for that income.'

Football clubs have three traditional revenue streams: matchday income (tickets, food, programmes), media income (TV money, from a centrally negotiated pot in the case of English clubs) and commercial income (including merchandise and sponsorshhip). None of these has yet proved sustainably lucrative for foreign clubs in

China, even for Manchester United, who, according to their own statistics, have 94 million fans, 40 million of them in Asia and 20 million of those in China. But that is actually a 'name recognition' statistic, not an allegiance as Western football knows it. In any case, cheap imitation merchandise undermines the market for high-price 'real' gear. Neither have Chinese fans been persuaded to part with cash for content being offered on Chinese-language websites. Numerous Western clubs have tried this route, with United, Arsenal, Liverpool and leading Italian and German sides among them. These clubs have taken lump sums from a Chinese website provider. United were paid about £350,000 for a three-year deal from 2005. The provider – China.com in United's case – hopes to recoup that money from subscriptions, advertising, SMS services and so on. But there is scepticism in the industry in China that these sites will break even in the near future, let alone make profits.

The potential is there, of course, but building any business takes time, effort and luck, as the history of American basketball in China shows. It took 20 years of foresight, investment, patience and good fortune to make NBA basketball the most popular sport in China, and the emergence of a Chinese basketball superstar, Yao Ming, who moved to the NBA in 2002, was a significant step.

The NBA is now screened by 14 separate broadcasters in China, including state television. There are 600 official retail outlets, and a Chinese language website. Direct NBA profits from China per year are around £10 million, but with potential to burgeon as China becomes richer. The commercial partners are reaping their own rewards, which will also trickle back into NBA coffers. Nurturing basketball as a sport, not as a pure profit opportunity, underpinned the NBA's success in China.

Lessons from Yao Ming

Ultimately, no matter what corporate activity goes on around them, the players – whether in basketball or football – are the attraction. That is how it should be. Yao Ming, 7ft 6in tall, and literally of massive significance to the NBA's global expansion, can be seen as a perfect example of how one person can cause an explosion of interest. First and foremost, he had the talent to succeed. That's why Houston

Rockets hired him. But his impact in America fuelled interest in basketball in China where it is the number one sport in TV viewing figures, and massive in participation terms. So the game grows, and the standard improves, and the likelihood of further export of Chinese players increases.

If, by 2006, English football had a figure who was talismanic throughout Asia, then it was the Chinese international, Sun Jihai, then at Manchester City. In a *Forbes* magazine celebrity list, he ranked 23rd in the whole of China, across all fields including sport, music, film and television. Yao Ming was no. 1. But Sun Jihai did not bring Manchester City riches, which perplexed the club. They even sought advice in 2006 from a specialist consultancy about why they had not made vast profits from Sun's fame at home. 'Lower your shirt prices in China and you might,' was the gist of what they were told. But that was not possible, for any number of reasons relating to bottom lines, manufacturers' mark-ups and too much inflexibility to deal with different countries in vastly different ways.

Sun Jihai was probably never going to be the man to change the landscape for East Asian players in England. He did not possess star status within England or Europe, nor did he have the particular blend of skills and attributes to acquire it. He was a decent player, for City, and flexible in what he could offer. 'Sun Jihai can play in either full-back position, central defence or central midfield,' said Stuart Pearce, not long after becoming City manager. 'He is a great asset to have because he is so comfortable on both feet.' But he was not a star, nor a glamour figure; not a prolific goalscorer or match winner.

Dong Fangzhou, who turned 21 in January 2006, is the kind of player, if he fulfils his potential, who *could* be that type of player. He signed for Manchester United in January 2004 from Dalian Shide for an initial fee of £500,000, rising to £3.5 million depending on appearances. He had a trial at United in September 2003, and Sir Alex Ferguson bought him on the basis of that, although not for immediate use at United. He was still raw, and he had no chance of getting a work permit. Instead, he was sent on indefinite loan to Belgium's Royal Antwerp, a club with a 'twinning' agreement with United. Young United players were often sent there for first-team experience; in Dong's case, he was sent there effectively to become a naturalised European. After a few years of residence, the theory went, he would be able to move on to England, if good enough.

Was United's interest purely sporting, or was there a business angle too? No lesser figure than Sir Bobby Charlton answered that in December 2003, when he told China's Xinhua news agency: 'I would very much hope to have a Chinese player in the club.' When asked whether it was a commercial or sporting move to sign Dong, Charlton said: 'It is both . . . first of all we want a good player. When you have a good player, the commercial side comes into it.' Even then, the agency reported that: 'No matter how the talks on Dong go, United will not stop their efforts to tap the Chinese market.' Sir Bobby was in China to attend the opening ceremony at United's themed cafe in Chengdu.

Dong's United debut, albeit not in a competitive game, came during the Asia tour of 2005, when he played against a Hong Kong XI and scored in a 2–0 win. By February 2006, while still playing his club football at Antwerp, he had stepped up a level in the international arena. He starred for China against Palestine in a 2–0 win in Asian Cup qualifying. Though he missed a penalty, he made amends by setting up the second goal. The scorer, of all people, was Li Weifeng, the one-time Everton reject who was about to start the new China Super League season with Shanghai Shenhua. After the win over Palestine, Dong told Xinhua: 'I'm sure that I can play for the national team much more and can get the work permit as soon as possible.' No doubt the Glazer family were hoping that would be the case, as long as Sir Alex Ferguson agreed that the youngster had the calibre to be part of United's first-team set-up.

To the lands of rising sons?

Over at Bolton, the most distinguished Japanese player to have appeared in England, Hidetoshi Nakata, played dozens of times in 2005–06. His compatriot predecessors – including Junichi Inamoto (with Arsenal, Fulham, West Brom and Cardiff), Akinori Nishizawa (Bolton), Yoshikatsu Kawaguchi (Portsmouth) and Kazuyuki Toda (Tottenham) – had by then spent generally unexceptional stints in the English game. Spurs had tried to sign a Chinese striker, Qu Bo, in 2003, but were unable to get a work permit. They had greater success with South Korea's Yong-Pyo Lee, who joined in 2005. South Korea and Japan had both qualified for the 2006 World Cup in Germany, having reached the semi-finals and first knockout stage respectively when co-hosting the 2002 event. There was every chance that further players from those nations would be heading to Europe, and England, in the months and years after the tournament.

Scottish football had already provided an example in 2005–06 of how an East Asian star could add to a club's success on and off the pitch. Japan's skilful playmaker, Shunsuke Nakamura, aka 'the Japanese David Beckham', was one of Gordon Strachan's first signings when he took over at Celtic Park in the summer of 2005. Celtic wrapped up the 2005–06 title with six games to spare, in many of which Nakamura had been hugely influential. Towards the end of that triumphant first season, Strachan opined: 'He has a touch of an angel.' Celtic's bank manager probably agreed. The player reportedly earned Celtic £400,000 in direct commercial spin-offs in his first eight months at the club.

And if proof were needed of how Nakamura was broadening the mindset in the East End of Glasgow, on and off the pitch, one need look no further than the toilet door in the media room. A Japanese-language sign had been put up to guide the dozens of Japanese journalists who visited that year. Even the old-timer Glaswegian doormen were capable of basic phrases in Japanese. Small gestures, maybe, but significant, and replicated across Britain in different ways at different clubs because of a multinational cast of characters.

This was, and is, a good thing: football, the global game, bringing people together. On the pitch, too, it can be argued that such a mentality can only, in the long term, make international competition more evenly balanced. Many observers have looked at topsy-turvy results in major competitions of recent years (the World Cup of 2002, where 'minnows' bit back, and Euro 2004, won by Greece, are always held up as examples), and say that the early exits of some of the strong favourites and biggest nations are down to too much football. This is partially true, but not the whole story.

It is arguable that what happened in Korea and Japan in the summer of 2002 was not just a fluke of exhaustion but a result of the internationalisation of the game. Due mainly to television, players and coaches are more familiar than ever before with the day-to-day details of leagues around the world. But most significantly a huge number of players who featured in the World Cups of 2002 and 2006 had played alongside or against their opponents at club level. More than 100 players at that event played club football in England, whose clubs also contributed more players (102) than any other country to the 2006 World Cup finals. Taking the argument to its logical conclusion, such familiarity is bound to start levelling the playing field.

The basic case for restricting the numbers of foreign players in any domestic league, including England, has moved on from the simplistic line that 'they take our jobs'. Instead the national interest is invoked, with claims that national teams will suffer if the leading club sides are staffed primarily by overseas players. Scotland is often used as an example. UEFA's quota rules, in force from the 2006–07 season, were introduced for that very reason – to encourage local production of talent, on however limited a basis.

As Sir Bobby Robson said in an interview for this book: 'We [English football] have brought in players for the sake of bringing in a player, probably got him a bit cheaper than an English player but not better than what we've got and that's what we've got to guard against. Because obviously if we are denying English players a chance of playing English football that will ultimately affect the English side. If we shorten the base, that's less players being produced for England.'

Ultimately he is, though, a huge fan of any great player, regardless of nationality. 'The best foreign players have enhanced our Premiership. No doubt about it. They've made it better, more attractive, better football, spurred us on and entertained the crowds. It's been great for the public. Henry, Vieira, Bergkamp, Van Nistelrooy, all the top players . . .'

In little more than a decade, these and many others have transformed English football, domestically at least. The best of the foreign players are exemplary professionals who prepare meticulously, eat properly, and don't arrive with the baggage of a drink culture that for generations has been an integral part of the British game, and still persists in some places. If ever there was a single figure who led by example – dining on healthy food, drinking occasionally and sensibly, applying himself with the utmost dedication and sense of fair play – it was Gianfranco Zola at Chelsea. At times he spoke of his surprise at English football culture, booze and all, but never judgementally. He just got on with doing things his way, and others copied.

Across the game, the pattern has been replicated. David Beckham was inspired to incessant practice by watching the perfectionist Eric

Cantona. Beckham in turn has inspired many others. Foreign players have no monopoly on superb technical skills but foreign players have brought these skills and incorporated them more often into the traditional British game. Dennis Bergkamp, stalwart and stylist at Arsenal for a decade until his final season of 2005–06, was a prime exponent. English football, after a century of closed minds and closed doors, has now accepted the most progressive thinkers and the best ideas from wherever in the world they hail, be it the powerhouses of Europe and South America or one of the emerging nations.

And for the future? We can only hope it involves the best of what the rest of the world can offer, and the education of home-grown players so that proper preparation and technical advancement become the norm not the exception. Only then can English football really claim to have come home, to a home frequented by foreign visitors for almost as long as the game has existed.

ALL-TIME BESTS

By the end of the 2005–06 season, 2,125 foreign-born players from 126 countries outside Britain and Ireland had played first-team football for English League clubs. There are many subjective ways of determining the 'best' of them, including the number of times each has been voted 'Footballer of the Year'. By 2006, that honour had been given to an overseas-born player 13 times in the 59 years since Blackpool's Stanley Matthews first won in 1948. More significantly in the story of foreign players' dominance in the Premier League age, it went to a foreign player nine times in 12 years between 1995 and 2006. France's Thierry Henry, winning for a third time in 2006, became the first man, of any nationality, to bag the hat-trick. The other overseas-born players to win were Germany's Bert Trautmann (1956), the Netherlands Frans Thijssen (1981), England's Jamaica-born striker John Barnes (1988, 1990), Germany's Jurgen Klinsmann (1995), France's Eric Cantona (1996), Italy's Gianfranco Zola (1997), the Netherlands' Dennis Bergkamp (1998), France's David Ginola (1999), and France's Robert Pires (2002). Henry won in 2003, 2004 and 2006.

The best: by trophies

One objective barometer of the best is hard evidence of success: major trophies won while playing in England. Measured by that, the best foreign players by 2006 were:

1 Bruce Grobbelaar   *13 major trophies, all with Liverpool*
The South African-born Zimbabwean international goalkeeper won the league title (the old First Division) six times (1982, 1983, 1984, 1986, 1988, 1990), the FA Cup three times (1986, 1989 and 1992), the League Cup three times (1982, 1983, 1984) and the European Cup (1984).

2 Peter Schmeichel   *10 major trophies, all with Manchester United*
The Danish international goalkeeper won the Premier League five times (1993, 1994, 1996, 1997, 1999), the FA Cup three times (1994, 1996, 1999), the League Cup once (1992) and the European Cup (1999).

3 Craig Johnston   *9 major trophies, all with Liverpool*
The South African-born Australian, a versatile midfielder who could also play in attack, won the league title five times (1982, 1983, 1984, 1986, 1988), the FA Cup once (1986), the League Cup twice (1983, 1984) and the European Cup (1984).

4 Ole Gunnar Solskjaer   *8 major trophies, all with Manchester United*
Up to 2006, the Norwegian international striker had won the Premier League five times (1997, 1999, 2000, 2001, 2003), the FA Cup twice (1999, 2004) and the European Cup (1999).

5 Eric Cantona   *7 major trophies, one with Leeds, six with Manchester United*
The French international striker won the league title five times, once with Leeds

(the last old First Division title in 1992) and four times with Manchester United (the Premier League in 1993, 1994, 1996, 1997), and the FA Cup twice (1994, 1996)

6= Dennis Bergkamp   *6 major trophies, all with Arsenal*
Premier League: 1998, 2002, 2004. FA Cup: 2002, 2003, 2005.
6= Dietmar Hamann   *6 major trophies by 2006, all with Liverpool*
FA Cup: 2001, 2006. League Cup: 2001, 2003. Uefa Cup: 2001. European Cup: 2005.
6= Sami Hyypia *6 major trophies by 2006, all with Liverpool*
FA Cup: 2001, 2006. League Cup: 2001, 2003. Uefa Cup: 2001. European Cup: 2005.
6= Patrick Vieira   *6 major trophies, all with Arsenal*
Premier League: 1998, 2002, 2004. FA Cup: 1998, 2002, 2005.
6= Dwight Yorke *6 major trophies, 5 with Manchester United, 1 with Aston Villa*
Premier League: 1999, 2000, 2001. FA Cup: 1999. European Cup: 1999. League Cup: 1996 (with Villa).

The best: by goals

Another objective measurement of the best is those players who have scored the most goals, and had the longevity to sustain their prowess over numerous seasons. The most prolific foreign-born goal scorers in English football up to 2006 were:

1 Gordon Hodgson   *304 goals*
Born and raised in South Africa. Later played for England. Played for Liverpool, Aston Villa and Leeds United in the 1920s and 1930s. Scored 231 League goals for Liverpool alone, including 17 hat-tricks, a record. Played 469 League games altogether, scoring 294 League goals at a ratio of 0.63 per game. Played 23 other first-team games, scoring 10 goals (0.43 per game). Overall strike rate: 0.62 per game.

2 Shaun Goater   *258 goals*
Born and raised in Bermuda. Played for Bermuda. Between 1989 and 2006 he played for Rotherham, Notts County, Bristol City, Manchester City, Reading, Coventry and Southend, scoring 217 League goals in 552 League games at a ratio of 0.39 per game. Played 106 other first-team games, scoring 41 goals (0.39 per game). Overall strike rate: 0.39 per game.

3 Luther Blissett   *244 goals*
Born in Jamaica. Later played for England. Between 1975 and 1994, he played for Watford (in three separate spells), Bournemouth, West Bromwich Albion, Bury and Mansfield, scoring 207 League goals in 554 League games at a ratio of 0.37 goals per game. Played 98 other first-team games, scoring 37 goals (0.38 per game). Overall strike rate: 0.37 per game.

4 Alf Ackerman   *215 goals*
Born and raised in South Africa. Between 1950 and 1959, he played for Hull (in two separate spells), Norwich, Derby, Carlisle and Millwall, scoring 197 League goals in 372 League games at a ratio of 0.53 goals per game. Played 28 other first-team games, scoring 18 goals (0.64 per game). Overall strike rate: 0.54 per game.

5 Thierry Henry   *214 goals*
Born and raised in France. He signed for Arsenal in 1999 and by the end of the 2005–06 season had scored 164 Premier League goals in 237 Premier League games for Arsenal at a ratio of 0.69 goals per game. He had also played 106 other first-team games, scoring 50 goals (0.47 per game). Overall strike rate: 0.62 per game, and fractionally better than Gordon Hodgson's strike rate. By the end of 2005–06, Henry had also won four major trophies with Arsenal: the Premier League twice (2002, 2004) and the FA Cup twice (2002, 2003).

The most cosmopolitan clubs

As the club who fielded the first all-foreign XI in an English League match and who hired a string of foreign managers who hastened the truly cosmopolitan 'melting pot' era in English football, it is not surprising that by the end of the 2005–06 season, Chelsea had had more foreign players than any other club in the country, with 84 overseas-born footballers appearing in first-team matches for them at some stage in their history. Of these, 22 had arrived in the four-year 'World Cup cycle' between the end of the 2002 World Cup and before the start of the 2006 World Cup, at an average of 5.5 new foreign players per year. A more remarkable statistic is that Portsmouth, at No. 2 in the list of most cosmopolitan clubs, with 83 foreign players in their history, had hired an average of 11 foreign players each year in the same period, or 44 altogether between summer 2002 and summer 2006. No other club came close to that increase.

Most foreign-born players between 1888 and summer 2006

Total number of foreign players per club, with the increase since summer 2002

1	Chelsea	84	+22
2	Portsmouth	83	+44
3	Arsenal	79	+27
4	Coventry	75	+23
5	Man City	72	+20
6	Liverpool	71	+21
7	West Ham	68	+31
8	Bolton	66	+27
9=	Derby	64	+17
9=	Fulham	64	+22

The major sources of foreign players

Courtesy of France, English football has benefited down the years from the respective flair, goals, crowd-pleasing talents and eccentricities of Thierry Henry, Eric Cantona, Patrick Vieira, Robert Pires, David Ginola, Nicolas Anelka, Emmanuel Petit, Didier Deschamps, Marcel Desailly, William Gallas, Claude

Makelele and another 236 footballers who were either born in France or qualified to play for her. By summer 2006, some 247 players allied to France had played first-team football for English League clubs (209 of them born in France, 38 born elsewhere with French nationality), making France by far and away the No. 1 provider of foreign players in English League history. In second place were the Dutch, with 147 players (126 born in the Netherlands and another 21 born elsewhere of Dutch nationality) followed by South Africa (126+1), Australia (114+6) and Denmark (99+4).

Major sources of foreign players to the English Leagues: 1888 to summer 2006

	Country	Players	First player	Year	Club
1	France	247	Eugene Langenove	1922	Walsall
2	The Netherlands	147	Gerry Keizer	1930	Arsenal
3	South Africa	127	Wilfred Waller	1900	Bolton
4	Australia	120	John Cuffe	1905	Glossop
5	Denmark	103	Nils Middleboe	1913	Chelsea
6	Germany	87	Max Seeburg	1907	Tottenham
7	Norway	82	Karl Hansen	1949	Huddersfield
8	Italy	75	Rolando Ugolini	1948	Middlesbrough
9	Sweden	67	Dan Ekner	1949	Portsmouth
10	USA	66	Billy Andrews	1908	Oldham
11	Spain	57	Emilio Aldecoa	1945	Coventry
12	Nigeria	55	Tesilim Balogun	1956	QPR
13=	Canada	53	Walter Bowman*	1891	Accrington
13=	Portugal	53	Jose Dominguez	1994	Birmingham

*the first foreign footballer in the English League

BIBLIOGRAPHY

Cantona, Eric, and Alex Fynn, *Cantona On Cantona*, London: Manchester United Books, 1996

Di Canio, Paolo and Gabriele Marcotti, *Paolo Di Canio: The Autobiography*, London: Collins Willow, 2000

Egbers, Tom, *Twaalf Gestolen Jaren*, Amsterdam: Uitgeverij Thomas Rap, 2002

Ferguson, Alex and Hugh McIlvanney, *Managing My Life: My Autobiography*, London: Hodder & Stoughton, 1999

Firmani, Eddie, *Football with the Millionaires*, London: Sportsmans Book Club, 1960

Freddi, Cris, *Complete Book of the World Cup 2002*, London: Collins Willow, 2002

Harding, John, *For the Good of the Game: The Official History of the PFA*, London: Robson Books, 1991

Horrie, Chris, *Premiership: Lifting the Lid on a National Obsession*, London: Pocket Books, 2002

Hugman, Barry, *The PFA Premier & Football League Players' Records 1946–1998*, Herts: Queen Anne Press, 1998

Jelinek, Radovan and Jiri Tomes, *The First World Atlas of Football*, Prague: Infokart, 2000

Joyce, Michael, *Football League Players' Records: 1888 to 1939*, Nottingham: SoccerData Publications, 2002

Kelly, Graham and Bob Harris, *Sweet F.A: A Fascinating Insight into Football's Corridors of Power*, London: Collins Willow, 1999

Lanfranchi, Pierre and Matthew Taylor, *Moving with the Ball: The Migration of Professional Footballers*, Oxford: Berg, 2001

Lovejoy, Joe, *Sven Goran Eriksson*, London: Collins Willow, 2002

Molby, Jan and Grahame Lloyd, *Jan The Man: From Anfield to Vetch Field*, London: Orion, 1999

Palmer, Mark, *The Professor: Arsène Wenger at Arsenal*, London: Virgin Books, 2002

Roberts, John, *Everton: The Official Centenary History*, London: Mayflower Books, 1978

Rothmans Football Yearbooks (1970–71 to 2002–03 inclusive), Herts: Queen Anne Press (until 1992) and then London: Headline.

Rowlands, Alan, *Trautmann: The Biography*, Derby: Breedon Books, 1990

Schmeichel, Peter and Egon Balsby, *Schmeichel: The Autobiography*, London: Virgin Books, 2000

Seed, Jimmy, *The Jimmy Seed Story*, London: Sportsmans Book Club, 1958

Shaw, Phil, *The Book of Football Quotations*, London: Ebury Press, 2003

Trautmann, Bert, *Steppes to Wembley*, London: Sportsmans Book Club, 1957

Tyler, Martin, *The Story of Football*, London: Marshall Cavendish, 1976

Vasili, Phil, *Colouring Over the White Line: The History of Black Footballers in Britain*, Edinburgh: Mainstream, 2000

—*The First Black Footballer: Arthur Wharton 1865–1930*, London: Frank Cass, 1998

APPENDICES: FOREIGN PLAYERS IN ENGLAND SINCE 1888

These appendices record all overseas-born players in English League history by country of origin in chronological order of arrival/first appearance (1888–May 2006 inclusive). They include all players to have featured in at least one first-team match, but not those who, while signed, have not actually played.

Key
DOB = date of birth
Nat = nationality/footballing nationality

Notes
1) These appendices do not include any players born within Britain or Ireland, for example players who are British nationals but represent countries outside Britain and Ireland.
2) If an overseas-born player has represented one of the home nations or is otherwise identifiable as English, Scottish, Welsh or Northern Irish as opposed to simply British, it is specified.
3) Joined/first played, in this context, means the month from which the player was employed by the club, usually the month in which he signed his contract. In some cases (loans, non-contract deals, instances when it has not been possible to establish precisely when the contract was signed) the month given here refers to the player's debut. In many instances, a player left one club on loan, played for another and returned to play for his original club. This is listed as two separate spells at the original club only when the player has severed his ties and then returned.
4) The number in brackets after each country is the number of players born there. (+1) denotes how many other players born outside that country have the nationality of that country.

APPENDIX 1: COUNTRY BY COUNTRY

Name	DOB	Place of birth	Nat	Club(s) (joined/first played)
ALBANIA (2)				
Kuqi, Shefki	10 Nov 1976	Vushtrri	Alb/Fin	Stockport (Jan 2001); Sheff Wed (Jan 2002); Ipswich (Sep 2003); Blackburn (Jun 2005)
Kuqi, Njazi	25 Mar 1983	Vushtrri	Alb/Fin	Blackpool (Jan 2006); Peterborough (Mar 2006)
ALGERIA (3+3)				
Saib, Moussa	5 Mar 1969	Theniet-el-Had	Alg	Tottenham (Feb 1998)
Benarbia, Ali	8 Oct 1968	Oran	Alg	Man City (Sep 2001)
Ferrari, Matteo	5 Dec 1979		Aflou It	Everton (Aug 2005)
Qualified for Algeria but born outside Algeria				
Belmadi, Djamel	27 Mar 1976	Champigny,	Fr Alg	Man City (Jan 2003); Southampton (Aug 2005)
Mansouri, Yazid	25 Feb 1978	Revin,	Fr Alg	Coventry (Aug 2003)
Bougherra, Madjid	7 Oct 1982	Dijon,	Fr Alg	Crewe (Jan 2006)
ANGOLA (7)				
Paulo, Pedro	21 Nov 1973	Angola	Por	Darlington (Aug 1995)
Quitongo, Jose	18 Nov 1974	Luanda	Ang	Darlington (Sep 1995)
Helder, Rodrigues	21 Mar 1971	Luanda	Por	Newcastle (Nov 1999)
Batista, Jordao	30 Aug 1971	Malanje	Por	WBA (Aug 2000)
Da Silva, Lourenco	5 Jun 1983	Luanda	Por	Bristol C (Mar 2001); Oldham (Aug 2002)
Garrocho, Carlos	26 Jan 1974	Benguela	Ang	Walsall (Jul 2001)
Marques, Rui	3 Sep 1977	Luanda	Ang	Leeds (Jul 2005); Hull (Mar 2006)
ANTIGUA (1)				
Carr, Everton	11 Jan 1961	Antigua	Ant	Leicester (Jan 1979); Halifax (Aug 1981); Rochdale (Mar 1983)
ARGENTINA (50+1)				
Peed, Frank	27 Jul 1905	Vernado Tuerto	Brit	B&B Ath (Jun 1930); Norwich (Oct 1930); Newport (Aug 1931); Barrow (Nov 1933)
Ardiles, Ossie	3 Aug 1952	Cordoba	Arg	Tottenham (Jul 1978); Blackburn (Mar 1988); QPR (Aug 1988); Swindon (Jul 1989)
Villa, Ricky	18 Aug 1952	Buenos Aires	Arg	Tottenham (Jul 1978)
Sabella, Alex	5 Nov 1954	Buenos Aires	Arg	Sheff Utd (Aug 1978); Leeds (Jun 1980)
Tarantini, Alberto	3 Dec 1955	Buenos Aires	Arg	Birmingham (Oct 1978)
Verde, Pedro	12 Mar 1952	Buenos Aires	Arg	Sheff Utd (Aug 1979)
Marangoni, Claudio	17 Nov 1954	Rosario	Arg	Sunderland (Dec 1979)
Lorenzo, Nestor	28 Feb 1966	Buenos Aires	Arg	Swindon (Oct 1990)
Taricco, Mauricio	10 Mar 1973	Buenos Aires	Arg	Ipswich (Sep 1994); Tottenham (Dec 1998); West Ham (Nov 2004)
Mendez, Gabriel	12 Mar 1973	Buenos Aires	Aus	Notts Co (Mar 1997)
Di Lella, Gustavo	6 Oct 1973	Buenos Aires	Arg	Darlington (Dec 1997); Hartlepool (Mar 1998)
Carbonari, Horacio	2 May 1973	Rosario	Arg	Derby (Jul 1998); Coventry (Mar 2002)
Cobian, Juan	11 Sep 1975	Buenos Aires	Arg	Sheff Wed (Aug 1998); Swindon (Jul 2000)
Vivas, Nelson	18 Oct 1969	San Nicolas	Arg	Arsenal (Aug 1998)
Del Rio, Walter	16 Jun 1976	Buenos Aires	Arg	C Palace (Sep 1998)
Caballero, Fabian	31 Jan 1978	Misiones	Arg	Arsenal (Oct 1998)
Otta, Walter	20 Dec 1973	Cordoba	Arg	Walsall (Nov 1998)
Fuertes, Esteban	26 Dec 1976	Colonel Dorredo	Arg	Derby (Aug 1999)
Marinelli, Carlos	28 Aug 1980	Buenos Aires	Arg	Middlesbrough (Oct 1999)

Name	DOB	Place of birth	Nat	Club(s) (joined/first played)
Padula, Gino	11 Jul 1976	Buenos Aires	Arg	Walsall (Nov 1999); Wigan Ath (Jul 2000); QPR (Aug 2002); Nottm For (Jul 2005)
Bassedas, Chistian	16 Feb 1973	Buenos Aires	Arg	Newcastle (Jul 2000)
Arca, Julio	31 Jan 1981	Quilmes Bernal	Arg	Sunderland (Aug 2000)
Cordone, Daniel	6 Nov 1974	General Rodriguez	Arg	Newcastle (Aug 2000)
Mazzina, Nicolas	31 Jan 1979	Buenos Aires	Arg	Swansea (Jul 2001); York (Sep 2002)
Veron, Juan	9 Mar 1975	La Plata	Arg	Man Utd (Jul 2001); Chelsea (Aug 2003)
Bonvin, Pablo F	15 Apr 1981	Concepcion	Arg	Sheff Wed (Aug 2001)
Peralta, Sixto	16 Apr 1979	Chubut	Arg	Ipswich (Aug 2001)
Caceres, Adrian	20 Jan 1982	Buenos Aires	Aus	Brentford (Sep 2001), Hull (Mar 2002); Yeovil (Jul 2004); Wycombe (Mar 2005)
Zavagno, Luciano	6 Aug 1977	Rosario	Arg	Derby (Oct 2001)
Biagini, Leo	13 Apr 1977	Arroyo Seco	Arg	Portsmouth (Feb 2002)
Colusso, Cristian	7 Feb 1977	Rosario	Arg	Oldham (Feb 2002)
Sava, Facundo	3 Jul 1974	Ituzaingo	Arg	Fulham (Jul 2002)
Medina, Nicolas	17 Feb 1982	Buenos Aires	Arg	Sunderland (Jan 2003)
Sara, Juan	13 Oct 1978	Buenos Aires	Arg	Coventry (Jan 2003)
Herrera, Martin	13 Sep 1970	Rio Puerto	Arg	Fulham (Feb 2003)
Crespo, Hernan	5 Jul 1975	Buenos Aires	Arg	Chelsea (Aug 2003)
Figueroa, Luciano	19 May 1981	Santa Fe	Arg	Birmingham (Aug 2003)
Heinze, Gabriel	19 Mar 1978	Crespo	Arg	Man Utd (Jun 2004)
Scartiscini, Leandro	30 Jan 1985	Buenos Aires	Arg	Darlington (Jul 2004)
Speroni, Julian	18 May 1979	Buenos Aires	Arg	C Palace (Jul 2004)
Cominelli, Lucas	25 Dec 1976	Buenos Aires	Arg	Oxford (Jan 2005)
Pellegrino, Mauricio	5 Oct 1971	Leones	Arg	Liverpool (Jan 2005)
Raponi, Juan Pablo	7 May 1980	Santa Fe	Arg	Oxford (Feb 2005)
Larossa, Ruben Dario	4 Dec 1979	Buenos Aires	Arg	Walsall (Jul 2005)
Alvarez, Luciano	30 Nov 1978	Buenos Aires	Arg	Yeovil (Aug 2005)
Bastianini, Pablo	9 Nov 1982	Zarate	Arg	Yeovil (Aug 2005)
Torres, Sergio	11 Jul 1981	Mar Del Plata	Arg	Wycombe (Aug 2005)
Turienzo, Federico	2 Jun 1983	La Plata	Arg	Brighton (Aug 2005)
D'Alessandro, Andres	15 Apr 1981	Buenos Aires	Arg	Portsmouth (Jan 2006)
Scaloni, Lionel	16 May 1978	Rosario	Arg	West Ham (Jan 2006)

Other players qualified for Argentina but born outside Argentina

Name	DOB	Place of birth	Nat	Club(s) (joined/first played)
Corbo, Mateo	21 Apr 1976	Montevideo, Uru	Arg	Barnsley (Aug 2000)

AT SEA (1)

Name	DOB	Place of birth	Nat	Club(s) (joined/first played)
Wilcox, Tom	1879	At sea	Brit	Blackpool (May 1906); Man Utd (Aug 1907); Huddersfield (Jan 1911)

AUSTRALIA (114+6)

Name	DOB	Place of birth	Nat	Club(s) (joined/first played)
Cuffe, John	26 Jun 1880	Sydney	Aus	Glossop (Jul 1905)
Higginbotham, Harry	27 Jul 1897	Sydney	Aus	South Shields (Aug 1919); Luton (Jul 1920); Clapton O (Feb 1923); Nelson (Oct 1923); Reading (May 1924)
Baines, Peter	11 Sep 1919	Australia	Aus	Wrexham (Apr 1943); Crewe (Nov 1946); Hartlepool (Jun 1947); N Brighton (Oct 1947)
Mitchell, Frank	3 Jun 1922	Goulbourn	Aus	Birmingham (Sep 1943); Chelsea (Jan 1949); Watford (Aug 1952)
Grieves, Ken	27 Aug 1925	Sydney	Aus	Bury (Apr 1947); Bolton (Dec 1951); Stockport (Jul 1957)
Horsfall, George	19 Sep 1924	Perth	Aus	Southampton (May 1947); Southend (Jun 1949)

Name	DOB	Place of birth	Nat	Club(s) (joined/first played)
Cornock, Wally	1 Jan 1921	Bondi	Aus	Rochdale (Nov 1947)
Marston, Joe	7 Jan 1926	Sydney	Aus	Preston (Feb 1950)
Fraser, Willie	24 Feb 1929	Melbourne	Sco	Sunderland (Mar 1954); Nottm For (Dec 1958)
Tolson, Max	18 Jul 1945	Wollongong	Aus	Workington (Feb 1966)
Roberts, John	24 Mar 1944	Cessnock	Aus	Blackburn (Apr 1966); Chesterfield (Aug 1967); Bradford (Aug 1968); Southend (Jan 1971); Northampton (Jul 1972)
Kosmina, John	17 Aug 1956	Adelaide	Aus	Arsenal (Mar 1978)
Dorigo, Tony	31 Dec 1965	Melbourne	Eng	A Villa (Jul 1983); Chelsea (Jul 1987); Leeds (Jun 1991); Derby (Oct 1998); Stoke (Jul 2000)
Davidson, Alan	1 Jun 1960	Melbourne	Aus	Nottm For (Nov 1984)
Oldfield, David	30 May 1968	Perth	Eng	Luton (May 1986); Man City (Mar 1989); Leicester (Jan 1990); Millwall (Feb 1995); Luton (Jul 1995); Stoke (Jul 1998); Peterborough (Mar 2000); Oxford (Aug 2002)
Bernal, Andy	16 May 1966	Canberra	Aus	Ipswich (Sep 1987); Reading (Jul 1994)
Kearton, Jason	9 Jul 1969	Ipswich	Aus	Everton (Oct 1988); Blackpool (Jan 1992); Stoke (Aug 1991); Notts Co (Jan 1995); Crewe (Oct 1996)
Petterson, Andy	26 Sep 1969	Fremantle	Aus	Luton (Dec 1988); Ipswich (Mar 1993); Charlton (Jul 1994); Bradford (Dec 1994); Ipswich (Sep 1995); Plymouth (Jan 1996); Colchester (Mar 1996); Portsmouth (Jul 1999); Torquay (Mar 2001); Brighton (Aug 2002); Southend (Sep 2003); Walsall (Jan 2004)
Bosnich, Mark	13 Jan 1972	Fairfield	Aus	Man Utd (Jun 1989); A Villa (Feb 1992); Man Utd (Jun 1999); Chelsea (Jan 2001)
Hughes, Zacari	6 Jun 1971	Bentley	Aus	Rochdale (Aug 1989)
Edwards, Alistair	21 Jun 1968	Whyalla	Aus	Brighton (Nov 1989); Millwall (Dec 1994)
Greer, Ross	23 Sep 1967	Perth	Aus	Chester (Nov 1989)
Bradley, Pat	27 Apr 1972	Sydney	Aus	Bury (Jul 1990)
Lovell, Stuart	9 Jan 1972	Sydney	Aus	Reading (Jul 1990)
Farina, Frank	5 Sep 1964	Queensland	Aus	Notts Co (Mar 1992)
Johnson, Richard	27 Jul 1974	Kurri Kurri	Aus	Watford (May 1992); Northampton (Feb 2003); Colchester (Oct 2003); Stoke (Nov 2003); QPR (Feb 2004); MKD (Oct 2004)
Ollerenshaw, Scott	9 Feb 1968	Sydney	Aus	Walsall (Aug 1992)
Murphy, Shaun	5 Nov 1970	Sydney	Aus	Notts Co (Sep 1992); WBA (Dec 1996); Sheff Utd (Jul 1999); C Palace (Feb 2002)
Talia, Frank	20 Jul 1972	Melbourne	Aus	Hartlepool (Dec 1992); Swindon (Sep 1995); Sheff Utd (Sep 2000); Wycombe (Aug 2002)
Filan, John	8 Feb 1970	Sydney	Aus	Cambridge (Mar 1993); Coventry (Mar 1995); Blackburn (Jul 1997); Wigan Ath (Dec 2001)
Hodgson, Doug	27 Feb 1969	Frankston	Aus	Sheff Utd (Jul 1994); Plymouth (Aug 1995); Burnley (Oct 1996); Oldham (Feb 1997); Northampton (Oct 1998)
Veart, Carl	21 May 1970	Whyalla	Aus	Sheff Utd (Jul 1994); C Palace (Mar 1996); Millwall (Dec 1997)
Van Blerk, Jason	16 Mar 1968	Sydney	Aus	Millwall (Sep 1994); Man City (Aug 1997); WBA (Mar 1998); Hull (Jan 2002); Stockport (Aug 2001); Shrewsbury (Aug 2002)
Seal, David	26 Jan 1972	Penrith	Aus	Bristol C (Oct 1994); Northampton (Aug 1997)
Agostino, Paul	9 Jun 1975	Woodville	Aus	Bristol C (Jul 1995)

Name	DOB	Place of birth	Nat	Club(s) (joined/first played)
Corica, Steve	24 Mar 1973	Cairns	Aus	Leicester (Aug 1995); Wolves (Feb 1996); Walsall (Feb 2002)
Knight, Jason	16 Sep 1974	Melbourne	Aus	Doncaster (Aug 1995)
McDermott, Andy	24 Mar 1977	Sydney	Aus	QPR (Aug 1995); WBA (Mar 1997); Notts Co (Aug 2000)
Zelic, Ned	4 Jul 1971	Australia	Aus	QPR (Aug 1995)
Lazaridis, Stan	16 Aug 1972	Perth	Aus	West Ham (Sep 1995); Birmingham (Jul 1999)
Kalac, Zeljko	16 Dec 1972	Sydney	Aus	Leicester (Oct 1995)
Neill, Lucas	9 Mar 1978	Sydney	Aus	Millwall (Nov 1995); Blackburn (Sep 2001)
Kewell, Harry	22 Sep 1978	Smithfield	Aus	Leeds (Dec 1995); Liverpool (Jul 2003)
Coyne, Chris	20 Dec 1978	Brisbane	Aus	West Ham (Jan 1996); Brentford (Aug 1998); Southend (Mar 1999); Luton (Sep 2001)
Johnson, Glenn	16 Jul 1972	Sydney	Aus	Cardiff (Mar 1996)
Mautone, Steve	10 Aug 1970	Myrtleford	Aus	West Ham (Mar 1996); Crewe (Sep 1996); Reading (Feb 1997); C Palace (Nov 1999); Gillingham (Mar 2000)
Riches, Steve	6 Aug 1976	Sydney	Aus	Orient (Sep 1996)
Schwarzer, Mark	6 Oct 1972	Sydney	Aus	Bradford (Nov 1996); Middlesbrough (Feb 1997)
Cahill, Tim	6 Dec 1979	Sydney	Aus	Millwall (Jul 1997); Everton (Jul 2004)
Harries, Paul	19 Nov 1977	Sydney	Aus	Carlisle (Jul 1997); Portsmouth (Sep 1997); Torquay (Feb 1999); Exeter (Sep 2002)
Aloisi, John	5 Feb 1976	Adelaide	Aus	Portsmouth (Aug 1997); Coventry (Dec 1998)
Kalogeracos, Vas	21 Mar 1975	Perth	Aus	Stockport (Aug 1997)
Thorp, Hamilton	21 Aug 1973	Darwin	Aus	Portsmouth (Aug 1997)
Zabica, Robert	9 Apr 1964	Perth	Aus	Bradford (Aug 1997)
Foster, Craig	15 Apr 1969	Melbourne	Aus	Portsmouth (Sep 1997); C Palace (Oct 1998)
Enes, Robbie	22 Aug 1975	Victoria	Aus	Portsmouth (Oct 1997)
Ilic, Sasa	18 Jul 1972	Melbourne	Yug	Charlton (Oct 1997); West Ham (Feb 2000); Portsmouth (Sep 2001); Barnsley (Aug 2003); Blackpool (Jul 2004)
Kyratzoglou, Alex	27 Aug 1974	Armitale	Aus	Oldham (Oct 1997)
Robertson, Mark	6 Apr 1977	Sydney	Aus	Burnley (Oct 1997); Swindon (Aug 2000); Stockport (Jan 2004)
Tiatto, Danny	22 May 1973	Melbourne	Aus	Stoke (Nov 1997); Man City (Jul 1998); Leicester (Jul 2004)
Edds, Gareth	3 Feb 1981	Sydney	Aus	Nottm For (Feb 1998); Swindon (Aug 2002); Bradford (Jul 2003); MKD (Jul 2004)
Zois, Peter	21 Apr 1978	Melbourne	Aus	Cardiff (Feb 1998)
Brady, Jon	14 Jan 1975	Newcastle	Aus	Rushden (Jul 1998)
Miotto, Simon	5 Sep 1969	Tasmania	Aus	Hartlepool (Jul 1998)
Rizzo, Nicky	9 Jun 1979	Sydney	Aus	C Palace (Jul 1998); MKD (Nov 2004)
Allsopp, Danny	10 Aug 1978	Melbourne	Aus	Man City (Aug 1998); Notts Co (Nov 1999); Wrexham (Feb 2000); Bristol R (Oct 2000); Notts Co (Nov 2000); Hull (May 2003)
Wilkshire, Luke	2 Oct 1981	Wollongong	Aus	Middlesbrough (Aug 1998); Bristol C (Aug 2003)
Garcia, Richard	4 Sep 1981	Perth	Aus	West Ham (Sep 1998); Orient (Aug 2000); Colchester (Sep 2004)
Moore, Craig	12 Dec 1975	Canterbury	Aus	C Palace (Oct 1998); Newcastle (Jul 2005)
Howells, Lee	14 Oct 1968	Freemantle	Aus	Cheltenham (Aug 1999)
Panopoulos, Mike	9 Oct 1976	Melbourne	Grk	Portsmouth (Sep 1999)
Viduka, Mark	9 Oct 1975	Melbourne	Aus	Leeds (Jul 2000); Middlesbrough (Jul 2004)

Name	DOB	Place of birth	Nat	Club(s) (joined/first played)
Blatsis, Con	6 Jul 1977	Melbourne	Aus	Derby (Aug 2000); Sheff Wed (Dec 2000); Colchester (Mar 2002)
Burns, Jacob	21 Apr 1978	Sydney	Aus	Leeds (Aug 2000); Barnsley (Oct 2003)
Invincible, Danny	31 Mar 1979	Brisbane	Aus	Swindon (Aug 2000)
Jones, Brad	19 Feb 1982	Armadale	Aus	Middlesbrough (Aug 2000); Stockport (Dec 2002); Blackpool (Nov 2003)
McDonald, Scott	21 Aug 1983	Melbourne	Aus	Southampton (Aug 2000); Huddersfield (Aug 2002); Bournemouth (Mar 2003); MKD (Aug 2003)
Okon, Paul	5 Apr 1972	Sydney	Aus	Middlesbrough (Aug 2000); Watford (Jan 2002); Leeds (Nov 2002)
Stergiopoulos, Marcus	12 Jun 1973	Melbourne	Grk	Lincoln (Aug 2000)
Mansley, Chad	13 Nov 1980	Newcastle	Aus	Orient (Nov 2000)
Foxe, Hayden	23 Jun 1977	Canberra	Aus	West Ham (Mar 2001); Portsmouth (Aug 2002)
Guyett, Scott	20 Jan 1976	Ascot	Aus	Oxford (May 2001); Yeovil (Jul 2004)
Colosimo, Simon	8 Jan 1979	Melbourne	Aus	Man City (Jul 2001)
Popovic, Tony	4 Jul 1973	Sydney	Aus	C Palace (Aug 2001)
Hews, Chay	30 Sep 1976	Belmont	Aus	Carlisle (Sep 2001)
Pogliacomi, Les	3 May 1976	Australia	Aus	Oldham (Aug 2002); Blackpool (Aug 2005)
Zdrilic, David	14 Apr 1974	Sydney	Aus	Walsall (Aug 2002)
McMaster, Jamie	29 Nov 1982	Sydney	Aus	Leeds (Sep 2002); Coventry (Nov 2002); Chesterfield (Jan 2004); Swindon (Sep 2004); Peterborough (Jan 2005); Chesterfield (Mar 2005)
Reid, Paul	6 Jul 1979	Sydney	Aus	Bradford (Sep 2002); Brighton (Mar 2004)
Vidmar, Tony	15 Apr 1969	Adelaide	Aus	Middlesbrough (Sep 2002); Cardiff (Jul 2003)
Young, Jamie	25 Aug 1985	Brisbane	Aus	Reading (Sep 2002); Rushden (Jul 2005)
Cansdell-Sheriff, Shane	10 Nov 1982	Sydney	Aus	Rochdale (Nov 2002)
Milosevic, Danny	26 Jun 1978	Carlton	Aus	Plymouth (Nov 2002); Crewe (Jan 2003)
Theoklitos, Michael	11 Feb 1981	Melbourne	Aus	Blackpool (Nov 2002)
Cooney, Sean	31 Oct 1983	Perth	Aus	Coventry (Apr 2003)
Davies, Clint	24 Apr 1983	Perth	Aus	Bradford (Jul 2003)
Emerton, Brett	22 Feb 1979	Bankstown	Aus	Blackburn (Jul 2003)
Harnwell, Jamie	21 Jul 1977	Perth	Aus	Orient (Jul 2003)
McClenahan, Trent	4 Feb 1985	Sydney	Aus	West Ham (Jul 2003); MKD (Mar 2005)
Carney, Dave	30 Nov 1983	Sydney	Aus	Oldham (Aug 2003)
Porter, Joel	25 Dec 1978	Adelaide	Aus	Hartlepool (Nov 2003)
Bojic, Pedj	9 Apr 1984	Sydney	Aus	Northampton (Jul 2004)
Danze, Anthony	15 Mar 1984	Perth	Aus	C Palace (Jul 2004); MKD (Dec 2004)
Wesolowski, James	25 Aug 1987	Sydney	Aus	Leicester (Jul 2004)
Downes, Aaron	5 May 1985	Mudgee	Aus	Chesterfield (Aug 2004)
Henderson, Paul	22 Apr 1976	Sydney	Aus	Bradford (Aug 2004); Leicester (May 2005)
Zadkovich, Ruben	23 May 1986	Wollongong	Aus	Notts Co (Mar 2005)
Kisnorbo, Patrick	24 Mar 1981	Melbourne	Aus	Leicester (Apr 2005)
Elrich, Ahmed	30 May 1981	Sydney	Aus	Fulham (Jun 2005)
Nix, Kyle	21 Jan 1986	Sydney	Eng	Sheff Utd (Jul 2005)
Hughes, Adam	14 Jul 1982	Woolongong	Aus	Doncaster (Aug 2005)
Skoko, Josip	10 Dec 1975	Mt Gambier	Aus	Wigan (Aug 2005); Stoke (Feb 2006)
Griffiths, Adam	21 Aug 1979	Sydney	Aus	Bournemouth (Jan 2006)
Griffiths, Joel	21 Aug 1979	Sydney	Aus	Leeds (Jan 2006)

Other players qualified for Australia but born outside Australia

Johnston, Craig	8 Dec 1960	Johannesburg	Aus	Middlesbrough (Feb 1978); Liverpool (Apr 1981)

Name	DOB	Place of birth	Nat	Club(s) (joined/first played)
Banovic, Yakka	12 Nov 1956	Bihac (Bos, ex-Yug)	Aus	Derby (Sep 1980)
Bozinoski, Vlado	30 Mar 1964	Skopje, Mac	Aus	Ipswich (Dec 1992)
Kulcsar, George	12 Aug 1967	Budapest, Hun	Aus	Bradford (Mar 1997); QPR (Dec 1997)
Mendez, Gabriel	12 Mar 1973	Buenos Aires, Arg	Aus	Notts Co (Mar 1997)
Caceres, Adrian	20 Jan 1982	Buenos Aires, Arg	Aus	Brentford (Sep 2001), Hull (Mar 2002); Yeovil (Jul 2004); Wycombe (Mar 2005)

AUSTRIA (12)

Name	DOB	Place of birth	Nat	Club(s) (joined/first played)
Manninger, Alex	4 Jun 1977	Salzburg	Aut	Arsenal (Jun 1997)
Hiden, Martin	11 Mar 1973	Stainz	Aut	Leeds (Oct 1997)
Dorner, Mario	21 Mar 1970	Baden	Aut	Darlington (Oct 1997)
Resch, Franz	4 May 1969	Vienna	Aut	Darlington (Oct 1997)
Mayrleb, Christian	8 Jun 1972	Leonding	Aut	Sheff Wed (Jan 1998)
Laudrup, Brian	22 Feb 1969	Vienna	Den	Chelsea (Jun 1998)
Macho, Jurgen	24 Aug 1977	Vienna	Aut	Sunderland (Jul 2000)
Breitenfelder, Friedrich	16 Jun 1980	Vienna	Aut	Luton (Aug 2000)
Haas, Bernt	8 Apr 1978	Vienna	Swit	Sunderland (Aug 2001); WBA (Jul 2003)
Lipa, Andreas	26 Apr 1971	Vienna	Aut	Port Vale (Dec 2004)
Pogatetz, Emanuel	16 Jan 1983	Graz	Aut	Middlesbrough (Jun 2005)
Scharner, Paul	11 Mar 1980	Scheibbs	Aut	Wigan (Jan 2006)

BARBADOS (5)

Name	DOB	Place of birth	Nat	Club(s) (joined/first played)
Kingsley, Alf	25 Oct 1891	Barbados	Bar	Charlton (Jul 1921); Fulham (Jan 1922); Millwall (Sep 1923)
Alleyne, Andy	19 May 1951	Springtown	Bar	Reading (Nov 1972)
Corbin, Kirk	12 Mar 1955	Barbados	Bar	Cambridge (Jan 1978)
Welch, Micky	21 May 1958	Barbados	Bar	Wimbledon (Nov 1984); Southend (Feb 1985)
Goodridge, Greg	10 Jul 1971	Barbados	Bar	Torquay (Mar 1994); QPR (Aug 1995); Bristol C (Aug 1996); Cheltenham (Feb 2001); Torquay (Nov 2001)

BELARUS (6)

Name	DOB	Place of birth	Nat	Club(s) (joined/first played)
Gotsmanov, Sergei	17 Mar 1959	Minsk (then USSR)	USSR	Brighton (Feb 1990); Southampton (Aug 1990)
Gurinovich, Igor	5 Mar 1960	Minsk (then USSR)	USSR	Brighton (Nov 1990)
Yanushevski, Victor	23 Jan 1960	Minsk (then USSR)	USSR	Aldershot (Mar 1991)
Kachouro, Petr	2 Aug 1972	Minsk (then USSR)	Blr	Sheff Utd (Jul 1996)
Shtaniuk, Sergei	11 Jan 1972	Minsk (then USSR)	Blr	Stoke (Jul 2001)
Hleb, Aleksandr	1 May 1981	Minsk (then USSR)	Blr	Arsenal (Jul 2005)

BELGIUM (35+3)

Name	DOB	Place of birth	Nat	Club(s) (joined/first played)
Van Den Eynden, Ike	1890	Belgium	Bel	Clapton O (Feb 1914)
Bryant, Billy	1 Mar 1899	Belgium	Bel	Millwall (Jul 1925)
Gaillard, Marcel	15 Jan 1927	Charleris	Bel	C Palace (Feb 1948); Portsmouth (Feb 1951)
Van Den Hauwe, Pat	16 Dec 1960	Dendermonde	Wal	Birmingham (Aug 1978); Everton (Sep 1984); Tottenham (Aug 1989); Millwall (Sep 1993)
McDonough, Darron	7 Nov 1962	Antwerp	Brit	Oldham (Jan 1980); Luton (Sep 1986); Newcastle (Mar 1992)
Van Gool, Roger	1 Jun 1950	Belgium	Bel	Coventry (Mar 1980)
Van der Elst, Francois	1 Dec 1954	Opwyk	Bel	West Ham (Dec 1981)
Claesen, Nico	1 Oct 1962	Leut	Bel	Tottenham (Oct 1986)
Albert, Philippe	10 Aug 1967	Bouillon	Bel	Newcastle (Aug 1994); Fulham (Jan 1999)
Degryse, Marc	4 Sep 1965	Roeslare	Bel	Sheff Wed (Aug 1995)
Genaux, Reggie	31 Aug 1973	Charleroi	Bel	Coventry (Aug 1996)
Clement, Philippe	22 Mar 1974	Antwerp	Bel	Coventry (Jul 1998)

Name	DOB	Place of birth	Nat	Club(s) (joined/first played)
Ngonge, Michel	10 Jan 1967	Huy	DRC	Watford (Jul 1998); Huddersfield (Mar 2000); QPR (Dec 2000)
Vaesen, Nico	28 Sep 1969	Hasselt	Bel	Huddersfield (Jul 1998); Birmingham (Jun 2001); Gillingham (Dec 2003); Bradford (Feb 2004); C Palace (Mar 2004)
Walschaerts, Wim	5 Nov 1972	Antwerp	Bel	Orient (Jul 1998)
Delorge, Laurent	21 Jul 1979	Leuven	Bel	Coventry (Nov 1998)
Bakalli, Adrian	22 Nov 1976	Brussels	Bel	Watford (Jan 1999); Swindon (Mar 2001)
De Bilde, Gilles	9 Jun 1971	Zellik	Bel	Sheff Wed (Jul 1999); A Villa (Oct 2000)
Gysbrechts, Davy	20 Sep 1972	Heusden	Bel	Sheff Utd (Aug 1999)
Camilieri-Gioia, Carlo	14 May 1975	Brussels	Bel	Mansfield (Sep 1999)
Roussel, Cedric	6 Jan 1978	Mons	Bel	Coventry (Oct 1999); Wolves (Feb 2001)
Kinet, Christophe	31 Dec 1974	Huy	Bel	Millwall (Feb 2000)
Nilis, Luc	25 May 1967	Hasselt	Bel	A Villa (Jul 2000)
Peeters, Tom	25 Sep 1978	Bornem	Bel	Sunderland (Jul 2000)
Verhoene, Kenny	14 Apr 1973	Ghent	Bel	C Palace (Mar 2001)
Malbranque, Steed	6 Jan 1980	Mouscron	Fr	Fulham (Aug 2001)
Van Deurzen, Jurgen	26 Jan 1974	Genk	Bel	Stoke (Aug 2001)
Blondel, Jonathan	3 Apr 1984	Belgium	Bel	Tottenham (Aug 2002)
Bulent, Akin	28 Aug 1979	Brussels	Tur	Bolton (Oct 2002)
Oyen, Davy	17 Jul 1975	Bilzen	Bel	Nottm For (Feb 2003)
Peeters, Bob	10 Jan 1974	Lier	Bel	Millwall (Aug 2003)
Van Buyten, Daniel	7 Feb 1978	Chimay	Bel	Man City (Jan 2004)
Van Damme, Jelle	10 Oct 1983	Lokeren	Bel	Southampton (Jun 2004)
Hoefkens, Carl	6 Oct 1978	Lier	Bel	Stoke (Jul 2005)
Moussa, Franck	10 Aug 1989	Brussels	Bel	Southend (Jan 2006)

Other players qualified for Belgium but born outside Belgium

Smeets, Axel	12 Jul 1974	Karawa, DRC	Bel	Sheff Utd (Jul 1999)
Strupar, Branko	9 Feb 1970	Zagreb, Cro	Bel	Derby (Dec 1999)
Mbuyi, Gabriel	1 Jun 1982	Kinshasa, DRC	Bel	Stoke (Jul 2005)

BERMUDA (8)

Woollard, Arnold	24 Aug 1930	Bermuda	Ber	Northampton (Jun 1949); Newcastle (Dec 1952); B&B Ath (Jun 1956); Northampton (Mar 1962)
Symonds, Calvin	29 Mar 1932	Bermuda	Ber	Rochdale (Oct 1954)
Mallory, Richard	10 Aug 1942	Bermuda	Ber	Cardiff (May 1963)
Best, Clyde	24 Feb 1951	Bermuda	Ber	West Ham (Mar 1969)
Goater, Shaun	25 Feb 1970	Hamilton	Ber	Rotherham (Oct 1989); Notts Co (Nov 1993); Bristol C (Jul 1996); Man City (Mar 1998); Reading (Mar 2005); Coventry (Mar 2005); Southend (Aug 2005)
Jennings, Jed	15 Oct 1971	Bermuda	Ber	Hereford (Aug 1991)
Wade, Meshach	23 Jan 1973	Bermuda	Ber	Hereford (Aug 1991)
Lightbourne, Kyle	29 Sep 1968	Bermuda	Ber	Scarborough (Dec 1992); Walsall (Sep 1993); Coventry (Jul 1997); Fulham (Jan 1998); Stoke (Feb 1998); Cardiff (Feb 2001); Swindon (Jan 2001); Macclesfield (Jul 2001); Hull (Mar 2002)

BOLIVIA (1)

Moreno, Jaime	19 Jan 1974	Santa Cruz	Bol	Middlesbrough (Sep 1994) & (Dec 1997)

Name	DOB	Place of birth	Nat	Club(s) (joined/first played)
BOSNIA-HERZEGOVINA (10)				
Jankovic, Bozo	22 May 1951	Sarajevo (Bos, then Yug)	Yug	Middlesbrough (Feb 1979)
Banovic, Yakka	12 Nov 1956	Bihac (Bos, then Yug)	Aus	Derby (Sep 1980)
Rajkovic, Anto	17 Aug 1952	Sarajevo (Bos, then Yug)	Yug	Swansea (Mar 1981)
Milosevic, Savo	2 Sep 1973	Bijeljina (Bos, then Yug)	Yug	A Villa (Jul 1995)
Mavrak, Darko	19 Jan 1969	Mostar (Bos, then Yug)	Bos	Walsall (Jan 1999)
Konjic, Muhamed	14 May 1970	Tuzla (Bos, then Yug)	Bos	Coventry (Feb 1999)
Stanic, Mario	10 Apr 1972	Sarajevo (Bos, then Yug)	Cro	Chelsea (Jul 2000)
Boksic, Alen	21 Jan 1970	Makarska (Herz, then Yug)	Cro	Middlesbrough (Aug 2000)
Kuduzovic, Fahrudin	10 Oct 1984	Sarajevo (Bos, then Yug)	Bos	Notts Co (Sep 2004)
Koroman, Ognjen	19 Sep 1978	Sarajevo (Bos, then Yug)	SM	Portsmouth (Jan 2006)
BRAZIL (31)				
Laxton, Edward	1896	Brazil	Brit	Norwich (Dec 1919)
Mirandinha, Francisco	2 Jul 1959	Fortaleza	Bra	Newcastle (Aug 1987)
Isaias, Marques	17 Nov 1963	Rio de Janeiro	Por	Coventry (Aug 1995)
Juninho	22 Feb 1973	Sao Paulo	Bra	Middlesbrough (Oct 1995); (Sep 1999); (Aug 2002)
Branco	4 Apr 1964	Bage	Bra	Middlesbrough (Mar 1996)
Emerson	12 Apr 1972	Rio de Janeiro	Bra	Middlesbrough (Jun 1996)
Edinho, Amaral	21 Feb 1967	Brazil	Bra	Bradford (Feb 1997)
Moreira, Fabio	14 Mar 1972	Rio de Janeiro	Bra	Middlesbrough (Feb 1997)
Marcelo	11 Oct 1969	Niteroi	Bra	Sheff Utd (Oct 1997); Birmingham (Oct 1999); Walsall (Feb 2002)
Thome, Emerson	30 Mar 1972	Porto Alegre	Bra	Sheff Wed (Mar 1998); Chelsea (Dec 1999); Sunderland (Sep 2000); Bolton (Aug 2003); Wigan (Aug 2004); Derby (Oct 2005)
Fumaca, Jose	15 Jul 1976	Belem	Bra	Colchester (Mar 1999); C Palace (Sep 1999); Newcastle (Sep 1999)
Miglioranzi, Stefani	20 Sep 1977	Pocos de Caldas	USA	Portsmouth (Jun 1999); Swindon (Aug 2002)
Silvinho, Silvio	12 Apr 1974	Sao Paulo	Bra	Arsenal (Jul 1999)
Di Giuseppe, Bica	12 Mar 1972	Sao Paulo	Bra	Sunderland (Sep 1999); Walsall (Oct 1999)
Edu	16 May 1978	Sao Paulo	Bra	Arsenal (Jan 2001)
Herivelto, Moreira	23 Aug 1975	Tres Rios	Bra	Walsall (Jul 2001)
Duarte, Juan Maldondo	6 Feb 1982	Sao Paulo	Bra	Arsenal (Aug 2001); Millwall (Aug 2003)
Ferrari, Carlos	19 Feb 1979	Londrina	Bra	Birmingham (Aug 2001)
Silva, Gilberto	7 Oct 1976	Lagoa da Prata	Bra	Arsenal (Aug 2002)
Carvalho, Rogerio	28 May 1980	Brazil	Bra	York (Aug 2002)
Gaia, Marcio	8 Sep 1978	Sao Mateus	Bra	Exeter (Aug 2002)
Junior, Jose Luis	15 Jun 1979	Fortaleza	Bra	Walsall (Aug 2002); Derby (Aug 2003); Rotherham (Oct 2004)
Rodrigo, Juliano	7 Aug 1976	Santos	Bra	Everton (Aug 2002)
Doriva, Guidoni	28 May 1972	Landeara	Bra	Middlesbrough (Apr 2003)

Name	DOB	Place of birth	Nat	Club(s) (joined/first played)
Jardel, Mario	18 Sep 1973	Fortaleza	Bra	Bolton (Aug 2003)
Kleberson	19 Jun 1979	Urai	Bra	Man Utd (Aug 2003)
Roque Junior	31 Aug 1976	Santa Rita do Sapucai	Bra	Leeds (Sep 2003)
Vieira, Magno	13 Feb 1985	Brazil	Bra	Northampton (Jan 2004)
Cesar, Julio	18 Nov 1978	Maranhao	Bra	Bolton (Jul 2004)
Rochemback, Fabio	10 Dec 1981	Soledade	Bra	Middlesbrough (Aug 2005)
Basso, Adriano	18 Apr 1975	Jundiai	Bra	Bristol C (Oct 2005)

BULGARIA (4)

Name	DOB	Place of birth	Nat	Club(s) (joined/first played)
Guentchev, Bontcho	7 Jul 1964	Tchoshevo	Bul	Ipswich (Dec 1992); Luton (Aug 1995)
Mikhailov, Bobby	12 Feb 1963	Sofia	Bul	Reading (Sep 1995)
Kishishev, Radostin	30 Jul 1974	Burgas	Bul	Charlton (Aug 2000)
Todorov, Svetoslav	30 Aug 1978	Dobrich	Bul	West Ham (Jan 2001); Portsmouth (Mar 2002)

BURMA (1)

Name	DOB	Place of birth	Nat	Club(s) (joined/first played)
Mitten, Charlie	17 Jan 1921	Rangoon	Brit	Man Utd (Jan 1938); Fulham (Jan 1952); Mansfield (Feb 1956)

CAMEROON (27+3)

Name	DOB	Place of birth	Nat	Club(s) (joined/first played)
Pagal, Jean-Claude	15 Sep 1964	Cameroon	Cam	Carlisle (Feb 1998)
Misse-Misse, Jean-Jacques	7 Aug 1968	Yaounde	Cam	Chesterfield (Mar 1998)
Ipoua, Guy	14 Jan 1976	Douala	Fr	Bristol R (Aug 1998); Scunthorpe (Aug 1999); Gillingham (Mar 2001); Doncaster (Jul 2004); Mansfield (Oct 2004); Lincoln (Feb 2005)
Foe, Marc-Vivien	1 May 1975	Nkolo	Cam	West Ham (Jan 1999); Man City (Aug 2002)
Song, Rigobert	1 Jul 1976	Nkenlicock	Cam	Liverpool (Jan 1999); West Ham (Nov 2000)
Lauren	19 Jan 1977	Lodhji Kribi	Cam	Arsenal (Jun 2000)
Mamoun, Blaise	25 Dec 1979	Bamenda	Cam	Scunthorpe (Aug 2000)
Medou-Otye, Parfait	29 Nov 1976	Ekoundendi	Cam	Kidderminster (Nov 2000)
Suffo, Patrick	17 Jan 1978	Ebolowa	Cam	Sheff Utd (Nov 2000); Coventry (Jul 2003)
Mettomo, Lucien	19 Apr 1977	Douala	Cam	Man City (Sep 2001)
Atangana, Simon	10 Jul 1979	Yaounde	Cam	Port Vale (Jan 2002); Colchester (Nov 2002)
Mboma, Patrick	15 Nov 1970	Douala	Cam	Sunderland (Feb 2002)
Geremi	20 Dec 1978	Batousam	Cam	Middlesbrough (Aug 2002); Chelsea (Jul 2003)
Pericard, Vincent	3 Oct 1982	Efok	Fr	Portsmouth (Aug 2002); Sheff Utd (Sep 2005); Plymouth (Feb 2006)
Wome, Pierre	23 Mar 1979	Douala	Cam	Fulham (Sep 2002)
Djemba-Djemba, Eric	4 May 1981	Douala	Cam	Man Utd (Jul 2003); A Villa (Jan 2005)
Olembe, Saloman	8 Dec 1980	Yaounde	Cam	Leeds (Aug 2003)
Atouba, Thimothee	17 Feb 1982	Douala	Cam	Tottenham (Aug 2004)
Elokobi, George	31 Jan 1986	Douala	Cam	Colchester (Aug 2004); Chester (Jan 2005)
Mbome, Kingsley	21 Nov 1981	Yaounde	Cam	Cambridge (Aug 2004)
Branco, Serge	11 Oct 1980	Douala	Cam	QPR (Sep 2004)
Boumsong, Jean Alain	14 Dec 1979	Douala	Fr	Newcastle (Jan 2005)
Pensee-Bilong, Michel	16 Jun 1973	Yaounde	Cam	MKD (Jan 2005)
Madjo, Guy	1 Jun 1984	Cameroon	Cam	Bristol C (Aug 2005)
Priso, Carl	10 Jul 1979	Yaounde	Fr	Torquay (Aug 2005)
Songo'o, Frank	14 May 1987	Yaounde	Fr	Portsmouth (Sep 2005)
Song Billong, Alexandre	9 Apr 1987	Douala	Cam	Arsenal (Sep 2005)

Other players qualified for Cameroon but born outside Cameroon

Name	DOB	Place of birth	Nat	Club(s) (joined/first played)
Job, Joseph-Desire	1 Dec 1977	Venissieux, Fr	Cam	Middlesbrough (Aug 2000)
Moreau, Fabrice	7 Oct 1967	Paris, Fr	Cam	Notts Co (Mar 2001)

Name	DOB	Place of birth	Nat	Club(s) (joined/first played)
Mezague, Valery	8 Dec 1983	Marseille, Fr	Cam	Portsmouth (Aug 2004)
CANADA (49+4)				
Bowman, Walter W	11 Aug 1870	Waterloo, Ont	Can	Accrington (Aug 1891); Ardwick (Feb 1893)
Dalton, James	c.1865	Ontario	Can	Sunderland (Sep 1891)
Fursdon, Roy	1 Sep 1918	Saskatchewan	Can	Torquay (Aug 1938)
McMahon, Doug	c.1915	Winnipeg	Can	Wolves (Aug 1938)
Whittaker, Fred	12 Oct 1923	Vancouver	Can	Notts Co (Aug 1946)
Killin, Roy	18 Jul 1929	Toronto	Can	Lincoln (Aug 1952)
Kirk, John	13 Mar 1930	Winnipeg	Can	Acc Stanley (Mar 1953)
Burgess, Mike	17 Apr 1932	Montreal	Can	Orient (Jul 1953); Newport (Feb 1956); B&B Ath (Jun 1957); Halifax (Jul 1961); Gillingham (Mar 1963); Aldershot (Nov 1965)
Pidcock, Fred	29 Jun 1933	Canada	Can	Walsall (Sep 1953)
Crossan, Errol	6 Oct 1930	Montreal	Can	Gillingham (Jul 1955); Southend (Aug 1957); Norwich (Sep 1958); Orient (Jan 1961)
Newman, Mick	2 Apr 1932	London, Ont	Can	West Ham (Feb 1957)
Sharp, Ronnie	22 Nov 1932	Montreal	Can	Doncaster (Oct 1958)
Emmerson, Wayne	2 Nov 1947	Canada	Can	Crewe (Jul 1968)
Johnson, Glenn	22 Apr 1951	Vancouver	Can	WBA (Oct 1969)
Twamley, Bruce	23 May 1952	Victoria	Can	Ipswich (Oct 1969)
Lenarduzzi, Bob	1 May 1955	Vancouver	Can	Reading (May 1973)
Nicholl, Jimmy	28 Dec 1956	Hamilton	N Ire	Man Utd (Feb 1974); Sunderland (Dec 1981); WBA (Nov 1984)
Sweetzer, Gordon	27 Jan 1957	Toronto	Can	Brentford (Jul 1975); Cambridge (Apr 1978); Brentford (Jan 1982)
Ferguson, Don	2 Jan 1963	Toronto	Can	Wrexham (Jan 1986)
Kerr, John	6 Mar 1965	Toronto	USA	Portsmouth (Aug 1987); Peterborough (Dec 1987); Millwall (Feb 1993); Walsall (Nov 1995)
Forrest, Craig	20 Sep 1967	Vancouver	Can	Colchester (Mar 1988); Ipswich (Aug 1988); Chelsea (Mar 1997); West Ham (Jul 1997)
Sharp, Kevin	19 Sep 1974	Sarnia, Ont	Can	Leeds (Oct 1992); Wigan Ath (Nov 1995); Wrexham (Oct 2001); Huddersfield (Aug 2002); Scunthorpe (Jun 2003); Shrewsbury (Jul 2005)
Peschisolido, Paul	25 May 1971	Pickering, Ont	Can	Birmingham (Nov 1992); Stoke (1994-95); Birmingham (Mar 1996); WBA (Jul 1996); Fulham (Oct 1997); QPR (Nov 2000); Sheff Utd (Jan 2001); Norwich (Mar 2001); Sheff Utd (Jul 2001); Derby (Mar 2004)
Aunger, Geoff	4 Feb 1968	Red Deer	Can	Luton (Sep 1993); Chester (Dec 1994); Stockport (Dec 1997)
Watson, Mark	8 Sep 1970	Vancouver	Can	Watford (Nov 1993); Oxford (Dec 1998); Oldham (Sep 2000)
Corazzin, Carlo	25 Dec 1971	New Westminster	Can	Cambridge (Dec 1993); Plymouth (Mar 1996); Northampton (Jul 1998); Oldham (Jul 2000)
Brennan, Jim	8 May 1977	Toronto	Can	Bristol C (Oct 1994); Nottm For (Oct 1999); Huddersfield (Mar 2001); Norwich (Jul 2003); Southampton (Jan 2006)
Heald, Oliver	13 Mar 1975	Vancouver	Can	Scarborough (Aug 1995);
De Vos, Jason	2 Jan 1974	Appin, Ont	Can	Darlington (Nov 1996); Wigan Ath (Jul 2001); Ipswich (May 2004)
Nash, Martin	27 Dec 1975	Regina	Can	Stockport (Nov 1996); Chester (Sep 1999); Macclesfield (Jan 2003)

Name	DOB	Place of birth	Nat	Club(s) (joined/first played)
Dickinson, Patrick	6 May 1978	Vancouver	Can	Hull (Jul 1997)
Papaconstantinou, Loukas	10 May 1974	Toronto	Can	Darlington (Jul 1997)
Giumarra, Willy	26 Aug 1971	Ontario	Can	Darlington (Aug 1997)
Larkin, Jim	23 Oct 1975	Ontario	Can	Cambridge (Jan 1998)
Xausa, Davide	10 Mar 1976	Vancouver	Can	Stoke (Feb 1998)
Rogers, Mark	3 Nov 1975	Guelph	Can	Wycombe (Dec 1998)
Dunfield, Terry	20 Feb 1982	Vancouver	Can	Man City (May 1999); Bury (Aug 2002)
Busby, Hubert	18 Jun 1969	Kingston	Can	Oxford (Aug 2000)
Hume, Iain	31 Oct 1983	Brampton	Can	Tranmere (Nov 2000); Leicester (Aug 2005)
Bent, Jason	8 Mar 1977	Bramton	Can	Plymouth (Sep 2001)
Lynch, Simon	19 May 1982	Montreal	Sco	Preston (Jan 2003); Stockport (Dec 2003); Blackpool (Dec 2004)
Hirschfeld, Lars	17 Oct 1978	Edmonton	Can	Luton (Feb 2003); Gillingham (Feb 2004); Leicester (Jan 2005)
Godfrey, Elliott	22 Feb 1983	Toronto	Can	Watford (Mar 2003)
Thompson, Justin	9 Jan 1981	Prince Rupert	Can	Bury (Nov 2003)
Rayner, Simon	8 Jul 1983	Langley	Can	Lincoln (Aug 2004)
Serioux, Adrian	12 May 1979	Scarborough	Can	Millwall (Aug 2004)
Simpson, Josh	15 May 1983	Vancouver	Can	Millwall (Aug 2004)
Stalteri, Paul	18 Oct 1977	Etobicoke	Can	Tottenham (May 2005)
Peters, Jaime	4 May 1987	Pickering, Ont	Can	Ipswich (July 2005)

Other players qualified for Canada but born outside Canada

Bunbury, Alex	18 Jun 1967	Guyana	Can	West Ham (Dec 1992)
Hooper, Lyndon	30 May 1966	Guyana	Can	Birmingham (Sep 1993)
Samuel, Randy	23 Dec 1963	Trinidad	Can	Port Vale (Nov 1995)
Radzinski, Tomasz	14 Dec 1973	Poznan, Pol	Can	Everton (Jul 2001); Fulham (Jul 2004)

CAPE VERDE ISLANDS (0+1)

Qualified for CVI but born outside CVI

Santos, Georges	15 Aug 1970	Marseille	CVI	Tranmere (Jul 1998); WBA (Mar 2000); Sheff Utd (Jul 2000); Grimsby (Oct 2002); Ipswich (Jul 2003); QPR (Jul 2004)

CENTRAL AFRICAN REPUBLIC (1)

Youga, Kelly	22 Sep 1985	Bangui	Fr	Bristol C (Oct 2005)

CHILE (4)

Robledo, George	14 Apr 1926	Iquique	Chi	Barnsley (Apr 1943); Newcastle (Jan 1949)
Robledo, Ted	26 Jul 1928	Iquique	Chi	Barnsley (Mar 1946); Newcastle (Jan 1949); Notts Co (Sep 1957)
Margas, Javier	10 May 1969	Santiago	Chi	West Ham (Aug 1998)
Acuna, Clarence	8 Feb 1975	Coya Rancagua	Chi	Newcastle (Oct 2000)

CHINA (6)

Jihai, Sun	30 Sep 1977	Dalian	Chn	C Palace (Sep 1998); Man City (Feb 2002)
Zhiyi, Fan	22 Jan 1970	Shanghai	Chn	C Palace (Sep 1998); Cardiff (Dec 2002)
Enhua, Zhang	28 Apr 1973	Dalian	Chn	Grimsby (Dec 2000)
Li Tie	18 Sep 1977	Liaoning	Chn	Everton (Aug 2002)
Li Weifeng	26 Jan 1978	Shenzhen	Chn	Everton (Nov 2002)
Haidong, Hao	9 May 1970	Qingdao	Chn	Sheff Utd (Jan 2005)

Name	DOB	Place of birth	Nat	Club(s) (joined/first played)

COLOMBIA (4)

Name	DOB	Place of birth	Nat	Club(s) (joined/first played)
Asprilla, Faustino	10 Nov 1969	Tulua	Col	Newcastle (Feb 1996)
Ricard, Hamilton	12 Jan 1974	Choco	Col	Middlesbrough (Mar 1998)
Angel, Juan Pablo	24 Oct 1975	Medellin	Col	A Villa (Jan 2001)
Viafara, John	27 Oct 1978	Robles	Col	Portsmouth (Jul 2005)

COSTA RICA (2)

Name	DOB	Place of birth	Nat	Club(s) (joined/first played)
Wanchope, Paulo	31 Jan 1976	Heredia	CoRi	Derby (Mar 1997); West Ham (Jul 1999); Man City (Aug 2000)
Solis, Mauricio	13 Dec 1972	Heredia	CoRi	Derby (Mar 1997)

CROATIA (13+3)

Name	DOB	Place of birth	Nat	Club(s) (joined/first played)
Stimac, Igor	6 Sep 1967	Metkovic	Cro	Derby (Oct 1995); West Ham (Sep 1999)
Bilic, Slaven	11 Sep 1968	Split	Cro	West Ham (Feb 1996); Everton (Jul 1997)
Asanovic, Aljosa	14 Dec 1965	Split	Cro	Derby (Jun 1996)
Jerkan, Nikola	8 Dec 1964	Sinj	Cro	Nottm For (Jun 1996)
Maric, Silvio	20 Mar 1975	Zagreb	Cro	Newcastle (Feb 1999)
Suker, Davor	1 Jan 1968	Osijek	Cro	Arsenal (Aug 1999); West Ham (Jul 2000)
Brkovic, Ahmet	23 Sep 1974	Dubrovnik	Cro	Orient (Oct 1999); Luton (Oct 2001)
Strupar, Branko	9 Feb 1970	Zagreb	Bel	Derby (Dec 1999)
Biscan, Igor	4 May 1978	Zagreb	Cro	Liverpool (Dec 2000)
Bunjevcevic, Goran	17 Feb 1973	Karlovac	Yug	Tottenham (Jun 2001)
Balaban, Bosko	15 Oct 1978	Rijeka	Cro	A Villa (Aug 2001)
Zivkovic, Boris	15 Nov 1975	Zivinice	Cro	Portsmouth (Jun 2003)
Mornar, Ivica	12 Jan 1974	Split	Cro	Portsmouth (Jan 2004)

Other players qualified for Croatia but born outside Croatia

Name	DOB	Place of birth	Nat	Club(s) (joined/first played)
Stanic, Mario	10 Apr 1972	Sarajevo, then Yug	Cro	Chelsea (Jul 2000)
Boksic, Alen	21 Jan 1970	Makarska, Herz	Cro	Middlesbrough (Aug 2000)
Prosinecki, Robert	12 Jan 1969	Schweminger, Ger	Cro	Portsmouth (Aug 2001)

CYPRUS (8)

Name	DOB	Place of birth	Nat	Club(s) (joined/first played)
Orhan, Yilmaz	13 Mar 1955	Nicosia	Cyp	West Ham (Oct 1972)
Young, Charlie	14 Feb 1958	Nicosia	Brit	A Villa (Nov 1975); Gillingham (Mar 1978)
Salman, Danis	12 Mar 1960	Famagusta	Eng	Brentford (Aug 1977); Millwall (Aug 1986); Plymouth (Mar 1990); Peterborough (Mar 1992); Torquay (Sep 1992)
Goss, Jerry	11 May 1965	Oekolia	Wal	Norwich (Mar 1983)
Bedrossian, Ara	2 Jun 1967	Nicosia	Cyp	Fulham (Mar 1993)
O'Sullivan, Wayne	25 Feb 1974	Akrotiri	Ire	Swindon (May 1993); Cardiff (Aug 1997); Plymouth (Jul 1999)
Papavasiliou, Nicky	31 Aug 1970	Limassol	Cyp	Newcastle (Jul 1993)
Constantinou, Costas	24 Sep 1968	Limassol	Cyp	Barnet (Oct 1996)

CZECH REPUBLIC (15)

Name	DOB	Place of birth	Nat	Club(s) (joined/first played)
Miklosko, Ludek	9 Dec 1961	Ostrava	CzRep	West Ham (Feb 1990); QPR (Oct 1998)
Stejskal, Jan	15 Jan 1962	Czechoslavakia	CzRep	QPR (Oct 1990)
Srnicek, Pavel	10 Mar 1968	Ostrava	CzRep	Newcastle (Feb 1991); Sheff Wed (Nov 1998); Portsmouth (Sep 2003); West Ham (Feb 2004)
Poborsky, Karel	30 Mar 1972	Jindrihuv-Hradec	CzRep	Man Utd (Jul 1996)
Berger, Patrik	10 Nov 1973	Prague	CzRep	Liverpool (Aug 1996); Portsmouth (Jun 2003); A Villa (Jul 2005)
Smicer, Vladimir	24 May 1973	Decin	CzRep	Liverpool (Jul 1999)
Repka, Tomas	2 Jan 1974	Slavicin Zlin	CzRep	West Ham (Sep 2001)
Baros, Milan	28 Oct 1981	Valassake Mezirici	CzRep	Liverpool (Dec 2001); A Villa (Aug 2005)
Papadopulos, Michal	14 Apr 1985	Ostrava	CzRep	Arsenal (Aug 2003)

Name	DOB	Place of birth	Nat	Club(s) (joined/first played)
Cech, Petr	20 May 1982	Plzen	CzRep	Chelsea (Jun 2004)
Jarosik, Jiri	27 Oct 1977	Usti Nad Lebem	CzRep	Chelsea (Jan 2005); Birmingham (Aug 2005)
Cerny, Radek	18 Feb 1974	Prague	CzRep	Tottenham (Jan 2005)
Kolar, Martin	18 Sep 1983	Prague	CzRep	Stoke (Jul 2005)
Mikolanda, Petr	12 Sep 1984	Prague	CzRep	Northampton (Sep 2005); Swindon (Nov 2005); Rushden (Jan 2006)
Latka, Martin	28 Sep 1984	Prague	CzRep	Birmingham (Jan 2006)

DEMOCRATIC REPUBLIC OF CONGO (Formerly ZAIRE) (21+1)

Name	DOB	Place of birth	Nat	Club(s) (joined/first played)
Kandol, Tresor	30 Aug 1981	Banga	Brit	Luton (Sep 1998); Cambridge (Aug 2001); Bournemouth (Oct 2001); Darlington (Nov 2005); Barnet (Jan 2006)
Lua-Lua, Lomana	28 Dec 1980	Kinshasa	DRC	Colchester (Sep 1998); Newcastle (Sep 2000); Portsmouth (Feb 2004)
Smeets, Axel	12 Jul 1974	Karawa	Bel	Sheff Utd (Jul 1999)
Bolima, Cedric	26 Sep 1979	Kinshasa	DRC	Rotherham (Oct 2000)
Itonga, Carlin	11 Dec 1982	Kinshasa	DRC	Arsenal (Aug 2001)
M'Bombo, Doudou	11 Sep 1980	Kinshasa	DRC	QPR (Aug 2001); Oxford (Jan 2005)
Yulu, Christian	26 Jan 1978	Kinshasa	Fr	Coventry (Feb 2003)
Zakuani, Gaby	31 May 1986	Kinshasa	DRC	Orient (Mar 2003)
Kangana, Ndiwa	28 Feb 1984	Kinshasa	DRC	Oldham (Jul 2003); Rochdale (Feb 2004)
Zola, Calvin	31 Dec 1984	Kinshasa	DRC	Oldham (Aug 2003); Tranmere (May 2004)
Makelele, Claude	18 Feb 1973	Kinshasa	Fr	Chelsea (Sep 2003)
N'Dumbu-Nsungu, Guylain	26 Dec 1982	Kinshasa	DRC	Sheff Wed (Sep 2003); Preston (Sep 2004); Colchester (Jan 2005); Darlington (Aug 2005); Cardiff (Jan 2006)
Manangu, Eric	9 Sep 1985	Kinshasa	DRC	Rushden (Nov 2003)
N'Toya, Tcham	3 Nov 1983	Kinshasa	Fr	Chesterfield (Mar 2004); Oxford (Mar 2006)
Makofo, Serge	3 Sep 1986	Kinshasa	DRC	MKD (Nov 2004)
Musampa, Kiki	20 Jul 1977	Kinshasa	DRC	Man City (Jan 2005)
Lambu, Goma	10 Nov 1984	Kinshasa	DRC	Mansfield (Feb 2005)
Kanyuka, Patrick	19 Jul 1987	Kinshasa	DRC	QPR (Apr 2005)
Kamudimba, Jean-Paul	16 Mar 1982	Luashi	DRC	Grimsby (Jul 2005)
Mbuyi, Gabriel	1 Jun 1982	Kinshasa	Bel	Stoke (Jul 2005)
Muamba, Fabrice	6 Apr 1988	Kinshasa	Eng	Arsenal (Jul 2005)

Other players qualified for DRC but born outside DRC

Name	DOB	Place of birth	Nat	Club(s) (joined/first played)
Ngonge, Michel	10 Jan 1967	Huy, Bel	DRC	Watford (Jul 1998); Huddersfield (Mar 2000); QPR (Dec 2000)

DENMARK (99+4)

Name	DOB	Place of birth	Nat	Club(s) (joined/first played)
Middleboe, Nils	5 Oct 1887	Copenhagen	Den	Chelsea (Nov 1913)
Hansen, Edvin	21 Jan 1920	Koge	Den	Grimsby (Dec 1946)
Jensen, Viggo	29 Mar 1921	Skagen	Den	Hull (Oct 1948)
Arentoft, Ben	1 Nov 1942	Copenhagen	Den	Newcastle (Mar 1969); Blackburn (Sep 1971)
Thorup, Borge	4 Oct 1943	Copenhagen	Den	C Palace (Mar 1969)
Bartram, Per	8 Jan 1944	Odense	Den	C Palace (Aug 1969)
Jacobsen, Viggo	11 Aug 1953	Denmark	Den	Charlton (Nov 1979)
Ostergaard, Johnny	6 Feb 1955	Denmark	Den	Charlton (Nov 1979)
Simonsen, Allan	15 Dec 1952	Vejle	Den	Charlton (Nov 1982)
Olsen, Jesper	20 Mar 1961	Fakse	Den	Man Utd (Jul 1984)
Molby, Jan	4 Jul 1963	Kolding	Den	Liverpool (Aug 1984); Barnsley (Sep 1995); Norwich (Dec 1995); Swansea (Feb 1996)
Christensen, Tommy	20 Jul 1961	Aarhus	Den	Leicester (Nov 1985); Portsmouth (Nov 1985)
Bakholt, Kurt	12 Aug 1963	Odense	Den	QPR (Jan 1986)

Name	DOB	Place of birth	Nat	Club(s) (joined/first played)
Sivebaek, John	25 Oct 1961	Vejle	Den	Man Utd (Feb 1986)
Pingel, Frank	9 May 1964	Resskov	Den	Newcastle (Jan 1989)
Kristensen, Bjorn	10 Oct 1963	Malling	Den	Newcastle (Mar 1989); Bristol C (Mar 1993); Portsmouth (Nov 1992)
Nielsen, Kent	28 Dec 1961	Frederiksberg	Den	A Villa (Jun 1989)
Elstrup, Lars	24 Mar 1963	Rarby	Den	Luton (Aug 1989)
Mortensen, Henrik	12 Feb 1968	Odder	Den	Norwich (Oct 1989)
Schmeichel, Peter	18 Nov 1968	Gladsaxe	Den	Man Utd (Aug 1991); A Villa (Jul 2001); Man City (Aug 2002)
Lydersen, Pal	10 Sep 1965	Odense	Nor	Arsenal (Nov 1991)
Jensen, John	3 May 1965	Copenhagen	Den	Arsenal (Aug 1992)
Piechnik, Torben	21 May 1963	Copenhagen	Den	Liverpool (Sep 1992)
Rieper, Marc	5 Jun 1968	Rodoure	Den	West Ham (Jun 1994)
Thomsen, Claus	31 May 1970	Aarhus	Den	Ipswich (Jun 1994); Everton (Jan 1997)
Ekelund, Ronnie	21 Aug 1972	Glostrup	Den	Southampton (Sep 1994); Coventry (Dec 1995); Man City (Dec 1995); Walsall (Dec 2000)
Vilstrup, Johnny	27 Feb 1969	Copenhagen	Den	Luton (Sep 1995)
Haddaoui, Riffi	24 Mar 1971	Copenhagen	Den	Torquay (Mar 1996)
Laursen, Jacob	6 Oct 1971	Vejle	Den	Derby (Jul 1996); Leicester (Jan 2002)
Frandsen, Per	6 Feb 1970	Copenhagen	Den	Bolton (Aug 1996); Blackburn (Sep 1999); Bolton (Jul 2000); Wigan (Jun 2004)
Gall, Benny	14 Mar 1971	Copenhagen	Den	Shrewsbury (Aug 1996)
Johansen, Michael	22 Jul 1972	Golstrup	Den	Bolton (Aug 1996)
Nielsen, Tommy	25 Mar 1972	Aarhus	Den	Shrewsbury (Aug 1996)
Beck, Mikkel	12 May 1973	Aarhus	Den	Middlesbrough (Sep 1996); Derby (Mar 1999); Nottm For (Nov 1999); QPR (Feb 2000)
Nielsen, Allan	13 Mar 1971	Esbjerg	Den	Tottenham (Sep 1996); Wolves (Mar 2000); Watford (Aug 2000)
Nielsen, John	7 Apr 1972	Aarhus	Den	Southend (Sep 1996)
Dursun, Peter	8 Jan 1975	Aarhus	Den	Southend (Nov 1996)
Pedersen, Per	30 Mar 1969	Aalborg	Den	Blackburn (Feb 1997)
Willer-Jensen, Thomas	19 Sep 1968	Copenhagen	Den	Swansea (Mar 1997)
Johansen, Martin	22 Jul 1972	Golstrup	Den	Coventry (Jun 1997)
Tomasson, Jon Dahl	29 Aug 1976	Copenhagen	Den	Newcastle (Jun 1997)
Koogi, Anders	8 Sep 1979	Roskilde	Den	Peterborough (Jul 1997)
Nielsen, Martin	24 Mar 1973	Aarhus	Den	Huddersfield (Mar 1998)
Andersen, Soren	31 Jan 1970	Aarhus	Den	Bristol C (Jul 1998)
Jensen, Claus	29 Apr 1977	Nykobing	Den	Bolton (Jul 1998); Charlton (Jul 2000); Fulham (Jul 2004)
Sorensen, Thomas	12 Jun 1976	Fredericia	Den	Sunderland (Aug 1998); A Villa (Aug 2003)
Thogersen, Thomas	2 Apr 1968	Copenhagen	Den	Portsmouth (Aug 1998); Walsall (Oct 2001)
Dabelsteen, Thomas	6 Mar 1973	Copenhagen	Den	Scarborough (Nov 1998)
Goldbaek, Bjarne	6 Oct 1968	Nykobing Falster	Den	Chelsea (Nov 1998); Fulham (Jan 2000)
Andersen, Bo	26 Mar 1976	Slagelse	Den	Bristol C (Dec 1998)
Degn, Peter	6 Apr 1977	Aarhus	Den	Everton (Feb 1999)
Hansen, Bo	16 Jun 1972	Jutland	Den	Bolton (Feb 1999)
Fredgaard, Carsten	20 May 1976	Hillesod	Den	Sunderland (Jul 1999); WBA (Feb 2000); Bolton (Nov 2000)
Hogh, Jes	7 May 1966	Aalborg	Den	Chelsea (Jul 1999)
Hyldgaard, Morten	26 Jan 1978	Herning	Den	Coventry (Jul 1999); Scunthorpe (Jan 2000); Coventry (Aug 2002); Luton (Jan 2004)
Jorgensen, Claus	27 Apr 1976	Holstebro	Den	Bournemouth (Jul 1999); Bradford (Jul 2001);

Name	DOB	Place of birth	Nat	Club(s) (joined/first played)
				Coventry (Aug 2003); Bournemouth (Jan 2004)
Skovbjerg, Thomas	25 Oct 1974	Esbjerg	Den	Kidderminster (Aug 1999)
Hjorth, Jesper	3 Apr 1975	Odense	Den	Darlington (Nov 1999)
Jensen, Brian	8 Jun 1975	Copenhagen	Den	WBA (Mar 2000); Burnley (Jun 2003)
Nedergaard, Steen	25 Feb 1970	Aalborg	Den	Norwich (Jul 2000)
Gravesen, Thomas	11 Mar 1976	Vejle	Den	Everton (Aug 2000)
Heiselberg, Kim	21 Sep 1977	Tarm	Den	Swindon (Aug 2000)
Risom, Henrik	24 Jul 1968	Vildbjerg	Den	Stoke (Aug 2000)
Svard, Sebastian	15 Jan 1983	Hvidovre	Den	Arsenal (Aug 2000); Stoke (Dec 2003)
Jorgensen, Henrik	12 Jan 1979	Bogense	Den	Notts Co (Oct 2000)
Nielsen, David	1 Dec 1976	Sonderberg	Den	Grimsby (Oct 2000); Wimbledon (Mar 2001); Norwich (Dec 2001)
Bidstrup, Stefan	24 Feb 1975	Helsinger	Den	Wigan Ath (Nov 2000)
Gronkjaer, Jesper	12 Aug 1977	Nuuk	Den	Chelsea (Dec 2000); Birmingham (Jul 2004)
Moller, Peter	23 Mar 1972	Gistrup	Den	Fulham (Jan 2001)
Johnsson, Julian	24 Feb 1975	Denmark	Far	Hull (Jun 2001)
Pedersen, Henrik	10 Jun 1975	Copenhagen	Den	Bolton (Jul 2001)
Gaardsoe, Thomas	23 Nov 1979	Randers	Den	Ipswich (Aug 2001); WBA (Jul 2003)
Sand, Peter	19 Jul 1972	Aalborg	Den	Barnsley (Oct 2001)
Henriksen, Bo	7 Feb 1975	Roskilde	Den	Kidderminster (Nov 2001); Bristol R (Mar 2004)
Jensen, Niclas	17 Aug 1974	Copenhagen	Den	Man City (Jan 2002); Fulham (Jul 2005)
Tofting, Stig	14 Aug 1969	Aarhus	Den	Bolton (Feb 2002)
Ellegaard, Kevin	23 May 1983	Charlottenlund	Den	Man City (Jul 2002); Blackpool (Jan 2005)
Bischoff, Mikkel	3 Mar 1982	Copenhagen	Den	Man City (Sep 2002); Wolves (Sep 2004); Sheff Wed (Mar 2006)
Timm, Mads	31 Oct 1984	Odense	Den	Man Utd (Oct 2002); Walsall (Jan 2006)
Christiansen, Jesper	18 Jun 1980	Odense	Den	Kidderminster (Jan 2003)
Skoubo, Morten	30 Jun 1980	Holstebro	Den	WBA (Jan 2004)
Olsen, Kim	11 Feb 1979	Herning	Den	Sheff Wed (Feb 2004)
Andersen, Stephan	26 Nov 1981	Copenhagen	Den	Charlton (May 2004)
Laursen, Martin	26 Jul 1977	Silkeborg	Den	A Villa (May 2004)
Albrechtsen, Martin	31 Mar 1980	Copenhagen	Den	WBA (Jun 2004)
Bisgaard, Morten	25 Jun 1975	Randers	Den	Derby (Jun 2004)
Dakinah, Kofi	1 Feb 1980	Copenhagen	Den	Walsall (Jul 2004)
Helveg, Thomas	24 Jun 1971	Odense	Den	Norwich (Jul 2004)
Rommedahl, Dennis	22 Jul 1978	Copenhagen	Den	Charlton (Jul 2004)
Budtz, Jan	20 Apr 1979	Frederiksborg	Den	Doncaster (May 2005)
Kroldrup, Per	31 Jul 1979	Farso	Den	Everton (Jun 2005)
Nygaard, Marc	1 Sep 1976	Copenhagen	Den	QPR (Jul 2005)
Pedersen, Rune	9 Oct 1979	Copenhagen	Den	Nottm For (Jul 2005)
Priske, Brian	14 May 1977	Stensballe	Den	Portsmouth (Aug 2005)
Bendtner, Nicklas	16 Jan 1988	Copenhagen	Den	Arsenal (Oct 2005)
Agger, Daniel	12 Dec 1984	Hvidovre	Den	Liverpool (Jan 2006)
Madsen, Peter	26 Apr 1978	Roskilde	Den	Southampton (Jan 2006)
Schmeichel, Kasper	5 Nov 1985	Copenhagen	Den	Darlington (Jan 2006); Bury (Feb 2006)
Youssouf, Sammy	7 Sep 1976	Copenhagen	Den	QPR (Jan 2006)

Other players qualified for Denmark but born outside Denmark

Name	DOB	Place of birth	Nat	Club(s) (joined/first played)
Kjeldbjerg, Jakob	21 Oct 1969	Fredrikstad, Nor	Den	Chelsea (Aug 1993)
Melvang, Lars	3 Apr 1969	Seattle, USA	Den	Watford (Aug 1997)
Laudrup, Brian	22 Feb 1969	Vienna, Aut	Den	Chelsea (Jun 1998)
Hansen, John	17 Sep 1973	Mannheim, Ger	Den	Cambridge (Feb 2000)

Name	DOB	Place of birth	Nat	Club(s) (joined/first played)
DOMINICA (2)				
Cooke, Joe	15 Feb 1955	Dominica	Dom	Bradford (May 1972); Peterborough (Jan 1979); Oxford (Aug 1979); Exeter (Jun 1981); Bradford (Jan 1982); Rochdale (Jul 1984); Wrexham (Jul 1986)
Henry, Liburd	29 Aug 1967	Roseau	Dom	Watford (Nov 1987); Halifax (Sep 1988); Maidstone Utd (Jun 1990); Gillingham (Jun 1992); Peterborough (Aug 1994)
ECUADOR (3)				
Delgado, Agustin	23 Dec 1974	Ibarra	Ecu	Southampton (Nov 2001)
De La Cruz, Ulises	2 Aug 1974	Piqulucho	Ecu	A Villa (Aug 2002)
Kaviedes, Ivan	24 Oct 1977	Santo Domingo	Ecu	C Palace (Aug 2004)
EGYPT (4)				
Hegazi, Hassan	14 Sep 1891	Cairo	Egy	Fulham (Nov 1911)
Abdallah, Tewfik	23 Jun 1897	Cairo	Egy	Derby (Sep 1920); Hartlepools (Mar 1924)
Georgeson, Roddy	31 Jul 1948	Shubra	Brit	Port Vale (Jan 1966)
Mido	23 Feb 1983	Cairo	Egy	Tottenham (Jan 2005)
ESTONIA (1)				
Poom, Mart	3 Feb 1972	Tallinn	Est	Portsmouth (Aug 1994); Derby (Mar 1997); Sunderland (Apr 2003)
FAROES (0+1)				
Qualified for the Faroes but born outside the Faroes				
Johnsson, Julian	24 Feb 1975	Denmark	Far	Hull (Jun 2001)
FINLAND (31+5)				
Rintanen, Mauno	28 Apr 1925	Helsinki	Fin	Hull (Sep 1956)
Jantunen, Pertti	25 Jun 1952	Lahti	Fin	Bristol C (Mar 1979)
Lahtinen, Aki	31 Oct 1958	Oulu	Fin	Notts Co (Sep 1981)
Rantanen, Jari	31 Dec 1961	Helsinki	Fin	Leicester (Sep 1987)
Paatelainen, Mixu	3 Feb 1967	Helsinki	Fin	Bolton (Jul 1994); Wolves (Aug 1997)
Moilanen, Tepi	12 Dec 1973	Oulu	Fin	Preston (Dec 1995); Scarborough (Dec 1996); Darlington (Jan 1997)
Kottila, Mika	22 Sep 1974	Helsinki	Fin	Hereford (Nov 1996)
Vanhala, Jari	29 Aug 1965	Helsinki	Fin	Bradford (Dec 1996)
Jaaskelainen, Jussi	17 Apr 1975	Mikkeli	Fin	Bolton (Nov 1997)
Heinola, Antti	20 Mar 1973	Helsinki	Fin	QPR (Jan 1998)
Enckelman, Peter	10 Mar 1977	Turku	Fin	A Villa (Feb 1999); Blackburn (Jan 2004)
Viljanen, Ville	2 Feb 1971	Helsinki	Fin	Port Vale (Feb 1999)
Hyypia, Sami	7 Oct 1973	Porvoo	Fin	Liverpool (Jul 1999)
Vanninen, Jukka	31 Jan 1977	Riihimaki	Fin	Exeter (Dec 1999)
Valakari, Simo	28 Apr 1973	Helsinki	Fin	Derby (Jul 2000)
Wiss, Jarkko	17 Apr 1972	Tampere	Fin	Stockport (Aug 2000)
Tuomela, Marko	3 Mar 1972	Helsinki	Fin	Swindon (Sep 2000)
Helin, Petri	13 Dec 1969	Helsinki	Fin	Luton (Nov 2000); Stockport (Jul 2001)
Salli, Janne	14 Dec 1977	Seinajoki	Fin	Barnsley (Nov 2000)
Tihinen, Hannu	1 Jul 1976	Keminmaa	Fin	West Ham (Dec 2000)
Litmanen, Jari	20 Feb 1971	Lahti	Fin	Liverpool (Jan 2001)
Pilvi, Tero	21 Feb 1976	Vihti	Fin	Cambridge (Mar 2001)
Riihilahti, Aki	9 Sep 1976	Helsinki	Fin	C Palace (Mar 2001)
Viander, Jani	18 Aug 1975	Tuusula	Fin	Bolton (Nov 2001)
Niemi, Antti	31 May 1972	Oulu	Fin	Southampton (Sep 2002); Fulham (Jan 2006)

Name	DOB	Place of birth	Nat	Club(s) (joined/first played)
Petrescu, Tomi	24 Jul 1986	Jyvaskyla	Fin	Leicester (May 2003)
Pasanen, Petri	24 Sep 1980	Lahti	Fin	Portsmouth (Jan 2004)
Kolkka, Joonas	28 Sep 1974	Lahti	Fin	C Palace (Jul 2004)
Koskela, Toni	16 Mar 1983	Helsinki	Fin	Cardiff (Feb 2005)
Tainio, Teemu	27 Nov 1979	Tornio	Fin	Tottenham (Jul 2005)
Kopteff, Peter	10 Apr 1979	Helsinki	Fin	Stoke (Jan 2006)

Other players qualified for Finland but born outside Finland

Name	DOB	Place of birth	Nat	Club(s) (joined/first played)
Forssell, Mikael	15 Mar 1981	Steinfurt, Ger	Fin	Chelsea (Dec 1998); C Palace (Feb 2000); Birmingham (Aug 2003)
Johansson, Jonatan	16 Aug 1975	Stockholm, Swe	Fin	Charlton (Aug 2000); Norwich (Jan 2006)
Kuqi, Shefki	10 Nov 1976	Vuqitern, Kosovo	Alb/Fin	Stockport (Jan 2001); Sheff Wed (Jan 2002); Ipswich (Sep 2003); Blackburn (Jun 2005)
Heikkinen, Markus	13 Oct 1978	Katrineholm, Swe	Fin	Portsmouth (Feb 2003); Luton (Jul 2005)
Kuqi, Njazi	25 Mar 1983	Vushtrri, Alb	Alb/Fin	Blackpool (Jan 2006); Peterborough (Mar 2006)

FRANCE (209+38)

Name	DOB	Place of birth	Nat	Club(s) (joined/first played)
Langenove, Eugene	1898	Paris	Fr	Walsall (Oct 1922)
Praski, Josef	22 Jan 1926	France	Fr	Notts Co (Mar 1949)
Six, Didier	21 Aug 1954	Lille	Fr	A Villa (Oct 1984)
Bernardeau, Olivier	19 Aug 1962	Bourges	Fr	Chesterfield (Aug 1986)
Cantona, Eric	24 May 1966	Nimes	Fr	Leeds (Feb 1992); Man Utd (Nov 1992)
Cantona, Joel	26 Oct 1967	Paris	Fr	Stockport (Mar 1994)
Ginola, David	25 Jan 1967	Gossin	Fr	Newcastle (Jul 1995); Tottenham (Jul 1997); A Villa (Aug 2000); Everton (Feb 2002)
Rolling, Franck	23 Aug 1968	Colmar	Fr	Leicester (Sep 1995); Bournemouth (Aug 1997); Gillingham (Sep 1998)
Prunier, William	14 Aug 1967	Montreuil	Fr	Man Utd (Dec 1995)
Leboeuf, Frank	22 Jan 1968	Marseille	Fr	Chelsea (Jul 1996)
Darras, Frederic	19 Aug 1966	Calais	Fr	Swindon (Aug 1996)
Garde, Remi	3 Apr 1966	L'Arbresle	Fr	Arsenal (Aug 1996)
Perez, Lionel	24 Apr 1967	Bagnols Ceze	Fr	Sunderland (Aug 1996); Scunthorpe (Oct 1999); Cambridge (Jun 2000)
Pounewatchy, Stephane	10 Feb 1968	Paris	Fr	Carlisle (Aug 1996); Port Vale (Aug 1998); Colchester (Feb 1999)
Romano, Serge	25 May 1964	Metz	Fr	Wolves (Aug 1996)
Barbara, Daniel	12 Oct 1974	France	Fr	Darlington (Dec 1996)
Anelka, Nicolas	14 Mar 1979	Versailles	Fr	Arsenal (Mar 1997); Liverpool (Dec 2001); Man City (Aug 2002)
Laurent, Pierre	13 Dec 1970	Tulle	Fr	Leeds (Mar 1997)
Blondeau, Patrick	27 Jan 1968	Marseille	Fr	Sheff Wed (Jun 1997); Watford (Jul 2001)
Grimandi, Gilles	11 Nov 1970	Gap	Fr	Arsenal (Jun 1997)
Petit, Emmanuel	22 Sep 1970	Dieppe	Fr	Arsenal (Jun 1997); Chelsea (Jul 2001)
Terrier, David	4 Aug 1973	Verdun	Fr	West Ham (Jun 1997)
Valery, Patrick	3 Jul 1969	Brignoles	Fr	Blackburn (Jun 1997)
Bonalair, Thierry	14 Jun 1966	Paris	Fr	Nottm For (Jul 1997)
Remy, Christophe	6 Aug 1971	Besancon	Fr	Oxford (Jul 1997)
Cuervo, Phillipe	13 Aug 1969	Ris-Orangis	Fr	Swindon (Aug 1997)
Peron, Jeff	11 Oct 1965	St Omer	Fr	Walsall (Aug 1997); Portsmouth (Sep 1998); Wigan Ath (Nov 1999)
Coulbault, Regis	12 Aug 1972	Brignoles	Fr	Southend (Oct 1997)
Croci, Laurent	8 Feb 1964	Montbeliard	Fr	Carlisle (Oct 1997)
Lama, Bernard	7 Apr 1963	St-Symphorien	Fr	West Ham (Dec 1997)

Name	DOB	Place of birth	Nat	Club(s) (joined/first played)
Madar, Mickael	8 May 1968	Paris	Fr	Everton (Dec 1997)
Charvet, Laurent	8 May 1973	Beziers	Fr	Chelsea (Jan 1998); Newcastle (Jul 1998); Man City (Oct 2000)
Ismael, Valerien	28 Sep 1975	Strasbourg	Fr	C Palace (Jan 1998)
Sissoko, Habib	24 May 1971	Juvisy-sur-Orge	Fr	Preston (Feb 1998); Torquay (Aug 2000)
Eydelie, Jean-Jacques	3 Feb 1966	Angouleme	Fr	Walsall (Mar 1998)
Tholot, Didier	2 Apr 1964	Feurs	Fr	Walsall (Mar 1998)
Dacourt, Olivier	25 Sep 1974	Montreuil-sous-Bois	Fr	Everton (Jun 1998); Leeds (Jul 2000)
D'Jaffo, Laurent	5 Nov 1970	Bazas	Fr	Bury (Jul 1998); Stockport (Aug 1999); Sheff Utd (Feb 2000); Mansfield (Mar 2004)
Grondin, David	8 May 1980	Paris	Fr	Arsenal (Jul 1998)
Guivarc'h, Stephane	6 Sep 1970	Concameau	Fr	Newcastle (Jul 1998)
Keller, Marc	14 Jan 1968	Colmar	Fr	West Ham (Jul 1998); Blackburn (Jan 2001); Portsmouth (Sep 2000)
Perez, Sebastien	24 Nov 1973	Saint-Chamond	Fr	Blackburn (Jul 1998)
Santos, Georges	15 Aug 1970	Marseille	CVl	Tranmere (Jul 1998); WBA (Mar 2000); Sheff Utd (Jul 2000); Grimsby (Oct 2002); Ipswich (Jul 2003); QPR (Jul 2004)
Wallemme, Jean-Guy	10 Aug 1967	Naubeuge	Fr	Coventry (Jul 1998)
Bacque, Herve	13 Jul 1976	Bordeaux	Fr	Luton (Aug 1998)
Leoni, Stephane	1 Sep 1976	Metz	Fr	Bristol R (Aug 1998)
Mirankov, Alex	2 Dec 1967	Grenoble	Fr	Scarborough (Aug 1998)
Garcia, Tony	18 Mar 1972	Pierre Patte	Fr	Notts Co (Sep 1998)
Louis-Jean, Mathieu	22 Feb 1976	Mont St Aignan	Fr	Nottm For (Sep 1998); Norwich (Jun 2005)
Thetis, Manuel	5 Nov 1971	Dijon	Fr	Ipswich (Sep 1998); Wolves (Aug 2000); Sheff Utd (Mar 2001)
Simba, Amara	23 Dec 1961	Paris	Fr	Orient (Oct 1998)
Bonnot, Alex	31 Jul 1973	Boissy	Fr	Watford (Nov 1998); QPR (Aug 2001)
Horlaville, Christophe	1 Mar 1969	Rouen	Fr	Port Vale (Nov 1998)
Colleter, Patrick	6 Nov 1965	Brest	Fr	Southampton (Dec 1998)
Ferri, Jean-Michel	7 Feb 1969	Lyon	Fr	Liverpool (Dec 1998)
Keller, Francois	27 Oct 1973	Colmar	Fr	Fulham (Dec 1998)
L'Helgoualch, Cyrille	25 Sep 1970	St Nazaire	Fr	Mansfield (Dec 1998)
Diawara, Kaba	16 Dec 1975	Toulon	Fr	Arsenal (Jan 1999); Blackburn (Aug 2000); West Ham (Sep 2000)
Domi, Didier	2 May 1979	Sarcelles	Fr	Newcastle (Jan 1999); Leeds (Aug 2003)
Saha, Louis	8 Aug 1978	Paris	Fr	Newcastle (Jan 1999); Fulham (Jun 2000); Man Utd (Jan 2004)
Traore, Djimi	1 Mar 1980	St Ouen	Fr	Liverpool (Feb 1999)
Germain, Steve	22 Jun 1981	Cannes	Fr	Colchester (Mar 1999)
Huck, Willie	11 Mar 1979	Paris	Fr	Bournemouth (Mar 1999)
Richard, Fabrice	16 Aug 1973	Saintes	Fr	Colchester (Mar 1999)
Simb, Jean-Pierre	4 Sep 1974	Paris	Fr	Torquay (Mar 1999)
Anselin, Cedric	24 Jul 1977	Lens	Fr	Norwich (Apr 1999); Cambridge (Nov 2004)
Deschamps, Didier	15 Oct 1968	Bayonne	Fr	Chelsea (Jun 1999)
Dumas, Franck	9 Jan 1968	Bayeux	Fr	Newcastle (Jun 1999)
De Blasiis, Jean-Yves	25 Sep 1973	Bordeaux	Fr	Norwich (Jul 1999)
Diaf, Farid	19 Apr 1971	Carcassonne	Fr	Preston (Jul 1999)
Goma, Alain	5 Oct 1972	Sault	Fr	Newcastle (Jul 1999); Fulham (Mar 2001)
Luntala, Tresor	31 May 1982	Dreux	Fr	Birmingham (Jul 1999)
Pinault, Thomas	4 Dec 1981	Grasse	Fr	Colchester (Jul 1999); Grimsby (Jul 2004)
Henry, Thierry	17 Aug 1977	Paris	Fr	Arsenal (Aug 1999)

Name	DOB	Place of birth	Nat	Club(s) (joined/first played)
Roy, Eric	26 Sep 1967	Nice	Fr	Sunderland (Aug 1999)
Pamarot, Noe	14 Apr 1979	Paris	Fr	Portsmouth (Sep 1999); Tottenham (Aug 2004); Portsmouth (Jan 2006)
Pollet, Ludo	18 Jun 1970	Vieux-Conde	Fr	Wolves (Sep 1999); Walsall (Nov 2002)
Rodriguez, Bruno	25 Dec 1972	Bastia	Fr	Bradford (Sep 1999)
Silvestre, Mickael	9 Aug 1977	Chambray-les-Tours	Fr	Man Utd (Sep 1999)
Bossu, Bert	14 Oct 1980	Calais	Fr	Barnet (Oct 1999); Gillingham (Sep 2003); Torquay (Aug 2004); Oldham (Oct 2004); Darlington (Aug 2005)
Fradin, Karim	2 Feb 1972	St Martin d'Hyeres	Fr	Stockport (Nov 1999)
Gravelaine, Xavier	5 Oct 1968	Tours	Fr	Watford (Nov 1999)
Passi, Franck	28 Mar 1966	Bergerac	Fr	Bolton (Nov 1999)
Kaprielian, Mickael	6 Oct 1980	Marseille	Fr	Bolton (Jan 2000)
Aliadiere, Jeremie	30 Mar 1983	Rambouillet	Fr	Arsenal (Mar 2000); West Ham (Aug 2005); Wolves (Jan 2006)
Kanoute, Frederic	2 Sep 1977	Sainte Foy-les-Lyon	Mli	West Ham (Mar 2000); Tottenham (Aug 2003)
Barthez, Fabien	28 Jun 1971	Lavelanet	Fr	Man Utd (Jun 2000)
Diomede, Bernard	23 Jan 1974	Saint-Douichard	Fr	Liverpool (Jul 2000)
Pires, Robert	29 Oct 1973	Reims	Fr	Arsenal (Jul 2000)
Bassila, Christian	5 Oct 1977	Paris	Fr	West Ham (Aug 2000); Sunderland (Aug 2005)
Bouanane, Emad	22 Nov 1976	Paris	Fr	Wrexham (Aug 2000)
Fernandes, Fabrice	29 Oct 1979	Aubervilliers	Fr	Fulham (Aug 2000); Southampton (Dec 2001); Bolton (Aug 2005)
Javary, Jean-Phillipe	10 Jan 1978	Montpelier	Fr	Brentford (Aug 2000); Plymouth (Feb 2001); Sheff Utd (Mar 2002)
Job, Joseph-Desire	1 Dec 1977	Venissieux	Cam	Middlesbrough (Aug 2000)
Mawene, Youl	16 Jul 1979	Caen	Fr	Derby (Aug 2000); Preston (Jul 2004)
Menetrier, Mickael	23 Sep 1978	Reims	Fr	Bournemouth (Aug 2000)
Weber, Nicolas	28 Oct 1970	Metz	Fr	Sheff Utd (Aug 2000)
Wiltord, Sylvain	10 May 1974	Neuilly-sur-Marne	Fr	Arsenal (Aug 2000)
Dagnogo, Moussa	30 Jan 1972	Paris	Fr	Bristol R (Sep 2000)
Lemarchand, Stephane	6 Aug 1971	Saint-Lo	Fr	Carlisle (Sep 2000); Rotherham (Nov 2000)
Vignal, Gregory	19 Jul 1981	Montpelier	Fr	Liverpool (Sep 2000); Portsmouth (Jul 2005)
Zeghdane, Lehit	3 Oct 1977	Revin	Fr	Darlington (Sep 2000)
Bernard, Olivier	14 Oct 1979	Paris	Fr	Newcastle (Oct 2000); Darlington (Mar 2001); Southampton (Jan 2005)
Cadiou, Frederic	20 Apr 1969	Paris	Fr	Orient (Oct 2000)
Romo, David	7 Aug 1978	Nimes	Fr	Swansea (Oct 2000)
Sahnoun, Nicolas	3 Sep 1980	Bordeaux	Fr	Fulham (Oct 2000)
Friio, David	17 Feb 1973	Thionville	Fr	Plymouth (Nov 2000), Nottm For (Feb 2005)
Larrieu, Romain	31 Aug 1976	Mont-de-Marsan	Fr	Plymouth (Nov 2000)
Martin, Lilian	28 May 1971	Valreas	Fr	Derby (Nov 2000)
Schemmel, Sebastien	2 Jun 1975	Nancy	Fr	West Ham (Jan 2001); Portsmouth (Aug 2003)
Vasseur, Emmanuel	3 Sep 1976	Calais	Fr	Orient (Jan 2001)
Fabiano, Nicolas	8 Feb 1981	Courbevoie	Fr	Swansea (Feb 2001)
Opinel, Sacha	9 Apr 1977	Bourg-Saint-Maurice	Fr	Orient (Feb 2001)
Verschave, Matthias	24 Dec 1977	Lille	Fr	Swansea (Feb 2001)
Carteron, Patrice	30 Jul 1970	St Brieux	Fr	Sunderland (Mar 2001)
Cau, Jean-Michel	27 Oct 1980	Ajaccio	Fr	Darlington (Mar 2001)
Epesse-Titi, Steeve	5 Sep 1979	Bordeuax	Fr	Exeter (Mar 2001)

Name	DOB	Place of birth	Nat	Club(s) (joined/first played)
Forge, Nicolas	13 May 1977	Roanne	Fr	Orient (Mar 2001)
Jeannin, Alex	30 Dec 1977	Troyes	Fr	Darlington (Mar 2001); Bristol R (May 2005)
Moreau, Fabrice	7 Oct 1967	Paris	Cam	Notts Co (Mar 2001)
Gallas, William	17 Aug 1977	Asnieres	Fr	Chelsea (May 2001)
Laslandes, Lilian	4 Sep 1971	Pauillac	Fr	Sunderland (Jun 2001)
Sabin, Eric	22 Jan 1975	Sarcelles	Fr	Swindon (Jun 2001); QPR (Jul 2003); Boston (Mar 2004); Northampton (Mar 2004); Oxford (Aug 2005)
Bellion, David	27 Nov 1982	Paris	Fr	Sunderland (Jul 2001); Man Utd (Jul 2003); West Ham (Aug 2005)
Libbra, Marc	5 Aug 1972	Toulon	Fr	Norwich (Jul 2001)
Ben Askar, Aziz	30 Mar 1976	Chateau Gontier	Fr	QPR (Aug 2001)
Biancalani, Frederic	21 Jul 1974	Villerupt	Fr	Walsall (Aug 2001)
Blanc, Laurent	19 Nov 1965	Ales	Fr	Man Utd (Aug 2001)
Courtois, Laurent	11 Sep 1978	Lyon	Fr	West Ham (Aug 2001)
Legwinski, Sylvain	10 Jun 1973	Clermont-Ferrand	Fr	Fulham (Aug 2001)
Marlet, Steve	1 Oct 1974	Pithiviers	Fr	Fulham (Aug 2001)
Distin, Sylvain	16 Dec 1977	Bagnolet	Fr	Newcastle (Sep 2001); Man City (Aug 2002)
N'Gotty, Bruno	10 Jun 1971	Lyon	Fr	Bolton (Sep 2001)
One, Armand	15 Mar 1983	Paris	Fr	Cambridge (Sep 2001); Northampton (Sep 2003); Wrexham (Sep 2003)
Valois, Jean-Louis	15 Oct 1973	Saint-Priest	Fr	Luton (Sep 2001); Burnley (Sep 2004)
Baudet, Julien	13 Jan 1979	Grenoble	Fr	Oldham (Oct 2001); Rotherham (Aug 2003); Notts Co (Jun 2004)
Ducrocq, Pierre	18 Dec 1976	Pontoise	Fr	Derby (Oct 2001)
Queudrue, Franck	27 Aug 1978	Paris	Fr	Middlesbrough (Oct 2001)
Skora, Eric	20 Aug 1981	Metz	Fr	Preston (Oct 2001); Walsall (Nov 2005)
Grenet, Francois	8 Mar 1975	Bordeaux	Fr	Derby (Nov 2001)
Le Pen, Ulrich	21 Jan 1974	Auray	Fr	Ipswich (Nov 2001)
Carasso, Cedric	30 Dec 1981	Avignon	Fr	C Palace (Dec 2001)
Debeve, Mickael	1 Dec 1970	Abbeville	Fr	Middlesbrough (Feb 2002)
Djorkaeff, Youri	9 Mar 1968	Lyon	Fr	Bolton (Feb 2002); Blackburn (Sep 2004)
Espartero, Mario	17 Jan 1978	Frejus	Fr	Bolton (Feb 2002)
Sofiane, Youssef	8 Jul 1984	Lyon	Fr	West Ham (Jun 2002); Notts Co (Sep 2004); Coventry (Oct 2005)
Le Tallec, Anthony	3 Oct 1984	Hennebont	Fr	Liverpool (Jul 2002); Sunderland (Aug 2005)
Cheyrou, Bruno	10 May 1978	Suresnes	Fr	Liverpool (Aug 2002)
Cisse, Edouard	30 Mar 1978	Pau	Fr	West Ham (Aug 2002)
Mendy, Bernard	20 Aug 1981	Evreux	Fr	Bolton (Aug 2002)
Cygan, Pascal	19 Apr 1974	Lens	Fr	Arsenal (Sep 2002)
Berthelin, Cedric	25 Dec 1976	Courriers	Fr	Luton (Oct 2002); C Palace (Jan 2003)
Lopes, Osvaldo	6 Apr 1980	Frejus	Fr	Plymouth (Sep 2002); Torquay (Jan 2005)
Debec, Fabien	18 Jan 1976	Lyon	Fr	Coventry (Sep 2002)
Dugarry, Christophe	24 Mar 1972	Bordeaux	Fr	Birmingham (Jan 2003)
Belmadi, Djamel	27 Mar 1976	Champigny	Alg	Man City (Jan 2003); Southampton (Aug 2005)
Andre, Pierre-Yves	14 May 1974	Lannion	Fr	Bolton (Feb 2003)
Laville, Florent	7 Aug 1973	Valence	Fr	Bolton (Feb 2003); Coventry (Oct 2004)
Antoine-Curier, Mickael	5 Mar 1983	Orsay	Fr	Brentford (Mar 2003), Oldham (Jul 2003); Kidderminster (Sep 2003); Rochdale (Sep 2003); Sheff Wed (Nov 2003); Notts Co (Feb 2004); Grimsby (Mar 2004)
Bouazza, Hameur	22 Feb 1985	Evry	Fr	Watford (Jun 2003); Swindon (Oct 2005)
Camara, Zoumana	3 Apr 1979	Colombes	Fr	Leeds (Jul 2003)

Name	DOB	Place of birth	Nat	Club(s) (joined/first played)
Griffit, Leandre	21 May 1984	Maubeuge	Fr	Southampton (Jul 2003); Leeds (Jan 2005); Rotherham (Mar 2005)
Nalis, Lilian	29 Sep 1971	Nogent sur Marne	Fr	Leicester (Jul 2003); Sheff Utd (May 2005); Coventry (Oct 2005); Plymouth (Jan 2006)
Priet, Nicolas	31 Jan 1983	Lyon	Fr	Leicester (Jul 2003); Doncaster (Jul 2004)
Ruster, Sebastien	6 Sep 1982	Marseille	Fr	Swindon (Jul 2003)
Bonnissel, Jerome	16 Apr 1973	Montpellier	Fr	Fulham (Aug 2003)
Bossy, Fabian	1 Oct 1977	Marseille	Fr	Darlington (Aug 2003)
Chapuis, Cyril	21 Mar 1979	Lyon	Fr	Leeds (Aug 2003)
Clichy, Gael	26 Jul 1985	Paris	Fr	Arsenal (Aug 2003)
Cozic, Bertrand	18 May 1978	Quimper	Fr	Cheltenham (Aug 2003); Northampton (Jul 2004); Kidderminster (Jan 2005)
Dalmat, Stephane	16 Feb 1979	Joue-le-Tours	Fr	Tottenham (Aug 2003)
El Kholti, Abdou	17 Oct 1980	Annesse	Mor	Yeovil (Aug 2003); Cambridge (Jul 2004); Chester (Jul 2005)
Fofana, Aboubaka	4 Oct 1982	Paris	Fr	Millwall (Aug 2003)
Mansouri, Yazid	25 Feb 1978	Revin	Alg	Coventry (Aug 2003)
Sibierski, Antoine	5 Aug 1974	Lille	Fr	Man City (Aug 2003)
Luzi, Patrice	8 Jul 1980	Ajaccio	Fr	Liverpool (Sep 2003)
Deloumeaux, Eric	12 May 1973	Montbeliard	Fr	Coventry (Jan 2004)
Carole, Sebastien	8 Sep 1982	Pontoise	Fr	West Ham (Feb 2004); Brighton (Aug 2005)
Ntimban-Zeh, Harry	26 Sep 1973	Aubervilliers	Fr	MKD (Mar 2004)
Doumbe, Mathias Fred	28 Oct 1979	Paris	Fr	Plymouth (Jun 2004)
Advice-Desruisseaux,	12 Jan 1983	Paris	Fr	Kidderminster (Jul 2004)
Cisse, Djibril	12 Aug 1981	Arles	Fr	Liverpool (Jul 2004)
Flamini, Mathieu	7 Mar 1984	Marseille	Fr	Arsenal (Jul 2004)
Herve, Laurent	19 Jun 1976	Quimper	Fr	MKD (Jul 2004)
Hornuss, Julien	12 Jun 1986	Paris	Fr	MKD (Jul 2004)
Mirza, Nicolas	21 Jul 1985	Paris	Fr	Yeovil (Jul 2004)
Berson, Mathieu	23 Feb 1980	Vannes	Fr	Aston Villa (Aug 2004)
Kamara, Diomansy	8 Nov 1980	Paris	Sen	Portsmouth (Aug 2004); WBA (Jul 2005)
Mezague, Valery	8 Dec 2004	Marseille	Cam	Portsmouth (Aug 2004)
N'Zogbia, Charles	28 May 1986	Gennevilliers	Fr	Newcastle (Aug 2004)
Sanokho, Amadou	1 Sep 1979	Paris	Fr	Burnley (Sep 2004); Oldham (Mar 2005)
Candela, Vincent	24 Oct 1973	Bedarieux	Fr	Bolton (Jan 2005)
Juan, Jimmy	10 Jun 1983	Valence	Fr	Ipswich (Jan 2005)
Nafti, Mehdi	28 Nov 1978	Toulouse	Tun	Birmingham (Jan 2005)
Dje, Ludovic	22 Jul 1977	Paris	Fr	Stockport (Mar 2005)
Karam, Amine	3 Jan 1984	Besancon	Fr	Oxford (Mar 2005)
Diagouraga,Toumani	10 Jun 1987	Corbeil-Essones	Fr	Watford (Jul 2005); Swindon (Mar 2006)
Diarra, Lassana	10 Mar 1985	Paris	Fr	Chelsea (Jul 2005)
Fernandez, Vincent	19 Sep 1986	Paris	Fr	Nottm For (Jul 2005)
Sako, Malike	17 Nov 1981	Paris	Fr	Torquay (Jul 2005)
Sissoko, Mohamed	22 Jan 1985	Rouen	Mli	Liverpool (Jul 2005)
Wolski, Mickael	5 Mar 1979	Moulins	Fr	Stockport (Jul 2005)
Chaigneau, Florent	21 Mar 1984	La Roche-sur-Yon	Fr	Brighton (Aug 2005)
Frutos, Alexandre	23 Apr 1982	Vitry-le-François	Fr	Brighton (Aug 2005)
Baradji, Sekou	24 Apr 1984	Paris	Fr	Reading (Sep 2005)
Christanval, Philippe	31 Aug 1978	Paris	Fr	Fulham (Sep 2005)
Bougherra, Madjid	7 Oct 1982	Dijon	Alg	Crewe (Jan 2006)
Diaby, Abou	11 May 1986	Paris	Fr	Arsenal (Jan 2006)
Ehui, Ismael	10 Dec 1986	Lille	Fr	Scunthorpe (Feb 2006)

Name	DOB	Place of birth	Nat	Club(s) (joined/first played)

Other players qualified for France but born outside France

Vieira, Patrick	23 Jun 1976	Dakar, Sen	Fr	Arsenal (Aug 1996)
Horace, Alain	4 Dec 1971	Madagascar	Fr	Hartlepool (Oct 1996)
Lambourde, Bernard	11 May 1971	Pointe-a-Pitre, Guad	Fr	Chelsea (Jul 1997); Portsmouth (Sep 2000)
Arphexad, Pegguy	18 May 1973	Abymes, Guad	Fr	Leicester (Aug 1997); Liverpool (Jul 2000); Stockport (Sep 2001)
Boli, Roger	26 Sep 1965	Adjame, IvCo	Fr	Walsall (Aug 1997); Bournemouth (Oct 1998)
Abou, Samassi	4 Aug 1973	Gagnoa, IvCo	Fr	West Ham (Nov 1997); Ipswich (Dec 1998); Walsall (Oct 1999)
Berthe, Mohamed	12 Sep 1972	Conakry, Gui	Fr	Bournemouth (Jul 1998)
Darcheville, Jean-Claude	25 Jul 1975	Sinnamary, FrGu	Fr	Nottm For (Jul 1998)
Desailly, Marcel	17 Sep 1968	Accra, Gha	Fr	Chelsea (Jul 1998)
Ipoua, Guy	14 Jan 1976	Douala, Cam	Fr	Bristol R (Aug 1998); Scunthorpe (Aug 1999); Gillingham (Mar 2001)
Allou, Bernard	19 Jun 1975	Cocody, IvCo	Fr	Nottm For (Mar 1999)
Hodouto, Kwami	31 Oct 1974	Lome, Tgo	Fr	Huddersfield (Sep 1999)
Sigere, Jean-Michel	26 Jan 1977	Martinique	Fr	Rushden (Mar 2000)
Gueret, Willy	3 Aug 1973	St Claude, Guad	Fr	Millwall (Jul 2000); Swansea (Jul 2004)
Joseph, David	22 Nov 1976	Guad	Fr	Notts Co (Aug 2000)
Karembeu, Christian	3 Dec 1970	Lifou, Ncal	Fr	Middlesbrough (Aug 2000)
Gope-Fenepej, John	6 Nov 1978	Noumea, Ncal	Fr	Bolton (Sep 2000)
Sidibe, Mamady	18 Dec 1979	Mali	Fr	Swansea (Jul 2001); Gillingham (Aug 2002)
Gnohere, Arthur	20 Nov 1978	Yamoussoukro, IvCo	Fr	Burnley (Aug 2001); QPR (Sep 2003)
Malbranque, Steed	6 Jan 1980	Mouscron, Bel	Fr	Fulham (Aug 2001)
Robert, Laurent	21 May 1975	Saint-Benoit, Reu	Fr	Newcastle (Aug 2001); Portsmouth (Jun 2005)
Negouai, Christian	20 Jan 1975	Fort-de-France, Mrt	Fr	Man City (Nov 2001); Coventry (Jan 2005)
Sinama-Pongolle, Florent	20 Oct 1984	Saint-Pierre, Reu	Fr	Liverpool (Jul 2002); Blackburn (Jan 2006)
Pericard, Vincent	3 Oct 1982	Efok, Cam	Fr	Portsmouth (Aug 2002); Sheff Utd (Sep 2005); Plymouth (Feb 2006)
Djetou, Martin	15 Feb 1972	Brokohio, IvCo	Fr	Fulham (Oct 2002); Bolton (Oct 2005)
Sommeil, David	10 Aug 1974	Point-a-Pitre, Guad	Fr	Man City (Jan 2003)
Yulu, Christian	26 Jan 1978	Kinshasa, DRC	Fr	Coventry (Feb 2003)
Folly, Yoann	6 Jun 1985	Lome, Tgo	Fr/Tgo	Southampton (Jul 2003); Nottm For (Jan 2005); Preston (Mar 2005); Sheff Wed (Jan 2006)
Ba, Ibrahim	12 Jan 1973	Dakar, Sen	Fr	Bolton (Sep 2003)
Makelele, Claude	18 Feb 1973	Kinshasa, DRC	Fr	Chelsea (Sep 2003)
N'Toya, Tcham	3 Nov 1983	Kinshasa, DRC	Fr	Chesterfield (Mar 2004)
Boumsong, Jean Alain	14 Dec 1979	Douala, Cam	Fr	Newcastle (Jan 2005)
Sow, Mamadou	22 Aug 1981	Clarmont, Swit	Fr	Torquay (Jun 2005)
Chimbonda, Pascal	21 Feb 1979	Les Abymes, Guad	Fr	Wigan (Jul 2005)
Priso, Carl	10 Jul 1979	Yaounde, Cam	Fr	Torquay (Aug 2005)
Songo'o, Frank	14 May 1987	Yaounde, Cam	Fr	Portsmouth (Sep 2005)
Youga, Kelly	22 Sep 1985	Bangui, CAR	Fr	Bristol C (Oct 2005)
Evra, Patrice	15 May 1981	Dakar, Sen	Fr	Man Utd (Jan 2006)

FRENCH GUYANA (2)

Regis, Cyrille	9 Feb 1958	Mariapousoula	Eng	WBA (May 1977); Coventry (Oct 1984); A Villa (Jul 1991); Wolves (Aug 1993); Wycombe (Aug

Name	DOB	Place of birth	Nat	Club(s) (joined/first played)
				1994); Chester (Aug 1995)
Darcheville, Jean-Claude	25 Jul 1975	Sinnamary	Fr	Nottm For (Jul 1998)

GABON (1)

Name	DOB	Place of birth	Nat	Club(s) (joined/first played)
Nzamba, Guy	13 Jul 1970	Port Gentil	Gab	Southend (Sep 1997)

GEORGIA (7)

Name	DOB	Place of birth	Nat	Club(s) (joined/first played)
Kinkladze, Georgi	6 Jul 1973	Tbilisi	Geo	Man City (Aug 1995); Derby (Jun 2000)
Kavelashvili, Mikhail	22 Jul 1971	Tbilisi	Geo	Man City (Mar 1996)
Ketsbaia, Temuri	18 Mar 1968	Gali	Geo	Newcastle (Jul 1997); Wolves (Aug 2000)
Shelia, Murtaz	25 Mar 1969	Tbilisi	Geo	Man City (Nov 1997)
Tskhadadze, Kakhaber	7 Sep 1968	Rustavi	Geo	Man City (Feb 1998)
Aleksidze, Rati	3 Aug 1978	Tbilisi	Geo	Chelsea (Feb 2000)
Khizanishvili, Zurab	6 Nov 1981	Tblisi	Geo	Blackburn (Aug 2005)

GERMANY (84+3)

Name	DOB	Place of birth	Nat	Club(s) (joined/first played)
Seeburg, Max	19 Sep 1884	Leipzig	Ger	Tottenham (May 1907); Burnley (Jan 1910); Grimsby (Jul 1911)
Gunn, Alf	11 Jul 1924	Germany	Ger	Nottm For (Feb 1947)
Eisentrager, Alec	20 Jul 1927	Hamburg	Ger	Bristol C (Jul 1949)
Trautmann, Bert	22 Oct 1923	Bremen	Ger	Man City (Oct 1949)
Bruck, Dietmar	19 Apr 1944	Danzig	Ger	Coventry (May 1962); Charlton (Oct 1970); Northampton (Jun 1972)
Smit(h), Wilf	3 Sep 1946	Neumunster	Ger	Shef Wed (Sep 1963); Coventry (Aug 1970); Brighton (Oct 1974); Millwall (Jan 1975); Bristol R (Mar 1975); Chesterfield (Nov 1976)
Tunks, Roy	21 Jan 1951	Wuppertall	Brit	Rotherham (Mar 1968); York (Jan 1969); Preston (Nov 1974); Wigan Ath (Nov 1981); Hartlepool (Jul 1988); Preston (Nov 1988)
Berry, George	19 Nov 1957	Rostrup	Wal	Wolves (Nov 1975); Stoke (Aug 1982); Doncaster (Aug 1984); Peterborough (Jul 1990); Preston (Aug 1991); Aldershot (Nov 1991)
MacDonald, Ian	30 Aug 1953	Rinteln	Brit	Carlisle (May 1976)
Lee, Alan	19 Jun 1960	Wegburg	Brit	Leicester (Feb 1979)
Casey, Paul	6 Oct 1961	Rinteln	Brit	Sheff Utd (Jun 1979); Lincoln (Mar 1988)
Phillips, David	29 Jul 1963	Wegburg	Brit	Plymouth (Aug 1981); Man City (Aug 1984); Coventry (Jun 1986); Norwich (Jul 1989); Nottm For (Aug 1993); Huddersfield (Nov 1997); Lincoln (Mar 1999)
Rober, Jurgen	25 Dec 1953	Gernrode	Ger	Nottm For (Dec 1981)
Galloway, Steve	13 Feb 1963	Hanover	Brit	C Palace (Oct 1984); Cambridge (Mar 1986)
Sanderson, Mike	26 Oct 1966	Germany	Brit	Darlington (Mar 1986)
Kruszynski, Detsi	14 Oct 1961	Divschav	Ger	Wimbledon (Dec 1988); Brentford (Aug 1992); Coventry (Sep 1993); Peterborough (Dec 1993)
Short, Chris	9 May 1970	Munster	Brit	Scarborough (Jul 1988); Notts Co (Sep 1990); Huddersfield (Dec 1994); Sheff Utd (Dec 1995); Stoke (Jul 1998)
Hauser, Thomas	10 Apr 1965	Schopfhain	Ger	Sunderland (Feb 1989)
Taylor, Robin	14 Jan 1971	Rinteln	Brit	Wigan Ath (Oct 1989)
Barnard, Darren	30 Nov 1971	Rinteln	Wal	Chelsea (Jul 1990); Reading (Nov 1994); Bristol C (Oct 1995); Barnsley (Aug 1997); Grimsby (Apr 2003)
Lomas, Steve	18 Jan 1974	Hanover	N Ire	Man City (Jan 1991); West Ham (Mar 1997);

Name	DOB	Place of birth	Nat	Club(s) (joined/first played)
				QPR (Aug 2005)
Neilson, Alan	26 Sep 1972	Wegburg	Wal	Newcastle (Feb 1991); Southampton (Jun 1995); Fulham (Nov 1997); Grimsby (Oct 2001); Luton (Feb 2002)
Moylon, Craig	16 Oct 1972	Munster	Brit	Preston (Jul 1991)
Beinlich, Stefan	13 Jan 1972	Berlin	Ger	A Villa (Oct 1991)
Breitkreutz, Matthias	12 May 1971	Crivitz	Ger	A Villa (Oct 1991)
Tierling, Lee	25 Oct 1972	Wegburg	Brit	Fulham (May 1992)
Kitchen, Sam	11 Jun 1967	Rinteln	Brit	Orient (Aug 1992); Doncaster (Feb 1994)
Craven, Peter	30 Jun 1968	Hanover	Ger	Halifax (Mar 1993)
Thirlby, Anthony	4 Mar 1976	Berlin	Brit	Exeter (Jul 1993); Torquay (Feb 1997)
Hartenberger, Uwe	1 Feb 1968	Leuterecken	Ger	Reading (Sep 1993)
Rosler, Uwe	15 Nov 1968	Attenburg	Ger	Man City (Feb 1994); Southampton (Jul 2000); WBA (Oct 2001)
Karl, Steffen	3 Feb 1970	Hohenm-Oelsen	Ger	Man City (Mar 1994)
Klinsmann, Jurgen	30 Jul 1964	Goppingen	Ger	Tottenham (Aug 1994); Tottenham (Dec 1997)
Gaudino, Maurizio	12 Dec 1966	Brule	Ger	Man City (Dec 1994)
Fuchs, Uwe	23 Jul 1966	Kaiserslautern	Ger	Middlesbrough (Jan 1995); Millwall (Jul 1995)
Taylor, Maik	4 Sep 1971	Hildesheim	N Ire	Barnet (Jun 1995); Southampton (Jan 1997); Fulham (Nov 1997); Birmingham (Aug 2003)
Jones, Ian	26 Aug 1976	Germany	Brit	Cardiff (Jul 1995)
Immel, Eike	27 Nov 1960	Marburg Lahn	Ger	Man City (Aug 1995)
Frontzeck, Michael	26 Mar 1964	Moenchengladbach	Ger	Man City (Jan 1996)
Lenhart, Sascha	16 Dec 1973	Cologne	Ger	Leicester (Sep 1996)
Dowe, Jens	1 Jun 1968	Rostock	Ger	Wolves (Oct 1996)
Hey, Tony	19 Sep 1970	Berlin	Ger	Birmingham (Jun 1997)
Leese, Lars	18 Aug 1969	Cologne	Ger	Barnsley (Jul 1997)
Mendez, Alberto	24 Oct 1974	Nuremburg	Sp	Arsenal (Jul 1997)
Riedle, Karl-Heinz	16 Sep 1965	Weiler	Ger	Liverpool (Aug 1997); Fulham (Sep 1999)
Newell, Justin	8 Feb 1980	Germany	Ger	Torquay (Sep 1997)
Sobiech, Jorg	15 Jan 1969	Gelsenkirchen	Ger	Stoke (Mar 1998)
Schnoor, Stefan	24 Apr 1971	Neumunster	Ger	Derby (Jul 1998)
Hamann, Dietmar	27 Aug 1973	Waldasson	Ger	Newcastle (Aug 1998); Liverpool (Jul 1999)
Hebel, Dirk	24 Nov 1972	Cologne	Ger	Brentford (Aug 1998)
Lehmann, Dirk	16 Aug 1971	Aachen	Ger	Fulham (Aug 1998); Brighton (Jun 2001)
Forssell, Mikael	15 Mar 1981	Steinfurt	Fin	Chelsea (Dec 1998); C Palace (Feb 2000); Birmingham (Aug 2003)
Freund, Steffen	19 Jan 1970	Brandenburg	Ger	Tottenham (Dec 1998); Leicester (Feb 2004)
Unger, Lars	30 Sep 1972	Eutin	Ger	Southend (Feb 1999)
Jermyn, Mark	16 Apr 1981	Germany	Ger	Torquay (Mar 1999)
Wright, Ben	1 Jul 1980	Munster	Ire	Bristol C (Mar 1999)
Helmer, Thomas	21 Apr 1965	Herford	Ger	Sunderland (Jul 1999)
Malz, Stefan	15 Jun 1972	Ludwigshafen	Ger	Arsenal (Jul 1999)
Ziege, Christian	1 Jan 1972	Berlin	Ger	Middlesbrough (Aug 1999); Liverpool (Aug 2000); Tottenham (Jul 2001)
Schwinkendorf, Jorn	27 Jan 1971	Hamburg	Ger	Cardiff (Nov 1999)
Volz, Moritz	21 Jan 1983	Siegen	Ger	Arsenal (Jan 2000); Wimbledon (Feb 2003); Fulham (Aug 2003)
Hansen, John	17 Sep 1973	Mannheim	Den	Cambridge (Feb 2000)
Babbel, Markus	8 Sep 1972	Munich	Ger	Liverpool (Jul 2000); Blackburn (Aug 2003)
Hitzlsperger, Thomas	5 Apr 1982	Munich	Ger	A Villa (Aug 2000); Chesterfield (Oct 2001)
Macdonald, Gary	25 Oct 1979	Iselone	Brit	Peterborough (Feb 2001)
Cennamo, Luigi	7 Feb 1980	Munich	It	Burnley (Jul 2001)

Name	DOB	Place of birth	Nat	Club(s) (joined/first played)
Canham, Marc	11 Sep 1982	Wefburg	Brit	Colchester (Aug 2001)
Formann, Pascal	16 Nov 1982	Werne	Ger	Nottm For (Aug 2001)
Prosinecki, Robert	12 Jan 1969	Schweminger	Cro	Portsmouth (Aug 2001)
Huth, Robert	18 Aug 1984	Berlin	Ger	Chelsea (Feb 2002)
Konstantinidis, Kostas	31 Aug 1972	Schorndorf	Gre	Bolton (Mar 2002)
Pelzer, Marc	24 Sep 1980	Trier	Ger	Blackburn (Jun 2002)
Herzig, Nico	10 Dec 1983	Pobneck	Ger	Wimbledon (Aug 2002)
Camara, Ben	19 Jun 1985	Bonn	Brit	Torquay (Mar 2003)
Lehmann, Jens	10 Nov 1969	Essen	Ger	Arsenal (Jul 2003)
Tarnat, Michael	27 Oct 1969	Hilden	Ger	Man City (Jun 2003)
Reich, Marco	30 Dec 1977	Meisenheim	Ger	Derby (Jan 2004); C Palace (Sep 2005)
Scoffham, Steve	12 Jul 1983	Munster	Brit	Notts Co (Feb 2004)
Smeltz, Shane	20 Sep 1980	Goppingen	NZ	Mansfield (Jan 2005)
Yelldell, David	1 Oct 1981	Stuttgart	USA	Brighton (Jan 2005)
Cowan, Gavin	24 May 1981	Hanover	Brit	Shrewsbury (Mar 2005)
Peter, Sergio	12 Oct 1986	Ludwigshafen	Ger	Blackburn (Jul 2005)
Bastians, Felix	9 May 1988	Bochum	Ger	Nottm For (Oct 2005)

Other players qualified for Germany but born outside Germany

Niestroj, Robert	2 Dec 1974	Oppeln, Pol	Ger	Wolves (Nov 1998)
Bopp, Eugene	5 Sep 1983	Kiev, Ukr	Ger	Nottm For (Aug 2001)
Bobic, Fredi	30 Oct 1971	Maribor, Slo	Ger	Bolton (Jan 2002)

GHANA (15)

Wharton, Arthur	28 Oct 1865	Accra	Gha	Rotherham T (Jul 1893); Sheff Utd (Jul 1894); Rotherham T (Jul 1895); Stockport (Jul 1901)
Laryea, Benny	20 Mar 1962	Ghana	Gha	Torquay (Mar 1984)
Grant, Kim	25 Sep 1972	Sekondi-Takaradi	Gha	Charlton (Mar 1991); Luton (Mar 1996); Millwall (Aug 1997); Notts Co (Dec 1998); Scunthorpe (Aug 2001)
Okai, Stephen	3 Dec 1973	Ghana	Brit	Orient (Apr 1992)
Lamptey, Nii	10 Dec 1974	Accra	Gha	A Villa (Aug 1994); Coventry (Aug 1995)
Yeboah, Tony	6 Jun 1966	Kumasi	Gha	Leeds (Jan 1995)
Agogo, Junior	1 Aug 1979	Accra	Gha	Sheff Wed (Oct 1996); Oldham (Jul 1999); Chester (Sep 1999); Chesterfield (Nov 1999); Lincoln (Dec 1999); QPR (Aug 2001); Bristol R (Jun 2003)
Boateng, George	5 Sep 1975	Nkawkaw	Neth	Coventry (Dec 1997); A Villa (Jul 1999); Middlesbrough (Aug 2002); QPR (Aug 2001); Bristol R (Jun 2003)
Desailly, Marcel	17 Sep 1968	Accra	Fr	Chelsea (Jul 1998)
Hammond, Elvis	6 Oct 1980	Accra	Gha	Fulham (Jul 1999); Bristol R (Aug 2001); Norwich (Aug 2003); Leicester (Aug 2005)
Nyarko, Alex	15 Oct 1973	Accra	Gha	Everton (Aug 2000)
Asamoah, Derek	1 May 1981	Accra	Brit	Northampton (Jul 2001); Mansfield (Jul 2004); Lincoln (Mar 2005); Chester (Jan 2006)
Awuah, Jones	10 Jul 1983	Ghana	Gha	Gillingham (Sep 2002)
Buari, Malik	21 Jan 1984	Accra	Gha	Fulham (Jul 2003)
Essien, Michael	3 Dec 1982	Accra	Gha	Chelsea (Aug 2005)

GIBRALTAR (5)

Hill, Reg	1907	Gibraltar	Brit	Carlisle (Jul 1930); Tranmere (Dec 1932); Hartlepools (Jan 1933); Darlington (Feb 1937)
Macedo, Tony	22 Feb 1938	Gibraltar	Brit	Fulham (Oct 1955); Colchester (Sep 1968)
Devereux, Tony	6 Jan 1940	Gibraltar	Brit	Aldershot (Nov 1958)

Name	DOB	Place of birth	Nat	Club(s) (joined/first played)
Houston, Graham	24 Feb 1960	Gibraltar	Brit	Preston (Mar 1978); Wigan (Aug 1986); Carlisle (Oct 1987)
McEvoy, Ricky	6 Aug 1967	Gibraltar	Ire	Luton (Aug 1985); Cambridge (Feb 1987)

GREECE (18+5)

Name	DOB	Place of birth	Nat	Club(s) (joined/first played)
Donis, George	29 Oct 1969	Greece	Grk	Blackburn (Jul 1996); Sheff Utd (Mar 1999); Huddersfield (Jun 1999)
Borbokis, Vassilis	10 Feb 1969	Serres	Grk	Sheff Utd (Jul 1997); Derby (Mar 1999)
Dellas, Traianos	31 Jan 1976	Salonika	Grk	Sheff Utd (Aug 1997)
Zagorakis, Theo	17 Oct 1971	Kavala	Grk	Leicester (Feb 1998)
Dabizas, Nicos	3 Aug 1973	Ptolemaida	Grk	Newcastle (Mar 1998); Leicester (Jan 2004)
Vlachos, Michalis	20 Sep 1967	Athens	Grk	Portsmouth (Jun 1998); Walsall (Feb 2000)
Kyzeridis, Nicos	20 Apr 1971	Salonika	Grk	Portsmouth (Jul 1998)
Georgiadis, Georgios	8 Mar 1972	Kavala	Grk	Newcastle (Aug 1998)
Michopoulos, Nik	20 Feb 1970	Karditsa	Grk	Burnley (Aug 2000); C Palace (Sep 2002)
Syros, George	8 Feb 1976	Athens	Grk	Bury (Aug 2001)
Tavlaridis, Stathis	25 Jan 1980	Serres	Grk	Arsenal (Sep 2001); Portsmouth (Jan 2003)
Koumantarakis, George	27 Mar 1974	Athens	SA	Preston (Jan 2003)
Giannakopoulos, Stelios	12 Jul 1974	Athens	Grk	Bolton (May 2003)
Konstantopoulos, Dimi	29 Nov 1978	Salonika	Grk	Hartlepool (Oct 2003)
Lakis, Vassilis	10 Sep 1976	Salonika	Grk	C Palace (Sep 2004)
Chalkias, Konstantinos	30 May 1974	Larissa	Grk	Portsmouth (Jan 2005)
Skopelitis, Giannis	2 Mar 1978	Athens	Grk	Portsmouth (Jan 2005)
Samaras, Giorgios	21 Feb 1985	Heraklion	Grk	Man City (Jan 2006)

Other players qualified for Greece but born outside Greece

Name	DOB	Place of birth	Nat	Club(s) (joined/first played)
Panopoulos, Mike	9 Oct 1976	Melbourne, Aus	Grk	Portsmouth (Sep 1999)
Stergiopoulos, Marcus	12 Jun 1973	Melbourne, Aus	Grk	Lincoln (Aug 2000)
Bertos, Leo	20 Dec 1981	Wellington, NZ	Grk	Barnsley (Sep 2000); Rochdale (Jul 2003); Chester (Aug 2005)
Papadopoulos, Dimitrios	20 Sep 1981	Kazakhstan	Grk	Burnley (Jul 2001)
Konstantinidis, Kostas	31 Aug 1972	Schorndorf, Ger	Grk	Bolton (Mar 2002)

GRENADA (1)

Name	DOB	Place of birth	Nat	Club(s) (joined/first played)
Batson, Brendan	6 Feb 1953	St George's	Eng	Arsenal (Jun 1971); Cambridge (Jan 1974); WBA (Feb 1978)

GUADELOUPE (6)

Name	DOB	Place of birth	Nat	Club(s) (joined/first played)
Lambourde, Bernard	11 May 1971	Pointe-a-Pitre	Fr	Chelsea (Jul 1997); Portsmouth (Sep 2000)
Arphexad, Pegguy	18 May 1973	Abymes	Fr	Leicester (Aug 1997); Liverpool (Jul 2000); Stockport (Sep 2001); Coventry (Aug 2003); Notts Co (Mar 2004)
Gueret, Willy	3 Aug 1973	St Claude	Fr	Millwall (Jul 2000); Swansea (Jul 2004)
Joseph, David	22 Nov 1976	Guadeloupe	Fr	Notts Co (Aug 2000)
Sommeil, David	10 Aug 1974	Point-a-Pitre	Fr	Man City (Jan 2003)
Chimbonda, Pascal	21 Feb 1979	Les Abymes	Fr	Wigan (Jul 2005)

GUINEA (5+2)

Name	DOB	Place of birth	Nat	Club(s) (joined/first played)
Berthe, Mohamed	12 Sep 1972	Conakry	Fr	Bournemouth (Jul 1998)
Camara, Titi	7 Nov 1972	Donka	Gui	Liverpool (Jun 1999); West Ham (Dec 2000)
Camara, Mohamed	25 Jul 1975	Conakry	Gui	Wolves (Aug 2000); Burnley (Jun 2003)
Oulare, Souleymane	16 Oct 1972	Conakry	Gui	Stoke (Dec 2001)
Bangoura, Sambegou	3 Apr 1983	Conakry	Gui	Stoke (Oct 2005)

Other players qualified for Guinea but born outside Guinea

Name	DOB	Place of birth	Nat	Club(s) (joined/first played)
Diallo, Drissa	4 Jan 1973	Nouadhibou, Mau	Gui	Burnley (Jan 2003); Ipswich (Jun 2003); Sheff Wed (Jul 2005)

Name	DOB	Place of birth	Nat	Club(s) (joined/first played)
Sylla, Mohammed	13 Mar 1977	Bouake, IvCo	Gui	Leicester (Jun 2005)

GUINEA BISSAU (1)

Forbes, Boniek	30 Sep 1983	Guinea Bissau	GuB	Orient (Sep 2002)

GUYANA (5)

Maynard, Mike	7 Jan 1947	Guyana	Brit	Peterborough (Jul 1967)
Quamina, Mark	25 Nov 1969	Guyana	Guy	Wimbledon (Jul 1988); Plymouth (Jul 1991)
Griffith, Cohen	26 Dec 1962	Georgetown	Brit	Cardiff (Oct 1989)
Bunbury, Alex	18 Jun 1967	Plaisance	Can	West Ham (Dec 1992)
Hooper, Lyndon	30 May 1966	Georgetown	Can	Birmingham (Sep 1993)

HONDURAS (3)

Nunez, Milton	30 Oct 1972	Zambocreek	Hon	Sunderland (Mar 2000)
Guerrero, Ivan	30 Nov 1977	Comayagua	Hon	Coventry (Oct 2000)
Martinez, Jairo	14 May 1978	Yoro	Hon	Coventry (Oct 2000)

HONG KONG (6)

Edwards, Gerald	c.1919	Hong Kong	Brit	Luton (Jan 1931)
Harris, Alex	22 Oct 1934	Hong Kong	Brit	Blackpool (Nov 1951)
Cheung, Chi Doy	30 Jul 1941	Hong Kong	Brit	Blackpool (Oct 1960)
Anderson, Doug	29 Aug 1963	Hong Kong	Brit	Oldham (Sep 1980); Tranmere (Aug 1984); Plymouth (Aug 1987); Cambridge (Sep 1988); Northampton (Dec 1988)
Hunter, Chris	18 Jan 1964	Hong Kong	Brit	Preston (Sep 1981); Preston (Sep 1984)
Williamson, Davey	15 Dec 1975	Hong Kong	Brit	Cambridge (Aug 1996)

HUNGARY (15)

Nagy, Mick	1 May 1929	Budapest	Hun	Swindon (Aug 1951)
Olah, Bela	8 Jun 1938	Oyd	Hun	Northampton (Dec 1958)
Haasz, Johnny	7 Jul 1934	Budapest	Hun	Swansea Town (Sep 1960); Workington (Jul 1961)
Kozma, Istvan	3 Dec 1964	Paszto	Hun	Liverpool (Feb 1992)
Kulcsar, George	12 Aug 1967	Budapest	Aus	Bradford (Mar 1997); QPR (Dec 1997)
Sebok, Vilmos	13 Jun 1973	Budapest	Hun	Bristol C (Jan 1999)
Bukran, Gabor	16 Nov 1975	Eger	Hun	Walsall (Aug 1999); Wigan Ath (Aug 2001)
Gera, Zoltan	22 Apr 1979	Pecs	Hun	WBA (Jul 2004)
Kiraly, Gabor	1 Apr 1976	Szombathely	Hun	C Palace (Jul 2004)
Buzsaky, Akos	7 May 1982	Budapest	Hun	Plymouth (Jan 2005)
Gyepes, Gabor	26 Jun 1981	Budapest	Hun	Wolves (Jul 2005)
Torghelle, Sandor	5 May 1982	Budapest	Hun	C Palace (Aug 2005)
Fulop, Marton	3 May 1983	Budapest	Hun	Chesterfield (Mar 2005); Coventry (Oct 2005)
Kovacs, Janos	11 Sep 1985	Budapest	Hun	Chesterfield (Aug 2005)
Rosa, Denes	7 Apr 1977	Budapest	Hun	Wolves (Jan 2006)

ICELAND (33)

Gudmundsson, Albert	5 Oct 1923	Reykjavik	Ice	Arsenal (Sep 1946)
Jonsson, Siggi	27 Sep 1966	Akranes	Ice	Sheff Wed (Feb 1985); Barnsley (Jan 1986); Arsenal (Jul 1989)
Bergsson, Gudni	21 Jul 1965	Reykjavik	Ice	Tottenham (Dec 1988); Bolton (Mar 1995)
Orlygsson, Toddi	2 Aug 1966	Odense	Ice	Nottm For (Dec 1989); Stoke (Aug 1993); Oldham (Dec 1995)
Torfason, Gunnar	13 Dec 1961	Westann Isles	Ice	Doncaster (Jul 1994)
Sigurdsson, Larus	4 Jun 1973	Akuveyni	Ice	Stoke (Oct 1994); WBA (Sep 1999)
Gunnlaugsson, Arnie	6 Mar 1973	Akranes	Ice	Bolton (Aug 1997); Leicester (Feb 1999); Stoke (Mar 2000)

Name	DOB	Place of birth	Nat	Club(s) (joined/first played)
Hreidarsson, Hermann	11 Jul 1974	Reykjavik	Ice	C Palace (Aug 1997); Brentford (Sep 1998); Wimbledon (Oct 1999); Ipswich (Aug 2000); Charlton (Mar 2003)
Gislason, Valur	8 Sep 1977	Reykjavik	Ice	Brighton (Oct 1997)
Gudmundsson, Johann	7 Dec 1977	Reykjavik	Ice	Watford (Mar 1998); Cambridge (Nov 2000)
Gudjohnsen, Eidur	15 Sep 1978	Reykjavik	Ice	Bolton (Aug 1998); Chelsea (Jul 2000)
Larusson, Bjarni	11 Mar 1976	Vestmannaeyjar	Ice	Walsall (Sep 1998); Scunthorpe (Sep 2000)
Danielsson, Helgi	13 Jul 1981	Reykjavik	Ice	Peterborough (Oct 1998)
Eyjolfsson, Siggi	1 Dec 1973	Reykjavik	Ice	Walsall (Jan 1999); Chester (Jan 2000)
Gunnlaugsson, Bjarke	6 Mar 1973	Akranes	Ice	Preston (Sep 1999)
Ingimarsson, Ivar	20 Aug 1977	Reykjavik	Ice	Torquay (Oct 1999); Brentford (Nov 1999); Wolves (Aug 2002); Brighton (Feb 2003); Reading (Oct 2003)
Danielsson, Einer	19 Jan 1970	Reykjavik	Ice	Stoke (Nov 1999)
Gislason, Siggi	25 Jun 1968	Akranes	Ice	Stoke (Nov 1999)
Einarsson, Gunnar	7 Jul 1976	Reykjavik	Ice	Brentford (Jan 2000)
Gunnarsson, Brynjar	16 Oct 1975	Reykjavik	Ice	Stoke (Jan 2000); Nottm Forest (Aug 2003); Watford (Jul 2004); Reading (Jul 2005)
Helguson, Heidar	22 Aug 1977	Akureyri	Ice	Watford (Jan 2000), Fulham (Jun 2005)
Gudjonsson, Bjarni	26 Feb 1979	Akranes	Ice	Stoke (Mar 2000); Coventry (Jan 2004); Plymouth (Dec 2004)
Thordarson, Stefan	27 Mar 1975	Reykjavik	Ice	Stoke (Jun 2000)
Gottskalksson, Ole	12 Mar 1968	Keflavik	Ice	Brentford (Jul 2000); Torquay (Sep 2004)
Dadason, Rikki	26 Apr 1972	Reykjavik	Ice	Stoke (Oct 2000)
Kristinsson, Birkir	15 Aug 1964	Vestmannaeyjar	Ice	Stoke (Nov 2000)
Gudjonsson, Thordur	14 Oct 1973	Akranes	Ice	Derby (Mar 2001); Preston (Jan 2002); Stoke (Jan 2005)
Marteinsson, Petur	14 Jul 1973	Reykjavic	Ice	Stoke (Nov 2001)
Arason, Arni	7 May 1975	Reykjavik	Ice	Man City (Jan 2003)
Gudjonsson, Joey	25 May 1980	Akranes	Ice	A Villa (Jan 2003); Wolves (Aug 2003); Leicester (Aug 2004)
Skulason, Olafur Ingi	1 Apr 1983	Reykjavik	Ice	Arsenal (Jul 2003); Brentford (Jun 2005)
Einarsson, Gylfi	27 Oct 1978	Reykjavik	Ice	Leeds (Jan 2005)
Sigurdsson, Hannes	10 Apr 1983	Reykjavik	Ice	Stoke (Aug 2005)

INDIA (40)

Name	DOB	Place of birth	Nat	Club(s) (joined/first played)
Pass, Jimmy	6 Nov 1883	Juffulpore	Brit	Stockport (Aug 1903)
Donaghy, Charles	c.1885	India	Brit	Chelsea (Aug 1905)
Hunter, George	Aug 1886	Peshawar	Brit	A Villa (Feb 1908); Oldham (Jan 1912); Chelsea (Feb 1913); Man Utd (Mar 1914)
Dolby, Hugh	c.1885	Agra	Brit	Chelsea (Jul 1908)
O'Donnell, Rudolph	Aug 1888	Madras	Brit	Fulham (Dec 1909)
Chandler, Robert	Sep 1894	Calcutta	Brit	A Villa (Aug 1913)
Wagstaffe, Thomas	c.1890	Dinapore	Brit	Sunderland (Mar 1923); Crewe (Sep 1926)
Quantrill, Alf	22 Jan 1897	Punjab	Eng	Derby (Aug 1914); Preston (Jul 1921) Bradford PA (Sep 1924); Nottm For (May 1930)
Mills, Paddy	23 Feb 1900	Multan	Brit	Hull (Aug 1920); Notts Co (Mar 1926); Birmingham (Feb 1929); Hull (Dec 1929)
Armand, Jack	11 Aug 1898	Sabathu	Brit	Leeds (Dec 1922); Swansea Town (May 1929); Newport (Aug 1932)
Preedy, Charlie	11 Jan 1900	Neemuch	Brit	Charlton (Dec 1922); Wigan Bor (Jul 1928); Arsenal (May 1929); Bristol R (Jul 1933); Luton (Aug 1934)

Name	DOB	Place of birth	Nat	Club(s) (joined/first played)
Bellis, George	8 Jun 1904	Khadki	Brit	Southport (Aug 1923); Wrexham (May 1927); Wolves (Jun 1929); Burnley (Dec 1932); B&B Ath (Jul 1935)
Ashton, Hubert	13 Feb 1898	Calcutta	Brit	Bristol R (Jul 1924); Clapton O (Aug 1926)
Tricker, Reg	5 Oct 1905	Karachi	Brit	Luton (Jul 1924); Charlton (Aug 1925); Arsenal (Mar 1927); Clapton O (Feb 1929)
Price, Johnny	4 Dec 1903	Mhow	Brit	Brentford (Apr 1928); Fulham (Jun 1928); Port Vale (May 1937)
Callachan, Harry	9 Apr 1903	Madras	Brit	Leicester (Sep 1929)
Mills, Arthur	1906	Karachi	Brit	Luton (Jul 1932); Gillingham (Jul 1933)
McDowall, Les	25 Oct 1912	Gunga Pur	Brit	Sunderland (Dec 1932); Man City (Mar 1938); Wrexham (Nov 1949)
Dugnolle, Jack	24 Mar 1914	Peshawar	Brit	Brighton (Oct 1934); Plymouth (Feb 1939); Brighton (Aug 1946)
Lancelotte, Eric	26 Feb 1917	India	Brit	Charlton (May 1935); Brighton (Feb 1948)
Court, Dick	23 Oct 1916	India	Brit	Aldershot (Jun 1937)
Dolding, Len	13 Dec 1922	Nundydroog	Brit	Chelsea (Jul 1945); Norwich (Jul 1948)
Garwood, Len	28 Jul 1923	Ranikwet	Brit	Tottenham (May 1946)
Leslie, Maurice	19 Aug 1923	India	Brit	Swindon (Jun 1947)
Pickett, Reg	6 Jan 1927	India	Brit	Portsmouth (Mar 1949); Ipswich (Jun 1957)
Bluck, Dave	31 Jan 1930	India	Brit	Aldershot (Aug 1951)
Stiffle, Nelson	30 Jul 1928	India	Brit	Chester (Dec 1951); Chesterfield (Mar 1954); B&B Ath (May 1955); Exeter (Mar 1958); Coventry (Jul 1960)
Fleming, Mike	23 Feb 1928	India	Brit	Tranmere (Sep 1953)
Smith, Roy	19 Mar 1936	Rawalpindi	Brit	West Ham (Jun 1955); Portsmouth (Jan 1962)
Houghton, Bud	1 Sep 1936	Madras	Brit	Bradford PA (Oct 1955); Birmingham (Oct 1957); Southend (Oct 1958); Oxford (Mar 1961); Lincoln (Oct 1963)
Huggins, Joe	24 Feb 1930	India	Brit	Aldershot (Dec 1955)
Porteous, Jack	12 Jan 1933	India	Brit	Aldershot (Dec 1955)
Keelan, Kevin	5 Jan 1941	Calcutta	Brit	A Villa (Jul 1958); Stockport (Apr 1961); Wrexham (Nov 1961); Norwich (Jul 1963)
Thorpe, Arthur	31 Jul 1939	Lucknow	Brit	Scunthorpe (Sep 1960); Bradford (Jul 1963)
Chadwick, Dave	19 Aug 1943	Ooctamund	Brit	Southampton (Oct 1960); Middlesbrough (Jul 1966); Halifax (Jan 1970); Bournemouth (Feb 1972); Torquay (Dec 1972); Gillingham (Sep 1974)
Heppolette, Ricky	8 Apr 1949	Bhusawal	Brit	Preston (Sep 1964); Orient (Dec 1972); C Palace (Oct 1976); Chesterfield (Feb 1977); Peterborough (Aug 1979)
Methven, Colin	10 Dec 1955	India	Brit	Wigan Ath (Oct 1979); Blackpool (Jul 1986); Carlisle (Sep 1990); Walsall (Nov 1990)
Payne, Mark	2 Sep 1966	Bombay	Brit	Swindon (Sep 1984)
Cooper, Neale	24 Nov 1963	Darjeeling	Sco	A Villa (Jul 1986); Reading (Jul 1991)
Bhutia, Baichung	15 Jun 1976	Gangtok	Ind	Bury (Sep 1999)
IRAN (1)				
Bagheri, Karim	20 Feb 1974	Abbasi	Iran	Charlton (Aug 2000)
IRAQ (1)				
Fayadh, Jassim	16 Dec 1975	Baghdad	Irq	Macclesfield (Aug 2004)

Name	DOB	Place of birth	Nat	Club(s) (joined/first played)
ISRAEL (17)				
Cohen, Avi	14 Nov 1956	Tel Aviv	Isr	Liverpool (Jul 1979)
Gariani, Moshe	18 Jun 1957	Tiberias	Isr	Brighton (Jun 1980)
Cohen, Jacob	25 Sep 1956	Israel	Isr	Brighton (Oct 1980)
Fadida, Aharon	20 Sep 1961	Israel	Isr	Aldershot (Dec 1985)
Pisanti, David	27 May 1962	Israel	Isr	QPR (Sep 1987)
Rosenthal, Ronny	4 Oct 1963	Haifa	Isr	Liverpool (Jun 1990); Tottenham (Jan 1994); Watford (Aug 1997)
Berkovic, Eyal	2 Apr 1972	Haifa	Isr	Southampton (Oct 1996); West Ham (Jun 1997); Blackburn (Feb 2001); Man City (Jul 2001); Portsmouth (Jan 2004)
Zohar, Itzhak	31 Oct 1970	Tel Aviv	Isr	C Palace (Aug 1997)
Hazan, Alon	14 Sep 1967	Ashdod	Isr	Watford (Jan 1998)
Amsalem, David	4 Sep 1971	Israel	Isr	C Palace (Aug 1998)
Badir, Walid	12 Mar 1974	Kafr Kasm	Isr	Wimbledon (Aug 1999)
Ghrayib, Naguyan	30 Jan 1974	Nazareth	Isr	A Villa (Aug 1999)
Nimni, Avi	26 Apr 1972	Tel Aviv	Isr	Derby (Nov 1999)
Tal, Idan	13 Sep 1975	Petach-Tikva	Isr	Everton (Oct 2000)
Ben Haim, Tal	31 Mar 1982	Rishon Le Zion	Isr	Bolton (Jul 2004)
Benayoun, Yossi	5 May 1980	Beer-Sheva	Isr	West Ham (Jul 2005)
Katan, Yaniv	27 Jan 1981	Haifa	Isr	West Ham (Jan 2006)
ITALY (70+5)				
Ugolini, Rolando	4 Jun 1924	Lucca	It	Middlesbrough (May 1948); Wrexham (Jun 1957)
Besagni, Remo	22 Apr 1935	Italy	It	C Palace (Oct 1952)
Kemp, Fred	27 Feb 1946	Salerno	Brit	Wolves (Jun 1963); Southampton (Jun 1965); Blackpool (Nov 1970); Halifax (Dec 1971); Hereford (Jul 1974)
Derko, Franco	22 Dec 1946	Italy	It	Mansfield (Jan 1965)
Sartori, Carlo	10 Feb 1948	Calderzone	It	Man Utd (Feb 1965)
Chinaglia, Giorgio	24 Jan 1947	Carrara	It	Swansea Town (Apr 1965)
Masiello, Luciano	2 Jan 1951	Italy	It	Charlton (Jan 1969)
Fiocca, Paul	13 Jan 1955	Italy	It	Swindon (Jan 1973)
Sperti, Franco	28 Jan 1955	Italy	It	Swindon (Jan 1973)
Ponte, Raimondo	4 Apr 1954	Naples	It	Nottm For (Aug 1980)
Silenzi, Andrea	10 Feb 1966	Rome	It	Nottm For (Aug 1995)
Bonetti, Ivano	1 Aug 1964	Brescia	It	Grimsby (Sep 1995); Tranmere (Aug 1996); C Palace (Oct 1997)
Bolesan, Mirko	6 May 1975	Genoa	It	Cardiff (Oct 1995)
Gambaro, Enzo	23 Feb 1966	Genoa	It	Grimsby (Mar 1996)
Ravanelli, Fabrizio	11 Dec 1968	Perugia	It	Middlesbrough (Jun 1996); Derby (Jul 2001)
Vialli, Gianluca	9 Jul 1964	Cremona	It	Chelsea (Jul 1996)
Carbone, Benito	14 Aug 1971	Bagnara Calabra	It	Sheff Wed (Oct 1996); A Villa (Oct 1999); Bradford (Aug 2000); Derby (Oct 2001); Middlesbrough (Feb 2002)
Zola, Gianfranco	5 Jul 1966	Oliena	It	Chelsea (Nov 1996)
Festa, Gianluca	15 Mar 1969	Cagliari	It	Middlesbrough (Jan 1997); Portsmouth (Aug 2002)
Eranio, Stefano	29 Dec 1968	Genoa	It	Derby (Jul 1997)
Pistone, Alessandro	27 Jul 1975	Milan	It	Newcastle (Jul 1997); Everton (Jul 2000)
Baiano, Francesco	24 Feb 1968	Naples	It	Derby (Aug 1997)
Lombardo, Attilio	6 Jan 1966	St Maria la Fossa	It	C Palace (Aug 1997)

Name	DOB	Place of birth	Nat	Club(s) (joined/first played)
Di Canio, Paolo	9 Jul 1968	Rome	It	Sheff Wed (Aug 1997); West Ham (Jan 1999); Charlton (Aug 2003)
Padovano, Michele	28 Aug 1966	Turin	It	C Palace (Nov 1997)
Berti, Nicola	14 Apr 1967	Salsomaggiore Terme	It	Tottenham (Jan 1998)
Branca, Marco	6 Jan 1965	Grosseto	It	Middlesbrough (Feb 1998)
Bruno, Pasquale	19 Jun 1962	Lecce	It	Wigan Ath (Feb 1998)
Billio, Patrizio	19 Apr 1974	Treviso	It	C Palace (Mar 1998)
Sanetti, Francesco	11 Jan 1979	Rome	It	Sheff Wed (Apr 1998)
Fabio, Ferraresi	25 May 1979	Fano	It	A Villa (Jun 1998)
Tramezzani, Paolo	30 Jul 1970	Reggio-Emilia	It	Tottenham (Jun 1998)
Casiraghi, Pierluigi	4 Mar 1969	Monza	It	Chelsea (Jul 1998)
Materazzi, Marco	19 Aug 1973	Perugia	It	Everton (Jul 1998)
Bortolazzi, Mario	10 Jan 1965	Verona	It	WBA (Aug 1998)
Maresca, Enzo	10 Feb 1980	Pontecagnano	It	WBA (Aug 1998)
Percassi, Luca	25 Aug 1980	Milan	It	Chelsea (Aug 1998)
Pinamonte, Lorenzo	9 May 1978	Verona	It	Bristol C (Sep 1998); Brentford (Feb 2000); Brighton (Dec 1999); Orient (Feb 2000)
Dalla Bona, Sam	6 Feb 1981	San Dona di Piave	It	Chelsea (Oct 1998)
Marcolin, Dario	28 Oct 1971	Brescia	It	Blackburn (Oct 1998)
Gioacchini, Stefano	25 Nov 1976	Rome	It	Coventry (Jan 1999)
Cudicini, Carlo	6 Sep 1973	Milan	It	Chelsea (Jun 1999)
Nuzzo, Raffaele	21 Feb 1973	Monza	It	Coventry (Jul 1999)
Ambrosetti, Gabriele	7 Aug 1973	Varese	It	Chelsea (Aug 1999)
Mannini, Moreno	15 Aug 1962	Imola	It	Nottm For (Aug 1999)
Matrecano, Salvatore	5 Oct 1970	Naples	It	Nottm For (Aug 1999)
Petrachi, Gianluca	14 Jan 1969	Lecce	It	Nottm For (Aug 1999)
Taibi, Massimo	18 Feb 1970	Palermo	It	Man Utd (Sep 1999)
Di Piedi, Michele	4 Dec 1980	Palermo	It	Sheff Wed (Aug 2000); Bristol R (Feb 2003)
Panucci, Christian	12 Apr 1973	Savona	It	Chelsea (Aug 2000)
Morini, Emanuele	31 Jan 1982	Rome	It	Bolton (Sep 2000)
Mancini, Roberto	27 Nov 1964	Jesi	It	Leicester (Jan 2001)
Grabbi, Corrado	29 Jul 1975	Turin	It	Blackburn (Jun 2001)
Galli, Filippo	19 May 1963	Monza	It	Watford (Jul 2001)
Zamperini, Alessandro	15 Aug 1982	Rome	It	Portsmouth (Jul 2001)
Daino, Daniele	8 Sep 1979	Alessandria	It	Derby (Aug 2001)
Sereni, Matteo	11 Feb 1975	Parma	It	Ipswich (Aug 2001)
Maccarone, Massimo	9 Sep 1979	Galliate	It	Middlesbrough (Aug 2002)
Ambrosio, Marco	30 May 1973	Brescia	It	Chelsea (Jun 2003)
Amoruso, Lorenzo	28 Jun 1971	Palese	It	Blackburn (Jul 2003)
Baggio, Dino	24 Jul 1971	Camposampiero	It	Blackburn (Aug 2003)
Lupoli, Arturo	24 Jun 1987	Brescia	It	Arsenal (Jul 2004)
Ventola, Nicola	24 May 1978	Bari	It	C Palace (Aug 2004)
Gabrieli, Emanuele	31 Dec 1980	L'Aquila	It	Sheff Utd (Sep 2004); Boston (Feb 2005)
Rossi, Generoso	3 Jan 1979	Naples	It	QPR (Jan 2005)
Diaz, Emiliano	22 Jun 1983	Naples	It	Oxford (Feb 2005)
Ferretti, Andrea	18 Sep 1986	Parma	It	Cardiff (Jul 2005)
Milanese, Mauro	17 Sep 1971	Trieste	It	QPR (Aug 2005)
Ukah, Ugo	18 Jan 1984	Parma	Nig	QPR (Aug 2005)
Guatelli, Andrea	5 May 1984	Parma	It	Oxford (Mar 2006)
Qualified for Italy but born outside Italy				
Di Matteo, Roberto	29 May 1970	Sciaffusa, Swit	It	Chelsea (Jul 1996)
Cennamo, Luigi	7 Feb 1980	Munich, Ger	It	Burnley (Jul 2001)

Name	DOB	Place of birth	Nat	Club(s) (joined/first played)
Molango, Maheta	24 Jul 1982	St Imier, Swit	It	Brighton (Jul 2004); Lincoln (Jul 2005)
Rossi, Giuseppe	1 Feb 1987	New Jersey, USA	It	Man Utd (Nov 2004)
Ferrari, Matteo	5 Dec 1979	Aflou, Alg	It	Everton (Aug 2005)

IVORY COAST (18)

Name	DOB	Place of birth	Nat	Club(s) (joined/first played)
Boli, Roger	26 Sep 1965	Adjame	Fr	Walsall (Aug 1997); Bournemouth (Oct 1998)
Abou, Samassi	4 Aug 1973	Gagnoa	Fr	West Ham (Nov 1997); Ipswich (Dec 1998); Walsall (Oct 1999)
Bakayoko, Ibrahima	31 Dec 1976	Seguela	IvCo	Everton (Oct 1998)
Zahana-Oni, Landry	8 Aug 1976	Abidjan	IvCo	Luton (Jan 1999)
Allou, Bernard	19 Jun 1975	Cocody	Fr	Nottm For (Mar 1999)
Tebily, Olivier	19 Dec 1975	Abidjan	IvCo	Sheff Utd (Mar 1999); Birmingham (Mar 2002)
Gnohere, Arthur	20 Nov 1978	Yamoussoukro	Fr	Burnley (Aug 2001); QPR (Sep 2003)
Toure, Kolo	19 Mar 1981	Abidjan	IvCo	Arsenal (Aug 2002)
Djetou, Martin	15 Feb 1972	Brogohio	Fr	Fulham (Oct 2002); Bolton (Oct 2005)
Diabate, Lassina	16 Sep 1974	Bouake	IvCo	Portsmouth (Oct 2002)
Dadi, Eugene	20 Aug 1973	Abidjan	IvCo	Tranmere (Aug 2003); Nottm For (Aug 2005); Notts Co (Jan 2006)
Drogba, Didier	11 Mar 1978	Abidjan	IvCo	Chelsea (Jul 2004)
Latte-Yedo, Igor	14 Dec 1978	Dabou	IvCo	Cambridge (Jul 2004)
Djourou, Johan	18 Jan 1987	Abidjan	Swit	Arsenal (Aug 2004)
Eboue, Emmanuel	4 Jun 1983	Abidjan	IvCo	Arsenal (Jan 2005)
Sylla, Mohammed	13 Mar 1977	Bouake	Gui	Leicester (Jun 2005)
Nade, Raphael	18 Oct 1980	Abidjan	IvCo	Carlisle (Jul 2005)
Yao, Sosthene	7 Aug 1987	Abidjan	Brit	Cheltenham (Aug 2005)

JAMAICA (30)

Name	DOB	Place of birth	Nat	Club(s) (joined/first played)
Delapenha, Lindy	25 May 1927	Kingston	Jam	Portsmouth (Apr 1948); Middlesbrough (Apr 1950); Mansfield (Jun 1958)
Phillips, Brendon	16 Jul 1954	St Catherine	Jam	Peterborough (Aug 1973); Mansfield (Aug 1980)
Gardner, Don	30 Aug 1955	Kingston	Jam	Wolves (Aug 1973)
Blissett, Luther	1 Feb 1958	Falmouth	Eng	Watford (Jul 1975); Watford (Aug 1984); Bournemouth (Nov 1988); Watford (Aug 1991); WBA (Oct 1992); Bury (Aug 1993); Mansfield (Dec 1993)
Williams, Everton	1 Feb 1957	Blackrod	Jam	Wrexham (Jul 1975)
Richards, Lloyd	11 Feb 1958	Kingston	Jam	Notts Co (Feb 1976); York (Jun 1980)
Streete, Floyd	5 May 1959	Kingston	Jam	Cambridge (Jul 1976); Derby (Oct 1984); Wolves (Oct 1985); Reading (Jul 1990)
Hazell, Bob	14 Jun 1959	Kingston	Eng	Wolves (Mar 1977); QPR (Sep 1979); Leicester (Sep 1983); Wolves (Sep 1985); Reading (Nov 1986); Port Vale (Dec 1986)
Cunningham, Tony	12 Nov 1957	Kingston	Brit	Lincoln (May 1979); Barnsley (Sep 1982); Sheff Wed (Nov 1983); Man City (Jul 1984); Newcastle (Feb 1985); Blackpool (Jul 1987); Bury (Jul 1989); Bolton (Mar 1991); Rotherham (Aug 1991); Doncaster (Jul 1993); Wycombe (Mar 1994)
Blake, Noel	12 Jan 1962	Kingston	Brit	A Villa (Aug 1979); Shrewsbury (Mar 1982); Birmingham (Sep 1982); Portsmouth (Apr 1984); Leeds (Jul 1988); Stoke (Feb 1990); Bradford (Jul 1992); Exeter (Aug 1995)
Barnes, John	7 Nov 1963	Kingston	Eng	Watford (Jul 1981); Liverpool (Jun 1987);

Name	DOB	Place of birth	Nat	Club(s) (joined/first played)
Richards, Carl	1 Dec 1960	St Mary's	Brit	Newcastle (Aug 1997); Charlton (Feb 1999) Bournemouth (Jul 1986); Birmingham (Oct 1988); Peterborough (Jul 1989); Blackpool (Jan 1990); Maidstone (Oct 1991)
Johnson, David	15 Aug 1976	Kingston	Jam	Bury (Jul 1995); Ipswich (Nov 1997); Nottm For (Jan 2001); Sheff Wed (Feb 2002); Burnley (Mar 2002); Sheff Utd (Mar 2005)
Jack, Rodney	28 Sep 1972	Kingston	StV	Torquay (Oct 1995); Crewe (Aug 1998); Rushden (Jun 2003); Oldham (Jul 2004)
Moncrieffe, Prince	27 Feb 1977	Kingston	Jam	Doncaster (Jul 1997)
Gardner, Ricardo	25 Sep 1978	St Andrews	Jam	Bolton (Aug 1998)
Boyd, Walter	1 Jan 1972	Kingston	Jam	Swansea (Oct 1999)
Goodison, Ian	21 Nov 1972	St James	Jam	Hull (Oct 1999); Tranmere (Feb 2004)
Whitmore, Theo	21 Nov 1972	St James	Jam	Hull (Oct 1999); Tranmere (Jun 2004)
Fuller, Ricardo	31 Oct 1979	Kingston	Jam	C Palace (Feb 2001); Preston (Aug 2002); Portsmouth (Aug 2004); Southampton (Jul 2005); Ipswich (Feb 2006)
Lowe, Onandi	2 Dec 1973	Kingston	Jam	Port Vale (Feb 2001); Rushden (Nov 2001); Coventry (Mar 2004)
Johnson, Jermaine	25 Jun 1980	Kingston	Jam	Bolton (Sep 2001); Oldham (Nov 2003)
Davis, Claude	6 Mar 1979	Kingston	Jam	Preston (Jul 2003)
Robinson, Trevor	20 Sep 1984	St Catherines	Jam	Millwall (Jul 2003)
Daley, Omar	25 Apr 1981	Kingston	Jam	Reading (Aug 2003); Preston (Jul 2004)
Jackson, Simeon	28 Mar 1987	Kingston	Jam	Rushden (Aug 2004)
Ricketts, Donovan	7 Jun 1977	St James	Jam	Bradford (Aug 2004)
Stewart, Damion	8 Aug 1980	Kingston	Jam	Bradford (Jun 2005)
Joseph, Ricardo	17 Jan 1987	Kingston	Jam	Rushden (Jul 2005)
Francino, Francis	8 Jan 1987	Kingston	Jam	Watford (Aug 2005)
JAPAN (6)				
Atkins, Arthur	21 Feb 1925	Tokyo	Brit	Birmingham (Nov 1948); Shrewsbury (Jun 1954)
Inamoto, Junichi	18 Sep 1979	Kagoshima	Jap	Arsenal (Jul 2001); Fulham (Jul 2002); WBA (Aug 2004); Cardiff (Dec 2004)
Nishizawa, Akinori	18 Jun 1976	Shizuoka	Jap	Bolton (Jul 2001)
Kawaguchi, Yoshikatsu	15 Aug 1975	Shizuoka	Jap	Portsmouth (Oct 2001)
Toda, Kazuyuki	30 Dec 1977	Tokyo	Jap	Tottenham (Apr 2003)
Nakata, Hidetoshi	22 Jan 1977	Yamanashi	Jap	Bolton (Aug 2005)
KAZAKHSTAN (1)				
Papadopoulos, Dimitrios	20 Sep 1981	Kazakhstan	Grk	Burnley (Jul 2001)
KENYA (5)				
Thompson, Peter	25 Jul 1942	Kenya	Brit	Peterborough (Mar 1964)
McBride, Andy	15 Mar 1954	Kenya	Brit	C Palace (Oct 1971)
Rafferty, Kevin	9 Nov 1960	Kenya	Brit	Crewe (Nov 1978)
Johnstone, Glenn	5 Jun 1967	Kenya	Brit	Preston (Jan 1993)
Osano, Curtis	8 Mar 1987	Nakuru	Ken	Reading (Jul 2005)
LATVIA (8)				
Freimanis, Eddie	22 Feb 1920	Latvia	Lat	Northampton (May 1948)
Pahars, Marian	5 Aug 1976	Riga	Lat	Southampton (Mar 1999)
Astafjevs, Vitalis	3 Apr 1971	Riga	Lat	Bristol R (Jan 2000)
Bleidelis, Imants	16 Aug 1975	Latvia	Lat	Southampton (Feb 2000)
Kolinko, Alex	18 Jun 1975	Latvia	Lat	C Palace (Sep 2000)

Name	DOB	Place of birth	Nat	Club(s) (joined/first played)
Stepanovs, Igors	21 Jan 1976	Ogre	Lat	Arsenal (Sep 2000)
Rubins, Andrejs	26 Nov 1978	Latvia	Lat	C Palace (Oct 2000)
Stolcers, Andrejs	8 Jul 1974	Latvia	Lat	Fulham (Dec 2000)

LIBERIA (5)

Name	DOB	Place of birth	Nat	Club(s) (joined/first played)
Wreh, Christopher	14 May 1975	Monrovia	Lbr	Arsenal (Aug 1997); Birmingham (Oct 1999)
Andreasson, Marcus	13 Jul 1978	Monrovia	Swe	Bristol R (Jul 1998)
Sarr, Mass	6 Feb 1973	Unification Town	Lbr	Reading (Jul 1998)
Weah, George	1 Oct 1966	Monrovia	Lbr	Chelsea (Jan 2000); Man City (Aug 2000)
John, Collins	17 Oct 1985	Zwedru	Neth	Fulham (Jan 2004)

LIBYA (1)

Name	DOB	Place of birth	Nat	Club(s) (joined/first played)
Muntasser, Jehad	26 Jul 1978	Tripoli	Lby	Arsenal (Jun 1997)

LITHUANIA (2+1)

Name	DOB	Place of birth	Nat	Club(s) (joined/first played)
Bookman, Louis	1890	Zagaren	Brit	Bradford City (Jul 1911); WBA (Feb 1914); Luton (Aug 1920); Port Vale (Jul 1923)
Tereskinas, Andrejus	10 Jul 1970	Telsiai	Lith	Macclesfield (Nov 2000)

Qualified for Lithuania but born outside Lithuania

Name	DOB	Place of birth	Nat	Club(s) (joined/first played)
Danilevicius, Tomas	18 Jul 1978	Moscow, Rus	Lith	Arsenal (Sep 2000)

LUXEMBOURG (1)

Name	DOB	Place of birth	Nat	Club(s) (joined/first played)
Gillet, Stephane	20 Aug 1977	Luxembourg	Lux	Chester (Jan 2006)

MACEDONIA (4)

Name	DOB	Place of birth	Nat	Club(s) (joined/first played)
Bozinoski, Vlado	30 Mar 1964	Skopje	Aus	Ipswich (Dec 1992)
Hristov, Georgi	30 Jan 1976	Bitola	Mac	Barnsley (Jul 1997)
Sedloski, Goce	10 Apr 1974	Golemo Konjari	Mac	Sheff Wed (Mar 1998)
Sakiri, Artim	23 Sep 1973	Struga	Mac	WBA (Jul 2003)

MADAGASCAR (1)

Name	DOB	Place of birth	Nat	Club(s) (joined/first played)
Horace, Alain	4 Dec 1971	Madagascar	Fr	Hartlepool (Oct 1996)

MALAYSIA (3)

Name	DOB	Place of birth	Nat	Club(s) (joined/first played)
Mordey, Henry	4 May 1911	Kuala Lumpur	Brit	Charlton (Jul 1936)
Cruickshank, George	22 Jul 1931	Malaysia	Brit	Carlisle (Aug 1957)
Edge, Declan	18 Sep 1965	Malacca	NZ	Notts Co (Dec 1985)

MALI (4+2)

Name	DOB	Place of birth	Nat	Club(s) (joined/first played)
Sidibe, Mamady	18 Dec 1979	Mali	Fr	Swansea (Jul 2001); Gillingham (Aug 2002); Stoke (Jun 2005)
Berthe, Sekou	7 Oct 1977	Bamako	Mli	WBA (Sep 2003)
Konte, Amadou	23 Jan 1981	Bamako	Mli	Cambridge (Oct 2004)
Sissoko, Noe	2 Jun 1983	Bamako	Mli	Notts Co (Feb 2006)

Other players qualified for Mali but born outside Mali

Name	DOB	Place of birth	Nat	Club(s) (joined/first played)
Kanoute, Frederic	2 Sep 1977	Sainte Foy-les-Lyon, Fr	Mli	West Ham (Mar 2000); Tottenham (Aug 2003)
Sissoko, Mohamed	22 Jan 1985	Rouen, Fr	Mli	Liverpool (Jul 2005)

MALTA (15)

Name	DOB	Place of birth	Nat	Club(s) (joined/first played)
Hogan, Cornelius	1878	Malta	Brit	NB Tower (May 1899); Burnley (Nov 1901)
Dwane, Eddie	17 Jul 1896	Malta	Brit	Lincoln (Jul 1920)
McNeill, Hamilton	13 May 1910	Malta	Brit	Hull (May 1937); Bury (Feb 1939)
Shanks, Wally	1 May 1923	Malta	Brit	Luton (Dec 1946)
Cini, Joe	20 Nov 1936	Malta	Mal	QPR (Aug 1959)
Cutbush, John	28 Jun 1949	Malta	Brit	Fulham (Jul 1972); Sheff Utd (Mar 1977); Sheff Utd (Aug 1979)

Name	DOB	Place of birth	Nat	Club(s) (joined/first played)
Liddle, David	21 May 1957	Malta	Brit	Northampton (May 1975)
Eames, Billy	20 Sep 1957	Malta	Brit	Portsmouth (Sep 1975); Brentford (Aug 1978)
Strutt, Brian	21 Sep 1959	Malta	Mal	Sheff Wed (Sep 1977)
Geard, Glen	25 Feb 1960	Malta	Brit	Brighton (Feb 1978)
Stevens, Ian	21 Oct 1966	Malta	Brit	Preston (Nov 1984); Bolton (Mar 1987); Stockport (Oct 1986); Bury (Jul 1991); Shrewsbury (Aug 1994); Carlisle (May 1997); Cheltenham (Mar 2000); Wrexham (Jul 1999); Carlisle (Aug 2000)
Buttigieg, John	15 Oct 1963	Malta	Mal	Brentford (Nov 1988); Swindon (Sep 1990)
Kerr, Dylan	14 Jan 1967	Malta	Brit	Leeds (Feb 1989); Blackpool (Dec 1991); Doncaster (Aug 1991); Reading (Jul 1993); Carlisle (Sep 1996); Kidderminster (Sep 2000); Exeter (Aug 2001)
Tisdale, Paul	14 Jan 1973	Malta	Brit	Southampton (Jun 1991); Northampton (Mar 1992); Huddersfield (Nov 1996); Bristol C (Jun 1997); Exeter (Dec 1997)
Dimech, Luke	11 Jan 1977	Malta	Mal	Mansfield (Aug 2003); Chester (Jul 2005)

MARTINIQUE (2)

Name	DOB	Place of birth	Nat	Club(s) (joined/first played)
Sigere, Jean-Michel	26 Jan 1977	Martinique	Fr	Rushden (Mar 2000)
Negouai, Christian	20 Jan 1975	Fort-de-France	Fr	Man City (Nov 2001); Coventry (Jan 2005)

MAURITANIA (1)

Name	DOB	Place of birth	Nat	Club(s) (joined/first played)
Diallo, Drissa	4 Jan 1973	Nouadhibou	Gui	Burnley (Jan 2003); Ipswich (Jun 2003); Sheff Wed (Jul 2005)

MEXICO (3)

Name	DOB	Place of birth	Nat	Club(s) (joined/first played)
Burton, Frank	1891	Luapagno	Brit	West Ham (Aug 1919); Charlton (Jul 1921)
Lopez, Carlos	18 Apr 1970	Mexico City	Mex	Wycombe (Jan 2002)
Borgetti, Jared	14 Aug 1973	Culiacán	Mex	Bolton (Jul 2005)

MOLDOVA (1)

Name	DOB	Place of birth	Nat	Club(s) (joined/first played)
Tistimetanu, Ivan	27 Apr 1974	Moldova	Mol	Bristol C (Dec 1998)

MOROCCO (12+2)

Name	DOB	Place of birth	Nat	Club(s) (joined/first played)
Nayim, Mohamed	5 Nov 1968	Ceuta	Mor	Tottenham (Nov 1988)
Mettioui, Ahmed	3 Nov 1965	Tangier	Mor	Crewe (Jul 1992)
Moussaddik, Chuck	23 Feb 1970	Meknes	Mor	Wycombe (Sep 1995)
Kachloul, Hassan	19 Feb 1973	Agadir	Mor	Southampton (Oct 1998); A Villa (Jun 2001); Wolves (Sep 2003)
Chippo, Youssef	10 Jun 1973	Boujaad	Mor	Coventry (Jul 1999)
Hadji, Mustapha	16 Nov 1971	Ifrane	Mor	Coventry (Aug 1999); A Villa (Jul 2001)
El Khalej, Tahar	16 Jun 1968	Marrakesh	Mor	Southampton (Mar 2000); Charlton (Feb 2003)
Chalqi, Khalid	28 Apr 1971	Oujda	Mor	Torquay (Nov 2000)
Ouaddou, Abdeslam	1 Nov 1978	Ksar-Askour	Mor	Fulham (Aug 2001)
Safri, Youssef	1 Mar 1977	Casablanca	Mor	Coventry (Aug 2001); Norwich (Jul 2004)
El Karkouri, Talal	8 Jul 1976	Casablanca	Mor	Sunderland (Feb 2003); Charlton (Jul 2004)
Naybet, Noureddine	10 Feb 1979	Casablanca	Mor	Tottenham (Aug 2004)

Other players qualified for Morocco but born outside Morocco

Name	DOB	Place of birth	Nat	Club(s) (joined/first played)
El Kholti, Abdou	17 Oct 1980	Annesse, Fr	Mor	Yeovil (Aug 2003); Cambridge (Jul 2004); Chester (Jul 2005)
El Hamdaoui, Mounir	14 Jul 1984	Rotterdam, Neth	Mor	Derby (Sep 2005)

MOZAMBIQUE (2)

Name	DOB	Place of birth	Nat	Club(s) (joined/first played)
Xavier, Abel	30 Nov 1972	Nampula	Por	Everton (Sep 1999); Liverpool (Jan 2002);

Name	DOB	Place of birth	Nat	Club(s) (joined/first played)
				Middlesbrough (Aug 2005)
Cadete, Jorge	27 Aug 1968	Porto Amélia	Por	Bradford (Feb 2000)

THE NETHERLANDS (126+21)

Name	DOB	Place of birth	Nat	Club(s) (joined/first played)
Keizer, Gerry	18 Aug 1910	Amsterdam	Neth	Arsenal (Aug 1930); Charlton (Jul 1931)
Warburton, George	1916	Netherlands	Brit	Chester (Nov 1938)
Schroeder, Nico	19 Nov 1947	Netherlands	Neth	Swansea (Jul 1976)
Muhren, Arnold	2 Jun 1951	Volendam	Neth	Ipswich (Aug 1978); Man Utd (Aug 1982)
Thijssen, Frans	23 Jan 1952	Heumen	Neth	Ipswich (Feb 1979); Nottm For (Oct 1983)
Meijer, Geert	15 Mar 1951	Amsterdam	Neth	Bristol C (Mar 1979)
Ursem, Loek	7 Jan 1958	Amsterdam	Neth	Stoke (Jul 1979); Sunderland (Mar 1982)
De Goey, Len	29 Feb 1952	Amsterdam	Neth	Sheff Utd (Aug 1979)
Koenen, Frans	4 Nov 1958	Waalwijk	Neth	Newcastle (Aug 1980)
Brocken, Bud	12 Sep 1957	Tilburg	Neth	Birmingham (Aug 1981)
Kaiser, Rudi	26 Dec 1960	Amsterdam	Neth	Coventry (Aug 1981)
Otto, Heine	24 Aug 1954	Amsterdam	Neth	Middlesbrough (Aug 1981)
Van Mierlo, Toine	24 Aug 1957	Sorendonk	Neth	Birmingham (Aug 1981)
Jol, Martin	16 Jan 1956	Den Haag	Neth	WBA (Oct 1981); Coventry (Jul 1984)
Lohman, Jan	18 Feb 1959	Dussen	Neth	Watford (Oct 1981)
Van Breukelen, Hans	4 Oct 1956	Utrecht	Neth	Nottm For (Sep 1982)
Van Wijk, Dennis	16 Dec 1962	Oostzaan	Neth	Norwich (Oct 1982)
Kraay, Hans	22 Dec 1959	Utrecht	Neth	Brighton (Feb 1984)
Metgod, Johnny	27 Feb 1958	Amsterdam	Neth	Nottm For (Aug 1984); Tottenham (Jul 1987)
Segers, Hans	30 Oct 1961	Eindhoven	Neth	Nottm For (Aug 1984); Stoke (Feb 1987); Sheff Utd (Nov 1987); Wimbledon (Sep 1988); Wolves (Feb 1998); Tottenham (Aug 1998)
Cheetham, Mike	30 Jun 1967	Amsterdam	Brit	Ipswich (Oct 1988); Cambridge (Oct 1989); Colchester (Mar 1995); Chesterfield (Jul 1994)
Atteveld, Ray	8 Sep 1966	Amsterdam	Neth	Everton (Aug 1989); Bristol C (Mar 1992); West Ham (Feb 1992)
Van der Laan, Robin	5 Sep 1968	Schiedam	Neth	Port Vale (Feb 1991); Derby (Aug 1995); Wolves (Oct 1996); Barnsley (Jul 1998)
Jalink, Nico	22 Jun 1964	Rotterdam	Neth	Port Vale (Jul 1991)
Essers, Pierre	20 Feb 1959	Holland	Neth	Walsall (Sep 1991)
Hoekman, Danny	21 Sep 1964	Nijmegen	Neth	Man City (Oct 1991)
Van Rossum, Erik	27 Mar 1963	Nijmegen	Neth	Plymouth (Jan 1992)
Vonk, Michel	28 Oct 1968	Alkmaar	Neth	Man City (Mar 1992); Oldham (Dec 1995); Sheff Utd (Nov 1995)
Dijkstra, Meindert	28 Feb 1967	Eindhoven	Neth	Notts Co (Aug 1992)
Goulooze, Richard	16 Nov 1967	Alkmaar	Neth	Derby (Sep 1992)
Keizerweerd, Orpheo	2 Nov 1968	Holland	Neth	Oldham (Mar 1993)
Groenendijk, Alfons	17 May 1964	Leiden	Neth	Man City (Jul 1993)
Nijholt, Luc	29 Jul 1961	Zaandam	Neth	Swindon (Jul 1993)
Boere, Jeroen	18 Nov 1967	Arnheim	Neth	Portsmouth (Mar 1994); West Ham (Sep 1993); WBA (Sep 1994); C Palace (Sep 1995); Southend (Mar 1996)
Dijkstra, Sieb	20 Oct 1966	Kerkrade	Neth	QPR (Jul 1994); Bristol C (Sep 1995); Wycombe (Mar 1996)
Roy, Bryan	12 Feb 1969	Amsterdam	Neth	Nottm For (Aug 1994)
Sneekes, Richard	30 Oct 1968	Amsterdam	Neth	Bolton (Aug 1994); WBA (Mar 1996); Hull (Nov 2001); Stockport (Sep 2001)
Van Heusden, Arjan	11 Dec 1972	Alphen	Neth	Port Vale (Aug 1994); Oxford (Sep 1997); Cambridge (Aug 1998); Exeter (Jul 2000);

Name	DOB	Place of birth	Nat	Club(s) (joined/first played)
				Mansfield (Sep 2002); Torquay (Nov 2002)
De Wolf, John	10 Dec 1962	Schiedam	Neth	Wolves (Dec 1994)
Helder, Glenn	28 Oct 1968	Leiden	Neth	Arsenal (Feb 1995)
Witschge, Richard	20 Sep 1969	Amsterdam	Neth	Blackburn (Mar 1995)
Bergkamp, Dennis	18 May 1969	Amsterdam	Neth	Arsenal (Jul 1995)
Boogers, Marco	12 Jan 1967	Dordrecht	Neth	West Ham (Jul 1995)
Holwyn, Jermaine	16 Apr 1973	Amsterdam	Neth	Port Vale (Jul 1995)
Willems, Ron	20 Sep 1966	Epe	Neth	Derby (Jul 1995)
De Zeeuw, Arjan	16 Apr 1970	Castricum	Neth	Barnsley (Nov 1995); Wigan Ath (Jul 1999); Portsmouth (Aug 2002); Wigan (Aug 2005)
Griemink, Bart	29 Mar 1972	Groningen	Neth	Birmingham (Nov 1995); Peterborough (Oct 1996); Swindon (Mar 2000); Southend (Jun 2004)
Bos, Gijsbert	22 Mar 1973	Spakenburg	Neth	Lincoln (Mar 1996); Rotherham (Aug 1997)
Ten Heuvel, Laurens	6 Jun 1976	Duivendrecht	Neth	Barnsley (Mar 1996); Sheff Utd (Aug 2002); Bradford (Mar 2003); Grimsby (Aug 2003)
Van der Velden, Carel	3 Aug 1972	Arnhem	Neth	Barnsley (Mar 1996); Scarborough (Aug 1997)
Petta, Bobby	6 Aug 1974	Rotterdam	Neth	Ipswich (Jun 1996); Fulham (Dec 2003); Darlington (Feb 2005); Bradford (Jun 2005)
Regtop, Erik	16 Feb 1968	Emmen	Neth	Bradford (Jul 1996)
Sas, Marco	16 Feb 1971	Vlaardingden	Neth	Bradford (Jul 1996)
Van der Gouw, Raimond	24 Mar 1963	Oldenzaal	Neth	Man Utd (Jul 1996)
Cruyff, Jordi	9 Feb 1974	Amsterdam	Neth	Man Utd (Aug 1996)
Trustfull, Orlando	4 Aug 1970	Amsterdam	Neth	Sheff Wed (Aug 1996)
Molenaar, Robert	27 Feb 1969	Zaandam	Neth	Leeds (Jan 1997); Bradford (Dec 2000)
Koordes, Rogier	13 Jun 1972	Haarlem	Neth	Port Vale (Feb 1997)
Van Hooijdonk, Pierre	29 Nov 1969	Steenbergen	Neth	Nottm For (Mar 1997)
Gentile, Marco	24 Aug 1968	Den Haag	Neth	Burnley (Jun 1997)
Schreuder, Jan-Dirk	2 Aug 1971	Barneveld	Neth	Stoke (Jun 1997)
Sepp, Dennis	5 Jun 1973	Apeldoorn	Neth	Bradford (Jun 1997)
Zoetebier, Ed	7 May 1970	Purmerend	Neth	Sunderland (Jun 1997)
Overmars, Marc	29 Mar 1973	Emst	Neth	Arsenal (Jul 1997)
De Goey, Ed	20 Dec 1966	Gouda	Neth	Chelsea (Jul 1997); Stoke (Aug 2003)
Wiekens, Gérard	25 Feb 1973	Tolhuiswyk	Neth	Man City (Jul 1997)
Van Dulleman, Ray	6 May 1973	Gravenhage	Neth	Northampton (Aug 1997)
Snijders, Mark	12 Mar 1972	Alkmaar	Neth	Port Vale (Sep 1997)
Smeets, Jorg	5 Nov 1970	Bussum	Neth	Wigan Ath (Oct 1997); Chester (Mar 1999)
Holster, Marco	4 Dec 1971	Weesp	Neth	Ipswich (Jul 1998)
Stam, Jaap	17 Jul 1972	Kampen	Neth	Man Utd (Jul 1998)
Jonk, Wim	12 Oct 1966	Volendam	Neth	Sheff Wed (Aug 1998)
Kromheer, Elroy	15 Jan 1970	Amsterdam	Neth	Reading (Aug 1998)
Van der Kwaak, Peter	12 Oct 1968	Haarlem	Neth	Reading (Aug 1998); Carlisle (Feb 2000)
Achterberg, John	8 Jul 1971	Utrecht	Neth	Tranmere (Sep 1998)
Zwijnenberg, Clemens	18 May 1970	Enschede	Neth	Bristol C (Sep 1998)
Korsten, Willem	21 Jan 1975	Baxtel	Neth	Leeds (Jan 1999); Tottenham (Jul 1999)
Kuipers, Michel	26 Jun 1974	Amsterdam	Neth	Bristol R (Jan 1999); Brighton (Jul 2000); Hull (Aug 2003); Boston (Nov 2005)
Westerveld, Sander	23 Oct 1974	Enschede	Neth	Liverpool (Jun 1999); Portsmouth (Jul 2005); Everton (Feb 2006)
Meijer, Erik	2 Aug 1969	Meersen	Neth	Liverpool (Jul 1999); Preston (Oct 2000)
Melchiot, Mario	4 Nov 1976	Amsterdam	Neth	Chelsea (Jul 1999); Birmingham (Jul 2004)
Sibon, Gerald	19 Apr 1974	Dalen	Neth	Sheff Wed (Jul 1999)
Karelse, John	17 May 1970	Kapelle	Neth	Newcastle (Aug 1999)

Name	DOB	Place of birth	Nat	Club(s) (joined/first played)
Derveld, Fernando	22 Oct 1976	Vlissingen	Neth	Norwich (Mar 2000); WBA (Feb 2001)
De Waard, Raimond	27 Mar 1973	Rotterdam	Neth	Norwich (Mar 2000)
Reuser, Martijn	1 Feb 1975	Amsterdam	Neth	Ipswich (Jun 2000)
Abidallah, Nabil	5 Aug 1982	Amsterdam	Neth	Ipswich (Jul 2000), Northampton (Jan 2004)
Kaak, Tom	31 Mar 1978	Winterswijk	Neth	Darlington (Jul 2000)
Van der Geest, Frank	30 Apr 1973	Beverwijk	Neth	Darlington (Aug 2000)
Van der Linden, Antoine	10 Mar 1976	Rotterdam	Neth	Swindon (Aug 2000)
Bogarde, Winston	22 Oct 1970	Rotterdam	Neth	Chelsea (Sep 2000)
Hernandez, Dino	27 May 1971	Amersfoort	Neth	Wigan Ath (Nov 2000)
Willems, Menno	3 Oct 1977	Amsterdam	Neth	Grimsby (Nov 2000)
Van Nistelrooy, Ruud	1 Jul 1976	Oss	Neth	Man Utd (Apr 2001)
Van Bronckhorst, Giovanni	5 Feb 1975	Rotterdam	Neth	Arsenal (Jun 2001)
Cas, Marcel	30 Apr 1972	Breda	Neth	Notts Co (Jul 2001); Sheff Utd (Feb 2003); Grimsby (Jun 2003)
Hoekstra, Peter	4 Apr 1973	Assen	Neth	Stoke (Jul 2001)
Busscher, Robbie	23 Nov 1982	Leichendan	Neth	Grimsby (Aug 2001)
De Vogt, Wilko	17 Sep 1975	Breda	Neth	Sheff Utd (Aug 2001)
Moor, Reinier	12 Jun 83	The Hague	Ire	Exeter (Aug 2001)
Van der Sar, Edwin	29 Oct 1970	Voorhout	Neth	Fulham (Aug 2001); Man Utd (Jun 2005)
Zenden, Boudewijn	15 Aug 1976	Maastricht	Neth	Chelsea (Aug 2001); Middlesbrough (Aug 2003); Liverpool (Jul 2005)
Evans, Michael	21 Jul 1976	Venlo	Neth	York (Sep 2001)
Ommel, Sergio	2 Sep 1977	The Hague	Neth	Bristol R (Nov 2001)
Postma, Stefan	10 Jun 1976	Utrecht	Neth	A Villa (Jul 2002); Wolves (Aug 2005)
Loran, Tyrone	29 Jun 1981	Amsterdam	Neth	Tranmere (Jan 2003); Port Vale (Dec 2004)
Bosvelt, Paul	26 Mar 1970	Doetinchem	Neth	Man City (Jul 2003)
Owusu-Abeyie, Quincy	15 Apr 1986	Amsterdam	Neth	Arsenal (Jul 2003)
Wapenaar, Harald	10 Apr 1970	Vlaardingen	Neth	Portsmouth (Jul 2003)
Volmer, Joost	7 Mar 1974	Enschede	Neth	WBA (Aug 2003)
Boussatta, Dries	23 Dec 1972	Amsterdam	Neth	Sheff Utd (Nov 2003)
Van Persie, Robin	6 Aug 1983	Rotterdam	Neth	Arsenal (May 2004)
Kluivert, Patrick	1 Jul 1976	Amsterdam	Neth	Newcastle (Jul 2004)
Reiziger, Michael	3 May 1973	Amstelveen	Neth	Middlesbrough (Jul 2004)
Robben, Arjan	23 Jan 1984	Bedum	Neth	Chelsea (Jul 2004)
Waterreus, Ronald	25 Aug 1970	Lemiers	Neth	Man City (Aug 2004)
Stam, Stefan	14 Sep 1979	Amersfoort	Neth	Oldham (Feb 2005)
Colin, Jurgen	20 Jan 1981	Utrecht	Neth	Norwich (Jul 2005)
Loovens, Glenn	22 Oct 1983	Doetinchem	Neth	Cardiff (Jul 2005)
Martis, Shelton	29 Nov 1982	Rotterdam	Neth	Darlington (Jul 2005)
Bouma, Wilfred	15 June 1978	Helmond	Neth	A Villa (Aug 2005)
Carrilho, Mirano	17 Jul 1975	Amsterdam	Neth	MKD (Aug 2005)
Van der Meyde, Andy	30 Sep 1979	Arnhem	Neth	Everton (Aug 2005)
El Hamdaoui, Mounir	14 Jul 1984	Rotterdam	Mor	Derby (Sep 2005)
Kromkamp, Jan	17 Aug 1980	Makkinga	Neth	Liverpool (Jan 2006)
Powel, Berry	2 May 1980	Utrecht	Neth	Millwall (Jan 2006)

Other players qualified for The Netherlands but born outside The Netherlands

Name	DOB	Place of birth	Nat	Club(s) (joined/first played)
Zondervan, Romeo	4 Mar 1959	Surinam	Neth	WBA (Mar 1982); Ipswich (Mar 1984)
Wilson, Ulrich	5 May 1964	Surinam	Neth	Ipswich (Dec 1987)
Monkou, Ken	29 Nov 1964	Surinam	Neth	Chelsea (Mar 1989); Southampton (Aug 1992); Huddersfield (Aug 1999)
Verveer, Etienne	22 Sep 1967	Surinam	Neth	Millwall (Dec 1991); Bradford (Feb 1995)
De Freitas, Fabian	28 Jul 1972	Surinam	Neth	Bolton (Aug 1994); WBA (Aug 1998)

Name	DOB	Place of birth	Nat	Club(s) (joined/first played)
Gullit, Ruud	1 Sep 1962	Surinam	Neth	Chelsea (Jul 1995)
Uhlenbeek, Gus	28 Aug 1970	Surinam	Neth	Ipswich (Aug 1995); Fulham (Jul 1998); Sheff Utd (Aug 2000); Walsall (Mar 2002); Bradford (Aug 2002); Chesterfield (Aug 2003); Wycombe (Jul 2004); Mansfield (Jun 2005)
Blinker, Regi	4 Jun 1969	Surinam	Neth	Sheff Wed (Mar 1996)
Van Gobbel, Ulrich	16 Jan 1971	Surinam	Neth	Southampton (Oct 1996)
Wilsterman, Brian	19 Nov 1966	Surinam	Neth	Oxford (Feb 1997); Rotherham (Jul 1999)
Hasselbaink, Jimmy Floyd	27 Mar 1972	Surinam	Neth	Leeds (Jul 1997); Chelsea (Jul 2000); Middlesbrough (Jul 2004)
Boateng, George	5 Sep 1975	Nkawkaw, Gha	Neth	Coventry (Dec 1997); A Villa (Jul 1999); Middlesbrough (Aug 2002)
Wijnhard, Clyde	9 Nov 1973	Surinam	Neth	Leeds (Jul 1998); Huddersfield (Jul 1999); Preston (Mar 2002); Oldham (Aug 2002); Darlington (Oct 2004); Macclesfield (Oct 2005)
Wilnis, Fabian	23 Aug 1970	Surinam	Neth	Ipswich (Jan 1999)
Faerber, Winston	23 Jul 1971	Surinam	Neth	Cardiff (Aug 1999)
Gorre, Dean	10 Sep 1970	Surinam	Neth	Huddersfield (Sep 1999); Barnsley (Jul 2001); Blackpool (Sep 2004)
Wooter, Nordin	24 Aug 1976	Surinam	Neth	Watford (Sep 1999)
Koejoe, Sammy	17 Aug 1974	Surinam	Neth	QPR (Nov 1999)
John, Collins	17 Oct 1985	Zwedru, Lib	Neth	Fulham (Jan 2004)
De Vries, Mark	24 Aug 1975	Surinam	Neth	Leicester (Jan 2005)
Davids, Edgar	13 Mar 1973	Surinam	Neth	Tottenham (Aug 2005)

NEW CALEDONIA (2)

Name	DOB	Place of birth	Nat	Club(s) (joined/first played)
Karembeu, Christian	3 Dec 1970	Lifou, NCal	Fr	Middlesbrough (Aug 2000)
Gope-Fenepej, John	6 Nov 1978	Noumea, Ncal	Fr	Bolton (Sep 2000)

NEW ZEALAND (19+2)

Name	DOB	Place of birth	Nat	Club(s) (joined/first played)
Moorhead, George	27 May 1895	Christchurch	Ire	Southampton (Aug 1920); Brighton (Aug 1922)
Rush, Jon	13 Oct 1961	Wellington	NZ	Blackpool (Nov 1979)
Herbert, Ricki	10 Apr 1961	Auckland	NZ	Wolves (Oct 1984)
Evans, Ceri	2 Oct 1963	Christchurch	NZ	Oxford (Feb 1989)
Ngata, Harry	24 Aug 1971	Wanganui	NZ	Hull (Jul 1989)
Zoricich, Chris	3 May 1969	Auckland	NZ	Orient (Feb 1990)
Smith, Scott	6 Mar 1975	Christchurch	NZ	Rotherham (Oct 1993)
Norfolk, Lee	17 Oct 1975	Dunedin	NZ	Ipswich (Jul 1994)
Viljoen, Nik	3 Dec 1976	Auckland	NZ	Rotherham (Jun 1995)
Fallon, Rory	20 Mar 1982	Gisborne	NZ	Barnsley (Mar 1999); Shrewsbury (Dec 2001); Swindon (Nov 2003); Yeovil (Feb 2005); Swansea (Jan 2006)
Killen, Chris	8 Oct 1981	Wellington	NZ	Man City (Mar 1999); Wrexham (Sep 2000); Port Vale (Sep 2001); Oldham (Aug 2002)
Hay, Danny	15 May 1975	Auckland	NZ	Leeds (Aug 1999); Walsall (Aug 2002)
Bertos, Leo	20 Dec 1981	Wellington	Grk	Barnsley (Sep 2000); Rochdale (Jul 2003); Chester (Aug 2005)
Christie, Jeremy	22 May 1983	Whangarie	NZ	Barnsley (Dec 2001)
Pearce, Allan	7 Apr 1983	Wellington	NZ	Lincoln (Dec 2002)
Paston, Mark	13 Dec 1976	Hawke's Bay	NZ	Bradford (Aug 2003); Walsall (Jun 2004)
Webster, Adrian	11 Oct 1980	Hawke's Bay	NZ	Darlington (Oct 2004)
Nelsen, Ryan	18 Oct 1977	Christchurch	NZ	Blackburn (Jan 2005)
Elliott, Simon	6 Oct 1976	Wellington	NZ	Fulham (Jan 2006)

Name	DOB	Place of birth	Nat	Club(s) (joined/first played)

Qualified for New Zealand but born outside New Zealand

Name	DOB	Place of birth	Nat	Club(s) (joined/first played)
Edge, Declan	18 Sep 1965	Malacca, Mly	NZ	Notts Co (Dec 1985)
Smeltz, Shane	20 Sep 1980	Goppingen, Ger	NZ	Mansfield (Jan 2005)

NIGERIA (54+1)

Name	DOB	Place of birth	Nat	Club(s) (joined/first played)
Balogun, Tesilim	27 Mar 1931	Lagos	Nig	QPR (Sep 1956)
Onyeali, Elkanah	7 Jun 1939	Port Harcourt	Nig	Tranmere (Aug 1960)
Coker, Ade	19 May 1954	Lagos	Nig	West Ham (Dec 1971); Lincoln (Dec 1974)
Chiedozie, John	18 Apr 1960	Owerri	Nig	Orient (Apr 1977); Notts Co (Aug 1981); Tottenham (Aug 1984); Derby (Aug 1988); Chesterfield (Mar 1990); Notts Co (Jan 1990)
Nwajiobi, Emeka	25 May 1959	Nibo Awka	Nig	Luton (Dec 1983)
Salako, John	11 Feb 1969	Lagos	Eng	C Palace (Nov 1986); Swansea (Aug 1989); Coventry (Aug 1995); Bolton (Mar 1998); Fulham (Jul 1998); Charlton (Aug 1999); Reading (Nov 2001); Brentford (Jul 2004)
Iorfa, Dominic	1 Oct 1968	Lagos	Nig	QPR (Mar 1990); Peterborough (Oct 1992); Southend (Aug 1994); Southend (Dec 1998)
Salako, Andy	8 Nov 1972	Lagos	Nig	Charlton (Apr 1991)
Okenla, Foley	9 Oct 1967	Nigeria	Nig	Birmingham (Aug 1991)
Adekola, David	18 May 1968	Lagos	Nig	Bury (Jan 1993); Exeter (Feb 1994); Bournemouth (Sep 1994); Wigan Ath (Oct 1994); Cambridge (Aug 1995); Brighton (Oct 1996)
Adebola, Dele	23 Jun 1975	Lagos	Nig	Crewe (Mar 1993); Birmingham (Feb 1998); Oldham (Mar 2002); C Palace (Aug 2002); Coventry (Jun 2003); Burnley (Mar 2004); Bradford (Aug 2004)
Obebo, Godfrey	16 Apr 1966	Lagos	Nig	Halifax (Mar 1993)
Okorie, Chima	8 Oct 1968	Izombe	Nig	Grimsby (Sep 1993); Torquay (Mar 1994)
Amokachi, Daniel	30 Dec 1972	Kaduna	Nig	Everton (Aug 1994)
Emenalo, Michael	14 Jul 1965	Aba	Nig	Notts Co (Aug 1994)
Omoyimni, Manny	28 Dec 1977	Nigeria	Nig	West Ham (May 1995); Bournemouth (Sep 1996); Orient (Mar 1999); Gillingham (Sep 1999); Scunthorpe (Dec 1999); Barnet (Feb 2000); Oxford (Jul 2000)
Ayorinde, Sammy	20 Oct 1974	Lagos	Nig	Orient (Apr 1996)
Bankole, Ade	9 Sep 1969	Abeokuta	Nig	Crewe (Sep 1996); QPR (Jul 1998); Crewe (Jul 2000); Brentford (Feb 2005)
Babayaro, Celestine	29 Aug 1978	Kaduna	Nig	Chelsea (Jun 1997); Newcastle (Jan 2005)
Okafor, Sam	17 Mar 1982	Xtiam	Nig	Colchester (Aug 1998)
Ameobi, Shola	12 Oct 1981	Zaria	Eng	Newcastle (Oct 1998)
Ifejiagwa, Emeka	30 Oct 1977	Aba	Nig	Brighton (Oct 1998)
Iroha, Ben	29 Nov 1969	Aba	Nig	Watford (Dec 1998)
Kanu, Nwankwo	1 Aug 1976	Owerri	Nig	Arsenal (Feb 1999); WBA (Jul 2004)
Opara, Kelechi	21 Dec 1981	Oweri	Nig	Colchester (Aug 1999); Orient (Dec 2000)
Abbey, George	20 Oct 1978	Port Harcourt	Nig	Macclesfield (Aug 1999); Port Vale (Dec 2004)
Etuhu, Dixon	8 Jun 1982	Kano	Nig	Man City (Dec 1999); Preston (Jan 2002); Norwich (Nov 2005)
Odejayi, Kay	21 Feb 1982	Ibadon	Brit	Bristol C (Jul 2000); Cheltenham (May 2003)
Olaoye, Dele	17 Oct 1982	Lagos	Nig	Port Vale (Aug 2000)
West, Taribo	26 Mar 1974	Port Harcourt	Nig	Derby (Nov 2000); Plymouth (Jul 2005)
Shittu, Danny	2 Sep 1980	Lagos	Nig	Blackpool (Feb 2001); QPR (Oct 2001)

Name	DOB	Place of birth	Nat	Club(s) (joined/first played)
Ofodile, Adolphus	15 Dec 1979	Fungu	Nig	Walsall (Jul 2001)
George, Finidi	15 Apr 1971	Port Harcourt	Nig	Ipswich (Aug 2001)
Okocha, Jay-Jay	14 Aug 1973	Enugu	Nig	Bolton (Aug 2002)
Okoli, James	11 Jan 1976	Lagos	Nig	York (Aug 2002)
Yobo, Joseph	6 Sep 1980	Kano	Nig	Everton (Sep 2002)
Ayegbini, Yakubu	22 Nov 1982	Benin City	Nig	Portsmouth (Jan 2003); Middlesbrough (Jul 2005)
Okuonghae, Magnus	16 Feb 1986	Nigeria	Eng	Rushden (Jan 2003)
Udeze, Ifeanyi	21 Jul 1980	Lagos	Nig	WBA (Jan 2003)
Ashikodi, Moses	27 Jun 1987	Lagos	Nig	Millwall (Feb 2003); West Ham (Aug 2004); Gillingham (Aug 2005)
Okoronkwo, Isaac	1 May 1978	Nbela	Nig	Wolves (Jul 2003)
Kanu, Chris	4 Dec 1979	Owerri	Nig	Peterborough (Aug 2003)
Olugbodi, Jide	29 Nov 1977	Lagos	Nig	Brentford (Oct 2003)
Onibuje, Fola	25 Sep 1984	Lagos	Nig	Huddersfield (Nov 2003); Barnsley (Jul 2004); Peterborough (Mar 2005)
Odubade, Yemi	4 Jul 1984	Lagos	Nig	Yeovil (Jul 2004); Oxford (Jan 2006)
Olofinjana, Seyi	30 Jun 1980	Lagos	Nig	Wolves (Jul 2004)
Kaku, Blessing	5 Mar 1978	Ughelli	Nig	Bolton (Aug 2004); Derby (Nov 2004)
Oyedele, Shola	14 Sep 1984	Kano	Nig	MKD (Mar 2004)
Onuoha, Nedum	12 Nov 1986	Warri	Eng	Man City (Aug 2004)
Echanomi, Efe	27 Sep 1986	Lagos	Nig	Orient (Dec 2004)
Olisadebe, Emmanuel	22 Dec 1978	Warri	Pol	Portsmouth (Jan 2005)
Anichebe, Victor	23 Apr 1988	Lagos	Nig	Everton (Jul 2005)
Chilaka, Chibuzor	21 Oct 1986	Lagos	Nig	Notts Co (Oct 2005)
Obinna, Eric	10 Jun 1981	Owerri	Nig	Reading (Jan 2006)
Other players qualified for Nigeria but born outside Nigeria				
Ukah, Ugo	18 Jan 1984	Parma, It	Nig	QPR (Aug 2005)

NORWAY (80+2)

Name	DOB	Place of birth	Nat	Club(s) (joined/first played)
Hansen, Karl	4 Jul 1921	Denmark	Nor	Huddersfield (Jan 1949)
Aas, Einar	12 Oct 1955	Moss	Nor	Nottm For (Mar 1981)
Hareide, Aage	23 Sep 1953	Hareide	Nor	Man City (Oct 1981); Norwich (Jun 1983)
Osvold, Kjetil	5 Jun 1961	Aalesund	Nor	Nottm For (Mar 1987); Leicester (Dec 1987)
Thorstvedt, Erik	28 Oct 1962	Stavanger	Nor	Tottenham (Dec 1988)
Andersen, Vetle	20 Apr 1964	Kristiansand	Nor	WBA (Dec 1989)
Johnsen, Erland	5 Apr 1967	Fredrikstad	Nor	Chelsea (Dec 1989)
Halle, Gunnar	11 Aug 1965	Larvik	Nor	Oldham (Feb 1991); Leeds (Dec 1996); Bradford (Jun 1999); Wolves (Mar 2002)
Bjornebye, Stig Inge	11 Dec 1969	Elverum	Nor	Liverpool (Dec 1992); Blackburn (Jun 2000)
Berg, Henning	1 Sep 1969	Eidsvell	Nor	Blackburn (Jan 1993); Man Utd (Aug 1997); Blackburn (Sep 2000)
Ingebrigtsen, Kaare	11 Nov 1965	Rosenborg	Nor	Man City (Jan 1993)
Strandli, Frank	16 May 1972	Norway	Nor	Leeds (Jan 1993)
Fjortoft, Jan Aage	10 Jan 1967	Aalesund	Nor	Swindon (Jul 1993); Middlesbrough (Mar 1995); Sheff Utd (Jan 1997); Barnsley (Jan 1998)
Flo, Jostein	3 Oct 1964	Eid	Nor	Sheff Utd (Aug 1993)
Kjeldbjerg, Jakob	21 Oct 1969	Fredrikstad	Den	Chelsea (Aug 1993)
Pedersen, Tore	29 Sep 1969	Fredrikstad	Nor	Oldham (Oct 1993); Blackburn (Sep 1997); Wimbledon (Jun 1999)
Bohinen, Lars	8 Sep 1969	Vadso	Nor	Nottm For (Nov 1993); Blackburn (Oct 1995); Derby (Mar 1998)

Name	DOB	Place of birth	Nat	Club(s) (joined/first played)
Nilsen, Roger	8 Aug 1969	Tromso	Nor	Sheff Utd (Nov 1993); Tottenham (Mar 1999)
Haaland, Alf-Inge	23 Nov 1972	Stavanger	Nor	Nottm For (Jan 1994); Leeds (Jul 1997); Man City (Jun 2000)
Hansen, Vergard	8 Aug 1969	Drammen	Nor	Bristol C (Nov 1994)
Leonhardsen, Oyvind	17 Aug 1970	Kristiansund	Nor	Wimbledon (Nov 1994); Liverpool (Jun 1997); Tottenham (Aug 1999); A Villa (Sep 2002)
Hovi, Tom	15 Jan 1972	Gjovik	Nor	Charlton (Jan 1995)
Riseth, Vidar	21 Apr 1972	Levanger	Nor	Luton (Oct 1995)
Rushfeldt, Siggi	11 Dec 1972	Vadso	Nor	Birmingham (Oct 1995)
Belsvik, Petter	2 Oct 1967	Lillehammer	Nor	Southend (Nov 1995)
Andersen, Leif	19 Apr 1971	Fredrikstad	Nor	C Palace (Jan 1996)
Johnsen, Ronny	10 Jun 1969	Sandefjord	Nor	Man Utd (Jul 1996); A Villa (Sep 2002); Newcastle (Sep 2004)
Solskjaer, Ole Gunnar	26 Feb 1973	Kristiansund	Nor	Man Utd (Jul 1996)
Grodas, Frode	24 Oct 1964	Sogndal	Nor	Chelsea (Sep 1996)
Ostenstad, Egil	2 Jan 1972	Haugesund	Nor	Southampton (Oct 1996); Blackburn (Aug 1999); Man City (Feb 2001)
Henriksen, Tony	25 Apr 1973	Hammel	Nor	Southend (Oct 1996)
Knarvik, Tommy	1 Nov 1979	Bergen	Nor	Leeds (Nov 1996)
Lundekvam, Claus	22 Feb 1973	Austevoll	Nor	Southampton (Nov 1996)
Sundgot, Ole	21 Mar 1972	Olsumd	Nor	Bradford (Nov 1996)
Heidenstrom, Bjorn	15 Jan 1968	Porsgrunn	Nor	Orient (Dec 1996)
Iversen, Steffen	10 Nov 1976	Oslo	Nor	Tottenham (Dec 1996); Wolves (Aug 2003)
Kvarme, Bjorn Tore	17 Jun 1972	Trondheim	Nor	Liverpool (Jan 1997)
Nevland, Erik	10 Nov 1977	Stavanger	Nor	Man Utd (Jul 1997)
Soltvedt, Trond Egil	15 Feb 1967	Voss	Nor	Coventry (Jul 1997); Southampton (Aug 1999); Sheff Wed (Feb 2001)
Flo, Tore Andre	15 Jun 1973	Stryn	Nor	Chelsea (Aug 1997); Sunderland (Nov 2002)
Hjelde, Jon Olav	30 Jul 1972	Levanger	Nor	Nottm For (Aug 1997); Mansfield (Aug 2005)
Pedersen, Jan Ove	12 Nov 1968	Oslo	Nor	Hartlepool (Oct 1997)
Rudi, Petter	17 Sep 1973	Kristiansund	Nor	Sheff Wed (Oct 1997)
Solbakken, Stale	27 Feb 1968	Kongsvinger	Nor	Wimbledon (Oct 1997)
Fuglestad, Erik	13 Aug 1974	Randaberg	Nor	Norwich (Nov 1997)
Hollund, Martin	11 Aug 1974	Stord	Nor	Hartlepool (Nov 1997)
Myhre, Thomas	16 Oct 1973	Sarpsborg	Nor	Everton (Nov 1997); Birmingham (Mar 2000); Tranmere (Nov 2000); Sunderland (Oct 2002); C Palace (Oct 2003); Charlton (Aug 2005)
Larsen, Stig Olav	29 Sep 1973	Bergen	Nor	Hartlepool (Dec 1997)
Johansen, Stig	13 Jun 1972	Svolvær	Nor	Bristol C (Feb 1998); Southampton (Aug 1997)
Heggem, Vegard	13 Jul 1975	Trondheim	Nor	Liverpool (Jul 1998)
Alsaker, Paul	6 Nov 1973	Stord	Nor	Stockport (Aug 1998)
Kval, Frank	17 Jul 1974	Bergen	Nor	Burnley (Oct 1998)
Vindheim, Rune	18 May 1972	Hoyanguer	Nor	Burnley (Oct 1998); Hartlepool (Sep 1999)
Berntsen, Robin	10 Jul 1970	Tromso	Nor	Port Vale (Nov 1998)
Andreassen, Svein	3 Jul 1968	Hadsel	Nor	Portsmouth (Dec 1998)
Jacobsen, Anders	18 Apr 1968	Oslo	Nor	Sheff Utd (Dec 1998); Stoke (Aug 1999); Notts Co (Sep 2000)
Flo, Havard	4 Apr 1970	Volda	Nor	Wolves (Jan 1999)
Kippe, Frode	17 Jan 1978	Oslo	Nor	Liverpool (Jan 1999); Stoke (Dec 1999)
Stensaas, Stale	7 Jul 1971	Trondheim	Nor	Nottm For (Jan 1999)
Bakke, Eirik	13 Sep 1977	Sogndal	Nor	Leeds (Jul 1999); A Villa (Aug 2005)
Andersen, Trond	6 Jan 1975	Kristiansund	Nor	Wimbledon (Aug 1999)
Normann, Runar	1 Mar 1978	Harstad	Nor	Coventry (Aug 1999)

Name	DOB	Place of birth	Nat	Club(s) (joined/first played)
Tennebo, Thomas	19 Mar 1975	Bergen	Nor	Hartlepool (Aug 1999)
Bergersen, Kent	8 Feb 1967	Oslo	Nor	Stockport (Sep 1999)
Andresen, Martin	2 Feb 1977	Oslo	Nor	Wimbledon (Oct 1999); Blackburn (Feb 2004)
Berntsen, Tommy	18 Dec 1973	Oslo	Nor	Portsmouth (Nov 1999)
Tessem, Jo	28 Feb 1972	Orlandet	Nor	Southampton (Nov 1999); Millwall (Sep 2004)
Lund, Andreas	7 May 1975	Kristiansand	Nor	Wimbledon (Feb 2000)
Bragstad, Bjorn Otto	5 Jan 1971	Trondheim	Nor	Derby (Aug 2000); Birmingham (Sep 2001)
Sperrevik, Tim	2 Mar 1976	Bergen	Nor	Hartlepool (Aug 2000)
Fostervold, Anders	4 Oct 1971	Molde	Nor	Grimsby (Nov 2000)
Johansen, Rune	1 Apr 1978	Oslo	Nor	Bristol R (Nov 2000)
Karlsen, Kent	17 Feb 1973	Oslo	Nor	Luton (Nov 2000)
Soma, Ragnvald	10 Nov 1979	Bryne	Nor	West Ham (Jan 2001)
Riise, John Arne	29 Sep 1980	Molde	Nor	Liverpool (Jun 2001)
Rovde, Marius	26 Jun 1972	Trondheim	Nor	Wrexham (Jan 2002)
Capaldi, Tony	12 Aug 1981	Porsgrunn	N Ire	Plymouth (May 2003)
Pedersen, Morten G.	8 Sep 1981	Vadso	Nor	Blackburn (Aug 2004)
Karadas, Azar	9 Aug 1981	Bergen	Nor	Portsmouth (Jul 2005)
Brekke-Skard, Vemund	11 Sep 1980	Hedmark	Nor.	Ipswich (Jan 2006)

Other players qualified for Norway but born outside Norway

Name	DOB	Place of birth	Nat	Club(s) (joined/first played)
Lydersen, Pal	10 Sep 1965	Odense, Den	Nor	Arsenal (Nov 1991)
Baardsen, Espen	7 Dec 1977	San Rafael, USA	Nor	Tottenham (Jul 1996); Watford (Aug 2000); Everton (Jan 2003)

OMAN (1)

Collins, Patrick	4 Feb 1985	Oman	Eng	Sheff Wed (May 2004); Swindon (Aug 2005)

PARAGUAY (1)

Gavilan, Diego	1 Mar 1980	Ascuncion	Par	Newcastle (Feb 2000)

PERU (3)

Solano, Nolberto	12 Dec 1974	Lima	Per	Newcastle (Aug 1998); A Villa (Jan 2004); Newcastle (Aug 2005)
Zuniga, Ysrael	27 Aug 1976	Lima	Per	Coventry (Mar 2000)
Labarthe, Gianfranco	20 Sep 1984	Lima	Per	Huddersfield (Feb 2003); Derby (Jul 2003)

POLAND (29+2)

Kubicki, Eryk	18 Aug 1925	Hadjuki	Pol	York (Oct 1946)
Wojtczak, Edouard	29 Apr 1921	Poland	Pol	York (Oct 1946)
Gerula, Stan	21 Feb 1914	Dzikow	Pol	Orient (May 1948)
Kapler, Konrad	25 Feb 1925	Tychy	Pol	Rochdale (May 1949)
Starocsik, Felix	20 May 1920	Silesia	Pol	Northampton (Jul 1951)
Wasilewski, Adam	1925	Poland	Pol	Rochdale (Jul 1953)
Deyna, Kazimierz	23 Oct 1947	Starograd	Pol	Man City (Nov 1978)
Nowak, Tadeusz	28 Nov 1948	Trzcinsko	Pol	Bolton (Mar 1979)
Kowenicki, Ryszard	22 Dec 1948	Lodz	Pol	Oldham (Dec 1979)
Musial, Adam	18 Dec 1948	Wieliczka	Pol	Hereford (Aug 1980)
Warzycha, Robert	20 Jun 1963	Wielun	Pol	Everton (Mar 1991)
Kubicki, Dariusz	6 Jun 1963	Kozuchow	Pol	A Villa (Aug 1991); Sunderland (Mar 1994); Tranmere (Mar 1998); Wolves (Aug 1997); Carlisle (Jul 1998); Darlington (Oct 1998)
Dziekanowski, Jackie	30 Sep 1962	Warsaw	Pol	Bristol C (Jan 1992)
Wdowczyk, Dariusz	21 Sep 1962	Warsaw	Pol	Reading (Aug 1994)
Niestroj, Robert	2 Dec 1974	Oppeln	Ger	Wolves (Nov 1998)
Radzinski, Tomasz	14 Dec 1973	Poznan	Can	Everton (Jul 2001); Fulham (Jul 2004)
Dudek, Jerzy	23 Mar 1973	Rybnik	Pol	Liverpool (Aug 2001)

Name	DOB	Place of birth	Nat	Club(s) (joined/first played)
Adamczuk, Darius	20 Oct 1969	Szczecinek	Pol	Wigan (Aug 2001)
Bak, Arkadiusz	6 Jan 1974	Szczecinek	Pol	Birmingham (Dec 2001)
Swierczewski, Piotr	8 Apr 1972	NowySacz	Pol	Birmingham (Feb 2003)
Olszar, Sebastian	16 Dec 1981	Warsaw	Pol	Portsmouth (Feb 2004); Coventry (Mar 2004)
Kuszczak, Tomasz	20 Mar 1982	Krosno Odrzanskie	Pol	WBA (Jul 2004)
Tarachulski, Bartosz	14 May 1975	Warsaw	Pol	Yeovil (Jul 2004)
Rasiak, Grzegorz	12 Jan 1979	Szczecin	Pol	Derby (Sep 2004); Tottenham (Aug 2005); Southampton (Feb 2006)
Hajto, Tomasz	16 Oct 1972	Krakow	Pol	Southampton (Jul 2005); Derby (Jan 2006)
Kosowski, Kamil	30 Aug 1977	Ostrowiec Swietokrzyski	Pol	Southampton (Aug 2005)
Fojut, Jaroslaw	17 Oct 1987	Legionowo	Pol	Bolton (Sep 2005)
Bialkowski, Bartosz	6 Jul 1987	Braniewo	Pol	Southampton (Jan 2006)
Frankowski, Tomasz	16 Aug 1974	Bialystok	Pol	Wolves (Jan 2006)
Kus, Marcin	2 Sep 1981	Warsaw	Pol	QPR (Jan 2006)

Qualified for Poland but born outside Poland

Name	DOB	Place of birth	Nat	Club(s) (joined/first played)
Kloner, Hymie	23 May 1929	Jo-burg, SA	Pol	Birmingham (Nov 1950)
Olisadebe, Emmanuel	22 Dec 1978	Warri, Nig	Pol	Portsmouth (Jan 2005)

PORTUGAL (46+7)

Name	DOB	Place of birth	Nat	Club(s) (joined/first played)
Dominguez, Jose	16 Feb 1974	Lisbon	Por	Birmingham (Mar 1994); Tottenham (Aug 1997)
Andrade, Jose-Manuel	1 Jun 1970	Gaboverde	Por	Stoke (Mar 1995); Stoke (Aug 1997)
Neves, Rui	10 Mar 1965	Vinhais	Por	Darlington (Aug 1995)
Carvalho, Dani	2 Nov 1976	Lisbon	Por	West Ham (Feb 1996)
Futre, Paulo	26 Feb 1966	Montijo	Por	West Ham (Jun 1996)
Moreira, Joao	30 Jun 1970	Oporto	Por	Swansea (Jun 1996)
Nelson, Fernando	5 Nov 1971	Lisbon	Por	A Villa (Jun 1996)
Cavaco, Luis Miguel	1 Mar 1972	Almada	Por	Stockport (Aug 1996)
Da Costa, Hugo	4 Nov 1973	Tramagal	Por	Stoke (Aug 1996)
Porfirio, Hugo	29 Sep 1973	Lisbon	Por	West Ham (Sep 1996); Nottm For (Jan 1999)
Pinto, Sergio	8 Jan 1973	Escudos	Por	Bradford (Oct 1996)
Kiko, Manuel	24 Oct 1976	Cedofeita	Por	Stockport (Dec 1996)
Oliveira, Raul	26 Aug 1972	Lisbon	Por	Bradford (Mar 1997)
Boa Morte, Luis	4 Aug 1977	Lisbon	Por	Arsenal (Jun 1997); Southampton (Aug 1999); Fulham (Jun 2001)
Ribeiro, Bruno	22 Oct 1975	Setubal	Por	Leeds (Jul 1997); Sheff Utd (Oct 1999)
Alves, Paulo	10 Feb 1969	Mateus Villareal	Por	West Ham (Nov 1997)
Rodrigues, Dani	3 Mar 1980	Madeira	Por	Bournemouth (Oct 1998); Southampton (Mar 1999); Bristol C (Oct 2000); Walsall (Aug 2002); Yeovil (Mar 2004); Bournemouth (Jul 2004)
Costa, Ricardo	10 Jan 1973	Lisbon	Por	Darlington (Jan 1999)
Almeida, Marco	4 Apr 1977	Lisbon	Por	Southampton (Jul 1999)
Rocha, Carlos	4 Dec 1974	Lisbon	Por	Bury (Aug 1999)
Leitao, Jorge	14 Jan 1974	Oporto	Por	Walsall (Aug 2000)
Andre, Carlos	28 Nov 1971	Lisbon	Por	Walsall (Aug 2001)
Miranda, Jose	2 Apr 1974	Lisbon	Por	Rotherham (Sep 2001)
Costa, Jorge	14 Oct 1971	Oporto	Por	Charlton (Dec 2001)
Viana, Hugo	15 Jan 1983	Barcelos	Por	Newcastle (Aug 2002)
De Oliveira, Filipe	27 May 1984	Braga	Por	Chelsea (Sep 2002); Preston (Dec 2004)
Postiga, Helder	25 Jun 2003	Vila do Conde	Por	Tottenham (Jun 2003)
Costa, Candido	30 Apr 1981	Sao Joao da Madeira	Por	Derby (Jul 2003)

Name	DOB	Place of birth	Nat	Club(s) (joined/first played)
Fernandes, Silas	1 Sep 1976	Lisbon	Por	Wolves (Jul 2003)
Rodrigues, Hugo	22 Nov 1979	Santa Maria de Feira	Por	Yeovil (Jul 2003)
Ronaldo, Cristiano	5 Feb 1985	Madeira	Por	Man Utd (Aug 2003)
Vaz Te, Ricardo	1 Oct 1986	Lisbon	Por	Bolton (Aug 2003)
Batista, Ricardo	19 Nov 1986	Setubal	Por	Fulham (Jul 2004); MKD (Jan 2006)
Carvalho, Ricardo	18 May 1978	Amarante	Por	Chelsea (Jul 2004)
Ferreira, Paulo	18 Jan 1979	Cascais	Por	Chelsea (Jul 2004)
Mendes, Pedro	26 Feb 1979	Guimaraes	Por	Tottenham (Jul 2004); Portsmouth (Jan 2006)
Tiago, Cardoso	2 May 1981	Viana do Castelo	Por	Chelsea (Jul 2004)
Meirelles, Bruno	23 Feb 1982	Leiria	Por	Torquay (Aug 2004)
Nuno Morais	29 Jan 1984	Penafiel	Por	Chelsea (Aug 2004)
Andrade, Diogo	23 Jul 1985	Lisbon	Por	Bournemouth (Sep 2004)
Leite, Sergio	16 Aug 1979	Oporto	Por	Hull (Jun 2005)
Mendes, Nuno	7 Apr 1978	Guimaraes	Por	Plymouth (Jul 2005)
Fangueiro, Carlos	19 Dec 1976	Matosinhos	Por	Millwall (Aug 2005)
Valente, Nuno	12 Sep 1974	Lisbon	Por	Everton (Aug 2005)
Maniche, Nuno	11 Nov 1977	Lisbon	Por	Chelsea (Jan 2006)
Morais, Filipe	21 Nov 1985	Lisbon	Por	MKD (Jan 2006)

Other players qualified for Portugal but born outside Portugal

Name	DOB	Place of birth	Nat	Club(s) (joined/first played)
Isaias, Marques	17 Nov 1963	Rio de Janeiro, Bra	Por	Coventry (Aug 1995)
Paulo, Pedro	21 Nov 1973	Angola	Por	Darlington (Aug 1995)
Xavier, Abel	30 Nov 1972	Nampula, Moz	Por	Everton (Sep 1999); Liverpool (Jan 2002); Middlesbrough (Aug 2005)
Helder, Rodrigues	21 Mar 1971	Luanda, Ang	Por	Newcastle (Nov 1999)
Cadete, Jorge	27 Aug 1968	Porto Amélia, Moz	Por	Bradford (Feb 2000)
Batista, Jordao	30 Aug 1971	Malanje, Ang	Por	WBA (Aug 2000)
Da Silva, Lourenco	5 Jun 1983	Luanda, Ang	Por	Bristol C (Mar 2001); Oldham (Aug 2002)

QATAR (1)

Name	DOB	Place of birth	Nat	Club(s) (joined/first played)
Hussein, Yasser	19 Jan 1984	Doha	Qtr	Man City (Jul 2005)

REPUBLIC OF THE CONGO (aka Congo-Brazzaville) (1)

Name	DOB	Place of birth	Nat	Club(s) (joined/first played)
Lita, Leroy	28 Dec 1984	Brazzaville	Con	Bristol C (Aug 2002); Reading (Jul 2005)

REUNION (2)

Name	DOB	Place of birth	Nat	Club(s) (joined/first played)
Robert, Laurent	21 May 1975	Saint-Benoit	Fr	Newcastle (Aug 2001); Portsmouth (Jun 2005)
Sinama-Pongolle Florent	20 Oct 1984	Saint-Pierre	Fr	Liverpool (Jul 2002); Blackburn (Jan 2006)

ROMANIA (9)

Name	DOB	Place of birth	Nat	Club(s) (joined/first played)
Iovan, Stefan	23 Aug 1960	Bucharest	Rom	Brighton (Mar 1991)
Dumitrescu, Ilie	6 Jan 1969	Bucharest	Rom	Tottenham (Aug 1994); West Ham (Mar 1996)
Petrescu, Dan	22 Dec 1967	Bucharest	Rom	Sheff Wed (Aug 1994); Chelsea (Nov 1995); Southampton (Aug 2000); Bradford (Aug 2000)
Popescu, Gica	9 Oct 1967	Calafat	Rom	Tottenham (Sep 1994)
Raducioiu, Florin	17 Mar 1970	Bucharest	Rom	West Ham (Jun 1996)
Moldovan, Viorel	8 Jul 1972	Bistrita	Rom	Coventry (Jan 1998)
Mutu, Adrian	8 Jan 1979	Pitesti	Rom	Chelsea (Aug 2003)
Ganea, Ionel	10 Aug 1973	Fagaras	Rom	Wolves (Dec 2003)
Contra, Cosmin	15 Dec 1975	Timisoara	Rom	WBA (Aug 2004)

RUSSIA (4)

Name	DOB	Place of birth	Nat	Club(s) (joined/first played)
Kharine, Dimitri	16 Aug 1968	Moscow	Rus	Chelsea (Dec 1992)
Kulkov, Vasili	11 Jun 1966	Moscow	Rus	Millwall (Jan 1996)

Name	DOB	Place of birth	Nat	Club(s) (joined/first played)
Danilevicius, Tomas	18 Jul 1978	Moscow	Lith	Arsenal (Sep 2000)
Smertin, Alexei	1 May 1975	Barnaul	Rus	Chelsea (Aug 2003); Portsmouth (Aug 2003); Charlton (Jul 2005)

SAUDI ARABIA (1)

| Al-Jaber, Sami | 11 Dec 1972 | Riyadh | Sau | Wolves (Sep 2000) |

SENEGAL (24+1)

Vieira, Patrick	23 Jun 1976	Dakar	Fr	Arsenal (Aug 1996)
Dia, Ali	20 Aug 1965	Dakar	Sen	Southampton (Nov 1996)
N'Diaye, Sada	27 Mar 1975	Dakar	Sen	Southend (Oct 1997)
Diop, Pape Seydou	12 Jan 1979	Dakar	Sen	Norwich (Aug 1999)
Mendy, Jules	4 Sep 1973	Pikine	Sen	Torquay (Aug 2000)
N'Diaye, Seyni	1 Jun 1973	Dakar	Sen	Tranmere (Mar 2001)
Diawara, Djibril	3 Jan 1975	Dakar	Sen	Bolton (Jun 2001)
Sall, Abdou	1 Nov 1980	Dakar	Sen	Kidderminster (Aug 2001); Oxford (Dec 2002)
Diallo, Cherif	28 Aug 1971	Dakar	Sen	Exeter (Sep 2001)
Cisse, Aliou	24 Mar 1976	Ziguinchor	Sen	Birmingham (Aug 2002); Portsmouth (Aug 2004)
Diao, Salif	10 Jan 1977	Kedougou	Sen	Liverpool (Aug 2002); Birmingham (Jan 2005); Portsmouth (Aug 2005)
Diouf, El Hadji	15 Jan 1981	Dakar	Sen	Liverpool (Aug 2002); Bolton (Aug 2004)
Sonko, Ibrahima	22 Jan 1981	Bignona	Sen	Brentford (Aug 2002); Reading (Jul 2004)
Coly, Ferdinand	10 Sep 1973	Dakar	Sen	Birmingham (Jan 2003)
Camara, Henri	10 May 1977	Dakar	Sen	Wolves (Aug 2003); Southampton (Jan 2005); Wigan (Aug 2005)
Faye, Amdy	12 Mar 1977	Dakar	Sen	Portsmouth (Aug 2003); Newcastle (Jan 2005)
N'Dour, Alassane	12 Dec 1981	Dakar	Sen	WBA (Aug 2003)
Sakho, Lamine	28 Sep 1977	Louga	Sen	Leeds (Aug 2003)
Ba, Ibrahim	12 Jan 1973	Dakar	Fr	Bolton (Sep 2003)
Diop, Pape Bouba	28 Jan 1978	Dakar	Sen	Fulham (Jul 2004)
Diop, Youssou	5 May 1980	Ziguinchor	Sen	Kidderminster (Aug 2004)
Fadiga, Khalilou	30 Dec 1974	Dakar	Sen	Bolton (Sep 2004); Derby (Sep 2005)
Faye, Abdoulaye	26 Feb 1978	Dakar	Sen	Bolton (Jul 2005)
Evra, Patrice	15 May 1981	Dakar	Fr	Man Utd (Jan 2006)

Qualified for Senegal but born outside Senegal

| Kamara, Diomansy | 8 Nov 1980 | Paris, Fr | Sen | Portsmouth (Aug 2004); WBA (Jul 2005) |

SERBIA & MONTENEGRO (7)

NB: Prior to February 2003, Serbia & Montenegro players played as part of the national side formerly known as Yugoslavia. See Yugoslavia for relevant players arriving in England before that point. Players here have arrived in England, or changed clubs in England, since Yugoslavia became S&M.

Stefanovic, Dejan	28 Oct 1974	Belgrade	SM	Sheff Wed (Dec 1995); Portsmouth (Jul 2003)
Kezman, Mateja	12 Apr 1979	Zemun	SM	Chelsea (Jul 2004)
Grabovac, Zarko	16 Mar 1983	Ruma	SM	Blackpool (Jan 2005)
Predic, Uros	11 Aug 1973	Novi Sad	SM	Doncaster (Aug 2005)
Vukic, Zvonimir	19 Jul 1979	Zrenjanin	SM	Portsmouth (Aug 2005)
Koroman, Ognjen	19 Sep 1978	Sarajevo, Bos	SM	Portsmouth (Jan 2006)
Vidic, Nemanja	21 Oct 1981	Uzice	SM	Man Utd (Jan 2006)

SEYCHELLES (1)

| Betsy, Kevin | 20 Mar 1978 | Seychelles | Sey | Fulham (Sep 1998); Bournemouth (Sep 1999); Hull (Nov 1999); Barnsley (Mar 2002); Hartlepool (Jul 2004); Oldham (Sep 2004); Wycombe (Jun 2005) |

Name	DOB	Place of birth	Nat	Club(s) (joined/first played)
SIERRA LEONE (5)				
Dillsworth, Eddie	16 Apr 1946	Freetown	SiLe	Lincoln (Mar 1967)
Bart-Williams, Chris	16 Jun 1974	Freetown	Brit	Orient (Jul 1990); Sheff Wed (Nov 1991); Nottm For (Jul 1995); Charlton (Dec 2001); Ipswich (Sep 2003)
Jarrett, Albert	23 Oct 1984	Freetown	Brit	MKD (Jul 2003); Brighton (Aug 2004); Swindon (Jan 2006)
Deen, Ahmed	30 Jun 1985	Freetown	SiLe	Peterborough (Sep 2004)
Bangura, Al	24 Jan 1988	Freetown	SiLe	Watford (Apr 2005)
SINGAPORE (6)				
Twissell, Charlie	16 Dec 1932	Singapore	Eng	Plymouth (Aug 1955); York (Nov 1958)
Butcher, Terry	28 Dec 1958	Singapore	Eng	Ipswich (Aug 1976); Coventry (Nov 1990); Sunderland (Jul 1992)
Callaghan, Nigel	12 Sep 1962	Singapore	Eng	Watford (Jul 1979); Derby (Feb 1987); A Villa (Feb 1989); Derby (Sep 1990); Watford (Mar 1991); Huddersfield (Jan 1992)
Young, Eric	25 Mar 1960	Changi	Wal	Brighton (Nov 1982); Wimbledon (Jul 1987); C Palace (Aug 1990); Wolves (Sep 1995)
Atkinson, Paddy	22 May 1970	Singapore	Brit	Hartlepool (Aug 1988); York (Nov 1995); Scarborough (Aug 1998)
Carmichael, Matt	13 May 1964	Singapore	Brit	Lincoln (Aug 1989); Scunthorpe (Jul 1993); Barnet (Sep 1994); Preston (Mar 1995); Darlington (Feb 1996); Doncaster (Aug 1995); Mansfield (Aug 1995)
SLOVAKIA (8)				
Kinder, Vladimir	9 Mar 1969	Bratislava	Svk	Middlesbrough (Jan 1997)
Varga, Stanislav	8 Oct 1972	Lipany	Svk	Sunderland (Aug 2000); WBA (Mar 2002)
Balis, Igor	5 Jan 1970	Zalozinik	Svk	WBA (Dec 2000)
Nemeth, Szilard	8 Aug 1977	Komarno	Svk	Middlesbrough (Jul 2001)
Labant, Vladimir	8 Jun 1974	Zilina	Svk	West Ham (Jan 2002)
Gresko, Vratislav	24 Jul 1977	Pressburg	Svk	Blackburn (Jan 2003)
Suhaj, Pavel	16 Apr 1981	Lipany	Svk	Crewe (Jul 2005)
Kozak, Jan	24 Apr 1980	Bratislava	Svk	WBA (Jan 2006)
SLOVENIA (6+1)				
Krizan, Ales	25 Jul 1971	Maribor	Slo	Barnsley (Jul 1997)
Rudonja, Mladen	26 Jul 1971	Koper	Slo	Portsmouth (Aug 2000)
Karic, Amir	31 Dec 1973	Oramovica Ponja	Slo	C Palace (Mar 2001); Ipswich (Sep 2000)
Bobic, Fredi	30 Oct 1971	Maribor	Ger	Bolton (Jan 2002)
Acimovic, Milenko	15 Feb 1977	Ljubljana	Slo	Tottenham (Aug 2002)
Seremet, Dino	16 Aug 1980	Ljubljana	Slo	Luton (Jul 2004); Doncaster (Nov 2005); Tranmere (Jan 2006)
Qualified for Slovenia but born outside Slovenia				
Rodic, Alexsander	26 Dec 1979	Belgrade, Yug	Slo	Portsmouth (Jan 2005)
SOUTH AFRICA (126+1)				
Waller, Wilfred	27 Jul 1877	South Africa	SA	Bolton (Mar 1900)
Bell, Alec	1882	Cape Town	Sco	Man Utd (Jan 1903); Blackburn (Jul 1913)
Whitson, Anthony	c.1880	Cape Town	SA	Newcastle (Feb 1905)
Gibson, Fred	8 Dec 1888	Pilgrim's Rest	SA	Sunderland (May 1909); Coventry (May 1919)
Mackrill, Percy	19 Oct 1894	Wynberg	SA	Coventry (Jul 1919); Halifax (Jul 1921); Torquay (Jul 1925)
Osborne, Frank	14 Oct 1896	Wynberg	Eng	Fulham (Nov 1921); Tottenham (Jan 1924);

Name	DOB	Place of birth	Nat	Club(s) (joined/first played)
				Southampton (Jun 1931)
Osborne, Reg	23 Jul 1898	Wynberg	Eng	Leicester (Feb 1923)
King, Charlie	18 May 1897	Johannesburg	SA	Southport (May 1923)
Osborne, Harold	2 Apr 1904	Wynberg	SA	Norwich (Sep 1924)
Riley, Arthur	26 Dec 1903	Boksburg	SA	Liverpool (Jul 1925)
Murray, David	1902	Wynberg	SA	Everton (Aug 1925); Bristol C (Oct 1926); Bristol R (1928); Swindon (Jun 1930); Rochdale (Aug 1931)
Hodgson, Gordon	16 Apr 1904	Johannesburg	Eng	Liverpool (Nov 1925); A Villa (Jan 1936); Leeds (Mar 1937)
Martin, Sydney	c.1910	Durban	SA	Gillingham (Jul 1929)
Mandy, Aubrey	c.1910	Transvaal	SA	Leicester (Oct 1929)
Crawford, Ronald	c.1910	South Africa	SA	Thames (Jul 1930); Rotherham (Jul 1931)
Richardson, John	1909	Johannesburg	SA	Bristol R (Aug 1930)
Carr, Lance	18 Feb 1910	Johannesburg	SA	Liverpool (Aug 1933); Newport (Oct 1936); Newport (Jul 1938); Bristol R (Aug 1946)
Nieuwenhuys, Berry	5 Nov 1911	Boksburg	SA	Liverpool (Sep 1933)
Bunch, Arthur	30 Sep 1909	Bloemfontein	SA	Aldershot (Jun 1934)
Clarke, Bruce	4 Oct 1910	Johannesburg	SA	Fulham (Jun 1934)
Brown, Lennox	24 Nov 1910	South Africa	SA	Millwall (Nov 1935)
Kemp, Dick	15 Oct 1913	Cape Town	SA	Liverpool (Jul 1936)
Van Den Berg, Herman	21 Mar 1918	Cape Town	SA	Liverpool (Jul 1937)
Wienand, Tolley	1912	East London	SA	Huddersfield (Jul 1937); Hull (Oct 1938)
Lindsay, Denis	1916	Benoni	SA	Huddersfield (Aug 1937)
Woolf, Levi	28 Jan 1916	Johannesburg	SA	Southampton (Sep 1937)
Fish, Kenneth	c.1915	Cape Town	SA	Port Vale (Nov 1937)
Milligan, Dudley	7 Nov 1916	Johannesburg	N Ire	Chesterfield (Nov 1938); B&B Ath (Aug 1947); Walsall (Oct 1948)
Malan, Norman	23 Nov 1923	Johannesburg	SA	Middlesbrough (Oct 1945); Scunthorpe (Jun 1950); Bradford PA (Jul 1956)
Priday, Bob	29 Mar 1925	Cape Town	SA	Liverpool (Dec 1945); Blackburn (Mar 1949); Acc Stanley (Dec 1952); Rochdale (Aug 1953)
Strauss, Bill	6 Jan 1916	Transvaal	SA	Plymouth (Jul 1946)
Kelly, Pat	9 Apr 1918	Johannesburg	N Ire	Barnsley (Oct 1946); Crewe (Feb 1952)
Forbes, Dudley	19 Apr 1926	Cape Town	SA	Charlton (Dec 1947)
O'Linn, Syd	5 May 1927	Oudtschoorn	SA	Charlton (Dec 1947)
Havenga, Willie	6 Nov 1924	Bloemfontein	SA	Birmingham (Jul 1948); Luton (May 1950); Ipswich (Jan 1952)
Arnison, Joseph	27 Jun 1924	Johannesburg	SA	Luton (Aug 1948)
Uytenbogaardt, Albert	5 Mar 1930	Cape Town	SA	Charlton (Oct 1948)
Nielson, Norman	6 Nov 1928	Johannesburg	SA	Charlton (Jul 1949); Derby (Sep 1951); Bury (May 1954); Hull (Apr 1957)
Williams, Stan	1 May 1919	South Africa	SA	Plymouth (Aug 1949)
Falconer, Andy	27 Jun 1925	South Africa	SA	Blackpool (Sep 1949)
Hewie, John	13 Dec 1927	Pretoria	Sco	Charlton (Oct 1949)
Perry, Bill	10 Sep 1930	Johannesburg	SA	Blackpool (Nov 1949); Southport (Jun 1962)
Firmani, Eddie	7 Aug 1933	Cape Town	SA	Charlton (Feb 1950); Charlton (Oct 1963); Southend (Jun 1965); Charlton (Mar 1967)
Leary, Stuart	30 Apr 1933	Cape Town	SA	Charlton (Feb 1950); QPR (Dec 1962)
Ackerman, Alf	5 Jan 1929	Pretoria	SA	Hull (Jul 1950); Norwich (Aug 1951); Hull (Oct 1953); Derby (Mar 1955); Carlisle (Nov 1956); Millwall (Jan 1959)
Purdon, Ted	1 Mar 1930	Johannesburg	SA	Birmingham (Aug 1950); Sunderland (Jan

Name	DOB	Place of birth	Nat	Club(s) (joined/first played)
				1954); Workington (Mar 1957); Barrow (Mar 1958); Bristol R (Aug 1960)
Carr, John	10 Jun 1926	Durban	SA	Huddersfield (Oct 1950)
Kloner, Hymie	23 May 1929	Johannesburg	Pol	Birmingham (Nov 1950)
Miller, George	17 Oct 1927	South Africa	SA	Leeds (Nov 1950); Workington (Mar 1952)
Stuart, Eddie	12 May 1931	Johannesburg	SA	Wolves (Jan 1951); Stoke (Jul 1962); Tranmere (Aug 1964); Stockport (Jul 1966)
Davies, Roy	23 Aug 1924	Cape Town	SA	Luton (May 1951)
Kirsten, Ken	28 Oct 1922	South Africa	SA	Aldershot (Aug 1951)
Oelofse, Ralph	12 Nov 1926	Johannesburg	SA	Chelsea (Oct 1951); Watford (Jul 1953)
Stewart, Gordon	7 Aug 1927	Durban	SA	Leeds (Oct 1951)
Chamberlain, Ken	30 Jun 1926	Durban	SA	Charlton (Oct 1951)
Foreman, Denis	1 Feb 1933	Cape Town	SA	Brighton (Mar 1952)
Gerhardt, Hugh	5 May 1933	South Africa	SA	Liverpool (Aug 1952)
Hastie, Ken	6 Sep 1928	Cape Town	SA	Leeds (Aug 1952)
Miller, Graham	25 Aug 1927	South Africa	SA	Workington (Dec 1952)
Firmani, Peter	14 Feb 1936	Cape Town	SA	Charlton (Sep 1953)
Oosthuizen, Ron	16 Mar 1936	South Africa	SA	Charlton (Sep 1953); Carlisle (Sep 1959)
Tulloch, Roland	15 Jul 1932	South Africa	SA	Hull (Dec 1953)
McEwan, Peter	23 May 1933	Roodepoort	SA	Luton (Feb 1954)
Rudham, Doug	3 May 1926	Johannesburg	SA	Liverpool (Nov 1954)
Hauser, Peter	20 Apr 1934	Kimberley	SA	Blackpool (Nov 1955); Chester (Aug 1963)
Hewkins, Ken	30 Oct 1929	Pretoria	SA	Fulham (Nov 1955)
Kennon, Sandy	26 Nov 1933	Johannesburg	Zim	Huddersfield (Aug 1956); Norwich (Feb 1959); Colchester (Mar 1965)
Hodge, Eric	3 Apr 1933	Cape Town	SA	Brighton (Oct 1956); Aldershot (Jun 1959)
Mokone, Steve	23 Mar 1932	Pretoria	SA	Coventry (Oct 1956); Cardiff (Jun 1959); Barnsley (Aug 1961)
Peterson, Brian	20 Oct 1936	Durban	SA	Blackpool (Oct 1956)
Horne, Des	12 Dec 1939	Johannesburg	SA	Wolves (Dec 1956); Blackpool (Mar 1961)
Lightening, Arthur	1 Aug 1936	Durban	SA	Nottm For (Dec 1956); Coventry (Nov 1958); Middlesbrough (Aug 1962)
Le Roux, Daniel	25 Nov 1933	Port Shepstone	SA	Arsenal (Feb 1957)
Durandt, Cliff	16 Apr 1940	Johannesburg	SA	Wolves (Jun 1957); Charlton (Mar 1963)
Cubie, Neil	3 Nov 1932	South Africa	SA	Hull (Jul 1957)
Francis, Gerry	6 Dec 1933	Johannesburg	SA	Leeds (Jul 1957); York (Oct 1961)
Kichenbrand, Don	13 Aug 1933	Johannesburg	SA	Sunderland (Mar 1958)
Tennant, Roy	12 Sep 1936	Durban	SA	Workington (Jul 1958)
Hubbard, John	16 Dec 1930	Pretoria	SA	Bury (Apr 1959)
Tocknell, Brian	21 May 1937	Pretoria	SA	Charlton (Jul 1959)
Smethurst, Peter	8 Aug 1940	Durban	SA	Blackpool (Feb 1960)
Johanneson, Albert	12 March 1940	Johannesburg	SA	Leeds (Apr 1961); York (Jul 1970)
Viljoen, Colin	20 Jun 1948	Johannesburg	SA	Ipswich (Mar 1967); Man City (Aug 1978); Chelsea (Mar 1980)
Smethurst, Derek	24 Oct 1947	Durban	SA	Chelsea (Dec 1968); Millwall (Sep 1971)
Collins, Mike	27 Jul 1953	Johannesburg	SA	Swindon (Jul 1973)
Vernon, John	2 Mar 1956	South Africa	SA	Stockport (Apr 1975)
Backos, Des	13 Nov 1950	Wynberg	SA	Stoke (Oct 1977)
Stein, Brian	19 Oct 1957	Cape Town	Eng	Luton (Oct 1977); Luton (Jul 1991); Barnet (Aug 1992)
Johnston, Craig	8 Dec 1960	Johannesburg	Aus	Middlesbrough (Feb 1978); Liverpool (Apr 1981)
Parkinson, Andy	5 May 1959	Johannesburg	SA	Newcastle (Mar 1978); Peterborough (Aug 1979)

Name	DOB	Place of birth	Nat	Club(s) (joined/first played)
D'Avray, Mich	19 Feb 1962	Johannesburg	Eng	Ipswich (May 1979); Leicester (Feb 1987)
Grobbelaar, Bruce	6 Oct 1957	Durban	Zim	Crewe (Dec 1979); Liverpool (Mar 1981); Stoke (Mar 1993); Southampton (Aug 1994); Plymouth (Aug 1996); Oldham (Dec 1997); Bury (Sep 1998); Lincoln (Dec 1998)
Nebbeling, Gavin	15 May 1963	Johannesburg	SA	C Palace (Aug 1981); Northampton (Oct 1985); Fulham (Jul 1989); Hereford (Dec 1991); Preston (Jul 1993)
Stein, Edwin	28 Jun 1955	Cape Town	Brit	Barnet (Jul 1982)
Stein, Mark	28 Jan 1966	Cape Town	Eng	Luton (Jan 1984); Aldershot (Jan 1986); QPR (Jun 1988); Oxford (Sep 1989); Stoke (Nov 1991); Chelsea (Oct 1993); Stoke (Aug 1996); Bournemouth (June 1998); Ipswich (Aug 1997); Luton (Jul 2000)
Wegerle, Roy	19 Mar 1964	Johannesburg	USA	Chelsea (Jun 1986); Swindon (Mar 1988); Luton (Jul 1988); QPR (Dec 1989); Blackburn (Mar 1992); Coventry (Mar 1993)
McMillan, Andy	22 Jun 1968	Bloemfontein	SA	York (Oct 1987)
Paskin, John	1 Feb 1962	Cape Town	SA	WBA (Aug 1988); Wolves (Jun 1989); Stockport (Sep 1991); Birmingham (Nov 1991); Shrewsbury (Feb 1992); Wrexham (Feb 1992); Bury (Jul 1994)
Leitch, Grant	31 Oct 1972	South Africa	SA	Blackpool (Aug 1990)
Aspinall, Brendan	22 Jul 1975	Johannesburg	SA	Mansfield (Jul 1994)
Masinga, Phil	28 Jun 1969	Johannesburg	SA	Leeds (Aug 1994)
Radebe, Lucas	12 Apr 1969	Johannesburg	SA	Leeds (Sep 1994)
Stephenson, Ashlyn	6 Jul 1974	South Africa	SA	Darlington (Sep 1995)
Williams, Mark	11 Aug 1966	Johannesburg	SA	Wolves (Sep 1995)
Goodhind, Warren	16 Aug 1977	Johannesburg	SA	Barnet (Jul 1996); Cambridge (Sep 2001); Rochdale (Sep 2005); Oxford (Feb 2006)
Harris, Andy	26 Feb 1977	Springs	Brit	Southend (Jul 1996); Orient (Jul 1999); Chester (Jun 2003)
Tinkler, Eric	30 Jul 1970	Roodepoort	SA	Barnsley (Jul 1997)
Arendse, Andre	27 Jun 1967	Cape Town	SA	Fulham (Aug 1997); Oxford (Jul 1999)
Fish, Mark	14 Mar 1974	Cape Town	SA	Bolton (Sep 1997); Charlton (Nov 2000); Ipswich (Aug 2005)
Dundee, Sean	7 Dec 1972	Durban	SA	Liverpool (Jun 1998)
Arber, Mark	9 Oct 1977	Johannesburg	Brit	Barnet (Sep 1998); Peterborough (Dec 2002); Oldham (Jun 2004); Peterborough (Dec 2004)
O'Brien, Burton	10 Jun 1981	South Africa	Brit	Blackburn (Feb 1999); Sheff Wed (Jul 2005)
Fortune, Quinton	21 May 1977	Cape Town	SA	Man Utd (Aug 1999)
Hardy, Adam	22 Feb 1983	Uitenhage	SA	Bradford (Sep 2000)
Bartlett, Shaun	31 Oct 1972	Cape Town	SA	Charlton (Dec 2000)
Byrne, Paul	26 Nov 1982	Natal	Brit	Port Vale (Apr 2001)
Greyling, Anton	5 Dec 1977	Pretoria	SA	Torquay (Aug 2001)
Thorrington, John	17 Oct 1979	Johannesburg	USA	Huddersfield (Aug 2001); Grimsby (Mar 2004)
Issa, Pierre	11 Aug 1975	Johannesburg	SA	Watford (Sep 2001)
Roberts, Sean	2 Jan 1983	Johannesburg	SA	Sheff Wed (Oct 2001)
Miller, Justin	16 Dec 1980	Johannesburg	SA	Orient (Sep 2002)
Evans, Paul	28 Dec 1973	Newcastle	SA	Sheff Wed (Mar 2003); Rushden (Oct 2003)
Mabizela, Mbulelo	16 Sep 1980	Pietermaritzburg	SA	Tottenham (Aug 2003)
Surman, Andrew	20 Aug 1986	Johannesburg	SA	Southampton (Jul 2004); Walsall (Jan 2005); Bournemouth (Aug 2005)

Name	DOB	Place of birth	Nat	Club(s) (joined/first played)
Mokoena, Aaron	25 Nov 1980	Johannesburg	SA	Blackburn (Jan 2005)
Pattison, Matty	27 Oct 1986	Johannesburg	SA	Newcastle (Feb 2006)
Other players qualified for South Africa but born outside South Africa				
Koumantarakis, George	27 Mar 1974	Athens, Grk	SA	Preston (Jan 2003)

SOUTH KOREA (3)

Name	DOB	Place of birth	Nat	Club(s) (joined/first played)
Seol, Ki-Hyeon	8 Jan 1979	Jeongseon	SK	Wolves (Aug 2004)
Park, Ji-Sung	25 Feb 1981	Seoul	SK	Man Utd (Jul 2005)
Lee, Yong-Pyo	23 Apr 1977	Hongcheon	SK	Tottenham (Aug 2005)

SPAIN (56+1)

Name	DOB	Place of birth	Nat	Club(s) (joined/first played)
Aldecoa, Emilio	30 Nov 1922	Bilbao	Sp	Coventry (Dec 1945)
Gallego, Jose	8 Apr 1923	San Sebastian	Sp	Brentford (Jan 1947); Southampton (May 1948); Colchester (Aug 1950)
Gallego, Tony	2 Jun 1924	San Sebastian	Sp	Norwich (Mar 1947)
Diaz, Isidro	15 May 1972	Valencia	Sp	Wigan Ath (Jul 1995); Wolves (Aug 1997); Wigan Ath (Aug 1997); Rochdale (Aug 1998)
Martinez, Roberto	13 Jul 1973	Balaguer Lerida	Sp	Wigan Ath (Jul 1995); Walsall (Aug 2002); Swansea (Feb 2003)
Seba, Jesus	11 Apr 1974	Zaragoza	Sp	Wigan Ath (Aug 1995)
Mateu, Jose-Luis	15 Jan 1966	Castellon	Sp	Torquay (Sep 1995)
Doncel, Antonio	31 Jan 1967	Lugo	Sp	Hull (Aug 1996)
San Miguel, Xavier	7 May 1971	Bilbao	Sp	Cambridge (Aug 1996)
Calvo-Garcia, Alex	1 Jan 1972	Ordizia	Sp	Scunthorpe (Oct 1996)
Segura, Victor	30 Mar 1973	Zaragoza	Sp	Norwich (Aug 1997)
Garcia Sanjuan, Jesus	22 Aug 1971	Zaragoza	Sp	Wolves (Sep 1997)
Merino, Carlos	15 Mar 1980	Bilbao	Sp	Nottm For (Sep 1997)
Ferrer, Albert	6 Jun 1970	Barcelona	Sp	Chelsea (Aug 1998)
Gomez, Fernando	11 Sep 1965	Valencia	Sp	Wolves (Aug 1998)
Matias, Pedro	11 Oct 1973	Madrid	Sp	Macclesfield (Dec 1998); Tranmere (Aug 1999); Walsall (Oct 1999); Blackpool (Mar 2004); Kidderminster (Nov 2004)
Mori Cuesta, Francisco	10 Nov 1970	Canea de Onis	Sp	Barnsley (Mar 1999)
Elena, Marcelino	26 Sep 1971	Gijon	Sp	Newcastle (Jul 1999)
Aranalde, Zigor	28 Feb 1973	Guipuzcoa	Sp	Walsall (Aug 2000); Sheff Wed (Mar 2005); Carlisle (Jul 2005)
Counago, Pablo	9 Aug 1979	Potevedra	Sp	Ipswich (May 2001)
Juanjo, Carricondo	4 May 1977	Barcelona	Sp	Bradford (Oct 2001)
Sanchez-Lopez, Carlos	22 Jul 1979	Madrid	Sp	Bristol R (Feb 2002)
Yordi	14 Sep 1974	San Fernando	Sp	Blackburn (Feb 2002)
De Lucas, Enrique	17 Aug 1978	Llobregat	Sp	Chelsea (Aug 2002)
Dixon, Jonny	16 Jan 1984	Muria	Brit	Wycombe (Aug 2002)
Campo, Ivan	21 Feb 1974	San Sebastian	Sp	Bolton (Sep 2002)
Lopez, Ricardo	30 Dec 1971	Madrid	Sp	Man Utd (Sep 2002)
Ballesta, Salva	22 May 1975	Paese	Sp	Bolton (Feb 2003)
Bravo, Raul	14 Apr 1981	Gandia	Sp	Coventry (Feb 2003)
Fabregas, Cesc	4 May 1987	Arenys de Mar	Sp	Arsenal (Jul 2003)
Mendieta, Gaizka	27 Mar 1974	Bilbai	Sp	Middlesbrough (Aug 2003)
Martinez, Manel	11 Mar 1973	Barcelona	Sp	Derby (Jan 2004)
Moreno, Javi	10 Sep 1974	Silla	Sp	Bolton (Jan 2004)
Reyes, Jose	1 Sep 1983	Utrera	Sp	Arsenal (Jan 2004)
Adaggio, Marco	6 Oct 1987	Malaga	Sp	Shrewsbury (Jul 2004)
Almunia, Manuel	19 May 1977	Pamplona	Sp	Arsenal (Jul 2004)
De Pedro, Javier	4 Aug 1973	Logrono	Sp	Blackburn (Jul 2004)

Name	DOB	Place of birth	Nat	Club(s) (joined/first played)
Hierro, Fernando	23 Mar 1968	Velez	Sp	Bolton (Jul 2004)
Idiakez, Inigo	8 Nov 1973	San Sebastian	Sp	Derby (Jul 2004)
Josemi	15 Sep 1979	Malaga	Sp	Liverpool (Jul 2004)
Alonso, Xabi	25 Nov 1981	San Sebastian	Sp	Liverpool (Aug 2004)
Garcia, Luis	24 Jun 1978	Barcelona	Sp	Liverpool (Aug 2004)
Nunez, Antonio	15 Jan 1979	Madrid	Sp	Liverpool (Aug 2004)
Pique, Gerard	2 Feb 1987	Barcelona	Sp	Man Utd (Oct 2004)
Ugarte, Juan	7 Nov 1980	San Sebastian	Sp	Wrexham (Nov 2004); Crewe (Jul 2005); Wrexham (Oct 2005)
Arteta, Mikel	26 Mar 1982	San Sebastian	Sp	Everton (Jan 2005)
Morientes, Fernando	5 Apr 1976	Caceres	Sp	Liverpool (Jan 2005)
Valero, Xavi	28 Feb 1973	Castellon	Sp	Wrexham (Jan 2005)
Del Horno, Asier	19 Jan 1981	Vizcaya	Sp	Chelsea (Jun 2005)
Barragan, Antonio	12 Jun 1987	Seville	Sp	Liverpool (Jul 2005)
Reina, Jose	31 Aug 1982	Madrid	Sp	Liverpool (Jul 2005)
Sito, Castro	21 May 1980	La Coruna	Sp	Ipswich (Jul 2005)
Luque, Alberto	12 Mar 1978	Barcelona	Sp	Newcastle (Aug 2005)
Riera, Albert	15 Apr 1982	Manacor	Sp	Man City (Jan 2006)
Other players qualified for Spain but born outside Spain				
Mendez, Alberto	24 Oct 1974	Nuremburg, Ger	Sp	Arsenal (Jul 1997)

SRI LANKA (1)

Butler, Jack	14 Aug 1894	Colombo	Brit	Arsenal (Jan 1914); Torquay (May 1930)

ST KITTS-NEVIS (4)

Podd, Ces	7 Aug 1952	St Kitts	StK	Bradford (Aug 1970); Halifax (Aug 1984); Scarborough (Jul 1986)
Bowery, Bert	29 Oct 1954	St Kitts	StK	Nottm For (Jan 1975); Lincoln (Feb 1976)
Benjamin, Tristan	1 Apr 1957	St Kitts	StK	Notts Co (Mar 1975); Chesterfield (Jul 1987)
Walwyn, Keith	17 Feb 1956	Nevis	Brit	Chesterfield (Nov 1979); York (Jul 1981); Blackpool (Jun 1987); Carlisle (Jul 1989)

ST LUCIA (2)

Marshall, Dwight	3 Oct 1965	St Lucia	Brit	Plymouth (Aug 1991); Middlesbrough (Mar 1993); Luton (Jul 1994); Plymouth (Oct 1998)
Jean, Earl	9 Oct 1971	St Lucia	StL	Ipswich (Dec 1996); Rotherham (Jan 1997); Plymouth (Aug 1997)

ST VINCENT (2+1)

Ambrose, Leroy	22 Jun 1960	St Vincent	StV	Charlton (Aug 1979)
Kelly, Errington	8 Apr 1958	Sandy Bay	StV	Bristol R (Sep 1981); Lincoln (Jan 1983); Bristol C (Feb 1983); Peterborough (Mar 1984); Peterborough (Dec 1986)
Other players qualified for St Vincent but born outside St Vincent				
Jack, Rodney	28 Sep 1972	Kingston, Jam	StV	Torquay (Oct 1995); Crewe (Aug 1998); Rushden (Jun 2003); Oldham (Jul 2004)

SURINAM (19)

Zondervan, Romeo	4 Mar 1959	Surinam	Neth	WBA (Mar 1982); Ipswich (Mar 1984)
Wilson, Ulrich	5 May 1964	Surinam	Neth	Ipswich (Dec 1987)
Monkou, Ken	29 Nov 1964	Surinam	Neth	Chelsea (Mar 1989); Southampton (Aug 1992); Huddersfield (Aug 1999)
Verveer, Etienne	22 Sep 1967	Surinam	Neth	Millwall (Dec 1991); Bradford (Feb 1995)
De Freitas, Fabian	28 Jul 1972	Surinam	Neth	Bolton (Aug 1994); WBA (Aug 1998)
Gullit, Ruud	1 Sep 1962	Surinam	Neth	Chelsea (Jul 1995)

Name	DOB	Place of birth	Nat	Club(s) (joined/first played)
Uhlenbeek, Gus	28 Aug 1970	Surinam	Neth	Ipswich (Aug 1995); Fulham (Jul 1998); Sheff Utd (Aug 2000); Walsall (Mar 2002); Bradford (Aug 2002); Chesterfield (Aug 2003); Wycombe (Jul 2004); Mansfield (Jun 2005)
Blinker, Regi	4 Jun 1969	Surinam	Neth	Sheff Wed (Mar 1996)
Van Gobbel, Ulrich	16 Jan 1971	Surinam	Neth	Southampton (Oct 1996)
Wilsterman, Brian	19 Nov 1966	Surinam	Neth	Oxford (Feb 1997); Rotherham (Jul 1999)
Hasselbaink, Jimmy Floyd	27 Mar 1972	Surinam	Neth	Leeds (Jul 1997); Chelsea (Jul 2000); Middlesbrough (Jul 2004)
Wijnhard, Clyde	9 Nov 1973	Surinam	Neth	Leeds (Jul 1998); Huddersfield (Jul 1999); Oldham (Aug 2002); Darlington (Oct 2004); Macclesfield (Oct 2005)
Wilnis, Fabian	23 Aug 1970	Surinam	Neth	Ipswich (Jan 1999)
Faerber, Winston	23 Jul 1971	Surinam	Neth	Cardiff (Aug 1999)
Gorre, Dean	10 Sep 1970	Surinam	Neth	Huddersfield (Sep 1999); Barnsley (Jul 2001); Blackpool (Sep 2004)
Wooter, Nordin	24 Aug 1976	Surinam	Neth	Watford (Sep 1999)
Koejoe, Sammy	17 Aug 1974	Surinam	Neth	QPR (Nov 1999)
De Vries, Mark	24 Aug 1975	Surinam	Neth	Leicester (Jan 2005)
Davids, Edgar	13 Mar 1973	Surinam	Neth	Tottenham (Aug 2005)

SWEDEN (64+3)

Name	DOB	Place of birth	Nat	Club(s) (joined/first played)
Ekner, Dan	5 Feb 1927	Sweden	Swe	Portsmouth (1949-50)
Jeppson, Hans	10 May 1925	Gothenburg	Swe	Charlton (Jan 1951)
Moller, Jan	17 Sep 1953	Malmo	Swe	Bristol C (Dec 1980)
Gough, Richard	5 Apr 1962	Stockholm	Sco	Tottenham (Aug 1986); Nottm For (Mar 1999); Everton (Jun 1999)
Rehn, Stefan	22 Sep 1966	Stockholm	Swe	Everton (Jun 1989)
Hysen, Glenn	30 Oct 1959	Gothenburg	Swe	Liverpool (Jul 1989)
Nilsson, Roland	27 Nov 1963	Helsingborg	Swe	Sheff Wed (Nov 1989); Coventry (Jul 1997) & (Jul 2001)
Limpar, Anders	24 Sep 1965	Solna	Swe	Arsenal (Aug 1990); Everton (Mar 1994); Birmingham (Jan 1997)
Andersson, Patrik	18 Aug 1971	Borgeby	Swe	Blackburn (Dec 1992)
Shail, Mark	15 Oct 1963	Sandviken	Brit	Bristol C (Mar 1993); Kidderminster (Jul 2000)
Wirmola, Jonas	17 Jul 1969	Vaxjo	Swe	Sheff Utd (Aug 1993)
Schwarz, Stefan	18 Apr 1969	Malmo	Swe	Arsenal (May 1994); Sunderland (Aug 1999)
Ingesson, Klas	20 Aug 1968	Odeshog	Swe	Sheff Wed (Sep 1994)
Brolin, Tomas	29 Nov 1969	Hudiksvall	Swe	Leeds (Nov 1995); C Palace (Jan 1998)
Kaamark, Pontus	5 Apr 1969	Vasteras	Swe	Leicester (Nov 1995)
Sahlin, Dan	18 Apr 1967	Falum	Swe	Birmingham (Nov 1995)
Gudmundsson, Niklas	29 Feb 1972	Sweden	Swe	Blackburn (Dec 1995); Ipswich (Mar 1997)
Pehrsson, Magnus	25 May 1976	Malmo	Swe	Bradford (Oct 1996)
Jansson, Jan	26 Jan 1968	Kalmar	Swe	Port Vale (Nov 1996)
Svensson, Mathias	24 Sep 1974	Boras	Swe	Portsmouth (Dec 1996); C Palace (Sep 1998); Charlton (Jan 2000); Derby (Aug 2003); Norwich (Dec 2003)
Ottosson, Ulf	2 Jul 1968	Degefors	Swe	Norwich (Jan 1997)
Eriksson, Jan	24 Aug 1967	Sundsvall	Swe	Sunderland (Jan 1997)
Rahmberg, Marino	7 Aug 1974	Orebro	Swe	Derby (Jan 1997)
Andersson, Anders	15 Mar 1974	Tomelilla	Swe	Blackburn (Jun 1997)
Dahlin, Martin	16 Apr 1968	Udevalla	Swe	Blackburn (Jul 1997)
Hedman, Magnus	19 Mar 1973	Stockholm	Swe	Coventry (Jul 1997)

Name	DOB	Place of birth	Nat	Club(s) (joined/first played)
Steiner, Rob	20 Jun 1973	Finsprong	Swe	Bradford (Jul 1997); QPR (Jul 1998); Walsall (Mar 1999); QPR (Jul 1999)
Markstedt, Peter	11 Jan 1972	Vasteras	Swe	Barnsley (Nov 1997)
Alexandersson, Niclas	29 Dec 1971	Halmstad	Swe	Sheff Wed (Dec 1997); Everton (Jul 2000); West Ham (Sep 2003)
Andersson, Andreas	10 Apr 1974	Osterhoninge	Swe	Newcastle (Jan 1998)
Blomqvist, Jesper	5 Feb 1974	Tavelsjo	Swe	Man Utd (Jul 1998); Everton (Nov 2001); Charlton (Sep 2002)
Ljungberg, Freddie	16 Apr 1977	Halmstad	Swe	Arsenal (Sep 1998)
Mattsson, Jesper	18 Apr 1968	Visby	Swe	Nottm For (Dec 1998)
Pringle, Martin	18 Nov 1970	Gothenburg	Swe	Charlton (Jan 1999); Grimsby (Feb 2002)
Lundin, Pal	21 Nov 1964	Osby	Swe	Oxford (Mar 1999)
Axeldahl, Jonas	2 Sep 1970	Holm	Swe	Ipswich (Jul 1999); Cambridge (Aug 2000)
Bengtsson, Robert	4 Jun 1968	Gothenburg	Swe	Barnsley (Nov 1999)
Gustafsson, Tomas	7 May 1973	Stockholm	Swe	Coventry (Dec 1999)
Hansson, Mikael	15 Mar 1968	Norrkoping	Swe	Stoke (Dec 1999)
Bryngelsson, Fredrik	10 Apr 1975	Sweden	Swe	Stockport (Jul 2000)
Johansson, Jonatan	16 Aug 1975	Stockholm	Fin	Charlton (Aug 2000); Norwich (Jan 2006)
Karlsson, Par	29 May 1978	Gothenburg	Swe	Wimbledon (Sep 2000)
Traore, Demba	22 Apr 1982	Stockholm	Swe	Cambridge (Dec 2000)
Svensson, Anders	17 Jul 1976	Gothenburg	Swe	Southampton (Jun 2001)
Mellberg, Olof	3 Sep 1977	Gullspang	Swe	A Villa (Jul 2001)
Johansson, Nils-Eric	13 Jan 1980	Stockholm	Swe	Blackburn (Oct 2001); Leicester (Jul 2005)
Mild, Hakan	14 Jun 1971	Trollhattan	Swe	Wimbledon (Nov 2001)
Bjorklund, Joachim	15 Mar 1971	Vaxjo	Swe	Sunderland (Jan 2002); Wolves (Aug 2004)
Linderoth, Tobias	21 Apr 1979	Stockholm	Swe	Everton (Jan 2002)
Allback, Marcus	5 Jul 1973	Gothenburg	Swe	A Villa (Jul 2002)
Svensson, Michael	25 Nov 1975	Sweden	Swe	Southampton (Aug 2002)
Shaaban, Rami	30 Jun 1975	Stockholm	Swe	Arsenal (Nov 2002); Brighton (Feb 2005)
Lucic, Teddy	15 Apr 1973	Biskopsgaard	Swe	Leeds (Oct 2002)
Tidman, Ola	11 May 1979	Malmo	Swe	Stockport (Jan 2003); Sheff Wed (Jun 2003)
Heikkinen, Markus	13 Oct 1978	Katrineholm	Fin	Portsmouth (Feb 2003); Luton (Jul 2005)
Baxter, Lee	17 Jul 1976	Helsingborg	Swe	Sheff Utd (Jul 2004)
Edman, Erik	11 Nov 1978	Huskvarna	Swe	Tottenham (Jul 2004)
Nilsson, Mikael	24 Jun 1978	Kristianstad	Swe	Southampton (Jul 2004)
Jakobsson, Andreas	6 Oct 1972	Helsingborg	Swe	Southampton (Aug 2004)
Jonson, Mattias	16 Jan 1974	Orebro	Swe	Norwich (Aug 2004)
Larsson, Sebastian	6 Jun 1985	Eskilstuna	Swe	Arsenal (Aug 2004)
Johansson, Andreas	5 Jul 1978	Vanersborg	Swe	Wigan (Jan 2005)
Gerrbrand, Patrik	27 Apr 1981	Stockholm	Swe	Leicester (Jul 2005)
Ostlund, Alexander	2 Nov 1978	Akersberga	Swe	Southampton (Jan 2006)

Other players qualified for Sweden but born outside Sweden

Name	DOB	Place of birth	Nat	Club(s) (joined/first played)
Andreasson, Marcus	13 Jul 1978	Monrovia, Lbr	Swe	Bristol R (Jul 1998)
Avdiu, Kemajl	22 Dec 1976	Kosovo, Yug	Swe	Bury (Aug 1998)
Djordjic, Bojan	6 Feb 1982	Belgrade, Yug	Swe	Man Utd (Feb 1999); Sheff Wed (Dec 2001); Plymouth (May 2005)

SWITZERLAND (14+2)

Name	DOB	Place of birth	Nat	Club(s) (joined/first played)
Steffen, Willi	17 Mar 1925	Berne	Swit	Chelsea (Nov 1946)
Hottiger, Marc	7 Nov 1967	Lausanne	Swit	Newcastle (Aug 1994); Everton (Mar 1996)
Mazzarelli, Giuseppe	14 Aug 1972	Uster	Swit	Man City (Mar 1996)
Di Matteo, Roberto	29 May 1970	Sciaffusa	It	Chelsea (Jul 1996)
Vega, Ramon	14 Jun 1971	Olten	Swit	Tottenham (Jan 1997); Watford (Jun 2001)

Name	DOB	Place of birth	Nat	Club(s) (joined/first played)
Pascolo, Marco	9 May 1966	Sion	Swit	Nottm For (Jun 1997)
Henchoz, Stephane	7 Sep 1974	Billens	Swit	Blackburn (Jul 1997); Liverpool (Jul 1999); Wigan (Jul 2005)
Giallanza, Gaetano	6 Jun 1974	Dornach	Swit	Bolton (Mar 1998); Norwich (Mar 2000)
Konde, Oumar	19 Aug 1979	Binnengen	Swit	Blackburn (Nov 1998)
Foletti, Patrick	27 May 1974	Sorengo	Swit	Derby (Feb 2002)
Senderos, Philippe	14 Feb 1985	Geneva	Swit	Arsenal (Jul 2003)
Molango, Maheta	24 Jul 1982	Saint Imier	It	Brighton (Jul 2004); Lincoln (Jul 2005)
Ziegler, Reto	16 Jan 1986	Servette	Swit	Tottenham (Aug 2004); Wigan (Jan 2006)
Sow, Mamadou	22 Aug 1981	Clarmont	Fr	Torquay (Jun 2005)

Other players qualified for Switzerland but born outside Switzerland

Name	DOB	Place of birth	Nat	Club(s) (joined/first played)
Haas, Bernt	8 Apr 1978	Vienna, Aut	Swit	Sunderland (Aug 2001); WBA (Jul 2003)
Djourou, Johan	18 Jan 1987	Abidjan, IvCo	Swit	Arsenal (Aug 2004)

TANZANIA (2)

Name	DOB	Place of birth	Nat	Club(s) (joined/first played)
Chine, Athumani	12 Mar 1967	Dar es Salaam	Tan	Walsall (Mar 1992)
Anaclet, Eddie	31 Aug 1985	Arusha	Tan	Chester (Dec 2004)

TOGO (3)

Name	DOB	Place of birth	Nat	Club(s) (joined/first played)
Hodouto, Kwami	31 Oct 1974	Lome	Fr	Huddersfield (Sep 1999)
Folly, Yoann	6 Jun 1985	Lome	Fr/Tgo	Southampton (Jul 2003); Nottm For (Jan 2005); Preston (Mar 2005); Sheff Wed (Jan 2006)
Adebayor, Emmanuel	26 Feb 1984	Lome	Tgo	Arsenal (Jan 2006)

TRINIDAD AND TOBAGO (20)

Name	DOB	Place of birth	Nat	Club(s) (joined/first played)
Charles, Alf	11 Jul 1909	Trinidad	Trin	Southampton (Jan 1937)
Auguste, Joe	24 Nov 1955	Trinidad	Trin	Exeter (Jun 1981)
Granville, John	6 May 1956	Tobago	Trin	Millwall (Oct 1985); Aldershot (Aug 1991)
Yorke, Dwight	3 Dec 1971	Canaan	Trin	A Villa (Dec 1989); Man Utd (Aug 1998); Blackburn (Jul 2002); Birmingham (Aug 2004)
Samuel, Randy	23 Dec 1963	Trinidad	Can	Port Vale (Nov 1995)
Marcelle, Clint	9 Nov 1968	Port of Spain	Trin	Barnsley (Aug 1996); Scunthorpe (Oct 1999); Hull (Sep 2000); Darlington (Feb 2001); Grimsby (Aug 2004)
Rougier, Tony	17 Jul 1971	Tobago	Trin	Port Vale (Jan 1999); Reading (Aug 2000); Brighton (Feb 2003); Brentford (Aug 2003); Bristol C (Mar 2004)
Ince, Clayton	13 Jul 1972	Trinidad	Trin	Crewe (Sep 1999); Coventry (Jul 2005)
Samuel, J Lloyd	29 Mar 1981	Trinidad	Brit	A Villa (Feb 1999); Gillingham (Oct 2001)
John, Stern	30 Oct 1976	Tunapuna	Trin	Nottm For (Nov 1999); Birmingham (Feb 2002); Coventry (Sep 2004); Derby (Sep 2005)
Eve, Angus	23 Feb 1972	Trinidad	Trin	Chester (Dec 1999)
Laird, Kamu	23 Dec 1975	Port of Spain	Trin	Chester (Dec 1999)
Pierre, Nigel	2 Jun 1979	Port of Spain	Trin	Bristol R (Feb 2000)
Edwards, Carlos	24 Oct 1978	Port of Spain	Trin	Wrexham (Aug 2000); Luton (May 2005)
Sam, Hector	25 Feb 1978	Mount Murray	Trin	Wrexham (Aug 2000); Port Vale (Jun 2005)
Lawrence, Denis	1 Aug 1974	Port of Spain	Trin	Wrexham (Mar 2001)
Norville, Jason	9 Sep 1983	Trinidad	Trin	Watford (Oct 2001); Barnet (Jul 2005)
Rahim, Brent	8 Aug 1978	Diego Martin	Trin	Northampton (Jan 2003)
Jones, Kenwyne	5 Oct 1984	Trinidad	Trin	Southampton (Jul 2004); Sheff Wed (Sep 2004); Stoke (Feb 2005)
Sancho, Brent	13 Mar 1977	Port of Spain	Trin	Gillingham (Aug 2005)

Name	DOB	Place of birth	Nat	Club(s) (joined/first played)
TUNISIA (2+1)				
Karaa, Roch	3 Apr 1964	Tunisia	Tun	Darlington (Mar 1985)
Jaidi, Radhi	30 Aug 1975	Tunis	Tun	Bolton (Jul 2004)
Other players qualified for Tunisia but born outside Tunisia				
Nafti, Mehdi	28 Nov 1978	Toulouse, Fr	Tun	Birmingham (Jan 2005)
TURKEY (5+1)				
Alpay Ozalan	29 May 1973	Karisyaled	Tur	A Villa (Jul 2000)
Tugay Kerimoglu	24 Aug 1970	Istanbul	Tur	Blackburn (Jul 2001)
Hakan Unsal	14 May 1973	Sinop	Tur	Blackburn (Mar 2002)
Hakan Sukur	1 Sep 1971	Sakarya	Tur	Blackburn (Dec 2002)
Emre Belozoglu	7 Sep 1980	Istanbul	Tur	Newcastle (Jul 2005)
Other players qualified for Turkey but born outside Turkey				
Bulent, Akin	28 Aug 1979	Brussels, Bel	Tur	Bolton (Oct 2002)
UGANDA (3)				
Baugh, John	23 Feb 1956	Uganda	Uga	Exeter (Feb 1977)
Iga, Andrew	9 Dec 1977	Kampala	Brit	Millwall (Jun 1995)
Kitamirike, Joel	5 Apr 1984	Kampala	Uga	Chelsea (Apr 2001); Brentford (Sep 2003); Mansfield (Dec 2004)
UKRAINE (8)				
Baltacha, Sergei	17 Feb 1958	Kiev	USSR	Ipswich (Jan 1989)
Kanchelskis, Andrei	23 Jan 1969	Kirowograd	Ukr	Man Utd (Mar 1991); Everton (Aug 1995); Man City (Jan 2001); Southampton (Sep 2002)
Yuran, Sergei	11 Jun 1969	Kiev	Ukr	Millwall (Jan 1996)
Evtushok, Alex	11 Jan 1970	Kiev	Ukr	Coventry (Feb 1997)
Luzhny, Oleg	5 Aug 1968	Kiev	Ukr	Arsenal (Jul 1999); Wolves (Jul 2003)
Rebrov, Sergei	3 Jun 1974	Gorlovka	Ukr	Tottenham (Jun 2000); West Ham (Jul 2004)
Bopp, Eugene	5 Sep 1983	Kiev	Ger	Nottm For (Aug 2001)
Baltacha, Sergei Jnr	28 Jul 1979	Kiev	Sco	Millwall (Jan 2003)
URUGUAY (11)				
Villazan, Rafael	19 Jul 1956	Montevideo	Uru	Wolves (May 1980)
Perdomo, Jose	6 Jan 1965	Montevideo	Uru	Coventry (Aug 1990)
Paz, Adrian	9 Sep 1968	Montevideo	Uru	Ipswich (Sep 1994)
Poyet, Gustavo	15 Nov 1967	Montevideo	Uru	Chelsea (Jul 1997); Tottenham (Jul 2001)
Corbo, Mateo	21 Apr 1976	Montevideo	Arg	Barnsley (Aug 2000); Oxford (Jan 2005)
Forlan, Diego	19 May 1979	Montevideo	Uru	Man Utd (Jan 2002)
Sorondo, Gonzalo	9 Oct 1979	Montevideo	Uru	C Palace (Aug 2004); Charlton (Jul 2005)
Pandiani, Walter	27 Apr 1976	Montevideo	Uru	Birmingham (Jan 2005)
Silva, Dario	2 Nov 1972	Treinta y Tres	Uru	Portsmouth (Aug 2005)
Melono, Gabriel	27 Apr 1977	Montevideo	Uru	Yeovil (Sep 2005)
Martinez, Williams	18 Dec 1982	Montevideo	Uru	WBA (Jan 2006)
USA (60+6)				
Andrews, Billy	1886	Kansas City	N Ire	Oldham (Aug 1908); Stockport (Mar 1909); Grimsby Town (Jul 1912)
Lester, Hugh	1891	USA	Brit	Liverpool (Aug 1911); Oldham (Aug 1914)
Gibson, Jock	23 Mar 1898	Philadelphia	Sco	Sunderland (Nov 1920); Hull (May 1922); Sheff Utd (Mar 1929); Luton (Jul 1933)
Donoghue, John	22 Jan 1903	New York	USA	Wrexham (Jul 1930)
Aspinall, Wilf	22 Sep 1910	Hartford	USA	Stockport (Jun 1934); Southport (Jul 1935)
McLaughlin, William	31 Jan 1918	USA	USA	Crewe (Oct 1946)
Kirkby, John	29 Nov 1929	USA	USA	Stoke (Dec 1946); Wrexham (Aug 1951)

Name	DOB	Place of birth	Nat	Club(s) (joined/first played)
Boyd, John	10 Sep 1926	USA	USA	Bristol C (Dec 1950)
Turner, Alf	26 Dec 1929	USA	Brit	N Brighton (Feb 1951)
Clelland, Crawford	3 Dec 1930	New Jersey	USA	Plymouth (Jun 1955)
Baker, Gerry	11 Apr 1938	New York	Brit	Man City (Nov 1960); Ipswich (Dec 1963); Coventry (Nov 1967); Brentford (Oct 1969)
Potts, Steve	7 May 1967	Hartford	Eng	West Ham (May 1984)
Goulet, Brent	19 Jun 1964	Tacoma	USA	Crewe (Jan 1988); Bournemouth (Nov 1987)
Pittman, Steve	18 Jul 1967	North Carolina	USA	Shrewsbury (Mar 1989)
Bruce, Marcelle	15 Mar 1971	Detroit	USA	Colchester (Jul 1989)
Meola, Tony	21 Feb 1969	Belleville	USA	Brighton (Aug 1990)
Harkes, John	8 Mar 1967	Kearny	USA	Sheff Wed (Oct 1990); Derby (Aug 1993); West Ham (Oct 1995); Nottm For (Jan 1999)
Sommer, Jurgen	27 Feb 1964	New York	USA	Luton (Sep 1991); Brighton (Nov 1991); Torquay (Oct 1992); QPR (Aug 1995); Bolton (Feb 2001)
Keller, Kasey	27 Nov 1969	Washington	USA	Millwall (Feb 1992); Leicester (Aug 1996); Tottenham (Aug 2001); Southampton (Nov 2004)
Murray, Bruce	25 Jan 1966	Washington	USA	Millwall (Aug 1993); Stockport (Mar 1994)
Barada, Taylor	14 Aug 1972	Charlottesville	USA	Colchester (Mar 1994)
Stackman, Scott	16 Nov 1975	Arizona	USA	Northampton (Mar 1994)
McDougald, Junior	12 Jan 1975	Big Spring	Brit	Brighton (May 1994); Chesterfield (Mar 1996); Rotherham (Jul 1996); Millwall (Jul 1998); Orient (Oct 1998)
Ammann, Mike	8 Feb 1971	California	USA	Charlton (Jul 1994)
Jones, Cobi	16 Jun 1970	Detroit	USA	Coventry (Sep 1994)
Feuer, Ian	20 May 1971	Las Vegas	USA	Peterborough (Feb 1995); Luton (Sep 1995); West Ham (Feb 2000); Wimbledon (Jun 2000); Derby (Oct 2001); Tranmere (Aug 2002)
Crawford, Jimmy	1 May 1973	Chicago	Ire	Newcastle (Mar 1995); Rotherham (Sep 1996); Reading (Mar 1998)
Lapper, Mike	28 Aug 1970	California	USA	Southend (Aug 1995)
Santos, Ali	30 Jul 1975	New Jersey	USA	Bournemouth (Aug 1995)
Caldwell, Garrett	6 Nov 1973	Princeton	USA	Colchester (Sep 1995)
Baardsen, Espen	7 Dec 1977	San Rafael	Nor	Tottenham (Jul 1996); Watford (Aug 2000); Everton (Jan 2003)
Melvang, Lars	3 Apr 1969	Seattle	Den	Watford (Aug 1997)
Friedel, Brad	18 May 1971	Lakewood	USA	Liverpool (Dec 1997); Blackburn (Nov 2000)
Hahnemann, Marcus	15 Jun 1972	Seattle	USA	Fulham (Jul 1999); Rochdale (Oct 2001); Reading (Dec 2001)
Rachubka, Paul	21 May 1981	San Luis Obispo	USA	Man Utd (Jul 1999); Oldham (Nov 2001); Huddersfield (Mar 2004); MK Dons (Aug 2004); Northampton (Sep 2004); Huddersfield (Nov 2004)
Carver, Joe	11 Jun 1971	Illinois	USA	Chester (Sep 1999)
Moore, Joe-Max	23 Feb 1971	Tulsa	USA	Everton (Dec 1999)
Lewis, Eddie	17 May 1974	Cerritos	USA	Fulham (Mar 2000); Preston (Sep 2002); Leeds (Jun 2005)
McBride, Brian	19 Jun 1972	Arlington Heights	USA	Preston (Sep 2000); Everton (Jan 2003); Fulham (Jan 2004)
Olsen, Ben	3 May 1977	Harrisburg	USA	Nottm For (Oct 2000)
Berhalter, Gregg	8 Jan 1973	Tenafly	USA	C Palace (Feb 2001)
Joy, Ian	14 Jul 1981	San Diego	USA	Kidderminster (Aug 2001)

Name	DOB	Place of birth	Nat	Club(s) (joined/first played)
Kirovski, Jovan	18 Mar 1976	Escondido	USA	C Palace (Aug 2001); Birmingham (Sep 2002)
Reyna, Claudio	20 Jul 1973	New Jersey	USA	Sunderland (Dec 2001); Man City (Aug 2003)
Myhill, Boaz	9 Nov 1982	California	Eng	Bradford (Nov 2002); Macclesfield (Aug 2003); Stockport (Nov 2003); Hull (Dec 2003)
Sagere, Jake	5 Apr 1980	USA	USA	Grimsby (Apr 2003)
Howard, Tim	3 Jun 1979	New Jersey	USA	Man Utd (Jul 2003)
Simek, Frankie	13 Oct 1984	St Louis	USA	Arsenal (Jul 2003); QPR (Oct 2003); Bournemouth (Mar 2005); Sheff Wed (Jul 2005)
Whitbread, Zak	10 Jan 1984	Houston	USA	Liverpool (Jul 2003)
Bocanegra, Carlos	25 May 1979	Alta Loma, CA	USA	Fulham (Jan 2004)
Spector, Jonathan	1 Mar 1986	Arlington Heights	USA	Man Utd (May 2004); Charlton (Jul 2005)
Convey, Bobby	27 May 1983	Philadelphia	USA	Reading (Jul 2004)
De Merit, Jay	4 Dec 1979	Green Bay	USA	Watford (Jul 2004)
Johnson, Jemal	3 May 1985	New Jersey	USA	Blackburn (Jul 2004); Preston (Oct 2005); Darlington (Mar 2006)
Karbassiyoon, Daniel	10 Aug 1984	Virginia	USA	Arsenal (Aug 2004); Ipswich (Dec 2004); Burnley (Jun 2005)
Gregorio, Adolfo	1 Oct 1982	Turlock, CA	USA	Darlington (Sep 2004)
Rossi, Giuseppe	1 Feb 1987	New Jersey	It	Man Utd (Nov 2004)
Cooper, Kenny	21 Oct 1984	Baltimore	USA	Oldham (Jan 2005)
Denny, Jay	6 Jan 1986	Los Angeles	USA	Shrewsbury (Jun 2005)
Pittman, Jon-Paul	24 Oct 1986	Oklahoma City	USA	Nottm For (Jul 2005); Hartlepool (Jan 2006)

Other players qualified for USA but born outside USA

Name	DOB	Place of birth	Nat	Club(s) (joined/first played)
Wegerle, Roy	19 Mar 1964	Johannesburg, SA	USA	Chelsea (Jun 1986); Swindon (Mar 1988); Luton (Jul 1988); QPR (Dec 1989); Blackburn (Mar 1992); Coventry (Mar 1993)
Kerr, John	6 Mar 1965	Toronto, Can	USA	Portsmouth (Aug 1987); Peterborough (Dec 1987); Millwall (Feb 1993); Walsall (Nov 1995)
Radosavljevic, Preki	24 Jun 1963	Belgrade, Yug	USA	Everton (Aug 1992); Portsmouth (Jul 1994)
Miglioranzi, Stefani	20 Sep 1977	Pocos de Caldas, Bra	USA	Portsmouth (Jun 1999); Swindon (Aug 2002)
Thorrington, John	17 Oct 1979	Jo'burg, SA	USA	Huddersfield (Aug 2001); Grimsby (Mar 2004)
Yelldell, David	1 Oct 1981	Stuttgart, Ger	USA	Brighton (Jan 2005)

USSR (8)

Five of these players also listed under Belarus

Name	DOB	Place of birth	Nat	Club(s) (joined/first played)
Baltacha, Sergei	17 Feb 1958	Kiev (then USSR)	USSR	Ipswich (Jan 1989)
Cherednik, Alexei	12 Dec 1960	Pamir (then USSR)	USSR	Southampton (Feb 1990)
Gotsmanov, Sergei	17 Mar 1959	Minsk (then USSR)	USSR/Blr	Brighton (Feb 1990); Southampton (Aug 1990)
Gurinovich, Igor	5 Mar 1960	Minsk (then USSR)	USSR/Blr	Brighton (Nov 1990)
Yanushevski, Victor	23 Jan 1960	Minsk (then USSR)	USSR/Blr	Aldershot (Mar 1991)
Kachouro, Petr	2 Aug 1972	Minsk (then USSR)	Blr	Sheff Utd (Jul 1996)
Shtaniuk, Sergei	11 Jan 1972	Minsk (then USSR)	Blr	Stoke (Jul 2001)
Hleb, Aleksandr	1 May 1981	Minsk (then USSR)	Blr	Arsenal (Jul 2005)

VENEZUELA (3)

Name	DOB	Place of birth	Nat	Club(s) (joined/first played)
De Ornelas, Fernando	29 Jul 1976	Caracas	Ven	C Palace (Sep 1999); QPR (Oct 2001)
Savarese, Giovanni	14 Jul 1971	Caracas	Ven	Swansea (Oct 2000); Millwall (Jul 2001)
Nacca, Franco	9 Nov 1982	Venezuela	Ven	Cambridge (Sep 2002)

YUGOSLAVIA (33+1)

Some of these players also listed under Bosnia-Herzogovina

Name	DOB	Place of birth	Nat	Club(s) (joined/first played)
Golac, Ivan	15 Jun 1950	Kuprivnica	Yug	Southampton (Nov 1978); Bournemouth (Nov

Name	DOB	Place of birth	Nat	Club(s) (joined/first played)
				1982); Man City (Mar 1983); Southampton (Mar 1984); Portsmouth (Jan 1985)
Jankovic, Bozo	22 May 1951	Sarajevo (Bos, then Yug)	Yug	Middlesbrough (Feb 1979)
Borota, Petar	5 Mar 1952	Belgrade	Yug	Chelsea (Mar 1979)
Avramovic, Raddy	29 Nov 1949	Rijeka	Yug	Notts Co (Aug 1979); Coventry (Sep 1983)
Stepanovic, Dragoslav	30 Aug 1948	Rekovac	Yug	Man City (Aug 1979)
Jovanovic, Nikola	18 Sep 1952	Cetinje	Yug	Man Utd (Jan 1980)
Katalinic, Ivan	17 May 1951	Yugoslavia	Yug	Southampton (Feb 1980)
Antic, Raddy	22 Nov 1949	Zitiste	Yug	Luton (Jul 1980)
Hadziabdic, Dzemal	25 Jul 1953	Yugoslavia	Yug	Swansea (Aug 1980)
Banovic, Yakka	12 Nov 1956	Bihac (Bos, then Yug)	Aus	Derby (Sep 1980)
Muzinic, Drazen	25 Jan 1953	Yugoslavia	Yug	Norwich (Sep 1980)
Mirocevic, Ante	6 Aug 1952	Titograd	Yug	Sheff Wed (Oct 1980)
Dusan, Nikolic	23 Jan 1953	Belgrade	Yug	Bolton (Oct 1980)
Rajkovic, Anto	17 Aug 1952	Sarajevo (Bos, then Yug)	Yug	Swansea (Mar 1981)
Petrovic, Vladimir	1 Jul 1955	Belgrade	Yug	Arsenal (Dec 1982)
Radosavljevic, Preki	24 Jun 1963	Belgrade	USA	Everton (Aug 1992); Portsmouth (Jul 1994)
Milosevic, Savo	2 Sep 1973	Bijeljina (Bos, then Yug)	Yug	A Villa (Jul 1995)
Curcic, Sasa	14 Feb 1972	Belgrade	Yug	Bolton (Oct 1995); A Villa (Aug 1996); C Palace (Mar 1998)
Stefanovic, Dejan	28 Oct 1974	Belgrade	Yug	Sheff Wed (Dec 1995); Portsmouth (Jul 2003)
Kovacevic, Darko	18 Nov 1973	Kovin	Yug	Sheff Wed (Dec 1995)
Bosancic, Jovo	7 Aug 1970	Novi Sad	Yug	Barnsley (Aug 1996)
Avdiu, Kemajl	22 Dec 1976	Kosovo	Swe	Bury (Aug 1998)
Petric, Gordan	30 Jul 1969	Belgrade	Yug	C Palace (Nov 1998)
Mavrak, Darko	19 Jan 1969	Mostar (Bos, then Yug)	Bos	Walsall (Jan 1999)
Konjic, Muhamed	14 May 1970	Tuzla (Bos, then Yug)	Bos	Coventry (Feb 1999); Derby (May 2004)
Djordjic, Bojan	6 Feb 1982	Belgrade	Swe	Man Utd (Feb 1999); Sheff Wed (Dec 2001); Plymouth (May 2005)
Milovaijevic, Goran	11 Apr 1967	Kraljevo	Yug	Chester (Sep 1999)
Stanic, Mario	10 Apr 1972	Sarajevo (Bos, then Yug)	Cro	Chelsea (Jul 2000)
Boksic, Alen	21 Jan 1970	Makarska (Herz, then Yug)	Cro	Middlesbrough (Aug 2000)
Jokanovic, Slavisa	16 Aug 1968	Novi Sad	Yug	Chelsea (Oct 2000)
Bunjevcevic, Goran	17 Feb 1973	Karlovac (Cro, then Yug)	Yug	Tottenham (Jun 2001)
Kuduzovic, Fahrudin	10 Oct 1984	Sarajevo (Bos, then Yug)	Bos	Notts Co (Sep 2004)
Rodic, Alexsander	26 Dec 1979	Belgrade	Slo	Portsmouth (Jan 2005)

Qualified for Yugoslavia but born outside Yugoslavia

Name	DOB	Place of birth	Nat	Club(s) (joined/first played)
Ilic, Sasa	18 Jul 1972	Melbourne, Aus	Yug	Charlton (Oct 1997); West Ham (Feb 2000); Portsmouth (Sep 2001); Barnsley (Aug 2003); Blackpool (Jul 2004)

NB: From February 2003, the Yugoslavia national team became Serbia & Montenegro. See Serbia & Montenegro for players arriving in England after that point.

Name	DOB	Place of birth	Nat	Club(s) (joined/first played)
ZAMBIA (10)				
Mwila, Freddie	6 Jul 1946	Kasama	Zam	A Villa (Jun 1969)
Kapengwe, Emment	27 Mar 1943	Zambia	Zam	A Villa (Sep 1969)
Hesford, Iain	4 Mar 1960	Ndola	Eng	Blackpool (Aug 1977); Fulham (Jan 1985); Notts Co (Nov 1985); Sunderland (Aug 1986); Hull (Dec 1988); Maidstone United (Aug 1991)
Gregory, Neil	7 Oct 1972	Ndola	Brit	Chesterfield (Feb 1994); Scunthorpe (Aug 1994); Ipswich (Mar 1995); Torquay (Nov 1996); Peterborough (Nov 1997); Colchester (Jan 1998)
Rice, Gary	29 Sep 1975	Zambia	Brit	Exeter (Jul 1994)
Whitley, Jim	14 Apr 1975	Ndola	N Ire	Man City (Aug 1994); Blackpool (Aug 1999); Norwich (Aug 2000); Swindon (Dec 2000); Northampton (Feb 2001); Wrexham (Oct 2001)
Whitley, Jeff	28 Jan 1979	Ndola	N Ire	Man City (Feb 1996); Wrexham (Jan 1999); Notts Co (Mar 2002); Sunderland (Aug 2003); Cardiff (Jun 2005)
Earnshaw, Robert	6 Apr 1981	Mufulira	Wal	Cardiff (Aug 1997); WBA (Aug 2004); Norwich (Jan 2006)
Haarhoff, Jimmy	27 May 1981	Lusaka	Zam	Birmingham (Jun 1998)
Mbesuma, Collins	3 Feb 1984	Luanshya	Zam	Portsmouth (Aug 2005)
ZIMBABWE (8+2)				
Law, Cecil	10 Mar 1930	Salisbury	Brit	Derby (Aug 1951); Bury (May 1954)
Gibbs, Peter	24 Aug 1956	Chingola	Brit	Watford (Jul 1975)
Statham, Brian	21 May 1969	Harare	Eng	Tottenham (Aug 1987); Reading (Mar 1991); Bournemouth (Nov 1991); Brentford (Jan 1992); Gillingham (Aug 1997)
Robinson, John	29 Aug 1971	Bulawayo	Wal	Brighton (Apr 1989); Charlton (Sep 1992); Cardiff (Jul 2003); Gillingham (Oct 2004)
Ndlovu, Peter	25 Feb 1973	Bulawayo	Zim	Coventry (Aug 1991); Birmingham (Jul 1997); Huddersfield (Dec 2000); Sheff Utd (Feb 2001)
McKop, Henry	8 Jul 1967	Bulawayo	Zim	Bristol C (Feb 1994)
Deeney, David	12 Jan 1987	Bulawayo	Brit	Luton (Aug 2002)
Mwaruwari, Benjani	13 Aug 1978	Bulawayo	Zim	Portsmouth (Jan 2006)
Other players qualified for Zimbabwe but born outside Zimbabwe				
Kennon, Sandy	26 Nov 1933	Johannesburg, SA	Zim	Huddersfield (Aug 1956); Norwich (Feb 1959); Colchester (Mar 1965)
Grobbelaar, Bruce	6 Oct 1957	Durban, SA	Zim	Crewe (Dec 1979); Liverpool (Mar 1981); Stoke (Mar 1993); Southampton (Aug 1994); Plymouth (Aug 1996); Oldham (Dec 1997); Bury (Sep 1998); Lincoln (Dec 1998)

APPENDIX 2: CLUB BY CLUB

This appendix lists overseas-born players in English League history (Football League and Premier League), club by club, in chronological order of arrival.

Key
LgAp = league starts + substitute appearances
LgG = league goals
OthAp = all other competitive appearances, including FA Cup, League Cup, play-off matches and European club games
OthG = all other goals
Born = country of birth (nationality, where it differs, in brackets after surname)
Pos = playing position (gk = goalkeeper; fb = full-back; ch = centre-half; d = defender; wh = wing-half; w = winger; m = midfielder; f = forward)
From = month of signing or month of first appearance.
(1) (2) (3) Numbers in brackets next to a player's name denote separate playing spells at the club.

Name	Born	Pos	From	LgAp	LgG	OthAp	OthG
ACCRINGTON (1)							
Bowman, Walter	Can	wh	Aug 1891	5	3	0	0
ACCRINGTON STANLEY (2)							
Priday, Bob	SA	w	Dec 1952	5	0	0	0
Kirk, John	Can	f	Mar 1953	14	1	0	0
ALDERSHOT (14)							
Bunch, Arthur	SA	f	Jun 1934	16	3	4	2
Court, Dick (Brit)	Ind	f	Jun 1937	10	1	3	3
Bluck, Dick (Brit)	Ind	wh	Aug 1951	1	0	0	0
Kirsten, Ken	SA	fb	Aug 1951	5	0	0	0
Huggins, Joe (Brit)	Ind	f	Dec 1955	6	5	0	0
Porteous, Jack (Brit)	Ind	f	Feb 1956	1	0	0	0
Devereux, Tony (Brit)	Gib	fb	Nov 1958	132	0	14	0
Hodge, Eric	SA	ch	Jul 1959	17	0	1	0
Burgess, Mike	Can	f/ch	Nov 1965	6	0	1	0
Fadida, Aharon	Isr	f	Dec 1985	9+5	6	1	0
Stein, Mark (Eng)	SA	f	Jan 1986	2	1	0	0
Yanushevski, Victor	USSR	d	Mar 1991	6	1	0	0
Granville, John	Trin	gk	Aug 1991	30	0	3	0
Berry, George (Wal)	Ger	d	Nov 1991	25	1	1	0
ARSENAL (79)							
Butler, Jack (Eng)	SL	ch	Jan 1914	267	7	29	1
Tricker, Reg (Brit)	Ind	f	Mar 1927	12	5	0	0
Preedy, Reg (Brit)	Ind	gk	May 1929	37	0	2	0
Keizer, Gerry	Neth	gk	Aug 1930	12	0	0	0
Gudmundsson, Albert	Ice	f	Sep 1946	2	0	0	0
Le Roux, Daniel	SA	w	Feb 1957	5	0	0	0
Batson, Brendan (Eng)	Grn	fb	Jun 1971	6+4	0	0	0

Name	Born	Pos	From	LgAp	LgG	OthAp	OthG
Kosmina, John	Aus	f	Mar 1978	0+1	0	1+2	0
Petrovic, Vladimir	Yug	m	Dec 1982	10+3	2	9	1
Jonsson, Siggi	Ice	m	Jul 1989	2+6	1	1+1	0
Limpar, Anders	Swe	w	Aug 1990	76+20	17	19	3
Lydersen, Pal (Nor)	Den	fb	Nov 1991	12+3	0	1	0
Jensen, John	Den	m	Aug 1992	93+5	1	35+3	0
Schwarz, Stefan	Swe	m	May 1994	34	2	13	2
Helder, Glenn	Neth	f	Feb 1995	27+12	1	6+4	0
Bergkamp, Dennis	Neth	f	Jul 1995	253+62	87	92+16	34
Garde, Remi	Fr	m	Aug 1996	19+12	0	8+4	0
Vieira, Patrick (Fr)	Sen	m	Aug 1996	272+7	29	125+3	5
Anelka, Nicolas	Fr	f	Mar 1997	50+15	23	22+2	4
Manninger, Alex	Aut	gk	Jun 1997	38+1	0	24	0
Boa Morte, Luis	Por	f	Jun 1997	6+19	0	7+5	4
Grimandi, Gilles	Fr	d	Jun 1997	85+29	4	42+12	2
Petit, Emmanuel	Fr	m	Jun 1997	82+3	9	30+1	2
Muntasser, Jehad	Lby	m	Jun 1997	0	0	0+1	0
Overmars, Marc	Neth	w	Jul 1997	91+9	25	35+6	15
Mendez, Alberto (Sp)	Ger	m	Jul 1997	1+3	0	5+2	2
Wreh, Christopher	Lbr	f	Aug 1997	10+18	3	8+9	1
Grondin, David	Fr	d	Jul 1998	1	0	3	0
Vivas, Nelson	Arg	d	Aug 1998	14+26	0	15+14	1
Ljungberg, Freddie	Swe	m	Sep 1998	172+26	46	101+13	24
Caballero, Fabian	Arg	f	Oct 1998	0+1	0	0+2	0
Diawara, Kaba	Fr	f	Jan 1999	2+10	0	1+2	0
Kanu, Nwankwo	Nig	f	Feb 1999	63+56	30	41+38	14
Luzhny, Oleg	Ukr	d	Jul 1999	58+17	0	33+1	0
Malz, Stefan	Ger	m	Jul 1999	2+4	1	4+4	1
Silvinho, Silvio	Bra	fb	Jul 1999	46+9	3	19+5	2
Henry, Thierry	Fr	f	Aug 1999	219+18	164	95+11	50
Suker, Davor	Cro	f	Aug 1999	8+14	8	7+10	3
Volz, Moritz	Ger	d	Jan 2000	0	0	1+1	0
Aliadiere, Jeremie	Fr	f	Mar 2000	3+15	1	4+6	4
Lauren	Cam	m	Jun 2000	152+7	7	75+7	3
Pires, Robert	Fr	m	Jul 2000	159+30	62	79+16	22
Svard, Sebastian	Den	d	Aug 2000	0	0	2+2	0
Wiltord, Sylvain	Fr	f	Aug 2000	78+28	31	46+23	18
Stepanovs, Igors	Lat	d	Sep 2000	17	0	12+2	1
Danilevicius, Tomas (Lith)	Rus	f	Dec 2000	0+2	0	0+1	0
Edu	Bra	m	Jan 2001	41+38	7	35+13	8
Van Bronckhorst, Giovanni	Neth	m	Jun 2001	22+19	2	17+6	0
Inamoto, Junichi	Jap	m	Jul 2001	0	0	2+2	0
Duarte, Juan M	Bra	d	Aug 2001	0	0	2	0
Itonga, Carlin	DRC	f	Aug 2001	0	0	0+1	0
Tavlaridis, Stathis	Grk	d	Sep 2001	0+1	0	7	0
Silva, Gilberto	Bra	m	Aug 2002	107+6	6	40+6	6
Toure, Kolo	IvCo	d	Aug 2002	113+18	3	51+9	4
Cygan, Pascal	Fr	d	Sep 2002	52+11	3	28+7	0
Shaaban, Rami	Swe	gk	Nov 2002	3	0	2	0
Fabregas, Cesc	Sp	m	Jul 2003	54+14	5	23+8	4
Lehmann, Jens	Ger	gk	Jul 2003	104	0	38	0
Owusu-Abeyie, Quincy	Neth	f	Jul 2003	1+4	0	7+11	2
Senderos, Philippe	Swit	d	Jul 2003	31+2	2	25	0
Simek, Frankie	USA	d	Jul 2003	0	0	0+1	0

Name	Born	Pos	From	LgAp	LgG	OthAp	OthG
Skulason Olafur, Ingi	Ice	d	Jul 2003	0	0	0+1	0
Clichy, Gael	Fr	d	Aug 2003	19+15	0	16+7	0
Papadopulos, Michal	CzRep	f	Aug 2003	0	0	0+1	0
Reyes, Jose	Sp	f	Jan 2004	54+15	16	35+6	7
Van Persie, Robin	Neth	f	May 2004	25+25	10	14+15	11
Almunia, Manuel	Sp	gk	Jul 2004	10	0	18+1	0
Flamini, Mathieu	Fr	m	Jul 2004	28+24	1	25+4	0
Lupoli, Arturo	It	f	Jul 2004	0+1	0	6+2	3
Djourou, Johan (IvCo)	Swit	d	Aug 2004	6+1	0	7+1	0
Karbassiyoon, Daniel	USA	f	Aug 2004	0	0	1+2	1
Larsson, Sebastian	Swe	m	Aug 2004	2+1	0	5+4	0
Eboue, Emmanuel	IvCo	d	Jan 2005	11+8	0	15+2	1
Hleb, Aleksandr	Blr	m	Jul 2005	17+8	3	13+2	0
Muamba, Fabrice (Eng)	DRC	m	Jul 2005	0	0	2	0
Song Billong, Alexandre	Cam	m	Sep 2005	3+2	0	3+1	0
Bendtner, Nicklas	Den	f	Oct 2005	0+0	0	0+3	0
Adebayor, Emmanuel	Tgo	f	Jan 2006	12+1	4	0	0
Diaby, Abou	Fr	m	Jan 2006	9+3	1	2+2	0

ASTON VILLA (55)

Name	Born	Pos	From	LgAp	LgG	OthAp	OthG
Hunter, George (Brit)	Ind	wh	Feb 1908	91	1	6	0
Chandler, Robert (Brit)	Ind	gk	Aug 1913	1	0	0	0
Hodgson, Gordon (Eng)	SA	f	Jan 1936	28	11	0	0
Keelan, Kevin (Brit)	Ind	gk	Jul 1958	5	0	0	0
Mwila, Freddie	Zam	f	Jun 1969	1	0	0	0
Kapengwe, Emment	Zam	f	Sep 1969	3	0	0	0
Young, Charlie (Brit)	Cyp	d	Nov 1975	9+1	0	1	0
Blake, Noel (Brit)	Jam	d	Aug 1979	4	0	0	0
Dorigo, Tony (Eng)	Aus	fb	Jul 1983	106+5	1	21+1	0
Six, Didier	Fr	w	Oct 1984	13+3	2	1+1	0
Cooper, Neale (Sco)	Ind	m	Jul 1986	19+1	0	2	1
Callaghan, Nigel (Eng)	Sing	w	Feb 1989	24+2	1	3+2	0
Nielsen, Kent	Den	d	Jun 1989	74+5	4	16+1	1
Yorke, Dwight	Trin	f	Dec 1989	195+36	73	51+4	24
Regis, Cyrille (Eng)	FrGu	f	Jul 1991	46+6	12	8+3	0
Kubicki, Dariusz	Pol	fb	Aug 1991	24+1	0	7+1	0
Beinlich, Stefan	Ger	m	Oct 1991	7+9	1	0	0
Breitkreutz, Matthias	Ger	m	Oct 1991	10+3	0	0+1	0
Bosnich, Mark	Aus	gk	Feb 1992	179	0	48+1	0
Lamptey, Nii	Gha	m	Aug 1994	1+5	0	2+1	3
Milosevic, Savo	Yug	f	Jul 1995	84+6	28	26+1	5
Nelson, Fernando	Por	d	Jun 1996	54+5	0	11+4	0
Curcic, Sasa	Yug	m	Aug 1996	20+9	0	3+2	1
Fabio, Ferraresi	It	m	Jun 1998	0	0	0+1	0
Enckelman, Peter	Fin	gk	Feb 1999	51+1	0	14+1	0
Samuel, J Lloyd (Brit)	Trin	d	Feb 1999	142+23	2	26+3	1
Boateng, George (Neth)	Gha	m	Jul 1999	96+7	4	31+1	1
Ghrayib, Naguyan	Isr	d	Aug 1999	1+4	0	1	0
Carbone, Benito	It	f	Oct 1999	22+2	3	6	5
Nilis, Luc	Bel	f	Jul 2000	3	1	2	1
Ozalan, Alpay	Tur	d	Jul 2000	56+2	1	13	0
Ginola, David	Fr	w	Aug 2000	14+18	3	5+4	2
Hitzlsperger, Thomas	Ger	m	Aug 2000	74+25	8	8+7	4
De Bilde, Gilles	Bel	f	Oct 2000	4	0	0	0

Name	Born	Pos	From	LgAp	LgG	OthAp	OthG
Angel, Juan Pablo	Col	f	Jan 2001	116+36	40	20+6	15
Kachloul, Hassan	Mor	m	Jun 2001	17+5	2	8+2	0
Hadji, Mustapha	Mor	m	Jul 2001	24+11	2	6+5	1
Schmeichel, Peter	Den	gk	Jul 2001	29	1	7	0
Mellberg, Olof	Swe	d	Jul 2001	160	5	25	0
Balaban, Bosko	Cro	f	Aug 2001	0+8	0	2+1	0
Allback, Marcus	Swe	f	Jul 2002	16+19	6	4+5	1
Postma, Stefan	Neth	gk	Jul 2002	7+4	0	3	0
De La Cruz, Ulises	Ecu	d/m	Aug 2002	66+23	1	8+2	1
Johnsen, Ronny	Nor	d	Sep 2002	46+3	1	6+1	0
Leonhardsen, Oyvind	Nor	m	Sep 2002	13+6	3	3+1	0
Gudjonsson, Joey	Ice	m	Jan 2003	9+2	2	0	0
Sorensen, Thomas	Den	gk	Aug 2003	110	0	17	0
Solano, Nolberto	Per	m	Jan 2004	44+5	8	3	1
Laursen, Martin	Den	d	May 2004	13	1	0	0
Berson, Mathieu	Fr	m	Aug 2004	7+4	0	0+2	0
Djemba-Djemba, Eric	Cam	m	Jan 2005	4+6	0	0	0
Berger, Patrik	CzRep	m	Jul 2005	3+5	0	1	0
Baros, Milan	CzRep	f	Aug 2005	24+1	8	5	1
Bakke, Eirik	Nor	m	Aug 2005	8+6	0	0	0
Bouma, Wilfred	Neth	d	Aug 2005	20	0	1	0

BARNET (11)

Name	Born	Pos	From	LgAp	LgG	OthAp	OthG
Stein, Edwin (Brit)	SA	m	Jul 1982	0+1	0	0	0
Stein, Brian (Eng)	SA	f	Aug 1992	17+23	8	2	0
Carmichael, Matt (Brit)	Sing	f	Sep 1994	2+1	0	0	0
Taylor, Maik (N Ire)	Ger	gk	Jun 1995	70	0	12	0
Goodhind, Warren	SA	d	Jul 1996	73+20	3	9+2	1
Constantinou, Costas	Cyp	d	Oct 1996	1	0	0	0
Arber, Mark (Brit)	SA	d	Sep 1998	123+2	15	9	1
Bossu, Bert	Fr	gk	Oct 1999	0	0	0+1	0
Omoyimni, Manny	Nig	f	Feb 2000	1+5	0	0	0
Norville, Jason	Trin	f	Jul 2005	7+15	2	3+2	1
Kandol, Tresor (Brit)	DRC	f	Jan 2006	13	4	0	0

BARNSLEY (33)

Name	Born	Pos	From	LgAp	LgG	OthAp	OthG
Robledo, George	Chi	f	Apr 1943	105	45	9	2
Robledo, Ted	Chi	wh	Mar 1946	5	0	0	0
Kelly, Pat (N Ire)	SA	gk	Oct 1946	144	0	3	0
Mokone, Steve	SA	w	Aug 1961	0	0	1	0
Cunningham, Tony (Brit)	Jam	f	Sep 1982	40+2	11	3	0
Jonsson, Siggi	Ice	m	Jan 1986	5	0	0	0
Molby, Jan	Den	m	Sep 1995	5	0	0	0
De Zeeuw, Arjan	Neth	d	Nov 1995	138	7	26	0
Ten Heuvel, Laurens	Neth	f	Mar 1996	1+7	0	0+1	0
Van der Velden, Carel	Neth	m	Mar 1996	7+2	0	1	0
Bosancic, Jovo	Yug	m	Aug 1996	30+12	3	8+2	0
Marcelle, Clint	Trin	f	Aug 1996	37+32	8	9+6	1
Hristov, Georgi	Mac	f	Jul 1997	18+27	8	4+7	3
Krizan, Ales	Slo	d	Jul 1997	13	0	6	0
Tinkler, Eric	SA	m	Jul 1997	78+21	9	18+1	1
Leese, Lars	Ger	gk	Jul 1997	16+1	0	4	0
Barnard, Darren (Wal)	Ger	m	Aug 1997	151+19	28	28+3	8
Markstedt, Peter	Swe	f	Nov 1997	8+1	0	1+1	0
Mori Cuesta, Francisco	Sp	m	Mar 1999	2	0	0	0

Name	Born	Pos	From	LgAp	LgG	OthAp	OthG
Fjortoft, Jan Aage	Nor	f	Jan 1998	21+13	9	5+1	4
Van der Laan, Robin	Neth	m	Jul 1998	52+15	5	11+2	4
Fallon, Rory	NZ	f	Mar 1999	33+19	11	4+1	0
Bengtsson, Robert	Swe	d	Nov 1999	0	0	2	0
Corbo, Mateo	Uru	d	Aug 2000	10+8	0	2+1	1
Bertos, Leo (Grk)	NZ	f	Sep 2000	4+8	1	0+1	0
Salli, Janne	Fin	d	Nov 2000	6+1	0	1	0
Gorre, Dean (Neth)	Sur	m	Jul 2001	48+17	9	5	1
Sand, Peter	Den	m	Oct 2001	4+2	1	1+1	0
Christie, Jeremy	NZ	m	Dec 2001	0+1	0	0+1	0
Betsy, Kevin	Sey	m	Mar 2002	84+10	16	11	0
Ilic, Sasa (Yug)	Aus	gk	Aug 2003	25	0	8	0
Burns, Jacob	Aus	m	Oct 2003	81+8	6	11+4	2
Oninuije, Fola	Nig	f	Jul 2004	0+3	0	0+1	0

BARROW (2)

Name	Born	Pos	From	LgAp	LgG	OthAp	OthG
Peed, Frank (Brit)	Arg	f	Nov 1933	38	15	0	0
Purdon, Ted	SA	f	Mar 1958	37	12	0	0

BIRMINGHAM CITY (53)

Name	Born	Pos	From	LgAp	LgG	OthAp	OthG
Mills, Paddy (Brit)	Ind	f	Feb 1929	13	3	0	0
Mitchell, Frank	Aus	wh	Sep 1943	93	6	13	2
Havenga, Willie	SA	f	Jul 1948	1	0	0	0
Atkins, Arthur (Brit)	Jap	ch	Nov 1948	97	0	8	0
Purdon, Ted	SA	f	Aug 1950	64	27	6	3
Kloner, Hymie (Pol)	SA	wh	Nov 1950	1	0	0	0
Houghton, Bud (Brit)	Ind	f	Oct 1957	4	1	0	0
Van Den Hauwe, Pat (Wal)	Bel	fb	Aug 1978	119+4	1	17	0
Tarantini, Alberto	Arg	d	Oct 1978	23	1	1	0
Brocken, Bud	Neth	m	Aug 1981	17	0	2	0
Van Mierlo, Toine	Neth	w	Aug 1981	44	4	3	0
Blake, Noel (Brit)	Jam	d	Sep 1982	76	5	20	0
Richards, Carl (Eng)	Jam	f	Oct 1988	18+1	2	0	0
Okenla, Foley	Nig	m	Aug 1991	2+5	1	1+3	0
Paskin, John	SA	f	Nov 1991	8+2	3	0+1	0
Peschisolido, Paul (1)	Can	f	Nov 1992	37+6	16	2+1	1
Hooper, Lyndon (Can)	Guy	m	Sep 1993	1+4	0	1	0
Dominguez, Jose	Por	w	Mar 1994	15+10	3	3+3	0
Rushfeldt, Siggi	Nor	f	Oct 1995	3+4	0	1	1
Griemink, Bart	Neth	gk	Nov 1995	20	0	4	0
Sahlin, Dan	Swe	f	Nov 1995	0+1	0	0	0
Peschisolido, Paul (2)	Can	f	Mar 1996	7+2	1	0	0
Limpar, Anders	Swe	w	Jan 1997	3+1	0	1	0
Hey, Tony	Ger	m	Jun 1997	8+1	0	2	1
Ndlovu, Peter	Zim	f	Jul 1997	78+29	22	22+5	5
Adebola, Dele	Nig	f	Feb 1998	86+43	31	16+7	11
Haarhoff, Jimmy	Zam	f	Jun 1998	0+1	0	0	0
Luntala, Tresor	Fr	d/m	Jul 1999	9+6	0	1	0
Lazaridis, Stan	Aus	w	Jul 1999	142+49	8	20+11	0
Wreh, Christopher	Lbr	f	Oct 1999	6+1	1	0	0
Marcelo	Bra	f	Oct 1999	47+30	24	6+9	2
Myhre, Thomas	Nor	gk	Mar 2000	7	0	2	0
Vaesen, Nico	Bel	gk	Jun 2001	53+1	0	9	0
Ferrari, Carlos	Bra	f	Aug 2001	0+4	0	0	0
Bragstad, Bjorn Otto	Nor	d	Sep 2001	3	0	0	0

Name	Born	Pos	From	LgAp	LgG	OthAp	OthG
Bak, Arkadiusz	Pol	m	Dec 2001	2+2	0	1	0
John, Stern	Tri	f	Feb 2002	42+31	16	6+2	5
Tebily, Olivier	IvCo	d	Mar 2002	57+20	0	8+3	0
Cisse, Aliou	Sen	m	Aug 2002	26	10	1+1	0
Kirovski, Jovan	USA	f	Sep 2002	5+18	2	2+3	0
Coly, Ferdinand	Sen	d	Jan 2003	1	0	1	0
Dugarry, Christophe	Fr	f	Jan 2003	28+2	6	0+1	0
Swierczewski, Piotr	Pol	m	Feb 2003	0+1	0	0	0
Figueroa, Luciano	Arg	f	Aug 2003	0+1	0	0+1	0
Forssell, Mikael (Fin)	Ger	f	Aug 2003	46+17	20	9+4	7
Taylor, Maik (N Ire)	Ger	gk	Aug 2003	106	0	16	0
Gronkjaer, Jesper	Den	m	Jul 2004	13+3	0	2	1
Melchiot, Mario	Neth	d	Jul 2004	55+1	2	10	0
Yorke, Dwight	Trin	f	Aug 2004	4+9	2	2+1	0
Diao, Salif	Sen	m	Jan 2005	2+0	0	0	0
Nafti, Mehdi (Tun)	Fr	m	Jan 2005	8+3	0	0	0
Pandiani, Walter	Uru	f	Jan 2005	20+11	6	2+2	0
Jarosik, Jiri	CzRep	m	Aug 2005	19+5	5	6+2	3
Latka, Martin	CzRep	d	Jan 2006	6	0	1	0

BLACKBURN ROVERS (56)

Name	Born	Pos	From	LgAp	LgG	OthAp	OthG
Bell, Alec (Sco)	SA	wh	Jul 1913	11	0	1	0
Priday, Bob	SA	w	Mar 1949	44	11	1	0
Roberts, John	Aus	gk	Apr 1966	3	0	0	0
Arentoft, Ben	Den	m	Sep 1971	94	3	14	0
Ardiles, Ossie	Arg	m	Mar 1988	5	0	1+1	0
Wegerle, Roy (USA)	SA	f	Mar 1992	20+14	6	7+4	6
Andersson, Patrik	Swe	d	Dec 1992	7+5	5	3	1
Berg, Henning (1)	Nor	d	Jan 1993	154+5	4	34	0
Witschge, Richard	Neth	m	Mar 1995	1	0	0	0
Bohinen, Lars	Nor	m	Oct 1995	40+18	7	5+3	2
Gudmundsson, Niklas	Swe	f	Dec 1995	1+5	0	0	0
Donis, George	Grk	m	Jul 1996	11+11	2	2+1	0
Pedersen, Per	Den	f	Feb 1997	6+5	1	1+1	0
Andersson, Anders	Swe	m	Jun 1997	1+3	0	3+1	1
Valery, Patrick	Fr	d	Jun 1997	14+1	0	3+1	0
Filan, John	Aus	gk	Jul 1997	61+1	0	11	0
Henchoz, Stephane	Swit	d	Jul 1997	70	0	11+1	0
Dahlin, Martin	Swe	f	Jul 1997	13+13	4	2+2	2
Pedersen, Tore	Nor	d	Sep 1997	3+2	0	3	0
Perez, Sebastien	Fr	m	Jul 1998	4+1	1	3	1
Marcolin, Dario	It	m	Oct 1998	5+5	1	5	0
Konde, Oumar	Swit	d/m	Nov 1998	0	0	0+1	0
O'Brien, Burton (Brit)	SA	f	Feb 1999	0	0	0+1	0
Ostenstad, Egil	Nor	f	Aug 1999	38+24	12	10+9	2
Frandsen, Per	Den	m	Sep 1999	26+5	5	4	1
Bjornebye, Stig Inge	Nor	d	Jun 2000	53+3	1	11+1	0
Diawara, Kaba	Fr	f	Aug 2000	1+4	0	1	1
Berg, Henning (2)	Nor	d	Sep 2000	90+1	3	10+1	0
Friedel, Brad	USA	gk	Nov 2000	211	1	44	0
Keller, Marc	Fr	m	Jan 2001	0+2	0	0+3	0
Berkovic, Eyal	Isr	m	Feb 2001	4+7	2	3	0
Grabbi, Corrado	It	f	Jun 2001	11+19	2	5+6	3
Tugay, Kerimoglu	Tur	m	Jul 2001	130+24	7	33+4	1

Name	Born	Pos	From	LgAp	LgG	OthAp	OthG
Neill, Lucas	Aus	d/m	Sep 2001	164+4	5	33	2
Johansson, Nils-Eric	Swe	d	Oct 2001	59+27	0	20+4	2
Yordi	Sp	f	Feb 2002	5+3	2	0+1	0
Hakan Unsal	Tur	m	Mar 2002	7+1	0	0	0
Pelzer, Marc	Ger	d	Jun 2002	0	0	1	0
Hakan, Sukur	Tur	f	Dec 2002	7+2	2	0	0
Yorke, Dwight	Trin	f	Jul 2002	42+18	12	12+2	7
Gresko, Vratislav	Svk	m	Jan 2003	35+5	2	5	0
Amoruso, Lorenzo	It	d	Jul 2003	16+2	3	3	0
Emerton, Brett	Aus	m	Jul 2003	81+22	7	10+7	3
Babbel, Markus	Ger	d	Aug 2003	23+2	3	3	0
Baggio, Dino	It	m	Aug 2003	0+9	1	1+2	0
Enckelman, Peter	Fin	gk	Jan 2004	2	0	1	0
Andresen, Martin	Nor	m	Feb 2004	11	0	0	0
Johnson, Jemal	USA	f	Jul 2004	0+6	0	1+3	1
De Pedro, Javier	Sp	f	Jul 2004	1+1	0	1	0
Pedersen, Morten Gamst	Nor	m	Aug 2004	53	13	13+3	5
Djorkaeff, Youri	Fr	f	Sep 2004	3	0	0	0
Mokoena, Aaron	SA	d	Jan 2005	20+18	0	6+4	0
Nelsen, Ryan	NZ	d	Jan 2005	46	0	9+1	0
Kuqi, Shefki (Fin)	Alb	f	Jun 2005	15+18	7	5+3	1
Peter, Sergio	Ger	m	Jul 2005	1+7	0	1+1	0
Khizanishvili, Zurab	Geo	d	Aug 2005	24+2	1	4	1
Sinama-Pongolle, Florent (Fr)	Reu	f	Jan 2006	8+2	1	0	0
BLACKPOOL (31)							
Wilcox, Tom (Brit)	At sea	gk	May 1906	37	0	1	0
Falconer, Andy	SA	f	Sep 1949	4	0	0	0
Perry, Bill	SA	w	Nov 1949	397	119	42	10
Harris, Alex (Brit)	HK	w	Nov 1951	15	4	0	0
Hauser, Peter	SA	wh	Nov 1955	83	10	14	1
Peterson, Brian	SA	f	Oct 1956	101	16	8	1
Smethurst, Peter	SA	f	Feb 1960	1	0	0	0
Cheung, Chi Doy	HK	f	Oct 1960	2	1	0	0
Horne, Des	SA	w	Mar 1961	117+1	17	19	4
Kemp, Fred (Brit)	It	m	Nov 1970	19+2	1	3	0
Hesford, Iain (Eng)	Zam	gk	Aug 1977	202	0	28	0
Rush, Jon	NZ	gk	Nov 1979	11	0	0	0
Methven, Colin (Brit)	Ind	d	Jul 1986	166+7	11	26+1	2
Walwyn, Keith (Brit)	Jam	f	Jun 1987	51+18	16	10+2	1
Cunningham, Tony (Brit)	Jam	f	Jul 1987	71	17	13	5
Richards, Carl (Eng)	Jam	f	Jan 1990	32+9	8	2+2	0
Leitch, Grant	SA	f	Aug 1990	13+12	1	1+1	0
Kerr, Dylan (Brit)	Mal	d	Dec 1991	12	1	0	0
Kearton, Jason	Aus	gk	Jan 1992	14	0	0	0
Whitley, Jim (N Ire)	Zam	m	Aug 1999	7+1	0	1	0
Shittu, Danny	Nig	m	Feb 2001	15+2	2	2	0
Theoklitos, Michael	Aus	gk	Nov 2002	2	0	1	0
Jones, Brad	Aus	gk	Nov 2003	17	0	2	0
Matias, Pedro	Sp	m	Mar 2004	7	1	0	0
Ilic, Sasa (Yug)	Aus	gk	Jul 2004	3	0	2	0
Gorre, Dean (Neth)	Sur	m	Sep 2004	0+1	0	0	0
Lynch, Simon	Can	f	Dec 2004	5+2	0	2	0
Ellegaard, Kevin	Den	gk	Jan 2005	2	0	1	0

Name	Born	Pos	From	LgAp	LgG	OthAp	OthG
Grabovac, Zarko	SM	f	Jan 2005	1+2	0	0	0
Pogliacomi, Les	Aus	gk	Aug 2005	15	0	5	0
Kuqi, Njazi (Fin)	Alb	f	Jan 2006	1+3	0	0	0
BOLTON WANDERERS (66)							
Waller, Wilfred	SA	gk	Mar 1900	6	0	0	0
Grieves, Ken	Aus	gk	Dec 1951	49	0	1	0
Nowak, Tadeusz	Pol	w	Mar 1979	22+2	1	1+2	0
Dusan, Nikolic	Yug	w	Oct 1980	22	2	3	0
Stevens, Ian (Brit)	Mal	f	Mar 1987	26+21	7	5+3	2
Cunningham, Tony (Brit)	Jam	f	Mar 1991	9	4	3	0
Paatelainen, Mixu	Fin	f	Jul 1994	58+11	15	12+2	3
Sneekes, Richard	Neth	m	Aug 1994	51+4	7	13+1	4
De Freitas, Fabian (Neth)	Sur	f	Aug 1994	24+16	7	3+6	2
Bergsson, Gudni	Ice	d	Mar 1995	263+7	23	43+4	4
Curcic,Sasa	Yug	m	Oct 1995	28	4	5	3
Frandsen, Per (1)	Den	m	Aug 1996	129+1	17	22+2	5
Johansen, Michael	Den	m	Aug 1996	112+25	16	28+5	5
Gunnlaugsson, Arnie	Ice	m	Aug 1997	24+18	13	7+4	2
Fish, Mark	SA	d	Sep 1997	102+1	3	23+1	1
Jaaskelainen, Jussi	Fin	gk	Nov 1997	278+1	0	34	0
Giallanza, Gaetano	Swit	f	Mar 1998	0+3	0	0	0
Salako, John (Eng)	Nig	m	Mar 1998	0+7	0	0	0
Jensen, Claus	Den	d	Jul 1998	85+1	8	23	2
Gudjohnsen, Eidur	Ice	f	Aug 1998	48+7	18	16+2	8
Gardner, Ricardo	Jam	m	Aug 1998	209+30	15	43+8	4
Hansen, Bo	Den	m	Feb 1999	64+32	15	14+9	2
Passi, Franck	Fr	m	Nov 1999	21+17	0	9+2	0
Kaprielian, Mickael	Fr	m	Jan 2000	0+1	0	0	0
Frandsen, Per (2)	Den	m	Jul 2000	116+19	13	10+5	1
Morini, Emanuele	It	m	Sep 2000	1+1	0	1	0
Gope-Fenepej, John (Fr)	NCal	d	Sep 2000	0+2	0	0	0
Fredgaard, Carsten	Den	m	Nov 2000	1+4	0	0	0
Sommer, Jurgen	USA	gk	Feb 2001	0	0	1	0
Diawara, Djibril	Sen	d	Jun 2001	4+5	0	2	0
Nishizawa, Akinori	Jap	f	Jul 2001	0	0	3	1
Pedersen, Henrik	Den	f	Jul 2001	83+42	21	15+10	7
Johnson, Jermaine	Jam	m	Sep 2001	4+8	0	4+1	0
N'Gotty, Bruno	Fr	d	Sep 2001	143+5	5	21+3	2
Viander, Jani	Fin	gk	Nov 2001	0	0	1	0
Bobic, Fredi (Ger)	Slo	f	Jan 2002	14+2	4	0	0
Tofting, Stig	Den	m	Feb 2002	8+6	0	3	0
Djorkaeff, Youri	Fr	f	Feb 2002	72+3	20	5+1	1
Espartero, Mario	Fr	m	Feb 2002	0+3	0	0	0
Konstantinidis, Kostas (Grk)	Ger	m	Mar 2002	3	0	0	0
Mendy, Bernard	Fr	d	Aug 2002	20+1	0	2	0
Okocha, Jay-Jay	Nig	m	Aug 2002	106+18	14	17+4	4
Campo, Ivan	Sp	d	Sep 2002	93+18	8	12+2	0
Bulent, Akin (Tur)	Bel	m	Oct 2002	0+1	0	2	0
Andre, Pierre-Yves	Fr	f	Feb 2003	0+9	0	0	0
Ballesta, Salva	Sp	f	Feb 2003	1+5	0	0	0
Laville, Florent	Fr	d	Feb 2003	15	0	0	0
Giannakopoulos, Stelios	Grk	m	May 2003	74+25	18	21+3	6
Jardel, Mario	Bra	f	Aug 2003	0+7	0	4+1	3

Name	Born	Pos	From	LgAp	LgG	OthAp	OthG
Thome, Emerson	Bra	d	Aug 2003	25+1	0	6	0
Vaz Te, Ricardo	Por	f	Aug 2003	7+23	3	5+9	4
Ba, Ibrahim (Fr)	Sen	m	Sep 2003	0+9	0	6+1	0
Moreno, Javi	Sp	f	Jan 2004	1+7	0	0+2	0
Ben Haim Tal	Isr	d	Jul 2004	51+5	1	20	0
Cesar, Julio	Bra	d	Jul 2004	4+1	0	2	1
Hierro, Fernando	Sp	d	Jul 2004	15+14	1	6	0
Jaidi, Radhi	Tun	d	Jul 2004	35+8	8	8+1	0
Diouf, El Hadji	Sen	f	Aug 2004	40+7	12	7+5	1
Kaku, Blessing	Nig	m	Aug 2004	0+1	0	1+1	0
Fadiga, Khalilou	Sen	m	Sep 2004	5+8	1	7+1	0
Candela, Vincent	Fr	d	Jan 2005	9+1	0	1+1	0
Borgetti, Jared	Mex	f	Jul 2005	5+14	2	7+6	5
Faye, Abdoulaye	Sen	m	Jul 2005	23+4	1	10	0
Fernandes, Fabrice	Fr	m	Aug 2005	0+1	0	3+1	0
Nakata, Hidetoshi	Jap	m	Aug 2005	14+7	1	10+1	0
Fojut, Jaroslaw	Pol	d	Sep 2005	0+1	0	0+1	0
Djetou, Martin (Fr)	IvCo	m	Oct 2005	1+2	0	1+1	0

BOSTON UNITED (3)

Name	Born	Pos	From	LgAp	LgG	OthAp	OthG
Sabin, Eric	Fr	f	Mar 2004	2	0	0	0
Gabrieli, Emanuele	It	d	Feb 2005	4	0	0	0
Kuipers, Michel	Neth	gk	Nov 2005	15	0	0	0

BOURNEMOUTH (30)

Name	Born	Pos	From	LgAp	LgG	OthAp	OthG
Peed, Frank (Brit)	Arg	f	Jun 1930	2	0	0	0
Bellis, George (Brit)	Ind	ch	Jul 1935	56	0	4	0
Milligan, Dudley (N Ire)	SA	f	Aug 1947	45	25	3	2
Stiffle, Nelson (Brit)	Ind	w	May 1955	36	7	6	1
Woollard, Arnold	Ber	fb	Jun 1956	157	0	15	0
Burgess, Mike	Can	f/ch	Jun 1957	104	34	9	2
Chadwick, Dave (Brit)	Ind	w	Feb 1972	29+7	4	1	0
Golac, Ivan	Yug	fb	Nov 1982	9	0	1	0
Richards, Carl (Eng)	Jam	f	Jul 1986	57+14	16	9+3	2
Goulet, Brent	USA	f	Nov 1987	1+2	0	0	0
Blissett, Luther (Eng)	Jam	f	Nov 1988	121	56	18	4
Statham, Brian (Eng)	Zim	d/m	Nov 1991	2	0	0	0
Adekola, David	Nig	f	Sep 1994	0	0	0+1	0
Santos, Ali	USA	f	Aug 1995	0+3	0	0	0
Omoyimni, Manny	Nig	f	Sep 1996	5+2	0	0	0
Rolling, Franck	Fr	d	Aug 1997	26+4	4	2+2	1
Stein, Mark (Eng)	SA	f	Jun 1998	90	30	17	9
Berthe, Mohamed (Fr)	Gui	m	Jul 1998	12+3	2	5	0
Boli, Roger (Fr)	IvCo	f	Oct 1998	5+1	0	0+3	0
Rodrigues, Dani (1)	Por	f	Oct 1998	0+5	0	0	0
Huck, Willie	Fr	m	Mar 1999	11+29	0	0+6	1
Jorgensen, Claus (1)	Den	m	Jul 1999	77+10	14	12	1
Betsy, Kevin	Sey	m	Sep 1999	1+4	0	0	0
Menetrier, Mickael	Fr	gk	Aug 2000	12+1	0	5	0
Kandol, Tresor (Brit)	DRC	f	Oct 2001	3+9	0	0+2	0
McDonald, Scott	Aus	f	Mar 2003	3+4	1	0+1	0
Jorgensen, Claus (2)	Den	m	Jan 2004	16+1	0	0	0
Rodrigues, Dani (2)	Por	f	Jul 2004	23+29	6	5+3	1
Andrade, Diogo	Por	m	Sep 2004	0	0	0+2	0
Simek, Frankie	USA	d	Mar 2005	8	0	0	0

Name	Born	Pos	From	LgAp	LgG	OthAp	OthG
Surman, Andrew	SA	m	Aug 2005	24	6	4	0
Griffiths, Adam	Aus	d	Jan 2006	6+1	1	0	0
BRADFORD CITY (43)							
Bookman, Louis (Brit)	Lith	w	Jul 1911	32	2	2	0
Thorpe, Arthur (Brit)	Ind	w	Jul 1963	81	17	9	0
Roberts, John	Aus	gk	Aug 1968	44	0	4	0
Podd, Ces	StK	fb	Aug 1970	494+8	3	63+1	1
Cooke, Joe (1)	Dom	d/f	May 1972	184+20	62	25+1	9
Cooke, Joe (2)	Dom	d/f	Jan 1982	61+1	6	10	2
Blake, Noel (Brit)	Jam	d	Jul 1992	44+1	3	7+1	1
Petterson, Andy	Aus	gk	Dec 1994	3	0	0	0
Verveer, Etienne (Neth)	Sur	m	Feb 1995	9	1	0	0
Regtop, Erik	Neth	f	Jul 1996	5+3	1	2	0
Sas, Marco	Neth	d	Jul 1996	31	3	3	0
Pehrsson, Magnus	Swe	m	Oct 1996	1	0	0	0
Pinto, Sergio	Por	m	Oct 1996	7+11	0	1+1	0
Schwarzer, Mark	Aus	gk	Nov 1996	13	0	3	0
Sundgot, Ole	Nor	f	Nov 1996	11+14	6	0+1	0
Vanhala, Jari	Fin	f	Dec 1996	0+1	0	0	0
Edinho, Amaral	Bra	f	Feb 1997	50+9	15	3+1	1
Oliveira, Raul	Por	d	Mar 1997	2	0	0	0
Kulcsar, George (Aus)	Hun	d	Mar 1997	23+3	1	0	0
Sepp, Dennis	Neth	f	Jun 1997	0+3	0	0	0
Steiner, Rob	Swe	f	Jul 1997	40+12	14	5	2
Zabica, Robert	Aus	gk	Aug 1997	3	0	1	0
Halle, Gunnar	Nor	d	Jun 1999	78+5	1	9+1	1
Rodriguez, Bruno	Fr	f	Sep 1999	0+2	0	1+2	0
Cadete, Jorge (Por)	Moz	f	Feb 2000	2+5	0	0	0
Carbone, Benito	It	f	Aug 2000	39+3	10	3+1	2
Petrescu, Dan	Rom	m	Aug 2000	16+1	1	2+1	0
Hardy, Adam	SA	m	Sep 2000	0	0	0+1	0
Molenaar, Robert	Neth	d	Dec 2000	70+1	2	5+1	0
Jorgensen, Claus	Den	m	Jul 2001	41+9	12	3+1	0
Juanjo, Carricondo	Sp	f	Oct 2001	7+19	1	2+1	0
Uhlenbeek, Gus (Neth)	Sur	d	Aug 2002	42	1	2	0
Reid, Paul	Aus	m	Sep 2002	7+1	2	0	0
Myhill, Boaz (Eng)	USA	gk	Nov 2002	2	0	0	0
Ten Heuvel, Laurens	Neth	f	Mar 2003	4+1	0	0	0
Davies, Clint	Aus	gk	Jul 2003	1+1	0	0	0
Edds, Gareth	Aus	m	Jul 2003	19+4	0	1	0
Paston, Mark	NZ	gk	Aug 2003	13	0	1	0
Vaesen, Nico	Bel	gk	Feb 2004	6	0	0	0
Adebola, Dele	Nig	f	Aug 2004	14+1	3	1	1
Henderson, Paul	Aus	gk	Aug 2004	40	0	3	0
Ricketts, Donovan	Jam	gk	Aug 2004	40	0	3	0
Petta, Bobby	Neth	m	Jun 2005	23+4	4	4	0
Stewart, Damion	Jam	d	Jun 2005	20+3	1	1+2	0
BRADFORD PARK AVENUE (3)							
Quantrill, Alf (Eng)	Ind	w	Sep 1924	191	58	11	1
Houghton, Bud (Brit)	Ind	f	Oct 1955	28	7	3	3
Malan, Norman	SA	gk	Jul 1956	24	0	2	0

BRENTFORD (26)

Name	Born	Pos	From	LgAp	LgG	OthAp	OthG
Price, Johnny (Brit)	Ind	f	Apr 1928	1	1	0	0
Gallego, Jose	Sp	w	Jan 1947	6	0	0	0
Baker, Gerry (Brit)	USA	f	Oct 1969	8	2	0	0
Sweetzer, Gordon (1)	Can	f	Jul 1975	68+4	40	7	4
Salman, Danis (Eng)	Cyp	d	Aug 1977	316+9	8	34+2	0
Eames, Billy (Brit)	Mal	f	Aug 1978	2	1	0	0
Sweetzer, Gordon (2)	Can	f	Jan 1982	8+1	1	0	0
Buttigieg, John	Mal	d	Nov 1988	24+16	0	3+2	0
Statham, Brian (Eng)	Zim	d/m	Jan 1992	148+18	1	23	0
Kruszynski, Detsi	Ger	m	Aug 1992	13+1	0	1	0
Coyne, Chris	Aus	d	Aug 1998	7	0	1	0
Hebel, Dirk	Ger	m	Aug 1998	6+9	0	2+1	0
Hreidarsson, Hermann	Ice	d	Sep 1998	41	6	4	1
Ingimarsson, Ivar	Ice	m	Nov 1999	109+4	10	12	0
Einarsson, Gunnar	Ice	d	Jan 2000	1+2	0	0	0
Pinamonte, Lorenzo	It	f	Feb 2000	8+15	2	1+1	1
Gottskalksson, Ole	Ice	gk	Jul 2000	73	0	9	0
Javary, Jean-Phillipe	Fr	m	Aug 2000	4+2	0	2	0
Caceres, Adrian (Aus)	Arg	m	Sep 2001	5	0	0	0
Sonko, Ibrahima	Sen	d	Aug 2002	79+1	8	11	1
Antoine-Curier, Mickael	Fr	f	Mar 2003	11	3	0	0
Rougier, Tony	Trin	m	Aug 2003	29+2	4	3	1
Kitamirike, Joel	Uga	d	Sep 2003	21+1	0	3	0
Olugbodi, Jide	Nig	f	Oct 2003	0+2	0	1+2	0
Salako, John (Eng)	Nig	f	Jul 2004	30+5	4	8+1	1
Bankole, Ade	Nig	gk	Feb 2005	5	0	1	0
Skulason, Olafur-Ingi	Ice	d	Jun 2005	2	0	0	0

BRIGHTON & HOVE ALBION (37)

Name	Born	Pos	From	LgAp	LgG	OthAp	OthG
Moorhead, George (Ire)	NZ	ch	Aug 1922	1	0	0	0
Dugnolle, Jack (Brit) (1)	Ind	ch	Oct 1934	7	0	0	0
Dugnolle, Jack (Brit) (2)	Ind	ch	Aug 1946	59	0	6	0
Lancelotte, Eric (Brit)	Ind	f	Feb 1948	60	14	1	0
Foreman, Denis	SA	w	Mar 1952	211	63	8	6
Hodge, Eric	SA	ch	Oct 1956	4	0	0	0
Smit(h), Wilf	Ger	fb	Oct 1974	5	0	0	0
Geard, Glen	Mal	m	Feb 1978	0	0	1	0
Gariani, Moshe	Isr	m	Jun 1980	0+1	0	0	0
Cohen, Jacob	Isr	d	Oct 1980	3+3	0	0	0
Young, Eric (Wal)	Sing	d	Nov 1982	126	10	19+1	1
Kraay, Hans	Neth	m/d	Feb 1984	19+4	3	0	0
Robinson, John (Wal)	Zim	m	Apr 1989	57+5	6	7+3	2
Edwards, Alistair	Aus	f	Nov 1989	1	0	0	0
Gotsmanov, Sergei (Blr)	USSR	f	Feb 1990	14+2	4	0	0
Meola, Tony	USA	gk	Aug 1990	1	0	1	0
Gurinovich, Igor (Blr)	USSR	f	Nov 1990	3+1	1	1	0
Iovan, Stefan	Rom	d	Mar 1991	4+2	0	3	0
Sommer, Jurgen	USA	gk	Nov 1991	1	0	0	0
McDougald, Junior (Brit)	USA	f	May 1994	71+7	14	12	5
Adekola, David	Nig	f	Oct 1996	1	0	0	0
Gislason, Valur	Ice	m	Oct 1997	7	0	0	0
Ifejiagwa, Emeka	Nig	d	Oct 1998	2	1	0	0
Pinamonte, Lorenzo	It	f	Dec 1999	8+1	2	0	0
Kuipers, Michel	Neth	gk	Jul 2000	138+1	0	17	0

Name	Born	Pos	From	LgAp	LgG	OthAp	OthG
Lehmann, Dirk	Ger	f	Jun 2001	3+4	0	1+1	0
Petterson, Andy	Aus	gk	Aug 2002	6+2	0	2	0
Ingimarsson, Ivar	Ice	m	Feb 2003	15	0	0	0
Rougier, Tony	Trin	m/f	Feb 2003	5+1	2	0	0
Reid, Paul	Aus	m	Mar 2004	73+4	4	4+2	0
Molango, Maheta (It)	Swit	f	Jul 2004	4+1	1	1	0
Jarrett, Albert (Eng)	SiLe	m	Aug 2004	12+11	1	1+1	0
Yelldell, David (USA)	Ger	gk	Jan 2005	3	0	0	0
Shaaban, Rami	Swe	gk	Feb 2005	6	0	0	0
Carole, Sebastien	Fr	m	Aug 2005	34+6	2	2	0
Chaigneau, Florent	Fr	gk	Aug 2005	1	0	2	0
Frutos, Alexandre	Fr	m	Aug 2005	27+9	3	1	0
Turienzo, Federico	Arg	f	Aug 2005	1+3	0	0	0

BRISTOL CITY (38)

Name	Born	Pos	From	LgAp	LgG	OthAp	OthG
Murray, David	SA	f	Oct 1926	16	0	0	0
Eisentrager, Alec	Ger	f	Jul 1949	228	47	11	0
Boyd, John	USA	w	Dec 1950	31	6	1	0
Jantunen, Pertti	Fin	m	Mar 1979	7+1	1	3+1	1
Meijer, Geert	Neth	w	Mar 1979	12+3	2	1+1	0
Moller, Jan	Swe	gk	Dec 1980	48	0	13	0
Kelly, Errington	StV	w	Feb 1983	4+1	1	0	0
Dziekanowski, Jackie	Pol	f	Jan 1992	40+3	7	5+1	2
Atteveld, Ray	Neth	d/m	Mar 1992	9+5	1	0	0
Kristensen, Bjorn	Den	d	Nov 1992	4	0	0	0
Shail, Mark (Brit)	Swe	d	Mar 1993	117+11	4	18+1	1
McKop, Henry	Zim	d	Feb 1994	2+3	0	0	0
Brennan, Jim	Can	fb	Oct 1994	51+4	3	7	0
Seal, David	Aus	f	Oct 1994	24+27	10	5+2	3
Hansen, Vergard	Nor	fb	Nov 1994	36+1	0	7	0
Agostino, Paul	Aus	f	Jul 1995	63+21	19	10+3	7
Dijkstra, Sieb	Neth	gk	Sep 1995	8	0	0	0
Barnard, Darren (Wal)	Ger	m	Oct 1995	77+1	15	12	2
Goater, Shaun	Ber	f	Jul 1996	67+8	40	14	2
Goodridge, Greg	Bar	w	Aug 1996	76+43	14	15+7	2
Tisdale, Paul (Brit)	Mal	m	Jun 1997	2+3	0	2+1	0
Johansen, Stig	Nor	f	Feb 1998	2+1	0	0	0
Andersen, Soren	Den	f	Jul 1998	26+13	10	3+1	1
Pinamonte, Lorenzo	It	f	Sep 1998	3+4	1	1+2	0
Zwijnenberg, Clemens	Neth	d	Sep 1998	1+2	0	1	0
Andersen, Bo	Den	gk	Dec 1998	10	0	0	0
Tistimetanu, Ivan	Mol	d	Dec 1998	23+12	2	4+1	0
Sebok, Vilmos	Hun	d	Jan 1999	18+5	0	4	0
Wright, Ben (Ire)	Ger	f	Mar 1999	0+2	0	0	0
Odejayi, Kay (Brit)	Nig	f	Jul 2000	0+6	0	0	0
Rodrigues, Dani	Por	f	Oct 2000	3+5	0	0	0
Da Silva, Lourenco (Por)	Ang	m	Mar 2001	1+2	1	0	0
Lita, Leroy (Eng)	Con	f	Aug 2002	44+41	31	7+8	9
Wilkshire, Luke	Aus	m	Aug 2003	90+20	17	12+2	1
Rougier, Tony	Trin	m	Mar 2004	5+1	1	3	1
Madjo, Guy	Cam	f	Aug 2005	1+4	0	0+1	1
Basso, Adriano	Bra	gk	Oct 2005	29	0	0	0
Youga, Kelly (Fr)	CAR	d	Oct 2005	4	0	1	0

BRISTOL ROVERS (25)

Name	Born	Pos	From	LgAp	LgG	OthAp	OthG
Ashton, Hubert (Brit)	Ind	d	1924	1	0	0	0
Murray, David	SA	f	1928	39	12	5	1
Richardson, John	SA	f	1930	8	0	0	0
Preedy, Charlie (Brit)	Ind	gk	1933	39	0	3	0
Carr, Lance	SA	f	Aug 1946	42	8	1	0
Purdon, Ted	SA	f	Aug 1960	4	1	2	0
Smit(h), Wilf	Ger	d	Mar 1975	54	2	8	0
Kelly, Errington	StV	m	Sep 1981	12+6	3	2+1	0
Andreasson, Marcus	Swe	d	Jul 1998	14+1	1	4	0
Ipoua, Guy (Fr)	Cam	f	Aug 1998	15+9	3	4+2	0
Leoni, Stephane	Fr	m	Aug 1998	27+11	0	5+1	1
Kuipers, Michels	Neth	gk	Jan 1999	1	0	0	0
Astafjevs, Vitalis	Lat	m	Jan 2000	87+22	16	14+1	1
Pierre, Nigel	Trin	f	Feb 2000	1+2	0	0	0
Andreasson, Marcus	Swe	d	Mar 2000	9	1	2	0
Dagnogo, Moussa	Fr	f	Sep 2000	0+2	0	0	0
Allsopp, Danny	Aus	f	Oct 2000	4+2	0	0	0
Johansen, Rune	Nor	m	Nov 2000	0+2	0	1	0
Hammond, Elvis	Gha	f	Aug 2001	3+4	0	0+1	0
Ommel, Sergio	Neth	f	Nov 2001	18+5	8	2+1	1
Sanchez-Lopez, Carlos	Sp	m	Feb 2002	5	0	0	0
Di Piedi, Michele	It	m	Feb 2003	3+2	0	0	0
Agogo, Junior	Gha	f	Jun 2003	106+17	41	11+3	4
Henriksen, Bo	Den	f	Mar 2004	1+3	0	0	0
Jeannin, Alex	Fr	d	May 2005	1	0	0	0

BURNLEY (20)

Name	Born	Pos	From	LgAp	LgG	OthAp	OthG
Hogan, Cornelius (Brit)	Mal	f	Nov 1901	43	17	3	2
Seeburg, Max	Ger	f	Jan 1910	17	0	1	0
Bellis, George (Brit)	Ind	ch	Dec 1932	86	0	5	0
Hodgson, Doug	Aus	d	Oct 1996	1	0	0	0
Gentile, Marco	Neth	d	Jun 1997	0	0	1	0
Robertson, Mark	Aus	m	Oct 1997	27+9	1	1+2	0
Vindheim, Rune	Nor	m	Oct 1998	8	2	1	0
Kval, Frank	Nor	gk	Oct 1998	0	0	1	0
Michopoulos, Nik	Grk	gk	Aug 2000	85	0	8	0
Cennamo, Luigi (It)	Ger	gk	Jul 2001	0	0	0+1	0
Papadopoulos, Dimitrios (Grk)	Khz	f	Jul 2001	7+33	3	2+6	3
Gnohere, Arthur (Fr)	IvCo	d	Aug 2001	74+7	6	11	0
Johnson, David	Jam	f	Mar 2002	8	5	0	0
Diallo, Drissa (Gui)	Mau	m	Jan 2003	14	1	4	1
Camara, Mo	Gui	d	Jun 2003	90	0	13+1	1
Jensen, Brian	Den	gk	Jun 2003	110+2	0	14	0
Adebola, Dele	Nig	f	Mar 2004	0+3	1	0	0
Sanokho, Amadou	Fr	d	Sep 2004	0+3	0	1	0
Valois, Jean-Louis	Fr	f	Sep 2004	18+12	3	5+2	1
Karbassiyoon, Daniel	USA	f	Jun 2005	0+5	0	0+1	0

BURY (21)

Name	Born	Pos	From	LgAp	LgG	OthAp	OthG
McNeill, Hamilton (Brit)	Mal	f	Feb 1939	18	7	0	0
Grieves, Ken	Aus	gk	Apr 1947	59	0	4	0
Law, Cecil	Zim	w	May 1954	44	5	3	0
Nielson, Norman	SA	ch	May 1954	100	5	7	0
Hubbard, John	SA	w	Apr 1959	109	29	11	3
Cunningham, Tony (Brit)	Jam	f	Jul 1989	55+3	17	7	1

Name	Born	Pos	From	LgAp	LgG	OthAp	OthG
Bradley, Pat	Aus	d	Jul 1990	0+1	0	0	0
Stevens, Ian	Mal	f	Jul 1991	100+10	38	7+3	0
Adekola, David	Nig	f	Jan 1993	21+14	12	3+1	0
Blissett, Luther (Eng)	Jam	f	Aug 1993	8+2	1	2	1
Paskin, John	SA	f	Jul 1994	15+23	8	4+3	1
Johnson, David	Jam	f	Jul 1995	72+25	18	9+3	4
D'Jaffo, Laurent	Fr	f	Jul 1998	35+2	8	5+1	1
Avdiu, Kemajl (Swe)	Yug	m	Aug 1998	8+19	1	0+2	0
Grobbelaar, Bruce (Zim)	SA	gk	Sep 1998	1	0	0	0
Rocha, Carlos	Por	f	Aug 1999	0+3	0	0	0
Bhutia, Baichung	Ind	m	Sep 1999	20+17	3	4+3	0
Syros, George	Grk	d	Aug 2001	9+1	1	0+1	0
Dunfield, Terry	Can	m	Aug 2002	63+11	5	6+2	1
Thompson, Justin	Can	d	Nov 2003	1	0	2	1
Schmeichel, Kasper	Den	gk	Feb 2006	15	0	0	0

CAMBRIDGE UNITED (30)

Name	Born	Pos	From	LgAp	LgG	OthAp	OthG
Batson, Brendan (Eng)	Grn	fb	Jan 1974	162+1	6	17	0
Streete, Floyd (Brit)	Jam	d	Jul 1976	111+14	19	13+4	1
Sweetzer, Gordon	Can	f	Apr 1978	9	3	0	0
Corbin, Kirk	Bar	fb	Jan 1978	3	0	0	0
Galloway, Steve (Brit)	Ger	f	Mar 1986	0+1	0	0	0
McEvoy, Ricky (Ire)	Gib	m	Feb 1987	10+1	1	0	0
Anderson, Doug (Brit)	HK	m	Sep 1988	8	2	0	0
Cheetham, Mike	Neth	m	Oct 1989	123+9	22	30+1	4
Filan, John	Aus	gk	Mar 1993	68	0	9	0
Corazzin, Carlo	Can	f	Dec 1993	104+1	39	9	2
Adekola, David	Nig	f	Aug 1995	1+4	1	2	0
San Miguel, Xavier	Sp	m	Aug 1996	0+1	0	1	0
Larkin, Jim	Can	gk	Jan 1998	1	0	0	0
Williamson, Davey (Brit)	HK	d	Aug 1996	2+4	0	2	0
Van Heusden, Arjan	Neth	gk	Aug 1998	41+1	0	7	0
Hansen, John (Den)	Ger	m	Feb 2000	19+9	3	1+2	1
Perez, Lionel	Fr	gk	Jun 2000	87+1	0	7	0
Axeldahl, Jonas	Swe	f	Aug 2000	12+6	2	3	1
Gudmundsson, Johann	Ice	m	Nov 2000	3	0	0	0
Traore, Demba	Swe	f	Dec 2000	2+6	0	1	0
Pilvi, Tero	Fin	m	Mar 2001	3+2	0	0	0
Kandol, Tresor (Brit)	DRC	f	Aug 2001	2+2	0	0	0
Goodhind, Warren	SA	d	Sep 2001	95+8	0	16+3	0
One, Armand	Fr	f	Sep 2001	18+14	4	0+2	0
Nacca, Franco	Ven	d	Sep 2002	11+15	0	4+9	0
El Kholti, Abdou (Mor)	Fr	m	Jul 2004	13+2	0	3+1	0
Latte-Yedo, Igor	IvCo	d	Jul 2004	5+6	0	1	0
Mbome, Kingsley	Cam	m	Aug 2004	12+1	1	2	0
Konte, Amadou	Mli	f	Oct 2004	6+3	3	0	0
Anselin, Cedric	Fr	m	Nov 2004	2	0	0	0

CARDIFF CITY (21)

Name	Born	Pos	From	LgAp	LgG	OthAp	OthG
Mokone, Steve	SA	w	Jun 1959	3	1	0	0
Mallory, Richard	Ber	w	May 1963	3	0	1	0
Griffith, Cohen (Brit)	Guy	m/f	Oct 1989	205+29	39	27+2	5
Jones, Ian (Brit)	Ger	d	Jul 1995	3	0	0	0
Bolesan, Mirko	It	f	Oct 1995	0+1	0	0	0
Johnson, Glenn	Aus	f	Mar 1996	1+4	0	0	0

Name	Born	Pos	From	LgAp	LgG	OthAp	OthG
Earnshaw, Robert (Wal)	Zam	f	Aug 1997	141+37	85	22+5	20
O'Sullivan, Wayne (Ire)	Cyp	m	Aug 1997	78+7	4	11+2	1
Zois, Peter	Aus	gk	Feb 1998	1	0	0	0
Faerber, Winston (Neth)	Sur	d	Aug 1999	31+2	1	8+1	0
Schwinkendorf, Jorn	Ger	m	Nov 1999	5	0	1	0
Lightbourne, Kyle	Ber	f	Feb 2001	2+1	0	0	0
Zhiyi, Fan	Chn	d	Dec 2002	6	0	0	0
Robinson, John (Wal)	Zim	m	Jul 2003	39+3	3	0+1	0
Vidmar, Tony	Aus	d	Jul 2003	68+5	2	7+1	0
Inamoto, Junichi	Jap	m	Dec 2004	13+1	0	2	0
Koskela, Toni	Fin	m	Feb 2005	0+2	0	0+1	0
Whitley, Jeff (N Ire)	Zam	m	Jun 2005	32+2	1	4	0
Ferretti, Andrea	It	f	Jul 2005	0+4	0	0+3	0
Loovens, Glenn	Neth	d	Jul 2005	32+1	2	3	0
N'Dumbu-Nsungu, Guylain	DRC	f	Jan 2006	4+7	0	0	0

CARLISLE UNITED (20)

Hill, Reg (Brit)	Gib	wh	Jul 1930	5	0	0	0
Ackerman, Alf	SA	f	Nov 1956	97	61	10	12
Cruickshank, George (Brit)	Mly	w	Aug 1957	14	0	0	0
Oosthuizen, Ron	SA	w	Sep 1959	1	0	0	0
MacDonald, Ian (Brit)	Ger	d	May 1976	186+1	7	32	2
Houston, Graham	Gib	m	Oct 1987	8+8	1	0	0
Walwyn, Keith (Brit)	Jam	f	Jul 1989	59+3	15	8	2
Methven, Colin (Brit)	Ind	d	Sep 1990	12	0	3	0
Pounewatchy, Stephane	Fr	d	Aug 1996	81	3	12	0
Kerr, Dylan (Brit)	Mal	d	Sep 1996	0+1	0	0	0
Stevens, Ian (1)	Mal	f	May 1997	64+14	26	4	1
Harries, Paul	Aus	f	Jul 1997	6+14	2	1	1
Croci, Laurent	Fr	m	Oct 1997	1	0	0	0
Pagal, Jean-Claude	Cam	d	Feb 1998	1	0	0	0
Kubicki, Dariusz	Pol	fb	Jul 1998	7	0	2	0
Van der Kwaak, Peter	Neth	gk	Feb 2000	2	0	0	0
Stevens, Ian (2)	Mal	f	Aug 2000	64+3	19	8	5
Lemarchand, Stephane	Fr	f	Sep 2000	4+1	1	0	0
Hews, Chay	Aus	m	Sep 2001	4+1	2	0	0
Aranalde, Zigor	Sp	d	Jul 2005	38+1	5	7	0
Nade, Raphael	IvCo	f	Jul 2005	10+12	2	4+1	0

CHARLTON ATHLETIC (56)

Burton, Frank (Brit)	Mex	fb	Jul 1921	97	0	10	0
Kingsley, Alf	Bar	w	Jul 1921	20	2	0	0
Preedy, Charlie (Brit)	Ind	gk	Dec 1922	131	0	9	0
Tricker, Reg (Brit)	Ind	f	Aug 1925	41	17	2	1
Keizer, Gerry	Neth	gk	Jul 1931	17	0	0	0
Lancelotte, Eric (Brit)	Ind	f	May 1935	40	6	1	1
Mordey, Henry (Brit)	Mly	fb	Jul 1936	10	0	1	0
O'Linn, Syd	SA	f	Dec 1947	187	32	7	1
Forbes, Dudley	SA	wh	Dec 1947	57	1	3	0
Uytenbogaardt, Albert	SA	gk	Oct 1948	6	0	0	0
Nielson, Norman	SA	ch	Jul 1949	1	0	0	0
Hewie, John (Sco)	SA	fb	Oct 1949	495	37	35	1
Firmani, Eddie (1)	SA	f	Feb 1950	100	50	6	1
Leary, Stuart (Eng)	SA	f	Feb 1950	376	153	27	10
Jeppson, Hans	Swe	f	Jan 1951	11	9	0	0

Name	Born	Pos	From	LgAp	LgG	OthAp	OthG
Chamberlain, Ken	SA	ch	Oct 1951	42	0	2	0
Firmani, Peter	SA	fb	Sep 1953	31	2	4	0
Oosthuizen, Ron	SA	w	Sep 1953	1	0	0	0
Tocknell, Brian	SA	wh	Jul 1959	199	14	21	1
Durandt, Cliff	SA	w	Mar 1963	36	4	0	0
Firmani, Eddie (2)	SA	f	Oct 1963	55	32	6	0
Firmani, Eddie (3)	SA	f	Mar 1967	10	6	0	0
Masiello, Luciano	It	w	Jan 1969	6	0	2	1
Bruck, Dietmar	Ger	fb	Oct 1970	54+2	0	6	0
Ambrose, Leroy	StV	m	Aug 1979	28+5	1	1	0
Jacobsen, Viggo	Den	m	Nov 1979	9	0	0	0
Ostergaard, Johnny	Den	f	Nov 1979	8+4	1	0+2	0
Simonsen, Allan	Den	f	Nov 1982	16	9	1	0
Grant, Kim	Gha	f	Mar 1991	74+49	18	11+14	6
Salako, Andy	Nig	d	Apr 1991	1	0	1+1	0
Robinson, John (Wal)	Zim	m	Sep 1992	296+36	35	39+8	8
Petterson, Andy	Aus	gk	Jul 1994	68+4	0	11	0
Ammann, Mike	USA	gk	Jul 1994	28+2	0	1	0
Hovi, Tom	Nor	m/d	Jan 1995	0+2	0	0	0
Ilic, Sasa (Yug)	Aus	gk	Oct 1997	51	0	8	0
Pringle, Martin	Swe	f	Jan 1999	28+30	8	5	0
Barnes, John (Eng)	Jam	f	Feb 1999	2+10	0	0	0
Salako, John (Eng)	Nig	f	Aug 1999	10+37	2	4+6	1
Svensson, Mathias	Swe	f	Jan 2000	42+28	8	2+6	1
Jensen, Claus	Den	m	Jul 2000	113+10	16	11	1
Bagheri, Karim	Iran	m	Aug 2000	0+1	0	0	0
Johansson, Jonatan (Fin)	Swe	f	Aug 2000	90+58	27	14+5	6
Kishishev, Radostin	Bul	d	Aug 2000	143+22	2	14+3	0
Fish, Mark	SA	d	Nov 2000	101+1	2	8+1	0
Bartlett, Shaun	SA	f	Dec 2000	95+28	24	14+2	2
Bart-Williams, Chris (Brit)	SiLe	m	Dec 2001	17+12	2	3+1	0
Costa, Jorge	Por	d	Dec 2001	22+2	0	2	0
Blomqvist, Jesper	Swe	m	Sep 2002	0+3	0	1	0
El Khalej, Tahar	Mor	d	Feb 2003	2+1	0	0	0
Hreidarsson, Hermann	Ice	d	Mar 2003	100+1	3	15	1
Di Canio, Paolo	It	f	Aug 2003	23+8	4	1+1	1
Andersen, Stephan	Den	gk	May 2004	17	0	1	0
El Karkouri, Talal	Mor	d	Jul 2004	32+10	5	6	0
Rommedahl, Dennis	Den	f	Jul 2004	38+9	4	4+1	2
Smertin, Alexei	Rus	m	Jul 2005	18	0	3+1	0
Sorondo, Gonzalo	Uru	d	Jul 2005	7	0	1	0
Spector, Jonathan	USA	d	Jul 2005	13+7	0	3+1	0
Myhre, Thomas	Nor	gk	Aug 2005	20	0	6	0
CHELSEA (84)							
Donaghy, Charles (Brit)	Ind	w	Aug 1905	2	1	1	0
Dolby, Hugh (Brit)	Ind	w	Jul 1908	2	0	0	0
Hunter, George (Brit)	Ind	wh	Feb 1913	30	2	2	0
Middleboe, Nils	Den	hb	Nov 1913	41	0	5	0
Dolding, Len (Brit)	Ind	w	Jul 1945	26	2	1	0
Steffen, Willi	Swit	fb	Nov 1946	15	0	5	0
Mitchell, Frank	Aus	wh	Jan 1949	75	1	10	0
Oelofse, Ralph	SA	wh	Oct 1951	8	0	0	0
Smethurst, Derek	SA	f	Dec 1968	14	4	4+1	1

Name	Born	Pos	From	LgAp	LgG	OthAp	OthG
Borota, Petar	Yug	gk	Mar 1979	107	0	7	0
Viljoen, Colin	SA	m	Mar 1980	19+1	0	3	0
Wegerle, Roy (USA)	SA	f	Jun 1986	15+8	3	1+1	1
Dorigo, Tony (Eng)	Aus	fb	Jul 1987	146	11	21	0
Monkou, Ken (Neth)	Sur	d	Mar 1989	92+2	2	15	0
Johnsen, Erland	Nor	d	Dec 1989	135+10	1	31+3	0
Barnard, Darren (Wal)	Ger	m	Jul 1990	18+11	2	2+2	0
Kharine, Dimitri	Rus	gk	Dec 1992	118	0	28	0
Kjeldbjerg, Jakob (Den)	Nor	d	Aug 1993	52	2	13+1	0
Stein, Mark (Eng)	SA	f	Oct 1993	46+4	21	11+2	4
Gullit, Ruud (Neth)	Sur	m	Jul 1995	37+12	4	13+2	3
Petrescu, Dan	Rom	m	Nov 1995	134+16	18	52+5	6
Di Matteo, Roberto (It)	Swit	m	Jul 1996	108+11	15	44+9	11
Leboeuf, Frank	Fr	d	Jul 1996	142+2	17	55+2	7
Vialli, Gianluca	It	f	Jul 1996	46+12	21	23+6	19
Grodas, Frode	Nor	gk	Sep 1996	20+1	0	6	0
Zola, Gianfranco	It	f	Nov 1996	185+44	59	72+8	21
Forrest, Craig	Can	gk	Mar 1997	2+1	0	0	0
Babayaro, Celestine	Nig	d	Jun 1997	118+14	5	59+6	3
Lambourde, Bernard (Fr)	Guad	d	Jul 1997	29+11	2	14+6	1
Poyet, Gustavo	Uru	m	Jul 1997	79+26	36	29+8	12
De Goey, Ed	Neth	gk	Jul 1997	123	0	52+1	0
Flo Andre, Tore	Nor	f	Aug 1997	59+53	34	35+15	16
Charvet, Laurent	Fr	d	Jan 1998	7+4	2	0+2	0
Laudrup, Brian (Den)	Aut	f	Jun 1998	5+2	0	3	1
Casiraghi, Pierluigi	It	f	Jul 1998	10	1	2+2	0
Desailly, Marcel (Fr)	Gha	d	Jul 1998	156+2	6	63+1	1
Percassi, Luca	It	d	Aug 1998	0	0	0+2	0
Ferrer, Albert	Sp	d	Aug 1998	71+5	0	33+3	1
Dalla Bona, Sam	It	m	Oct 1998	42+13	6	9+9	0
Goldbaek, Bjarne	Den	m	Nov 1998	15+14	5	6+5	0
Forssell, Mikael (Fin)	Ger	f	Dec 1998	6+27	5	6+14	7
Cudicini, Carlo	It	gk	Jun 1999	119+3	0	59+1	0
Deschamps, Didier	Fr	m	Jun 1999	24+3	0	20	1
Hogh, Jes	Den	d	Jul 1999	6+3	0	5+3	0
Melchiot, Mario	Neth	d	Jul 1999	117+13	4	32+3	1
Ambrosetti, Gabriele	It	f	Aug 1999	9+7	0	2+5	1
Thome, Emerson	Bra	d	Dec 1999	19+2	0	1	0
Weah, George	Lbr	f	Jan 2000	9+2	3	4	2
Aleksidze, Rati	Geo	m	Feb 2000	0+2	0	0+1	0
Gudjohnsen, Eidur	Ice	f	Jul 2000	126+60	54	51+26	24
Hasselbaink, Jimmy (Neth)	Sur	f	Jul 2000	119+17	70	37+4	18
Stanic, Mario (Cro)	Yug	m	Jul 2000	39+20	7	15+6	3
Panucci, Christian	It	d	Aug 2000	7+1	0	2	1
Bogarde, Winston	Neth	d	Sep 2000	2+7	0	2+1	0
Jokanovic, Slavisa	Yug	m	Oct 2000	19+20	0	9+5	0
Gronkjaer, Jesper	Den	m	Dec 2000	56+32	7	21+10	4
Bosnich, Mark	Aus	gk	Jan 2001	5	0	2	0
Gallas, William	Fr	d	May 2001	147+12	12	66	2
Kitamirike, Joel	Uga	d	Apr 2001	0	0	1	0
Petit, Emmanuel	Fr	m	Jul 2001	52+3	2	19+2	1
Zenden, Boudewijn	Neth	m	Aug 2001	24+19	4	6+10	0
Huth, Robert	Ger	d	Feb 2002	23+19	0	9+11	2
De Lucas, Enrique	Sp	m	Aug 2002	17+8	0	4+2	0

Name	Born	Pos	From	LgAp	LgG	OthAp	OthG
De Oliveira, Filipe	Por	f	Sep 2002	0+5	0	0+3	0
Ambrosio, Marco	It	gk	Jun 2003	8	0	4	0
Geremi	Cam	m	Jul 2003	33+20	3	18+9	0
Crespo, Hernan	Arg	f	Aug 2003	33+16	20	14+10	5
Mutu, Adrian	Rom	f	Aug 2003	21+6	6	9+2	4
Smertin, Alexei	Rus	m	Aug 2003	11+5	0	8+1	1
Veron, Juan Sebastian	Arg	m	Aug 2003	5+2	1	6+1	0
Makelele, Claude (Fr)	DRC	m	Sep 2003	91+6	1	39+1	0
Cech, Petr	CzRep	gk	Jun 2004	69	0	21	0
Carvalho, Ricardo	Por	d	Jul 2004	44+5	2	25	2
Drogba, Didier	IvCo	f	Jul 2004	38+17	22	21+6	10
Ferreira, Paulo	Por	d	Jul 2004	47+3	0	21+3	1
Kezman, Mateja	SM	f	Jul 2004	6+18	4	8+8	3
Robben, Arjan	Neth	f	Jul 2004	35+11	13	15+8	3
Tiago, Cardoso	Por	m	Jul 2004	21+13	4	10+8	0
Nuno, Morais	Por	d	Aug 2004	0+2	0	1+1	0
Jarosik, Jiri	CzRep	m	Jan 2005	3+11	0	3+3	0
Del Horno, Asier	Sp	d	Jun 2005	25	1	7+2	0
Diarra, Lassana	Fr	m	Jul 2005	2+1	0	2+2	0
Essien, Michael	Gha	m	Aug 2005	27+4	2	10+1	0
Maniche, Nuno	Por	m	Jan 2006	3+5	0	2+1	0

CHELTENHAM TOWN (6)

Name	Born	Pos	From	LgAp	LgG	OthAp	OthG
Howells, Lee	Aus	f	Aug 1999	119+2	6	22	3
Stevens, Ian (Brit)	Mal	f	Mar 2000	1	0	0	0
Goodridge, Greg	Bar	w	Feb 2001	10+1	1	0	0
Odejayi, Kay	Nig	f	May 2003	62+41	17	14+6	2
Cozic, Bertrand	Fr	m	Aug 2003	7	1	0+1	0
Yao, Sosthene (Brit)	IvCo	m	Aug 2005	0+3	0	0	0

CHESTER CITY (22)

Name	Born	Pos	From	LgAp	LgG	OthAp	OthG
Warburton, George	Neth	w	Nov 1938	11	3	0	0
Stiffle, Nelson (Brit)	Ind	w	Dec 1951	7	2	0	0
Hauser, Peter	SA	wh	Aug 1963	117+4	3	16	0
Greer, Ross	Aus	f	Nov 1989	2	0	1	0
Aunger, Geoff	Can	d/m	Dec 1994	1+4	0	0	0
Regis, Cyrille (Eng)	FrGu	f	Aug 1995	29	7	4	0
Smeets, Jorg	Neth	m	Mar 1999	1+2	0	0	0
Agogo, Junior	Gha	f	Sep 1999	10	6	0	0
Carver, Joe	USA	f	Sep 1999	1+1	0	0	0
Eve, Angus	Trin	f	Dec 1999	9+5	4	0	0
Laird, Kamu	Trin	f	Dec 1999	2+1	1	0	0
Milovaijevic, Goran	Yug	m	Sep 1999	11+1	0	5	0
Nash, Martin	Can	m	Sep 1999	12+4	0	3+1	0
Eyjolfsson, Siggi	Ice	f	Jan 2000	9	3	0	0
Harris, Andy (Brit)	SA	d/m	Jun 2003	19+13	0	5+1	0
Anaclet, Eddie	Tan	f	Dec 2004	0	0	0+1	0
Elokobi, George	Cam	d	Jan 2005	4+1	0	0	0
Dimech, Luke	Mal	d	Jul 2005	27+3	0	5	0
El Kholti, Abdou (Mor)	Fr	m	Jul 2005	7+15	0	1+4	0
Bertos, Leo (Grk)	NZ	m	Aug 2005	2+3	0	1+1	0
Asamoah, Derek	Gha	f	Jan 2006	14+3	8	0	0
Gillet, Stephane	Lux	gk	Jan 2006	8	0	2	0

CHESTERFIELD (21)

Name	Born	Pos	From	LgAp	LgG	OthAp	OthG
Milligan, Dudley (N Ire)	SA	f	Nov 1938	49	19	4	1
Stiffle, Nelson (Brit)	Ind	w	Mar 1954	38	9	1	0
Roberts, John	Aus	gk	Aug 1967	46	0	3	0
Smit(h), Wilf	Ger	fb	Nov 1976	26+1	2	0+1	0
Heppolette, Ricky (Brit)	Ind	m	Feb 1977	46+1	3	5	1
Walwyn, Keith (Brit)	Jam	f	Nov 1979	3	2	1+2	0
Bernardeau, Olivier	Fr	m	Aug 1986	5+4	0	0+1	0
Benjamin, Tristan	StK	d	Jul 1987	32+2	0	0	0
Chiedozie, John	Nig	w	Mar 1990	5+2	0	3	1
Gregory, Neil (Brit)	Zam	f	Feb 1994	2+1	1	0	0
Cheetham, Mike	Neth	m	Jul 1994	5	0	2	1
McDougald, Junior (Brit)	USA	f	Mar 1996	9	3	0	0
Misse-Misse, Jean-Jacques	Cam	f	Mar 1998	1	0	0	0
Agogo, Junior	Gha	f	Nov 1999	3+1	0	0	0
Hitzlsperger, Thomas	Ger	m	Oct 2001	5	0	0	0
Uhlenbeek, Gus (Neth)	Sur	d	Aug 2003	36+1	0	1	0
McMaster, Jamie	Aus	m	Jan 2004	10+4	2	0	0
N'Toya, Tcham (Fr)	DRC	m	Mar 2004	22+26	8	1+4	0
Downes, Aaron	Aus	d	Aug 2004	27+4	2	1	0
Fulop, Marton	Hun	gk	Mar 2005	7	0	0	0
Kovacs, Janos	Hun	d	Aug 2005	9	0	1	0

COLCHESTER UNITED (25)

Gallego, Jose	Sp	w	Aug 1950	4	0	0	0
Kennon, Sandy	SA	gk	Mar 1965	76	0	6	0
Macedo, Tony (Brit)	Gib	gk	Sep 1968	38	0	2	0
Forrest, Craig	Can	gk	Mar 1988	11	0	0	0
Bruce, Marcelle	USA	gk	Jul 1989	28+1	1	2	0
Barada, Taylor	USA	gk	Mar 1994	1	0	0	0
Cheetham, Mike (Brit)	Neth	m	Mar 1995	33+4	3	3	1
Caldwell, Garrett	USA	gk	Sep 1995	6	0	2	0
Petterson, Andy	Aus	gk	Mar 1996	5	0	0	0
Gregory, Neil (Brit)	Zam	f	Jan 1998	41+12	11	5	0
Okafor, Sam	Nig	m	Aug 1998	0+1	0	0	0
Lua-Lua, Lomana	DRC	f	Sep 1998	37+24	15	5	5
Pounewatchy, Stephane	Fr	d	Feb 1999	15	1	0	0
Fumaca, Jose	Bra	m	Mar 1999	1	0	0	0
Richard, Fabrice	Fr	d	Mar 1999	23+1	0	1+1	0
Germain, Steve	Fr	f	Mar 1999	2+7	0	0	0
Pinault, Thomas	Fr	m	Jul 1999	104+29	5	22+2	2
Opara, Kelechi	Nig	f	Aug 1999	2+17	0	1	0
Canham, Marc (Brit)	Ger	m	Aug 2001	2+2	0	0	0
Blatsis, Con	Aus	d	Mar 2002	7	0	0	0
Atangana, Simon	Cam	f	Nov 2002	1+5	0	0+1	0
Johnson, Richard	Aus	m	Oct 2003	0	0	0+1	0
Garcia, Richard	Aus	f	Sep 2004	29+17	9	12+3	5
Elokobi, George	Cam	d	Jan 2005	10+2	1	4+1	1
N'Dumbu-Nsungu, Guylain	DRC	f	Jan 2005	2+6	1	0+1	0

COVENTRY CITY (75)

Gibson, Fred	SA	w	May 1919	54	5	0	0
Mackrill, Percy	SA	fb	Jul 1919	1	0	0	0
Aldecoa, Emilio	Sp	w	Dec 1945	29	0	2	0
Mokone, Steve	SA	w	Oct 1956	4	1	0	0
Lightening, Arthur	SA	gk	Nov 1958	150	0	10	0

Name	Born	Pos	From	LgAp	LgG	OthAp	OthG
Stiffle, Nelson (Brit)	Ind	w	Jul 1960	15	2	3	0
Bruck, Dietmar	Ger	fb	May 1962	181+8	7	27+1	1
Baker, Gerry	USA	f	Nov 1967	27+4	5	3	1
Smit(h), Wilf	Ger	fb	Aug 1970	132+3	1	18	1
Van Gool, Roger	Bel	w	Mar 1980	17	0	2	0
Kaiser, Rudi	Neth	w	Aug 1981	11+5	3	3	0
Avramovic, Raddy	Cro	gk	Sep 1983	18	0	6	0
Jol Martin	Neth	m	Jul 1984	15	0	0	0
Regis, Cyrille (Eng)	FrGu	f	Oct 1984	231+6	47	39+1	15
Phillips, David (Brit)	Ger	m	Jun 1986	93+7	8	17	1
Perdomo, Jose	Uru	m	Aug 1990	4	0	2	0
Butcher, Terry (Eng)	Sing	d	Nov 1990	6	0	1	0
Ndlovu, Peter	Zim	f	Aug 1991	141+36	37	15+4	4
Wegerle, Roy (USA)	SA	f	Mar 1993	46+7	9	8+2	2
Kruszynski, Detsi	Ger	m	Sep 1993	1+1	0	1	0
Jones, Cobi	USA	m	Sep 1994	16+5	2	2+2	0
Filan, John	Aus	gk	Mar 1995	15+1	0	2	0
Isaias, Marques (Por)	Bra	m	Aug 1995	9+3	2	2	0
Lamptey, Nii	Gha	f	Aug 1995	3+3	0	3+2	2
Salako, John (Eng)	Nig	f	Aug 1995	68+4	4	13	4
Genaux, Reggie	Bel	d	Aug 1996	3+1	0	0	0
Evtushok, Alex	Ukr	d	Feb 1997	3	0	0	0
Johansen, Martin	Den	m/f	Jun 1997	0+2	0	1	0
Hedman, Magnus	Swe	gk	Jul 1997	134	0	17	0
Lightbourne, Kyle	Ber	f	Jul 1997	1+6	0	3	0
Nilsson, Roland (1)	Swe	fb	Jul 1997	60	0	9	0
Soltvedt, Trond Egil	Nor	m	Jul 1997	47+10	3	6+6	1
Boateng, George	Gha	m	Dec 1997	43+4	5	11	2
Moldovan, Viorel	Rom	f	Jan 1998	5+5	1	2+2	1
Clement, Philippe	Bel	m	Jul 1998	6+6	0	2+2	0
Wallemme, Jean-Guy	Fr	d	Jul 1998	4+2	0	2	0
Chippo, Youssef	Mor	m/f	Jul 1999	100+22	6	10+1	4
Delorge, Laurent	Bel	f	Nov 1998	23+7	4	1+3	0
Aloisi, John	Aus	f	Dec 1998	18+24	10	2+3	3
Gioacchini, Stefano	It	f	Jan 1999	0+3	0	0	0
Konjic, Muhamed	Bos	d	Feb 1999	130+8	4	16+1	0
Hyldgaard, Morten	Den	gk	Jul 1999	27	0	4	0
Hadji, Mustapha	Mor	m/f	Aug 1999	61+1	12	7+1	1
Normann, Runar	Nor	m	Aug 1999	3+10	1	1+1	0
Nuzzo, Raffaele	It	gk	Jul 1999	0	0	1	0
Roussel, Cedric	Bel	f	Oct 1999	28+11	8	3+1	3
Gustafsson, Tomas	Swe	d	Dec 1999	10+5	0	1+2	0
Zuniga, Ysrael	Per	f	Mar 2000	11+18	3	2	1
Guerrero, Ivan	Hon	d	Oct 2000	6+1	0	1	0
Martinez, Jairo	Hon	f	Oct 2000	5+6	3	1+1	0
Nilsson, Roland (2)	Swe	fb	Jul 2001	9	0	1	0
Safri, Youssef	Mor	m	Aug 2001	87+4	1	7	0
Carbonari, Horacio	Arg	d	Mar 2002	5	0	0	0
Debec, Fabien	Fr	gk	Sep 2002	11	0	2	0
McMaster, Jamie	Aus	m	Nov 2002	2	0	0	0
Sara, Juan	Arg	f	Jan 2003	1+2	1	0+1	0
Engongam, Vincente	Sp	m	Feb 2003	5+3	0	0	0
Yulu, Christian (Fr)	DRC	m	Feb 2003	1+2	0	0	0
Cooney, Sean	Aus	d	Apr 2003	0+1	0	0	0

Name	Born	Pos	From	LgAp	LgG	OthAp	OthG
Adebola, Dele	Nig	f	Jun 2003	72+25	19	7+4	2
Suffo, Patrick	Cam	f	Jul 2003	22+26	10	3+3	2
Arphexad, Pegguy (Fr)	Guad	gk	Aug 2003	5	0	0	0
Jorgensen, Claus	Den	m	Aug 2003	30+22	6	3+6	0
Mansouri, Yazid (Alg)	Fr	m	Aug 2003	9+5	0	1	0
Deloumeaux, Eric	Fr	d	Jan 2004	20+1	1	3	0
Gudjonsson, Bjarni	Ice	m	Jan 2004	20+8	3	4+1	0
Lowe, Onandi	Jam	f	Mar 2004	1+1	1	0	0
Olszar, Sebastian	Pol	f	Mar 2004	1+4	0	0	0
John, Stern	Trin	f	Sep 2004	46+9	21	7	2
Laville, Florent	Fr	d	Oct 2004	5+1	0	0	0
Negouai, Christian (Fr)	Mart	m	Jan 2005	1	0	1	0
Goater, Shaun	Ber	f	Mar 2005	4+2	0	0	0
Ince, Clayton	Trin	gk	Jul 2005	1	0	3	0
Fulop, Marton	Hun	gk	Oct 2005	31	0	2	0
Nalis, Lilian	Fr	m	Oct 2005	5+1	2	0	0
Sofiane, Youssef	Fr	f	Oct 2005	0+1	0	0	0

CREWE ALEXANDRA (19)

Name	Born	Pos	From	LgAp	LgG	OthAp	OthG
Wagstaffe, Thomas (Brit)	India	f	Sep 1926	3	1	0	0
McLaughlin, William	USA	wh	Oct 1946	1	0	0	0
Baines, Peter	Aus	f	Nov 1946	8	0	0	0
Kelly, Pat (N Ire)	SA	gk	Feb 1952	38	0	0	0
Emmerson, Wayne	Can	f	Jul 1968	6+2	1	1	1
Rafferty, Kevin (Brit)	Ken	gk	Nov 1978	22	0	4	0
Grobbelaar, Bruce (Zim)	SA	gk	Dec 1979	24	1	0	0
Goulet, Brent	USA	f	Jan 1988	2+1	3	0	0
Mettioui, Ahmed	Mor	m	Jul 1992	1+2	0	1	0
Adebola, Dele	Nig	f	Mar 1993	98+26	39	18+5	5
Bankole, Ade (1)	Nig	gk	Sep 1996	6	0	1	0
Mautone, Steve	Aus	gk	Sep 1996	3	0	0	0
Kearton, Jason	Aus	gk	Oct 1996	190+1	0	25	0
Jack, Rodney (StV)	Jam	f	Aug 1998	140+23	33	20+2	5
Ince, Clayton	Trin	gk	Sep 1999	120+3	0	14	0
Bankole, Ade (2)	Nig	gk	Jul 2000	51+1	0	10+2	0
Milosevic, Danny	Aus	gk	Jan 2003	1	0	0	0
Ugarte, Juan	Sp	f	Jul 2005	0+2	0	1	0
Suhaj, Pavel	Svk	f	Jul 2005	1+5	0	0	0
Bougherra, Madjid (Alg)	Fr	d	Jan 2006	11	1	0	0

CRYSTAL PALACE (61)

Name	Born	Pos	From	LgAp	LgG	OthAp	OthG
Gaillard, Marcel	Bel	w	Feb 1948	21	3	0	0
Besagni, Remo	It	f	Oct 1952	2	0	0	0
Thorup, Borge	Den	fb	Mar 1969	0+1	0	0	0
Bartram, Per	Den	f	Aug 1969	8+2	2	1+1	1
McBride, Andy (Brit)	Ken	d	Oct 1971	1	0	0	0
Heppolette, Ricky (Brit)	Ind	m	Oct 1976	13+2	0	3	0
Nebbeling, Gavin	SA	d	Aug 1981	145+6	8	13+1	0
Galloway, Steve (Brit)	Ger	f	Oct 1984	3+2	1	0+1	0
Salako, John (Eng)	Nig	f	Nov 1986	172+43	23	39+5	9
Young, Eric (Wal)	Sing	d	Aug 1990	161	15	35	1
Boere, Jeroen	Neth	f	Sep 1995	0+8	1	0	0
Andersen, Leif	Nor	d	Jan 1996	19+11	1	5	0
Veart, Carl	Aus	m	Mar 1996	41+16	6	8+3	5
Hreidarsson, Hermann	Ice	d	Aug 1997	32+5	2	11	1

Name	Born	Pos	From	LgAp	LgG	OthAp	OthG
Zohar, Itzy	Isr	m	Aug 1997	2+4	0	2	0
Lombardo, Attilio	It	m	Aug 1997	40+3	8	5	2
Bonetti, Ivano	It	m	Oct 1997	0+2	0	0	0
Padovano, Michele	It	f	Nov 1997	8+4	1	0	0
Brolin, Tomas	Swe	m	Jan 1998	13	0	3	0
Ismael, Valerien	Fr	m	Jan 1998	13	0	3	0
Billio, Patrizio	It	m	Mar 1998	1+2	0	0	0
Curcic, Sasa	Yug	m	Mar 1998	10+13	5	3	0
Rizzo, Nicky	Aus	m	Jul 1998	15+21	1	2+3	1
Amsalem, David	Isr	d	Aug 1998	6+4	0	1+1	0
Del Rio, Walter	Arg	d	Sep 1998	1+1	0	0+1	0
Jihai, Sun	Chn	d	Sep 1998	22+1	0	2	0
Svensson, Mathias	Swe	f	Sep 1998	26+6	10	3	0
Zhiyi, Fan	Chn	d	Sep 1998	87+1	4	14	2
Moore, Craig	Aus	d	Oct 1998	23	3	1	0
Foster, Craig	Aus	m	Oct 1998	47+5	3	2	0
Petric, Gordan	Yug	d	Nov 1998	18	1	0	0
Fumaca, Jose	Bra	m	Sep 1999	2+1	0	2	0
De Ornelas, Fernando	Ven	m	Sep 1999	5+4	0	0	0
Mautone, Steve	Aus	gk	Nov 1999	2	0	0	0
Forssell, Mikael (Fin)	Ger	f	Feb 2000	44+8	16	9+1	2
Kolinko, Alex	Lat	gk	Sep 2000	79+3	0	17	0
Rubins, Andrejs	Lat	m	Oct 2000	17+14	0	5+1	2
Berhalter, Gregg	USA	d	Feb 2001	10+9	1	1+1	0
Fuller, Ricardo	Jam	f	Feb 2001	2+6	0	0	0
Karic, Amir	Slo	d	Mar 2001	3	0	0	0
Riihilahti, Aki	Fin	m	Mar 2001	130+27	13	16+5	1
Verhoene, Kenny	Bel	d	Mar 2001	0+1	0	0	0
Kirovski, Jovan	USA	f	Aug 2001	25+11	5	3	0
Popovic, Tony	Aus	d	Aug 2001	121+2	6	21	2
Carasso, Cedric	Fr	g	Dec 2001	0+1	0	0	0
Murphy, Shaun	Aus	d	Feb 2002	11	0	0	0
Adebola, Dele	Nig	f	Aug 2002	32+7	5	9	2
Michopoulos, Nik	Grk	gk	Sep 2002	5	0	1+1	0
Berthelin, Cedric	Fr	gk	Jan 2003	26	0	6+1	0
Myhre, Thomas	Nor	gk	Oct 2003	15	0	1	0
Vaesen, Nico	Bel	gk	Mar 2004	10	0	3	0
Danze, Anthony	Aus	m	Jul 2004	0	0	2	0
Kiraly, Gabor	Hun	gk	Jul 2004	75	0	7	0
Kolkka, Joonas	Fin	m	Jul 2004	21+5	3	2	0
Speroni, Julian	Arg	gk	Jul 2004	9+1	0	6	0
Kaviedes, Ivan	Ecu	f	Aug 2004	1+3	0	0+2	0
Sorondo, Gonzalo	Uru	d	Aug 2004	16+4	0	2	0
Torghelle, Sandor	Hun	f	Aug 2004	3+9	0	3	1
Ventola, Nicola	It	f	Aug 2004	0+3	1	0	0
Lakis, Vassilis	Grk	m	Sep 2004	6+12	0	1+1	0
Reich, Marco	Ger	f	Sep 2005	14+7	2	2+3	2
DARLINGTON (38)							
Hill, Reg (Brit)	Gib	wh	Feb 1937	12	0	0	0
Karaa, Roch	Tun	gk	Mar 1985	1	0	0	0
Sanderson, Mike (Brit)	Ger	m	Mar 1986	1	0	0	0
Neves, Rui	Por	f	Aug 1995	3+2	0	2	0
Paulo, Pedro	Por	m	Aug 1995	4+2	0	1+1	0

Name	Born	Pos	From	LgAp	LgG	OthAp	OthG
Quitongo, Jose	Ang	f	Sep 1995	1	0	0	0
Stephenson, Ashlyn	SA	gk	Sep 1995	1	0	0	0
Carmichael, Matt (Brit)	Sing	f	Feb 1996	11+2	2	2+1	0
De Vos, Jason	Can	d	Nov 1996	43+1	5	7	1
Barbara, Daniel	Fr	f	Dec 1996	1+5	1	0	0
Moilanen, Tepi	Fin	gk	Jan 1997	16	0	0	0
Papaconstantinou, Loukas	Can	gk	Jul 1997	1	0	0	0
Giumarra, Willy	Can	m	Aug 1997	0+4	0	0	0
Resch, Franz	Aut	d	Oct 1997	15+2	1	1+2	0
Dorner, Mario	Aut	f	Oct 1997	34+15	13	6+1	2
Di Lella, Gustavo	Arg	m	Dec 1997	0+5	0	0	0
Kubicki, Dariusz	Pol	d	Oct 1998	2+1	0	0	0
Costa, Ricardo	Por	f	Jan 1999	0+3	1	0	0
Hjorth, Jesper	Den	f	Nov 1999	16+29	7	6+4	0
Kaak, Tom	Neth	f	Jul 2000	7+1	2	0+2	0
Van der, Geest Frank	Neth	gk	Aug 2000	2	0	2	0
Zeghdane, Lehit	Fr	f	Sep 2000	1+2	0	0+2	0
Marcelle, Clint	Trin	f	Feb 2001	8+7	0	0	0
Bernard, Olivier	Fr	m	Mar 2001	9+1	2	0	0
Cau, Jean-Michel	Fr	f	Mar 2001	0+1	0	0	0
Jeannin, Alex	Fr	d	Mar 2001	22	0	0	0
Bossy, Fabien	Fr	d	Aug 2003	4+2	0	2	0
Scartiscini, Leandro	Arg	f	Jul 2004	0	0	0+1	0
Gregorio, Adolfo	USA	m	Sep 2004	19+5	2	1	0
Webster, Adrian	NZ	m	Oct 2004	22+13	1	3	0
Wijnhard, Clyde (Neth)	Sur	f	Oct 2004	36+3	15	3	0
Petta, Bobby	Neth	m	Feb 2005	12	1	0	0
Martis, Shelton	Neth	m	Jul 2005	39+1	2	3	0
Bossu, Bert	Fr	gk	Aug 2005	9	0	1	0
N'Dumbu-Nsungu, Guylain	DRC	f	Aug 2005	11+10	10	1+1	0
Kandol, Tresor (Brit)	DRC	f	Nov 2005	6+1	2	0	0
Schmeichel, Kasper	Den	gk	Jan 2006	4	0	0	0
Johnson, Jemal	USA	f	Mar 2006	9	3	0	0
DERBY COUNTY (64)							
Quantrill, Alf (Eng)	Ind	w	Aug 1914	72	5	4	0
Abdallah, Tewfik	Egy	f	Sep 1920	15	1	0	0
Law, Cecil (Brit)	Zim	w	Aug 1951	33	2	0	0
Nielson, Norman	SA	ch	Sep 1951	57	8	3	1
Ackerman, Alf	SA	f	Mar 1955	36	21	0	0
Banovic, Yakka (Yug)	Aus	gk	Sep 1980	35	0	3	0
Streete, Floyd (Brit)	Jam	d	Oct 1984	35	0	5	0
Callaghan, Nigel (Eng) (1)	Sing	w	Feb 1987	76	10	7	1
Chiedozie, John	Nig	w	Aug 1988	2	0	0	0
Callaghan, Nigel (Eng) (2)	Sing	w	Sep 1990	12	1	0	0
Goulooze, Richard	Neth	d	Sep 1992	7+5	0	1+1	0
Harkes, John	USA	m	Aug 1993	67+7	2	8	0
Willems, Ron	Neth	f	Jul 1995	41+18	13	6+2	3
Van der Laan, Robin	Neth	m	Aug 1995	61+4	8	9+3	3
Stimac, Igor	Cro	d	Oct 1995	84	3	9	0
Asanovic, Aljosa	Cro	m	Jun 1996	37+1	7	5	0
Laursen, Jacob	Den	d/m	Jul 1996	135+2	3	16	0
Rahmberg, Marino	Swe	f	Jan 1997	0+1	0	0	0
Poom, Mart	Est	gk	Mar 1997	143+3	0	20	0

Name	Born	Pos	From	LgAp	LgG	OthAp	OthG
Solis, Mauricio	CoRi	m	Mar 1997	3+8	0	1+2	0
Wanchope, Paulo	CoRi	f	Mar 1997	65+7	23	10+1	5
Eranio, Stefano	It	m	Jul 1997	83+12	7	13	3
Baiano, Francesco	It	f	Aug 1997	52+12	16	11	3
Bohinen, Lars	Nor	m	Mar 1998	47+9	1	5	0
Carbonari, Horacio	Arg	d	Jul 1998	89+1	9	12	0
Schnoor, Stefan	Ger	d	Jul 1998	48+12	2	7+2	0
Dorigo, Tony (Eng)	Aus	fb	Oct 1998	37+4	1	8	2
Beck, Mikkel	Den	f	Mar 1999	11+7	2	2+1	1
Borbokis, Vassilis	Grk	d	Mar 1999	9+7	0	4	1
Fuertes, Esteban	Arg	f	Aug 1999	8	1	2	1
Nimni, Avi	Isr	m	Nov 1999	2+2	1	1	0
Strupar, Branko (Bel)	Cro	f	Dec 1999	32+9	16	2	0
Kinkladze, Georgi	Geo	m	Jun 2000	60+33	7	5+2	1
Valakari, Simo	Fin	m	Jul 2000	34+12	3	5	0
Blatsis, Con	Aus	d	Aug 2000	2	0	0	0
Bragstad, Bjorn Otto	Nor	d	Aug 2000	10+2	0	4	2
Mawene, Youl	Fr	d	Aug 2000	54+1	1	6	0
Martin, Lilian	Fr	d	Nov 2000	7+2	0	2+1	0
West, Taribo	Nig	d	Nov 2000	18	0	2	0
Gudjonsson, Thordur	Ice	m	Mar 2001	2+8	1	0	0
Ravanelli, Fabrizio	It	f	Jul 2001	46+4	14	3	2
Daino, Daniele	It	d	Aug 2001	2	0	1+1	0
Carbone, Benito	It	f	Oct 2001	13	1	1	0
Ducrocq, Pierre	Fr	m	Oct 2001	19	0	0	0
Feuer, Ian	USA	gk	Oct 2001	2	0	0	0
Zavagno, Luciano	Arg	d	Oct 2001	48+4	3	2+1	0
Grenet, Francois	Fr	d	Nov 2001	14+4	0	1	0
Foletti, Patrick	Swit	gk	Feb 2002	1+1	0	0	0
Costa, Candido	Por	m	Jul 2003	23+11	1	1	0
Labarthe, Gianfranco	Per	f	Jul 2003	0+3	0	1	0
Junior, Jose Luis	Bra	f	Aug 2003	11+19	4	0+2	1
Svensson, Mathias	Swe	f	Aug 2003	9+1	3	0	0
Martinez, Manel	Sp	f	Jan 2004	12+3	3	1	0
Reich, Marco	Ger	f	Jan 2004	36+14	7	4+1	0
Peschisolido, Paul	Can	f	Mar 2004	35+42	17	6+1	3
Konjic, Muhamed	Bos	d	May 2004	13+3	0	3	0
Bisgaard, Morten	Den	m	Jun 2004	56+13	8	6	0
Idiakez, Inigo	Sp	m	Jul 2004	82+1	20	7	2
Rasiak, Grzegorz	Pol	f	Sep 2004	41	18	3+1	1
John, Stern	Trin	f	Sep 2005	6+1	0	0	0
Kaku, Blessing	Nig	m	Nov 2004	3+1	0	0	0
Fadiga, Khalilou	Sen	m	Sep 2005	2+2	0	0	0
Thome, Emerson	Bra	d	Oct 2005	3+1	0	0	0
El Hamdaoui, Mounir (Mor)	Neth	f	Sep 2005	5+4	3	0	0
Hajto, Tomasz	Pol	d	Jan 2006	5	0	1	0
DONCASTER ROVERS (15)							
Sharp, Ronnie	Can	w	Oct 1958	58	11	8	3
Berry, George (Wal)	Ger	d	Aug 1984	1	0	1	0
Kerr, Dylan (Brit)	Mal	d	Aug 1991	7	1	0	0
Cunningham, Tony (Brit)	Jam	f	Jul 1993	19+6	1	3+1	0
Kitchen, Sam (Brit)	Ger	d	Feb 1994	21+1	1	1	0
Torfason, Gunnar	Ice	f	Jul 1994	1+3	0	1+1	1

Name	Born	Pos	From	LgAp	LgG	OthAp	OthG
Carmichael, Matt (Brit)	Sing	f	Aug 1995	19+8	4	0+2	1
Knight, Jason	Aus	m	Aug 1995	1+3	0	0	0
Moncrieffe, Prince	Jam	f	Jul 1997	30+8	8	3	0
Ipoua, Guy	Cam	f	Jul 2004	1+8	0	1+1	0
Priet, Nicolas	Fr	d	Jul 2004	7	0	3	0
Hughes, Adam	Aus	m	Aug 2005	4+2	0	2+1	1
Predic, Uros	SM	m	Aug 2005	3+3	0	2	0
Budtz, Jan	Den	gk	May 2005	20	0	4+2	0
Seremet, Dino	Slo	gk	Nov 2005	1	0	1	0

EVERTON (45)

Name	Born	Pos	From	LgAp	LgG	OthAp	OthG
Murray, David	SA	f	Aug 1925	3	1	0	0
Van Den Hauwe, Pat (Wal)	Bel	fb	Sep 1984	134+1	2	55	1
Kearton, Jason	Aus	gk	Oct 1988	3+3	0	2	0
Rehn, Stefan	Swe	w	Jun 1989	1+3	0	1+1	0
Atteveld, Ray	Neth	d/m	Aug 1989	41+10	1	12+2	1
Warzycha, Robert	Pol	w	Mar 1991	51+21	6	5+5	0
Radosavljevic, Preki (US)	Yug	w	Aug 1992	22+24	4	3+4	0
Limpar, Anders	Swe	w	Mar 1994	51+15	5	12+3	1
Amokachi, Daniel	Nig	f	Aug 1994	34+9	10	8+3	4
Kanchelskis, Andrei	Ukr	w	Aug 1995	52	20	8	2
Hottiger, Marc	Swit	fb	Mar 1996	13+4	1	1	0
Thomsen, Claus	Den	m	Jan 1997	17+7	1	1	0
Bilic, Slaven	Cro	d	Jul 1997	26+2	0	4	0
Myhre, Thomas	Nor	gk	Nov 1997	70	0	12	0
Madar, Mickael	Fr	f	Dec 1997	17+2	6	0+1	0
Dacourt, Olivier	Fr	m	Jun 1998	28+2	2	6	1
Materazzi, Marco	It	d	Jul 1998	26+1	1	6	1
Bakayoko, Ibrahima	IvCo	f	Oct 1998	17+6	4	3+2	3
Degn, Peter	Den	m	Feb 1999	0+4	0	1	0
Gough, Richard (Sco)	Swe	d	Jun 1999	38	1	3+1	0
Xavier, Abel (Por)	Moz	d	Sep 1999	39+4	0	6	0
Moore, Joe-Max	USA	f	Dec 1999	22+30	8	5+7	2
Alexandersson, Niclas	Swe	m	Jul 2000	49+9	4	6+2	1
Pistone, Alessandro	It	d	Jul 2000	94+9	1	12+2	0
Gravesen, Thomas	Den	m	Aug 2000	131+10	11	12+2	1
Nyarko, Alex	Gha	m	Aug 2000	26+7	1	5	0
Tal, Idan	Isr	m	Oct 2000	13+16	2	1+3	0
Radzinski, Tomasz (Can)	Pol	f	Jul 2001	78+13	25	7+3	1
Blomqvist, Jesper	Swe	m	Nov 2001	10+5	1	2+1	0
Linderoth, Tobias	Swe	m	Jan 2002	29+11	0	4+2	1
Ginola, David	Fr	w	Feb 2002	2+3	0	2	0
Li Tie	Chn	m	Aug 2002	32+2	0	4+2	0
Rodrigo, Juliano	Bra	m	Aug 2002	0+4	0	0	0
Yobo, Joseph	Nig	d	Sep 2002	97+11	3	15+1	1
Li, Weifeng	Chn	d	Nov 2002	1	0	1	0
Baardsen, Espen (Nor)	USA	gk	Jan 2003	1	0	0	0
McBride, Brian	USA	f	Jan 2003	7+1	4	0	0
Cahill, Tim	Aus	m	Jul 2004	65	17	10+2	3
Arteta, Mikel	Sp	m	Jan 2005	37+4	2	9	2
Anichebe, Victor	Nig	f	Jul 2005	0+2	1	0+1	0
Ferrari, Matteo (It)	Alg	d	Aug 2005	6+2	0	5	0
Kroldrup, Per	Den	d	Jun 2005	1	0	0+1	0
Valente, Nuno	Por	d	Aug 2005	20	0	6	0

Name	Born	Pos	From	LgAp	LgG	OthAp	OthG
Van der Meyde, Andy	Neth	f	Aug 2005	7+3	0	0+1	0
Westerveld, Sander	Neth	gk	Feb 2006	2	0	0	0
EXETER CITY (17)							
Stiffle, Nelson (Brit)	Ind	w	Mar 1958	94	17	4	2
Baugh, John	Uga	gk	Feb 1977	20	0	4	0
Cooke Joe	Dom	d/f	Jun 1981	17	3	4	2
Auguste, Joe	Trin	f	Sep 1983	7+3	0	1	0
Thirlby, Anthony (Brit)	Ger	m	Jul 1993	27+12	2	2+3	0
Adekola, David	Nig	f	Feb 1994	1+2	1	0	0
Rice, Gary (Brit)	Zam	d	Jul 1994	31+13	0	3	0
Blake, Noel (Brit)	Jam	d	Aug 1995	135+12	10	12	0
Tisdale, Paul (Brit)	Mal	m	Dec 1997	10	1	0	0
Vanninen, Jukka	Fin	m	Dec 1999	3+2	0	0	0
Van Heusden, Arjan	Neth	gk	Jul 2000	74	0	6	0
Epesse-Titi, Steeve	Fr	d	Mar 2001	5+1	0	0	0
Kerr, Dylan (Brit)	Mal	d	Aug 2001	5	1	1	0
Moor, Reinier (Ire)	Neth	f	Aug 2001	2+17	3	1+3	1
Diallo, Cherif	Sen	f	Sep 2001	0+2	0	0	0
Gaia, Marcio	Bra	d	Aug 2002	33	1	5	1
Harries, Paul	Aus	f	Sep 2002	0+1	0	0+1	0
FULHAM (64)							
O'Donnell, Rudolph (Brit)	Ind	gk	Dec 1909	3	0	0	0
Hegazi, Hassan	Egy	f	Nov 1911	1	1	0	0
Kingsley, Alf	Bar	w	Jan 1922	29	2	2	0
Osborne, Frank (Eng)	SA	f	Nov 1921	67	18	3	0
Price, Johnny (Brit)	Ind	f	Jun 1928	189	49	15	4
Clarke, Bruce	SA	wh	Jun 1934	112	1	2	0
Mitten, Charlie (Brit)	Bur	wh	Jan 1952	154	32	6	1
Macedo, Tony (Brit)	Gib	gk	Oct 1955	346	0	45	0
Hewkins, Ken	SA	gk	Nov 1955	38	0	3	0
Cutbush, John (Brit)	Mal	fb	Jul 1972	131+3	3	26	0
Hesford, Iain (Eng)	Zam	gk	Jan 1985	3	0	0	0
Nebbeling, Gavin	SA	d	Jul 1989	85+3	2	8	0
Tierling, Lee (Brit)	Ger	m	May 1992	7+12	0	1	0
Bedrossian, Ara	Cyp	m	Mar 1993	34+8	1	1+1	0
Arendse, Andre	SA	gk	Aug 1997	6	0	3	0
Peschisolido, Paul	Can	f	Oct 1997	69+26	24	18+2	6
Neilson, Alan (Wal)	Ger	d	Nov 1997	24+5	2	8+2	0
Taylor, Maik (N Ire)	Ger	gk	Nov 1997	183+1	0	46	0
Lightbourne, Kyle	Ber	f	Jan 1998	4	2	0	0
Salako, John (Eng)	Nig	f	Jul 1998	7+3	1	4+2	1
Uhlenbeek, Gus (Neth)	Sur	d	Jul 1998	22+17	1	7+3	0
Lehmann, Dirk	Ger	f	Aug 1998	16+10	2	7+2	3
Betsy, Kevin (Brit)	Sey	m	Sep 1998	3+12	1	2+2	0
Keller, Francois	Fr	m	Dec 1998	0+1	0	0	0
Albert, Philippe	Bel	d	Jan 1999	12+1	2	0	0
Hahnemann, Marcus	USA	gk	Jul 1999	2	0	2	0
Hammond, Elvis	Gha	f	Jul 1999	3+7	0	0+1	0
Riedle, Karl-Heinz	Ger	f	Sep 1999	16+19	6	1	0
Goldbaek, Bjarne	Den	m	Jan 2000	73+12	6	12+5	1
Lewis, Eddie	USA	f	Mar 2000	8+8	0	6	1
Saha, Louis	Fr	f	Jun 2000	100+17	53	18+8	10
Fernandes, Fabrice	Fr	m	Aug 2000	23+6	2	5+2	2

Name	Born	Pos	From	LgAp	LgG	OthAp	OthG
Sahnoun, Nicolas	Fr	m	Oct 2000	2+5	0	2	0
Stolcers, Andrejs	Lat	f	Dec 2000	8+17	2	3+4	2
Moller, Peter	Den	f	Jan 2001	2+3	1	0	0
Goma, Alain	Fr	d	Mar 2001	115+2	0	33+2	0
Boa Morte, Luis	Por	f	Jun 2001	157+33	44	37+8	10
Legwinski, Sylvain	Fr	m	Aug 2001	116+12	8	32+4	4
Malbranque, Steed (Fr)	Bel	m	Aug 2001	160+12	32	35+4	12
Marlet, Steve	Fr	f	Aug 2001	50+5	11	20+3	8
Ouaddou, Abdeslam	Mor	d	Aug 2001	13+8	0	15+2	0
Van der Sar, Edwin	Neth	gk	Aug 2001	126+1	0	27	0
Inamoto, Junichi	Jap	m	Jul 2002	24+17	4	9+8	5
Sava, Facundo	Arg	f	Jul 2002	13+13	6	11+5	1
Wome, Pierre	Cam	m	Sep 2002	13+1	1	3+2	0
Djetou, Martin (Fr)	IvCo	d	Oct 2002	41+10	1	13+2	0
Herrera, Martin	Arg	gk	Feb 2003	1+1	0	0	0
Buari, Malik	Gha	m	Jul 2003	1+2	0	2	0
Bonnissel, Jerome	Fr	m	Aug 2003	16	0	0	0
Volz, Moritz	Ger	d	Aug 2003	86+1	0	10+1	1
Petta, Bobby	Neth	m	Dec 2003	3+5	0	2+3	0
Bocanegra, Carlos	USA	d	Jan 2004	61+3	2	11+1	0
John, Collins (Neth)	Lib	f	Jan 2004	32+38	19	3+7	3
McBride, Brian	USA	f	Jan 2004	54+30	19	5+5	5
Batista, Ricardo	Por	gk	Jul 2004	0	0	1	0
Diop, Pape Bouba	Sen	m	Jul 2004	50+1	8	6+1	1
Jensen, Claus	Den	m	Jul 2004	21+2	2	1+2	1
Radzinski, Tomasz (Can)	Pol	f	Jul 2004	48+20	8	7+1	6
Elrich, Ahmed	Aus	m	Jun 2005	2+4	0	3	0
Helguson, Heidar	Ice	f	Jun 2005	15+12	8	2	2
Jensen, Niclas	Den	d	Jul 2005	14+2	0	1	0
Christanval, Philippe	Fr	d	Sep 2005	7+8	0	1	0
Elliott, Simon	NZ	m	Jan 2006	12	0	1	0
Niemi, Antti	Fin	gk	Jan 2006	9	0	0	0

GILLINGHAM (21)

Name	Born	Pos	From	LgAp	LgG	OthAp	OthG
Martin, Syd	SA	f	Jul 1929	2	0	1	0
Mills, Arthur (Brit)	Ind	w	Jul 1933	33	12	2	1
Crossan, Errol	Can	w	Jul 1955	76	16	4	1
Burgess, Mike	Can	f/ch	Mar 1963	109+1	2	10	0
Chadwick, Dave (Brit)	Ind	w	Sep 1974	35	3	1	0
Young, Charlie (Brit)	Cyp	d	Mar 1978	27+1	1	6	1
Henry, Liburd	Dom	f	Jun 1992	37+5	2	6+1	1
Statham, Brian (Eng)	Zim	d/m	Aug 1997	16+4	0	2	0
Rolling, Franck	Fr	d	Sep 1998	1	0	0	0
Omoyimni, Manny	Nig	f	Sep 1999	7+2	3	2	0
Mautone, Steve	Aus	gk	Mar 2000	1	0	0	0
Ipoua, Guy (Fr)	Cam	f	Mar 2001	42+40	12	6+6	3
Samuel, Jlloyd	Trin	d	Oct 2001	7+1	0	0	0
Sidibe, Mamady (Fr)	Mli	f	Aug 2002	80+26	10	7+2	3
Awuah, Jones	Gha	f	Sep 2002	1+3	0	0	0
Bossu, Bert	Fr	gk	Sep 2003	4+2	0	2	0
Vaesen, Nico	Bel	gk	Dec 2003	5	0	0	0
Hirschfeld, Lars	Can	gk	Feb 2004	2	0	0	0
Robinson, John (Wal)	Zim	m	Oct 2004	2+2	0	0	0
Ashikodi, Moses	Nig	f	Aug 2005	0+4	0	0	0

Name	Born	Pos	From	LgAp	LgG	OthAp	OthG
Sancho, Brent	Trin	d	Aug 2005	16+3	2	1+1	0
GLOSSOP (1)							
Cuffe, John	Aus	fb	Jul 1905	282	3	9	0
GRIMSBY TOWN (23)							
Seeburg, Max	Ger	f	Jul 1911	20	0	1	0
Andrews, Billy (N Ire)	USA	wh	Jul 1912	105	2	3	0
Hansen, Edvin	Den	f	Dec 1946	1	0	0	0
Okorie, Chima	Nig	f	Sep 1993	0+5	0	0+1	1
Bonetti, Ivano	It	m	Sep 1995	19	3	3	1
Gambaro, Enzo	It	d	Mar 1996	0+1	0	0	0
Nielsen, David	Den	f	Oct 2000	16+1	5	1+1	1
Fostervold, Anders	Nor	d	Nov 2000	9+1	0	0	0
Willems, Menno	Neth	f	Nov 2000	44+10	2	5	0
Enhua, Zhang	Chn	d	Dec 2000	16+1	3	0	0
Busscher, Robbie	Neth	m	Aug 2001	0+1	0	0	0
Neilson, Alan (Wal)	Ger	d	Oct 2001	8+2	0	2	0
Pringle, Martin	Swe	f	Feb 2002	2	0	0	0
Santos, Georges (CVI)	Fr	m	Oct 2002	24+2	1	1	1
Sagere, Jake	USA	f	Apr 2003	1	0	0	0
Barnard, Darren (Wal)	Ger	m	Apr 2003	55+8	4	5	0
Cas, Marcel	Neth	d	Jun 2003	13+6	2	2+2	1
Ten Heuvel, Laurens	Neth	f	Aug 2003	3+1	0	1	0
Antoine-Curier, Mickael	Fr	f	Mar 2004	3+2	0	0	0
Thorrington, John (USA)	SA	m	Mar 2004	2+1	0	0	0
Pinault, Thomas	Fr	m	Jul 2004	32+11	7	4	0
Marcelle, Clint	Trin	f	Aug 2004	0+3	0	1+1	0
Kamudimba, Jean-Paul	DRC	m	Jul 2005	14+7	5	4	1
HALIFAX TOWN (9)							
Mackrill, Percy	SA	fb	Jul 1921	57	0	5	0
Burgess, Mike	Can	f/ch	Jul 1961	34	3	2	0
Chadwick, Dave (Brit)	Ind	w	Jan 1970	95	15	8	1
Kemp, Fred (Brit)	It	m	Dec 1971	106+5	10	8	1
Carr, Everton	Ant	fb	Aug 1981	49+4	0	5	0
Podd, Ces	StK	fb	Aug 1984	52+5	0	6+1	0
Henry, Liburd	Dom	f	Sep 1988	1+4	0	0	0
Craven, Peter	Ger	w	Mar 1993	7	0	0	0
Obebo, Godfrey	Nig	f	Mar 1993	0+3	0	0	0
HARTLEPOOL UNITED (19)							
Abdallah, Tewfik	Egy	f	Mar 1924	11	1	0	0
Hill, Reg (Brit)	Gib	wh	Jan 1933	139	6	13	0
Baines, Peter	Aus	f	Jun 1947	9	1	0	0
Tunks, Roy (Brit)	Ger	gk	Jul 1988	5	0	0	0
Atkinson, Paddy (Brit)	Sing	fb	Aug 1988	9+12	3	2+2	0
Talia, Frank	Aus	gk	Dec 1992	14	0	0	0
Horace, Alain (Fr)	Mad	m	Oct 1996	0+1	0	0	0
Pedersen, Jan Ove	Nor	m	Oct 1997	17	1	1	1
Hollund, Martin	Nor	gk	Nov 1997	117	0	9	0
Larsen, Stig Olav	Nor	f	Dec 1997	0+4	0	0	0
Di Lella, Gustavo	Arg	m	Mar 1998	22+9	4	4+1	1
Miotto, Simon	Aus	gk	Jul 1998	5	0	0	0
Tennebo, Thomas	Nor	d	Aug 1999	6+7	0	1+2	0
Vindheim, Rune	Nor	m	Sep 1999	7	0	1	0

Name	Born	Pos	From	LgAp	LgG	OthAp	OthG
Sperrevik, Tim	Nor	f	Aug 2000	4+11	1	1	0
Konstantopoulos, Dimi	Grk	gk	Oct 2003	71	0	17	0
Porter, Joel	Aus	f	Nov 2003	60+14	20	13+4	4
Betsy, Kevin	Sey	m	Jul 2004	3+3	1	1	0
Pittman, Jon-Paul	USA	f	Jan 2006	2+1	0	0	0

HEREFORD UNITED (6)

Name	Born	Pos	From	LgAp	LgG	OthAp	OthG
Kemp, Fred (Brit)	It	m	Jul 1974	12+1	2	3	0
Musial, Adam	Pol	d	Aug 1980	44+2	0	2	0
Jennings, Jed	Ber	fb	Aug 1991	11+5	0	0	0
Wade, Meshach	Ber	m	Aug 1991	13+4	0	5	0
Nebbeling, Gavin	SA	d	Dec 1991	3	0	1	0
Kottila, Mika	Fin	f	Nov 1996	11+2	1	0	0

HUDDERSFIELD TOWN (26)

Name	Born	Pos	From	LgAp	LgG	OthAp	OthG
Wilcox, Tom (Brit)	At sea	gk	Jan 1911	2	0	0	0
Wienand, Tolley	SA	m	Jul 1937	28	3	4	0
Lindsay, Denis	SA	gk	Aug 1937	1	0	0	0
Hansen, Karl	Nor	f	Jan 1949	15	2	0	0
Carr, John	SA	w	Oct 1950	1	0	0	0
Kennon, Sandy	SA	gk	Aug 1956	78	0	2	0
Callaghan, Nigel (Eng)	Sing	w	Jan 1992	8	0	0	0
Short, Chris (Brit)	Ger	d	Dec 1994	6	0	0	0
Tisdale, Paul (Brit)	Mal	m	Nov 1996	1+1	0	0	0
Phillips, David (Brit)	Ger	m	Nov 1997	44+8	3	7	0
Nielsen, Martin	Den	d	Mar 1998	0+3	0	0	0
Vaesen, Nico	Bel	gk	Jul 1998	134	0	19	0
Donis, George	Grk	m	Jun 1999	10+10	0	3+2	0
Wijnhard, Clyde (Neth)	Sur	f	Jul 1999	51+11	16	8	1
Monkou, Ken (Neth)	Sur	d	Aug 1999	21	1	4	0
Gorre, Dean (Neth)	Sur	m	Sep 1999	49+13	6	5+1	1
Hodouto, Kwami (Fr)	Tgo	d	Sep 1999	1+1	0	1	0
Ngonge, Michel (DRC)	Bel	f	Mar 2000	0+4	0	0	0
Ndlovu, Peter	Zim	f	Dec 2000	6	4	0	0
Brennan, Jim	Can	d	Mar 2001	0+2	0	0	0
Thorrington, John (USA)	SA	m	Aug 2001	48+19	7	5+2	1
McDonald, Scott	Aus	f	Aug 2002	7+6	1	0+1	0
Sharp, Kevin	Can	d	Aug 2002	38+1	0	3	0
Labarthe, Gianfranco	Per	f	Feb 2003	0+3	0	0	0
Onibuje, Fola	Nig	f	Nov 2003	0+2	0	0	0
Rachubka, Paul	USA	gk	Mar 2004	76	0	11	0

HULL CITY (28)

Name	Born	Pos	From	LgAp	LgG	OthAp	OthG
Mills, Paddy (Brit) (1)	Ind	f	Aug 1920	173	76	11	7
Gibson, Jock	USA	fb	May 1922	210	0	8	0
Mills, Paddy (Brit) (2)	Ind	f	Dec 1929	96	25	11	2
McNeill, Hamilton (Brit)	Mal	f	May 1937	52	27	0	0
Wienand, Tolley	SA	w	Oct 1938	15	3	0	0
Jensen, Viggo	Den	d/m	Oct 1948	308	51	27	3
Ackerman, Alf (1)	SA	f	Jul 1950	34	21	3	0
Ackerman, Alf (2)	SA	f	Oct 1953	58	28	8	2
Tulloch, Roland	SA	wh	Dec 1953	3	0	0	0
Rintanen, Mauno	Fin	gk	Sep 1956	4	0	0	0
Nielson, Norman	SA	ch	Apr 1957	25	0	3	0
Cubie, Neil	SA	wh	Jul 1957	4	0	0	0

Name	Born	Pos	From	LgAp	LgG	OthAp	OthG
Hesford, Iain (Eng)	Zam	gk	Dec 1988	91	0	9	0
Ngata, Harry	NZ	f	Jul 1989	8+17	0	1+1	0
Doncel, Antonio	Sp	d	Aug 1996	30+8	2	6+1	0
Dickinson, Patrick	Can	m	Jul 1997	2+2	0	1	0
Goodison, Ian	Jam	d	Oct 1999	67+3	1	9+1	0
Whitmore, Theo	Jam	m	Oct 1999	63+14	9	10+1	1
Betsy, Kevin	Sey	m	Nov 1999	1+1	0	0	0
Marcelle, Clint	Trin	f	Sep 2000	16+7	2	2	0
Johnsson, Julian (Far)	Den	m	Jun 2001	38+2	4	4	1
Sneekes, Richard	Neth	m	Nov 2001	17+5	0	0+1	0
Van Blerk, Jason	Aus	m	Jan 2002	10	1	0	0
Caceres, Adrian (Aus)	Arg	m	Mar 2002	1+3	0	0	0
Lightbourne, Kyle	Ber	f	Mar 2002	3+1	0	0	0
Allsopp, Danny	Aus	f	May 2003	45+19	22	2+1	0
Kuipers, Michel	Neth	gk	Aug 2003	3	0	0	0
Myhill, Boaz	USA	gk	Dec 2003	113	0	5	0
Leite, Sergio	Por	gk	Jun 2005	0	0	1	0
Marques, Rui	Ang	d	Mar 2006	1	0	0	0

IPSWICH TOWN (56)

Name	Born	Pos	From	LgAp	LgG	OthAp	OthG
Havenga, Willie	SA	f	Jan 1952	19	3	0	0
Pickett, Reg (Brit)	Ind	wh	Jul 1957	140	3	6	0
Baker, Gerry	USA	f	Dec 1963	135	58	16	8
Viljoen, Colin	SA	m	Mar 1967	303+2	45	59+3	9
Twamley, Bruce	Can	fb	Oct 1969	2	0	0	0
Butcher, Terry (Eng)	Sing	d	Aug 1976	271	16	80	5
Muhren, Arnold	Neth	m	Aug 1978	161	21	53	8
Thijssen, Frans	Neth	m	Feb 1979	123+2	10	44+1	6
D'Avray, Mich (Eng)	SA	f	May 1979	170+41	37	29+10	9
Zondervan, Romeo (Neth)	Sur	m	Mar 1984	270+4	13	37+2	5
Bernal, Andy	Aus	d	Sep 1987	4+5	0	0	0
Wilson, Ulrich (Neth)	Sur	d	Dec 1987	5+1	0	0	0
Baltacha, Sergei (Ukr)	USSR	d	Jan 1989	22+6	1	1	0
Cheetham, Mike	Neth	m	Oct 1988	1+3	0	0+1	0
Forrest, Craig	Can	gk	Aug 1988	263	0	35	0
Bozinoski, Vlado (Aus)	Mac	m	Dec 1992	3+6	0	1+2	0
Guentchev, Bontcho	Bul	m	Dec 1992	39+22	6	12+2	5
Petterson, Andy (1)	Aus	gk	Mar 1993	1	0	0	0
Gregory, Neil (Brit)	Zam	f	Aug 1994	18+27	9	3+5	0
Norfolk, Lee	NZ	m	Jul 1994	1+2	0	0	0
Paz, Adrian	Uru	f	Sep 1994	13+4	1	0+1	0
Taricco, Mauricio	Arg	fb	Sep 1994	134+3	4	30	3
Thomsen, Claus	Den	m	Jun 1994	77+4	7	13	1
Petterson, Andy (2)	Aus	gk	Sep 1995	1	0	0	0
Uhlenbeek, Gus (Neth)	Sur	d	Aug 1995	77+12	4	12+7	0
Gudmundsson, Niklas	Swe	f	Mar 1997	2+6	2	1+1	1
Jean, Earl	StL	f	Dec 1996	0+1	0	0	0
Petta, Bobby	Neth	m	Jun 1996	55+15	9	16+3	0
Johnson, David	Jam	f	Nov 1997	121+10	55	27	7
Stein, Mark (Eng)	SA	f	Aug 1997	6+1	2	3+1	1
Abou, Samassi (Fr)	IvCo	f	Dec 1998	5	1	0	0
Holster, Marco	Neth	m	Jul 1998	1+9	0	0+2	0
Thetis, Manuel	Fr	d	Sep 1998	44+3	2	9+1	1
Wilnis, Fabian (Neth)	Sur	d	Jan 1999	227+21	6	34+5	0

Name	Born	Pos	From	LgAp	LgG	OthAp	OthG
Axeldahl, Jonas	Swe	f	Jul 1999	1+15	0	0+4	0
Reuser, Martijn	Neth	f	Jun 2000	42+49	14	11+12	5
Abidallah, Nabil	Neth	m	Jul 2000	0+2	0	0+1	0
Hreidarsson, Hermann	Ice	d	Aug 2000	101+1	2	26	1
Karic, Amir	Slo	d	Sep 2000	0	0	0+3	0
Gaardsoe, Thomas	Den	m	Aug 2001	40+1	5	5+3	2
George, Finidi	Nig	f	Aug 2001	24+11	7	6+5	1
Counago, Pablo	Sp	f	May 2001	51+48	31	18+4	5
Le Pen, Ulrich	Fr	m	Nov 2001	0+1	0	0+2	0
Peralta, Sixto	Arg	m	Aug 2001	16+6	3	5+2	2
Sereni, Matteo	It	gk	Aug 2001	25	0	8	0
Diallo, Drissa (Gui)	Mau	m	Jun 2003	39+6	0	4	0
Santos, Georges (CVI)	Fr	m	Jul 2003	28+6	1	2	0
Bart-Williams, Chris (Brit)	SiLe	m	Sep 2003	23+3	2	1+1	0
Kuqi, Shefki (Fin)	Alb	f	Sep 2003	69+10	30	5+4	2
De Vos, Jason	Can	d	May 2004	86	6	5	0
Karbassiyoon, Danny	USA	f	Dec 2004	3+2	0	1	0
Juan, Jimmy	Fr	m	Jan 2005	24+10	5	1+1	0
Peters, Jaime	Can	m	Jul 2005	4+9	0	1	0
Sito, Castro	Sp	d	Aug 2005	31+7	0	1+1	0
Fish, Mark	SA	d	Aug 2005	1	0	0	0
Brekke-Skard, Vemund	Nor	m	Jan 2006	2+1	0	0	0
Fuller, Ricardo	Jam	f	Feb 2006	3	2	0	0

KIDDERMINSTER HARRIERS (13)

Name	Born	Pos	From	LgAp	LgG	OthAp	OthG
Skovbjerg, Thomas	Den	m	Aug 1999	7+5	1	0	0
Shail, Mark (Brit)	Swe	d	Jul 2000	40	1	5	0
Kerr, Dylan (Brit)	Mal	d	Sep 2000	0+1	0	0	0
Medou-Otye, Parfait	Cam	d	Nov 2000	18+1	0	1	0
Joy, Ian	USA	d	Aug 2001	15+7	0	0+1	0
Sall, Abdou	Sen	d	Aug 2001	50+2	2	4	1
Henriksen, Bo	Den	f	Nov 2001	74+10	30	7+3	0
Christiansen, Jesper	Den	f	Jan 2003	22+16	1	4+1	0
Antoine-Curier, Mickael	Fr	f	Sep 2003	0+1	0	0	0
Advice-Desruisseaux, Frederic	Fr	m	Jul 2004	9	0	1	0
Diop, Youssou	Sen	f	Aug 2004	7+3	0	0+1	0
Matias, Pedro	Sp	m	Nov 2004	4+1	1	0	0
Cozic, Bertrand	Fr	m	Jan 2005	13+2	0	0	0

LEEDS UNITED (49)

Name	Born	Pos	From	LgAp	LgG	OthAp	OthG
Armand, Jack (Brit)	Ind	f	Dec 1922	74	23	5	1
Hodgson, Gordon (Eng)	SA	f	Mar 1937	82	51	4	2
Miller, George	SA	f	Nov 1950	13	1	1	0
Stewart, Gordon	SA	f	Oct 1951	9	2	2	0
Hastie, Ken	SA	f	Aug 1952	4	2	0	0
Francis, Gerry	SA	w	Jul 1957	48	9	4	0
Johanneson, Albert	SA	w	Apr 1961	170+2	48	27+1	19
Sabella, Alex	Arg	m	Jun 1980	22+1	2	4	0
Blake, Noel (Brit)	Jam	d	Jul 1988	51	4	6+1	0
Kerr, Dylan (Brit)	Mal	d	Feb 1989	6+7	0	3	0
Dorigo, Tony (Eng)	Aus	fb	Jun 1991	168+3	5	35+1	0
Cantona, Eric	Fr	f	Feb 1992	18+10	9	6	2
Sharp, Kevin	Can	d	Oct 1992	11+6	0	0+1	0
Strandli, Frank	Nor	f	Jan 1993	5+9	2	1+1	0
Masinga, Phil	SA	f	Aug 1994	20+11	5	6+2	6

Name	Born	Pos	From	LgAp	LgG	OthAp	OthG
Radebe, Lucas	SA	d	Sep 1994	180+20	0	55+7	3
Yeboah, Tony	Gha	f	Jan 1995	44+3	24	17+2	8
Brolin, Tomas	Swe	m	Nov 1995	17+2	4	3+3	0
Kewell, Harry	Aus	m	Dec 1995	169+12	45	58+3	18
Knarvik, Tommy	Nor	m	Nov 1996	0	0	0+1	0
Halle, Gunnar	Nor	d	Dec 1996	65+5	4	13+2	0
Molenaar, Robert	Neth	d	Jan 1997	47+4	5	13+1	1
Laurent, Pierre	Fr	f	Mar 1997	2+2	0	0	0
Haaland, Alf-Inge	Nor	m	Jul 1997	57+17	8	15+3	0
Hasselbaink, Jimmy (Neth)	Sur	f	Jul 1997	66+3	34	18	8
Ribeiro, Bruno	Por	m	Jul 1997	35+7	4	8+2	2
Hiden, Martin	Aut	d	Feb 1998	25+1	0	6	0
Wijnhard, Clyde (Neth)	Sur	f	Jul 1998	11+7	3	3+4	1
Korsten, Willem	Neth	f	Jan 1999	4+3	2	2+1	0
Bakke, Eirik	Nor	m	Jul 1999	114+27	8	47+4	12
Hay, Danny	NZ	d	Aug 1999	2+2	0	1+1	0
Dacourt, Olivier	Fr	m	Jul 2000	53+4	3	25	0
Viduka, Mark	Aus	f	Jul 2000	126+4	59	36	13
Burns, Jacob	Aus	m	Aug 2000	5+1	0	4+1	0
McMaster, Jamie	Aus	m	Sep 2002	0+11	0	1+1	0
Lucic, Teddy	Swe	d	Oct 2002	16+1	1	3+1	0
Okon, Paul	Aus	d	Nov 2002	15	0	6	0
Bravo, Raul	Sp	d	Feb 2003	5	0	1	0
Camara, Zoumana	Fr	d	Jul 2003	13	1	2	0
Chapuis, Cyril	Fr	f	Aug 2003	0+1	0	1+1	0
Domi, Didier	Fr	d	Aug 2003	9+3	0	0+2	0
Olembe, Saloman	Cam	m	Aug 2003	8+4	0	2	0
Sakho, Lamine	Sen	f	Aug 2003	9+8	1	1+1	0
Roque, Junior	Bra	d	Sep 2003	5	0	2	2
Einarsson, Gylfi	Ice	m	Jan 2005	12+6	1	3+1	0
Griffit, Leandre	Fr	m	Jan 2005	0+1	0	0	0
Lewis, Eddie	USA	m	Jun 2005	43+1	5	4+1	1
Marques, Rui	Ang	d	Jul 2005	0	0	1	0
Griffiths, Joel	Aus	m	Jan 2006	0+2	0	0	0
LEICESTER CITY (39)							
Osborne, Reg (Eng)	SA	fb	Feb 1923	240	2	9	0
Callachan, Harry (Brit)	Ind	fb	Sep 1929	3	0	0	0
Mandy, Aubrey	SA	gk	Oct 1929	3	0	0	0
Carr, Everton	Ant	fb	Jan 1979	11+1	0	2	0
Lee, Alan (Brit)	Ger	w	Feb 1979	6	0	0	0
Hazell, Bob (Eng)	Jam	d	Sep 1983	41	2	5	0
Christensen, Tommy	Den	f	Nov 1985	1+1	0	0	0
D'Avray, Mich (Eng)	SA	f	Feb 1987	3	0	0	0
Rantanen, Jari	Fin	f	Sep 1987	10+3	3	2+1	1
Osvold, Kjetil	Nor	m	Dec 1987	3+1	0	0	0
Oldfield, David (Eng)	Aus	m/f	Jan 1990	163+25	26	20+5	4
Corica, Steve	Aus	m	Aug 1995	16	2	2	0
Rolling, Franck	Fr	d	Sep 1995	18	0	5+1	0
Kalac, Zeljko	Aus	gk	Oct 1995	1	0	1+1	0
Kaamark, Pontus	Swe	d	Nov 1995	60+5	0	11+1	0
Keller, Kasey	USA	gk	Aug 1996	99	0	27	0
Lenhart, Sascha	Ger	m	Sep 1996	0	0	0+1	0
Arphexad, Pegguy (Fr)	Guad	gk	Aug 1997	17+4	0	7+1	0

Name	Born	Pos	From	LgAp	LgG	OthAp	OthG
Zagorakis, Theo	Grk	m	Feb 1998	34+16	3	11+7	0
Gunnlaugsson, Arnie	Ice	m	Feb 1999	10+20	3	3+7	1
Mancini, Roberto	It	f	Jan 2001	3+1	0	1	0
Laursen, Jacob	Den	d/m	Jan 2002	10	0	0	0
Petrescu, Tomi	Fin	f	May 2003	0+1	0	0	0
Nalis, Lilian	Fr	m	Jul 2003	43+16	6	3+4	0
Priet, Nicolas	Fr	d	Jul 2003	0	0	0+1	0
Dabizas, Nicos	Grk	d	Jan 2004	51	1	6	1
Freund, Steffen	Ger	m	Feb 2004	13+1	0	0	0
Tiatto, Danny	Aus	d	Jul 2004	36+12	2	7	0
Wesolowski, James	Aus	m	Jul 2004	3+2	0	0	0
Gudjonsson, Joey	Ice	m	Aug 2004	66+11	10	12	1
De Vries, Mark (Neth)	Sur	f	Jan 2005	29+16	7	6+4	3
Hirschfeld, Lars	Can	gk	Jan 2005	1	0	0	0
Kisnorbo, Patrick	Aus	m	Apr 2005	36+1	1	2+2	0
Henderson, Paul	Aus	gk	May 2005	14+1	0	3	0
Sylla, Mohammed (Gui)	IvCo	d	Jun 2005	24+4	0	1+1	0
Gerrbrand, Patrik	Swe	d	Jul 2005	14+3	0	3	0
Johansson, Nils-Eric	Swe	d	Jul 2005	39	0	6	1
Hammond, Elvis	Gha	f	Aug 2005	15+18	3	4+1	0
Hume, Iain	Can	f	Aug 2005	28+9	9	1	0

LEYTON ORIENT (35)

Name	Born	Pos	From	LgAp	LgG	OthAp	OthG
Van Den Eynden, Ike	Bel	ch	Feb 1914	12	0	0	0
Higginbotham, Harry	Aus	f	Feb 1923	19	1	0	0
Ashton, Hubert (Brit)	Ind	fb	Aug 1926	5	0	0	0
Tricker, Reg (Brit)	Ind	f	Feb 1929	131	60	6	3
Gerula, Stan	Pol	gk	May 1948	30	0	1	0
Burgess, Mike	Can	f/ch	Jul 1953	31	12	5	2
Crossan, Errol	Can	w	Jan 1961	8	2	2	0
Heppolett, Ricky (Brit)	Ind	m	Dec 1972	113+10	9	0	0
Chiedozie, John	Nig	w	Apr 1977	131+14	20	15	3
Zoricich, Chris	NZ	d	Feb 1990	53+9	1	6+3	0
Bart-Williams, Chris (Brit)	SiLe	m	Jul 1990	34+2	2	4	0
Okai, Stephen (Brit)	Gha	m	Apr 1992	11+14	4	2+2	0
Kitchen, Sam (Brit)	Ger	d	Aug 1992	35+8	1	6	0
Ayorinde, Sammy	Nig	f	Apr 1996	7+6	2	2+1	0
Riches, Steve	Aus	m	Sep 1996	2+3	0	0	0
Heidenstrom, Bjorn	Nor	d/m	Dec 1996	3+1	0	0	0
Walschaerts, Wim	Bel	m	Jul 1998	120+5	9	22+1	2
McDougald, Junior (Brit)	USA	f	Oct 1998	3+5	0	1+1	0
Simba, Amara	Fr	f	Oct 1998	27+10	13	8+4	1
Omoyimni, Manny	Nig	f	Mar 1999	3+1	1	0	0
Harris, Andy (Brit)	SA	m	Jul 1999	143+6	2	21+1	0
Brkovic, Ahmet	Cro	m	Oct 1999	59+10	8	7+4	2
Garcia, Richard	Aus	f	Aug 2000	18	4	3	0
Cadiou, Frederic	Fr	f	Oct 2000	0+3	0	0	0
Mansley, Chad	Aus	f	Nov 2000	0+1	0	0+1	0
Opara, Kelechi	Nig	f	Dec 2000	3+3	0	2	0
Vasseur, Emmanuel	Fr	m	Jan 2001	0+2	0	0	0
Opinel, Sacha	Fr	d	Feb 2001	9+2	1	0	0
Pinamonte, Lorenzo	It	f	Feb 2001	5+6	2	0	0
Forge, Nicolas	Fr	d	Mar 2001	1	0	0	0
Forbes, Boniek	GuB	f	Sep 2002	0+13	0	1+2	0

Name	Born	Pos	From	LgAp	LgG	OthAp	OthG
Miller, Justin	SA	d	Sep 2002	123+9	3	18	1
Zakuani, Gaby	DRC	d	Mar 2003	84+3	3	11	0
Harnwell, Jamie	Aus	d	Jul 2003	1+2	0	0	0
Echanomi, Efe	Nig	f	Dec 2004	4+30	8	2+1	0

LINCOLN CITY (20)

Name	Born	Pos	From	LgAp	LgG	OthAp	OthG
Dwane, Eddie (Brit)	Mal	wh	Jul 1920	46	2	2	0
Killin, Roy	Can	fb	Aug 1952	7	0	3	0
Houghton, Bud (Brit)	Ind	f	Oct 1963	54	22	7	3
Dillsworth, Eddie	SL	wh	Mar 1967	2	0	0	0
Coker, Ade	Nig	f	Dec 1974	6	1	1	0
Bowery, Bert	StK	f	Feb 1976	2+2	1	0	0
Cunningham, Tony (Brit)	Jam	f	May 1979	111+12	32	18+1	8
Kelly, Errington	StV	w	Jan 1983	0+2	0	0	0
Casey, Paul (Brit)	Ger	d/m	Mar 1988	44+5	4	4	0
Carmichael, Matt (Brit)	Sing	f	Aug 1989	113+20	18	13+2	1
Bos, Gijsbert	Neth	m	Mar 1996	28+6	6	7	4
Grobbelaar, Bruce (Zim)	SA	gk	Dec 1998	2	0	0	0
Phillips, David (Brit)	Ger	m	Mar 1999	15+2	0	1+1	0
Agogo, Junior	Gha	f	Dec 1999	3	1	0	0
Stergiopoulos, Marcus (Grk)	Aus	m	Aug 2000	2+5	0	1+1	1
Pearce, Allan	NZ	f	Dec 2002	9+10	1	0+2	0
Rayner, Simon	Can	gk	Aug 2004	4	0	1	0
Ipoua, Guy	Cam	f	Feb 2005	0+6	0	0	0
Asamoah, Derek	Gha	f	Mar 2005	27+8	2	5+3	0
Molango, Maheta (It)	Swit	f	Jul 2005	5+5	0	2+2	1

LIVERPOOL (71)

Name	Born	Pos	From	LgAp	LgG	OthAp	OthG
Lester, Hugh	USA	wh	Aug 1911	2	0	0	0
Hodgson, Gordon (Eng)	SA	f	Nov 1925	359	232	19	8
Riley, Arthur	SA	gk	Jul 1925	322	0	16	0
Carr, Lance	SA	w	Aug 1933	31	8	2	0
Nieuwenhuys, Berry	SA	w	Sep 1933	239	74	21	5
Kemp, Dirk	SA	gk	Jul 1936	30	0	3	0
Van Den Berg, Herman	SA	w	Jul 1937	22	4	0	0
Priday, Bob	SA	w	Dec 1945	34	6	6	1
Gerhardt, Hugh	SA	f	Aug 1952	6	0	0	0
Rudham, Doug	SA	gk	Nov 1954	63	0	3	0
Cohen, Avi	Isr	fb	Jul 1979	16+2	1	5+1	0
Grobbelaar, Bruce (Zim)	SA	gk	Mar 1981	440	0	169	0
Johnston Craig, (Aus)	SA	w	Apr 1981	165+25	30	59+12	9
Molby, Jan	Den	m	Aug 1984	195+23	44	55+8	14
Barnes, John (Eng)	Jam	f	Jun 1987	310+4	84	89	22
Hysen, Glenn	Swe	d	Jul 1989	70+2	2	19	1
Rosenthal, Ronny	Isr	f	Jun 1990	32+42	21	8+13	1
Kozma, Istvan	Hun	m	Feb 1992	3+3	0	0+3	0
Piechnik, Torben	Den	d	Sep 1992	16+1	0	7	0
Bjornebe, Stig Inge	Nor	d	Dec 1992	132+7	2	43+2	2
Berger, Patrik	CzRep	f	Aug 1996	106+42	28	30+17	7
Kvarme, Bjorn Tore	Nor	d	Jan 1997	39+6	0	9	0
Leonhardsen, Oyvind	Nor	m	Jun 1997	34+3	7	8+4	0
Riedle, Karl-Heinz	Ger	f	Aug 1997	34+26	11	8+8	4
Friedel, Brad	USA	gk	Dec 1997	25	0	5+1	0
Dundee, Sean	SA	d	Jun 1998	0+3	0	0+2	0
Heggem, Vegard	Nor	d	Jul 1998	38+16	3	8+3	0

Name	Born	Pos	From	LgAp	LgG	OthAp	OthG
Ferri, Jean-Michel	Fr	d/m	Dec 1998	0+2	0	0	0
Kippe, Frode	Nor	d	Jan 1999	0	0	0+2	0
Song, Rigobert	Cam	d	Jan 1999	27+7	0	3+1	0
Traore, Djimi	Fr	d	Feb 1999	72+16	0	47+5	1
Camara, Titi	Gui	f	Jun 1999	22+11	9	2+2	1
Westerveld, Sander	Neth	gk	Jun 1999	75	0	26	0
Hamann, Dietmar	Ger	m	Jul 1999	174+17	8	79+12	3
Henchcz, Stephane	Swit	d	Jul 1999	132+3	0	89+1	0
Hyypia, Sami	Fin	d	Jul 1999	251+1	18	118	8
Meijer, Erik	Neth	f	Jul 1999	7+17	0	3	2
Smicer, Vladimir	CzRep	m	Jul 1999	69+52	10	41+22	9
Diomede, Bernard	Fr	m	Jul 2000	1+1	0	3	0
Arphexad, Pegguy (Fr)	Guad	gk	Jul 2000	1+1	0	4	0
Babbel, Markus	Ger	d	Jul 2000	42	3	27+1	3
Ziege, Christian	Ger	m	Aug 2000	11+5	1	9+7	1
Vignal, Gregory	Fr	d	Sep 2000	7+4	0	7+2	0
Biscan, Igor	Cro	m	Dec 2000	50+22	2	31+18	1
Litmanen, Jari	Fin	f	Jan 2001	12+14	5	7+10	4
Riise, John Arne	Nor	d	Jun 2001	145+27	20	79+5	8
Dudek, Jerzy	Pol	gk	Aug 2001	124+1	0	54+1	0
Anelka, Nicolas	Fr	f	Dec 2001	13+7	4	2	1
Baros, Milan	CzRep	f	Dec 2001	45+23	19	22+18	8
Xavier, Abel (Por)	Moz	d	Jan 2002	13+1	1	6	1
Le Tallec, Anthony	Fr	f	Jul 2002	5+12	0	8+7	1
Sinama-Pongolle, Florent (Fr)	Reu	f	Jul 2002	12+26	4	10+14	5
Cheyrou, Bruno	Fr	m	Aug 2002	17+14	2	11+6	3
Diao, Salif	Sen	m	Aug 2002	19+18	1	16+8	2
Diouf, El Hadji	Sen	f	Aug 2002	41+14	3	20+5	3
Kewell, Harry	Aus	m	Jul 2003	73+8	11	26+13	4
Whitbread, Zak	USA	d	Jul 2003	0	0	6+1	0
Luzi, Patrice	Fr	gk	Sep 2003	0+1	0	0	0
Cisse, Djibril	Fr	f	Jul 2004	29+20	13	13+16	11
Josemi	Sp	d	Jul 2004	16+5	0	11+2	0
Alonso, Xabi	Sp	m	Aug 2004	49+10	5	23+1	3
Garcia, Luis	Sp	m	Aug 2004	41+19	15	26+6	9
Nunez, Antonio	Sp	m	Aug 2004	8+10	0	5+4	0
Morientes, Fernando	Sp	f	Jan 2005	32+9	8	14+5	4
Pellegrino, Mauricio	Arg	d	Jan 2005	11+1	0	1	0
Barragan, Antonio	Sp	d	Jul 2005	0	0	0+1	0
Reina, Jose	Sp	gk	Jul 2005	33	0	18	0
Sissoko, Mohamed (Mli)	Fr	f	Jul 2005	21+5	0	14+3	0
Zenden, Bolo	Neth	m	Jul 2005	5+2	2	6+4	0
Agger, Daniel	Den	d	Jan 2006	4	0	0	0
Kromkamp, Jan	Neth	d	Jan 2006	6+7	0	1+3	0

LUTON TOWN (47)

Name	Born	Pos	From	LgAp	LgG	OthAp	OthG
Higginbotham, Harry	Aus	f	Jul 1920	80	26	8	4
Bookman, Louis (Brit)	Lith	w	Aug 1920	72	4	5	1
Tricker, Reg (Brit)	Ind	f	Jul 1924	4	0	1	0
Edwards, Gerald	HK	gk	Jan 1931	2	0	0	0
Mills, Arthur	Ind	w	Jul 1932	37	14	4	0
Gibson, Jock	USA	fb	Jul 1933	3	0	0	0
Preedy, Charlie (Brit)	Ind	gk	Aug 1934	5	0	0	0
Shanks, Wally (Brit)	Mal	wh	Dec 1946	264	6	11	0

Name	Born	Pos	From	LgAp	LgG	OthAp	OthG
Arnison, Joseph	SA	f	Aug 1948	44	19	2	2
Havenga, Willie	SA	f	May 1950	18	6	1	1
Davies, Roy	SA	w	May 1951	150	24	16	2
McEwan, Peter	SA	f	Feb 1954	26	11	0	0
Stein, Brian (Eng) (1)	SA	f	Oct 1977	378+10	126	63	21
Antic, Raddy	Yug	m	Jul 1980	54+40	9	5+3	1
Nwajiobi, Emeka	Nig	f	Dec 1983	59+13	17	11+4	3
Stein, Mark (Eng) (1)	SA	f	Jan 1984	41+13	19	13+1	3
McEvoy, Ricky (Brit)	Gib	m	Aug 1985	0+1	0	0	0
Oldfield, David (Eng) (1)	Aus	m/f	May 1986	21+8	4	4+3	2
McDonough, Darron (Brit)	Bel	d	Sep 1986	88+17	5	19+2	2
Wegerle, Roy (USA)	SA	f	Jul 1988	39+6	10	11	8
Petterson, Andy	Aus	gk	Dec 1988	16+3	0	2	0
Elstrup, Lars	Den	f	Aug 1989	50+10	19	7	7
Stein, Brian (Eng) (2)	SA	f	Jul 1991	32+7	3	2+1	0
Sommer, Jurgen	USA	gk	Sep 1991	82	0	17	0
Aunger, Geoff	Can	d/m	Sep 1993	5	1	0	0
Marshall, Dwight (Brit)	Jam	f	Jul 1994	90+38	28	16+4	7
Oldfield, David (Eng) (2)	Aus	m/f	Jul 1995	99+18	18	15	5
Guentchev, Bontcho	Bul	m	Aug 1995	40+22	10	7+4	0
Feuer, Ian	USA	gk	Sep 1995	97	0	15	0
Vilstrup, Johnny	Den	m	Sep 1995	6+1	0	0	0
Riseth, Vidar	Nor	d/m	Oct 1995	6+5	0	0	0
Grant, Kim	Gha	f	Mar 1996	18+17	5	4+3	2
Bacque, Herve	Fr	f	Aug 1998	2+5	0	1+2	0
Kandol, Tresor (Brit)	DRC	f	Sep 1998	9+12	3	3+1	2
Zahana-Oni, Landry	IvCo	f	Jan 1999	4+5	0	0	0
Stein, Mark (Eng) (2)	SA	f	Jul 2000	19+11	3	4+1	1
Breitenfelder, Friedrich	Aut	m	Aug 2000	2+3	0	0	0
Helin, Petri	Fin	d	Nov 2000	23	1	3	0
Karlsen, Kent	Nor	d	Nov 2000	4+2	0	2	0
Coyne, Chris	Aus	d	Sep 2001	178+7	13	20	2
Valois, Jean-Louis	Fr	m	Sep 2001	32+2	6	0	0
Brkovic, Ahmet	Cro	m	Oct 2001	148+25	28	21	7
Neilson, Alan (Wal)	Ger	d	Feb 2002	46+11	1	3+3	0
Deeney, David (Brit)	Zim	d	Aug 2002	0	0	1+1	1
Berthelin, Cedric	Fr	gk	Oct 2002	9	0	0	0
Hirschfeld, Lars	Can	gk	Feb 2003	5	0	0	0
Hyldgaard, Morten	Den	gk	Jan 2004	18	0	0	0
Seremet, Dino	Slo	gk	Jul 2004	6+1	0	2	0
Edwards, Carlos	Trin	m	May 2005	38+4	2	3	0
Heikkinen, Markus	Fin	d	Jul 2005	38+1	2	1	0

MACCLESFIELD TOWN (8)

Name	Born	Pos	From	LgAp	LgG	OthAp	OthG
Matias, Pedro	Sp	m	Dec 1998	21+1	2	1	0
Abbey, George	Nig	d	Aug 1999	79+21	1	12+5	0
Tereskinas, Andrejus	Lith	d	Nov 2000	0+1	0	0	0
Lightbourne, Kyle	Ber	f	Jul 2001	61+12	15	6	3
Nash, Martin	Can	m	Jan 2003	1+4	0	0	0
Myhill, Boaz	USA	gk	Aug 2003	15	0	1	0
Fayadh, Jassim	Irq	m	Aug 2004	0+1	0	0+1	0
Wijnhard, Clyde (Neth)	Sur	f	Oct 2005	19+1	8	6	4

MAIDSTONE UNITED (3)

Name	Born	Pos	From	LgAp	LgG	OthAp	OthG
Henry, Liburd	Dom	f	Jun 1990	61+6	9	3+1	1

Name	Born	Pos	From	LgAp	LgG	OthAp	OthG
Hesford, Iain (Eng)	Zam	gk	Aug 1991	42	1	4	0
Richards, Carl (Eng)	Jam	f	Oct 1991	4	2	0	0
MANCHESTER CITY (72)							
Bowman, WW	Can	ch	Feb 1893	47	3	2	0
McDowall, Les (Brit)	Ind	ch	Mar 1938	120	8	9	0
Trautmann, Bert	Ger	gk	Nov 1949	508	0	37	0
Baker, Gerry	USA	f	Nov 1960	37	14	2	0
Viljoen, Colin	SA	m	Aug 1978	25+2	0	10+1	1
Deyna, Kazimierz	Pol	f	Nov 1978	34+4	12	4+1	1
Stepanovic, Dragoslav	Yug	d	Aug 1979	14+1	0	4	0
Hareide, Aage	Nor	d	Oct 1981	17+7	0	0+1	0
Golac, Ivan	Yug	fb	Mar 1983	2	0	0	0
Cunningham, Tony (Brit)	Jam	f	Jul 1984	16+2	1	5+1	3
Phillips, David (Brit)	Ger	m	Aug 1984	81	13	13	0
Oldfield, David (Eng)	Aus	m/f	Mar 1989	18+8	6	2+1	2
Lomas, Steve (N Ire)	Ger	m	Jan 1991	102+9	8	25+1	3
Hoekman, Danny	Neth	m	Oct 1991	0+1	0	0+2	0
Vonk, Michel	Neth	d	Jun 1992	87+4	4	9+3	2
Ingebrigtsen, Kaare	Nor	m	Jan 1993	4+11	0	2	3
Groenendijk, Alfons	Neth	m	Jul 1993	9	0	3	0
Karl, Steffen	Ger	d/m	Mar 1994	4+2	1	0	0
Rosler, Uwe	Ger	f	Feb 1994	141+11	50	24+1	14
Whitley, Jim (N Ire)	Zam	m	Aug 1994	27+11	0	5+2	1
Gaudino, Maurizio	Ger	m	Dec 1994	17+3	3	4+1	1
Immel, Eike	Ger	gk	Aug 1995	42	0	8	0
Kinkladze, Georgi	Geo	m	Aug 1995	105+1	20	15	2
Ekelund, Ronnie	Den	f	Dec 1995	2+2	0	1+1	0
Frontzeck, Michael	Ger	d	Jan 1996	19+4	0	2	0
Whitley, Jeff (N Ire)	Zam	m	Feb 1996	96+27	8	14+3	0
Kavelashvili, Mikhail	Geo	f	Mar 1996	9+19	3	0+1	0
Mazzarelli, Giuseppe	Swit	m	Mar 1996	0+2	0	0	0
Wiekens, Gerard	Neth	d	Jul 1997	169+15	10	27+3	0
Van Blerk, Jason	Aus	fb	Aug 1997	10+9	0	0+2	0
Shelia, Murtaz	Geo	d	Nov 1997	15	2	2	0
Tskhadadze, Kakhaber	Geo	d	Feb 1998	12	2	1	1
Goater, Shaun	Ber	f	Mar 1998	164+20	84	25+3	19
Tiatto, Danny	Aus	d	Jul 1998	112+27	3	16+3	1
Allsopp, Danny	Aus	f	Aug 1998	3+26	4	0+8	1
Killen, Chris	NZ	f	Mar 1999	0+3	0	0	0
Dunfield, Terry	Can	m	May 1999	0+1	0	0	0
Etuhu, Dixon	Nig	m	Dec 1999	11+1	0	1	0
Haaland, Alf-Inge	Nor	m	Jun 2000	35+3	3	8+1	0
Wanchope, Paulo	CoRi	f	Aug 2000	51+13	27	8+3	2
Weah, George	Lbr	f	Aug 2000	5+2	1	2	3
Charvet, Laurent	Fr	d	Oct 2000	19+4	0	0+1	0
Kanchelskis, Andrei	Urk	w	Jan 2001	7+3	0	1	1
Ostenstad, Egil	Nor	f	Feb 2001	1+3	0	0	0
Berkovic, Eyal	Isr	m	Jul 2001	48+8	7	8+3	2
Colosimo, Simon	Aus	d	Jul 2001	0+6	0	1	0
Benarbia, Ali	Alg	m	Sep 2001	59+12	11	7	0
Mettomo, Lucien	Cam	d	Sep 2001	20+7	1	3+1	0
Negouai, Christian (Fr)	Mart	m	Nov 2001	2+4	1	2+2	1
Jensen, Niclas	Den	m	Jan 2002	48+3	2	5	0

Name	Born	Pos	From	LgAp	LgG	OthAp	OthG
Toure, Alioune	Fr	f	Sep 2001	0+1	0	0+1	0
Jihai, Sun	Chn	d	Feb 2002	76+27	3	18	1
Ellegaard, Kevin	Den	gk	Jul 2002	2+2	0	3	0
Anelka, Nicolas	Fr	f	Aug 2002	87+2	38	14	8
Distin, Sylvain	Fr	d	Aug 2002	141	3	22	1
Foe, Marc-Vivien	Cam	m	Aug 2002	35	9	3	0
Schmeichel, Peter	Den	gk	Aug 2002	29	0	2	0
Bischoff, Mikkel	Den	d	Sep 2002	1	0	1	0
Arason, Arni	Ice	gk	Jan 2003	0	0	2	0
Belmadi, Djamel (Alg)	Fr	m	Jan 2003	2+6	0	0	0
Sommeil, David (Fr)	Guad	d	Jan 2003	47+2	4	7+2	1
Tarnat, Michael	Ger	m	Jun 2003	32	3	9	1
Bosvelt, Paul	Neth	m	Jul 2003	50+3	2	11+1	1
Reyna, Claudio	USA	m	Aug 2003	57+5	4	7+2	0
Sibierski, Antoine	Fr	m	Aug 2003	64+28	11	10+5	4
Van Buyten, Daniel	Bel	d	Jan 2004	5	0	1	0
Onuoha, Nedum	Nig	d	Aug 2004	19+9	0	3	0
Waterreus, Ronald	Neth	gk	Aug 2004	0	0	2	0
Musampa, Kiki	DRC	m	Jan 2005	38+3	3	3+1	1
Hussein, Yasser	Qtr	m	Jan 2005	0	0	1	0
Riera, Albert	Sp	m	Jan 2006	12+3	1	4	0
Samaras, Giorgios	Grk	f	Jan 2006	10+4	4	2	1
MANCHESTER UNITED (51)							
Bell, Alec (Sco)	SA	wh	Jan 1903	278	10	28	0
Wilcox, Tom (Brit)	At sea	gk	Aug 1907	2	0	0	0
Hunter, George (Brit)	Ind	wh	Mar 1914	22	2	1	0
Mitten, Charlie (Brit)	Bur	w	Jan 1938	142	50	19	11
Sartori, Carlo	It	m	Feb 1965	26+13	4	14+2	2
Nicholl, Jimmy (N Ire)	Can	fb	Feb 1974	188+9	3	46+4	3
Jovanovic, Nikola	Yug	d	Jan 1980	20+1	4	5	0
Muhren, Arnold	Neth	m	Aug 1982	65+5	13	27	5
Olsen, Jesper	Den	f	Jul 1984	119+20	21	29+7	3
Sivebaek, John	Den	d	Feb 1986	29+2	1	3	0
Bosnich, Mark (1)	Aus	gk	Jun 1989	3	0	0	0
Kanchelskis, Andrei	Urk	w	Mar 1991	96+27	28	33+2	8
Schmeichel, Peter	Den	gk	Aug 1991	292	0	100	1
Cantona, Eric	Fr	f	Nov 1992	142+1	64	39	16
Prunier, William	Fr	d	Dec 1995	2	0	0	0
Poborsky, Karel	CzRep	m	Jul 1996	18+14	5	10+5	1
Johnsen, Ronny	Nor	d	Jul 1996	85+14	7	43+5	1
Solskjaer, Ole Gunnar	Nor	f	Jul 1996	142+74	85	60+59	32
Van der Gouw, Raimond	Neth	gk	Jul 1996	26+11	0	20+1	0
Cruyff, Jordi	Neth	m	Aug 1996	15+19	8	9+8	0
Nevland, Erik	Nor	f	Jul 1997	0+1	0	2+3	1
Berg, Henning	Nor	d	Aug 1997	49+17	2	29+4	1
Blomqvist, Jesper	Swe	m	Jul 1998	20+5	1	9+4	0
Stam, Jaap	Neth	d	Jul 1998	79	1	39+1	0
Yorke, Dwight	Trin	f	Aug 1998	80+16	48	37+13	16
Djordjic, Bojan (Swe)	Yug	m	Feb 1999	0+1	0	1	0
Bosnich, Mark (2)	Aus	gk	Jun 1999	23	0	8	0
Rachubka, Paul	USA	gk	Jul 1999	1	0	0+1	0
Fortune, Quinton	SA	m	Aug 1999	53+23	5	35+15	5
Silvestre, Mickael	Fr	d	Sep 1999	216+16	5	92+10	4

Name	Born	Pos	From	LgAp	LgG	OthAp	OthG
Taibi, Massimo	It	gk	Sep 1999	4	0	0	0
Barthez, Fabien	Fr	gk	Jun 2000	92	0	45	0
Veron, Juan Sebastian	Arg	m	Jul 2001	45+6	7	30+1	4
Van Nistelrooy, Ruud	Neth	f	Apr 2001	137+13	95	63+6	55
Blanc, Laurent	Fr	d	Aug 2001	44+4	1	27	3
Forlan, Diego	Uru	f	Jan 2002	23+40	10	14+21	7
Lopez, Ricardo	Sp	gk	Sep 2002	0+1	0	3+1	0
Timm, Mads	Den	f	Oct 2002	0	0	0+1	0
Bellion, David	Fr	f	Jul 2003	5+19	4	10+6	4
Djemba-Djemba, Eric	Cam	m	Jul 2003	13+7	0	14+5	2
Howard, Tim	USA	gk	Jul 2003	44+1	0	32	0
Kleberson	Bra	m	Aug 2003	16+4	2	8+2	0
Ronaldo, Cristiano	Por	m	Aug 2003	64+31	18	37+5	9
Saha, Louis	Fr	f	Jan 2004	28+17	15	13+8	9
Spector, Jonathan	USA	d	May 2004	2+1	0	2+3	0
Heinze, Gabriel	Arg	d	Jun 2004	28+2	1	15	2
Pique, Gerard	Sp	d	Oct 2004	1+2	0	4+3	0
Rossi, Giuseppe (It)	USA	f	Nov 2004	1+4	1	5+4	3
Van der Sar, Edwin	Neth	gk	Jun 2005	38	0	13	0
Park, Ji-Sung	SK	m	Jul 2005	23+10	1	4+7	1
Evra, Patrice (Fr)	Sen	d	Jan 2006	7+4	0	1+2	0
Vidic, Nemanja	SM	d	Jan 2006	9+2	0	2+2	0
MANSFIELD TOWN (19)							
Mitten, Charlie (Brit)	Bur	w	Feb 1956	100	25	6	2
Delapenha, Lindy	Jam	f	Jun 1958	115	27	5	0
Derko, Franco	It	fb	Jan 1965	1	0	0	0
Phillips, Brendon	Jam	m	Aug 1980	17	0	6	0
Blissett, Luther (Eng)	Jam	f	Dec 1993	4+1	1	0	0
Aspinall, Brendan	SA	d	Jul 1994	13+7	0	5+1	1
Carmichael, Matt (Brit)	Sing	f	Aug 1995	1	1	0	0
L'Helgoualch, Cyrille	Fr	m	Dec 1998	3+1	1	0	0
Camilieri-Gioia, Carlo	Bel	m	Sep 1999	0+2	0	0	0
Van Heusden, Arjan	Neth	gk	Sep 2002	5	0	0	0
Dimech, Luke	Mal	d	Aug 2003	36+9	1	7+1	0
D'Jaffo, Laurent	Fr	f	Mar 2004	4+4	1	0+3	0
Asamoah, Derek	Gha	f	Jul 2004	24+6	5	1+1	0
Ipoua, Guy	Cam	f	Oct 2004	4+1	0	0	0
Kitamirike, Joel	Uga	d	Dec 2004	7	0	0+1	0
Smeltz, Shane (NZ)	Ger	f	Jan 2005	1+4	0	0	0
Lambu, Goma	DRC	f	Feb 2005	1	0	0	0
Uhlenbeek, Gus (Neth)	Sur	d	Jun 2005	28+12	2	4	0
Hjelde Jon Olav	Nor	d	Aug 2005	30+1	1	3	0
MIDDLESBROUGH (49)							
Malan, Norman	SA	gk	Oct 1945	2	0	0	0
Ugolini, Rolando	It	gk	May 1948	320	0	15	0
Delapenha, Lindy	Jam	f	Apr 1950	260	90	10	3
Lightening, Arthur	SA	gk	Aug 1962	15	0	3	0
Chadwick, Dave (Brit)	Ind	w	Jul 1966	100+2	3	13+1	1
Johnston, Craig (Aus/Eng)	SA	w	Feb 1978	61+3	16	9+4	0
Jankovic, Bozo	Yug	f	Feb 1979	42+8	16	10+2	2
Otto, Heine	Neth	m	Aug 1981	163+3	24	21	4
Marshall, Dwight (Brit)	Jam	f	Mar 1993	0+3	0	0	0
Moreno, Jaime (1)	Bol	m	Sep 1994	8+13	1	3+1	0

Name	Born	Pos	From	LgAp	LgG	OthAp	OthG
Fuchs, Uwe	Ger	f	Jan 1995	13+2	9	0	0
Fjortoft, Jan Aage	Nor	f	Mar 1995	37+4	9	7+2	3
Juninho (1)	Bra	m	Oct 1995	54+2	14	18	3
Branco	Bra	f	Mar 1996	6+3	0	2	2
Emerson	Bra	m	Jun 1996	53	9	17	3
Ravanelli, Fabrizio	It	f	Jun 1996	35	17	15	15
Beck, Mikkel	Den	f	Sep 1996	66+25	24	19+6	7
Festa, Gianluca	It	d	Jan 1997	132+6	10	32+1	2
Kinder, Vladimir	Svk	d	Jan 1997	29+8	5	10+1	0
Schwarzer, Mark	Aus	gk	Feb 1997	297	0	68	0
Moreira, Fabio	Bra	m	Feb 1997	1	0	0	0
Moreno, Jaime (2)	Bol	m	Dec 1997	1+4	1	2	0
Branca, Marco	It	f	Feb 1998	11+1	9	2	1
Ricard, Hamilton	Col	f	Mar 1998	92+23	33	17+2	10
Juninho (2)	Bra	m	Sep 1999	24+4	4	5	1
Ziege, Christian	Ger	m	Aug 1999	29	6	4+1	1
Marinelli, Carlos	Arg	m	Oct 1999	18+25	3	6+4	1
Boksic, Alen (Cro)	Herz	f	Aug 2000	59+9	22	5+4	0
Job, Joseph-Desire (Cam)	Fr	f	Aug 2000	62+31	17	12+7	5
Jones, Brad	Aus	gk	Aug 2000	15	0	6+1	0
Karembeu, Christian (Fr)	Ncal	m	Aug 2000	31+2	4	2+1	0
Okon, Paul	Aus	d	Aug 2000	24+4	0	2	0
Nemeth, Szilard	Svk	f	Jul 2001	62+55	23	19+10	6
Wilkshire, Luke	Aus	m	Aug 2001	13+8	0	3	0
Queudrue, Franck	Fr	d	Oct 2001	145+5	11	42+6	1
Carbone, Benito	It	f	Feb 2002	13	1	0	0
Debeve, Mickael	Fr	m	Feb 2002	1+3	0	1+1	0
Boateng, George (Neth)	Gha	m	Aug 2002	113+1	5	30	1
Juninho (3)	Bra	m	Aug 2002	35+6	11	5+2	1
Maccarone, Massimo	It	f	Aug 2002	45+29	17	7+12	4
Geremi	Cam	d/m	Aug 2002	33	7	1	0
Vidmar, Tony	Aus	d	Sep 2002	9+3	0	3	0
Doriva, Guidoni	Bra	m	Apr 2003	56+23	0	27+3	1
Mendieta, Gaizka	Sp	m	Aug 2003	52+3	4	19+1	2
Zenden, Boudewyn	Neth	m	Aug 2003	67	9	19+2	6
Hasselbaink, Jimmy (Neth)	Sur	f	Jul 2004	48+10	23	26+4	11
Reiziger, Michael	Neth	d	Jul 2004	19+3	1	6+1	0
Viduka, Mark	Aus	f	Jul 2004	34+9	12	17+5	11
Pogatetz, Emanuel	Aut	d	Jun 2005	21+3	1	16+1	0
Yakubu, Ayegbeni	Nig	f	Jul 2005	29+5	13	13+9	6
Rochemback, Fabio	Bra	m	Aug 2005	22	2	8+1	1
Xavier, Abel (Por)	Moz	d	Aug 2005	4	0	2	0
MILLWALL (39)							
Kingsley, Alf	Bar	w	Sep 1923	44	2	3	0
Bryant, Billy	Bel	ch	Jul 1925	132	30	7	0
Brown, Lennox	SA	f	Nov 1935	1	0	0	0
Ackerman, Alf	SA	f	Jan 1959	81	35	3	0
Smethurst, Derek	SA	f	Sep 1971	66+4	9	7+2	4
Smit(h), Wilf	Ger	fb	Jan 1975	5	0	0	0
Granville, John	Trin	gk	Oct 1985	6	0	0	0
Salman, Danis (Eng)	Cyp	d	Aug 1986	85+8	4	12+1	1
Verveer, Etienne (Neth)	Sur	m	Dec 1991	46+10	7	6	2
Keller, Kasey	USA	gk	Feb 1992	176	0	24	0

Name	Born	Pos	From	LgAp	LgG	OthAp	OthG
Kerr, John (USA)	Can	f	Feb 1993	21+22	8	2+2	0
Murray, Bruce	USA	f	Aug 1993	7+6	2	0+1	1
Van Den Hauwe, Pat (Wal)	Bel	fb	Sep 1993	27	0	8	0
Van Blerk, Jason	Aus	fb	Sep 1994	68+5	2	11+1	0
Edwards, Alistair	Aus	f	Dec 1994	3+1	0	3+1	0
Oldfield, David (Eng)	Aus	m/f	Feb 1995	16+1	6	0	0
Iga, Andrew (Brit)	Uga	gk	Jun 1995	0+1	0	0	0
Fuchs, Uwe	Ger	f	Jul 1995	21+11	5	2+2	0
Neill, Lucas	Aus	d/m	Nov 1995	124+28	13	12+1	0
Kulkov, Vasili	Rus	d/m	Jan 1996	6	0	0	0
Yuran, Sergei	Ukr	f	Jan 1996	13	1	0	0
Cahill, Tim	Aus	m	Jul 1997	212+5	52	28+4	5
Grant, Kim	Gha	f	Aug 1997	35+20	11	3+1	1
Veart, Carl	Aus	m	Dec 1997	7+1	1	0	0
McDougald, Junior (Brit)	USA	f	Jul 1998	0+1	0	0	0
Kinet, Christophe	Bel	m	Feb 2000	39+28	7	6+7	1
Gueret, Willy (Fr)	Guad	gk	Jul 2000	13+2	0	5	0
Savarese, Giovanni	Ven	f	Jul 2001	0+1	0	0	0
Baltacha, Sergei Jnr (Sco)	Ukr	m	Jan 2003	1+1	0	0+1	0
Ashikodi, Moses	Nig	f	Feb 2003	0+5	0	0	0
Robinson, Trevor	Jam	m	Jul 2003	1+3	0	0	0
Fofana, Aboubaka	Fr	m	Aug 2003	9+7	0	0+1	0
Duarte, Juan M	Bra	d	Aug 2003	2+1	0	1	0
Peeters, Bob	Bel	f	Aug 2003	16+9	3	0	0
Serioux, Adrian	Can	d	Aug 2004	12+12	0	2	0
Simpson, Josh	Can	m	Aug 2004	30+13	2	4+1	0
Tessem, Jo	Nor	f	Sep 2004	11+1	1	1	0
Fangueiro, Carlos	Por	m	Aug 2005	1+8	0	0+3	1
Powel, Berry	Neth	f	Jan 2006	8+4	1	0	0

MILTON KEYNES DONS (formerly WIMBLEDON) (36)

Name	Born	Pos	From	LgAp	LgG	OthAp	OthG
Welch, Micky	Bar	f	Nov 1984	2+2	0	0	0
Young, Eric (Wal)	Sing	d	Jul 1987	96+3	9	19+1	1
Quamina, Mark	Guy	m/d	Jul 1988	1	0	0	0
Segers, Hans	Neth	gk	Sep 1988	265+2	0	48	0
Kruszynski, Detsi	Ger	m	Dec 1988	65+6	4	10+1	0
Leonhardsen, Oyvind	Nor	m	Nov 1994	73+3	13	24+2	3
Solbakken, Stale	Nor	m	Oct 1997	4+2	1	1+1	0
Pedersen, Tore	Nor	d	Jun 1999	6	0	0	0
Andersen, Trond	Nor	m	Aug 1999	136+10	6	21	2
Badir, Walid	Isr	m	Aug 1999	12+9	1	3+1	0
Andresen, Martin	Nor	m	Oct 1999	4+10	1	1+1	0
Hreidarsson, Hermann	Ice	d	Oct 1999	25	1	2	0
Lund, Andreas	Nor	f	Feb 2000	10+2	2	0	0
Karlsson, Par	Swe	m	Sep 2000	10+16	0	6	1
Nielsen, David	Den	f	Mar 2001	15+8	4	1	0
Feuer, Ian	USA	gk	Jun 2000	2+2	0	3	0
Mild, Hakan	Swe	m	Nov 2001	8+1	0	0	0
Herzig, Nico	Ger	m	Aug 2002	18+1	0	0	0
Volz, Moritz	Ger	d	Feb 2003	10	1	0	0
Jarrett, Albert	SiLe	m	Jul 2003	3+6	0	0+1	0
McDonald, Scott	Aus	f	Aug 2003	0+2	0	0	0
Ntimban-Zeh, Harry	Fr	d	Mar 2004	20+1	0	4+1	0
Oyedele, Shola	Nig	d	Mar 2004	29+8	0	4+1	0

Name	Born	Pos	From	LgAp	LgG	OthAp	OthG
Edds, Gareth	Aus	m	Jul 2004	69+11	8	13	2
Herve, Laurent	Fr	m	Jul 2004	15+5	0	5+1	0
Hornuss, Julien	Fr	f	Jul 2004	0+3	0	0+2	0
Rachubka, Paul	USA	gk	Aug 2004	4	0	0	0
Johnson, Richard	Aus	m	Oct 2004	2	0	0+1	0
Makofo, Serge	DRC	f	Nov 2004	0+1	0	0+1	1
Rizzo, Nicky	Aus	f	Nov 2004	28+19	4	6+2	1
Danze, Anthony	Aus	m	Dec 2004	2	0	0	0
Pensee-Bilong, Michel	Cam	d	Jan 2005	18	1	0	0
McClenahan, Trent	Aus	d	Mar 2005	31+6	0	5	0
Carrilho, Mirano	Neth	d	Aug 2005	1+2	0	0+1	0
Batista, Ricardo	Por	gk	Jan 2006	9	0	0	0
Morais, Filipe	Por	m	Jan 2006	11+2	0	0	0

NELSON (1)

Name	Born	Pos	From	LgAp	LgG	OthAp	OthG
Higginbotham, Harry	Aus	f	Oct 1923	4	0	0	0

NEW BRIGHTON (2)

Name	Born	Pos	From	LgAp	LgG	OthAp	OthG
Baines, Peter	Aus	f	Oct 1947	2	0	0	0
Turner, Alf	USA	f	Feb 1951	4	0	0	0

NEW BRIGHTON TOWER (1)

Name	Born	Pos	From	LgAp	LgG	OthAp	OthG
Hogan, Cornelius	Mal	f	May 1899	18	1	0	0

NEWCASTLE UNITED (60)

Name	Born	Pos	From	LgAp	LgG	OthAp	OthG
Whitson, Tony	SA	fb	Feb 1905	124	0	21	0
Robledo, George	Chi	f	Jan 1949	146	82	18	9
Robledo, Ted	Chi	wh	Feb 1949	37	0	8	0
Woollard, Arnold	Ber	fb	Dec 1952	8	0	2	0
Arentoft, Ben	Den	m	Mar 1969	46+4	2	13+1	1
Parkinson, Andy	SA	f	Mar 1978	0+3	0	0	0
Koenen, Frans	Neth	m	Aug 1980	11+1	1	2	0
Cunningham, Tony (Brit)	Jam	f	Feb 1985	37+10	4	3	2
Mirandinha, Francisco	Bra	f	Aug 1987	47+7	20	8+1	3
Pingel, Frank	Den	f	Jan 1989	13+1	1	0	0
Kristensen, Bjorn	Den	d	Mar 1989	69+11	4	11	0
Neilson, Alan (Wal)	Ger	d	Feb 1991	35+7	1	4	0
Srnicek, Pavel	CzRep	gk	Feb 1991	148+1	0	31+1	0
McDonough, Darron (Brit)	Bel	d	Mar 1992	2+1	0	0	0
Papavasiliou, Nicky	Cyp	m	Jul 1993	7	0	0	0
Albert, Philippe	Bel	d	Aug 1994	87+9	8	36+5	4
Hottiger, Marc	Swit	d	Aug 1994	38+1	1	14+1	1
Crawford, Jimmy (Ire)	USA	d/m	Mar 1995	0+2	0	0+1	0
Ginola, David	Fr	m	Jul 1995	54+4	6	16+1	1
Asprilla, Faustino	Col	f	Feb 1996	36+12	9	14	9
Tomasson, Jon Dahl	Den	f	Jun 1997	17+6	3	10+2	1
Ketsbaia, Temuri	Geo	f	Jul 1997	41+37	8	16+15	6
Pistone, Alessandro	It	d	Jul 1997	45+1	1	16+1	0
Barnes, John (Eng)	Jam	f	Aug 1997	22+5	6	11+2	1
Andersson, Andreas	Swe	f	Jan 1998	21+6	4	4+1	0
Dabizas, Nicos	Grk	d	Mar 1998	119+11	10	44+2	3
Charvet, Laurent	Fr	d	Jul 1998	37+3	1	13	0
Guivarc'h, Stephane	Fr	f	Jul 1998	2+2	1	0	0
Hamann, Dietmar	Ger	m	Aug 1998	22+1	4	8	1
Georgiadis, Georgios	Grk	m	Aug 1998	7+3	0	1+2	1
Solano, Nolberto (1)	Per	m	Aug 1998	158+14	29	55+6	9

Name	Born	Pos	From	LgAp	LgG	OthAp	OthG
Ameobi, Shola (Eng)	Nig	f	Oct 1998	84+66	25	36+20	16
Saha, Louis	Fr	f	Jan 1999	5+6	1	1	1
Domi, Didier	Fr	d	Jan 1999	44+11	3	11+4	1
Maric, Silvio	Cro	f	Feb 1999	12+11	0	5+3	2
Dumas, Franck	Fr	d	Jun 1999	6	0	1	0
Goma, Alain	Fr	d	Jul 1999	32+1	1	8	0
Elena, Marcelino	Sp	d	Jul 1999	15+2	0	4+1	0
Karelse, John	Neth	gk	Aug 1999	3	0	0	0
Fumaca, Jose	Bra	m	Sep 1999	1+4	0	0+1	0
Rodrigues, Helder (Por)	Ang	d	Nov 1999	8	1	4	0
Gavilan, Diego	Par	m	Feb 2000	2+5	1	0+1	0
Bassedas, Chistian	Arg	m	Jul 2000	18+6	1	7+2	0
Cordone, Daniel	Arg	f	Aug 2000	12+9	2	1+5	1
Lua-Lua, Lomana	DRC	f	Sep 2000	14+45	5	7+22	4
Acuna, Clarence	Chi	m	Oct 2000	35+11	6	9+4	1
Bernard, Olivier	Fr	m	Oct 2000	82+20	6	37+6	0
Robert, Laurent (Fr)	Reu	m	Aug 2001	110+19	22	45+7	10
Distin, Sylvain	Fr	d	Sep 2001	20+8	0	7	0
Viana, Hugo	Por	m	Aug 2002	16+23	2	12+10	2
Kluivert, Patrick	Neth	f	Jul 2004	15+10	6	8+2	7
Johnsen, Ronny	Nor	d	Sep 2004	3	0	2	0
Babayaro, Celestine	Nig	d	Jan 2005	33+2	0	13	1
Boumsong, Jean-Alain (Fr)	Cam	d	Jan 2005	44+3	0	12	0
Faye, Amdy	Sen	m	Jan 2005	22+9	0	13+1	0
Emre, Belozoglu	Tur	m	Jul 2005	19+1	2	3+2	0
Moore, Craig	Aus	d	Jul 2005	8	0	0+1	0
Luque, Alberto	Sp	f	Aug 2005	6+8	1	2+2	0
N'Zogbia, Charles	Fr	m	Aug 2004	35+11	5	9+5	0
Solano, Nolberto (2)	Per	m	Aug 2005	27+2	6	6	0
Pattison, Matty	SA	m	Feb 2006	2+1	0	0	0
NEWPORT COUNTY (4)							
Peed, Frank (Brit)	Arg	f	Aug 1931	13	4	1	0
Armand, Jack (Brit)	Ind	f	Aug 1932	3	1	1	0
Carr, Lance (1)	SA	f	Oct 1936	25	5	2	0
Carr, Lance (2)	SA	f	Jul 1938	39	9	10	1
Burgess, Mike	Can	f/ch	Feb 1956	24	7	0	0
NORTHAMPTON TOWN (27)							
Freimanis, Eddie	Lat	f	May 1948	19	4	0	0
Woollard, Arnold (1)	Ber	fb	Jun 1949	3	0	0	0
Starocsik, Felix	Pol	m	Jul 1951	49	19	1	0
Olah, Bela	Hun	m	Dec 1958	42	8	1	0
Woollard, Arnold (2)	Ber	fb	Mar 1962	28	0	3	0
Bruck, Dietmar	Ger	fb	Jun 1972	41	0	3	0
Roberts, John	Aus	gk	Jul 1972	13	0	0	0
Liddle, David (Brit)	Mal	d	May 1975	28+3	3	7	0
Nebbeling, Gavin	SA	d	Oct 1985	11	0	0	0
Anderson, Doug (Brit)	HK	m	Dec 1988	4+1	0	0	0
Tisdale, Paul (Brit)	Mal	m	Mar 1992	5	0	0	0
Stackman, Scott	USA	d	Mar 1994	0+1	0	0	0
Seal, David	Aus	f	Aug 1997	35+8	12	5+3	2
Van Dulleman, Ray	Neth	f	Aug 1997	0+1	0	0+1	0
Corazzin, Carlo	Can	f	Jul 1998	63+15	30	8+2	1
Hodgson, Doug	Aus	d	Oct 1998	7+1	1	2	0

Name	Born	Pos	From	LgAp	LgG	OthAp	OthG
Whitley, Jim (N Ire)	Zam	m	Feb 2001	13	0	0	0
Asamoah, Derek (Brit)	Gha	f	Jul 2001	27+85	10	11+9	3
One, Armand	Fr	f	Sep 2002	6	1	0+1	0
Rahim, Brent	Trin	m	Jan 2003	6	1	0	0
Johnson, Richard	Aus	m	Feb 2003	5+1	1	0	0
Abidallah, Nabil	Neth	m	Jan 2004	0+1	0	0+1	0
Vieira, Magno	Bra	f	Jan 2004	7+3	2	0	0
Sabin, Eric	Fr	f	Mar 2004	41+16	13	6+6	2
Bojic, Pedj	Aus	d	Jul 2004	43+28	4	13+1	2
Cozic, Bertrand	Fr	m	Jul 2004	8+6	0	3+2	0
Rachubka, Paul	USA	gk	Sep 2004	10	0	1	0
Mikolanda, Petr	CzRep	f	Sep 2005	2	0	1	0

NORWICH CITY (41)

Name	Born	Pos	From	LgAp	LgG	OthAp	OthG
Laxton, Edward	Bra	w	Dec 1919	16	0	0	0
Osborne, Harold	SA	w	Sep 1924	1	0	0	0
Peed, Frank (Brit)	Arg	f	Oct 1930	17	4	2	2
Gallego, Tony	Sp	gk	Mar 1947	1	0	0	0
Dolding, Len (Brit)	Ind	w	Jul 1948	12	1	0	0
Ackerman, Alf	SA	f	Aug 1951	66	31	4	4
Crossan, Errol	Can	w	Sep 1958	102	28	14	4
Kennon, Sandy	SA	gk	Feb 1959	213	0	42	0
Keelan, Kevin (Brit)	Ind	gk	Jul 1963	571	0	88	0
Muzinic, Drazen	Yug	d	Sep 1980	15+4	0	2+2	0
Van Wijk, Dennis	Neth	d/m	Oct 1982	109+9	3	31+1	1
Goss, Jerry (Wal)	Cyp	m	Mar 1983	155+33	14	34+7	6
Hareide, Aage	Nor	d	Jun 1983	38+2	1	14	1
Phillips, David (Brit)	Ger	m	Jul 1989	152	18	26	1
Mortensen, Henrik	Den	f	Oct 1989	12+6	0	0+1	1
Molby, Jan	Den	m	Dec 1995	3	0	2	1
Ottosson, Ulf	Swe	f	Jan 1997	4+3	1	0+1	0
Segura, Victor	Sp	d	Aug 1997	24+5	0	4	0
Fuglestad, Erik	Nor	d	Nov 1997	71+3	2	5+1	0
Anselin, Cedric	Fr	m	Apr 1999	22+4	1	3	0
De Blasiis, Jean-Yves	Fr	m	Jul 1999	28+7	0	2+1	0
Diop, Pape Seydou	Sen	d/m	Aug 1999	2+5	0	1+2	0
Derveld, Fernando	Neth	d	Mar 2000	20+2	1	3	0
De Waard, Raimond	Neth	m	Mar 2000	4+6	0	1+2	0
Giallanza, Gaetano	Swit	f	Mar 2000	7+7	2	3+1	3
Nedergaard, Steen	Den	d	Jul 2000	81+9	5	5+2	0
Whitley, Jim (N Ire)	Zam	m	Aug 2000	7+1	1	0	0
Peschisolido, Paul	Can	f	Mar 2001	3+2	0	0	0
Libbra, Marc	Fr	f	Jul 2001	17+17	7	3+1	0
Nielsen, David	Den	f	Dec 2001	35+23	14	7+1	0
Brennan, Jim	Can	d	Jul 2003	25+18	1	5	1
Hammond, Elvis	Gha	f	Aug 2003	0+4	0	0	0
Svensson, Mathias	Swe	f	Dec 2003	26+16	11	1+1	0
Helveg, Thomas	Den	m	Jul 2004	16+4	0	2+1	0
Safri, Youssef	Mor	m	Jul 2004	38+10	2	2+2	1
Jonson, Mattias	Swe	m	Aug 2004	19+9	0	2	0
Louis-Jean, Mathieu	Fr	d	Jun 2005	2	0	0	0
Colin, Jurgen	Neth	d	Jul 2005	24+1	0	1	0
Etuhu, Dixon	Nig	m	Nov 2005	15+4	0	1	0
Earnshaw, Robert (Wal)	Zam	f	Jan 2006	13+2	8	0	0

Name	Born	Pos	From	LgAp	LgG	OthAp	OthG
Johansson, Jonatan (Fin)	Swe	f	Jan 2006	6+6	3	0	0

NOTTINGHAM FOREST (55)

Name	Born	Pos	From	LgAp	LgG	OthAp	OthG
Quantrill, Alf (Eng)	Ind	m	May 1930	15	2	0	0
Gunn, Alf	Ger	f	Feb 1947	2	0	0	0
Lightening, Arthur	SA	gk	Dec 1956	6	0	0	0
Fraser, Willie (Sco)	Aus	gk	Dec 1958	2	0	0	0
Bowery, Bert	StK	f	Jan 1975	2	2	2	0
Ponte, Raimondo	It	m	Aug 1980	17+4	3	5+3	4
Aas, Einar	Nor	d	Mar 1981	20+1	1	3	0
Rober, Jurgen	Ger	m	Dec 1981	21+1	3	3	1
Van Breukelen, Hans	Neth	gk	Sep 1982	61	0	14	0
Thijssen, Frans	Neth	m	Oct 1983	17	3	2	0
Metgod, Johnny	Neth	m	Aug 1984	113+3	15	23	2
Segers, Hans	Neth	gk	Aug 1984	58	0	9	0
Davidson, Alan	Aus	fb	Nov 1984	3	0	2	0
Osvold, Kjetil	Nor	m	Mar 1987	5+2	0	0+1	0
Orlygsson, Toddi	Ice	m	Dec 1989	31+6	2	6+1	2
Phillips, David (Brit)	Ger	m	Aug 1993	116+10	5	29+3	0
Bohinen, Lars	Nor	m	Nov 1993	59+5	7	10+1	3
Haaland, Alf-Inge	Nor	m	Jan 1994	66+9	7	9+6	0
Roy, Bryan	Neth	f	Aug 1994	70+15	24	23+2	4
Bart-Williams, Chris (Brit)	SiLe	m	Jul 1995	200+7	30	37+1	5
Silenzi, Andrea	It	f	Aug 1995	4+8	0	4+4	2
Jerkan, Nikola	Cro	d	Jun 1996	14	0	0	0
Van Hooijdonk, Pierre	Neth	f	Mar 1997	68+3	36	4+2	5
Pascolo, Marco	Swit	gk	Jun 1997	5	0	1	0
Bonalair, Thierry	Fr	m	Jul 1997	58+13	5	7+2	0
Hjelde, Jon Olav (1)	Nor	d	Aug 1997	136+21	4	17+1	2
Merino, Carlos	Sp	m	Sep 1997	3+6	0	1+2	0
Edds, Gareth	Aus	m	Feb 1998	11+5	1	1	0
Darcheville, Jean-Claude (Fr)	FrGu	f	Jul 1998	14+2	2	1+2	0
Louis-Jean, Mathieu	Fr	d	Sep 1998	188+10	3	23+2	0
Mattsson, Jesper	Swe	d	Dec 1998	5+1	0	0	0
Harkes, John	USA	m	Jan 1999	3	0	0	0
Porfirio, Hugo	Por	m	Jan 1999	3+6	1	0	0
Stensaas, Stale	Nor	d	Jan 1999	6+1	0	0	0
Allou, Bernard (Fr)	IvCo	m	Mar 1999	1+5	1	2+2	1
Gough, Richard (Sco)	Swe	d	Mar 1999	7	0	0	0
Mannini, Moreno	It	d	Aug 1999	7+1	0	1	0
Matrecano, Salvatore	It	d	Aug 1999	11	0	2	0
Petrachi, Gianluca	It	m	Aug 1999	10+3	0	2	0
Brennan, Jim	Can	d	Oct 1999	117+6	1	14	0
Beck, Mikkel	Den	f	Nov 1999	5	1	0	0
John, Stern	Trin	f	Nov 1999	49+23	18	7+1	2
Olsen, Ben	USA	m	Oct 2000	14+4	2	0	0
Johnson, David	Jam	f	Jan 2001	120+28	46	15+2	4
Bopp, Eugene (Ger)	Ukr	m	Aug 2001	39+38	8	8+4	3
Oyen, Davy	Bel	d	Feb 2003	4+4	0	1	0
Gunnarsson, Brynjar	Ice	d	Aug 2003	9+4	0	1	0
Hjelde, Jon Olav (2)	Nor	d	Aug 2004	13+1	0	1	0
Folly, Yoann (Fr)	Tgo	m	Jan 2005	0+1	0	2	0
Friio, David	Fr	m	Feb 2005	16+6	1	0	0
Fernandez, Vincent	Fr	d	Jul 2005	0+1	0	1	0

Name	Born	Pos	From	LgAp	LgG	OthAp	OthG
Padula, Gino	Arg	d	Jul 2005	3	0	1	0
Pedersen, Rune	Den	gk	Jul 2005	17+1	0	2	0
Pittman, Jon-Paul	USA	f	Jul 2005	0	0	0+2	0
Dadi, Eugene	IvCo	f	Aug 2005	0+5	0	1	0
Bastians, Felix	Ger	m	Oct 2005	2+9	0	1+1	0

NOTTS COUNTY (39)

Name	Born	Pos	From	LgAp	LgG	OthAp	OthG
Mills, Paddy (Brit)	Ind	f	Mar 1926	76	35	3	1
Whittaker, Fred	Can	f	Aug 1946	10	2	0	0
Praski, Josef	Fr	w	Mar 1949	3	0	0	0
Robledo, Ted	Chi	wh	Sep 1957	2	0	0	0
Benjamin, Tristan	StK	d	Mar 1975	296+15	4	46+1	0
Richards, Lloyd	Jam	m	Feb 1976	7+2	0	1+1	0
Avramovic, Raddy	Cro	gk	Aug 1979	149	0	18	0
Chiedozie, John (1)	Nig	m	Aug 1981	110+2	15	19	4
Lahtinen, Aki	Fin	d	Sep 1981	37+8	2	7+1	0
Hesford, Iain (Eng)	Zam	gk	Nov 1985	10	0	0	0
Edge, Declan (NZ)	Mly	f	Dec 1985	7+3	2	3	0
Chiedozie, John (2)	Nig	m	Jan 1990	0+1	0	0	0
Short, Chris (Brit)	Ger	d	Sep 1990	77+17	2	13+1	0
Farina, Frank	Aus	f	Mar 1992	1+2	0	0	0
Dijkstra, Meindert	Neth	gk	Aug 1992	27+2	1	4+1	0
Murphy, Shaun	Aus	d	Sep 1992	100+9	5	14+2	0
Goater, Shaun	Ber	f	Nov 1993	1	0	0	0
Emenalo, Michael	Nig	d	Aug 1994	7	0	0	0
Kearton, Jason	Aus	gk	Jan 1995	10	0	0	0
Mendez, Gabriel (Aus)	Arg	m	Mar 1997	2+1	0	0	0
Garcia, Tony	Fr	m	Sep 1998	10+9	2	3+2	0
Grant, Kim	Gha	f	Dec 1998	6	1	0	0
Allsopp, Danny (1)	Aus	f	Nov 1999	3	1	0	0
Joseph, David (Fr)	Guad	f	Aug 2000	13+14	4	3+2	0
McDermott, Andy	Aus	m	Aug 2000	20+5	0	5	0
Jacobsen, Anders	Nor	d	Sep 2000	27+2	2	5	0
Jorgensen, Henrik	Den	d	Oct 2000	3+4	0	0+3	0
Allsopp, Danny (2)	Aus	f	Nov 2000	97+8	42	11	8
Moreau, Fabrice (Cam)	Fr	m	Mar 2001	2+3	0	0	0
Cas, Marcel	Neth	m	Jul 2001	49+9	8	6	0
Whitley, Jeff (N Ire)	Zam	m	Mar 2002	18	0	1	0
Antoine-Curier, Mickael	Fr	f	Feb 2004	4	1	0	0
Scoffham, Steve (Brit)	Ger	f	Feb 2004	29+23	7	1+1	0
Arphexad, Pegguy (Fr)	Guad	gk	Mar 2004	3	0	0	0
Baudet, Julien	Fr	d	Jun 2004	80+1	11	8	2
Kuduzovic, Fahrudin	Bos	m	Sep 2004	0+3	0	0	0
Sofiane, Youssef	Fr	f	Sep 2004	2+2	0	1	1
Zadkovich, Ruben	Aus	m	Mar 2005	6+3	1	0	0
Chilaka, Chibuzor	Nig	m	Oct 2005	0	0	1	0
Dadi, Eugene	IvCo	f	Jan 2006	9+2	2	0	0
Sissoko, Noe	Mli	m	Feb 2006	1+2	0	0	0

OLDHAM ATHLETIC (36)

Name	Born	Pos	From	LgAp	LgG	OthAp	OthG
Andrews, Billy (N Ire)	USA	wh	Aug 1908	9	3	0	0
Hunter, George (Brit)	Ind	wh	Jan 1912	40	1	6	0
Lester, Hugh	USA	wh	Aug 1914	1	0	0	0
Kowenicki, Ryszard	Pol	m	Dec 1979	40+2	5	5	1
McDonough, Darron (Brit)	Bel	d	Jan 1980	178+5	14	17	3

Name	Born	Pos	From	LgAp	LgG	OthAp	OthG
Anderson, Doug (Brit)	HK	m	Sep 1980	4+5	0	0+2	0
Halle, Gunnar	Nor	d	Feb 1991	185+3	17	24	4
Keizerweerd, Orpheo	Neth	f	Mar 1993	0+1	0	0	0
Pedersen, Tore	Nor	d	Oct 1993	7+3	0	1+1	0
Vonk, Michel	Neth	d	Nov 1995	5	1	0	0
Orlygsson, Toddi	Ice	m	Dec 1995	65+11	1	10+2	0
Hodgson, Doug	Aus	d	Feb 1997	33+8	4	3+2	0
Kyratzoglou, Alex	Aus	m	Oct 1997	0+1	0	0	0
Grobbelaar, Bruce (Zim)	SA	gk	Dec 1997	4	0	0	0
Agogo, Junior	Gha	f	Jul 1999	2	0	0	0
Corazzin, Carlo	Can	f	Jul 2000	82+27	21	11+7	3
Watson, Mark	Can	d	Sep 2000	1+1	0	1	0
Baudet, Julien	Fr	d	Oct 2001	34+10	3	4+2	0
Rachubka, Paul	USA	gk	Nov 2001	16	0	0	0
Colusso, Cristian	Arg	m	Feb 2002	6+7	2	0	0
Adebola, Dele	Nig	f	Mar 2002	5	0	0	0
Da Silva, Lourenco (Por)	Ang	m	Aug 2002	1+6	1	1+1	0
Killen, Chris	NZ	f	Aug 2002	53+25	17	9+3	6
Pogliacomi, Les	Aus	gk	Aug 2002	120	0	21	0
Wijnhard, Clyde (Neth)	Sur	f	Aug 2002	24+1	10	6	3
Antoine-Curier, Mickael	Fr	f	Jul 2003	5+3	2	2	0
Kangana, Ndiwa	DRC	d	Jul 2003	3+1	0	0	0
Carney, Dave	Aus	m	Aug 2003	0	0	0+1	0
Zola, Calvin	DRC	f	Aug 2003	21+4	5	3	2
Johnson, Jermaine	Jam	m	Nov 2003	31+8	9	4	1
Arber, Mark (Brit)	SA	d	Jun 2004	13+1	1	3	0
Jack, Rodney (StV)	Jam	f	Jul 2004	5+5	2	0+1	0
Betsy, Kevin	Sey	m	Sep 2004	34+2	5	8	0
Cooper, Kenny	USA	f	Jan 2005	5+2	3	1+1	0
Stam, Stefan	Neth	d	Feb 2005	20+6	0	0+1	0
Sanokho, Amadou	Fr	d	Mar 2005	0+1	0	0	0

OXFORD UNITED (26)

Name	Born	Pos	From	LgAp	LgG	OthAp	OthG
Houghton, Bud (Brit)	Ind	f	Mar 1961	53	17	5	2
Cooke, Joe	Dom	d/f	Aug 1979	71+1	13	7	0
Evans, Ceri	NZ	d	Feb 1989	113+3	3	14	0
Stein, Mark (Eng)	SA	f	Sep 1989	72+10	18	6+1	0
Wilsterman, Brian (Neth)	Sur	d	Feb 1997	28+14	2	3	0
Remy, Christophe	Fr	d	Jul 1997	23+5	1	5+3	0
Van Heusden, Arjan	Neth	gk	Sep 1997	11	0	2	0
Watson, Mark	Can	d	Dec 1998	57+1	0	10	0
Lundin, Pal	Swe	gk	Mar 1999	28+1	0	5	0
Arendse, Andre	SA	gk	Jul 1999	13	0	5+1	0
Omoyimni, Manny	Nig	f	Jul 2000	32+35	9	5+5	0
Busby, Hubert	Can	gk	Aug 2000	0+1	0	0	0
Guyett, Scott	Aus	d	May 2001	20+2	0	2	0
Oldfield, David	Aus	m/f	Aug 2002	20+11	2	4+2	1
Sall, Abdou	Sen	d	Dec 2002	0+1	0	0+1	0
Cominelli, Lucas	Arg	m	Jan 2005	11+5	1	0	0
Corbo, Mateo	Uru	d	Jan 2005	13	0	0	0
M'Bombo, Doudou	DRC	f	Jan 2005	0+1	0	0	0
Diaz, Emiliano	It	m	Feb 2005	2+5	0	0	0
Raponi, Juan Pablo	Arg	m	Feb 2005	5+5	0	0	0
Karam, Amine	Fr	m	Mar 2005	0+2	0	0	0

Name	Born	Pos	From	LgAp	LgG	OthAp	OthG
Sabin, Eric	Fr	f	Aug 2005	28+1	7	6	2
Goodhind, Warren	SA	d	Feb 2006	4+2	0	0	0
Guatelli, Andrea	It	gk	Mar 2006	4	0	0	0
N'Toya, Tcham (Fr)	DRC	m	Mar 2006	7+1	4	0	0
Odubade, Yemi	Nig	f	Jan 2006	4+4	1	0	0

PETERBOROUGH UNITED (28)

Name	Born	Pos	From	LgAp	LgG	OthAp	OthG
Thompson, Peter	Ken	w	Mar 1964	79+6	15	9	3
Maynard, Mike	Guy	fb	Jul 1967	2+1	0	1	0
Phillips, Brendon	Jam	m	Aug 1973	1	0	0	0
Cooke, Joe	Dom	d/f	Jan 1979	18	5	0	0
Heppolette, Ricky (Brit)	Ind	m	Aug 1979	5	0	3	0
Parkinson, Andy	SA	f	Aug 1979	12+1	5	5	1
Kelly, Errington (1)	StV	w	Mar 1984	59+13	22	9+2	4
Kelly, Errington (2)	StV	w	Dec 1986	36+10	6	3+2	1
Kerr, John (USA)	Can	f	Dec 1987	10	1	0	0
Richards, Carl (Eng)	Jam	f	Jul 1989	16+4	5	4+1	2
Berry, George (Wal)	Ger	d	Jul 1990	28+4	6	1	0
Salman, Danis (Eng)	Cyp	d	Mar 1992	1	0	0	0
Iorfa, Dominic	Nig	f	Oct 1992	27+33	9	5+3	0
Kruszynski, Detsi	Ger	m	Dec 1993	2+1	0	2	0
Henry, Liburd	Dom	f	Aug 1994	22+10	7	2+1	1
Feuer, Ian	USA	gk	Feb 1995	16	0	0	0
Griemink, Bart	Neth	gk	Oct 1996	58	0	5	0
Koogi, Anders	Den	m	Jul 1997	0+2	0	0	0
Gregory, Neil (Brit)	Zam	f	Nov 1997	2+1	1	0	0
Danielsson, Helgi	Ice	m	Oct 1998	38+17	2	4	1
Oldfield, David (Eng)	Aus	m/f	Mar 2000	68+10	4	14+2	1
Macdonald, Gary (Brit)	Ger	d	Feb 2001	13+4	1	3+1	0
Arber, Mark (Brit) (1)	SA	d	Dec 2002	67+2	5	6	0
Kanu, Chris	Nig	d	Aug 2003	25+9	0	6+2	0
Deen, Ahmed	SiLe	d	Sep 2004	4+1	0	0	0
Arber, Mark (Brit) (2)	SA	d	Dec 2004	67	2	8	1
McMaster, Jamie	Aus	m	Jan 2005	3	0	1	0
Onibuje, Fola	Nig	f	Mar 2005	0+2	0	0	0
Kuqi, Njazi (Fin)	Alb	f	Mar 2006	1	0	0	0

PLYMOUTH ARGYLE (32)

Name	Born	Pos	From	LgAp	LgG	OthAp	OthG
Dugnolle, Jack (Brit)	Ind	ch	Feb 1939	5	0	0	0
Strauss, Bill	SA	w	Jul 1946	158	40	8	2
Williams, Stan	SA	w	Aug 1949	35	4	2	1
Twissell, Charlie (Eng)	Sing	w	Apr 1955	41	9	1	0
Clelland, Crawford	USA	f	Jun 1955	2	0	0	0
Phillips, David (Brit)	Ger	m	Aug 1981	65+8	15	14+2	0
Anderson, Doug (Brit)	HK	m	Aug 1987	17+2	1	2	0
Salman, Danis (Eng)	Cyp	d	Mar 1990	71+3	4	8	1
Quamina, Mark	Guy	m/d	Jul 1991	4+1	0	0	0
Marshall, Dwight (Brit) (1)	StL	f	Aug 1991	93+6	27	17+2	6
Van Rossum, Erik	Neth	d	Jan 1992	9	0	0	0
Hodgson, Doug	Aus	d	Aug 1995	3+2	0	0	0
Petterson, Andy	Aus	gk	Jan 1996	6	0	0	0
Corazzin, Carlo	Can	f	Mar 1996	61+13	22	4+4	1
Grobbelaar, Bruce (Zim)	SA	gk	Aug 1996	36	0	5	0
Jean, Earl	StL	f	Aug 1997	37+28	7	9	2
Marshall, Dwight (Brit) (2)	StL	f	Oct 1998	25+3	12	1+2	0

Name	Born	Pos	From	LgAp	LgG	OthAp	OthG
O'Sullivan, Wayne (Ire)	Cyp	d	Jul 1999	83+2	3	11	0
Friio, David	Fr	m	Nov 2000	158+9	39	14+4	5
Larrieu, Romain	Fr	gk	Nov 2000	176+1	0	16	0
Javary, Jean-Phillipe	Fr	m	Feb 2001	4	0	0	0
Bent, Jason	Can	m	Sep 2001	52+12	5	8+2	1
Lopes, Osvaldo	Fr	m	Sep 2002	4+5	0	2	0
Milosevic, Danny	Aus	gk	Nov 2002	1	0	0	0
Capaldi, Tony (N Ire)	Nor	d	Mar 2003	92+18	12	5+2	0
Doumbe, Mathias	Fr	d	Jun 2004	67+2	3	4+1	0
Gudjonsson, Bjarni	Ice	m	Dec 2004	18+7	0	2	1
Buzsaky, Akos	Hun	m	Jan 2005	30+19	5	3	1
Djordjic, Bojan (Swe)	Yug	m	May 2005	9+13	1	1+2	0
Mendes, Nuno	Por	d	Jul 2005	2	0	1	0
West, Taribo	Nig	d	Jul 2005	4	0	1	0
Nalis, Lilian	Fr	m	Jan 2006	20	1	0	0
Pericard, Vincent (Cam)	Fr	f	Feb 2006	14+1	4	0	0
PORTSMOUTH (83)							
Delapenha, Lindy	Jam	f	Apr 1948	7	0	1	1
Pickett, Reg	Ind	wh	Mar 1949	123	3	2	0
Ekner, Dan	Swe	f	Nov 1949	5	0	0	0
Gaillard, Marcel	Bel	w	Feb 1951	58	7	6	6
Smith, Roy	Ind	f	Jan 1962	8	3	1	2
Eames, Billy (Brit)	Mal	f	Sep 1975	9+3	1	4+2	2
Blake, Noel (Brit)	Jam	d	Apr 1984	144	10	24	3
Golac, Ivan	Yug	fb	Jan 1985	8	0	0	0
Christensen, Tommy	Den	f	Nov 1985	3	2	1	0
Kerr, John (USA)	Can	f	Aug 1987	2+2	0	0+1	0
Kristensen, Bjorn	Den	d	Mar 1993	56+15	1	13+1	3
Boere, Jeroen	Neth	f	Mar 1994	4+1	0	0	0
Radosavljevic, Preki (USA)	Yug	w	Jul 1994	30+10	5	4+1	2
Poom, Mart	Est	gk	Aug 1994	4	0	3	0
Svensson, Mathias	Swe	f	Dec 1996	34+11	10	4+2	2
Aloisi, John	Aus	f	Aug 1997	55+5	25	7	3
Thorp, Hamilton	Aus	d	Aug 1997	0+7	0	1+1	1
Foster, Craig	Aus	m	Sep 1997	13+3	2	2	2
Harries, Paul	Aus	f	Sep 1997	0+1	0	0	0
Enes, Robbie	Aus	m	Oct 1997	1+4	0	0	0
Vlachos, Michalis	Grk	d	Jun 1998	55+2	0	7	1
Kyzeridis, Nicos	Grk	m	Jul 1998	2+2	0	2	0
Thogersen, Thomas	Den	m	Aug 1998	95+13	8	10+1	0
Peron, Jeff	Fr	m	Sep 1998	46+2	3	6	0
Andreassen, Svein	Nor	m	Dec 1998	0+2	0	1	0
Miglioranzi, Stefani (USA)	Bra	m	Jun 1999	25+10	2	3+4	0
Petterson, Andy	Aus	gk	Jul 1999	32	0	1+1	0
Pamarot, Noe (1)	Fr	d	Sep 1999	1+1	0	0+1	0
Panopoulos, Mike (Grk)	Aus	m	Sep 1999	45+9	7	4	0
Berntsen, Tommy	Nor	d	Nov 1999	1+1	0	0	0
Rudonja, Mladen	Slo	f	Aug 2000	4+10	0	2+2	0
Keller, Marc	Fr	gk	Sep 2000	3	0	0	0
Lambourde, Bernard (Fr)	Guad	d	Sep 2000	6	0	0	0
Zamperini, Alessandro	It	d	Jul 2001	16	2	1	0
Prosinecki, Robert (Cro)	Ger	m	Aug 2001	30+3	9	2	0
Ilic, Sasa (Yug)	Aus	gk	Sep 2001	7	0	0	0
Kawaguchi, Yoshikatsu	Jap	gk	Oct 2001	11+1	0	1	0

Name	Born	Pos	From	LgAp	LgG	OthAp	OthG
Biagini, Leo	Arg	f	Feb 2002	6+2	2	0	0
Todorov, Svetoslav	Bul	f	Mar 2002	53+20	31	3+3	0
De Zeeuw, Arjan	Neth	d	Aug 2002	103+3	5	12	0
Festa, Gianluca	It	d	Aug 2002	27	1	2	0
Foxe, Hayden	Aus	d	Aug 2002	38+4	2	3+1	0
Pericard, Vincent	Fr	f	Aug 2002	21+23	9	3+2	1
Diabate, Lassina	Iv Co	m	Oct 2002	16+9	0	1	0
Ayegbini, Yakubu	Nig	f	Jan 2003	76+5	36	8+3	4
Tavlaridis, Stathis	Grk	d	Jan 2003	3+1	0	1	0
Heikkinen, Markus	Fin	d	Feb 2003	0+2	0	0	0
Berger, Patrik	CzRep	m	Jun 2003	50+2	8	6+2	0
Zivkovic, Boris	Cro	d	Jun 2003	17+1	0	2	0
Stefanovic, Dejan	SM	d	Jul 2003	91+1	3	12+1	0
Wapenaar, Harald	Neth	gk	Jul 2003	5	0	3	0
Faye, Amdy	Sen	m	Aug 2003	44+3	0	4+1	0
Schemmel, Sebastien	Fr	d	Aug 2003	12+2	0	3+1	1
Smertin, Alexei	Rus	m	Aug 2003	23+3	0	7	0
Srnicek, Pavel	CzRep	g	Sep 2003	3	0	1	0
Berkovic, Eyal	Isr	m	Jan 2004	16+6	2	6	1
Mornar, Ivica	Cro	f	Jan 2004	4+6	1	2	0
Pasanen, Petri	Fin	d	Jan 2004	11+1	0	4	0
Lua-Lua, Lomana	DRC	f	Feb 2004	54+11	17	2	0
Olszar, Sebastian	Pol	f	Feb 2004	0	0	0+1	0
Cisse, Aliou	Sen	d	Aug 2004	14+9	0	4+1	0
Fuller, Ricardo	Jam	f	Aug 2004	13+18	1	4+2	0
Kamara, Diomansy (Sen)	Fr	f	Aug 2004	15+10	4	4	2
Mezague, Valery (Cam)	Fr	m	Aug 2004	3+8	0	3	0
Chalkias, Konstantinos	Grk	gk	Jan 2005	5	0	1	0
Olisadebe, Emmanuel (Pol)	Nig	f	Jan 2005	0+2	0	0	0
Rodic, Alexsander (Slo)	Bos	f	Jan 2005	1+3	0	0	0
Skopelitis, Giannis	Grk	m	Jan 2005	9+9	0	0	0
Robert, Laurent (Fr)	Reu	m	Jun 2005	13+4	1	0	0
Karadas, Azar	Nor	d	Jul 2005	4+13	1	1+2	0
Viafara, John	Col	m	Jul 2005	10+4	1	0+1	0
Vignal, Gregory	Fr	d	Jul 2005	13+1	0	3	0
Westerveld, Sander	Neth	gk	Jul 2005	6	0	1	0
Mbesuma, Collins	Zam	f	Aug 2005	0+4	0	0	0
Priske, Brian	Den	d	Aug 2005	26+4	0	2+1	0
Diao, Salif	Sen	m	Aug 2005	7+4	0	2	0
Silva, Dario	Uru	f	Aug 2005	13	2	2	1
Vukic, Zvonimir	SM	m	Aug 2005	6+3	1	0	0
Songo'o, Frank (Fr)	Cam	m	Sep 2005	0+2	0	0+1	0
D'Alessandro, Andres	Arg	m	Jan 2006	13	1	0	0
Koroman, Ognjen	S&M	m	Jan 2006	1+2	1	0	0
Mendes, Pedro	Por	m	Jan 2006	14	3	1	0
Mwaruwari, Benjani	Zim	f	Jan 2006	16	1	0	0
Pamarot, Noe (2)	Fr	d	Jan 2006	4+4	0	0	0

PORT VALE (27)

Name	Born	Pos	From	LgAp	LgG	OthAp	OthG
Bookman, Louis (Brit)	Lith	w	Jul 1923	10	0	1	0
Fish, Kenneth	SA	f	Nov 1937	5	1	1	0
Price, Johnny (Brit)	Ind	f	May 1937	13	2	0	0
Georgeson, Roddy	Egy	f	Jan 1966	26+1	6	1	0
Hazell, Bob (Eng)	Jam	d	Dec 1986	81	1	12	0
Van der Laan, Robin	Neth	m	Feb 1991	154+22	24	23+2	2

Name	Born	Pos	From	LgAp	LgG	OthAp	OthG
Jalink, Nico	Neth	m	Jul 1991	20+8	1	3	0
Van Heusden, Arjan	Neth	gk	Aug 1994	27	0	4	0
Holwyn, Jermaine	Neth	d	Jul 1995	5+2	0	0	0
Samuel, Randy (Can)	Trin	d	Nov 1995	9	1	0	0
Jansson, Jan	Swe	m	Nov 1996	37+14	6	3+1	0
Koordes, Rogier	Neth	m	Feb 1997	29+9	0	0+1	0
Snijders, Mark	Neth	d	Sep 1997	46+9	2	5	0
Pounewatchy, Stephane	Fr	d	Aug 1998	2	0	0	0
Berntsen, Robin	Nor	d	Nov 1998	1	0	0	0
Horlaville, Christophe	Fr	f	Nov 1998	1+1	0	0+1	0
Rougier, Tony	Trin	m/f	Jan 1999	41+10	8	3	1
Viljanen, Ville	Fin	f	Feb 1999	26+8	6	3	0
Olaoye, Dele	Nig	f	Aug 2000	0+1	0	0	0
Byrne, Paul (Brit)	SA	m	Apr 2001	8+3	0	0	0
Lowe, Onandi	Jam	f	Feb 2001	4+1	1	0	0
Atangana, Simon	Cam	f	Jan 2002	1+1	0	0	0
Killen, Chris	NZ	f	Sep 2001	8+1	6	0	0
Abbey, George	Nig	d	Dec 2004	35+3	0	2	0
Lipa, Andreas	Aut	d	Dec 2004	27+5	2	3	0
Loran, Tyrone	Neth	d	Dec 2004	6	0	1	0
Sam, Hector	Trin	f	Jun 2005	0+4	0	0+1	0
PRESTON NORTH END (33)							
Quantrill, Alf (Eng)	Ind	w	Jul 1921	64	7	1	0
Marston, Joe	Aus	ch	Feb 1950	185	0	15	0
Heppolette, Ricky (Brit)	Ind	m	Sep 1964	149+5	13	20	1
Tunks, Roy (Brit) (1)	Ger	gk	Nov 1974	277	0	36	0
Houston, Graham	Gib	m	Mar 1978	90+38	11	19+1	1
Hunter, Chris (1)	HK	f	Sep 1981	0+1	0	0	0
Hunter, Chris (2)	HK	f	Sep 1984	3+3	0	0+1	1
Stevens, Ian	Mal	f	Nov 1984	9+2	2	0	0
Tunks, Roy (Brit) (2)	Ger	gk	Nov 1988	25	0	1	0
Moylon, Craig (Brit)	Ger	m	Jul 1991	0+1	0	0	0
Berry, George (Wal)	Ger	d	Aug 1991	4	0	1+1	0
Johnstone, Glenn (Brit)	Ken	gk	Jan 1993	10	0	0	0
Nebbeling, Gavin	SA	d	Jul 1993	22	4	5	0
Carmichael, Matt (Brit)	Sing	f	Mar 1995	7+3	3	0	0
Moilanen, Tepi	Fin	gk	Dec 1995	155+3	0	23+1	0
Sissoko, Habib	Fr	f	Feb 1998	4+3	0	0	0
Diaf, Farid	Fr	m	Jul 1999	1+2	0	0+1	0
Gunnlaugsson, Bjarke	Ice	f	Sep 1999	17+28	2	3+4	1
McBride, Brian	USA	f	Sep 2000	8+1	1	2	0
Meijer, Erik	Neth	f	Oct 2000	9	0	0	0
Skora, Eric	Fr	f	Oct 2001	37+13	0	6+1	2
Gudjonsson, Thordur	Ice	m	Jan 2002	4+3	0	0+1	0
Wijnhard, Clyde (Neth)	Sur	f	Mar 2002	6	3	0	0
Etuhu, Dixon	Nig	m	Jan 2002	100+34	17	12+3	1
Fuller, Ricardo	Jam	f	Aug 2002	57+1	27	4+1	4
Lewis, Eddie	USA	f	Sep 2002	97+14	15	12+1	1
Koumantarakis, George (USA)	Grk	f	Jan 2003	11+6	4	2	1
Lynch, Simon	Can	f	Jan 2003	14+30	1	0+1	1
Davis, Claude	Jam	d	Jul 2003	74+20	4	14	0
Daley, Omar	Jam	m	Jul 2004	1+13	0	1+2	1
Mawene, Youl	Fr	d	Jul 2004	72+4	3	13	0
N'Dumbu-Nsungu, Guylain	DRC	f	Sep 2004	4+2	0	0	0

Name	Born	Pos	From	LgAp	LgG	OthAp	OthG
De Oliveira, Filipe	Por	f	Dec 2004	1+4	0	0	0
Folly, Yoann (Fr)	Tgo	m	Mar 2005	0+2	0	0	0
Johnson, Jemal	USA	f	Oct 2005	2+1	1	0	0
QUEENS PARK RANGERS (46)							
Balogun, Tesilim	Nig	f	Sep 1956	13	3	2	2
Cini, Joe	Mal	w	Aug 1959	7	1	0	0
Leary, Stuart (Eng)	SA	f	Dec 1962	94	29	10	3
Hazell, Bob (Eng)	Jam	d	Sep 1979	100+6	8	17+1	1
Bakholt, Kurt	Den	m	Jan 1986	0+1	0	0	0
Pisanti, David	Isr	m	Sep 1987	16+5	0	7+1	1
Stein, Mark (Eng)	SA	f	Jun 1988	20+13	4	6+1	3
Ardiles, Ossie	Arg	m	Aug 1988	4+4	0	2+1	0
Wegerle, Roy (USA)	SA	f	Dec 1989	71+4	29	16	2
Iorfa, Dominic	Nig	f	Mar 1990	1+7	0	1	0
Stejskal, Jan	CzRep	gk	Oct 1990	107+1	0	14	0
Dijkstra, Sieb	Neth	gk	Jul 1994	11	0	1	0
Goodridge, Greg	Bar	w	Aug 1995	0+7	1	0+2	0
Sommer, Jurgen	USA	gk	Aug 1995	66	0	5	0
Zelic, Ned	Aus	fb	Aug 1995	3+1	0	0	0
McDermott, Andy	Aus	m	Aug 1995	6	2	0	0
Kulcsar, George (Aus)	Hun	d	Dec 1997	42+14	1	2+2	0
Heinola, Antti	Fin	d	Jan 1998	23+11	0	4+1	0
Steiner, Rob	Swe	f	Jul 1998	29+7	9	3	0
Miklosko, Ludek	CzRep	gk	Oct 1998	57	0	6+2	0
Koejoe, Sammy (Neth)	Sur	f	Nov 1999	13+21	3	4+4	0
Bankole, Ade	Nig	gk	Jul 1998	0+1	0	0	0
Beck, Mikkel	Den	f	Feb 2000	10+1	4	0	0
Peschisolido, Paul	Can	f	Nov 2000	5	1	0	0
Ngonge, Michel (DRC)	Bel	f	Dec 2000	7+6	3	0+2	0
Agogo, Junior	Gha	f	Aug 2001	0+2	0	0	0
Ben Askar, Aziz	Fr	d	Aug 2001	18	0	1	0
Bonnot, Alex	Fr	m	Aug 2001	17+5	1	2	0
De Ornelas, Fernando	Ven	m	Oct 2001	1+1	0	0	0
M'Bombo, Doudou	DRC	f	Aug 2001	23+23	3	2+1	0
Shittu, Danny	Nig	d	Oct 2001	166+3	17	13	0
Padula, Gino	Arg	d	Aug 2002	81+9	4	10+3	1
Sabin, Eric	Fr	f	Jul 2003	3+7	1	3+3	0
Gnohere, Arthur (Fr)	IvCo	d	Sep 2003	20+1	0	2	1
Johnson, Richard	Aus	m	Feb 2004	16+1	0	1	0
Kanyuka, Patrick	DRC	d	Apr 2004	1	0	0	0
Santos, Georges (CVI)	Fr	m	Jul 2004	64+10	6	2+1	0
Branco, Serge	Cam	m	Sep 2004	3+4	0	2	0
Simek, Frankie	USA	d	Oct 2004	5	0	0	0
Rossi, Generoso	It	gk	Jan 2005	3	0	0	0
Nygaard, Marc	Den	d	Jul 2005	20+7	9	0	0
Lomas, Steve (N Ire)	Ger	m	Aug 2005	18+3	0	0	0
Milanese, Mauro	It	d	Aug 2005	22+4	0	2	0
Ukah, Ugo (Nig)	It	d	Aug 2005	0+1	0	1	0
Kus, Marcin	Pol	d	Jan 2006	3	0	0	0
Youssouf, Sammy	Den	f	Jan 2006	2+4	0	0	0
READING (33)							
Higginbotham, Harry	Aus	f	May 1924	24	3	1	0
Alleyne, Andy	Bar	fb	Nov 1972	46+2	2	5	0

Name	Born	Pos	From	LgAp	LgG	OthAp	OthG
Lenarduzzi, Bob	Can	d	May 1973	63+4	2	3+1	0
Hazell, Bob (Eng)	Jam	d	Nov 1986	4	1	0	0
Lovell, Stuart	Aus	f	Jul 1990	177+50	58	24+9	9
Streete, Floyd (Brit)	Jam	d	Jul 1990	38	0	5	0
Statham, Brian (Eng)	Zim	d/m	Mar 1991	8	0	0	0
Cooper, Neale (Sco)	Ind	m	Jul 1991	6+1	0	2	0
Kerr, Dylan (Brit)	Mal	d	Jul 1993	84+5	5	10+1	1
Hartenberger, Uwe	Ger	f	Sep 1993	8+16	4	0+2	0
Bernal, Andy	Aus	d	Jul 1994	179+8	2	34+2	1
Wdowczyk, Dariusz	Pol	d	Aug 1994	77+5	0	12+1	0
Barnard, Darren (Wal)	Ger	m	Nov 1994	3+1	0	0	0
Mikhailov, Bobby	Bul	gk	Sep 1995	24	0	4	0
Mautone, Steve	Aus	gk	Feb 1997	29	0	5	0
Crawford, Jimmy (Ire)	USA	d/m	Mar 1998	17+4	1	3+2	0
Sarr, Mass	Lbr	f	Jul 1998	18+13	3	2+2	0
Kromheer, Elroy	Neth	d	Aug 1998	11	0	1	0
Van der Kwaak, Peter	Neth	gk	Aug 1998	3+1	0	1	0
Rougier, Tony	Trin	m/f	Aug 2000	47+37	6	4+6	0
Salako, John (Eng)	Nig	f	Nov 2001	96+15	13	5+5	1
Hahnemann, Marcus	USA	gk	Dec 2001	174	0	17+1	0
Young, Jamie	Aus	gk	Sep 2002	0+1	0	0	0
Daley, Omar	Jam	m	Aug 2003	0+6	0	0+1	0
Goater, Shaun	Ber	f	Aug 2003	32+11	12	5+1	2
Ingimarsson, Ivar	Ice	m	Oct 2003	113+2	6	15	1
Convey, Bobby	USA	m	Jul 2004	49+14	7	3+1	0
Sonko, Ibrahima	Sen	d	Jul 2004	81+4	4	9	0
Gunnarsson, Brynjar	Ice	d	Jul 2005	19+10	4	4+1	0
Lita, Leroy (Eng)	Con	f	Jul 2005	22+4	11	3+3	4
Osano, Curtis	Ken	d	Jul 2005	0	0	0+1	0
Baradji, Sekou	Fr	d	Sep 2005	0+1	0	2	0
Obinna, Eric	Nig	f	Jan 2006	0+6	0	2	0

ROCHDALE (16)

Name	Born	Pos	From	LgAp	LgG	OthAp	OthG
Murray, David	SA	f	Aug 1931	22	3	1	1
Cornock, Wally	Aus	gk	Nov 1947	1	0	0	0
Kapler, Konrad	Pol	w	May 1949	4	0	0	0
Wasilewski, Adam	Pol	f	Jul 1953	4	1	0	0
Priday, Bob	SA	w	Aug 1953	5	1	0	0
Symonds, Calvin	Ber	f	Oct 1954	1	0	0	0
Carr, Everton	Ant	fb	Mar 1983	9	0	0	0
Cooke, Joe	Dom	d/f	Jul 1984	75	4	9	1
Hughes, Zacari	Aus	d	Aug 1989	2	0	1	0
Diaz, Isidro	Sp	m	Aug 1998	12+2	2	2+2	0
Hahnemann, Marcus	USA	gk	Oct 2001	5	0	0	0
Cansdell-Sheriff, Shane	Aus	d	Nov 2002	3	0	1	0
Bertos, Leo (Grk)	NZ	m	Jul 2003	73+9	13	6+1	1
Antoine-Curier, Mickael	Fr	f	Sep 2003	5+3	1	0+2	0
Kangana, Ndiwa	DRC	d	Feb 2004	0+1	0	0	0
Goodhind, Warren	SA	d	Sep 2005	10	0	2	0

ROTHERHAM TOWN (1)

Name	Born	Pos	From	LgAp	LgG	OthAp	OthG
Wharton, Arthur (1)	Gha	gk	Jul 1893	19	0	0	0
Wharton, Arthur (2)	Gha	gk	Jul 1895	15	0	0	0

ROTHERHAM UNITED (17)

Name	Born	Pos	From	LgAp	LgG	OthAp	OthG
Crawford, Ronald	SA	fb	Jul 1931	3	0	0	0
Tunks, Roy (Brit)	Ger	gk	Mar 1968	138	0	20	0
Goater, Shaun	Ber	f	Oct 1989	169+40	70	44+12	18
Cunningham, Tony (Brit)	Jam	f	Aug 1991	65+5	24	13	3
Smith, Scott	NZ	d	Oct 1993	30+6	0	4+1	0
Viljoen, Nik	NZ	f	Jun 1995	5+3	2	0	0
McDougald, Junior (Brit)	USA	f	Jul 1996	14+4	2	1	0
Crawford, Jimmy (Ire)	USA	d/m	Sep 1996	11	0	0	0
Jean, Earl	StL	f	Jan 1997	7+11	6	0	0
Bos, Gijsbert	Neth	m	Aug 1997	7+11	4	1+1	0
Wilsterman, Brian (Neth)	Sur	d	Jul 1999	47+5	4	5	0
Bolima, Cedric	DRC	f	Oct 2000	0+1	0	0	0
Lemarchand, Stephane	Fr	f	Nov 2000	0	0	0+1	0
Miranda, Jose	Por	m	Sep 2001	2	0	0+1	0
Baudet, Julien	Fr	d	Aug 2003	8+3	6	0+1	0
Junior, Jose Luis	Bra	f	Oct 2004	12	2	0	0
Griffit, Leandre	Fr	m	Mar 2005	1+1	0	0	0

RUSHDEN & DIAMONDS (11)

Brady, Jon	Aus	m	Jul 1998	9+13	1	3+2	0
Lowe, Onandi	Jam	f	Nov 2001	87+3	49	7+1	3
Sigere, Jean-Michel (Fr)	Mart	f	Mar 2000	4+3	1	1	0
Okuonghae, Magnus	Nig	m	Jan 2003	15+7	1	0+2	0
Jack, Rodney (StV)	Jam	f	Jun 2003	44+1	12	4	1
Evans, Paul	SA	gk	Oct 2003	2	0	2	0
Manangu, Eric	DRC	m	Nov 2003	0+1	0	0	0
Jackson, Simeon	Jam	m	Aug 2004	8+8	5	0	0
Joseph, Ricardo	Jam	d	Jul 2005	1	0	0	0
Young, Jamie	Aus	gk	Jul 2005	19+1	0	4	0
Mikolanda, Petr	CzRep	f	Jan 2006	7+2	1	0	0

SCARBOROUGH (9)

Podd, Cec	StK	fb	Jul 1986	3	0	0	0
Short, Chris (Brit)	Ger	d	Jul 1988	42+1	1	6	0
Lightbourne, Kyle	Ber	f	Dec 1992	11+8	3	1	0
Heald, Oliver	Can	m	Aug 1995	1+8	1	0+3	0
Moilanen, Tepi	Fin	gk	Dec 1996	4	0	0	0
Van der Velden, Carel	Neth	m	Aug 1997	5+3	1	2	0
Atkinson, Paddy (Brit)	Sing	d	Aug 1998	23+4	0	4	0
Mirankov, Alex	Fr	m	Aug 1998	22	4	3	0
Dabelsteen, Thomas	Den	m	Nov 1998	5	1	0	0

SCUNTHORPE UNITED (15)

Malan, Norman	SA	gk	Jun 1950	136	0	18	0
Thorpe, Arthur (Brit)	Ind	w	Sep 1960	27	5	1	0
Carmichael, Matt (Brit)	Sing	f	Jul 1993	51+11	20	5+4	2
Gregory, Neil (Brit)	Zam	f	Mar 1995	10	7	0	0
Calvo-Garcia, Alex	Sp	m	Oct 1996	208+28	33	38+3	11
Ipoua, Guy (Fr)	Cam	f	Aug 1999	50+15	23	5	4
Marcelle, Clint	Trin	f	Oct 1999	8+2	0	1	0
Perez, Lionel	Fr	gk	Oct 1999	13	0	0	0
Omoyimni, Manny	Nig	f	Dec 1999	6	1	0	0
Hyldgaard, Morten	Den	gk	Jan 2000	5	0	0	0
Mamoun, Blaise	Cam	m	Aug 2000	0+1	0	0	0
Larusson, Bjarni	Ice	m	Sep 2000	33	4	5	0

Name	Born	Pos	From	LgAp	LgG	OthAp	OthG
Grant, Kim	Gha	f	Aug 2001	3+1	1	1	0
Sharp, Kevin	Can	d	Jun 2003	41+5	2	11+1	0
Ehui, Ismael	Fr	f	Feb 2006	0+3	0	0	0

SHEFFIELD UNITED (48)

Name	Born	Pos	From	LgAp	LgG	OthAp	OthG
Wharton, Arthur	Gha	gk	Jul 1894	1	0	0	0
Gibson, Jock	USA	fb	Mar 1929	74	0	3	0
Cutbush, John (1)	Mal	fb	Mar 1977	79+2	1	2	0
Sabella, Alex	Arg	m	Aug 1978	76	8	6	0
Casey, Paul (Brit)	Ger	d/m	Jun 1979	23+2	1	0	0
Cutbush, John (2)	Mal	fb	Aug 1979	47+1	0	4	0
De Goey, Len	Neth	m	Aug 1979	33	5	3	0
Verde, Pedro	Arg	f	Aug 1979	9+1	3	2	0
Segers, Hans	Neth	gk	Nov 1987	10	0	0	0
Flo, Jostein	Nor	f	Aug 1993	74+10	19	5+1	3
Wirmola, Jonas	Swe	d	Aug 1993	8	0	1	0
Nilsen, Roger	Nor	d	Nov 1993	157+9	0	20+4	0
Hodgson, Doug	Aus	d	Jul 1994	24+6	0	4+2	0
Veart, Carl	Aus	m	Jul 1994	47+19	15	4+2	2
Short, Chris (Brit)	Ger	d	Dec 1995	40+4	0	11+2	0
Vonk, Michel	Neth	d	Dec 1995	37	2	6	2
Kachouro, Petr	Blr	f	Jul 1996	50+45	19	13+13	4
Fjortoft, Jan Aage	Nor	f	Jan 1997	30+4	19	6+2	4
Borbokis, Vassilis	Grk	d	Jul 1997	55	4	19	5
Dellas, Traianos	Grk	d	Aug 1997	14+12	3	2+3	0
Marcelo	Bra	f	Oct 1997	47+19	24	14+3	8
Jacobsen, Anders	Nor	d	Dec 1998	8+4	0	0+1	0
Donis, George	Grk	m	Mar 1999	5+2	1	0	0
Tebily, Olivier	IvCo	d	Mar 1999	7+1	0	0	0
Murphy, Shaun	Aus	d	Jul 1999	157+1	10	24	2
Smeets, Axel (Bel)	DRC	d	Jul 1999	2+3	0	2+1	0
Gysbrechts, Davy	Bel	d	Aug 1999	9+8	0	2	0
Ribeiro, Bruno	Por	m	Oct 1999	12+13	1	4+1	0
D'Jaffo, Laurent	Fr	f	Feb 2000	45+24	11	1+4	1
Santos, Georges (CVI)	Fr	m	Jul 2000	37+24	6	3+4	0
Uhlenbeek, Gus (Neth)	Sur	d	Aug 2000	47+4	0	8	0
Weber, Nicolas	Fr	d	Aug 2000	3+1	0	2	0
Talia, Frank	Aus	gk	Sep 2000	6	0	0	0
Suffo, Patrick	Cam	f	Nov 2000	16+20	5	0+2	1
Ndlovu, Peter	Zim	f	Feb 2001	114+21	25	16+3	4
Thetis, Manuel	Fr	d	Mar 2001	0+1	0	0	0
Peschisolido, Paul	Can	f	Jul 2001	39+45	18	6+12	5
De Vogt, Wilko	Neth	gk	Aug 2001	5+1	0	3	0
Javary, Jean-Phillipe	Fr	m	Mar 2002	8+5	1	0+1	0
Ten Heuvel, Laurens	Neth	f	Aug 2002	0+5	0	0+4	0
Cas, Marcel	Neth	m	Feb 2003	3+3	0	0	0
Baxter, Lee (Brit)	Swe	gk	Dec 2003	1	0	0	0
Boussatta, Dries	Neth	m	Nov 2003	3+3	0	1	0
Gabrieli, Emanuele	It	d	Sep 2004	0+1	0	0	0
Haidong, Hao	Chn	f	Jan 2005	0	0	0+1	0
Johnson, David	Jam	f	Mar 2005	0+4	0	0	0
Nalis, Lilian	Fr	m	May 2005	3+1	0	2	0
Nix, Kyle (Eng)	Aus	m	Jul 2005	0	0	0+2	0
Pericard, Vincent	Fr	f	Sep 2005	3+8	2	0	0

Name	Born	Pos	From	LgAp	LgG	OthAp	OthG
SHEFFIELD WEDNESDAY (51)							
Smit(h), Wilf	Ger	fb	Sep 1963	206	4	27	1
Strutt, Brian	Mal	f	Sep 1977	2	0	0	0
Mirocevic, Ante	Yug	m	Oct 1980	58+3	6	7+2	1
Cunningham, Tony (Brit)	Jam	f	Nov 1983	26+2	5	4+1	0
Jonsson, Siggi	Ice	m	Feb 1985	59+8	4	4+1	2
Nilsson, Roland	Swe	fb	Nov 1989	151	2	32+1	1
Harkes, John	USA	m	Oct 1990	59+22	7	33+1	4
Bart-Williams, Chris (Brit)	SiLe	m	Nov 1991	95+29	16	20+11	7
Petrescu, Dan	Rom	m	Aug 1994	28+9	3	3+2	1
Ingesson, Klas	Swe	m	Sep 1994	12+6	2	3	0
Degryse, Marc	Bel	m	Aug 1995	30+4	8	4	4
Kovacevic, Darko	Yug	f	Dec 1995	8+8	4	1	0
Stefanovic, Dejan	Yug	d	Dec 1995	59+7	4	6	1
Blinker, Regi (Neth)	Sur	f	Mar 1996	24+18	3	3	0
Trustfull, Orlando	Neth	m	Aug 1996	9+10	3	2+1	0
Carbone, Benito	It	f	Oct 1996	86+10	25	10+1	1
Agogo, Junior	Gha	f	Oct 1996	0+2	0	0+1	0
Blondeau, Patrick	Fr	d	Jun 1997	5+1	0	0	0
Di Canio, Paolo	It	f	Aug 1997	39+2	15	7	2
Rudi, Petter	Nor	m	Oct 1997	70+7	8	11+1	2
Alexandersson, Niclas	Swe	m	Dec 1997	73+2	8	12+1	4
Mayrleb, Christian	Aut	f	Jan 1998	0+3	0	0	0
Sedloski, Goce	Mac	d	Mar 1998	3+1	0	0	0
Thome, Emerson	Bra	d	Mar 1998	60+1	1	9+1	1
Sanetti, Francesco	It	f	Apr 1998	1+4	1	0+2	0
Cobian, Juan	Arg	d	Aug 1998	7+2	0	1	0
Jonk, Wim	Neth	m	Aug 1998	69+1	5	11	0
Srnicek, Pavel	CzRep	gk	Nov 1998	44	0	8	0
De Bilde, Gilles	Bel	f	Jul 1999	50+9	13	9	2
Sibon, Gerald	Neth	d	Jul 1999	98+31	36	18+3	7
Di Piedi, Michele	It	m	Aug 2000	9+30	5	1+4	2
Blatsis, Con	Aus	d	Dec 2000	6	0	2	0
Soltvedt, Trond Egil	Nor	m	Feb 2001	74	2	7	2
Bonvin, Pablo	Arg	m	Aug 2001	7+16	4	2+5	1
Roberts, Sean	SA	gk	Oct 2001	0+1	0	0	0
Djordjic, Bojan (Swe)	Yug	m	Dec 2001	4+1	0	0	0
Kuqi, Shefki (Fin)	Alb	f	Jan 2002	58+6	19	4	0
Johnson, David	Jam	f	Feb 2002	7	2	0	0
Evans, Paul	SA	gk	Mar 2003	7	0	0	0
Tidman, Ola	Swe	gk	Jun 2003	12+1	0	3	0
N'Dumbu-Nsungu, Guylain	DRC	f	Sep 2003	24+11	10	6+3	1
Antoine-Curier, Mickael	Fr	f	Nov 2003	0+1	0	0	0
Olsen, Kim	Den	f	Feb 2004	6+4	0	1+1	0
Collins, Patrick (Eng)	Om	d	May 2004	28+3	1	4+1	0
Jones, Kenwyne	Trin	f	Sep 2004	7	7	0	0
Aranalde, Zigor	Sp	d	Mar 2005	1+1	0	0	0
Diallo, Drissa (Gui)	Mau	m	Jul 2005	8+3	0	1	0
O'Brien, Burton	SA	f	Jul 2005	34+10	2	2+1	0
Simek, Frankie	USA	d	Jul 2005	42+1	1	2	0
Folly, Yoann (Fr)	Tgo	m	Jan 2006	14	0	0	0
Bischoff, Mikkel	Den	d	Mar 2006	4	0	0	0

Name	Born	Pos	From	LgAp	LgG	OthAp	OthG
SHREWSBURY TOWN (13)							
Atkins, Arthur (Brit)	Jap	ch	Jun 1954	16	0	1	0
Blake, Noel (Brit)	Jam	d	Mar 1982	6	0	0	0
Pittman, Steve	USA	fb	Mar 1989	31+1	2	4	0
Paskin, John	SA	f	Feb 1992	1	0	0	0
Stevens, Ian	Mal	f	Aug 1994	98+31	39	6+4	2
Gall, Benny	Den	gk	Aug 1996	34	0	4	0
Nielsen, Tommy	Den	fb	Aug 1996	19+3	1	1+2	0
Fallon, Rory	NZ	f	Dec 2001	8+3	0	0	0
Van Blerk, Jason	Aus	m	Aug 2002	17+6	1	3	1
Adaggio, Marco	Sp	f	Jul 2004	0+10	0	0+1	0
Cowan, Gavin (Brit)	Ger	d	Mar 2005	14+6	1	1	0
Denny, Jay	USA	m	Jun 2005	7+7	0	2+1	2
Sharp, Kevin	Can	d	Jul 2005	27+3	1	1+1	0
SOUTHAMPTON (62)							
Moorhead, George (Ire)	NZ	ch	Aug 1920	9	0	4	0
Osborne, Frank (Eng)	SA	f	Jun 1931	17	0	3	0
Charles, Alf	Trin	f	Jan 1937	1	0	0	0
Woolf, Levi	SA	f	Sep 1937	1	0	0	0
Horsfall, George	Aus	wh	May 1947	2	0	0	0
Gallego, Jose	Sp	w	May 1948	1	0	0	0
Chadwick, Dave (Brit)	Ind	w	Oct 1960	25	1	1	0
Kemp, Fred (Brit)	It	m	Jun 1965	58+3	10	10+1	1
Golac, Ivan (1)	Yug	fb	Nov 1978	143+1	4	28	0
Katalinic, Ivan	Yug	gk	Feb 1980	48	0	6	0
Golac, Ivan (2)	Yug	fb	Mar 1984	24	0	0	0
Cherednik, Alexei	USSR	d	Feb 1990	19+4	0	4	0
Gotsmanov, Sergei	USSR	f	Aug 1990	2+6	0	4	0
Monkou, Ken (Neth)	Sur	d	Aug 1992	190+8	10	33+1	3
Grobbelaar, Bruce (Zim)	SA	gk	Aug 1994	32	0	8	0
Ekelund, Ronnie	Den	f	Sep 1994	15+2	5	2+1	0
Tisdale, Paul (Brit)	Mal	m	Jun 1991	5+11	1	0+2	0
Neilson, Alan (Wal)	Ger	d	Jun 1995	42+13	0	8	0
Lundekvam, Claus	Nor	d	Sep 1996	317+7	2	53+3	0
Ostenstad, Egil	Nor	f	Oct 1996	80+16	28	12+1	5
Berkovic, Eyal	Isr	m	Oct 1996	26+2	4	6+1	2
Van Gobbel, Ulrich (Neth)	Sur	d	Oct 1996	25+2	1	7	1
Dia, Ali	Sen	f	Nov 1996	0+1	0	0	0
Taylor, Maik (N Ire)	Ger	gk	Jan 1997	18	0	0	0
Johansen, Stig	Nor	f	Aug 1997	3+3	0	1+1	0
Kachloul, Hassan	Mor	m	Oct 1998	73+13	14	9+2	1
Colleter, Patrick	Fr	d	Dec 1998	24	1	3	0
Rodrigues, Dani	Por	f	Mar 1999	0+2	0	0	0
Pahars, Marian	Lat	f	Mar 1999	110+27	43	17+2	2
Almeida, Marco	Por	d	Jul 1999	0+1	0	0	0
Boa Morte, Luis	Por	f	Aug 1999	6+8	1	1+2	0
Soltvedt, Trond Egil	Nor	m	Aug 1999	20+10	2	8+1	3
Tessem, Jo	Nor	m	Nov 1999	67+43	12	11+8	4
Bleidelis, Imants	Lat	m	Feb 2000	0+2	0	1+2	0
El Khalej, Tahar	Mor	d	Mar 2000	48+10	3	3+4	1
Rosler, Uwe	Ger	f	Jul 2000	9+15	0	1+4	1
McDonald, Scott	Aus	f	Aug 2000	0+2	0	1	0
Petrescu, Dan	Rom	m	Jan 2001	8+3	2	0	0
Svensson, Anders	Swe	m	Jun 2001	97+30	10	19+1	4

Name	Born	Pos	From	LgAp	LgG	OthAp	OthG
Delgado, Agustin	Ecu	f	Nov 2001	2+9	1	3+1	1
Fernandes, Fabrice	Fr	m	Dec 2001	76+15	5	12+3	1
Svensson, Michael	Swe	d	Aug 2002	66+1	4	15	2
Kanchelskis, Andrei	Ukr	m	Sep 2002	0+1	0	0+1	0
Niemi, Antti	Fin	gk	Sep 2002	106	0	17	0
Folly, Yoann (Fr)	Tgo	m	Jul 2003	12+2	0	2+2	0
Griffit, Leandre	Fr	m	Jul 2003	2+5	2	0+1	0
Van, Damme Jelle	Bel	d	Jun 2004	4+2	0	2+1	0
Jones, Kenwyne	Trin	f	Jul 2004	18+18	4	3+2	1
Nilsson, Mikael	Swe	m	Jul 2004	12+4	0	5	0
Surman, Andrew	SA	m	Jul 2004	11+1	2	0	0
Jakobsson, Andreas	Swe	d	Aug 2004	24+3	2	5+1	0
Keller, Kasey	USA	gk	Nov 2004	4	0	0	0
Bernard, Olivier	Fr	m	Jan 2005	12+1	0	3	0
Camara, Henri	Sen	f	Jan 2005	10+3	4	2+1	2
Fuller, Ricardo	Jam	f	Jul 2005	21+9	9	0+1	0
Hajto, Tomasz	Pol	d	Jul 2005	15+5	0	1	0
Belmadi, Djemal (Alg)	Fr	m	Aug 2005	21+1	3	1	0
Kosowski, Kamil	Pol	m	Aug 2005	12+6	1	0	0
Bialkowski, Bartosz	Pol	gk	Jan 2006	5	0	2	0
Brennan, Jim	Can	d	Jan 2006	13+1	0	2	0
Madsen, Peter	Den	f	Jan 2006	8+1	2	1	0
Ostlund, Alexander	Swe	d	Jan 2006	10+2	0	1	0
Rasiak, Grzegorz	Pol	f	Feb 2006	12+1	4	0	0

SOUTHEND UNITED (23)

Name	Born	Pos	From	LgAp	LgG	OthAp	OthG
Horsfall, George	Aus	wh	Jul 1949	1	0	0	0
Crossan, Errol	Can	w	Aug 1957	40	11	5	0
Houghton, Bud (Brit)	Ind	f	Oct 1958	68	32	5	1
Firmani, Eddie	SA	f	Jun 1965	55	24	7	4
Roberts, John	Aus	gk	Jan 1971	47	0	4	0
Welch, Micky	Bar	f	Feb 1985	4	0	0	0
Iorfa, Dominic (1)	Nig	f	Aug 1994	5+7	1	2	0
Lapper, Mike	USA	d	Aug 1995	46+6	1	3	0
Belsvik, Petter	Nor	f	Nov 1995	3	1	0	0
Boere, Jeroen	Neth	f	Mar 1996	61+12	25	5+2	0
Harris, Andy (Brit)	SA	m	Jul 1996	70+2	0	8	0
Nielsen, John	Den	m	Sep 1996	18+11	3	3	1
Dursun, Peter	Den	f	Nov 1996	0+1	0	0	0
Nzamba, Guy	Gab	f	Sep 1997	0+1	0	0	0
Coulbault, Regis	Fr	m	Oct 1997	30+4	4	2	0
Henriksen, Tony	Nor	gk	Oct 1996	0	0	0+1	0
N'Diaye, Sada	Sen	m	Oct 1997	15+2	2	1	0
Iorfa, Dominic (2)	Nig	f	Dec 1998	0+2	0	0	0
Unger, Lars	Ger	m	Feb 1999	14	0	0	0
Coyne, Chris	Aus	d	Mar 1999	0+1	0	0	0
Petterson, Andy	Aus	gk	Sep 2003	1	0	0	0
Griemink, Bart	Neth	gk	Jun 2004	22	0	4	0
Goater, Shaun	Ber	f	Aug 2005	28+6	11	3	0
Moussa, Franck	Bel	m	Jan 2006	0+1	0	0	0

SOUTHPORT (4)

Name	Born	Pos	From	LgAp	LgG	OthAp	OthG
King, Charlie	SA	ch	May 1923	35	1	4	0
Bellis, George (Brit)	Ind	ch	Aug 1923	41	4	1	0
Aspinall, Wilf	USA	f	Jul 1935	6	0	0	0
Perry, Bill	SA	w	Jun 1962	26	0	3	0

Name	Born	Pos	From	LgAp	LgG	OthAp	OthG
SOUTH SHIELDS (1)							
Higginbotham, Harry	Aus	f	Aug 1919	7	0	0	0
STOCKPORT COUNTY (35)							
Wharton, Arthur	Gha	gk	Jul 1901	6	0	0	0
Pass, George (Brit)	Ind	f	Aug 1903	59	18	7	1
Andrews, Billy (N Ire)	USA	wh	Mar 1909	13	0	0	0
Aspinall, Wilf	USA	f	Jun 1934	1	1	0	0
Grieves, Ken	Aus	gk	Jul 1957	39	0	4	0
Keelan, Kevin (Brit)	Ind	gk	Apr 1961	3	0	0	0
Stuart, Eddie	SA	d	Jul 1966	77	1	4	0
Vernon, John	SA	w	Apr 1975	4+2	0	0	0
Stevens, Ian	Mal	f	Oct 1986	1+1	0	0+1	0
Paskin, John	SA	f	Sep 1991	3+2	1	0	0
Cantona, Joel	Fr	m	Mar 1994	0+3	0	0	0
Murray, Bruce	USA	f	Mar 1994	2+1	0	0	0
Cavaco, Luis Miguel	Por	f	Aug 1996	19+10	5	10+2	2
Nash, Martin	Can	f	Nov 1996	0+11	0	0+1	0
Kiko, Manuel	Por	f	Dec 1996	0+3	0	0	0
Kalogeracos, Vas	Aus	f	Aug 1997	0+2	0	1	0
Aunger, Geoff	Can	d/m	Dec 1997	0+1	0	0	0
Alsaker, Paul	Nor	f	Aug 1998	1	0	1	0
D'Jaffo, Laurent	Fr	f	Aug 1999	20+1	7	2	1
Bergersen, Kent	Nor	m	Sep 1999	18+8	1	1	0
Fradin, Karim	Fr	m	Nov 1999	72+9	9	6+1	2
Bryngelsson, Fredrik	Swe	d	Jul 2000	7+1	0	2	0
Wiss, Jarkko	Fin	m	Aug 2000	34+7	6	4+2	1
Kuqi, Shefki (Fin)	Alb	f	Jan 2001	32+3	11	3	1
Helin, Petri	Fin	d	Jul 2001	10+3	0	1+2	0
Sneekes, Richard	Neth	m	Sep 2001	8+1	0	1	0
Arphexad, Pegguy (Fr)	Guad	gk	Sep 2001	3	0	0	0
Van Blerk, Jason	Aus	m	Aug 2001	13	0	1	0
Jones, Brad	Aus	gk	Dec 2002	1	0	0	0
Tidman, Ola	Swe	gk	Jan 2003	18	0	0	0
Myhill, Boaz	USA	gk	Nov 2003	2	0	1	0
Lynch, Simon	Can	f	Dec 2003	9	3	0	0
Robertsson, Mark	Aus	m	Jan 2004	27+5	1	4	0
Dje, Ludovic	Fr	d	Mar 2005	7+3	0	1	0
Wolski, Mickael	Fr	m	Jul 2005	14+6	1	2+2	1
STOKE CITY (54)							
Kirkby, John	USA	fb	Dec 1946	1	0	0	0
Stuart, Eddie	SA	d	Jul 1962	63	2	8	0
Backos, Des	SA	f	Oct 1977	1+1	0	0	0
Ursem, Loek	Neth	w	Jul 1979	32+8	7	4	0
Berry, George (Wal)	Ger	d	Aug 1982	229+8	27	23	1
Segers, Hans	Neth	gk	Feb 1987	1	0	0	0
Blake, Noel (Brit)	Jam	d	Feb 1990	74+1	3	11+1	0
Kearton, Jason	Aus	gk	Aug 1991	16	0	0	0
Stein, Mark (Eng) (1)	SA	f	Nov 1991	94	50	14	9
Grobbelaar, Bruce (Zim)	SA	gk	Mar 1993	4	0	0	0
Orlygsson, Toddi	Ice	m	Aug 1993	86+4	16	13	2
Peschisolido, Paul	Can	f	Aug 1994	59+7	19	9	3
Sigurdsson, Larus	Ice	d	Oct 1994	199+1	7	23+1	0
Andrade, Jose-Manuel (1)	Por	f	Mar 1995	2+2	1	0	0

Name	Born	Pos	From	LgAp	LgG	OthAp	OthG
Stein, Mark (Eng) (2)	SA	f	Aug 1996	11	4	0	0
Da Costa, Hugo	Por	d	Aug 1996	1+1	0	1+1	0
Schreuder, Jan-Dirk	Neth	f	Jun 1997	0	0	0+2	0
Andrade, Jose-Manuel (2)	Por	f	Aug 1997	4+8	1	2	0
Tiatto, Danny	Aus	d	Nov 1997	11+4	1	0	0
Xausa, Davide	Can	f	Feb 1998	1	0	0	0
Lightbourne, Kyle	Ber	f	Feb 1998	83+28	21	12	2
Sobiech, Jorg	Ger	d	Mar 1998	3	0	0	0
Oldfield, David (Eng)	Aus	m/f	Jul 1998	50+15	7	6+1	0
Short, Chris (Brit)	Ger	d	Jul 1998	33+2	0	5+1	0
Jacobsen, Anders	Nor	d	Aug 1999	29+4	2	5+1	0
Danielsson, Einer Thor	Ice	m	Nov 1999	3+5	1	0	0
Gislason, Siggi	Ice	m	Nov 1999	4+4	0	0	0
Hansson, Mikael	Swe	m	Dec 1999	60+5	2	9	0
Kippe, Frode	Nor	d	Dec 1999	30+4	1	2	0
Gunnarsson, Brynjar	Ice	d	Jan 2000	129+5	16	26+1	4
Gudjonsson, Bjarni	Ice	f	Mar 2000	119+13	11	21+2	3
Gunnlaugsson, Arnie	Ice	m	Mar 2000	19+3	5	4	1
Thordarson, Stefan	Ice	f	Jun 2000	18+33	8	7+3	2
Dorigo, Tony (Eng)	Aus	d	Jul 2000	34+2	0	5	0
Risom, Henrik	Den	m	Aug 2000	9+16	0	3+2	0
Dadason, Rikki	Ice	f	Oct 2000	19+20	10	1+6	1
Kippe, Frode	Nor	d	Oct 2000	15+4	0	2	0
Kristinsson, Birkir	Ice	gk	Nov 2000	18	0	0	0
Shtaniuk, Sergei	Blr	d	Jul 2001	84	5	11	0
Hoekstra, Peter	Neth	f	Jul 2001	66+12	11	5+3	1
Van Deurzen, Jurgen	Bel	m	Aug 2001	44+8	5	5+3	0
Marteinsson, Petur	Ice	m	Nov 2001	12+6	2	1+1	0
Oulare, Souleymane	Gui	f	Dec 2001	0+1	0	0+1	1
De Goey, Ed	Neth	gk	Aug 2003	55+1	0	1+1	0
Johnson, Richard	Aus	m	Nov 2003	3+4	0	1+1	0
Svard, Sebastian	Den	d	Dec 2003	9+4	1	0	0
Gudjonsson, Thordur	Ice	m	Jan 2005	0+2	0	0+1	0
Jones, Kenwyne	Trin	f	Feb 2005	13	3	0	0
Sidibe, Mamady (Fr)	Mli	f	Jun 2005	37+5	6	5	1
Hoefkens, Carl	Bel	d	Jul 2005	44	3	5	0
Mbuyi, Gabriel (Bel)	DRC	d	Jul 2005	16+6	0	1+1	0
Kolar, Martin	CzRep	m	Jul 2005	12+2	1	1	0
Sigurdsson, Hannes	Ice	f	Aug 2005	10+13	1	0+3	0
Bangoura, Sambegou	Gui	f	Oct 2005	23+1	9	1	0
Kopteff, Peter	Fin	m	Jan 2006	3+3	0	1+2	0
Skoko, Josip	Aus	m	Feb 2006	9	2	0	0

SUNDERLAND (45)

Name	Born	Pos	From	LgAp	LgG	OthAp	OthG
Dalton, James	Can	ch	Sep 1891	3	0	0	0
Gibson, Fred	SA	w	May 1909	1	0	0	0
Gibson, Jock	USA	fb	Nov 1920	4	0	1	0
Wagstaffe, Thomas (Brit)	Ind	f	Mar 1923	2	0	0	0
McDowall, Les	Ind	ch	Dec 1932	13	0	1	0
Purdon, Ted	SA	f	Jan 1954	90	3	96	3
Fraser, Willie (Sco)	Aus	gk	Mar 1954	127	0	16	0
Kichenbrand, Don	SA	f	Mar 1958	53	28	1	0
Marangoni, Claudio	Arg	m	Dec 1979	19+1	3	2	0
Ursem, Loek	Neth	w	Mar 1982	0+4	0	0	0

Name	Born	Pos	From	LgAp	LgG	OthAp	OthG
Nicholl, Jimmy (N Ire)	Can	fb	Sep 1982	32	0	8	0
Hesford, Iain (Eng)	Zam	gk	Aug 1986	97	0	9	0
Hauser, Thomas	Ger	f	Feb 1989	22+31	9	3+8	2
Butcher, Terry (Eng)	Sing	d	Jul 1992	37+1	0	4	1
Kubicki, Dariusz	Pol	fb	Jun 1994	135+1	0	14	0
Perez, Lionel	Fr	gk	Aug 1996	74+1	0	9	0
Eriksson, Jan	Swe	d	Jan 1997	1	0	0	0
Zoetebier, Ed	Neth	gk	Jun 1997	0	0	2	0
Sorensen, Thomas	Den	gk	Aug 1998	171	0	26	0
Fredgaard, Carsten	Den	m	Jul 1999	0+1	0	3+1	2
Helmer, Thomas	Ger	d	Jul 1999	1+1	0	0	0
Roy, Eric	Fr	m	Aug 1999	20+7	0	7	1
Schwarz, Stefan	Swe	m	Aug 1999	62+5	3	8	1
Di Giuseppe, Bica	Bra	f	Sep 1999	0	0	0+1	0
Nunez, Milton	Hon	f	Mar 2000	0+1	0	0+1	0
Arca, Julio	Arg	m	Aug 2000	145+12	17	20	4
Macho, Jurgen	Aut	gk	Jul 2000	20+2	0	4+1	0
Peeters, Tom	Bel	m	Jul 2000	0	0	1	0
Thome, Emerson	Bra	d	Sep 2000	43+1	2	9	0
Varga, Stanislav	Svk	d	Aug 2000	18+3	1	10+1	0
Carteron, Patrice	Fr	d	Mar 2001	8	1	0	0
Bellion, David	Fr	f	Jul 2001	5+15	1	3+1	0
Haas, Bernt (Swit)	Aut	d	Aug 2001	27	0	1+1	0
Laslandes, Lilian	Fr	f	Jun 2001	5+7	0	0+1	1
Reyna, Claudio	USA	m	Dec 2001	28	3	1	1
Bjorklund, Joachim	Swe	d	Jan 2002	49+8	0	6+2	0
Mboma, Patrick	Cam	f	Feb 2002	5+4	1	0	0
Myhre, Thomas	Nor	gk	Oct 2002	35+2	0	5	0
Flo, Tore Andre	Nor	f	Nov 2002	23+6	4	3+1	2
Medina, Nicolas	Arg	m	Jan 2003	0	0	1	0
El Karkouri, Talal	Mor	d	Feb 2003	8	0	0+1	0
Poom, Mart	Est	gk	Apr 2003	58	1	9+1	0
Whitley, Jeff (N Ire)	Zam	m	Aug 2003	65+3	2	9	0
Bassila, Christian	Fr	m	Aug 2005	12+1	0	1	0
Le Tallec, Anthony	Fr	f	Aug 2005	12+15	3	4+1	1
SWANSEA CITY (20)							
Armand, Jack (Brit)	Ind	f	May 1929	54	10	1	0
Haasz, Johnny	Hun	f	Sep 1960	1	0	0	0
Chinaglia, Giorgio	It	f	Apr 1965	4+1	1	1	0
Schroeder, Nico	Neth	gk	Jul 1976	1	0	0	0
Hadziabdic, Dzemal	Yug	fb	Aug 1980	87+2	1	14	1
Rajkovic, Anto	Yug	d	Mar 1981	79+1	2	14	1
Salako, John (Eng)	Nig	f	Aug 1989	13	3	2	1
Molby, Jan	Den	m	Feb 1996	39+2	8	2	0
Moreira, Joao	Por	d	Jun 1996	15	0	7+1	0
Willer-Jensen, Thomas	Den	d	Mar 1997	7	0	0	0
Boyd, Walter	Jam	f	Oct 1999	35+9	10	3+1	0
Romo, David	Fr	m	Oct 2000	31+12	1	2+1	0
Savarese, Giovanni	Ven	f	Oct 2000	28+3	12	0+1	0
Fabiano, Nicolas	Fr	m	Feb 2001	12+4	1	0	0
Verschave, Matthias	Fr	f	Feb 2001	12	3	0	0
Mazzina, Nicolas	Arg	m	Jul 2001	3	0	1	0
Sidibe, Mamady (Fr)	Mli	f	Jul 2001	26+5	7	2+1	1
Martinez, Roberto	Sp	m	Feb 2003	111+11	4	13+4	0

Name	Born	Pos	From	LgAp	LgG	OthAp	OthG
Gueret, Willy (Fr)	Guad	gk	Jul 2004	90	0	17	0
Fallon, Rory	NZ	f	Jan 2006	12+5	4	2	0
SWINDON TOWN (38)							
Murray, David	SA	f	Jun 1930	1	0	0	0
Leslie, Maurice (Brit)	Ind	fb	Jun 1947	1	0	0	0
Nagy, Mick	Hun	ch	Aug 1951	2	0	0	0
Fiocca, Paul	It	m	Jan 1973	1	0	0	0
Sperti, Franco	It	fb	Jan 1973	1	0	0	0
Collins, Mike	SA	f	Jul 1973	2+4	0	1	0
Payne, Mark (Brit)	Ind	w	Sep 1984	0+3	0	1	0
Wegerle, Roy (USA)	SA	f	Mar 1988	7	1	0	0
Ardiles, Ossie	Arg	m	Jul 1989	0+2	0	0	0
Buttigieg, John	Mal	d	Sep 1990	2+1	0	0+1	0
Lorenzo, Nestor	Arg	d	Oct 1990	20+4	2	3	0
O'Sullivan, Wayne (Ire)	Cyp	m	May 1993	65+24	3	12+3	1
Fjortoft, Jan Aage	Nor	f	Jul 1993	62+10	28	12+1	11
Nijholt, Luc	Neth	d	Jul 1993	66+1	1	14+2	1
Talia, Frank	Aus	gk	Sep 1995	107	0	11	0
Darras, Frederic	Fr	d	Aug 1996	42+7	0	6	0
Cuervo, Phillipe	Fr	m	Aug 1997	16+19	0	2+1	0
Cobian, Juan	Arg	d	Jul 2000	3+1	0	3	0
Griemink, Bart	Neth	gk	Mar 2000	122+2	0	20	0
Heiselberg, Kim	Den	m	Aug 2000	1	0	1	0
Invincible, Danny	Aus	m	Aug 2000	109+19	22	11+1	3
Van der Linden, Antoine	Neth	d	Aug 2000	17+16	1	3	0
Robertson, Mark	Aus	m	Aug 2000	4+6	1	2+1	0
Tuomela, Marko	Fin	d	Sep 2000	1+1	0	2	0
Whitley, Jim (N Ire)	Zam	m	Dec 2000	2	0	1	0
Lightbourne, Kyle	Ber	f	Jan 2001	2	0	0	0
Bakalli, Adrian	Bel	d	Mar 2001	1	0	0	0
Sabin, Eric	Fr	f	Jun 2001	60+13	9	7	0
Edds, Gareth	Aus	m	Aug 2002	8+6	0	1+1	0
Miglioranzi, Stefani (USA)	Bra	m	Aug 2002	111+12	8	10+1	1
Ruster, Sebastien	Fr	m	Jul 2003	0+2	0	0+1	0
Fallon, Rory	NZ	f	Nov 2003	43+32	21	8+6	4
McMaster, Jamie	Aus	m	Sep 2004	2+2	1	0	0
Collins, Patrick (Eng)	Om	d	Aug 2005	13	0	0	0
Bouazza, Hameur	Fr	f	Oct 2005	11+2	2	2	1
Mikolanda, Petr	CzRep	f	Nov 2005	1+4	0	0	0
Jarrett, Albert (Eng)	SiLe	m	Jan 2006	2+4	0	0	0
Diagouraga, Toumani	Fr	m	Mar 2006	5+3	0	0	0
THAMES (1)							
Crawford, Ronald	SA	fb	Jul 1930	3	0	0	0
TORQUAY UNITED (33)							
Mackrill, Percy	SA	fb	Jul 1925	6	0	0	0
Butler, Jack (Eng)	SL	d	May 1930	50	2	3	0
Fursdon, Roy	Can	w	Aug 1938	15	2	0	0
Chadwick, Dave (Brit)	Ind	m	Dec 1972	10	0	0	0
Laryea, Benny	Gha	f	Mar 1984	10+2	3	3	1
Salman, Danis (Eng)	Cyp	d	Sep 1992	20	0	2	0
Sommer, Jurgen	USA	gk	Oct 1992	10	0	0	0
Goodridge, Greg (1)	Bar	w	Mar 1994	32+6	4	8+1	2
Okorie, Chima	Nig	f	Mar 1994	32+4	6	8+1	1

Name	Born	Pos	From	LgAp	LgG	OthAp	OthG
Mateu, Jose-Luis	Sp	f	Sep 1995	5+5	1	0+3	1
Jack, Rodney (StV)	Jam	f	Oct 1995	82+5	24	15	4
Haddaoui, Riffi	Den	f	Mar 1996	0+2	0	0	0
Gregory, Neil (Brit)	Zam	f	Nov 1996	5	0	0	0
Thirlby, Anthony (Brit)	Ger	m	Feb 1997	1+2	0	0	0
Newell, Justin (Brit)	Ger	f	Sep 1997	0+1	0	0	0
Harries, Paul	Aus	f	Feb 1999	5	0	0	0
Simb, Jean-Pierre	Fr	f	Mar 1999	4+16	1	0+4	0
Jermyn, Mark (Brit)	Ger	d	Mar 1999	0+1	0	0	0
Ingimarsson, Ivar	Ice	m	Oct 1999	4	1	0	0
Mendy, Jules	Sen	m	Aug 2000	7+14	2	0+4	0
Sissoko, Habib	Fr	f	Aug 2000	7+7	2	2	0
Chalqi, Khalid	Mor	f	Nov 2000	20+1	1	2	1
Petterson, Andy	Aus	gk	Mar 2001	6	0	0	0
Greyling, Anton	SA	m	Aug 2001	0+2	0	0	0
Goodridge, Greg (2)	Bar	w	Nov 2001	9+8	1	0	0
Van Heusden, Arjan	Neth	gk	Nov 2002	47	0	5	0
Camara, Ben (Brit)	Ger	f	Mar 2003	0+2	0	0	0
Bossu, Bert	Fr	gk	Aug 2004	2	0	0	0
Meirelles, Bruno	Por	m	Aug 2004	5+4	0	2	0
Gottskalksson, Ole	Ice	gk	Sep 2004	15	0	2	0
Lopes, Osvaldo	Fr	m	Jan 2005	1	0	0	0
Sow, Mamadou	Fr	f	Jun 2005	9+2	0	0+1	0
Sako, Malike	Fr	f	Jul 2005	10+15	3	2+1	0
Priso, Carl (Fr)	Cam	f	Aug 2005	1+2	0	0	0

TOTTENHAM HOTSPUR (58)

Name	Born	Pos	From	LgAp	LgG	OthAp	OthG
Seeburg, Max	Ger	f	May 1907	1	0	0	0
Osborne, Frank (Eng)	SA	f	Jan 1924	210	78	10	4
Garwood, Len (Brit)	Ind	wh	May 1946	2	0	0	0
Ardiles, Ossie	Arg	m	Jul 1978	221+16	16	71+2	9
Villa, Ricky	Arg	m	Jul 1978	124+9	18	44+2	7
Chiedozie, John	Nig	w	Aug 1984	45+8	12	19+3	2
Gough, Richard (Sco)	Swe	d	Aug 1986	49	2	16	0
Claesen, Nico	Bel	f	Oct 1986	37+13	18	8+5	5
Metgod, Johnny	Neth	m	Jul 1987	5+7	0	2	0
Statham, Brian (Eng)	Zim	d/m	Aug 1987	20+4	0	2+1	0
Nayim, Mohamed	Mor	m	Nov 1988	95+17	11	23+9	6
Bergsson, Gudni	Ice	d	Dec 1988	51+20	2	11+5	0
Thorstvedt, Erik	Nor	gk	Dec 1988	171+2	0	45	0
Van Den Hauwe, Pat (Wal)	Bel	fb	Aug 1989	110+6	0	29	0
Rosenthal, Ronny	Isr	f	Jan 1994	55+33	4	10+2	7
Dumitrescu, Ilie	Rom	m	Aug 1994	16+2	4	2	1
Klinsmann, Jurgen (1)	Ger	f	Aug 1994	41	20	9	9
Popescu, Gica	Rom	m	Sep 1994	23	3	5	0
Baardsen, Espen (Nor)	USA	gk	Jul 1996	22+1	0	5+1	0
Nielsen, Allan	Den	m	Sep 1996	78+19	12	16+3	6
Iversen, Steffen	Nor	f	Dec 1996	112+31	36	25+9	11
Vega, Ramon	Swit	d	Jan 1997	53+11	7	17+3	1
Ginola, David	Fr	w	Jul 1997	100	12	26+1	9
Dominguez, Jose	Por	w	Aug 1997	12+33	4	4+9	1
Klinsmann, Jurgen (2)	Ger	f	Dec 1997	15	9	3	0
Berti, Nicola	It	m	Jan 1998	21	3	2	0
Saib, Moussa	Alg	m	Feb 1998	3+10	1	0	0
Segers, Hans	Neth	gk	Aug 1998	1	0	1	0

Name	Born	Pos	From	LgAp	LgG	OthAp	OthG
Freund, Steffen	Ger	m	Dec 1998	92+10	0	29	0
Taricco, Mauricio	Arg	fb	Dec 1998	125+5	2	24+2	0
Nilsen, Roger	Nor	d	Mar 1999	3	0	0	0
Tramezzani, Paolo	It	d	Jun 1998	6	0	1	0
Korsten, Willem	Neth	f	Jul 1999	12+11	3	1+3	0
Leonhardsen, Oyvind	Nor	m	Aug 1999	46+8	7	13+5	4
Rebrov, Sergei	Ukr	f	Jun 2000	37+22	10	11+5	6
Bunjevcevic, Goran	Yug	d	Jun 2001	41+10	0	6+1	2
Ziege, Christian	Ger	m	Jul 2001	44+3	7	8	3
Poyet, Gustavo	Uru	m	Jul 2001	66+16	18	14+2	5
Keller, Kasey	USA	gk	Aug 2001	85	0	14	0
Acimovic, Milenko	Slo	m	Aug 2002	4+13	0	1	0
Blondel, Jonathan	Bel	m	Aug 2002	0+2	0	1+1	0
Toda, Kazuyuki	Jap	m	Apr 2003	2+2	0	0	0
Postiga, Helder	Por	f	Jun 2003	9+10	1	3+2	1
Dalmat, Stephane	Fr	m	Aug 2003	12+10	3	3+3	0
Kanoute, Frederic (Mli)	Fr	f	Aug 2003	41+19	14	11+2	7
Mabizela, Mbulelo	SA	d	Aug 2003	1+6	1	1+1	0
Edman, Erik	Swe	d	Jul 2004	31	1	2+1	0
Mendes, Pedro	Por	m	Jul 2004	25+5	1	4+2	0
Atouba, Thimothee	Cam	d	Aug 2004	15+3	1	6	0
Naybet, Noureddine	Mor	d	Aug 2004	29+1	1	5	0
Pamarot, Noe	Fr	d	Aug 2004	23+2	1	5	1
Ziegler, Reto	Swit	m	Aug 2004	12+11	1	8	0
Cerny, Radek	CzRep	gk	Jan 2005	2+1	0	0	0
Mido	Egy	f	Jan 2005	28+8	13	0+2	1
Stalteri, Paul	Can	d	May 2005	33	1	2	1
Tainio, Teemu	Fin	m	Jul 2005	22+2	1	0+1	0
Davids, Edgar (Neth)	Sur	m	Aug 2005	28+3	1	0	0
Lee, Yong-Pyo	SK	d	Aug 2005	31	0	1	0
Rasiak, Grzegorz	Pol	f	Aug 2005	4+4	0	1	0
TRANMERE ROVERS (20)							
Hill, Reg (Brit)	Gib	wh	Dec 1932	1	0	0	0
Fleming, Mike (Brit)	Ind	f	Sep 1953	115	8	7	0
Onyeali, Elkanah	Nig	f	Aug 1960	13	8	3	1
Stuart, Eddie	SA	d	Aug 1964	83	2	6	0
Anderson, Doug (Brit)	HK	m	Aug 1984	125+1	15	13+1	3
Bonetti, Ivano	It	m	Aug 1996	9+4	1	2	1
Kubicki, Dariusz	Pol	fb	Mar 1998	12	0	0	0
Santos, Georges (CVI)	Fr	m	Jul 1998	46+1	2	7	0
Achterberg, John	Neth	gk	Sep 1998	238+3	0	50+1	0
Matias, Pedro	Sp	m	Aug 1999	1+3	0	0	0
Hume, Iain	Can	m	Nov 2000	100+49	32	18+9	5
Myhre, Thomas	Nor	gk	Nov 2000	3	0	1	0
N'Diaye, Seyni	Sen	f	Mar 2001	11+8	4	2+1	0
Feuer, Ian	USA	gk	Aug 2002	2	0	0	0
Loran, Tyrone	Neth	d	Jan 2003	42+5	0	4	0
Dadi, Eugene (Fr)	IvCo	f	Aug 2003	44+25	25	10+7	3
Goodison, Ian	Jam	d	Feb 2004	87+7	2	12	0
Zola, Calvin	DRC	f	May 2004	22+15	6	3+2	2
Whitmore, Theo	Jam	m	Jun 2004	17+20	5	3+2	0
Seremet, Dino	Slo	gk	Jan 2006	13	0	0	0

Name	Born	Pos	From	LgAp	LgG	OthAp	OthG
WALSALL (50)							
Langenove, Eugene	Fr	f	Oct 1922	2	0	0	0
Milligan, Dudley (N Ire)	SA	f	Oct 1948	5	1	0	0
Pidcock, Fred	Can	gk	Sep 1953	1	0	0	0
Methven, Colin (Brit)	Ind	d	Nov 1990	97	3	9+1	0
Essers, Pierre	Neth	f	Sep 1991	1	0	0	0
Chine, Athumani	Tan	m	Mar 1992	4+1	0	0	0
Ollerenshaw, Scott	Aus	f	Aug 1992	8+12	4	2+4	0
Lightbourne, Kyle	Ber	f	Sep 1993	158+7	65	24+2	14
Kerr, John (USA)	Can	f	Nov 1995	0+1	0	0+1	0
Boli, Roger (Fr)	IvCo	f	Aug 1997	41	12	10	6
Peron, Jeff	Fr	m	Aug 1997	38	1	9	0
Eydelie, Jean-Jacques	Fr	m	Mar 1998	10+1	0	0	0
Tholot, Didier	Fr	f	Mar 1998	13+1	4	0	0
Larusson, Bjarni	Ice	m	Sep 1998	45+14	3	4+1	1
Otta, Walter	Arg	f	Nov 1998	6+2	3	2	0
Eyjolfsson, Siggi	Ice	f	Jan 1999	1+22	2	1+5	3
Mavrak, Darko (Bos)	Cro	m	Jan 1999	13+4	2	1+2	0
Steiner, Rob	Swe	f	Mar 1999	10	3	0	0
Bukran, Gabor	Hun	m	Aug 1999	63+10	4	11+2	3
Abou, Samassi (Fr)	IvCo	f	Oct 1999	7+1	0	0	0
Di Giuseppe, Bica	Bra	f	Oct 1999	0+1	0	0	0
Matias, Pedro	Sp	m	Oct 1999	105+36	24	14+7	3
Padula, Gino	Arg	d	Nov 1999	23+2	0	2	0
Vlachos, Michalis	Grk	d	Feb 2000	11	1	0	0
Aranalde, Zigor	Sp	d	Aug 2000	183+12	5	29	1
Leitao, Jorge	Por	f	Aug 2000	190+40	57	31+1	14
Ekelund, Ronnie	Den	f	Dec 2000	2+7	1	0+1	0
Herivelto, Moreira	Bra	m	Jul 2001	10+10	3	2+1	1
Garrocho, Carlos	Ang	m	Jul 2001	2+2	0	0+1	0
Herivelto, Moreira	Bra	m	Jul 2001	11+17	5	3+2	1
Ofodile, Adolphus	Nig	f	Jul 2001	0+1	0	1	0
Biancalani, Frederic	Fr	d	Aug 2001	13+5	2	2+1	0
Thogersen, Thomas	Den	m	Oct 2001	7	2	0	0
Andre, Carlos	Por	m	Dec 2001	5	0	2	0
Corica, Steve	Aus	m	Feb 2002	63+10	9	7+2	0
Marcelo	Bra	f	Feb 2002	9	1	0	0
Uhlenbeek, Gus (Neth)	Sur	d	Mar 2002	5	0	0	0
Rodrigues, Dani	Por	f	Aug 2002	0+1	0	0	0
Hay, Danny	NZ	d	Aug 2002	40+5	0	6	0
Junior, Jose Luis	Bra	f	Aug 2002	28+8	15	6	1
Martinez, Roberto	Sp	m	Aug 2002	1+5	0	0	0
Zdrilic, David	Aus	f	Aug 2002	9+15	3	1+4	2
Pollet, Ludo	Fr	d	Nov 2002	5	0	0	0
Petterson, Andy	Aus	gk	Jan 2004	3	0	0	0
Paston, Mark	NZ	gk	Jun 2004	8+1	0	3	0
Dakinah, Kofi	Den	d	Jul 2004	1	0	0	0
Surman, Andrew	SA	m	Jan 2005	10+4	2	0	0
Larossa, Ruben Dario	Arg	f	Jul 2005	2+5	0	1+1	0
Skora, Eric	Fr	m	Nov 2005	4	2	1	0
Timm, Mads	Den	f	Jan 2006	6+3	1	3	0
WATFORD (36)							
Mitchell, Frank	Aus	wh	Aug 1952	193	0	12	0
Oelofse, Ralph	SA	wh	Jul 1953	15	0	0	0

Name	Born	Pos	From	LgAp	LgG	OthAp	OthG
Blissett, Luther (Eng) (1)	Jam	f	Jul 1975	222+24	95	43+1	16
Gibbs, Peter	Zim	gk	Jul 1975	4	0	0	0
Callaghan, Nigel (Eng) (1)	Sing	w	Jul 1979	209+13	41	51+4	8
Barnes, John (Eng)	Jam	f	Jul 1981	232+1	65	58	18
Lohman, Jan	Neth	m	Oct 1981	51+12	6	12+3	3
Blissett, Luther (Eng) (2)	Jam	f	Aug 1984	113+14	44	25+4	13
Henry, Liburd	Dom	f	Nov 1987	8+2	1	4	0
Callaghan, Nigel (Eng) (2)	Sing	w	Mar 1991	6+6	1	0	0
Blissett, Luther (Eng) (3)	Jam	f	Aug 1991	34+8	9	5	3
Johnson, Richard	Aus	m	May 1992	209+32	20	33+3	2
Watson, Mark	Can	d	Nov 1993	18	0	1+2	0
Melvang, Lars (Den)	USA	f	Aug 1997	4	1	1	0
Rosenthal, Ronny	Isr	f	Aug 1997	25+5	8	7+2	3
Hazan, Alon	Isr	m	Jan 1998	15+18	2	1+4	0
Gudmundsson, Johann	Ice	m	Mar 1998	7+15	2	1+3	0
Ngonge, Michel (DRC)	Bel	f	Jul 1998	29+18	9	7+3	2
Bonnot, Alex	Fr	m	Nov 1998	8+8	0	0	0
Iroha, Ben	Nig	d	Dec 1998	8+2	0	1	0
Bakalli, Adrian	Bel	d	Jan 1999	0+2	0	0	0
Wooter, Nordin (Neth)	Sur	m	Sep 1999	37+26	3	5+2	0
Gravelaine, Xavier	Fr	m	Nov 1999	7	2	0	0
Helguson, Heidar	Ice	f	Jan 2000	132+43	55	16+9	9
Baardsen, Espen (Nor)	USA	gk	Aug 2000	41	0	5	0
Nielsen, Allan	Den	m	Aug 2000	95+6	19	9+3	0
Blondeau, Patrick	Fr	d	Jul 2001	24+1	0	3	0
Vega, Ramon	Swit	d	Jun 2001	23+4	1	6	2
Galli, Filippo	It	d	Jul 2001	27+1	1	1	0
Issa, Pierre	SA	d	Sep 2001	12+3	1	3	0
Norville, Jason	Trin	f	Oct 2001	6+7	0	0+1	0
Okon, Paul	Aus	d	Jan 2002	14+1	0	0	0
Godfrey, Elliott	Can	f	Mar 2003	0+1	0	0	0
Bouazza, Hameur	Fr	f	Jun 2003	19+33	3	8+2	3
De Merit, Jay	USA	d	Jul 2004	50+7	6	11+1	0
Gunnarsson, Brynjar	Ice	d	Jul 2004	34+2	3	6+1	0
Bangura, Al	SiLe	m	Apr 2005	12+25	1	4+1	0
Francino, Francis	Jam	f	Aug 2005	0+1	0	1+1	0
Diagouraga, Toumani	Fr	m	Mar 2006	1	0	3	0
WEST BROMWICH ALBION (46)							
Bookman, Louis (Brit)	Lith	w	Feb 1914	16	1	0	0
Johnson, Glenn	Can	f	Oct 1969	2+2	0	0	0
Regis, Cyrille (Eng)	FrGu	f	May 1977	233+4	82	62+1	27
Batson, Brendan (Eng)	Gda	fb	Feb 1978	172	1	46	1
Jol, Martin	Neth	m	Oct 1981	63+1	4	15	0
Zondervan, Romeo (Neth)	Sur	m	Mar 1982	82+2	5	11	0
Nicholl, Jimmy (N Ire)	Can	fb	Nov 1984	56	0	9	0
Paskin, John	SA	f	Aug 1988	14+11	5	1+2	0
Andersen, Vetle	Nor	d	Dec 1989	0+1	0	0	0
Blissett, Luther (Eng)	Jam	f	Oct 1992	3	1	0	0
Boere, Jeroen	Neth	f	Sep 1994	5	0	0	0
Sneekes, Richard	Neth	m	Mar 1996	208+19	30	23+3	4
Peschisolido, Paul	Can	f	Jul 1996	36+9	18	5+1	3
Murphy, Shaun	Aus	d	Dec 1996	60+11	7	7	0
McDermott, Andy	Aus	fb	Mar 1997	49+3	1	4+1	1

Name	Born	Pos	From	LgAp	LgG	OthAp	OthG
Van Blerk, Jason	Aus	fb	Mar 1998	106+3	3	11+1	0
Bortolazzi, Mario	It	m	Aug 1998	25+10	2	1	0
De Freitas, Fabian (Neth)	Sur	f	Aug 1998	34+27	8	6+1	2
Maresca, Enzo	It	m	Aug 1998	28+19	5	3+3	0
Sigurdsson, Larus	Ice	d	Sep 1999	104+12	1	10+2	0
Fredgaard, Carsten	Den	m	Feb 2000	5	0	0	0
Jensen, Brian	Den	gk	Mar 2000	46	0	4	0
Santos, Georges (CVI)	Fr	m	Mar 2000	8	0	0	0
Batista, Jordao (Por)	Ang	m	Aug 2000	47+16	6	5+3	2
Balis, Igor	Svk	m	Dec 2000	60+9	4	3+3	0
Derveld, Fernando	Neth	d	Feb 2001	1+1	0	0	0
Rosler, Uwe	Ger	f	Oct 2001	5	1	0	0
Varga, Stanislav	Svk	d	Mar 2002	3+1	0	0	0
Udeze, Ifeanyi	Nig	d	Jan 2003	7+4	0	0	0
Gaardsoe, Thomas	Den	d	Jul 2003	77+4	4	8+2	0
Haas, Bernt (Swit)	Aut	d	Jul 2003	45+1	1	6	2
Sakiri, Artim	Mac	m	Jul 2003	8+20	1	3+2	0
N'Dour, Alassane	Sen	d	Aug 2003	2	0	1	0
Volmer, Joost	Neth	d	Aug 2003	10+5	0	2+1	0
Berthe, Sekou	Mli	d	Sep 2003	2+1	0	1	0
Skoubo, Morten	Den	f	Jan 2004	0+2	0	0	0
Albrechtsen, Martin	Den	d	Jun 2004	46+9	1	8	0
Gera, Zoltan	Hun	f	Jul 2004	43+10	8	4+1	1
Kanu, Nwankwo	Nig	f	Jul 2004	38+15	7	4+1	2
Kuszczak, Tomasz	Pol	gk	Jul 2004	30+1	0	3+1	0
Contra, Cosmin	Rom	d	Aug 2004	5	0	1	0
Earnshaw, Bernt (Wal)	Zam	f	Aug 2004	22+21	12	5+2	3
Inamoto, Junichi	Jap	m	Aug 2004	16+9	0	5	0
Kamara, Diomansy (Sen)	Fr	f	Jul 2005	21+5	1	3	1
Kozak, Jan	Svk	m	Jan 2006	4+2	0	0	0
Martinez, Williams	Uru	d	Jan 2006	1+1	1	0	0

WEST HAM (68)

Name	Born	Pos	From	LgAp	LgG	OthAp	OthG
Burton, Frank (Brit)	Mex	fb	Aug 1919	64	2	5	0
Smith, Roy (Brit)	Ind	f	Jun 1955	6	1	0	0
Newman, Mick	Can	f	Feb 1957	7	2	0	0
Best, Clyde	Ber	f	Mar 1969	178+8	47	32	11
Coker, Ade	Nig	f	Dec 1971	9+1	3	1	0
Orhan, Yilmaz	Cyp	f	Oct 1972	6+2	0	1	0
Van der Elst, Francois	Bel	m	Dec 1981	61+1	14	7+1	3
Potts, Steve (Eng)	USA	d	May 1984	362+37	1	87+5	0
Miklosko, Ludek	CzRep	gk	Feb 1990	315	0	50	0
Atteveld, Ray	Neth	d/m	Feb 1992	1	0	2	0
Bunbury, Alex (Can)	Guy	f	Dec 1992	2+2	0	0+1	0
Boere, Jeroen	Neth	f	Sep 1993	15+10	6	3+1	1
Rieper, Marc	Den	d	Jun 1994	83+7	5	10+1	0
Omoyimni, Manny	Nig	f	May 1995	1+8	2	1+3	0
Boogers, Marco	Neth	m	Jul 1995	0+4	0	0	0
Lazaridis, Stan	Aus	w	Sep 1995	53+16	3	15+3	0
Harkes, John	USA	m	Oct 1995	6+5	0	1+1	0
Coyne, Chris	Aus	d	Jan 1996	0+1	0	0	0
Bilic, Slaven	Cro	d	Feb 1996	48	2	6	1
Dumitrescu, Ilie	Rom	m	Mar 1996	5+5	0	2+1	0
Mautone, Steve	Aus	gk	Mar 1996	1	0	2	0
Carvalho, Dani	Por	f	Feb 1996	3+6	2	0	0

Name	Born	Pos	From	LgAp	LgG	OthAp	OthG
Futre, Paulo	Por	f	Jun 1996	4+5	0	0	0
Raducioiu, Florin	Rom	f	Jun 1996	6+5	2	1	1
Porfirio, Hugo	Por	m	Sep 1996	15+8	2	3+1	2
Lomas, Steve (N Ire)	Ger	m	Mar 1997	179+8	10	37+3	3
Berkovic, Eyal	Isr	m	Jun 1997	62+3	10	13+1	2
Terrier, David	Fr	m	Jun 1997	0+1	0	0	0
Forrest, Craig	Can	gk	Jul 1997	26+4	0	8	0
Abou, Samassi (Fr)	IvCo	f	Nov 1997	14+8	5	5+4	1
Alves, Paulo	Por	f	Nov 1997	0+4	0	0	0
Lama, Bernard	Fr	gk	Dec 1997	12	0	2	0
Keller, Marc	Fr	m	Jul 1998	36+8	5	11+1	2
Margas, Javier	Chi	d	Aug 1998	21+3	1	5+1	0
Garcia, Richard	Aus	f	Sep 1998	4+12	0	0+6	0
Di Canio, Paolo	It	f	Jan 1999	114+4	47	23	4
Foe, Marc-Vivien	Cam	m	Jan 1999	38	1	9+1	1
Wanchope, Paulo	CoRi	f	Jul 1999	33+2	12	10+2	3
Stimac, Igor	Cro	d	Sep 1999	43	1	9	0
Feuer, Ian	USA	gk	Feb 2000	3	0	0	0
Ilic, Sasa (Yug)	Aus	gk	Feb 2000	1	0	0	0
Kanoute, Frederic (Mli)	Fr	f	Mar 2000	79+5	29	8	4
Suker, Davor	Cro	f	Jul 2000	7+4	2	1+1	1
Bassila, Christian	Fr	d	Aug 2000	0+3	0	0+1	0
Diawara, Kaba	Fr	f	Sep 2000	6+5	0	0	0
Song, Rigobert	Cam	d	Nov 2000	23+1	0	3	0
Camara, Titi	Gui	f	Dec 2000	5+6	0	2+1	0
Tihinen, Hannu	Fin	d	Dec 2000	5+3	0	2	0
Schemmel, Sebastien	Fr	d	Jan 2001	60+3	1	9+1	0
Soma, Ragnvald	Nor	d	Jan 2001	3+4	0	1+1	0
Foxe, Hayden	Aus	d	Mar 2001	7+4	0	0+1	0
Todorov, Svetoslav	Bul	f	Jan 2001	4+10	1	1+1	1
Courtois, Laurent	Fr	m	Aug 2001	5+2	0	0+1	0
Repka, Tomas	CzRep	d	Sep 2001	164	0	23+1	0
Labant, Vladimir	Svk	d	Jan 2002	7+6	0	0+2	0
Sofiane, Youssef	Fr	f	Jun 2002	0+1	0	1	0
Cisse, Edouard	Fr	m	Aug 2002	18+7	0	0	0
McClenahan, Trent	Aus	d	Jul 2003	0+2	0	1	0
Alexandersson, Niclas	Swe	m	Sep 2003	5+3	0	0	0
Carole, Sebastien	Fr	m	Feb 2004	0+1	0	0	0
Srnicek, Pavel	CzRep	gk	Feb 2004	2+1	0	0	0
Rebrov, Sergei	Ukr	f	Jul 2004	12+14	1	3+3	1
Taricco, Mauricio	Arg	d	Nov 2004	1	0	0	0
Benayoun, Yossi	Isr	m	Jul 2005	30+4	5	6	0
Aliadiere, Jeremie	Fr	f	Aug 2005	1+6	0	0+1	0
Bellion, David	Fr	f	Aug 2005	2+6	0	1+1	1
Katan, Yaniv	Isr	f	Jan 2006	2+4	0	0+2	0
Scaloni, Lionel	Arg	d	Jan 2006	13	0	3+1	0
WIGAN ATHLETIC (30)							
Methven, Colin (Brit)	Ind	d	Oct 1979	295+1	21	45	7
Tunks, Roy (Brit)	Ger	gk	Nov 1981	245	0	41	0
Houston, Graham	Gib	m	Aug 1986	16+1	4	3	0
Taylor, Robin (Brit)	Ger	m	Oct 1989	0+1	0	0	0
Adekola, David	Nig	f	Oct 1994	1+3	0	0+1	0
Diaz, Isidro	Sp	m	Jul 1995	58+20	16	6+2	3

Name	Born	Pos	From	LgAp	LgG	OthAp	OthG
Martinez, Roberto	Sp	m	Jul 1995	148+39	17	26+4	5
Seba, Jesus	Sp	f	Aug 1995	8+13	3	2+3	0
Sharp, Kevin	Can	d	Nov 1995	156+22	10	21+5	1
Smeets, Jorg	Neth	m	Oct 1997	10+14	3	1+2	0
Bruno, Pasquale	It	d	Feb 1998	1	0	0	0
De Zeeuw, Arjan (1)	Neth	d	Jul 1999	126	6	20	0
Peron, Jeff	Fr	m	Nov 1999	19+4	0	1+1	0
Padula, Gino	Arg	d	Jul 2000	2+2	0	2+1	0
Bidstrup, Stefan	Den	m	Nov 2000	10+5	2	2	1
Hernandez, Dino	Neth	m	Nov 2000	0	0	1	0
Nuzzo, Raffaele	It	gk	Mar 2001	0	0	0	0
De Vos, Jason	Can	d	Jul 2001	87+3	15	8	0
Adamczuk, Darius	Pol	m	Aug 2001	3	0	1	0
Bukran, Gabor	Hun	m	Aug 2001	1	0	0	0
Filan, John	Aus	gk	Dec 2001	177	0	16+1	0
Frandsen, Per	Den	m	Jun 2004	9	1	0	0
Thome, Emerson	Bra	d	Aug 2004	11+4	0	5	0
Johansson, Andreas	Swe	m	Jan 2005	6+11	4	7+2	3
Chimbonda, Pascal (Fr)	Guad	d	Jul 2005	37	2	5+1	0
Henchoz, Stephane	Swit	d	Jul 2005	26	0	4+2	0
Camara, Henri	Sen	f	Aug 2005	25+4	12	2+1	0
De Zeeuw, Arjan (2)	Neth	d	Aug 2005	31	0	4	0
Skoko, Josip	Aus	m	Aug 2005	3+2	0	6	0
Scharner, Paul	Aut	d	Jan 2006	14+2	3	2+1	1
Ziegler, Reto	Swit	m	Jan 2006	5+5	0	1+2	0

WIGAN BOROUGH (1)

Name	Born	Pos	From	LgAp	LgG	OthAp	OthG
Preedy, Charlie (Brit)	Ind	gk	Jul 1928	41	0	0	0

WIMBLEDON
see Milton Keynes Dons

WOLVERHAMPTON WANDERERS (55)

Name	Born	Pos	From	LgAp	LgG	OthAp	OthG
Bellis, George (Brit)	Ind	ch	Jun 1929	42	0	1	0
McMahon, Doug	Can	f	Aug 1938	1	0	0	0
Stuart, Eddie	SA	d	Jan 1951	287	1	32	0
Horne, Des	SA	w	Dec 1956	40	16	11	2
Durandt, Cliff	SA	w	Jun 1957	43	9	5	0
Kemp, Fred (Brit)	It	m	Jun 1963	3	0	1	0
Gardner, Don	Jam	m	Aug 1973	1+2	0	0	0
Berry, George (Wal)	Ger	d	Nov 1975	124	4	36	2
Hazell, Bob (Eng) (1)	Jam	d	May 1977	32+1	1	3	0
Villazan, Rafael	Uru	d	May 1980	20+3	0	4	0
Herbert, Ricki	NZ	d	Oct 1984	44+1	0	3	0
Hazell, Bob (Eng) (2)	Jam	d	Sep 1985	1	0	0	0
Streete, Floyd (Brit)	Jam	d	Oct 1985	157+2	6	20	0
Paskin, John	SA	f	Jun 1989	21+13	3	4+1	0
Regis, Cyrille (Eng)	FrGu	f	Aug 1993	8+11	2	1+2	0
De Wolf, John	Neth	d	Dec 1994	27+1	5	5	0
Williams, Mark	SA	f	Sep 1995	5+7	0	3+1	1
Young, Eric (Wal)	Sing	d	Sep 1995	31	2	9	0
Corica, Steve	Aus	m	Feb 1996	80+20	5	8+2	0
Romano, Serge	Fr	d	Aug 1996	1+3	0	1	0
Dowe, Jens	Ger	m	Oct 1996	5+3	0	0	0
Van der Laan, Robin	Neth	m	Oct 1996	7	0	0	0
Diaz, Isidro	Sp	m	Aug 1997	1	0	0	0
Kubicki, Dariusz	Pol	fb	Aug 1997	12	0	4	0

Name	Born	Pos	From	LgAp	LgG	OthAp	OthG
Paatelainen, Mixu	Fin	f	Aug 1997	10+13	0	8+2	5
Garcia, Sanjuan Jesus	Sp	m	Sep 1997	4	0	2+1	1
Segers, Hans	Neth	gk	Feb 1998	11	0	2	0
Gomez, Fernando	Sp	f	Aug 1998	17+2	2	3	0
Niestroj, Robert (Ger)	Pol	m	Nov 1998	2+4	0	1	0
Flo, Havard	Nor	f	Jan 1999	27+11	9	3+2	1
Pollet, Ludo	Fr	d	Sep 1999	74+4	7	7+1	1
Nielsen, Allan	Den	m	Mar 2000	7	2	0	0
Camara, Mohamed	Gui	d	Aug 2000	27+18	0	5+2	0
Ketsbaia, Temuri	Geo	f	Aug 2000	14+10	3	4+1	1
Thetis, Manuel	Fr	d	Aug 2000	3	0	0	0
Al-Jaber, Sami	Sau	f	Sep 2000	0+4	0	1	0
Roussel, Cedric	Bel	f	Feb 2001	9+17	2	0+2	0
Halle, Gunnar	Nor	d	Mar 2002	4+1	0	2	0
Ingimarsson, Ivar	Ice	m	Aug 2002	10+3	2	2	0
Fernandes, Silas	Por	m	Jul 2003	2+7	0	3+2	0
Luzhny, Oleg	Ukr	d	Jul 2003	4+2	0	4	0
Okoronkwo, Isaac	Nig	d	Jul 2003	7	0	1	0
Camara, Henri	Sen	f	Aug 2003	29+1	7	2	0
Gudjonsson, Joey	Ice	m	Aug 2003	5+6	0	4+1	1
Iversen, Steffen	Nor	f	Aug 2003	11+5	4	3+1	0
Kachloul, Hassan	Mor	m	Sep 2003	0+4	0	0	0
Ganea, Ionel	Rom	f	Dec 2003	17+17	7	3+2	2
Olofinjana, Seyi	Nig	m	Jul 2004	47+8	5	4+1	0
Bjorklund, Joachim	Swe	d	Aug 2004	2+1	0	2	0
Seol, Ki-Hyeon	SK	f	Aug 2004	50+19	8	7	2
Bischoff, Mikkel	Den	d	Sep 2004	9+2	1	0	0
Gyepes, Gabor	Hun	d	Jul 2005	19+1	0	4	0
Postma, Stefan	Neth	gk	Aug 2005	29	0	3	0
Aliadiere, Jeremie	Fr	f	Jan 2006	12+2	2	0	0
Frankowski, Tomasz	Pol	f	Jan 2006	12+4	0	0+1	0
Rosa, Denes	Hun	m	Jan 2006	6+3	2	0+1	0
WORKINGTON (6)							
Miller, George	SA	f	Mar 1952	11	0	0	0
Miller, Graham	SA	f	Dec 1952	10	1	0	0
Purdon, Ted	SA	f	Mar 1957	33	9	3	1
Tennant, Roy	SA	ch	Jul 1958	151	1	13	0
Haasz, Johnny	Hun	f	Jul 1961	50	13	5	2
Tolson, Max	Aus	f	Feb 1966	29+2	6	4	0
WREXHAM (25)							
Bellis, George (Brit)	Ind	ch	May 1927	82	5	6	0
Donoghue, John	USA	wh	Jul 1930	67	2	4	0
Baines, Peter	Aus	f	Apr 1943	6	2	0	0
McDowall, Les	Ind	ch	Nov 1949	3	0	1	0
Kirkby, John	USA	fb	Aug 1951	5	0	0	0
Ugolini, Rolando	It	gk	Jun 1957	83	0	4	0
Keelan, Kevin (Brit)	Ind	gk	Nov 1961	68	0	4	0
Williams, Everton	Jam	f	Jul 1975	1+1	0	0	0
Ferguson, Don	Can	gk	Jan 1986	20	0	0	0
Cooke, Joe	Dom	d/f	Jul 1986	49+2	4	11	1
Paskin, John	SA	f	Feb 1992	28+23	11	1+3	2
Whitley, Jeff (N Ire) (1)	Zam	m	Jan 1999	9	2	0	0
Stevens, Ian	Mal	f	Jul 1999	14+2	4	3+1	0
Allsopp, Danny	Aus	f	Feb 2000	3	4	0	0

Name	Born	Pos	From	LgAp	LgG	OthAp	OthG
Bouanane, Emad	Fr	m	Aug 2000	13+4	0	1	0
Edwards, Carlos	Trin	m	Aug 2000	144+22	23	13+2	2
Sam, Hector	Trin	f	Aug 2000	77+73	35	16+10	5
Killen, Chris	NZ	f	Sep 2000	11+1	3	0	0
Lawrence, Denis	Trin	d	Mar 2001	187+8	14	17+1	2
Sharp, Kevin	Can	d	Oct 2001	12+3	0	0	0
Whitley, Jim (N Ire) (2)	Zam	m	Oct 2001	135+5	1	13+2	0
Rovde, Marius	Nor	g	Jan 2002	12	0	0	0
One, Armand	Fr	f	Sep 2003	2+1	0	0	0
Ugarte, Juan	Sp	f	Nov 2004	25+7	16	6+2	6
Valero, Xavi	Sp	gk	Jan 2005	3	0	0	0

WYCOMBE WANDERERS (12)

Name	Born	Pos	From	LgAp	LgG	OthAp	OthG
Cunningham, Tony (Brit)	Jam	f	Mar 1994	4+1	0	0	0
Regis, Cyrille (Eng)	FrGu	f	Aug 1994	30+5	9	3	1
Moussaddik, Chuck	Mor	gk	Sep 1995	1	0	0+1	0
Dijkstra, Sieb	Neth	gk	Mar 1996	13	0	0	0
Rogers, Mark	Can	d	Dec 1998	123+16	4	29+2	3
Lopez, Carlos	Mex	d	Jan 2002	1	0	0	0
Dixon, Jonny (Brit)	Sp	f	Aug 2002	20+43	6	3+4	2
Talia, Frank	Aus	gk	Aug 2002	132	0	16	0
Uhlenbeek, Gus (Neth)	Sur	d	Jul 2004	36+6	4	4	0
Caceres, Adrian (Aus)	Arg	m	Mar 2005	1+2	0	0	0
Betsy, Kevin	Sey	m	Jun 2005	41+1	8	7	0
Torres, Sergio	Arg	m	Aug 2005	13+11	1	3+2	0

YORK CITY (14)

Name	Born	Pos	From	LgAp	LgG	OthAp	OthG
Kubicki, Eryk	Pol	w	Oct 1946	5	0	0	0
Wojtczak, Edouard	Pol	gk	Oct 1946	8	0	0	0
Twissell, Charlie (Eng)	Sing	w	Nov 1958	53	8	3	0
Francis, Gerry	SA	w	Oct 1961	16	4	4	1
Tunks, Roy (Brit)	Ger	gk	Jan 1969	4	0	0	0
Johanneson, Albert	SA	w	Jul 1970	26	3	7	2
Richards, Lloyd	Jam	m	Jun 1980	17+1	1	4	1
Walwyn, Keith (Brit)	Jam	f	Jul 1981	245	119	42	20
McMillan, Andy	SA	fb	Oct 1987	409+12	5	50	0
Atkinson, Paddy (Brit)	Sing	fb	Nov 1995	36+5	0	3+1	0
Evans, Michael	Neth	f	Sep 2001	1+1	0	0	0
Carvalho, Rogerio	Bra	f	Aug 2002	0+4	0	0+1	0
Okoli, James	Nig	d	Aug 2002	1+2	0	0	0
Mazzina, Nicolas	Arg	m	Sep 2002	0+3	0	0	0

YEOVIL TOWN (13)

Name	Born	Pos	From	LgAp	LgG	OthAp	OthG
El Kholti, Abdou (Mor)	Fr	m	Sep 2002	33+16	4	3+3	0
Rodrigues, Hugo	Por	d	Jul 2003	23+11	1	4	0
Rodrigues, Dani	Por	f	Mar 2004	3+1	4	0	0
Caceres, Adrian (Aus)	Arg	m	Jul 2004	7+14	3	3+2	1
Guyett, Scott	Aus	d	Jul 2004	29+10	2	5	0
Mirza, Nicolas	Fr	m	Jul 2004	0+3	0	1	0
Odubade, Yemi	Nig	f	Jul 2004	0+4	0	0+2	1
Tarachulski, Bartosz	Pol	f	Jul 2004	27+14	10	7+1	3
Stolcers, Andrejs	Lat	f	Sep 2004	23+13	5	6+1	2
Fallon, Rory	NZ	f	Feb 2005	2+4	1	0	0
Alvarez, Luciano	Arg	f	Aug 2005	4	1	0+1	0
Bastianini, Pablo	Arg	f	Aug 2005	15+5	3	5+1	0
Melono, Gabriel	Uru	d	Sep 2005	1	0	1	0

APPENDIX 3: A–Z

League club(s) for each player in alphabetical, not chronological, order

Name (Born) (Nationality, if differs)	League club(s)	Name (Born) (Nationality, if differs)	League club(s)
A		Alsaker, Paul (Nor)	Stockport
Aas, Einar (Nor)	Nottm For	Alvarez, Luciano (Arg)	Yeovil
Abbey, George (Nig)	Macclesfield, Port Vale	Alves, Paulo (Por)	West Ham
Abdallah, Tewfik (Egy)	Derby, Hartlepool	Ambrose, Leroy (StV)	Charlton
Abidallah, Nabil (Neth)	Ipswich, Northampton	Ambrosetti, Gabriele (It)	Chelsea
Abou, Samassi (IvCo) (Fr)	Ipswich, Walsall, West Ham	Ambrosio, Marco (It)	Chelsea
		Ameobi, Shola (Nig) (Eng)	Newcastle
Achterberg, John (Neth)	Tranmere	Ammann, Mike (USA)	Charlton
Acimovic, Milenko (Slo)	Tottenham	Amokachi, Daniel (Nig)	Everton
Ackerman, Alf (SA)	Carlisle, Derby, Hull, Millwall, Norwich	Amoruso, Lorenzo (It)	Blackburn
		Amsalem, David (Isr)	C Palace
Acuna, Clarence (Chi)	Newcastle	Anaclet, Eddie (Tan)	Chester
Adaggio, Marco (Sp)	Shrewsbury	Andersen, Bo (Den)	Bristol C
Adamczuk, Dariusz (Pol)	Wigan	Andersen, Leif (Nor)	C Palace
Adebayor, Emmanuel (Tgo)	Arsenal	Andersen, Soren (Den)	Bristol C
Adebola, Dele (Nig)	Birmingham, Bradford, Burnley, Coventry, Crewe, C Palace, Oldham	Andersen, Stephan (Den)	Charlton
		Andersen, Trond (Nor)	Wimbledon
		Andersen, Vetle (Nor)	WBA
Adekola, David (Nig)	Bournemouth, Brighton, Bury, Cambridge, Exeter, Wigan	Anderson, Doug (HK) (Brit)	Cambridge, Northampton, Oldham, Plymouth, Tranmere
Advice-Desruisseaux, Fred (Fr)	Kidderminster	Andersson, Anders (Swe)	Blackburn
		Andersson, Andreas (Swe)	Newcastle
Agger, Daniel (Den)	Liverpool	Andersson, Patrik (Swe)	Blackburn
Agogo, Junior (Gha)	Bristol R, Chester, Chesterfield, Lincoln, Oldham, QPR, Sheff Wed	Andrade, Diogo (Por)	Bournemouth
		Andrade, Jose-Manuel (Por)	Stoke
		Andre, Carlos (Por)	Walsall
Agostino, Paul (Aus)	Bristol C	Andre, Pierre-Yves (Fr)	Bolton
Al-Jaber, Sami (Sau)	Wolves	Andreassen, Svein (Nor)	Portsmouth
Albert, Philippe (Bel)	Fulham, Newcastle	Andreasson, Marcus (Swe)	Bristol R
Albrechtsen, Martin (Den)	WBA	Andresen, Martin (Nor)	Blackburn, Wimbledon
Aldecoa, Emilio (Sp)	Coventry	Andrews, Billy (USA) (N Ire)	Grimsby, Oldham, Stockport
Aleksidze, Rati (Geo)	Chelsea		
Alexandersson, Niclas (Swe)	Everton, Sheff Wed, West Ham	Anelka, Nicolas (Fr)	Arsenal, Liverpool, Man City
Aliadiere, Jeremie (Fr)	Arsenal, West Ham, Wolves	Angel, Juan Pablo (Col)	A Villa
Allback, Marcus (Swe)	A Villa	Anichebe, Victor (Nig)	Everton
Alleyne, Andy (Bar)	Reading	Anselin, Cedric (Fr)	Cambridge, Norwich
Allou, Bernard (IvCo) (Fr)	Nottm For	Antic, Raddy (Yug)	Luton
Allsopp, Danny (Aus)	Bristol R, Hull, Man City, Notts Co, Wrexham	Antoine-Curier, Mickael (Fr)	Brentford, Grimsby, Kidderminster, Notts Co, Oldham, Rochdale, Sheff Wed
Almeida, Marco (Por)	Southampton		
Almunia, Manuel (Sp)	Arsenal		
Aloisi, John (Aus)	Coventry, Portsmouth	Aranalde, Zigor (Sp)	Carlisle, Sheff Wed, Walsall
Alonso, Xabi (Sp)	Liverpool		

Name (Born) (Nationality, if differs)	League club(s)	Name (Born) (Nationality, if differs)	League club(s)
Arason, Arni (Ice)	Man City	Baines, Peter (Aus)	Crewe, Hartlepool, N
Arber, Mark (SA) (Brit)	Barnet, Oldham,		Brighton, Wrexham
	Peterborough, Tottenham	Bak, Arkadiusz (Pol)	Birmingham
Arca, Julio (Arg)	Sunderland	Bakalli, Adrian (Bel)	Swindon, Watford
Ardiles, Ossie (Arg)	Blackburn, QPR, Swindon,	Bakayoko, Ibrahima (IvCo)	Everton
	Tottenham	Baker, Gerry (USA) (Brit)	Brentford, Coventry,
Arendse, Andre (SA)	Fulham, Oxford		Ipswich, Man City
Arentoft, Ben (Den)	Blackburn, Newcastle	Bakholt, Kurt (Den)	QPR
Armand, Jack (Ind) (Brit)	Leeds, Newport,	Bakke, Eirik (Nor)	A Villa, Leeds
	Southport, Swansea	Balaban, Bosko (Cro)	A Villa
	Town	Balis, Igor (Svk)	WBA
Arnison, Joseph (SA)	Luton	Ballesta, Salva (Sp)	Bolton
Arphexad, Pegguy (Guad) (Fr)	Coventry, Leicester,	Balogun, Tesilimi (Nig)	QPR
	Liverpool, Notts Co,	Baltacha, Sergei (USSR) (Ukr)	Ipswich
	Stockport	Baltacha, Sergei Jnr (Ukr)	Millwall
Arteta, Mikel (Sp)	Everton	(Sco)	
Asamoah, Derek (Gha) (Brit)	Chester, Lincoln,	Bangoura, Sambegou (Gui)	Stoke
	Mansfield, Northampton	Bangura, Al (SiLe)	Watford
Asanovic, Aljosa (Cro)	Derby	Bankole, Ade (Nig)	Brentford, Crewe, QPR
Ashikodi, Moses (Nig)	Gillingham, West Ham	Banovic, Yakka (Yug) (Aus)	Derby
Ashton, Hubert (Ind) (Brit)	Bristol R, Clapton O	Barada, Taylor (USA)	Colchester
Aspinall, Brendan (SA)	Mansfield	Baradji, Sekou (Fr)	Reading
Aspinall, Wilf (USA)	Southport, Stockport	Barbara, Daniel (Fr)	Darlington
Asprilla, Faustino (Col)	Newcastle	Barnard, Darren (Ger) (Wal)	Barnsley, Bristol C,
Astafjevs, Vitalis (Lat)	Bristol R		Chelsea, Grimsby, Reading
Atangana, Simon (Cam)	Colchester, Port Vale	Barnes, John (Jam) (Eng)	Charlton, Liverpool,
Atkins, Arthur (Jap) (Brit)	Birmingham, Shrewsbury		Newcastle, Watford
Atkinson, Paddy (Sing) (Brit)	Hartlepool, Scarborough,	Baros, Milan (CzRep)	A Villa, Liverpool
	Sheff Utd, York	Barragan, Antonio (Sp)	Liverpool
Atouba, Thimothee (Cam)	Tottenham	Bart-Williams, Chris (SiLe)	Charlton, Ipswich, Nottm
Atteveld, Ray (Neth)	Bristol C, Everton, West	(Brit)	For, Orient, Sheff Wed
	Ham	Barthez, Fabien (Fr)	Man Utd
Auguste, Joe (Trin)	Exeter	Bartlett, Shaun (SA)	Charlton
Aunger, Geoff (Can)	Chester, Luton, Stockport	Bartram, Per (Den)	C Palace
Avdiu, Kemajl (Yug) (Swe)	Bury	Bassedas, Chistian (Arg)	Newcastle
Avramovic, Raddy (Cro)	Coventry, Notts Co	Bassila, Christian (Fr)	Sunderland, West Ham
Awuah, Jones (Gha)	Gillingham	Basso, Adriano (Bra)	Bristol C
Axeldahl, Jonas (Swe)	Cambridge, Ipswich	Bastianini, Pablo (Arg)	Yeovil
Ayegbini, Yakubu (Nig)	Middlesbrough,	Bastians, Felix (Ger)	Nottm For
	Portsmouth	Batista, Jordao (Ang) (Por)	WBA
Ayorinde, Sammy (Nig)	Orient	Batista, Ricardo (Por)	Fulham, MKD
		Batson, Brendan (Grn) (Eng)	Arsenal, Cambridge, WBA
B		Baudet, Julien (Fr)	Notts Co, Oldham,
Ba, Ibrahim (Sen) (Fr)	Bolton		Rotherham
Baardsen, Espen (USA) (Nor)	Everton, Tottenham,	Baugh, John (Uga)	Exeter
	Watford	Baxter, Lee (Swe) (Brit)	Sheff Utd
Babayaro, Celestine (Nig)	Chelsea, Newcastle	Beck, Mikkel (Den)	Derby, Middlesbrough,
Babbel, Markus (Ger)	Blackburn, Liverpool		Nottm For, QPR
Backos, Des (SA)	Stoke	Bedrossian (Cyp)	Fulham
Bacque, Herve (Fr)	Luton	Beinlich, Stefan (Ger)	A Villa
Badir, Walid (Isr)	Wimbledon	Bell, Alec (SA) (Sco)	Blackburn, Man Utd
Bagheri, Karim (Irn)	Charlton	Bellion, David (Fr)	Man Utd, Sunderland,
Baiano, Francesco (It)	Derby		West Ham

Name (Born) (Nationality, if differs)	League club(s)	Name (Born) (Nationality, if differs)	League club(s)
Bellis, George (Ind) (Brit)	B&B Ath, Burnley, Southport, Wolves, Wrexham		Wolves
		Bisgaard, Morten (Den)	Derby
Belmadi, Djamel (Fr) (Alg)	Man City, Southampton	Bjorklund, Joachim (Swe)	Sunderland, Wigan
Belsvik, Petter (Nor)	Southend	Bjornebye, Stig Inge (Nor)	Blackburn, Liverpool
Ben Askar, Aziz (Fr)	QPR	Blake, Noel (Jam) (Brit)	A Villa, Birmingham,
Ben Haim, Tal (Isr)	Bolton		Bradford, Exeter, Leeds,
Benarbia, Ali (Alg)	Man City		Portsmouth, Shrewsbury,
Benayoun, Yossi (Isr)	West Ham		Stoke
Bendtner, Nicklas (Den)	Arsenal	Blanc, Laurent (Fr)	Man Utd
Bengtsson, Robert (Swe)	Barnsley	Blatsis, Con (Aus)	Derby, Sheff Wed
Benjamin, Tristan (StK)	Chesterfield, Notts Co	Bleidelis, Imants (Lat)	Southampton
Bent, Jason (Can)	Plymouth	Blinker, Regi (Sur) (Neth)	Sheff Wed
Berg, Henning (Nor)	Blackburn, Man Utd	Blissett, Luther (Jam) (Eng)	Bournemouth, Bury,
Berger, Patrik (Cz Rep)	A Villa, Liverpool, Portsmouth		Mansfield, WBA, Watford
		Blomqvist, Jesper (Swe)	Charlton, Everton, Man Utd
Bergersen, Kent (Nor)	Stockport	Blondeau, Patrick (Fr)	Sheff Wed, Watford
Bergkamp, Dennis (Neth)	Arsenal	Blondel, Jonathan (Bel)	Tottenham
Bergsson, Gudni (Ice)	Bolton, Tottenham	Bluck, Dave (Ind) (Brit)	Aldershot
Berhalter, Gregg (USA)	C Palace	Boa Morte, Luis (Por)	Arsenal, Fulham,
Berkovic, Eyal (Isr)	Blackburn, Man City, Portsmouth, Southampton, West Ham		Southampton
		Boateng, George (Gha) (Neth)	A Villa, Coventry, Middlesbrough
Bernal, Andy (Aus)	Ipswich, Reading	Bobic, Fredi (Slo) (Ger)	Bolton
Bernard, Olivier (Fr)	Darlington, Newcastle, Southampton	Bocanegra, Carlos (USA)	Fulham
		Boere, Jeroen (Neth)	C Palace, Portsmouth,
Bernardeau, Olivier (Fr)	Chesterfield		Southend, WBA, West Ham
Berntsen, Robin (Nor)	Port Vale	Bogarde, Winston (Neth)	Chelsea
Berntsen, Tommy (Nor)	Portsmouth	Bohinen, Lars (Nor)	Blackburn, Derby, Nottm
Berry, George (Ger) (Wal)	Aldershot, Doncaster, Peterborough, Preston, Stoke, Wolves		For
		Bojic, Pedj (Aus)	Northampton
		Boksic, Alen (Herz) (Cro)	Middlesbrough
		Bolesan, Mirko (It)	Cardiff
Berson, Mathieu (Fr)	Aston Villa	Boli, Roger (IvCo) (Fr)	Bournemouth, Walsall
Berthe, Mohamed (Gui) (Fr)	Bournemouth	Bolima, Cedric (DRC)	Rotherham
Berthe, Sekou (Mli)	WBA	Bonalair, Thierry (Fr)	Nottm For
Berthelin, Cedric (Fr)	C Palace, Luton	Bonetti, Ivano (It)	C Palace, Grimsby,
Berti, Nicola (It)	Tottenham		Tranmere
Bertos, Leo (NZ) (Grk)	Barnsley, Chester, Rochdale	Bonnissel, Jerome (Fr)	Fulham
		Bonnot, Alex (Fr)	QPR, Watford
Besagni, Remo (It)	C Palace	Bonvin, Pablo Facundo (Arg)	Sheff Wed
Best, Clyde (Ber)	West Ham	Boogers, Marco (Neth)	West Ham
Betsy, Kevin (Sey)	Barnsley, Bournemouth, Fulham, Hartlepool, Hull, Oldham, Wycombe	Bookman, Louis (Lith) (Ire)	Bradford City, Luton, Port Vale, WBA
		Bopp, Eugene (Ukr) (Ger)	Nottm For
Bhutia, Baichung (Ind)	Bury	Borbokis, Vassilis (Grk)	Derby, Sheff Utd
Biagini, Leo (Arg)	Portsmouth	Borota, Petar (Yug)	Chelsea
Bialkowski, Bartosz (Pol)	Southampton	Bortolazzi, Mario (It)	WBA
Biancalani, Frederic (Fr)	Walsall	Bos, Gijsbert (Neth)	Lincoln, Rotherham
Bidstrup, Stefan (Den)	Wigan	Bosancic, Jovo (Yug)	Barnsley
Bilic, Slaven (Cro)	Everton, West Ham	Bosnich, Mark (Aus)	A Villa, Chelsea, Man Utd
Billio, Patrizio (It)	C Palace	Bossu, Bert (Fr)	Barnet, Darlington,
Biscan, Igor (Cro)	Liverpool		Gillingham, Oldham,
Bischoff, Mikkel (Den)	Man City, Sheff Wed,		Torquay

Name (Born) (Nationality, if differs)	League club(s)
Bossy, Fabian (Fr)	Darlington
Bosvelt, Paul (Neth)	Man City
Bouanane, Emad (Fr)	Wrexham
Bouazza, Hameur (Fr)	Swindon, Watford
Bougherra, Madjid (Fr) (Alg)	Crewe
Bouma, Wilfred (Neth)	A Villa
Boumsong (Cam) (Fr)	Newcastle
Boussatta, Dries (Neth)	Sheff Utd
Bowery, Bert (StK)	Lincoln, Nottm For
Bowman, Walter W (Can)	Accrington, Ardwick
Boyd, John (USA)	Bristol C
Boyd, Walter (Jam)	Swansea
Bozinoski, Vlado (Mac) (Aus)	Ipswich
Bradley, Pat (Aus)	Bury
Brady, Jon (Aus)	Rushden
Bragstad, Bjorn Otto (Nor)	Birmingham, Derby
Branca, Marco (It)	Middlesbrough
Branco (Bra)	Middlesbrough
Branco, Serge (Cam)	QPR
Bravo, Raul (Sp)	Leeds
Breitenfelder, Friedrich (Aut)	Luton
Breitkreutz, Matthias (Ger)	A Villa
Brekke-Skard, Vemund (Nor)	Ipswich
Brennan, Jim (Can)	Bristol C, Huddersfield, Norwich, Nottm For, Southampton
Brkovic, Ahmet (Yug)	Luton, Orient
Brocken, Bud (Neth)	Birmingham
Brolin, Tomas (Swe)	C Palace, Leeds
Brown, Lennox (SA)	Millwall
Bruce, Marcelle (USA)	Colchester
Bruck, Dietmar (Ger)	Charlton, Coventry, Northampton
Bruno, Pasquale (It)	Wigan
Bryant, Billy (Bel)	Millwall
Bryngelsson, Fredrik (Swe)	Stockport
Buari, Malik (Gha)	Fulham
Budtz, Jan (Den)	Doncaster
Bukran, Gabor (Hun)	Walsall, Wigan
Bulent, Akin (Bel) (Tur)	Bolton
Bunbury, Alex (Guy) (Can)	West Ham
Bunch, Arthur (SA)	Aldershot
Bunjevcevic, Goran (Yug)	Tottenham
Burgess, Mike (Can)	Aldershot, B&B Ath, Gillingham, Halifax, Newport, Orient
Burns, Jacob (Aus)	Barnsley, Leeds
Burton, Frank (Mex) (Brit)	Charlton, West Ham
Busby, Hubert (Can)	Oxford
Busscher, Robbie (Neth)	Grimsby
Butcher, Terry (Sing) (Eng)	Coventry, Ipswich, Sunderland
Butler, Jack (Sri) (Eng)	Arsenal, Torquay

Name (Born) (Nationality, if differs)	League club(s)
Buttigieg, John (Mal)	Brentford, Swindon
Buzsaky, Akos (Hun)	Plymouth
Byrne, Paul (SA) (Brit)	Port Vale

C

Name (Born) (Nationality, if differs)	League club(s)
Caballero, Fabian (Arg)	Arsenal
Caceres, Adrian (Arg) (Aus)	Brentford, Hull, Wycombe, Yeovil
Cadete, Jorge (Moz) (Por)	Bradford
Cadiou, Frederic (Fr)	Orient
Cahill, Tim (Aus)	Everton, Millwall
Caldwell, Garrett (USA)	Colchester
Callachan, Harry (Ind) (Brit)	Leicester
Callaghan, Nigel (Sing) (Eng)	A Villa, Derby, Huddersfield, Watford
Calvo-Garcia, Alex (Sp)	Scunthorpe
Camara, Ben (Ger) (Brit)	Torquay
Camara, Henri (Sen)	Southampton, Wigan, Wolves
Camara, Mohamed (Gui)	Burnley, Wolves
Camara, Titi (Gui)	Liverpool, West Ham
Camara, Zoumana (Fr)	Leeds
Camilieri-Gioia, Carlo (Bel)	Mansfield, Sheff Utd
Campo, Ivan (Sp)	Bolton
Candela, Vincent (Fr)	Bolton
Canham, Mark (Ger) (Brit)	Colchester
Cansdell-Sheriff, Shane (Aus)	Rochdale
Cantona, Eric (Fr)	Leeds, Man Utd
Cantona, Joel (Fr)	Stockport
Capaldi, Tony (Nor) (N Ire)	Plymouth
Carasso, Cedric (Fr)	C Palace
Carbonari, Horacio (Arg)	Coventry, Derby
Carbone, Benito (It)	A Villa, Bradford, Derby, Middlesbrough, Sheff Wed
Carmichael, Matt (Sing) (Brit)	Barnet, Darlington, Doncaster, Lincoln, Mansfield, Preston, Scunthorpe
Carney, Dave (Aus)	Oldham
Carole, Sebastien (Fr)	Brighton, West Ham
Carr, Everton (Ant)	Halifax, Leicester, Rochdale
Carr, John (SA)	Huddersfield
Carr, Lance (SA)	Bristol R, Liverpool, Newport
Carrilho, Mirano (Neth)	MKD
Carteron, Patrice (Fr)	Sunderland
Carvalho, Dani (Por)	West Ham
Carvalho, Ricardo (Por)	Chelsea
Carvalho, Rogerio (Bra)	York
Carver, Joe (USA)	Chester
Cas, Marcel (Neth)	Grimsby, Notts Co, Sheff Utd

Name (Born) (Nationality, if differs)	League club(s)	Name (Born) (Nationality, if differs)	League club(s)
Casey, Paul (Ger) (Brit)	Lincoln, Sheff Utd	Collins, Patrick (Om) (Eng)	Sheff Wed, Swindon
Casiraghi, Pierluigi (It)	Chelsea	Colosimo, Simon (Aus)	Man City
Cau, Jean-Michel (Fr)	Darlington	Colusso, Cristian (Arg)	Oldham
Cavaco, Luis Miguel (Por)	Stockport	Coly, Ferdinand (Sen)	Birmingham
Cech, Petr (CzRep)	Chelsea	Cominelli, Lucas (Arg)	Oxford
Cennamo, Luigi (Ger) (It)	Burnley	Constantinou, Costas (Cyp)	Barnet
Cerny, Radek (CzRep)	Tottenham	Contra, Cosmin (Rom)	WBA
Cesar, Julio (Bra)	Bolton	Convey, Bobby (USA)	Reading
Chadwick, Dave (Ind) (Brit)	Bournemouth, Halifax, Gillingham, Middlesbrough, Southampton, Torquay	Cooke, Joe (Dom)	Bradford, Exeter, Oxford, Peterborough, Rochdale, Wrexham
Chaigneau, Florent (Fr)	Brighton	Cooney, Sean (Aus)	Coventry
Chalkias, Konstantinos (Grk)	Portsmouth	Cooper, Kenny (USA)	Oldham
Chalqi, Khalid (Mor)	Torquay	Cooper, Neale (Ind) (Brit)	A Villa, Reading
Chamberlain, Ken (SA)	Charlton	Corazzin, Carlo (Can)	Cambridge, Northampton, Oldham, Plymouth
Chandler, Robert (Ind) (Brit)	A Villa	Corbin, Kirk (Bar)	Cambridge
Chapuis, Cyril (Fr)	Leeds	Corbo, Mateo (Uru)	Barnsley, Oxford
Charles, Alf (Trin)	Southampton	Cordone, Daniel (Arg)	Newcastle
Charvet, Laurent (Fr)	Chelsea, Man City, Newcastle	Corica, Steve (Aus)	Leicester, Walsall, Wolves
		Cornock, Wally (Aus)	Rochdale
Cheetham, Mike (Neth) (Brit)	Cambridge, Chesterfield, Colchester, Ipswich	Costa, Candido (Por)	Derby
		Costa, Jorge (Por)	Charlton
Cherednik, Alexei (USSR)	Southampton	Costa, Ricardo (Por)	Darlington
Cheung, Chi Doy (HK)	Blackpool	Coulbault, Regis (Fr)	Southend
Cheyrou, Bruno (Fr)	Liverpool	Counago, Pablo (Sp)	Ipswich
Chiedozie, John (Nig)	Chesterfield, Derby, Notts Co, Orient, Tottenham	Court, Dick (Ind) (Brit)	Aldershot
		Courtois, Laurent (Fr)	West Ham
Chilaka, Chibuzor (Nig)	Notts Co	Cowan, Gavin (Ger) (Brit)	Shrewsbury
Chimbonda, Pascal (Guad) (Fr)	Wigan	Coyne, Chris (Aus)	Brentford, Luton, Southend, West Ham
Chinaglia, Giorgio (It)	Swansea Town		
Chine, Athumani (Tan)	Walsall	Cozic, Bertrand (Fr)	Cheltenham, Kidderminster, Northampton
Chippo, Youssef (Mor)	Coventry		
Christanval, Philippe (Fr)	Fulham		
Christensen, Tommy (Den)	Leicester, Portsmouth	Craven, Peter (Ger)	Halifax
Christiansen, Jesper (Den)	Kidderminster	Crawford, Jimmy (USA) (Ire)	Newcastle, Reading, Rotherham
Christie, Jeremy (NZ)	Barnsley		
Cini, Joe (Mal)	QPR	Crawford, Ronald (SA)	Rotherham, Thames
Cisse, Aliou (Sen)	Birmingham, Portsmouth	Crespo, Hernan (Arg)	Chelsea
Cisse, Djibril (Fr)	Liverpool	Croci, Laurent (Fr)	Carlisle
Cisse, Edouard (Fr)	West Ham	Crossan, Errol (Can)	Gillingham, Norwich, Orient, Southend
Claesen, Nico (Bel)	Tottenham		
Clarke, Bruce (SA)	Fulham	Cruickshank, George (Mly) (Brit)	Carlisle
Clelland, Crawford (USA)	Plymouth	Cruyff, Jordi (Neth)	Man Utd
Clement, Philippe (Bel)	Coventry	Cubie, Neil (SA)	Hull
Clichy, Gael (Fr)	Arsenal	Cudicini, Carlo (It)	Chelsea
Cobian, Juan (Arg)	Sheff Wed, Swindon	Cuervo, Phillipe (Fr)	Swindon
Cohen, Avi (Isr)	Liverpool	Cuffe, John (Aus)	Glossop
Cohen, Jacob (Isr)	Brighton	Cunningham, Tony (Jam) (Brit)	Barnsley, Blackpool, Bolton, Bury, Doncaster, Lincoln, Man City, Newcastle, Rotherham, Sheff Wed, Wycombe
Coker, Ade (Nig)	Lincoln, West Ham		
Colin, Jurgen (Neth)	Norwich		
Colleter, Patrick (Fr)	Southampton		
Collins, Mike (SA)	Swindon		

Name (Born) (Nationality, if differs)	League club(s)
Curcic, Sasa (Yug)	A Villa, Bolton, C Palace
Cutbush, John (Mal) (Brit)	Fulham, Sheff Utd, Tottenham
Cygan, Pascal (Fr)	Arsenal

D

Name (Born) (Nationality, if differs)	League club(s)
D'Alessandro, Andres (Arg)	Portsmouth
D'Avray, Mich (SA) (Eng)	Ipswich, Leicester
D'Jaffo, Laurent (Fr)	Bury, Sheff Utd, Stockport
Da Costa, Hugo (Por)	Stoke
Da Silva, Lourenco (Ang) (Por)	Bristol C, Oldham
Dabelsteen, Thomas (Den)	Scarborough
Dabizas, Nicos (Grk)	Leicester, Newcastle
Dacourt, Olivier (Fr)	Everton, Leeds
Dadason, Rikki (Ice)	Stoke
Dadi, Eugene (IvCo)	Nottm For, Notts Co, Tranmere
Dagnogo, Moussa (Fr)	Bristol R
Dahlin, Martin (Swe)	Blackburn
Daino, Daniele (It)	Derby
Dakinah, Kofi (Den)	Walsall
Daley, Omar (Jam)	Preston, Reading
Dalla Bona, Sam (It)	Chelsea
Dalmat, Stephane (Fr)	Tottenham
Dalton, James (Can)	Sunderland
Danielsson, Einer Thor (Ice)	Stoke
Danielsson, Helgi (Ice)	Peterborough
Danilevicius, Tomas (Rus) (Lith)	Arsenal
Danze, Anthony (Aus)	C Palace, MKD
Darcheville, Jean-Claude (FrGu) (Fr)	Nottm For
Darras, Frederic (Fr)	Swindon
Davids, Edgar (Sur) (Neth)	Tottenham
Davidson, Alan (Aus)	Nottm For
Davies, Clint (Aus)	Bradford
Davies, Roy (SA)	Luton
Davis, Claude (Jam)	Preston
De Bilde, Gilles (Bel)	A Villa, Sheff Wed
De Blasiis, Jean-Yves (Fr)	Norwich
De Freitas, Fabian (Sur) (Neth)	Bolton, WBA
De Goey, Ed (Neth)	Chelsea, Stoke
De Goey, Len (Neth)	Sheff Utd
De La Cruz, Ulises (Ecu)	A Villa
De Lucas, Enrique (Sp)	Chelsea
De Merit, Jay (USA)	Watford
De Oliveira, Filipe (Por)	Chelsea, Preston
De Ornelas, Fernando (Ven)	C Palace, QPR
De Pedro, Javier (Sp)	Blackburn
De Vogt, Wilko (Neth)	Sheff Utd
De Vos, Jason (Can)	Darlington, Ipswich, Wigan
De Vries, Mark (Sur) (Neth)	Leicester

Name (Born) (Nationality, if differs)	League club(s)
De Waard, Raimond (Neth)	Norwich
De Wolf, John (Neth)	Wolves
De Zeeuw, Arjan (Neth)	Barnsley, Portsmouth, Wigan
Debec, Fabien (Fr)	Coventry
Debeve, Mickael (Fr)	Middlesbrough
Deen, Ahmed (SiLe)	Peterborough
Deeney, David (Zim) (Brit)	Luton
Degn, Peter (Den)	Everton
Degryse, Marc (Bel)	Sheff Wed
Del Horno, Asier (Sp)	Chelsea
Del Rio, Walter (Arg)	C Palace
Delapenha, Lindy (Jam)	Mansfield, Middlesbrough, Portsmouth
Delgado, Agustin (Ecu)	Southampton
Dellas, Traianos (Grk)	Sheff Utd
Delorge, Laurent (Bel)	Coventry
Deloumeaux, Eric (Fr)	Coventry
Denny, Jay (USA)	Shrewsbury
Derko, Franco (It)	Mansfield
Derveld, Fernando (Neth)	Norwich, WBA
Desailly, Marcel (Gha) (Fr)	Chelsea
Deschamps, Didier (Fr)	Chelsea
Devereux, Tony (Gib) (Brit)	Aldershot
Deyna, Kazimierz (Pol)	Man City
Di Canio, Paolo (It)	Charlton, Sheff Wed, West Ham
Di Giuseppe, Bica (Bra)	Sunderland, Walsall
Di Lella, Gustavo (Arg)	Darlington, Hartlepool
Di Matteo, Roberto (Swit) (It)	Chelsea
Di Piedi, Michele (It)	Bristol R, Sheff Wed
Dia, Ali (Sen)	Southampton
Diabate, Lassina (IvCo)	Portsmouth
Diaby, Abou (Fr)	Arsenal
Diaf, Farid (Fr)	Preston
Diagouraga, Toumani (Fr)	Swindon, Watford
Diallo, Cherif (Sen)	Exeter
Diallo, Drissa (Mau) (Gui)	Burnley, Ipswich, Sheff Wed
Diao, Salif (Sen)	Birmingham, Liverpool, Portsmouth
Diarra, Lassana (Fr)	Chelsea
Diawara, Djibril (Sen)	Bolton
Diawara, Kaba (Fr)	Arsenal, Blackburn, West Ham
Diaz, Emiliano (It)	Oxford
Diaz, Isidro (Sp)	Rochdale, Wigan, Wolves
Dickinson, Patrick (Can)	Hull
Dijkstra, Meindert (Neth)	Notts Co
Dijkstra, Sieb (Neth)	Bristol C, QPR, Wycombe
Dillsworth, Eddie (SiLe)	Lincoln
Dimech, Luke (Mal)	Chester, Mansfield
Diomede, Bernard (Fr)	Liverpool

Name (Born) (Nationality, if differs)	League club(s)
Diop, Pape Bouba (Sen)	Fulham
Diop, Pape Seydou (Sen)	Norwich
Diop, Youssou (Sen)	Kidderminster
Diouf, El Hadji (Sen)	Bolton, Liverpool
Distin, Sylvain (Fr)	Man City, Newcastle
Dixon, Jonny (Sp) (Brit)	Wycombe
Dje, Ludovic (Fr)	Stockport
Djemba-Djemba, Eric (Cam)	A Villa, Man Utd
Djetou, Martin (IvCo) (Fr)	Bolton, Fulham
Djordjic, Bojan (Yug) (Swe)	Man Utd, Plymouth, Sheff Wed
Djorkaeff, Youri (Fr)	Blackburn, Bolton
Djourou, Johan (IvCo) (Swit)	Arsenal
Dolby, Hugh (Ind) (Brit)	Chelsea
Dolding, Len (Ind) (Brit)	Chelsea, Norwich
Domi, Didier (Fr)	Leeds, Newcastle
Dominguez, Jose (Por)	Birmingham, Tottenham
Donaghy, Charles (Ind) (Brit)	Chelsea
Doncel, Antonio (Sp)	Hull
Donis, George (Grk)	Blackburn, Huddersfield, Sheff Utd
Donoghue, John (USA)	Wrexham
Dorigo, Tony (Aus) (Eng)	A Villa, Chelsea, Derby, Leeds, Stoke
Doriva, Guidoni (Bra)	Middlesbrough
Dorner, Mario (Aut)	Darlington
Doumbe, Mathias (Fr)	Plymouth
Dowe, Jens (Ger)	Wolves
Downes, Aaron (Aus)	Chesterfield
Drogba, Didier (IvCo)	Chelsea
Duarte, Juan Maldondo (Bra)	Arsenal, Millwall
Ducrocq, Pierre (Fr)	Derby
Dudek, Jerzy (Pol)	Liverpool
Dugarry, Christophe (Fr)	Birmingham
Dugnolle, Jack (Ind) (Brit)	Brighton, Plymouth
Dumas, Franck (Fr)	Newcastle
Dumitrescu, Ilie (Rom)	Tottenham, West Ham
Dundee, Sean (SA)	Liverpool
Dunfield, Terry (Can)	Bury, Man City
Durandt, Cliff (SA)	Charlton, Wolves
Dursun, Peter (Den)	Southend
Dusan, Nikolic (Yug)	Bolton
Dwane, Eddie (Mal) (Brit)	Lincoln
Dziekanowski, Jackie (Pol)	Bristol C

E

Eames, Billy (Mal) (Brit)	Brentford, Portsmouth
Earnshaw, Robert (Zam) (Wal)	Cardiff, Norwich, WBA
Eboue, Emmanuel (IvCo)	Arsenal
Echanomi, Efe (Nig)	Orient
Edds, Gareth (Aus)	Bradford, MKD, Nottm For, Swindon
Edge, Declan (Mly) (NZ)	Notts Co

Name (Born) (Nationality, if differs)	League club(s)
Edinho, Amaral (Bra)	Bradford
Edman, Erik (Swe)	Tottenham
Edu (Bra)	Arsenal
Edwards, Alistair (Aus)	Brighton, Millwall
Edwards, Carlos (Trin)	Luton, Wrexham
Edwards, Gerald (HK) (Brit)	Luton
Einarsson, Gunnar (Ice)	Brentford
Einarsson, Gylfi (Ice)	Leeds
Eisentrager, Alec (Ger)	Bristol C
Ekelund, Ronnie (Den)	Coventry, Man City, Southampton, Walsall
Ekner, Dan (Swe)	Portsmouth
El Hamdaoui, Mounir (Neth) (Mor)	Derby
El Karkouri, Talal (Mor)	Charlton, Sunderland
El Khalej, Tahar (Mor)	Charlton, Southampton
El Kholti, Abdou (Fr) (Mor)	Cambridge, Chester, Yeovil
Elena, Marcelino (Sp)	Newcastle
Ellegaard, Kevin (Den)	Blackpool, Man City
Elliott, Simon (NZ)	Fulham
Elokobi, George (Cam)	Chester, Colchester
Elrich, Ahmed (Aus)	Fulham
Elstrup, Lars (Den)	Luton
Emenalo, Michael (Nig)	Notts Co
Emerson (Bra)	Middlesbrough
Emerton, Brett (Aus)	Blackburn
Emmerson, Wayne (Can)	Crewe
Emre Belozoglu (Tur)	Newcastle
Enckelman, Peter (Fin)	A Villa, Blackburn
Enes, Robbie (Aus)	Portsmouth
Engonga, Vincente (Sp)	Coventry
Enhua, Zhang (Chn)	Grimsby
Epesse-Titi, Steeve (Fr)	Exeter
Eranio, Stefano (It)	Derby
Eriksson, Jan (Swe)	Sunderland
Espartero, Mario (Fr)	Bolton
Essers, Pierre (Neth)	Walsall
Essien, Michael (Gha)	Chelsea
Etuhu, Dixon (Nig)	Man City, Norwich, Preston
Evans, Ceri (NZ)	Oxford
Evans, Michael (Neth)	York
Evans, Paul (SA)	Rushden, Sheff Wed
Eve, Angus (Trin)	Chester
Evra, Patrice (Sen) (Fr)	Man Utd
Evtushok, Alex (Ukr)	Coventry
Eydelie, Jean-Jacques (Fr)	Walsall
Eyjolfsson, Siggi (Ice)	Chester, Walsall

F

Fabiano, Nicolas (Fr)	Swansea
Fabio, Ferraresi (It)	A Villa
Fabregas, Cesc (Sp)	Arsenal

Name (Born) (Nationality, if differs)	League club(s)	Name (Born) (Nationality, if differs)	League club(s)
Fadida, Aharon (Isr)	Aldershot	Formann, Pascal (Ger)	Nottm For
Fadiga, Khalilou (Sen)	Bolton, Derby	Forrest, Craig (Can)	Chelsea, Colchester,
Faerber, Winston (Sur) (Neth)	Cardiff		Ipswich, West Ham
Falconer, Andy (SA)	Blackpool	Forssell, Mikael (Ger) (Fin)	Birmingham, Chelsea, C
Fallon, Rory (NZ)	Barnsley, Shrewsbury,		Palace
	Swansea, Swindon, Yeovil	Fortune, Quinton (SA)	Man Utd
Fangueiro, Carlos (Por)	Millwall	Foster, Craig (Aus)	C Palace, Portsmouth
Farina, Frank (Aus)	Notts Co	Fostervold, Anders (Nor)	Grimsby
Fayadh, Jassim (Irq)	Macclesfield	Foxe, Hayden (Aus)	Portsmouth, West Ham
Faye, Abdoulaye (Sen)	Bolton	Fradin, Karim (Fr)	Stockport
Faye, Amdy (Sen)	Newcastle, Portsmouth	Francino, Francis (Jam)	Watford
Ferguson, Don (Can)	Wrexham	Francis, Gerry (SA)	Leeds, York
Fernandes, Fabrice (Fr)	Bolton, Fulham,	Frandsen, Per (Den)	Bolton, Blackburn, Wigan
	Southampton	Frankowski, Tomasz (Pol)	Wolves
Fernandes, Silas (Por)	Wolves	Fraser, Willie (Aus) (Sco)	Nottm For, Sunderland
Fernandez, Vincent (Fr)	Nottm For	Fredgaard, Carsten (Den)	Bolton, Sunderland, WBA
Ferrari, Carlos (Bra)	Birmingham	Freimanis, Eddie (Lat)	Northampton
Ferrari, Matteo (Alg) (It)	Everton	Freund, Steffen (Ger)	Leicester, Tottenham
Ferreira, Paulo (Por)	Chelsea	Friedel, Brad (USA)	Blackburn, Liverpool
Ferrer, Albert (Sp)	Chelsea	Friio, David (Fr)	Nottm For, Plymouth
Ferretti, Andrea (It)	Cardiff	Frontzeck, Michael (Ger)	Man City
Ferri, Jean-Michel (Fr)	Liverpool	Frutos, Alexandre (Fr)	Brighton
Festa, Gianluca (It)	Middlesbrough,	Fuchs, Uwe (Ger)	Middlesbrough, Millwall
	Portsmouth	Fuertes, Esteban (Arg)	Derby
Feuer, Ian (USA)	Derby, Luton,	Fuglestad, Erik (Nor)	Norwich
	Peterborough, Tranmere,	Fuller, Ricardo (Jam)	C Palace, Ipswich,
	West Ham, Wimbledon		Portsmouth, Preston,
Figueroa, Luciano (Arg)	Birmingham		Southampton
Filan, John (Aus)	Blackburn, Cambridge,	Fulop, Marton (Hun)	Chesterfield, Coventry
	Coventry, Wigan	Fumaca, Jose (Bra)	Colchester, C Palace,
Fiocca, Paul (It)	Swindon		Newcastle
Firmani, Eddie (SA)	Charlton, Southend	Fursdon, Roy (Can)	Torquay
Firmani, Peter (SA)	Charlton	Futre, Paulo (Por)	West Ham
Fish, Kenneth (SA)	Port Vale		
Fish, Mark (SA)	Bolton, Charlton, Ipswich	**G**	
Fjortoft, Jan Aage (Nor)	Barnsley, Middlesbrough,	Gaardsoe, Thomas (Den)	Ipswich, WBA
	Sheff Utd, Swindon	Gabrieli, Emanuele (It)	Boston, Sheff Utd
Flamini, Mathieu (Fr)	Arsenal	Gaia, Marcio (Bra)	Exeter
Fleming, Mike (Ind) (Brit)	Tranmere	Gaillard, Marcel (Bel)	C Palace, Portsmouth
Flo, Havard (Nor)	Wolves	Gall, Benny (Den)	Shrewsbury
Flo, Jostein (Nor)	Sheff Utd	Gallas, William (Fr)	Chelsea
Flo, Tore Andre (Nor)	Chelsea, Sunderland	Gallego, Jose (Sp)	Brentford, Colchester,
Foe, Marc-Vivien (Cam)	Man City, West Ham		Southampton
Fofana, Aboubaka (Fr)	Millwall	Gallego, Tony (Sp)	Norwich
Fojut, Jaroslaw (Pol)	Bolton	Galli, Filippo (It)	Watford
Foletti, Patrick (Swit)	Derby	Galloway, Steve (Ger) (Brit)	Cambridge, C Palace
Folly, Yoann (Tgo) (Fr)	Nottm For, Preston, Sheff	Gambaro, Enzo (It)	Grimsby
	Wed, Southampton	Ganea, Ionel (Rom)	Wolves
Forbes, Boniek (GuB)	Orient	Garcia, Luis (Sp)	Liverpool
Forbes, Dudley (SA)	Charlton	Garcia, Richard (Aus)	Colchester, Orient, West
Foreman, Denis (SA)	Brighton		Ham
Forge, Nicolas (Fr)	Orient	Garcia, Sanjuan Jesus (Sp)	Wolves
Forlan, Diego (Uru)	Man Utd	Garcia, Tony (Fr)	Notts Co

Name (Born) (Nationality, if differs)	League club(s)	Name (Born) (Nationality, if differs)	League club(s)
Garde, Remi (Fr)	Arsenal	Gotsmanov, Sergei (USSR) (Blr)	Brighton, Southampton
Gardner, Don (Jam)	Wolves	Gottskalksson, Ole (Ice)	Brentford, Torquay
Gardner, Ricardo (Jam)	Bolton	Gough, Richard (Swe) (Sco)	Everton, Nottm For, Tottenham
Gariani, Moshe (Isr)	Brighton		
Garrocho, Carlos (Arg)	Walsall	Goulet, Brent (USA)	Bournemouth, Crewe
Garwood, Len (Ind) (Brit)	Tottenham	Goulooze, Richard (Neth)	Derby
Gaudino, Maurizio (Ger)	Man City	Grabbi, Corrado (It)	Blackburn
Gavilan, Diego (Par)	Newcastle	Grabovac, Zarko (SM)	Blackpool
Geard, Glen (Mal)	Brighton	Grant, Kim (Gha)	Charlton, Luton, Millwall, Notts Co, Scunthorpe
Genaux, Reggie (Bel)	Coventry		
Gentile, Marco (Neth)	Burnley	Granville, John (Trin)	Aldershot, Millwall
George, Finidi (Nig)	Ipswich	Gravelaine, Xavier (Fr)	Watford
Georgeson, Roddy (Egy) (Brit)	Port Vale	Gravesen, Thomas (Den)	Everton
Georgiadis, Georgios (Grk)	Newcastle	Greer, Ross (Aus)	Chester
Gera, Zoltan (Hun)	WBA	Gregorio, Adolfo (USA)	Darlington
Geremi (Cam)	Chelsea, Middlesbrough	Gregory, Neil (Zam) (Brit)	Chesterfield, Colchester, Ipswich, Peterborough, Scunthorpe, Torquay
Gerhardt, Hugh (SA)	Liverpool		
Germain, Steve (Fr)	Colchester		
Gerrbrand, Patrik (Swe)	Leicester		
Gerula, Stan (Pol)	Orient	Grenet, Francois (Fr)	Derby
Ghrayib, Naguyan (Isr)	A Villa	Gresko,Vratislav (Svk)	Blackburn
Giallanza, Gaetano (Swit)	Bolton, Norwich	Greyling, Anton (SA)	Torquay
Giannakopoulos, Stelios (Grk)	Bolton	Griemink, Bart (Neth)	Birmingham, Peterborough, Southend, Swindon
Gibbs, Peter (Zim)	Watford		
Gibson, Fred (SA)	Coventry, Sunderland		
Gibson, Jock (Brit)	Hull, Luton, Sheff Utd, Sunderland	Grieves, Ken (Aus)	Bolton, Bury, Stockport
		Griffit, Leandre (Fr)	Leeds, Rotherham, Southampton
Gillet, Stephane (Lux)	Chester		
Ginola, David (Fr)	A Villa, Everton, Newcastle, Tottenham	Griffith, Cohen (Guy) (Brit)	Cardiff
		Griffiths, Adam (Aus)	Bournemouth
Gioacchini, Stefano (It)	Coventry	Griffiths, Joel (Aus)	Leeds
Gislason, Siggi (Ice)	Stoke	Grimandi, Gilles (Fr)	Arsenal
Gislason, Valur (Ice)	Brighton	Grobbelaar, Bruce (SA) (Zim)	Bury, Crewe, Lincoln, Liverpool, Oldham, Plymouth, Southampton, Stoke
Giumarra, Willy (Can)	Darlington		
Gnohere, Arthur (IvCo) (Fr)	Burnley, QPR		
Goater, Shaun (Ber)	Bristol C, Coventry, Man City, Notts Co, Reading, Rotherham, Southend		
		Grodas, Frode (Nor)	Chelsea, Tottenham
		Groenendijk, Alfons (Neth)	Man City
Godfrey, Elliott (Can)	Watford	Grondin, David (Fr)	Arsenal
Golac, Ivan (Yug)	Bournemouth, Man City, Portsmouth, Southampton	Gronkjaer, Jesper (Den)	Birmingham, Chelsea
		Guatelli, Andrea (It)	Oxford
Goldbaek, Bjarne (Den)	Chelsea, Fulham	Gudjohnsen, Eidur (Ice)	Bolton, Chelsea
Goma, Alain (Fr)	Fulham, Newcastle	Gudjonsson, Bjarni (Ice)	Coventry, Plymouth, Stoke
Gomez, Fernando (Sp)	Wolves	Gudjonsson, Joey (Ice)	A Villa, Leicester, Wolves
Goodhind, Warren (SA)	Barnet, Cambridge, Oxford, Rochdale	Gudjonsson, Thordur (Ice)	Derby, Preston, Stoke
		Gudmundsson, Albert (Ice)	Arsenal
Goodison, Ian (Jam)	Hull, Tranmere	Gudmundsson, Johann (Ice)	Cambridge, Watford
Goodridge, Greg (Bar)	Bristol C, Cheltenham, QPR, Torquay	Gudmundsson, Niklas (Swe)	Blackburn, Ipswich
		Guentchev, Bontcho (Bul)	Ipswich, Luton
Gope-Fenepej, John (NCal) (Fr)	Bolton	Gueret, Willy (Guad) (Fr)	Millwall, Swansea
Gorre, Dean (Sur) (Neth)	Barnsley, Blackpool, Huddersfield	Guerrero, Ivan (Hon)	Coventry
		Guivarc'h, Stephane (Fr)	Newcastle
Goss, Jerry (Cyp) (Wal)	Norwich	Gullit, Ruud (Sur) (Neth)	Chelsea

Name (Born) (Nationality, if differs)	League club(s)	Name (Born) (Nationality, if differs)	League club(s)
Gunn, Alf (Ger)	Nottm For	Havenga, Willie (SA)	Birmingham, Ipswich, Luton
Gunnarsson, Brynjar (Ice)	Nottm For, Reading, Stoke, Watford	Hay, Danny (NZ)	Leeds, Walsall
Gunnlaugsson, Arnie (Ice)	Bolton, Leicester, Stoke	Hazan, Alon (Isr)	Watford
Gunnlaugsson, Bjarke (Ice)	Preston	Hazell, Bob (Jam) (Eng)	Leicester, Port Vale, QPR, Reading, Wolves
Gurinovich, Igor (USSR) (Blr)	Brighton		
Gustafsson, Tomas (Swe)	Coventry	Heald, Oliver (Can)	Scarborough
Guyett, Scott (Aus)	Oxford, Yeovil	Hebel, Dirk (Ger)	Brentford
Gyepes, Gabor (Hun)	Wolves	Hedman, Magnus (Swe)	Coventry
Gysbrechts, Davy (Bel)	Sheff Utd	Hegazi, Hassan (Egy)	Fulham
		Heggem, Vegard (Nor)	Liverpool
H		Heidenstrom, Bjorn (Nor)	Orient
Haaland, Alf-Inge (Nor)	Leeds, Man City, Nottm For	Heikkinen, Markus (Swe) (Fin)	Luton, Portsmouth
		Heinola, Antti (Fin)	QPR
Haarhoff, Jimmy (Zam)	Birmingham	Heinze, Gabriel (Arg)	Man Utd
Haas, Bernt (Aut)	Sunderland, WBA	Heiselberg, Kim (Den)	Swindon
Haasz, Johnny (Hun)	Swansea Town, Workington	Helder, Glenn (Neth)	Arsenal
		Helguson, Heidar (Ice)	Fulham, Watford
Haddaoui, Riffi (Den)	Torquay	Helin, Petri (Fin)	Luton, Stockport
Hadji, Mustapha (Mor)	A Villa, Coventry	Helmer, Thomas (Ger)	Sunderland
Hadziabdic, Dzemal (Yug)	Swansea	Helveg, Thomas (Den)	Norwich
Hahnemann, Marcus (USA)	Fulham, Reading, Rochdale	Henchoz, Stephane (Swit)	Blackburn, Liverpool, Wigan
Haidong, Hao (Chn)	Sheff Utd	Henderson, Paul (Aus)	Bradford, Leicester
Hajto, Tomasz (Pol)	Derby, Southampton	Henriksen, Tony (Nor)	Southend
Hakan Sukur (Tur)	Blackburn	Henriksen, Bo (Den)	Bristol R, Kidderminster
Hakan Unsal (Tur)	Blackburn	Henry, Liburd (Dom)	Gillingham, Halifax, Maidstone, Peterborough, Watford
Halle, Gunnar (Nor)	Bradford, Leeds, Oldham, Wolves		
Hamann, Dietmar (Ger)	Liverpool, Newcastle	Henry, Thierry (Fr)	Arsenal
Hammond, Elvis (Gha)	Bristol R, Fulham, Leicester, Norwich	Heppolette, Ricky (Ind) (Brit)	Chesterfield, C Palace, Orient, Peterborough, Preston
Hansen, Bo (Den)	Bolton		
Hansen, Edvin (Den)	Grimsby	Herbert, Ricki (NZ)	Wolves
Hansen, John (Ger) (Den)	Cambridge	Herivelto, Moreira (Bra)	Walsall
Hansen, Karl (Nor)	Huddersfield	Hernandez, Dino (Neth)	Wigan
Hansen, Vergard (Nor)	Bristol C	Herrera, Martin (Arg)	Fulham
Hansson, Mikael (Swe)	Stoke	Herve, Laurent (Fr)	MKD
Hardy, Adam (SA)	Bradford	Herzig, Nico (Ger)	Wimbledon
Hareide, Aage (Nor)	Man City, Norwich	Hesford, Iain (Zam) (Eng)	Blackpool, Fulham, Hull, Maidstone, Notts Co, Sunderland
Harkes, John (USA)	Derby, Nottm For, Sheff Wed, West Ham		
Harnwell, Jamie (Aus)	Orient	Hewie, John (SA) (Sco)	Charlton
Harries Paul (Aus)	Carlisle, Exeter, Portsmouth, Torquay	Hewkins, Ken (SA)	Fulham
		Hews, Chay (Aus)	Carlisle
Harris, Alex (HK) (Brit)	Blackpool	Hey, Tony (Ger)	Birmingham
Harris, Andy (SA) (Brit)	Chester, Orient, Southend	Hiden, Martin (Aut)	Leeds
Hartenberger, Uwe (Ger)	Reading	Hierro, Fernando (Sp)	Bolton
Hasselbaink, Jimmy Floyd (Sur) (Neth)	Chelsea, Leeds, Middlesbrough	Higginbotham, Harry (Aus)	Luton, Nelson, Orient, Reading, South Shields
Hastie, Ken (SA)	Leeds	Hill, Reginald (Gib) (Brit)	Carlisle, Darlington, Hartlepool, Tranmere
Hauser, Peter (SA)	Blackpool, Chester		
Hauser, Thomas (Ger)	Sunderland	Hirschfeld, Lars (Can)	Gillingham, Leicester,

Name (Born) (Nationality, if differs)	League club(s)	Name (Born) (Nationality, if differs)	League club(s)
	Luton	**I**	
Hitzlsperger, Thomas (Ger)	A Villa, Chesterfield	Idiakez, Inigo (Sp)	Derby
Hjelde, Jon Olav (Nor)	Mansfield, Nottm For	Ifejiagwa, Emeka (Nig)	Brighton
Hjorth, Jesper (Den)	Darlington	Iga, Andrew (Uga) (Brit)	Millwall
Hleb, Aleksandr (Blr)	Arsenal	Ilic, Sasa (Aus) (Yug)	Barnsley, Blackpool,
Hodge, Eric (SA)	Aldershot, Brighton		Charlton, Portsmouth,
Hodgson, Doug (Aus)	Burnley, Northampton,		West Ham
	Oldham, Plymouth, Sheff	Immel, Eike (Ger)	Man City
	Utd	Inamoto, Junichi (Jap)	Arsenal, Cardiff, Fulham,
Hodgson, Gordon (SA) (Eng)	A Villa, Leeds, Liverpool		WBA
Hodouto, Kwami (Tgo) (Fr)	Huddersfield	Ince, Clayton (Trin)	Coventry, Crewe
Hoefkens, Carl (Bel)	Stoke	Ingebrigtsen, Kaare (Nor)	Man City
Hoekman, Danny (Neth)	Man City	Ingesson, Klas (Swe)	Sheff Wed
Hoekstra, Peter (Neth)	Stoke	Ingimarsson, Ivar (Ice)	Brentford, Brighton,
Hogan, Cornelius (Mal)	Burnley, NB Tower		Reading, Torquay, Wolves
Hogh, Jes (Den)	Chelsea	Invincible, Danny (Aus)	Swindon
Hollund, Martin (Nor)	Hartlepool	Iorfa, Dominic (Nig)	Peterborough, QPR,
Holster, Marco (Neth)	Ipswich		Southend
Holwyn, Jermaine (Neth)	Port Vale	Iovan, Stefan (Rom)	Brighton
Hooper, Lyndon (Guy) (Can)	Birmingham	Ipoua, Guy (Cam) (Fr)	Bristol R, Doncaster,
Horace, Alain (Mad) (Fr)	Hartlepool		Gillingham, Lincoln,
Horlaville, Christophe (Fr)	Port Vale		Mansfield, Scunthorpe
Horne, Des (SA)	Blackpool, Wolves	Iroha, Ben (Nig)	Watford
Hornuss, Julien (Fr)	MKD	Isaias, Marques (Bra) (Por)	Coventry
Horsfall, George (Aus)	Southampton, Southend	Ismael, Valerien (Fr)	C Palace
Hottiger, Marc (Swit)	Everton, Newcastle	Issa, Pierre (SA)	Watford
Houghton, Brian (Ind) (Brit)	Birmingham, Bradford PA,	Itonga, Carlin (DRC)	Arsenal
	Lincoln, Oxford,	Iversen, Steffen (Nor)	Tottenham, Wolves
	Southend		
Houston, Graham (Gib) (Brit)	Carlisle, Preston, Wigan	**J**	
Hovi, Tom (Nor)	Charlton	Jaaskelainen, Jussi (Fin)	Bolton
Howard, Tim (USA)	Man Utd	Jack, Rodney (Jam) (StV)	Crewe, Oldham, Rushden,
Howells, Lee (Aus)	Cheltenham		Torquay
Hreidarsson, Hermann (Ice)	Brentford, Charlton, C	Jackson, Simeon (Jam)	Rushden
	Palace, Ipswich,	Jacobsen, Anders (Nor)	Notts Co, Sheff Utd, Stoke
	Wimbledon	Jacobsen, Viggo (Den)	Charlton
Hristov, Georgi (Mac)	Barnsley	Jaidi, Radhi (Tun)	Bolton
Hubbard, John (SA)	Bury	Jakobsson, Andreas (Swe)	Southampton
Huck, Willie (Fr)	Bournemouth	Jalink, Nico (Neth)	Port Vale
Huggins, Joe (Ind) (Brit)	Aldershot	Jankovic, Bozo (Yug)	Middlesbrough
Hughes, Adam (Aus)	Doncaster	Jansson, Jan (Swe)	Port Vale
Hughes, Zacari (Aus)	Rochdale	Jantunen, Pertti (Fin)	Bristol C
Hume, Iain (Can)	Leicester, Tranmere	Jardel, Mario (Bra)	Bolton
Hunter, Chris (HK) (Brit)	Preston	Jarosik, Jiri (CzRep)	Birmingham, Chelsea
Hunter, George (Ind) (Brit)	A Villa, Chelsea, Man Utd,	Jarrett, Albert (SiLe) (Brit)	Brighton, MKD, Swindon
	Oldham	Javary, Jean-Phillipe (Fr)	Brentford, Plymouth, Sheff
Hussein, Yasser (Qtr)	Man City		Utd
Huth, Robert (Ger)	Chelsea	Jean, Earl (StL)	Ipswich, Plymouth,
Hyldgaard, Morten (Den)	Coventry, Luton,		Rotherham
	Scunthorpe	Jeannin, Alex (Fr)	Bristol Rovers, Darlington
Hysen, Glenn (Swe)	Liverpool	Jennings, Jedd (Ber)	Hereford
Hyypia, Sami (Fin)	Liverpool	Jensen, Brian (Den)	Burnley, WBA
		Jensen, Claus (Den)	Bolton, Charlton, Fulham

Name (Born) (Nationality, if differs)	League club(s)
Jensen, John (Den)	Arsenal
Jensen, Niclas (Den)	Fulham, Man City
Jensen, Viggo (Den)	Hull
Jeppson, Hans (Swe)	Charlton
Jerkan, Nikola (Cro)	Nottm For
Jermyn, Mark (Ger) (Brit)	Torquay
Jihai, Sun (Chn)	C Palace, Man City
Job, Joseph-Desire (Fr) (Cam)	Middlesbrough
Johanneson, Albert (SA)	Leeds, York
Johansen, Martin (Den)	Coventry
Johansen, Michael (Den)	Bolton
Johansen, Rune (Nor)	Bristol R
Johansen, Stig (Nor)	Bristol C, Southampton
Johansson, Andreas (Swe)	Wigan
Johansson, Jonatan (Swe) (Fin)	Charlton, Norwich
Johansson, Nils-Eric (Den)	Blackburn, Leicester
John, Collins (Lib) (Neth)	Fulham
John, Stern (Trin)	Birmingham, Coventry, Derby, Nottm For
Johnsen, Erland (Nor)	Chelsea
Johnsen, Ronny (Nor)	A Villa, Man Utd, Newcastle
Johnson, David (Jam)	Burnley, Bury, Ipswich, Nottm For, Sheff Utd, Sheff Wed
Johnson, Glenn (Aus)	Cardiff
Johnson, Glenn (Can)	WBA
Johnson, Jemal (USA)	Blackburn, Darlington, Preston
Johnson, Jermaine (Jam)	Bolton, Oldham
Johnson, Richard (Aus)	Colchester, MKD, Northampton, QPR, Stoke, Watford
Johnsson, Julian (Den) (Far)	Hull
Johnston, Craig (SA) (Aus)	Liverpool, Middlesbrough
Johnstone, Glenn (Ken) (Brit)	Preston
Jokanovic, Slavisa (Yug)	Chelsea
Jol, Martin (Neth)	Coventry, WBA
Jones, Brad (Aus)	Blackpool, Middlesbrough, Stockport
Jones, Cobi (USA)	Coventry
Jones, Ian (Ger) (Brit)	Cardiff
Jones, Kenwyne (Trin)	Sheff Wed, Southampton, Stoke
Jonk, Wim (Neth)	Sheff Wed
Jonson, Mattias (Swe)	Norwich
Jonsson, Siggi (Ice)	Arsenal, Barnsley, Sheff Wed
Jorgensen, Claus (Den)	Bournemouth, Bradford, Coventry
Jorgensen, Henrik (Den)	Notts Co
Josemi (Sp)	Liverpool

Name (Born) (Nationality, if differs)	League club(s)
Joseph, David (Guad) (Fr)	Notts Co
Joseph, Ricardo (Jam)	Rushden
Jovanovic, Nikola (Yug)	Man Utd
Joy, Ian (USA)	Kidderminster
Juan, Jimmy (Fr)	Ipswich
Juanjo, Carricondo (Sp)	Bradford
Juninho (Bra)	Middlesbrough
Junior, Jose Luis (Bra)	Derby, Rotherham, Walsall

K

Kaak, Tom (Neth)	Darlington
Kaamark, Pontus (Swe)	Leicester
Kachloul, Hassan (Mor)	A Villa, Southampton, Wolves
Kachouro, Petr (Blr)	Sheff Utd
Kaiser, Rudi (Neth)	Coventry
Kaku, Blessing (Nig)	Bolton, Derby
Kalac, Zeljko (Aus)	Leicester
Kalogeracos, Vas (Aus)	Stockport
Kamara, Diomansy (Fr) (Sen)	Portsmouth, WBA
Kamudimba, Jean-Paul (DRC)	Grimsby
Kanchelskis, Andrei (Ukr)	Everton, Man City, Man Utd, Southampton
Kandol, Tresor (DRC) (Brit)	Barnet, Bournemouth, Cambridge, Darlington, Luton
Kangana, Ndiwa (DRC)	Oldham, Rochdale
Kanoute, Frederic (Fr) (Mli)	Tottenham, West Ham
Kanu, Chris (Nig)	Peterborough
Kanu, Nwankwo (Nig)	Arsenal, WBA
Kanyuka, Patrick (DRC)	QPR
Kapengwe, Emment (Zam)	A Villa
Kapler, Konrad (Pol)	Rochdale
Kaprielian, Mickael (Fr)	Bolton
Karaa, Roch (Tun)	Darlington
Karadas, Azar (Nor)	Portsmouth
Karam, Amine (Fr)	Oxford
Karbassiyoon, Daniel (USA)	Arsenal, Burnley, Ipswich
Karelse, John (Neth)	Newcastle
Karembeu, Christian (NCal) (Fr)	Middlesbrough
Karic, Amir (Slo)	C Palace, Ipswich
Karl, Steffen (Ger)	Man City
Karlsen, Kent (Nor)	Luton
Karlsson, Par (Swe)	Wimbledon
Katalinic, Ivan (Yug)	Southampton
Katan, Yaniv (Isr)	West Ham
Kavelashvili, Mikhail (Geo)	Man City
Kaviedes, Ivan (Ecu)	C Palace
Kawaguchi, Yoshikatsu (Jap)	Portsmouth
Kearton, Jason (Aus)	Blackpool, Crewe, Everton, Notts Co, Stoke
Keelan, Kevin (Ind) (Brit)	A Villa, Norwich, Stockport, Wrexham

Name (Born) (Nationality, if differs)	League club(s)
Keizer, Gerry (Neth)	Arsenal, Charlton
Keizerweerd, Orpheo (Neth)	Oldham
Keller, Francois (Fr)	Fulham
Keller, Kasey (USA)	Leicester, Millwall, Southampton, Tottenham
Keller, Marc (Fr)	Blackburn, Portsmouth, West Ham
Kelly, Errington (StV)	Bristol C, Bristol R, Lincoln, Peterborough
Kelly, Pat (SA) (N Ire)	Barnsley, Crewe
Kemp, Dirk (SA)	Liverpool
Kemp, Fred (It) (Brit)	Blackpool, Halifax, Hereford, Southampton, Wolves
Kennon, Sandy (SA)	Colchester, Huddersfield, Norwich
Kerr, Dylan (Mal) (Brit)	Blackpool, Carlisle, Doncaster, Exeter, Kidderminster, Leeds, Reading
Kerr, John (Can) (USA)	Millwall, Peterborough, Portsmouth, Walsall
Ketsbaia, Temuri (Geo)	Newcastle, Wolves
Kewell, Harry (Aus)	Leeds, Liverpool
Kezman, Mateja (SM)	Chelsea
Kharine, Dimitri (Rus)	Chelsea
Khizanishvili, Zurab (Geo)	Blackburn
Kichenbrand, Don (SA)	Sunderland
Kiko, Manuel (Por)	Stockport
Killen, Chris (NZ)	Man City, Oldham, Port Vale, Wrexham
Killin, Roy (Can)	Lincoln
Kinder, Vladimir (Svk)	Middlesbrough
Kinet, Christophe (Bel)	Millwall
King, Charlie (SA)	Southport
Kingsley, Alf (Bar)	Charlton, Fulham, Millwall
Kinkladze, Georgi (Geo)	Derby, Man City
Kippe, Frode (Nor)	Liverpool, Stoke
Kiraly, Gabor (Hun)	C Palace
Kirk, John (Can)	Acc Stanley, Portsmouth
Kirkby, John (USA)	Stoke, Wrexham
Kirovski, Jovan (USA)	Birmingham, C Palace
Kirsten, Ken (SA)	Aldershot
Kishishev, Radostin (Bul)	Charlton
Kisnorbo, Patrick (Aus)	Leicester
Kitamirike, Joel (Uga)	Brentford, Chelsea, Mansfield
Kitchen, Sam (Ger) (Brit)	Doncaster, Orient
Kjeldbjerg, Jakob (Nor) (Den)	Chelsea
Kleberson (Bra)	Man Utd
Klinsmann, Jurgen (Ger)	Tottenham
Kloner, Hymie (SA) (Pol)	Birmingham

Name (Born) (Nationality, if differs)	League club(s)
Kluivert, Patrick (Neth)	Newcastle
Knarvik, Tommy (Nor)	Leeds
Knight, Jason (Aus)	Doncaster
Koejoe, Sammy (Sur) (Neth)	QPR
Koenen, Frans (Neth)	Newcastle
Kolar, Martin (CzRep)	Stoke
Kolinko, Alex (Lat)	C Palace
Kolkka, Joonas (Fin)	C Palace
Konde, Oumar (Swit)	Blackburn
Konjic, Muhamed (Bos)	Coventry, Derby
Konstantinidis, Kostas (Ger) (Grk)	Bolton
Konstantopoulos, Dimi (Grk)	Hartlepool
Konte, Amadou (Mli)	Cambridge
Koogi, Anders (Den)	Peterborough
Koordes, Rogier (Neth)	Port Vale
Kopteff, Peter (Fin)	Stoke
Koroman, Ognjen (SM)	Portsmouth
Korsten, Willem (Neth)	Leeds, Tottenham
Koskela, Toni (Fin)	Cardiff
Kosmina, John (Aus)	Arsenal
Kosowski, Kamil (Pol)	Southampton
Kottila, Mika (Fin)	Hereford
Koumantarakis, George (Grk) (SA)	Preston
Kovacevic, Darko (Yug)	Sheff Wed
Kovacs, Janos (Hun)	Chesterfield
Kowenicki, Ryszard (Pol)	Oldham
Kozak, Jan (Svk)	WBA
Kozma, Istvan (Hun)	Liverpool
Kraay, Hans (Neth)	Brighton
Kristensen, Bjorn (Den)	Bristol C, Newcastle, Portsmouth
Kristinsson, Birkir (Ice)	Stoke
Krizan, Ales (Slo)	Barnsley
Kroldrup, Per (Den)	Everton
Kromheer, Elroy (Neth)	Reading
Kromkamp, Jan (Neth)	Liverpool
Kruszynski, Detsi (Ger)	Brentford, Coventry, Peterborough, Wimbledon
Kubicki, Dariusz (Pol)	A Villa, Carlisle, Darlington, Sunderland, Tranmere, Wolves
Kubicki, Eryk (Pol)	York
Kuduzovic, Fahrudin (Bos)	Notts Co
Kuipers, Michel (Neth)	Boston, Brighton, Bristol R, Hull
Kulcsar, George (Hun) (Aus)	Bradford, QPR
Kulkov, Vasili (Rus)	Millwall
Kuqi, Njazi (Alb) (Fin)	Blackpool, Peterborough
Kuqi, Shefki (Alb) (Fin)	Blackburn, Ipswich, Sheff Wed, Stockport
Kus, Marcin (Pol)	QPR

Name (Born) (Nationality, if differs)	League club(s)
Kuszczak, Tomasz (Pol)	WBA
Kval, Frank (Nor)	Burnley
Kvarme, Bjorn Tore (Nor)	Liverpool
Kyratzoglou, Alex (Aus)	Oldham
Kyzeridis, Nicos (Grk)	Portsmouth

L

Name (Born) (Nationality, if differs)	League club(s)
L'Helgoualch, Cyrille (Fr)	Mansfield, Walsall
Labant, Vladimir (Svk)	West Ham
Labarthe, Gianfranco (Per)	Derby, Huddersfield
Lahtinen, Aki (Fin)	Notts Co
Laird, Kamu (Trin)	Chester
Lakis, Vassilis (Grk)	C Palace
Lama, Bernard (Fr)	West Ham
Lambourde, Bernard (Guad) (Fr)	Chelsea, Portsmouth
Lambu, Goma (DRC)	Mansfield
Lamptey, Nii (Gha)	A Villa, Coventry
Lancelotte, Eric (Ind) (Brit)	Brighton, Charlton
Langenove, Eugene (Fr)	Walsall
Lapper, Mike (USA)	Southend
Larkin, Jim (Can)	Cambridge
Larossa, Ruben Dario (Arg)	Walsall
Larrieu, Romain (Fr)	Plymouth
Larsen, Stig Olav (Nor)	Hartlepool
Larsson, Sebastian (Swe)	Arsenal
Larusson, Bjarni (Ice)	Scunthorpe, Walsall
Laryea, Benny (Gha)	Torquay
Laslandes, Lilian (Fr)	Sunderland
Latka, Martin (CzRep)	Birmingham
Latte-Yedo, Igor (IvCo)	Cambridge
Laudrup, Brian (Aut) (Den)	Chelsea
Lauren, Etame-Mayer (Cam)	Arsenal
Laurent, Pierre (Fr)	Leeds
Laursen, Jacob (Den)	Derby, Leicester
Laursen, Martin (Den)	A Villa
Laville, Florent (Fr)	Bolton, Coventry
Law, Cecil (Zim) (Brit)	Bury, Derby
Lawrence, Denis (Trin)	Wrexham
Laxton, Edward (Bra) (Brit)	Norwich
Lazaridis, Stan (Aus)	Birmingham, West Ham
Le Pen, Ulrich (Fr)	Ipswich
Le Roux, Daniel (Fr)	Arsenal
Le Tallec, Anthony (Fr)	Liverpool, Sunderland
Leary, Stuart (SA)	Charlton, QPR
Leboeuf, Frank (Fr)	Chelsea
Lee, Alan (Ger) (Brit)	Leicester
Lee, Yong-Pyo (SK)	Tottenham
Leese, Lars (Ger)	Barnsley
Legwinski, Sylvain (Fr)	Fulham
Lehmann, Dirk (Ger)	Brighton, Fulham
Lehmann, Jens (Ger)	Arsenal
Leitao, Jorge (Por)	Walsall

Name (Born) (Nationality, if differs)	League club(s)
Leitch, Grant (SA)	Blackpool
Leite, Sergio (Por)	Hull
Lemarchand, Stephane (Fr)	Carlisle, Rotherham
Lenarduzzi, Bob (Can)	Reading
Lenhart, Sascha (Ger)	Leicester
Leonhardsen, Oyvind (Nor)	Liverpool, Tottenham, Wimbledon, A Villa
Leoni, Stephane (Fr)	Bristol R
Leslie, Maurice (Ind) (Brit)	Swindon
Lester, Hugh (USA) (Brit)	Liverpool, Oldham
Lewis, Eddie (USA)	Fulham, Leeds, Preston
Li Tie (Chn)	Everton
Li Weifeng (Chn)	Everton
Libbra, Marc (Fr)	Norwich
Liddle, David (Mal) (Brit)	Northampton
Lightbourne, Kyle (Ber)	Cardiff, Coventry, Fulham, Hull, Macclesfield, Scarborough, Stoke, Swindon, Walsall
Lightening, Arthur (SA)	Coventry, Middlesbrough, Nottm For
Limpar, Anders (Swe)	Arsenal, Birmingham, Everton
Linderoth, Tobias (Swe)	Everton
Lindsay, Denis (SA)	Huddersfield
Lipa, Andreas (Aut)	Port Vale
Lita, Leroy (Con)	Bristol C, Reading
Litmanen, Jari (Fin)	Liverpool
Ljungberg, Freddie (Swe)	Arsenal
Lohman, Jan (Neth)	Watford
Lomas, Steve (Ger) (N Ire)	Man City, QPR, West Ham
Lombardo, Attilio (It)	C Palace
Loovens, Glenn (Neth)	Cardiff
Lopes, Osvaldo (Fr)	Plymouth, Torquay
Lopez, Carlos (Mex)	Wycombe
Lopez, Ricardo (Sp)	Man Utd
Loran, Tyrone (Neth)	Port Vale, Tranmere
Lorenzo, Nestor (Arg)	Swindon
Louis-Jean, Mathieu (Fr)	Norwich, Nottm For
Lovell, Stuart (Aus)	Reading
Lowe, Onandi (Jam)	Coventry, Port Vale, Rushden
Lua-Lua, Lomana (DRC)	Colchester, Newcastle, Portsmouth
Lucic, Teddy (Swe)	Leeds
Lund, Andreas (Nor)	Wimbledon
Lundekvam, Claus (Nor)	Southampton
Lundin, Pal (Swe)	Oxford
Luntala, Tresor (Fr)	Birmingham
Lupoli, Arturo (It)	Arsenal
Luque, Alberto (Sp)	Newcastle
Luzhny, Oleg (Ukr)	Arsenal, Wolves
Luzi, Patrice (Fr)	Liverpool

Name (Born) (Nationality, if differs)	League club(s)
Lydersen, Pal (Den) (Nor)	Arsenal
Lynch, Simon (Can)	Blackpool, Preston, Stockport

M

Name (Born) (Nationality, if differs)	League club(s)
M'Bombo, Doudou (DRC)	Oxford, QPR
Mabizela, Mbulelo (SA)	Tottenham
Maccarone, Massimo (It)	Middlesbrough
Macdonald, Gary (Ger) (Brit)	Peterborough, Portsmouth
MacDonald, Ian (Ger) (Brit)	Carlisle
Macedo, Tony (Gib) (Brit)	Colchester, Fulham
Macho, Jurgen (Aut)	Sunderland
Mackrill, Percy (SA)	Coventry, Halifax, Torquay
Madar, Mickael (Fr)	Everton
Madjo, Guy (Cam)	Bristol C
Makelele, Claude (DRC) (Fr)	Chelsea
Malan, Norman (SA)	Bradford PA, Middlesbrough, Scunthorpe
Malbranque, Steed (Fr)	Fulham
Mallory, Richard (Ber)	Cardiff
Malz, Stefan (Ger)	Arsenal
Mamoun, Blaise (Cam)	Scunthorpe
Mancini, Roberto (It)	Leicester
Mandy, Aubrey (SA)	Leicester
Maniche, Nuno (Por)	Chelsea
Manninger, Alex (Aut)	Arsenal
Mannini, Moreno (It)	Nottm For
Mansley, Chad (Aus)	Orient
Mansouri, Yazid (Fr) (Alg)	Coventry
Marangoni, Claudio (Arg)	Sunderland
Marcelle, Clint (Trin)	Barnsley, Darlington, Grimsby, Hull, Scunthorpe
Marcelo, Cipriano (Bra)	Birmingham, Sheff Utd, Walsall
Marcolin, Dario (It)	Blackburn
Maresca, Enzo (It)	WBA
Margas, Javier (Chi)	West Ham
Maric, Silvio (Cro)	Newcastle
Marinelli, Carlos (Arg)	Middlesbrough
Markstedt, Peter (Swe)	Barnsley
Marlet, Steve (Fr)	Fulham
Marques, Rui (Ang)	Hull, Leeds
Marshall, Dwight (Jam) (Brit)	Luton, Middlesbrough, Plymouth
Marston, Joe (Aus)	Preston
Marteinsson, Petur (Ice)	Stoke
Martin, Lilian (Fr)	Derby
Martin, Sydney (SA)	Gillingham
Martinez, Jairo (Hon)	Coventry
Martinez, Manel (Sp)	Derby
Martinez, Roberto (Sp)	Swansea, Walsall, Wigan
Martinez, Williams (Uru)	WBA

Name (Born) (Nationality, if differs)	League club(s)
Martis, Shelton (Neth)	Darlington
Masiello, Luciano (It)	Charlton
Masinga, Phil (SA)	Leeds
Materazzi, Marco (It)	Everton
Mateu, Jose Luis (Sp)	Torquay
Matias, Pedro (Sp)	Blackpool, Kidderminster, Macclesfield, Tranmere, Walsall
Matrecano, Salvatore (It)	Nottm For
Mattsson, Jesper (Swe)	Nottm For
Mautone, Steve (Aus)	Crewe, C Palace, Gillingham, Reading, West Ham
Mavrak, Darko (Cro) (Bos)	Walsall
Mawene, Youl (Fr)	Derby, Preston
Maynard, Mike (Guy)	Peterborough
Mayrleb, Christian (Aut)	Sheff Wed
Mazzarelli, Giuseppe (Swit)	Man City
Mazzina, Nicolas (Arg)	Swansea, York
Mbesuma, Collins (Zam)	Portsmouth
Mboma, Patrick (Cam)	Sunderland
Mbome, Kingsley (Cam)	Cambridge
Mbuyi, Gabriel (Bel) (DRC)	Stoke
McBride, Andy (Ken) (Brit)	C Palace
McBride, Brian (USA)	Everton, Fulham, Preston
McClenahan, Trent (Aus)	MKD, West Ham
McDermott, Andy (Aus)	Notts Co, QPR, WBA
McDonald, Scott (Aus)	Bournemouth, Huddersfield, MKD, Southampton
McDonough, Darron (Bel) (Brit)	Luton, Newcastle, Oldham
McDougald, Junior (USA) (Brit)	Brighton, Chesterfield, Millwall, Orient, Rotherham
McDowall, Les (Ind) (Brit)	Man City, Sunderland, Wrexham
McEvoy, Ricky (Gib) (Ire)	Cambridge, Luton
McEwan, Peter (SA)	Luton
McKop, Henry (Zim)	Bristol C
McLaughlin, William (USA)	Crewe
McMahon, Doug (Can)	Wolves
McMaster, Jamie (Aus)	Chesterfield, Coventry, Leeds, Peterborough, Swindon
McMillan, Andy (SA)	York
McNeill, Hamilton (Mal) (Brit)	Bury, Hull
Medina, Nicolas (Arg)	Sunderland
Medou-Otye, Parfait (Cam)	Kidderminster
Meijer, Erik (Neth)	Liverpool, Preston
Meijer, Geert (Neth)	Bristol C
Meirelles, Bruno (Por)	Torquay

Name (Born) (Nationality, if differs)	League club(s)
Melchiot, Mario (Neth)	Birmingham, Chelsea
Mellberg, Olof (Swe)	A Villa
Melono, Gabriel (Uru)	Yeovil
Melvang, Lars (USA) (Den)	Watford
Mendes, Nuno (Por)	Plymouth
Mendes, Pedro (Por)	Portsmouth, Tottenham
Mendez, Alberto (Ger) (Sp)	Arsenal
Mendez, Gabriel (Arg) (Aus)	Notts Co
Mendieta, Gaizka (Sp)	Middlesbrough
Mendy, Bernard (Fr)	Bolton
Mendy, Jules (Sen)	Torquay
Menetrier, Mickael (Fr)	Bournemouth
Meola, Tony (USA)	Brighton
Merino, Carlos (Sp)	Nottm For
Metgod, Johnny (Neth)	Nottm For, Tottenham
Methven, Colin (Ind) (Brit)	Blackpool, Carlisle, Walsall, Wigan
Mettioui, Ahmed (Mor)	Crewe
Mettomo, Lucien (Cam)	Man City
Mezague, Valery (Fr) (Cam)	Portsmouth
Michopoulos, Nik (Grk)	Burnley, C Palace
Middleboe, Nils (Den)	Chelsea
Mido (Egy)	Tottenham
Miglioranzi, Stefani (Bra) (USA)	Portsmouth, Swindon
Mikhailov, Bobby (Bul)	Reading
Miklosko, Ludek (CzRep)	QPR, West Ham
Mikolanda, Petr (CzRep)	Northampton, Rushden, Swindon
Milanese, Mauro (It)	QPR
Mild, Hakan (Swe)	Wimbledon
Miller, George (SA)	Leeds, Workington
Miller, Graham (SA)	Workington
Miller, Justin (SA)	Orient
Milligan, Dudley (SA) (N Ire)	B&B Ath, Chesterfield, Walsall
Mills, Arthur (Ind) (Brit)	Gillingham, Luton, Notts Co
Mills, Paddy (Ind) (Brit)	Birmingham, Hull
Milosevic, Danny (Aus)	Crewe, Plymouth
Milosevic, Savo (Yug)	A Villa
Milovaijevic, Goran (Yug)	Chester
Miotto, Simon (Aus)	Hartlepool
Miranda, Jose (Por)	Rotherham
Mirandinha, Francisco (Bra)	Newcastle
Mirankov, Alex (Fr)	Scarborough
Mirocevic, Ante (Yug)	Sheff Wed
Mirza, Nicolas (Fr)	Yeovil
Misse-Misse, Jean-Jacques (Cam)	Chesterfield
Mitchell, Frank (Aus)	Birmingham, Chelsea, Watford
Mitten, Charlie (Bur) (Brit)	Fulham, Man Utd,

Name (Born) (Nationality, if differs)	League club(s)
	Mansfield
Moilanen, Tepi (Fin)	Darlington, Preston, Scarborough
Mokoena, Aaron (SA)	Blackburn
Mokone, Steve (SA)	Cardiff, Coventry
Molango, Maheta (Swit) (It)	Brighton, Lincoln
Molby, Jan (Den)	Barnsley, Liverpool, Norwich, Swansea
Moldovan, Viorel (Rom)	Coventry
Molenaar, Robert (Neth)	Bradford, Leeds
Moller, Jan (Swe)	Bristol C
Moller, Peter (Den)	Fulham
Moncrieffe, Prince (Jam)	Doncaster
Monkou, Ken (Sur) (Neth)	Chelsea, Huddersfield, Southampton
Moor, Reinier (Neth) (Ire)	Exeter
Moore, Craig (Aus)	C Palace, Newcastle
Moore, Joe-Max (USA)	Everton
Moorhead, George (NZ) (Ire)	Brighton, Southampton
Morais, Filipe (Por)	MKD
Mordey, Henry (Mly) (Brit)	Charlton
Moreau, Fabrice (Fr) (Cam)	Notts Co
Moreira, Fabio (Bra)	Middlesbrough
Moreira, Joao (Por)	Swansea
Moreno, Jaime (Bol)	Middlesbrough
Moreno, Javi (Sp)	Bolton
Mori Cuesta, Francisco (Sp)	Barnsley
Morientes, Fernando (Sp)	Liverpool
Morini, Emanuele (It)	Bolton
Mornar, Ivica (Cro)	Portsmouth
Mortensen, Henrik (Den)	Norwich
Moussaddik, Chuck (Mor)	Wycombe
Moylon, Craig (Ger) (Brit)	Preston
Muamba, Fabrice (DRC) (Eng)	Arsenal
Muhren, Arnold (Neth)	Ipswich, Man Utd
Muntasser, Jehad (Lby)	Arsenal
Murphy, Shaun (Aus)	C Palace, Notts Co, Sheff Utd, WBA
Murray, Bruce (USA)	Millwall, Stockport
Murray, David (SA)	Bristol C, Bristol R, Everton, Rochdale, Swindon
Musampa, Kiki (DRC)	Man City
Musial, Adam (Pol)	Hereford
Mutu, Adrian (Rom)	Chelsea
Muzinic, Drazen (Yug)	Norwich
Mwaruwari, Benjani (Zim)	Portsmouth
Mwila, Freddie (Zam)	A Villa
Myhill, Boaz (USA) (Eng)	Bradford, Hull, Macclesfield, Stockport
Myhre, Thomas (Nor)	Birmingham, Charlton, C Palace, Everton, Sunderland, Tranmere

Name (Born) (Nationality, if differs)	League club(s)	Name (Born) (Nationality, if differs)	League club(s)
N		Niestroj, Robert (Pol) (Ger)	Wolves
N'Diaye, Sada (Sen)	Southend	Nieuwenhuys, Berry (SA)	Liverpool
N'Diaye, Seyni (Sen)	Tranmere	Nijholt, Luc (Neth)	Swindon
N'Dour, Alassane (Sen)	WBA	Nilis, Luc (Bel)	A Villa
N'Dumbu-Nsungu, Guylain (DRC)	Cardiff, Colchester, Darlington, Preston, Sheff Wed	Nilson, Roger (Nor)	Sheff Utd, Tottenham
		Nilsson, Mikael (Swe)	Southampton
		Nilsson, Roland (Swe)	Coventry, Sheff Wed
N'Gotty, Bruno (Fr)	Bolton	Nimni, Avi (Isr)	Derby
N'Toya, Tcham (DRC) (Fr)	Chesterfield, Oxford	Nishizawa, Akinori (Jap)	Bolton
N'Zogbia, Charles (Fr)	Newcastle	Nix, Kyle (Aus) (Eng)	Sheff Utd
Nacca, Franco (Ven)	Cambridge	Norfolk, Lee (NZ)	Ipswich
Nade, Raphael (IvCo)	Carlisle	Normann, Runar (Nor)	Coventry
Nafti, Mehdi (Fr) (Tun)	Birmingham	Norville, Jason (Trin) (Brit)	Barnet, Watford
Nagy, Mick (Hun)	Swindon	Nowak, Tadeusz (Pol)	Bolton
Nakata, Hidetoshi (Jap)	Bolton	Ntimban-Zeh, Harry (Fr)	MKD
Nalis, Lilian (Fr)	Coventry, Leicester, Plymouth, Sheff Utd	Nunez, Antonio (Sp)	Liverpool
		Nunez, Milton (Hon)	Sunderland
Nash, Martin (Can)	Chester, Macclesfield, Stockport	Nuno Morais (Por)	Chelsea
		Nuzzo, Raffaele (It)	Coventry
Naybet, Noureddine (Mor)	Tottenham	Nwajiobi, Emeka (Nig)	Luton
Nayim, Mohamed (Mor)	Tottenham	Nyarko, Alex (Gha)	Everton
Ndlovu, Peter (Zim)	Birmingham, Coventry, Huddersfield, Sheff Utd	Nygaard, Marc (Den)	QPR
		Nzamba, Guy (Gab)	Southend
Nebbeling, Gavin (SA)	C Palace, Fulham, Hereford, Northampton, Preston	**O**	
		O'Brien, Burton (SA) (Brit)	Blackburn, Sheff Wed
Nedergaard, Steen (Den)	Norwich	O'Donnell, Rudolph (Ind) (Brit)	Fulham
Negouai, Christian (Mart) (Fr)	Coventry, Man City	O'Linn, Syd (SA)	Charlton
Neill, Lucas (Aus)	Blackburn, Millwall	O'Sullivan, Wayne (Cyp) (Ire)	Cardiff, Plymouth, Swindon
Neilson, Alan (Ger) (Wal)	Fulham, Grimsby, Luton, Newcastle, Southampton	Obebo, Godfrey (Nig)	Halifax
Nelsen, Ryan (NZ)	Blackburn	Obinna, Eric (Nig)	Reading
Nelson, Fernando (Por)	A Villa	Odejayi, Kay (Nig) (Brit)	Bristol C, Cheltenham
Nemeth, Szilard (Svk)	Middlesbrough	Odubade, Yemi (Nig)	Oxford, Yeovil
Neves, Rui (Por)	Darlington	Oelofse, Ralph (SA)	Chelsea, Watford
Nevland, Erik (Nor)	Man Utd	Ofodile, Adolphus (Nig)	Walsall
Newell, Justin (Ger) (Brit)	Torquay	Okafor, Sam (Nig)	Colchester
Newman, Mick (Can)	West Ham	Okai, Stephen (Gha) (Brit)	Orient
Ngata, Harry (NZ)	Hull	Okenla, Foley (Nig)	Birmingham
Ngonge, Michel (Bel) (DRC)	Huddersfield, QPR, Watford	Okocha, Jay-Jay (Nig)	Bolton
		Okoli, James (Nig)	York
Nicholl, Jimmy (Can) (N Ire)	Man Utd, Sunderland, WBA	Okon, Paul (Aus)	Leeds, Middlesbrough, Watford
Nielsen, Allan (Den)	Tottenham, Watford, Wolves	Okorie, Chima (Nig)	Grimsby, Torquay
Nielsen, David (Den)	Grimsby, Norwich, Wimbledon	Okoronkwo, Isaac (Nig)	Wolves
		Okuonghae, Magnus (Nig) (Eng)	Rushden
Nielsen, John (Den)	Southend		
Nielsen, Kent (Den)	A Villa	Olah, Bela (Hun)	Northampton
Nielsen, Martin (Den)	Huddersfield	Olaoye, Dele (Nig)	Port Vale
Nielsen, Tommy (Den)	Shrewsbury	Oldfield, David (Aus) (Eng)	Leicester, Luton, Man City, Millwall, Oxford, Peterborough, Stoke
Nielson, Norman (SA)	Bury, Charlton, Derby, Hull		
Niemi, Antti (Fin)	Fulham, Southampton	Olembe, Saloman (Cam)	Leeds

Name (Born) (Nationality, if differs)	League club(s)
Olisadebe, Emmanuel (Nig) (Pol)	Portsmouth
Oliveira, Raul (Por)	Bradford
Ollerenshaw, Scott (Aus)	Walsall
Olofinjana, Seyi (Nig)	Wolves
Olsen, Ben (USA)	Nottm For
Olsen, Jesper (Den)	Man Utd
Olsen, Kim (Den)	Sheff Wed
Olszar, Sebastian (Pol)	Coventry, Portsmouth
Olugbodi, Jide (Nig)	Brentford
Ommel, Sergio (Neth)	Bristol R
Omoyimni, Manny (Nig)	Barnet, Bournemouth, Gillingham, Orient, Oxford, Scunthorpe, West Ham
One, Armand (Fr)	Cambridge, Northampton, Wrexham
Onibuje, Fola (Nig)	Barnsley, Huddersfield, Peterborough
Onuoha, Nedum (Nig) (Eng)	Man City
Onyeali, Elkanah (Nig)	Tranmere
Oosthuizen, Ron (SA)	Carlisle, Charlton
Opara, Kelechi (Nig)	Colchester, Orient
Opinel, Sacha (Fr)	Orient
Orhan, Yilmaz (Cyp)	West Ham
Orlygsson, Toddi (Ice)	Nottm For, Oldham, Stoke
Osborne, Frank (SA) (Eng)	Fulham, Southampton, Tottenham
Osborne, Harold (SA) (Brit)	Norwich
Osborne, Reg (SA) (Eng)	Leicester
Ostenstad, Egil (Nor)	Blackburn, Man City, Southampton
Ostergaard, Johnny (Den)	Charlton
Ostlund, Alexander (Swe)	Southampton
Osvold, Kjetil (Nor)	Leicester, Nottm For
Otta, Walter (Arg)	Walsall
Otto, Heine (Neth)	Middlesbrough
Ottosson, Ulf (Swe)	Norwich
Ouaddou, Abdeslam (Mor)	Fulham
Oulare, Souleymane (Gui)	Stoke
Overmars, Marc (Neth)	Arsenal
Owusu-Abeyie, Quincy (Neth)	Arsenal
Oyedele, Shola (Nig)	MKD
Oyen, Davy (Bel)	Nottm For
Ozalan, Alpay (Tur)	A Villa

P

Paatelainen, Mixu (Fin)	Bolton, Wolves
Padovano, Michele (It)	C Palace
Padula, Gino (Arg)	Nottm For, QPR, Walsall, Wigan
Pagal, Jean-Claude (Cam)	Carlisle
Pahars, Marian (Lat)	Southampton
Pamarot, Louis Noe (Fr)	Portsmouth, Tottenham

Name (Born) (Nationality, if differs)	League club(s)
Pandiani, Walter (Uru)	Birmingham
Panopoulos, Mike (Aus) (Grk)	Portsmouth
Panucci, Christian (It)	Chelsea
Papaconstantinou, Loukas (Can)	Darlington
Papadopoulos, Dimitrios (Kaz) (Grk)	Burnley
Papadopulos, Michal (CzRep)	Arsenal
Papavasiliou, Nicky (Cyp)	Newcastle
Park, Ji-Sung (SK)	Man Utd
Parkinson, Andy (SA)	Newcastle, Peterborough
Pasanen, Petri (Fin)	Portsmouth
Pascolo, Marco (Swit)	Nottm For
Paskin, John (SA)	Birmingham, Bury, Shrewsbury, Stockport, WBA, Wolves, Wrexham
Pass, Jimmy (Ind) (Brit)	Stockport
Passi, Franck (Fr)	Bolton
Paston, Mark (NZ)	Bradford, Walsall
Pattison, Matty (SA)	Newcastle
Paulo, Pedro (Ang) (Por)	Darlington
Payne, Mark (Ind) (Brit)	Swindon
Paz, Adrian (Uru)	Ipswich
Pearce, Allan (NZ)	Lincoln
Pedersen, Henrik (Den)	Bolton
Pedersen, Jan Ove (Nor)	Hartlepool
Pedersen, Morten G (Nor)	Blackburn
Pedersen, Per (Den)	Blackburn
Pedersen, Rune (Den)	Nottm For
Pedersen, Tore (Nor)	Blackburn, Oldham, Wimbledon
Peed, Frank (Arg)	Barrow, B&B Ath, Newport, Norwich
Peeters, Bob (Bel)	Millwall
Peeters, Tom (Bel)	Sunderland
Pehrsson, Magnus (Swe)	Bradford
Pellegrino, Mauricio (Arg)	Liverpool
Pelzer, Marc (Ger)	Blackburn
Pensee-Bilong, Michel (Cam)	MKD
Peralta, Sixto (Arg)	Ipswich
Percassi, Luca (It)	Chelsea
Perdomo, Jose (Uru)	Coventry
Perez, Lionel (Fr)	Cambridge, Scunthorpe, Sunderland
Perez, Sebastien (Fr)	Blackburn
Pericard, Vincent (Fr)	Portsmouth, Sheff Utd
Peron, Jeff (Fr)	Portsmouth, Walsall, Wigan
Perry, Bill (SA)	Blackpool, Southport
Peschisolido, Paul (Can)	Birmingham, Derby, Fulham, Norwich, QPR, Sheff Utd, Stoke, WBA

Name (Born) (Nationality, if differs)	League club(s)	Name (Born) (Nationality, if differs)	League club(s)
Peter, Sergio (Ger)	Blackburn	Postma, Stefan (Neth)	A Villa, Wolves
Peters, Jaime (Can)	Ipswich	Potts, Steve (USA) (Eng)	West Ham
Peterson, Brian (SA)	Blackpool	Pounewatchy, Stephane (Fr)	Carlisle, Colchester, Port
Petit, Emmanuel (Fr)	Arsenal, Chelsea		Vale
Petrachi, Gianluca (It)	Nottm For	Powel, Berry (Neth)	Millwall
Petrescu, Dan (Rom)	Bradford, Chelsea, Sheff	Poyet, Gustavo (Uru)	Chelsea, Tottenham
	Wed, Southampton	Praski, Josef (Fr)	Notts Co
Petrescu, Tomi (Fin)	Leicester	Predic, Uros (SM)	Doncaster
Petric, Gordan (Yug)	C Palace	Preedy, Charlie (Ind) (Brit)	Arsenal, Bristol R,
Petrovic, Vladimir (Yug)	Arsenal		Charlton, Luton, Wigan
Petta, Bobby (Neth)	Bradford, Darlington,		Borough
	Fulham, Ipswich	Price, Johnny (Ind) (Brit)	Brentford, Fulham, Port
Petterson, Andy (Aus)	Bradford, Brighton,		Vale
	Charlton, Colchester,	Priday, Bob (SA)	Blackburn, Liverpool,
	Ipswich, Luton, Plymouth,		Rochdale, Acc Stanley
	Portsmouth, Southend,	Priet, Nicolas (Fr)	Doncaster, Leicester
	Torquay, Walsall	Pringle, Martin (Swe)	Charlton, Grimsby
Phillips, Brendon (Jam)	Mansfield, Peterborough	Priske, Brian (Den)	Portsmouth
Phillips, David (Ger) (Brit)	Coventry, Huddersfield,	Priso, Carl (Cam) (Fr)	Torquay
	Lincoln, Man City,	Prosinecki, Robert (Cro)	Portsmouth
	Norwich, Nottm For,	Prunier, William (Fr)	Man Utd
	Plymouth	Purdon, Ted (SA)	Barrow, Birmingham,
Pickett, Reg (Ind) (Brit)	Ipswich, Portsmouth		Bristol R, Sunderland,
Pidcock, Fred (Can)	Walsall		Workington
Piechnik, Torben (Den)	Liverpool		
Pierre, Nigel (Trin)	Bristol R	**Q**	
Pilvi, Tero (Fin)	Cambridge	Quamina, Mark (Guy)	Plymouth, Wimbledon
Pinamonte, Lorenzo (It)	Brentford, Brighton, Bristol	Quantrill, Alf (Ind) (Eng)	Bradford PA, Derby, Nottm
	C, Orient		For, Preston
Pinault, Thomas (Fr)	Colchester, Grimsby	Queudrue, Franck (Fr)	Middlesbrough
Pingel, Frank (Den)	Newcastle	Quitongo, Jose (Ang)	Darlington
Pinto, Sergio (Por)	Bradford		
Pique, Gerard (Sp)	Man Utd	**R**	
Pires, Robert (Fr)	Arsenal	Rachubka, Paul (USA)	Huddersfield, Man Utd, MK
Pisanti, David (Isr)	QPR		Dons, Northampton,
Pistone, Alessandro (It)	Everton, Newcastle		Oldham
Pittman, Jon-Paul (USA)	Hartlepool, Nottm For	Radebe, Lucas (SA)	Leeds
Pittman, Steve (USA)	Shrewsbury	Radosavljevic, Preki (Yug)	Everton, Portsmouth
Poborsky, Karel (CzRep)	Man Utd	(USA)	
Podd, Cyril (StK)	Bradford, Halifax,	Raducioiu, Florin (Rom)	West Ham
	Scarborough	Radzinski, Tomasz (Pol) (USA)	Everton, Fulham
Pogatetz, Emanuel (Aut)	Middlesbrough	Rafferty, Kevin (Ken) (Brit)	Crewe
Pogliacomi, Les (Aus)	Blackpool, Oldham	Rahim, Brent (Trin)	Northampton
Pollet, Ludo (Fr)	Walsall, Wolves	Rahmberg, Marino (Swe)	Derby
Ponte, Raimondo (It)	Nottm For	Rajkovic, Anto (Yug)	Swansea
Poom, Mart (Est)	Derby, Portsmouth,	Rantanen, Jari (Fin)	Leicester
	Sunderland	Raponi, Juan Pablo (Arg)	Oxford
Popescu, Gica (Rom)	Tottenham	Rasiak, Grzegorz (Pol)	Derby, Southampton,
Popovic, Tony (Aus)	C Palace		Tottenham
Porfirio, Hugo (Por)	Nottm For, West Ham	Ravanelli, Fabrizio (It)	Derby, Middlesbrough
Porteous, Jack (Ind) (Brit)	Aldershot	Rayner, Simon (Can)	Lincoln
Porter, Joel (Aus)	Hartlepool	Rebrov, Sergei (Ukr)	Tottenham, West Ham
Postiga, Helder (Por)	Tottenham	Regis, Cyrille (FrGui) (Eng)	A Villa, Chester, Coventry,

Name (Born) (Nationality, if differs)	League club(s)
	WBA, Wolves, Wycombe
Regtop, Erik (Neth)	Bradford
Rehn, Stefan (Swe)	Everton
Reich, Marco (Ger)	C Palace, Derby
Reid, Paul (Aus)	Bradford, Brighton
Reina, Jose (Sp)	Liverpool
Reiziger, Michael (Neth)	Middlesbrough
Remy, Christophe (Fr)	Oxford
Repka, Tomas (CzRep)	West Ham
Resch, Franz (Aut)	Darlington
Reuser, Martijn (Neth)	Ipswich
Reyes, Jose (Sp)	Arsenal
Reyna, Claudio (USA)	Man City, Sunderland
Ribeiro, Bruno (Por)	Leeds, Sheff Utd
Ricard, Hamilton (Col)	Middlesbrough
Rice, Gary (Zam) (Brit)	Exeter
Richard, Fabrice (Fr)	Colchester
Richards, Carl (Jam) (Brit)	Birmingham, Blackpool, Bournemouth, Maidstone, Peterborough
Richards, Lloyd (Jam)	Notts Co, York
Richardson, John (SA)	Bristol R
Riches, Steve (Aus)	Orient
Ricketts, Donovan (Jam)	Bradford
Riedle, Karl-Heinz (Ger)	Fulham, Liverpool
Rieper, Marc (Den)	West Ham
Riera, Albert (Sp)	Man City
Riihilahti, Aki (Fin)	C Palace
Riise, John Arne (Nor)	Liverpool
Riley, Arthur (SA)	Liverpool
Rintanen, Mauno (Fin)	Hull
Riseth, Vidar (Nor)	Luton
Risom, Henrik (Den)	Stoke
Rizzo, Nicky (Aus)	C Palace, MKD
Robben, Arjan (Neth)	Chelsea
Rober, Jurgen (Ger)	Nottm For
Robert, Laurent (Fr)	Newcastle, Portsmouth
Roberts, John (Aus)	Blackburn, Bradford, Chesterfield, Nothampton, Southend
Roberts, Sean (SA)	Sheff Wed
Robertson, Mark (Aus)	Burnley, Stockport, Swindon
Robinson, John (Zim) (Wal)	Brighton, Cardiff, Charlton, Gillingham
Robinson, Trevor (Jam)	Millwall
Robledo, George (Chi)	Barnsley, Newcastle
Robledo, Ted (Chi)	Barnsley, Newcastle, Notts Co
Rocha, Carlos (Por)	Bury
Rochemback, Fabio (Bra)	Middlesbrough
Rodic, Alexsander (Yug) (Slo)	Portsmouth
Rodrigo, Juliano (Bra)	Everton

Name (Born) (Nationality, if differs)	League club(s)
Rodrigues, Dani (Por)	Bournemouth, Bristol C, Southampton, Walsall, Yeovil
Rodrigues, Helder (Ang) (Por)	Newcastle
Rodrigues, Hugo (Por)	Yeovil
Rodriguez, Bruno (Fr)	Bradford
Rogers, Mark (Can)	Wycombe
Rolling, Franck (Fr)	Bournemouth, Gillingham, Leicester
Romano, Serge (Fr)	Wolves
Rommedahl, Dennis (Den)	Charlton
Romo, David (Fr)	Swansea
Ronaldo, Cristiano (Por)	Man Utd
Roque Junior (Bra)	Leeds
Rosa, Denes (Hun)	Wolves
Rosenthal, Ronny (Isr)	Liverpool, Tottenham, Watford
Rosler, Uwe (Ger)	Man City, Southampton, WBA
Rossi, Generoso (It)	QPR
Rossi, Giuseppe (USA) (It)	Man Utd
Rougier, Tony (Trin)	Brentford, Brighton, Bristol C, Reading, Port Vale
Roussel, Cedric (Bel)	Coventry, Wolves
Rovde, Marius (Nor)	Wrexham
Roy, Bryan (Neth)	Nottm For
Roy, Eric (Fr)	Sunderland
Rubins, Andrejs (Lat)	C Palace
Rudham, Doug (SA)	Liverpool
Rudi, Petter (Nor)	Sheff Wed
Rudonja, Mladen (Slo)	Portsmouth
Rush, Jon (NZ)	Blackpool
Rushfeldt, Siggi (Nor)	Birmingham
Ruster, Sebastien (Fr)	Swindon
S	
Sabella, Alex (Arg)	Leeds, Sheff Utd
Sabin, Eric (Fr)	Boston, Northampton, Oxford, QPR, Swindon
Safri, Youssef (Mor)	Coventry, Norwich
Sagere, Jake (USA)	Grimsby
Saha, Louis (Fr)	Fulham, Man Utd, Newcastle
Sahlin, Dan (Swe)	Birmingham
Sahnoun, Nicolas (Fr)	Fulham
Saib, Moussa (Alg)	Tottenham
Sakho, Lamine (Sen)	Leeds
Sakiri, Artim (Mac)	WBA
Sako, Malike (Fr)	Torquay
Salako, Andy (Nig)	Charlton
Salako, John (Nig) (Eng)	Bolton, Brentford, Charlton, Coventry,

Name (Born) (Nationality, if differs)	League club(s)	Name (Born) (Nationality, if differs)	League club(s)
	C Palace, Fulham, Reading, Swansea	Seremet, Dino (Slo)	Doncaster, Luton, Tranmere
Sall, Abdou (Sen)	Kidderminster, Oxford	Sereni, Matteo (It)	Ipswich
Salli, Janne (Fin)	Barnsley	Serioux, Adrian (Can)	Millwall
Salman, Danis (Cyp) (Eng)	Brentford, Millwall, Peterborough, Plymouth, Torquay	Shaaban, Rami (Swe)	Arsenal, Brighton
		Shail, Mark (Swe) (Brit)	Bristol C, Kidderminster
		Shanks, Wally (Mal) (Brit)	Luton
Sam, Hector (Trin)	Port Vale, Wrexham	Sharp, Kevin (Can)	Huddersfield, Leeds, Scunthorpe, Shrewsbury, Wigan, Wrexham
Samaras, Giorgios (Grk)	Man City		
Samuel, J Lloyd (Trin) (Brit)	A Villa, Gillingham		
Samuel, Randy (Trin) (Can)	Port Vale	Sharp, Ronnie (Can)	Doncaster
San Miguel, Xavier (Sp)	Cambridge	Shelia, Murtaz (Geo)	Man City
Sanchez-Lopez, Carlos (Sp)	Bristol R	Shittu, Danny (Nig)	Blackpool, QPR
Sancho, Brent (Trin)	Gillingham	Short, Chris (Ger) (Brit)	Huddersfield, Notts Co, Scarborough, Sheff Utd, Stoke
Sand, Peter (Den)	Barnsley		
Sanderson, Mike (Ger) (Brit)	Darlington		
Sanetti, Francesco (It)	Sheff Wed	Shtaniuk, Sergei (Blr)	Stoke
Sanokho, Amadou (Fr)	Burnley, Oldham	Sibierski, Antoine (Fr)	Man City
Santos, Ali (USA)	Bournemouth	Sibon, Gerald (Neth)	Sheff Wed
Santos, Georges (Fr) (CV)	Grimsby, Ipswich, QPR, Sheff Utd, Tranmere, WBA	Sidibe, Mamady (Mli) (Fr)	Gillingham, Stoke, Swansea
Sara, Juan (Arg)	Coventry	Sigere, Jean-Michel (Fr) (Mart)	Rushden
Sarr, Mass (Lbr)	Reading		
Sartori, Carlo (It)	Man Utd	Sigurdsson, Hannes (Ice)	Stoke
Sas, Marco (Neth)	Bradford	Sigurdsson, Larus (Ice)	Stoke, WBA
Sava, Facundo (Arg)	Fulham	Silenzi, Andrea (It)	Nottm For
Savarese, Giovanni (Ven)	Millwall, Swansea	Silva, Dario (Uru)	Portsmouth
Scaloni, Lionel (Arg)	West Ham	Silva, Gilberto (Bra)	Arsenal
Scartiscini, Leandro (Arg)	Darlington	Silvestre, Mickael (Fr)	Man Utd
Scharner, Paul (Aut)	Wigan	Silvinho, Silvio (Bra)	Arsenal
Schemmel, Sebastien (Fr)	Portsmouth, West Ham	Simb, Jean-Pierre (Fr)	Torquay
Schmeichel, Kasper (Den)	Bury, Darlington	Simba, Amara (Fr)	Orient
Schmeichel, Peter (Den)	A Villa, Man City, Man Utd	Simek, Frankie (USA)	Arsenal, Bournemouth, QPR, Sheff Wed
Schnoor, Stefan (Ger)	Derby		
Schreuder, Jan-Dirk (Neth)	Stoke	Simonsen, Allan (Den)	Charlton
Schroeder, Nico (Neth)	Swansea	Simpson, Josh (Can)	Millwall
Schwarz, Stefan (Swe)	Arsenal, Sunderland	Sinama-Pongolle, Florent (Reu) (Fr)	Blackburn, Liverpool
Schwarzer, Mark (Aus)	Bradford, Middlesbrough		
Schwinkendorf, Jorn (Ger)	Cardiff	Sissoko, Habib (Fr)	Preston, Torquay
Scoffham, Steve (Ger) (Brit)	Notts Co	Sissoko, Mohamed (Fr) (Mli)	Liverpool
Seal, David (Aus)	Bristol C, Northampton	Sito, Castro (Sp)	Ipswich
Seba, Jesus (Sp)	Wigan	Sivebaek, John (Den)	Man Utd
Sebok, Vilmos (Hun)	Bristol C	Six, Didier (Fr)	A Villa
Sedloski, Goce (Mac)	Sheff Wed	Skoko, Josip (Aus)	Stoke, Wigan
Seeburg, Max (Ger)	Burnley, Grimsby, Tottenham	Skopelitis, Giannis (Grk)	Portsmouth
		Skora, Eric (Fr)	Preston, Walsall
Segers, Hans (Neth)	Nottm For, Sheff Utd, Stoke, Tottenham, Wimbledon, Wolves	Skoubo, Morten (Den)	WBA
		Skovbjerg, Thomas (Den)	Kidderminster
		Skulason, Olafur Ingi (Ice)	Arsenal, Brentford
Segura, Victor (Sp)	Norwich	Smeets, Axel (DRC) (Bel)	Sheff Utd
Senderos, Philippe (Swit)	Arsenal	Smeets, Jorg (Neth)	Chester, Wigan
Seol, Ki-Hyeon (SK)	Wolves	Smeltz, Shane (Ger) (NZ)	Mansfield
Sepp, Dennis (Neth)	Bradford	Smertin, Alexei (Rus)	Charlton, Chelsea,

Name (Born) (Nationality, if differs)	League club(s)
	Portsmouth
Smethurst, Derek (SA)	Chelsea, Millwall
Smethurst, Peter (SA)	Blackpool
Smicer, Vladimir (CzRep)	Liverpool
Smit(h), Wilf (Ger) (Brit)	Brighton, Bristol R, Chesterfield, Coventry, Millwall, Sheff Wed
Smith, Roy (Ind) (Brit)	Portsmouth, West Ham
Smith, Scott (NZ)	Rotherham
Sneekes, Richard (Neth)	Bolton, Hull, Stockport, WBA
Snijders, Mark (Neth)	Port Vale
Sobiech, Jorg (Ger)	Stoke City
Sofiane, Youssef (Fr)	Coventry, Notts Co, West Ham
Solano, Nolberto (Per)	A Villa, Newcastle
Solbakken, Stale (Nor)	Wimbledon
Solis, Mauricio (CoRi)	Derby
Solskjaer, Ole Gunnar (Nor)	Man Utd
Soltvedt, Trond Egil (Nor)	Coventry, Sheff Wed, Southampton
Soma, Ragnvald (Nor)	West Ham
Sommeil, David (Guad) (Fr)	Man City
Sommer, Jurgen (USA)	Brighton, Bolton, Luton, QPR, Torquay
Song Billong, Alexandre (Cam)	Arsenal
Song, Rigobert (Cam)	Liverpool, West Ham
Songo'o, Frank (Cam) (Fr)	Portsmouth
Sonko, Ibrahima (Sen)	Brentford, Reading
Sorensen, Thomas (Den)	A Villa, Sunderland
Sorondo, Gonzalo (Uru)	Charlton, C Palace
Sow, Mamadou (Fr)	Torquay
Spector, Jonathan (USA)	Charlton, Man Utd
Speroni, Julian (Arg)	C Palace
Sperrevik, Tim (Nor)	Hartlepool
Sperti, Franco (It)	Swindon
Srnicek, Pavel (CzRep)	Portsmouth, Sheff Wed, Newcastle, West Ham
Stackman, Scott (USA)	Northampton
Stalteri, Paul (Can)	Tottenham
Stam, Jaap (Neth)	Man Utd
Stam, Stefan (Neth)	Oldham
Stanic, Mario (Yug) (Cro)	Chelsea
Starocsik, Felix (Pol)	Northampton
Statham, Brian (Zim) (Eng)	Bournemouth, Brentford, Gillingham, Reading, Tottenham
Stefanovic, Dejan (Yug)	Sheff Wed
Steffen, Willi (Swit)	Chelsea
Stein, Brian (SA) (Eng)	Barnet, Luton
Stein, Edwin (SA) (Brit)	Barnet
Stein, Mark (SA) (Eng)	Aldershot, Bournemouth,

Name (Born) (Nationality, if differs)	League club(s)
	Chelsea, Ipswich, Luton, Oxford, QPR, Stoke
Steiner, Rob (Swe)	Bradford, QPR, Walsall
Stejskal, Jan (CzRep)	QPR
Stensaas, Stale (Nor)	Nottm For
Stepanovic, Dragoslav (Yug)	Man City
Stepanovs, Igors (Lat)	Arsenal
Stephenson, Ashlyn (SA)	Darlington
Stergiopoulos, Marcus (Grk)	Lincoln
Stevens, Ian (Mal) (Brit)	Bolton, Bury, Carlisle, Cheltenham, Preston, Shrewsbury, Stockport, Wrexham
Stewart, Damion (Jam)	Bradford
Stewart, Gordon (SA)	Leeds
Stiffle, Nelson (Ind) (Brit)	B&B Ath, Chester, Chesterfield, Coventry, Exeter
Stimac, Igor (Cro)	Derby, West Ham
Stolcers, Andrejs (Lat)	Fulham
Strandli, Frank (Nor)	Leeds
Strauss, Bill (SA)	Plymouth
Streete, Floyd (Jam)	Cambridge, Derby, Reading, Wolves
Strupar, Branko (Cro) (Bel)	Derby
Strutt, Brian (Mal)	Sheff Wed
Stuart, Eddie (SA)	Stockport, Stoke, Tranmere, Wolves
Suffo, Patrick (Cam)	Coventry, Sheff Utd
Suhaj, Pavel (Svk)	Crewe
Suker, Davor (Cro)	Arsenal, West Ham
Sundgot, Ole (Nor)	Bradford
Surman, Andrew (SA)	Bournemouth, Southampton, Walsall
Svard, Sebastian (Den)	Arsenal, Stoke
Svensson, Anders (Swe)	Southampton
Svensson, Mathias (Swe)	Charlton, C Palace, Derby, Norwich, Portsmouth
Svensson, Michael (Swe)	Southampton
Sweetzer, Gordon (Can)	Brentford, Cambridge
Swierczewski, Piotr (Pol)	Birmingham
Sylla, Mohammed (IvCo) (Gui)	Leicester
Symonds, Calvin (Ber)	Rochdale
Syros, George (Grk)	Bury
T	
Taibi, Massimo (It)	Man Utd
Tainio, Teemu (Fin)	Tottenham
Tal, Idan (Isr)	Everton
Talia, Frank (Aus)	Hartlepool, Sheff Utd, Swindon, Wycombe
Tarachulski, Bartosz (Pol)	Yeovil
Tarantini, Alberto (Arg)	Birmingham

Name (Born) (Nationality, if differs)	League club(s)	Name (Born) (Nationality, if differs)	League club(s)
Taricco, Mauricio (Arg)	Ipswich, Tottenham, West Ham	Torres, Sergio (Arg)	Wycombe
		Toure, Alioune (Fr)	Man City
Tarnat, Michael (Ger)	Man City	Toure, Kolo (IvCo)	Arsenal
Tavlaridis, Stathis (Grk)	Arsenal, Portsmouth	Tramezzani, Paolo (It)	Tottenham
Taylor, Maik (Ger) (N Ire)	Barnet, Birmingham, Fulham, Southampton	Traore, Demba (Swe)	Cambridge
		Traore, Djimi (Fr)	Liverpool
Taylor, Robin (Ger) (Brit)	Wigan	Trautmann, Bert (Ger)	Man City
Tebily, Olivier (IvCo)	Birmingham, Sheff Utd	Tricker, Reg (Ind) (Brit)	Arsenal, Charlton, Luton, Orient
Ten Heuvel, Laurens (Neth)	Barnsley, Bradford, Grimsby, Sheff Utd		
		Trustfull, Orlando (Neth)	Sheff Wed
Tennant, Roy (SA)	Workington	Tskhadadze, Kakhaber (Geo)	Man City
Tennebo, Thomas (Nor)	Hartlepool	Tugay, Kerimoglu (Tur)	Blackburn
Tereskinas, Andrejus (Lith)	Macclesfield	Tulloch, Roland (SA)	Hull
Terrier, David (Fr)	West Ham	Tunks, Roy (Ger) (Brit)	Hartlepool, Preston, Rotherham, Wigan, York
Tessem, Jo (Nor)	Millwall, Southampton		
Theoklitos, Michael (Aus)	Blackpool	Tuomela, Marko (Fin)	Swindon
Thetis, Manuel (Fr)	Ipswich, Sheff Utd, Wolves	Turienzo, Federico (Arg)	Brighton
Thijssen, Frans (Neth)	Ipswich, Nottm For	Turner, Alf (USA)	N Brighton
Thirlby, Anthony (Ger) (Brit)	Exeter, Torquay	Twamley, Bruce (Can)	Ipswich
Thogersen, Thomas (Den)	Portsmouth, Walsall	Twissell, Charlie (Sing) (Eng)	Plymouth, York
Tholot, Didier (Fr)	Walsall		
Thome, Emerson (Bra)	Bolton, Chelsea, Derby, Sheff Wed, Sunderland, Wigan	**U**	
		Udeze, Ifeanyi (Nig)	WBA
		Ugarte, Juan (Sp)	Crewe, Wrexham
Thompson, Justin (Can)	Bury	Ugolini, Rolando (It)	Middlesbrough, Wrexham
Thompson, Peter (Ken) (Brit)	Peterborough	Uhlenbeek, Gus (Sur) (Neth)	Bradford, Chesterfield, Fulham, Ipswich, Mansfield, Sheff Utd, Walsall, Wycombe
Thomsen, Claus (Den)	Everton, Ipswich		
Thordarson, Stefan (Ice)	Stoke		
Thorp, Hamilton (Aus)	Portsmouth		
Thorpe, Arthur (Ind) (Brit)	Bradford, Scunthorpe	Ukah, Ugo (It) (Nig)	QPR
Thorrington, John (USA)	Grimsby, Huddersfield	Unger, Lars (Ger)	Southend
Thorstvedt, Erik (Nor)	Tottenham	Ursem, Loek (Neth)	Stoke, Sunderland
Thorup, Borge (Den)	C Palace	Uytenbogaardt, Albert (SA)	Charlton
Tiago, Cardoso (Por)	Chelsea		
Tiatto, Danny (Aus)	Leicester, Man City, Stoke	**V**	
Tidman, Ola (Swe)	Sheff Wed, Stockport	Vaesen, Nico (Bel)	Birmingham, Bradford, C Palace, Gillingham, Huddersfield
Tierling, Lee (Ger) (Brit)	Fulham		
Tihinen, Hannu (Fin)	West Ham		
Timm, Mads (Den)	Man Utd, Walsall	Valakari, Simo (Fin)	Derby
Tinkler, Eric (SA)	Barnsley	Valente, Nuno (Por)	Everton
Tisdale, Paul (Mal) (Brit)	Bristol C, Exeter, Huddersfield, Ipswich, Northampton, Southampton	Valero, Xavi (Sp)	Wrexham
		Valery, Patrick (Fr)	Blackburn
		Valois, Jean-Louis (Fr)	Burnley, Luton
		Van Blerk, Jason (Aus)	Hull, Man City, Millwall, Shrewsbury, Stockport, WBA
Tistimetanu, Ivan (Mol)	Bristol C		
Tocknell, Brian (SA)	Charlton		
Toda, Kazuyuki (Jap)	Tottenham	Van Breukelen, Hans (Neth)	Nottm For
Todorov, Svetoslav (Bul)	Portsmouth, West Ham	Van Bronckhorst, Giovanni (Neth)	Arsenal
Tofting, Stig (Den)	Bolton		
Tolson, Max (Aus)	Workington	Van Buyten, Daniel (Bel)	Man City
Tomasson, Jon Dahl (Den)	Newcastle	Van Damme, Jelle (Bel)	Southampton
Torfason, Gunnar (Ice)	Doncaster	Van Den Berg, Herman (SA)	Liverpool
Torghelle, Sandor (Hun)	C Palace	Van Den Eynden, Ike (Bel)	Clapton O

Name (Born) (Nationality, if differs)	League club(s)
Van Den Hauwe, Pat (Bel) (Wal)	Birmingham, Everton, Millwall, Tottenham
Van der Elst, Francois (Bel)	West Ham
Van der Geest, Frank (Neth)	Darlington
Van der Gouw, Raimond (Neth)	Man Utd
Van der Kwaak, Peter (Neth)	Carlisle, Reading
Van der Laan, Robin (Neth)	Barnsley, Derby, Port Vale, Wolves
Van der Linden, Antoine (Neth)	Swindon
Van der Meyde, Andy (Neth)	Everton
Van der Sar, Edwin (Neth)	Fulham, Man Utd
Van der Velden, Carel (Neth)	Barnsley, Scarborough
Van Dulleman, Ray (Neth)	Northampton
Van Gobbel, Ulrich (Sur) (Neth)	Southampton
Van Gool, Roger (Bel)	Coventry
Van Heusden, Arjan (Neth)	Cambridge, Exeter, Mansfield, Oxford, Port Vale, Torquay
Van Hooijdonk, Pierre (Neth)	Nottm For
Van Mierlo, Toine (Neth)	Birmingham
Van Nistelrooy, Ruud (Neth)	Man Utd
Van Persie, Robin (Neth)	Arsenal
Van Rossum, Erik (Neth)	Plymouth
Van Wijk, Dennis (Neth)	Norwich
Vandeurzen, Jurgen (Bel)	Stoke
Vanhala, Jari (Fin)	Bradford
Vanninen, Jukka (Fin)	Exeter
Varga, Stanislav (Svk)	Sunderland, WBA
Vasseur, Emmanuel (Fr)	Orient
Vaz Te, Ricardo (Por)	Bolton
Veart, Carl (Aus)	C Palace, Millwall, Sheff Utd
Vega, Ramon (Swit)	Tottenham, Watford
Ventola, Nicola (It)	C Palace
Verde, Pedro (Arg)	Sheff Utd
Verhoene, Kenny (Bel)	C Palace
Vernon, John (SA)	Stockport
Veron, Juan Sebastian (Arg)	Chelsea, Man Utd
Verschave, Matthias (Fr)	Swansea
Verveer, Etienne (Sur) (Neth)	Bradford, Millwall
Viafara, John (Col)	Portsmouth
Vialli, Gianluca (It)	Chelsea
Viana, Hugo (Por)	Newcastle
Viander, Jani (Fin)	Bolton
Vidic, Nemanja (SM)	Man Utd
Vidmar, Tony (Aus)	Cardiff, Middlesbrough
Viduka, Mark (Aus)	Leeds, Middlesbrough
Vieira, Magno (Bra)	Northampton
Vieira, Patrick (Sen) (Fr)	Arsenal
Vignal, Gregory (Fr)	Liverpool, Portsmouth
Viljanen, Ville (Fin)	Port Vale
Viljoen, Colin (SA)	Chelsea, Ipswich, Man City

Name (Born) (Nationality, if differs)	League club(s)
Viljoen, Nik (NZ)	Rotherham
Villa, Ricky (Arg)	Tottenham
Villazan, Rafael (Uru)	Wolves
Vilstrup, Johnny (Den)	Luton
Vindheim, Rune (Nor)	Burnley, Hartlepool
Vivas, Nelson (Arg)	Arsenal
Vlachos, Michalis (Grk)	Portsmouth, Walsall
Volmer, Joost (Neth)	WBA
Volz, Moritz (Ger)	Arsenal, Fulham, Wimbledon
Vonk, Michel (Neth)	Man City, Oldham, Sheff Utd
Vukic, Zvonimir (SM)	Portsmouth

W

Wade, Meshach (Ber)	Hereford
Wagstaffe, Thomas (Ind) (Brit)	Sunderland, Crewe
Wallemme, Jean-Guy (Fr)	Coventry
Waller, Wilfred (SA)	Bolton
Walschaerts, Wim (Bel)	Orient
Walwyn, Keith (Jam) (Brit)	Blackpool, Carlisle, Chesterfield, York
Wanchope, Paulo (CoRi)	Derby, Man City, West Ham
Wapenaar, Harald (Neth)	Portsmouth
Warburton, George (Neth)	Chester
Warzycha, Robert (Pol)	Everton
Wasilewski, Adam (Pol)	Rochdale
Waterreus, Ronald (Neth)	Man City
Watson, Mark (Can)	Oldham, Oxford, Watford
Wdowczyk, Dariusz (Pol)	Reading
Weah, George (Lbr)	Chelsea, Man City
Weber, Nicolas (Fr)	Sheff Utd
Webster, Adrian (NZ)	Darlington
Wegerle, Roy (SA) (USA)	Blackburn, Chelsea, Coventry, Luton, QPR, Sheff Utd, Swindon, Southend, Wimbledon
Welch, Micky (Bar)	
Wesolowski, James (Aus)	Leicester
West, Taribo (Nig)	Derby, Plymouth
Westerveld, Sander (Neth)	Everton, Liverpool, Portsmouth
Wharton, Arthur (Gha)	Rotherham, Sheff Utd, Stockport
Whitbread, Zak (USA)	Liverpool
Whitley, Jeff (Zam) (N Ire)	Cardiff, Man City, Notts Co, Sunderland, Wrexham
Whitley, Jim (Zam) (N Ire)	Blackpool, Man City, Northampton, Norwich, Swindon, Wrexham
Whitmore, Theo (Jam)	Hull, Tranmere
Whitson, Anthony (SA)	Newcastle
Whittaker, Fred (Can)	Notts Co

Name (Born) (Nationality, if differs)	League club(s)
Wiekens, Gerard (Neth)	Man City
Wienand, Tolley (SA)	Huddersfield, Hull
Wijnhard, Clyde (Sur) (Neth)	Darlington, Huddersfield, Leeds, Macclesfield, Oldham, Preston
Wilcox, Tom (At sea) (Brit)	Blackpool, Huddersfield, Man Utd
Wilkshire, Luke (Aus)	Bristol C, Middlesbrough
Willems, Menno (Neth)	Grimsby
Willems, Ron (Neth)	Derby
Willer-Jensen, Thomas (Den)	Swansea
Williams, Everton (Jam)	Wrexham
Williams, Mark (SA)	Wolves
Williams, Stan (SA)	Plymouth
Williamson, Davey (HK) (Brit)	Cambridge
Wilnis, Fabian (Sur) (Neth)	Ipswich
Wilson, Ulrich (Sur) (Neth)	Ipswich
Wilsterman, Brian (Sur) (Neth)	Oxford, Rotherham
Wiltord, Sylvain (Fr)	Arsenal
Wirmola, Jonas (Swe)	Sheff Utd
Wiss, Jarkko (Fin)	Stockport
Witschge, Richard (Neth)	Blackburn
Wojtczak, Edouard (Pol)	York City
Wolski, Mickael (Fr)	Stockport
Wome, Pierre (Cam)	Fulham
Woolf, Levi (SA)	Southampton
Woollard, Arnold (Ber)	B&B Ath, Newcastle, Northampton
Wooter, Nordin (Sur) (Neth)	Watford
Wreh, Christopher (Lbr)	Arsenal, Birmingham
Wright, Ben (Ger) (Ire)	Bristol C

X

Xausa, Davide (Can)	Stoke
Xavier, Abel (Moz) (Por)	Everton, Liverpool, Middlesbrough

Y

Yanushevski, Victor (Blr) (USSR)	Aldershot
Yao, Sosthene (IvCo) (Brit)	Cheltenham
Yeboah, Tony (Gha)	Leeds

Name (Born) (Nationality, if differs)	League club(s)
Yelldell, David (Ger) (USA)	Brighton
Yobo, Joseph (Nig)	Everton
Yordi (Sp)	Blackburn
Yorke, Dwight (Tri)	A Villa, Birmingham, Blackburn, Man Utd
Young, Charlie (Cyp) (Brit)	A Villa, Gillingham
Young, Eric (Sing) (Wal)	Brighton, C Palace, Wolves, Wimbledon
Young, Jamie (Aus)	Reading, Rushden
Youssouf, Sammy (Den)	QPR
Yulu, Christian (DRC) (Fr)	Coventry
Yuran, Sergei (Ukr)	Millwall

Z

Zabica, Robert (Aus)	Bradford
Zadkovich, Ruben (Aus)	Notts Co
Zagorakis, Theo (Grk)	Leicester
Zahana-Oni, Landry (IvCo)	Luton
Zakuani, Gaby (DRC)	Orient
Zamperini, Alessandro (It)	Portsmouth
Zavagno, Luciano (Arg)	Derby
Zdrilic, David (Aus)	Walsall
Zeghdane, Lehit (Fr)	Darlington
Zelic, Ned (Aus)	QPR
Zenden, Boudewijn (Neth)	Chelsea, Liverpool, Middlesbrough
Zhiyi, Fan (Chn)	Cardiff, C Palace
Ziege, Christian (Ger)	Liverpool, Middlesbrough, Tottenham
Ziegler, Reto (Swit)	Tottenham, Wigan
Zivkovic, Boris (Cro)	Portsmouth
Zoetebier, Ed (Neth)	Sunderland
Zohar, Itzhak (Isr)	C Palace
Zois, Peter (Aus)	Cardiff
Zola, Calvin (DRC)	Oldham, Tranmere
Zola, Gianfranco (It)	Chelsea
Zondervan, Romeo (Sur) (Neth)	Ipswich, WBA
Zoricich, Chris (NZ)	Orient
Zuniga, Ysrael (Per)	Coventry
Zwijnenberg, Clemens (Neth)	Bristol C

INDEX